THE ROUGH GUIDE TO

Korea

This third edition updated by

Norbert Paxton

ROUGH GUIDES

roughguides.com

Contents

Introduction to
Korea

Dangling off East Asia like a giant dewdrop, the Korean peninsula is a pleasingly underexplored mix of pine-clad mountains, misty archipelagos and rice paddies of emerald green, interspersed with urban pockets of incomparable *joie de vivre*. Surrounded by the global powerhouses of China, Japan and Russia, Korea's very existence is nothing short of miraculous; against all odds, and despite continued tension with its bellicose brother to the north, South Korea is turning into a little powerhouse of its own, and its traditions and customs have largely survived intact though troubled times. For visitors, this highly distinctive culture is an absolute joy to dive into, whether it's drinking ginseng infusions at a Seoul teahouse, peeking into a temple full of sutra-chanting monks, watching the spectacular ribbon-hatted "farmers' dance", or barbecuing *galbi* meat with new-found friends.

The two Koreas, now separated by the spiky twin frontiers of the Demilitarized Zone, went their separate ways in 1953 after the catastrophic **Korean War** – essentially a civil war, but one largely brought about by external forces, it left millions dead and flattened almost the whole peninsula. **North Korea** has armed itself to the teeth since 1953, stagnated in its pursuit of a local brand of **Communism**, and become one of the least accessible countries in the world. Unbelievably, many foreigners still seem to expect something similar of **South Korea**, which shows just how well kept a secret this fascinating place really is: despite the best efforts of *Gangnam Style*, relatively little except *kimchi* and taekwondo is known about the country in the outside world.

After the war, the South gradually embraced democracy and has since gone on to become a powerful and dynamic economy. Its **cities** are a pulsating feast of eye-searing neon, feverish activity and round-the-clock business. Here you can shop till you drop at markets that never close, feast on eye-wateringly spicy food, get giddy on a bottle or two of *soju*, then sweat out the day's exertions at a night-time

sauna. However, set foot outside the urban centres and your mere presence will cause quite a stir – in the remote **rural areas** life continues much as it did before the "Economic Miracle" of the 1970s, and pockets of **islands** exist where few foreigners have ever set foot.

And for all its new-found prosperity, the South remains a land steeped in **tradition**. Before being abruptly choked off by the Japanese occupation in 1910, an unbroken line of more than one hundred kings existed for almost two thousand years – their grassy burial mounds have yielded thousands of golden relics – and even the capital, Seoul, has a number of **palaces** dating back to the fourteenth century. The wooden *hanok* housing of decades gone by may have largely given way to rows of apartment blocks, but these traditional dwellings can still be found in places, and you'll never be more than a walk away from an immaculately painted **Buddhist temple**. Meanwhile, Confucian-style formal ceremonies continue to play an important part in local life, and some mountains still even host shamanistic rituals.

As for the **Korean people** themselves, they are a real delight: fiercely proud, and with a character almost as spicy as their food, they're markedly eager to please foreigners who come to live or holiday in their country. Within hours of arriving, you may well find yourself with new friends in tow, racing up a mountainside, lunching over a delicious barbecued *galbi*, throwing back rice beer until dawn, or singing the night away at a *noraebang*. Few travellers leave without tales of the kindness of Korean strangers, and all of them wonder why the country isn't a more popular stop on the international travel circuit.

Where to go

Korea is still something of a mystery to most non-natives, and more than half of all its visitors get no further than **Seoul**. One of the largest and most technically advanced cities in the world, the capital

FACT FILE

• The Korean peninsula is split in two by the 4km-wide Demilitarized Zone (DMZ). **North Korea's** population of around 24 million live in an area half the size of the UK. Slightly smaller **South Korea** has a population of 49 million, making it the world's 26th most populous country.

• Ethnic Koreans dominate both countries, making them two of the most **ethnically homogenous** societies on earth. Before splitting, both North and South Korea were traditionally Buddhist nations. Since then the North has followed Juche, a local brand of Communism, while Christianity has become the most popular religion in the South.

• There are over 7 million ethnic Koreans living overseas; famous **"gyopo"** include golfer Michelle Wie, Yunjin Kim of TV show *Lost*, Joe Hahn of nu-metal band Linkin Park and Woody Allen's wife Soonyi Previn.

• The **economies** of South and North Korea were almost equal in size until the mid-1970s. The "Economic Miracle" that followed in the South has propelled it to the cusp of the world's top ten economies, while the North languishes just above 100th place.

• Psy's **"Gangnam Style"** went ultra-viral in 2012, fast becoming the most popular video ever on YouTube – well over 2 billion views at the time of writing.

confounds many expectations by proving itself steeped in history. Here, fourteenth-century palaces, imperial gardens, teeming markets and secluded tearooms continue to exude charm among a maze of skyscrapers and shopping malls. From Seoul, anywhere in the country is reachable within a day, but the best day-trip by far is to the **DMZ**, the strip of land that separates the two Koreas from coast to coast.

Gyeonggi, the province that surrounds Seoul, is a largely unappealing area dissected by the roads and railways that snake their way into the capital, but two of its cities certainly deserve a visit: **Suwon**, home to a wonderful UNESCO-listed fortress dating from the late eighteenth century; and cosmopolitan **Incheon**, where you can eat some of the best food in the country before making your way to the **islands** of the West Sea. By contrast, the neighbouring province of **Gangwon** is unspoilt and stuffed full of attractions: in addition to a number of national parks, of which craggy **Seoraksan** is the most visited, you can head to the unspoilt beaches and colossal caves that surround the small city of **Samcheok**, or peek inside a genuine American warship and North Korean submarine north of the sleepy fishing village of **Jeongdongjin**.

THE CREATION OF HANGEUL

One thing that will strike you on a trip around Korea is **hangeul**, the peninsula's distinctive, almost Tetris-like alphabet. Amazingly, this was a royal creation, having been the brainchild of **King Sejong** in the 1440s. Most of this creative king's subjects were unable to read the

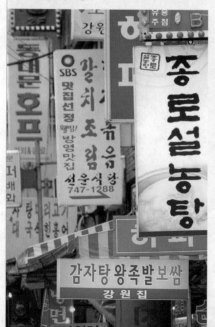

Chinese script used across the land at the time, so he devised a system that would be easier for ordinary people to learn. Sejong was forced to do much of his work in secret, as the plan did not go down well with the *yangban* – Confucian scholars who were even more powerful than royalty at the time. As the only truly educated members of society, the *yangban* argued fiercely against the change in an effort to maintain their monopoly over knowledge.

Hangeul experienced periodic bursts of popularity, but was almost erased entirely by the Japanese during their occupation of the peninsula (1910–45). However, it's now the **official writing system** in both North and South Korea, as well as a small autonomous Korean pocket in the Chinese province of Jilin.

The alphabet, while it appears complex, is surprisingly **easy to learn**, and demonstrating that you can read even a handful of simple words will generate gasps of admiration across Korea. Just a few hours of hard study should suffice – to get started, turn to the table of characters in the Language section (p.372).

Stretching down from Gangwon to the South Sea lie the markedly traditional **Gyeongsang** provinces, home to some of the peninsula's most popular attractions. Foremost among these is gorgeous **Gyeongju**; capital of the Silla dynasty for almost a thousand years, and extremely laidback by Korean standards, it's dotted with the grassy burial tombs of the many kings and queens who ruled here. There's enough in the surrounding area to fill at least a week of sightseeing – most notable are **Namsan**, a small mountain area peppered with trails, tombs and some intriguing Buddhas, and the sumptuously decorated **Bulguksa** temple, another sight on the UNESCO World Heritage list. Although less picturesque as a town, **Andong** is almost as relaxed as Gyeongju, and a superb base from which to access **Dosan Seowon**, a remote Confucian academy, and the charmingly dusty village of **Hahoe**, a functioning showcase of traditional Korean life. The region's rustic charm is actually best appreciated offshore on the windswept island of **Ulleungdo**, an extinct volcanic cone that rises precipitously from the East Sea, and where tiny fishing settlements cling barnacle-like to its coast. Thrills with a more urban flavour can be had in **Busan**, Korea's

GET YOUR MAK ON

Korea has plenty of local booze to get your teeth into (see box, p.41), but the milky-coloured rice beer known as **makgeolli** (막걸리) is by far the most interesting. Drinking *makgeolli* is not really a case of "when in Rome...", since Koreans themselves are far more partial to beer and *soju* (a clear spirit). However, this dynastic-era drink has been making a sustained comeback in recent years: trendy "mak-bars" have been opening up across Seoul (see p.42), with the wave now slowly spreading across the land. Some serve the drink mixed with fruit juice, which may be too faddish for purists, but breweries have long mixed the main constituent rice with local ingredients such as black bean, ginseng and berry juice. See the box on p.42 for some of the varieties to look out for on your way across Korea.

second city, which has an atmosphere markedly different from Seoul; as well as the most raucous nightlife outside the capital, it has the best fish market in the country, and a number of excellent beaches on its fringes.

Even more characterful are the **Jeolla** provinces, which make up the southwest of the peninsula. Left to stagnate by the government while Korea's economy kicked into gear in the 1970s, they have long played the role of the renegade, though this energy is now being rechannelled. Violent political protests took place in regional capital **Gwangju** as

TITLES AND TRANSLITERATION

The Korean peninsula is split into South Korea, officially known as the **Republic of Korea**; and North Korea, officially named the **Democratic People's Republic of Korea** (or DPRK for short). Most of this book is about the former, which is referred to throughout as "Korea"; this is how locals refer to their nation when talking to outsiders, though in Korean they use the term "*Hanguk*" (한국). North Korea has, where necessary, been referred to as such, or as "the DPRK"; North Koreans' own word for both country and peninsula is "*Choson*" (조선).

Also note that a uniform system of **transliteration** is used throughout this book. It's the best and most recent one, but as older generations have been schooled with different systems you may well spot a few varieties of the same word on your travels – see the Language section (p.373) for more information.

recently as 1980, though the city has reinvented itself to become one of the artiest and most business-savvy in the land. **Jeonju** has a similar feel, plus a delightful district of traditional *hanok* housing, and is justly famed for its wonderful, flavoursome cuisine. Earthy **Mokpo** is the hub for ferry trips to a mind-boggling number of **West Sea islands**, dotted with fishing communities where life has changed little in decades, while inland there are a clutch of excellent national parks.

The **Chungcheong** provinces at the centre of the country are bypassed by many travellers, but this is a shame, as they contain some fine sights. The old Baekje capitals of **Gongju** and **Buyeo** provide glimpses of a dynasty long dead, **Daecheon beach** hosts a rumbustious annual mud festival that may well be Korea's most enjoyable event, and there are temples galore: the gigantic golden Buddha at **Beopjusa** is surrounded by 1000m-high peaks, while the meandering trails and vivid colour schemes at **Guinsa** make it the most visually stimulating temple in the land.

THE TAEGEUKKI

South Korea's national flag – the **Taegeukki** – is one of the most distinctive around, and is heavily imbued with philosophical meaning. The design itself has changed a little since its first unveiling in the 1880s, though its fundamental elements remain the same: a red-and-blue circle surrounded by four black trigams, all set on a white background. The puritanical connotations of the white are obvious, whereas the circle and trigams offer greater food for thought. The four trigams make up half of the eight used in the *I Ching*, an ancient Chinese book of divination. Each can represent a number of different concepts: moving clockwise from the top-left of the flag, these may be read as spring, winter, summer and autumn; heaven, moon, earth and sun; father, son, mother and daughter; as well as many more besides.

The circle is split into the "Yin–Yang" shape (again, of Chinese origin), its two halves representing opposites such as light and dark, male and female, day and night. Though coincidental, connections with the divided Korean peninsula are easy to find, with two opposing halves forming part of the same whole – the red half is even on top.

Lying within a ferry ride of the mainland's southern shore is the island of **Jeju**, a popular honeymoon destination for Koreans. While it's undoubtedly touristy, it has its remote stretches and anyone who has climbed the volcanic cone of **Hallasan**, walked through the lava tubes of **Manjanggul** or watched the sun go down from **Yakcheonsa** temple will tell you the trip is more than worthwhile.

And finally, of course, there's **North Korea**. A visit to one of the world's most feared and most fascinating countries will instantly garner you some extra travel kudos – even experienced travellers routinely put the DPRK at the top of their "most interesting" list. Visits don't come cheap and can only be made as part of a guided tour, but the country's inaccessibility brings an epic quality to its few officially sanctioned sights.

When to go

Korea's year is split into **four distinct seasons**. **Spring** generally lasts from April to June, and is one of the best times to visit: flowers are in bloom, and a frothy spray of cherry blossom washes a brief wave of pinkish white from south to north. Locals head for the hills, making use of the country's many national parks, and the effects of the change in weather can also be seen in a number of interesting festivals.

Korea's **summer**, on the other hand, can be unbearably muggy, and you may find yourself leaping from one air-conditioned sanctuary to the next. It's best to avoid the **monsoon** season: more than half of the country's annual rain falls from early July to late August. In a neat reversal of history, Japan and China protect Korea from most of the area's typhoons, but one or two manage to get through the gap each year.

The very best time of the year to visit is **autumn** (Sept–Nov), when temperatures are mild, rainfall is generally low and festivals are easy to come across. Korea's mountains erupt in a magnificent array of reds, yellows and oranges, and locals flock to national parks to picnic under their fiery canopies. T-shirt weather can continue long into October, though you're likely to need some extra layers by then.

The Korean **winter** is long and cold, with the effects of the Siberian weather system more pronounced the further north you go. However, travel at this time is far from impossible – public transport services continue undaunted, underfloor *ondol* heating systems are cranked up, and the lack of rain creates photogenic contrasts between powdery snow, crisp blue skies, off-black pine trees and the earthy yellow of dead grass.

For more information on Korea's climate, including average monthly temperatures and rainfall, see p.49.

Author's picks

Our intrepid author has crisscrossed South Korea multiple times, and made several trips to reclusive North Korea, in a quest to better understand the workings of this fascinating peninsula. These are some of his own, favourite experiences.

Local booze Sample a fantastic selection of unique local tipples, some of which may actually improve your health – a cup of *makgeolli*, a sort of rice beer, contains more "friendly" bacteria than a pot of yoghurt; while whisky-coloured *baekseju* is made with ginseng, liquorice, cinnamon and ginger (p.41).

Shellfish barbies Korea is famed for its barbecued meat, but it's just as enjoyable to chuck a bunch of local shellfish on the flames instead. Those hauled from the west coast are best; try Daecheon beach (p.271).

Cycling Excellent bike paths have been laid out across the country, and it's now possible to cycle from Seoul (p.58) to Busan (p.197) in under a week.

Ferry rides There are almost 500 inhabited islands dotted around the South Korean mainland, and catching a ferry to one of them will give you both a pleasant ride and a trip back in time – islands such as Hongdo (p.234), Heuksando (p.234) and Ulleungdo (p.193) have changed little in decades.

The Farmers' Dance A dynastic tradition, with colourfully clad gents whirling super-long head-ribbons to a cacophony of clangs and drum beats – a real "this is Korea" sight. The Korean Folk Village (p.127) puts on daily shows.

Pyongyang Water Park A fun embodiment of the strides recently taken by the North Korean economy (and ignored by the Western press), this is one of the only places in the country in which you'll be allowed to chill – and take selfies – with "regular" locals (p.333).

> Our author recommendations don't end here. We've flagged up our favourite places – a perfectly sited hotel, an atmospheric café, a special restaurant – throughout the guide, highlighted with the ★ symbol.

FROM TOP PYONGYANG WATER PARK (P.333); HEUKSANDO (P.234)
LEFT PYONGYANG, NORTH KOREA (P.327)

25
things not to miss

It's not possible to see everything that Korea has to offer in a short trip – and we don't suggest you try. What follows, in no particular order, is a selective taste of the peninsula's highlights: idyllic islands, spectacular temples and delicious food. All entries have a page reference to take you straight into the Guide, where you can find out more.

1

1 GWANGJANG MARKET
Page 77
One of Korea's most earthily atmospheric places to eat, Gwangjang is a Seoul institution, with sights and smells redolent of decades gone by.

2 CHANGDEOKGUNG
Page 69
Saunter, as kings once did, though this dreamy, UNESCO-listed palace in central Seoul.

3 PAEKDUSAN
Page 339
The legendary birthplace of the Korean nation, this dormant volcano – the highest peak on the peninsula – rises up through the Chinese-North Korean border, its crater lake a preternatural blue when not frozen over.

4 INSADONG TEAROOMS
Page 106

Tea may have ceded ground to coffee across the nation, but Seoul's traditional Insadong district still has dozens of secluded places serving traditional brews.

5 DOSAN SEOWON
Page 172

The wonderfully unspoilt countryside surrounding the city of Andong is studded with gems, and this former Confucian academy is one of the best.

6 UDO
Page 297

This bucolic, beach-fringed island makes the ideal spot for a cycle ride – race past flower-filled fields whose borders are marked with walls of hand-stacked volcanic rock.

7 BORYEONG MUD FESTIVAL
Page 269

Korea's dirtiest, most enjoyable festival takes place each July on the west coast – even if you forget your soap, you can buy a bar made of mud right here.

8 GYEONGJU
Page 178

Dotted with the grassy burial mounds of Silla-dynasty royals, this ancient capital is the most traditional city in Korea, and should be on every visitor's itinerary.

9 HONGDAE
Page 107

If you're itching to dive into Korean nightlife, this Seoul 'burb is the place to head – it's like walking through an extremely noisy kaleidoscope, full of sozzled students.

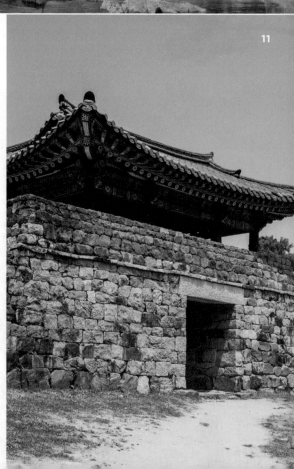

10 WEST SEA ISLANDS
Over three thousand islands are sprinkled like confetti around Korea's western coast – pick up a map in Mokpo, get on a ferry and lose track of time.

11 GONGSANSEONG
Overlooking the river in sleepy Gongju, the walls of this fortress follow an almost caldera-like course; in the middle you'll find dreamy pavilions and walking paths.

12 BARBECUED MEAT
A fire at the centre of your table and a plate of raw meat to fling onto it – could this be the world's most fun-to-eat dish?

13 ARIRANG MASS GAMES
Performers outnumber spectators at this feast of North Korean dance, music and acrobatics – one of the biggest and most spectacular events you're likely to see.

14 JEONGDONGJIN
Korea's most surreal village has a train station on the beach, a ship-hotel atop a cliff, an American warship and a North Korean spy submarine.

15 SOKCHO
Page 145

The harbourfront of this pleasant city is a grand place to eat – sample some of its signature squid sausage on tiny Abai island, accessible on a ferry that you have to pull along yourself.

16 WALKING THE JEJU OLLE TRAIL
Page 288

Get to know Korea's largest island by tackling part of this wonderful trail, which passes beaches, temples and mini-volcanoes on its circumnavigation of the island.

17 YAKCHEONSA
Page 304

This large, splendid temple on the southern coast of Jeju Island is almost unique among Korean temples in that it faces the sea – pop along for sundown and evening prayers.

18 MAKGEOLLI
Page 41

Get drunk the local way with *dongdongju* or *makgeolli*, both of which have undergone huge surges in popularity of late.

19 NORAEBANG
Page 86

A near-mandatory part of a Korean night out is a trip to a "singing room", the local take on Japan's karaoke bars.

20 JIRISAN NATIONAL PARK
Page 213

The largest of Korea's many national parks, Jirisan offers some superlative multi-day hiking possibilities.

21 BIBIMBAP
Pages 37 & 249

A delectable dish derived from the five principal colours of local Buddhism: red for the paste, yellow for the egg, white for the rice, blue for the meat and green for the veggies.

22 BEOPJUSA
Page 275

This delightful temple boasts one of the world's tallest bronze Buddhas – a 33m-high figure surrounded by mountains that just beg to be hiked across.

23 JEONJU HANOK VILLAGE
Page 244

In Jeonju, one of Korea's most agreeable cities, you can sleep in a traditional wooden *hanok* house, heated from underneath by gentle flames.

24 THE DMZ
Pages 129 & 337

Take a step inside the 4km-wide Demilitarized Zone separating North and South Korea: the world's frostiest remnant of the Cold War.

25 PYONGYANG
Page 327

The world's least-visited capital – a rhapsody of brutalist architecture, and red *hangeul* slogans extolling the virtues of the government and its leaders.

Itineraries

Despite Korea's relatively diminutive size, you'll need to do some planning if you're to make the most of the country. Seoul demands at least a couple of days, but with a little more time on your hands you could soon be racing up mountains, hopping between far-flung islands or tracking down the peninsula's best beaches and temples.

THE FULL MONTY

Korea's compact size and excellent public transportation makes it very simple to check off its main sights, and a couple of quirkier ones – even a week in the country is enough to give you a good idea of what Korea's all about. The number-one rule is to get out of Seoul – a great city it may be, but there's just so much else on offer across the land.

❶ **Seoul** Where to start with Korea's fascinating capital? Ancient palaces and shrines, a beguiling array of galleries, a national park on its doorstep and some of the best food and shopping in Asia – and that's just for starters. **See p.58**

❷ **Sokcho** This east-coast city offers day-trips into the mountains, as well as some simply fantastic restaurants – a great place to expand your waistline. **See p.145**

❸ **Seoraksan National Park** The undisputed number-one national park in a country full of mountains, Seoraksan delivers on lofty promises with a series of jagged, tremendously photogenic peaks. **See p.149**

❹ **Jeongdongjin** This small coastal village is perhaps Korea's best sunrise spot, and is also

home to the country's most distinctive hotel – a ship-shaped establishment perching atop a cliff. **See p.158**

❺ **Gyeongju** If you've only got time for one place outside Seoul, make it quiet Gyeongju, dynastic capital for almost a millennium and still home to a mind-boggling assortment of treasures, as well as some superb temples and hiking routes. **See p.178**

❻ **Busan** Korea's second city is an easy place to love – if the beaches and seafood don't get you, the nightlife will. **See p.197**

❼ **Jeju Island** An extinct volcano jutting out of the sea, Jeju is far more natural in feel than the mainland: think beaches, farmland, lava tubes and volcanic craters. And now you can walk around the whole island on the Jeju Olle Trail. **See p.282**

RIDING THE JUNGANG LINE

Bypass the high-speed KTX services linking Seoul and Busan, and take the Jungang line instead – slower it may be, but it'll take you to some beautiful places, and give you a far better perspective of Korea's history and traditions.

ABOVE GUINSA TEMPLE; BOATS IN SOKCHO HARBOUR

① Seoul Start out with a few days in Korea's dynamic, open-all-hours capital, before catching the train south. **See p.58**

② Danyang First stop, Danyang – a delightful town set along a lakeside and surrounded by mountains. Drink in the superb views, then drink down some local *makgeolli*. **See p.277**

③ Guinsa The most visually arresting temple in the land, shoehorned into a tight mountain valley a short bus ride from Danyang. **See p.280**

④ Andong Further down the Jungang line is Andong, a relaxing, traditionally minded city famed for its *soju*. **See p.169**

⑤ Hahoe Folk Village Step back in time at the quaint Hahoe Folk Village near Andong. Entirely made up of low-rise wooden buildings and surrounded by farmland, this charming village is a present-day sampler of Korea in dynastic times. **See p.171**

⑥ Gyeongju There are more echoes of the past in Gyeongju, the capital of the Silla dynasty for almost one thousand years. Explore the city's regal burial mounds by bike. **See p.178**

⑦ Oksan Seowon Established during the Goryeo dynasty, this shrine was once one of the most important Confucian academies in the land, and remains a fantastic draw on account of its beauty and idyllic location. **See p.190**

⑧ Haeundae, Busan The Jungang line comes to an end next to Haeundae, Korea's number-one beach – a fine place to kick back with seafood and cocktails after a rail journey across the country. **See p.201**

WEST SIDE STORY

Korea's west side is relatively off the radar, but features some of the most beguiling places in the land: national parks aplenty, ancient capitals, dazzling temples and more islands than you could ever count.

① Gongju The one-time capital of the Baekje dynasty boasts a giant fortress, several regal burial mounds, a district of wooden *hanok* housing and a museum full of ancient riches. **See p.262**

② Daecheon beach Not as pristine as Haeundae beach, but far more Korean in feel – come here to splash around in the sea and wolf down a yummy shellfish barbecue. Daecheon is also home to the Boryeong Mud Festival, by far the most popular festival in the country with international visitors. **See p.269**

③ Jeonju Most of Korea's traditional wooden housing has been flattened in the name of progress, but this earthy city boasts a whole swathe of it. It's also renowned for having the best food in the country. **See p.244**

④ Naejangsan National Park Achingly beautiful in the autumn, this national park's circle of modest peaks makes for some great hiking at any time of year. **See p.241**

⑤ Mokpo A pleasingly odd city surrounded by a spray of unspoiled islands, salty Mokpo is the best place to comprehend the provincial nuances of the Jeolla area. **See p.230**

⑥ Hongdo Essentially as far west as Korea goes, this tiny, beautiful island juts dramatically from the sea – an emphatic full stop to your journey. **See p.234**

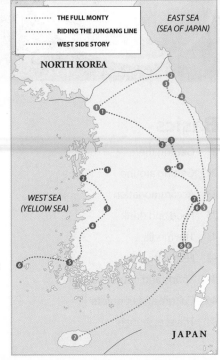

THE FULL MONTY

RIDING THE JUNGANG LINE

WEST SIDE STORY

EAST SEA (SEA OF JAPAN)

NORTH KOREA

WEST SEA (YELLOW SEA)

JAPAN

SIDE DISHES, GYEONGJU RESTAURANT

Basics

Getting there

With no way to travel to Korea by road or rail, the vast majority of travellers arrive at the gleaming Incheon International Airport; often referred to as "Seoul Incheon" on international departure boards, this offshore beast handles a large and ever-increasing number of international flights. The only other way in is by sea – there are services from both China and Japan.

Korean Air (W koreanair.com) and Asiana (W flyasiana.com) are the two big Korean **airlines**, operating direct flights from a number of destinations around the world. Seoul increasingly features as a stopover on round-the-world trips, and the country is well served by dozens of international carriers. **Fares** increase for travel in the summer months and at Christmas time. A **departure tax** applies when leaving Korea, but will almost certainly be factored in to your ticket price.

Flights from the UK and Ireland

Korean Air and Asiana have **direct** connections from **London Heathrow** to Incheon: Korean Air has a daily service, while Asiana has five per week. The journey takes eleven hours, with return fares costing around £600; this can rise to over £800 during summer and at Christmas, when it's common for all flights to be fully booked weeks in advance. You can save money by taking an **indirect flight**, with prices often dipping to around £400 return during low season; good options include Finnair via Helsinki (W finnair.com), Qatar Airways via Doha (W qatarairways.com), Aeroflot via Moscow (W aeroflot.ru) and Emirates via Dubai (W emirates.com). It's also worth checking deals with KLM (W klm.com) and Air France (W airfrance.com), whose routes are as close to direct as possible.

There are no direct flights to Korea from **Ireland** so you'll have to transfer in the UK or in mainland Europe.

Flights from the US and Canada

If you are coming from the **US** you have a number of options available to you: there are **direct** flights

to Incheon from New York, Dallas, Las Vegas, Los Angeles, San Francisco, Detroit, Seattle, Chicago, Atlanta, Houston, Washington and Honolulu; carriers include Delta (W delta.com) and United (W united.com), as well as Asiana and Korean Air. Sample low-season return fares are $1400 from New York (a journey of around 14hr), $1200 from Chicago (14hr) and $1150 from Los Angeles (13hr). In all cases you may save hundreds of dollars by transferring – Beijing and Tokyo are popular hubs. Fares on many routes can almost double during summer and Christmas time.

Korean Air has direct flights to Incheon from two **Canadian** cities, Vancouver and Toronto, but these can be very expensive when demand is high (over Can$2500); low-season prices can drop under Can$1000. Again, you're likely to save money by taking an indirect flight.

Flights from Australia, New Zealand and South Africa

From **Australia**, the only cities with direct connections to Korea are Sydney (10hr) and Brisbane (9hr). There have, in the past, also been direct flights from Melbourne and Cairns – check to see whether these connections have reappeared. The number of Koreans going to Australia means that bargain direct flights are few and far between, so check around for indirect flights via a Southeast Asian hub; return prices via Kuala Lumpur, Singapore or Hong Kong can often drop below Aus$1000. For those travelling from **New Zealand**, there are direct flights from Auckland (12hr), and a few from Christchurch, though indirect flights are cheaper. Keep your fingers crossed for a NZ$1400 fare, but assume you'll pay around NZ$1900. At the time of writing, there were no direct flights from **South Africa**.

Flights from other Asian countries

There are flights to Incheon from many cities across **Japan** (from $150 return) and **China** (around $250 to the major east-coast cities). If Seoul isn't your final destination, it may be worth checking for a connection to another Korean international airport: in decreasing order of importance, these include Busan's Gimhae Airport, Jeju, Daegu and Gwangju.

Unless otherwise stated, this Basics section is referring to South Korea, calling that country "Korea" as the locals do. For North Korea travel basics, see pp.314–319.

A BETTER KIND OF TRAVEL

At Rough Guides we are passionately committed to travel. We feel that travelling is the best way to understand the world we live in and the people we share it with – plus tourism has brought a great deal of benefit to developing economies around the world over the last few decades. But the growth in tourism has also damaged some places irreparably, and climate change is exacerbated by most forms of transport, especially flying. All Rough Guides' trips are carbon-offset, and every year we donate money to a variety of charities devoted to combating the effects of climate change.

There's also a handy, and extremely regular, connection between Seoul's Gimpo Airport and Tokyo Haneda, both of which are closer to the centre of their respective capitals than the larger hubs, Incheon and Narita.

China and Japan aside, Incheon is served by flights from an ever-increasing number of **other Asian countries**, and the good news is that many of these routes are run by budget airlines; local carriers Eastar Jet (Ⓦeastarjet.com), Jin Air (Ⓦjinair.com) and Jeju Air (Ⓦen.jejuair.net) have services from Thailand, the Philippines, Hong Kong, Vietnam, Laos, Cambodia, and more besides.

Ferries

Flights aside, access from the Asian continent takes the form of **ferries** from Japan or China, possibly via a ride on the Trans-Siberian Railway (see Ⓦseat61.com for more information). Note that if you're heading to or from China or Japan, you can make use of a **combined rail and ferry ticket** that gives substantial discounts on what you'd pay separately (see Ⓦletskorail.com for details).

There are several **ferry routes** from **China**'s eastern coast, all of which head to Incheon's international termini. All vessels have numerous classes of comfort, with one-way prices starting at around 850RMB. The most popular connections are Dalian and Qingdao, and Tianjin's port in Tanggu, which is most convenient if you're heading to or from

Beijing. See the box below for information on departure days and journey times.

Services from **Japan** run from Fukuoka, Osaka and Shimonoseki to Busan (see p.201), and arrive reasonably close to Busan train station, so you can be heading to other Korean destinations in no time. **Fukuoka** is by far the best choice, since there are, in fact, two different services to and from Korea – one a regular ferry, departing Fukuoka every day except Sunday (6hr; ¥9000), the other a faster jetfoil with at least five services per day (3hr; ¥13,000; Ⓦjrbeetle.co.jp). The longer ferry from **Osaka** (19hr; from ¥14,000) runs three days a week – a beautiful ride through Japan's island-studded inland sea.

Overland

Despite the fact that South Korea is part of the Eurasian landmass, and technically connected to the rest of it by rail, the Demilitarized Zone (DMZ) and North Korean red tape means that the country is currently **inaccessible by land**. Two old lines across the DMZ have been renovated, and 2007 saw trains rumble across the border as part of a peace ceremony, but overnight trains from Beijing to Seoul station remain a distant prospect.

INTERNATIONAL AGENTS

ebookers Ⓦebookers.com. Low fares on an extensive selection of scheduled flights and package deals.

FERRIES FROM CHINA

Chinese ports	Departure days and times	Journey times
Dalian	Mon, Wed & Fri 6pm	17hr
Dandong	Tues & Thurs 6pm; Sun 3pm	16hr
Qingdao	Mon, Wed & Fri 4pm	17hr
Qinhuangdao	Wed & Sun 1pm	24hr
Shidao	Tues, Thurs & Sun 6pm	14hr
Tanggu (Tianjin)	Thurs & Sun 11am	24hr
Weihai	Tues, Thurs & Sun 6pm	14hr
Yantai	Mon, Wed & Fri 6.30pm	14hr
Yingkou	Mon & Thurs 11am	24hr

North South Travel ⓦ northsouthtravel.co.uk. Friendly, competitive travel agency, offering discounted fares worldwide. Profits are used to support projects in the developing world, especially the promotion of sustainable tourism.

STA Travel ⓦ statravel.com. Worldwide specialists in independent travel; also student IDs, travel insurance, car rental, rail passes, and more. Good discounts for students and under-26s.

Trailfinders ⓦ trailfinders.com. One of the best-informed and most efficient agents for independent travellers.

LOCAL TOUR OPERATORS

Aju Tours ⓦ ajutours.co.kr. A few interesting additions to the regular Seoul tours and DMZ trips, including birdwatching, oriental health or a tour of shamanistic sites.

Grace Travel ⓦ english.triptokorea.com. Outfit offering a wide range of good-value tours, including ski trips, Jeju excursions, hiking adventures and a "Royal Relics" journey.

O'ngo ⓦ ongofood.com. Interesting food tours, mostly focused on Seoul but sometimes heading to the hinterlands; you'll be able to wrap up the experience with a cooking class or two.

Rye Tour ⓦ ryetour.com. In addition to a few Korea-only itineraries, this group also offers week-long tours which combine Seoul and Busan with Beijing, Shanghai or Tokyo.

Getting around

Travelling around the country is simple – even if the train won't take you where you want to go, there's almost always a bus that will; should you have a choice, it's usually faster but more expensive to take the train. Travel prices are reasonable by international standards, even if you choose to hop on one of the surprisingly numerous domestic flights. Korea is surrounded by islands, and should you take a ferry to one of these, it may well be the most pleasurable part of your visit. All cities have comprehensive (if slightly incomprehensible) bus networks, and many now have subway lines. Taxis are remarkably good value, and can even be feasible modes of transport from city to city.

Wherever you are, it's wise to avoid **peak travel seasons** if possible. During the two biggest holidays (Seollal and Chuseok; see p.43) it can often feel as if the whole country is on the move, as people rush to their home towns and back again – there's gridlock on the roads, it's hard to find a seat on trains or buses, and many shops and businesses (including some hotels) close down. Weekend or rush-hour train tickets can also be hard to come by

throughout the year. For **travel information**, it's best to ask at a tourist office, or call the English-speaking information line on ☎ 1330 (you'll need to add an area code if dialling from a mobile phone or abroad – see p.53).

By plane

For such a small country, Korea is surprisingly well served by **domestic flights**. The two **national carriers**, Korean Air (ⓦ koreanair.com) and Asiana (ⓦ flyasiana.com), have near-identical services – with near-identical fares – linking over a dozen airports across the nation, with the two main hubs being Gimpo in Seoul, and the holiday hotspot of Jeju Island. There's also a new mini-glut of **budget carriers** heading to Jeju from various Korean airports, including T'way (ⓦ twayair.com), Eastar Jet (ⓦ eastarjet.com), Jin (ⓦ jinair.com) and Jeju Air (ⓦ en.jejuair.net); hopefully, at least a couple will last the course. All this said, the country is so well covered by train and bus that only a trip to Jeju would see the average traveller need to use a domestic flight. Prices are reasonable – almost always between W50,000 and W100,000 – which is hardly surprising given that few trips take longer than an hour. Don't forget your **passport**, as you're likely to need it for identification purposes.

By ferry

With several thousand islands sprinkled around Korea's western and southern shores, no trip to the country would be complete without a **ferry ride**. Several towns and cities have connections, though the main ports of entry to Korea's offshore kingdom are Incheon, Mokpo, Wando, Yeosu and Busan, all of which embrace sizeable island communities. The choice from **Mokpo**, in particular, is incredible – some travellers have inadvertently made trailblazers

---

MOVING ON FROM INCHEON AIRPORT

Connections to Seoul from **Incheon Airport** are excellent (see p.121 for more details), but if you're headed elsewhere there's no need to transit in the capital. Express buses dash from the airport to all of the country's major cities at pleasingly regular intervals. Wherever you're going, useful signs help point the way, or you can ask at the information desk to find the most suitable route.

of themselves, finding their way onto islands that had never seen a foreign face. Popular **Jeju Island** is quite the opposite, and although the vast majority of Koreans travel here by plane, it has ferry connections to a number of south-coast mainland cities (see p.292 for details).

Fares, on the whole, are reasonable – short hops may cost as little as W5000, but for return fares to outlying islands such as Jeju, Hongdo, Ulleungdo or Dokdo you'll probably have to shell out at least ten times that. Only tickets to these destinations will be in much danger of selling out, and even then, only in high season; at these times, it's best to head to a Korean travel agency.

By train

A fleet of excellent **trains** ply the mainland provinces – sleek, affordable and punctual to a fault. There are two **main lines**, both starting in Seoul; these split in Daejeon, with one heading to Daegu and Busan to the southeast, and the other to Mokpo to the southwest. A third line, to Gangneung on the east coast, should open in 2017.

The highest of three main classes of train is the **KTX** – these high-speed machines can reach speeds of over 300km per hour. The Gyeongbu line runs from Seoul to Busan and connects the cities in around 2hr 45min (W58,800). The KTX has taken over from the previous lord of the tracks, the **Saemaeul**; though slower (Seoul to Busan takes over four hours), travelling on this class cuts KTX costs by around a third (W42,600 Seoul to Busan), and the greater legroom usually makes for a more comfortable journey. A third cheaper again is the network's third class of train, the **Mugunghwa**, which was forced to cede most of its schedule space to the KTX – a good thing, since the Seoul to Busan journey (W28,600) is now a haul of over five hours.

The line from Seoul to Mokpo also carries all three breeds of train, though the high-speed upgrade of the section from Daejeon to Mokpo will not be completed in full until 2017, when the Gangneung line also enters service.

There are other lines away from the inverted "Y"-shape ploughed by the high-speed trains. The south-coast line has irregular services, but can come in handy, while the Jungang line takes a

KOREAN ADDRESSES

First, the good news – almost all Korean road signs are dual-language, spelling the Korean *hangeul* out in Roman characters. The bad news is that the whole concept of **street names** remains alien to the majority of Koreans, since addresses in Korea were for a long time based on **city sections** rather than roads. The numbers of these sections often ran non-sequentially, making things a nightmare for local postmen, and anyone asking – or giving – directions.

In 2010 the government, in an attempt to bring order to the system, gave all of the roads in the country names (often, confusingly, featuring numbers); consequently, every address in Korea now has **two addresses**: one old, one new. It'll be a while before the new ones find common usage – many Koreans still don't even know what road they live on. This guide has listed the addresses used by each specific establishment (around half old, half new), since that's the one you're most likely to find on Internet search or mapping engines.

Alternative help is at hand. It's common for hotels and restaurants to include a small map on their **business cards**; wherever you're staying, pop one of their cards in your pocket, and it'll either help you find your way back, or enable locals to point you in the right direction. With a precise address, whether "new" or "old", taxi drivers will also be able to get you where you want to go – satnav systems have, understandably, become rather popular.

Despite the general confusion, addresses fit into a very rigid system. Unlike in the Western world, components are usually listed from largest to smallest when writing an address, the elements of which are discernable by their suffix. The country is split into nine **provinces** (도; –*do*), inside which you'll find **cities** (시; –*si*, pronounced "shee"), **towns** (읍; –*eup*) and **villages** (리; – *ri* or – *li*). The larger cities are split into a number of **districts** (구; –*gu*); the number will vary with the city's size (Seoul, for example, has 25 such sections), and these are further subdivided into **neighbourhoods** (동; *dong*). The new address system dispenses with the *dong* and replaces it with a **road name**; large roads end with 로 (–*no*, –*ro* or –*lo*), and smaller ones with –*gil* (길), and many of the latter are numbered. Finally, addresses end with the **number** of the house or establishment – under the new system, these run sequentially along the road. Happy hunting!

more rural route between Seoul and Busan, lassoing together some of Korea's most wonderful sights (see "Itineraries", pp.24–25).

All trains have **toilets**, and folk pushing trolleys of beer, peanuts, chocolate and *gimbap* for sale down the carriages with pleasing frequency. For fare and schedule information, check ⓦ letskorail.com.

Tickets

Almost all stations have English-language signs where necessary, and schedules can also be checked online. When buying your **tickets**, note that the bigger stations have special lanes for foreigners, though it doesn't really matter which one you use as the ticketing system is computerized and buying a ticket is easy. Simply state your destination and the class you require, and the cashier will swing a computer screen in your direction, showing the price and seat availability. If they're pointing at a zero and looking apologetic, you'll probably need another train. You'll be given a carriage and seat number: take your seat and not someone else's, otherwise it throws the seating system into disarray and may cause a domino-run of disgruntled passengers.

As trains are far less numerous than buses, they're far more likely to sell out quickly – on holidays or weekends, you'll need fortune on your side to walk into a station and find KTX tickets for the main routes. **Advance reservations** are highly recommended – tickets for all classes go on sale a month ahead of travel, and can be bought at any station. A **return ticket** costs the same as two single ones.

Subway trains

Six Korean cities now have **underground** networks: Busan, Daegu, Daejeon and Gwangju have independent systems, while Incheon's lines are linked to the marauding Seoul network; all are continuing to grow, and new networks are likely to be born in other cities. Prices start at about W1200 for a short hop, and increase with distance in the bigger cities, though even the full run through Seoul from Soyosan to Cheonan – about one-third of the country, and one of the longest metro routes in the world at three hours plus – will only set you back just over W3000. Signs are dual-language, and station maps easy to read.

By bus

There are a staggering number of **long-distance buses** in Korea – during rush hour, some scheduled services can run as often as every two minutes, with all of them departing on time. They come in two types: **express** (고속; *gosok*), and **intercity** (시외; *si-oe*, pronounced "shee-way"). Although the express services are more expensive and tend to be used for longer journeys, they are likely to run in tandem with intercity buses on many routes. Allied to this, the two bus types use **separate stations** in most cities, and even the locals don't always know which one to go to, or which one they'll be arriving at – very frustrating, though some cities are starting to see sense and group both bus stations into one building. Some cities have even more than two bus stations, so all in all it pays to keep a loose schedule when using buses, even more so if the highways are full.

Longer journeys are broken at **service stations**, housing fast-food bars and snack shops. You typically get fifteen minutes to make your purchases and use the **toilets** (there aren't any on the buses), but many a traveller has come a cropper after exiting the building to be confronted by forty near-identical vehicles, of which half-a-dozen may be heading to the same destination – your bus won't wait for you, so make sure that you know where it's parked.

Buses are so frequent that it's rare for them to sell out, though the last service of the day between major cities tends to be quite full. This can be surprisingly early: many services make their last trips at 7pm, though some have overnight connections. **Prices** are reasonable and usually lower than the trains, with intercity services slightly cheaper than express if the two coexist – Seoul to Busan is around W25,000 (5hr) on the former, W35,000 (4hr 30min) on the latter. Journeys take longer than the fastest trains, and are more prone to delays. Tickets are often checked at the start of the journey, but also at the end, so if possible try to avoid losing your ticket, lest the driver refuse to release you from his bus (which does happen).

City buses

With little English language on the signs or vehicles, Korea's **city bus** networks can be more than a little confusing for the first-time visitor. Once you are familiar with a route, city buses can be a good way of getting around – they're pleasingly frequent, and very affordable at around W1200 per ride.

Throw your money into the collection box next to the driver; change will be spat out just below – make sure that you've an ample supply of coins or W1000 notes with you, as higher-value bills are unlikely to be accepted (though foreigners in such situations may be waved on with a grin). The bigger cities have started to avoid these problems by introducing **pre-paid cards**, and in some cities (notably Seoul) you're no longer able to pay in cash at all. Cards work out cheaper per journey than paying by cash, and some are also valid on subway networks or longer-distance buses. They last for as long as you have credit, and can be topped up in increments of W1000 at kiosks or ticket booths.

By taxi

Korean **taxis** are pleasingly cheap for a developed country, and in any city you shouldn't have to wait long to spot one. Look for cars with illuminated blocks on top, usually something resembling a plastic pyramid. Those whose blocks aren't illuminated are taken or on call; others can be **waved down** from the roadside, though to make sure of being understood you'll have to do it the Korean way – arm out, palm to the ground, fingers dangling underneath. As few drivers speak English, it's a good idea to have your destination **written down**, if possible – even the cheapest motels have business cards with their address on.

Rates start at W3000. Over short distances, cab rides may work out cheaper than taking buses if you're in a group. All taxis are **metered** and though dishonesty is rarely an issue, when you start moving, check that the numbers are doing likewise. The only time that you may have to negotiate a fee is if you're using a **chong-al** – or "bullet" – taxi. Piloted by death-wish drivers, these hover like vultures around train and bus stations when tickets have sold out, or daily services have finished. Rides in such vehicles are not recommended for those of a nervous disposition, while others may find it quite a thrill.

By car and motorbike

Korea's public transport network is so good that few foreigners end up renting a car here – in many cases it would simply lose you time. If you do decide to drive, you will inevitably get snarled up in the traffic that blights the cities and highways, with exceptions being Jeju Island and rural Gangwon province in the northeast, where the roads are relatively calm and traffic-free.

To **hire a car** you will need an international driving licence, and to be at least 21 years of age. Rental offices can be found at all airports and many train stations, as well as around the cities. **Prices** usually start at W50,000 per day, though as insurance is compulsory, you should budget on a little extra. Vehicles usually drive on the right-hand side of the road (though not all the time; the pavement can be just as popular in some city areas).

Motorbikes

You'll be hard pushed to find two-wheeled vehicles above 125cc in the country, as the vast majority of oriental superbikes are exported for use in Europe or America. Despite this, though, a sizeable number of expats still don leather during their Korean stint. One good place to hunt for information or cycle partners is **Yongsan Motorcycle Club**, whose website (Ⓦ roaddragons.com) features a calendar of forthcoming trips and events.

Cycling

There are nowhere near as many **bikes** on the roads of Korea as there are in other Asian countries – so few, in fact, that Korean drivers would rarely think of checking for the presence of a bicycle alongside them. Not that you're much safer away from the street; cars regularly glide along the pavements looking for a place to park, and half of the country's road fatalities are **pedestrians** – an unusually high proportion.

There are, however, a few pleasant areas to cycle along rural roads; particular recommendations are the sparsely populated provinces of **Gangwon** and **Jeju Island**. Rides circumnavigating the latter take three or four days at a steady pace, and are becoming more and more commonplace. Those confined to a city will usually be able to go for a ride on a **riverbank**, with bikes available for hire at the most popular spots; at many such places foreigners are effectively barred from renting cycles, since a Korean ID card is required, though details have been included in this guide where appropriate.

In recent years, **long-distance bike routes** have been laid across the country; it's now possible to cycle much of the way from Seoul to Busan – a trip of up to one week – on dedicated cycle-and-walking paths. Other routes are set to follow – exciting times for Korean cyclists.

Hitching

Foreigners who attempt to cover long distances by **hitching rides** in Korea generally have a hard time of things. Even with your destination on a handwritten sign, and even after having confirmed to the smiling driver where it is that you want to go, you're likely to be dropped at the nearest bus or train station. After all, to Koreans, this is the only sensible way to travel if you don't have a vehicle of your own – hitching is almost unheard of as a money-saving or experiential device. **Short-distance** rides are a different proposition altogether; although the scope of Korea's public transport system means that you'd be very unfortunate to find yourself stuck without a bus or train, it can happen, and in such circumstances hitching a ride can be as easy as flagging down the first car that you see. Of course, accepting lifts with strangers isn't devoid of risk anywhere on Earth, but if you're ever determined to give it a try, there can be few easier and safer places to do it than the Korean countryside.

ONLINE TRAVEL RESOURCES

Incheon International Airport Ⓦ airport.or.kr. Information on flights into and out of Korea's main airport.

Korail Ⓦ letskorail.com. Information on train times and passes, including discounted combined train and ferry tickets to Japan.

Seoul Metropolitan Rapid Transport (SMRT) Ⓦ smrt.co.kr. Timetables, and a useful best-route subway map.

Visit Korea Ⓦ english.visitkorea.co.kr. Good for bus connections between major cities, with cursory information on trains and ferries.

Accommodation

Accommodation is likely to swallow up a large chunk of your travel budget, especially for those who favour Western-style luxuries, but for adventurous travellers there are ways to keep costs to a minimum. Finding a place is less likely to be a problem – Korea has an incredible number of places to stay, and one would be forgiven for thinking that there are actually more beds than there are people in the country. Do note, however, that most of these are on the cheaper side – only a few places around the country have top-drawer hotel facilities.

Luxury hotels can be found in all cities and major tourist areas, as well as a number of specially dedicated tourist hotels, though with space at such a premium, rooms are generally on the small side. At the lower end of the price scale, budget travellers can choose from thousands of motels and guesthouses – many of which have nicer rooms than the dedicated tourist hotels and at far lower prices – or even sleep in a *jjimjilbang* (a Korean sauna; see p.35). At these levels, there's so much

ACCOMMODATION PRICES

The **prices** given for all establishments listed in this guide are for the cheapest twin room, in high season, with all taxes and service charges included.

choice that reservations are almost unheard of. English is spoken to varying degrees in all top hotels, but elsewhere it pays to know a few keywords in Korean (or to have good miming skills).

Hotels

The big **hotel** (호텔) chains have dipped their toes into the Korean market, and there's at least one five-star option in every major city. You're most likely to pay full rack rates in July or August, though high season at national parks and ski resorts will be autumn and winter respectively. Standards are high, by and large, though even at the top end it's hard to find rooms of a decent size.

Korean hotels are split by **class**; from top to bottom, these are super-deluxe, deluxe, first-class, second-class and third-class. Categories are marked by a plaque at the front showing a number of flowers – five for super-deluxe down to one for third-class. Many **tourist hotels** were built as Korea was getting rich in the 1980s, and now offer questionable value; stained carpets, tiny bathrooms and curious smells have become the norm, and few have staff with English language skills. Indeed, some of the most recently built motels offer better rooms, and at much lower prices. Most hotels have "Western" or "Korean" rooms; there are no beds in the latter (the sandwich of blankets on a heated *ondol* floor represents the traditional Korean way to sleep), and prices for both are about the same.

When booking, bear in mind that the 10 percent **tax** levied on hotel rooms is not always factored into the quoted prices; in higher-end establishments, you're also likely to be hit with an additional 10 percent service charge.

Motels

Bearing little resemblance to their American counterparts, **motels** (모텔) are absolutely all over the place – in any urban centre, you should never be more than a walk from the nearest one. Most offer fairly uniform en-suite doubles for W30,000–50,000, and standard facilities include shampoo and shower gel, hairdryers, televisions, a water fountain and free cans of beer, coffee or "vitamin juice".

FIVE QUIRKY PLACES TO STAY

Sun Cruise, Jeongdongjin Ship-shape in a most literal sense, this hotel sits on top of a cliff overlooking the East Sea (p.160).

Rakkojae, Hahoe Folk Village A delightful wooden guesthouse, brooding away in one of Korea's prettiest, quietest villages (p.171).

Jelly Hotel, Seoul One of the country's most famous "love hotels" – take your pick of rooms featuring billiard tables, Persian-style canopies, Cinderella-style furnishings, and more (p.99).

Deungmeoeul, Biyangdo Basically the only inhabited building on this tiny islet, accessible from another tiny islet, which is accessible in turn by ferry from Jeju Island – a great place to get away from it all (p.298).

Jjimjilbang Not a specific place, but a concept: found by the dozen in every city, these bathhouses have communal sleeping rooms in which you can get a night's rest for next to nothing (see box opposite).

Extortion of foreigners is extremely rare, and you shouldn't be afraid to haggle the price down if you're travelling alone, especially outside summer.

Korean motels won't appeal to everybody, as they're generally used as a much-needed source of privacy by young couples (or those who would need to keep their relationship secret). A few would be more honestly described as "love hotels" – pink neon and Cinderella turrets are the most obvious giveaways, while the interior may feature heart-shaped beds, condom machines and more mirrors than you can shake a stick at. That said, the majority of establishments are quite tame, any seaminess is kept behind closed doors, and even for lone women most make acceptable places to stay – indeed, those that can put up with the decor will find them Korea's best-value accommodation option. The motels that have gone up since the turn of the century, in particular, often have cleaner rooms than the average tourist hotel, typically featuring huge flatscreen TVs and internet-ready computer terminals.

Guesthouses

Yeogwan (여관) are older, smaller, less polished versions of motels. Slightly cheaper, but often a little grubby, they once formed the backbone of Korea's budget travel accommodation, and can still be found in teams around bus and train stations. With whole streets full of them, it's easy to hunt around for the best deal – a double room usually costs W20,000–35,000, though prices are higher in Seoul, and tend to rise in high season. Single rooms do not exist, but almost all have en-suite bathrooms.

Minbak rooms (민박) are usually rented-out parts of a residential property, and are less likely to have private bathrooms. These are most commonly found on islands and by popular beaches or national parks,

and though the prices are comparable to *yeogwan* rates for much of the year they can quadruple if there's enough demand – summer is peak season for the beaches and islands, spring and autumn for the national parks.

Even cheaper rooms can be found at a **yeoinsuk** (여인숙) – around W15,000 per night. Slowly disappearing, these are a noisier, more spartan variation of the *yeogwan*, invariably found in older areas of town, with rooms containing nothing more than a couple of blankets, a television and a heated linoleum *ondol* floor to sleep on. Such wipe-clean minimalism generally makes for clean rooms, though some have a cockroach problem, and the communal toilets and showers can be quite off-putting; in addition, some of them are used by prostitutes and their clients.

Hostels

Hostels (호스텔) in Korea come in two distinct varieties: official and independent. The official hostels are created for, and primarily used by, the nation's youth, with the resultant atmosphere more boarding school than bohemian – none have been listed in this guide. The **independent hostels** will be much more familiar to international backpackers, and have really taken off of late – every major city now has one, and Seoul an almost countless number. However, they're not always great value: with W20,000 now normal for a dorm bed, you'd almost always be able to score a private motel room for a few dollars more, often in a far more convenient location. Many hostels also offer **private rooms**, though at W50,000–60,000, they're double the aforementioned motel prices. Still, if you're keen to socialize with other travellers, hostels remain a great way to go, and they're becoming ever more numerous.

STAYING AT A JJIMJILBANG

For travellers willing to take the plunge and bare all in front of curious strangers, sauna establishments (known locally as **jjimjilbang**; 찜질방) are some of the cheapest and most uniquely Korean places in which to get a night's sleep. Almost entirely devoid of the seedy reputations that may dog similar facilities abroad, *jjimjilbang* are large, round-the-clock venues primarily used by families escaping their homes for the night, businessmen who've worked or partied beyond their last trains, or teenage groups having a safe night out together. They can be found in any Korean city, typically costing W5000–8000, and consist of a shower and pool area, a sauna or steam room, and a large playschool-style quiet room or two for communal napping; most also have snack bars and internet terminals. Upon entry, guests are given a locker key for their shoes, another for their clothing, and matching T-shirts and shorts to change into – outside clothes are not allowed to be worn inside the complex, though it's OK to wear underwear beneath your robe. All must be sacrificed on entry to the pools, which are segregated by gender. The common rooms are uniformly clean but vary in style; some have TVs and hi-tech recliner chairs, others invite you to roll out a mini-mattress, but all will have a floorful of snoring Koreans – not the quietest night's sleep you'll ever have, but a wonderfully local experience.

Camping and mountain huts

Most national parks have at least one **campsite** to cater for the swarms of Korean hikers who spend their weekends in the mountains. Most are free, but those that charge (typically under W5000) have excellent toilet and shower facilities. Jirisan and Seoraksan, two of the largest parks, have well-signposted **shelters** or **huts** dotted around the hiking trails; these cost under W8000 per person, though they may only open from summer until autumn, and you're advised to book ahead – check the national park website (Ⓦ english.knps.or.kr). At both campsites and shelters, drinking water should always be available, and though simple snacks may also be on offer, it's best to bring your own food.

Templestays and hanok guesthouses

If you're looking for a more traditional experience, you could try staying at a **temple**. Though temples with sufficient room are pretty much obliged to take in needy travellers for the night, many offer interesting, prearranged **templestay programmes** for around W50,000 per night, some with the capacity for English-language translation (see Ⓦ eng.templestay.com for more details). A stay generally involves meditation, grounds-sweeping, a tea ceremony and a meal or two, but be prepared for spartan sleeping arrangements and a pre-dawn wake-up call.

If you're after something traditional but without the routine, try hunting down a **hanok**. These are traditional Korean buildings, replete with wooden frames, sliding doors and a woodfired underfloor heating system. Few such buildings cater for travellers, though some can be found at the traditional villages scattered around the country (Hahoe near Andong is the best; see p.171), and there are dedicated districts in Seoul (see box, p.68) and Jeonju (see p.244). Many include tea ceremonies and other activities such as *kimchi*-making in the cost.

ONLINE ACCOMMODATION RESOURCES

Ⓦ **asiarooms.com** An excellent discount site with interesting reviews of the hotel rooms on offer.

Ⓦ **eng.templestay.com** Information on the various templestay programmes around the country.

Ⓦ **english.knps.or.kr** Korea National Park Service site detailing available shelters.

Ⓦ **hostelworld.com** Good listings of Seoul's budget accommodation, and a few more choices from around the country.

Ⓦ **khrc.com** Website for the Korea Hotel Reservation Centre, worth a look for occasional special deals.

Ⓦ **stay.visitseoul.net** City-sponsored site featuring a range of cheap accommodation in Seoul, all at places deemed suitable for foreigners.

Ⓦ **trivago.com** User-friendly site that compares quotes from all the major hotel booking engines, and directs you to the cheapest.

Food and drink

Korean cuisine deserves greater international attention. A thrillingly spicy mishmash of simple but invariably healthy ingredients, it's prepared with consummate attention, then doled out in hearty portions at more restaurants than you could possibly count – even if

every single person in the country suddenly decided to go out for dinner simultaneously, there would probably still be some free tables. Most are open from early morning until late at night, and a full 24 hours a day in many cases. You can usually find a restaurant to suit your budget, and there will always be an affordable option close by, a fact attested to by the great number of foreigners that live here quite happily for weeks, months or even years on end without doing a single bit of cooking for themselves.

The traditional Korean **restaurant** is filled with low tables; diners are required to remove their footwear and sit on floor cushions. There are a number of rules of restaurant **etiquette** (see p.47) but a substantial amount of custom also surrounds the food itself; while what often appears to be a culinary free-for-all can draw gasps from foreign observers (eat the meal; boil off the soup; throw in some rice to fry up with the scraps; add some noodles), Korea's great on conformity, and you may well provoke chuckles of derision by performing actions that you deem quite sensible – it's best just to follow the Korean lead.

Korean eating establishments are hard to pigeon-hole. The lines between bar, restaurant, snack shop and even home are often blurry to say the least, and some places cover all bases: in provincial towns, you may well see children snoozing under empty tables.

Restaurant meals usually consist of communal servings of **meat** or **fish** around which are placed a bewildering assortment of **side dishes** (banchan; 반찬). Often, these are the best part of the meal – a range of fish, meat, vegetables and steamed egg broth, they're included in the price of the meal, and there may be as many as twenty of them on the table; when your favourite is finished, waitresses will scoot around with a free refill.

One common problem for visitors is the **spice** level of the food, an issue that has given Korea one of the world's highest rates of stomach cancer. It's not so much the spiciness of the individual dishes that causes problems (British travellers trained on curry, for example, rarely have any problems adjusting to Korean spice) as the fact that there's little respite from it – red pepper paste (gochujang; 고추장) is a component of almost every meal. Another common complaint by foreign visitors is the lack of attention paid to **vegetarians**, as such folk are extremely rare in Korea. Despite the high vegetable content of many meals, almost all have at least a little meat, and very few are cooked in meat-free environments. Most resort to asking for bibimbap without the meat, eating ramyeon (라면; instant noodles), or poking the bits of ham out of gimbap with a chopstick.

Many dishes are for **sharing**, a fantastic arrange-ment that fosters togetherness and increases mealtime variety, though this has adverse impli-cations for single travellers – Koreans don't like to eat alone, and are likely to fret about those who do. One other point worth mentioning is the incredible number of foodstuffs that are claimed to be "good for **sexual stamina**"; at times it feels as if food is an augmenter of male potency first, and a necessary means of sustenance second. Raw fish and dog meat, in particular, are said to be good for this.

KIMCHI

No country on Earth is as closely entwined with its national dish as Korea is with its beloved **kimchi**: a spicy mix of fermented vegetables, which is served as a complimentary **side dish** at pretty much every restaurant in the land. Many traditionally minded families still ferment their own in distinctive earthenware jars, but home-made or not it's an important part of breakfast, lunch and dinner in most Korean homes. Lots of families even have a dedicated kimchi fridge, quartered off to separate the four main types. The two most common varieties are **baechu kimchi**, made with cabbage, and **ggakdugi kimchi**, which are cubes of radish in a red-pepper sauce, but there are others made with cucumber or other vegetables.

Salt, garlic and a hearty dollop of **red-pepper paste** are almost mandatory in a good kimchi, though additional ingredients vary from home to home and restaurant to restaurant. Many of the best recipes are shrouded in secrecy and handed down through the generations, but some of the most popular components include onion, brine, ginger and fish paste. The effect on the breath can be dramatic, to say the least, but there are few better ways to endear yourself to the locals than by chowing down on a bowlful of kimchi.

Rice dishes

Many meals involve **rice** in various forms: one that proves a hit with many foreigners is **bibimbap**, a mixture of shoots, leaves and vegetables on a bed of rice, flecked with meat, then topped with an egg and spicy *gochujang* pepper sauce. *Bibimbap* was originally a religious dish derived from the five principal colours of Korean Buddhism – red for the paste, yellow for the egg yolk, white for the rice, blue for the meat and green for the vegetables – and is one of the easiest dishes to find in Korea. It can cost as little as W4000, though there are sometimes a few varieties to choose from. Some restaurants serve it in a heated stone bowl (*dolsot bibimbap*; 돌솥 비빔밥); those in the countryside may make it using only vegetables sourced from the surrounding mountains (*sanchae bibimbap*; 산채 비빔밥); and certain establishments in Jeonju have elevated the dish to an art form, serving it with a whole witch's cauldron of fascinating ingredients – including pine kernels, fern bracken and slices of jujube – and up to a dozen individual side dishes.

Other dishes to be served on a bed of rice include beef (*bulgogi deop-bap*; 불고기덮밥), highly spicy squid (*ojingeo deop-bap*; 오징어덮밥) or *donkasseu* (돈까스), a breaded pork cutlet dish imported from Japan that's particularly popular with those who want to avoid spice. Also fulfilling this need are rolls of **gimbap** (김밥): *gim* means laver seaweed, *bap* means rice, the former is rolled around the latter, which itself surrounds strips of egg, ham and pickled radish; the resulting tube is then cut into segments with a sharp knife to make the dish chopstick-friendly. The regular ones are filling and only cost W1500, but for a little more you'll usually have a variety of fillings to choose from, including tuna (*chamchi*; 참치), minced beef (*sogogi*; 소고기), processed cheese (*chi-jeu*; 치즈) and *kimchi*.

Noodle dishes

Noodles are used as a base in many dishes, and can be extremely cheap – a bowl of **ramyeon** (라면) can go for just W3000. This is a block of instant noodles boiled up in a spicy red-pepper soup, and usually mixed in with an egg and some onion. For a little more you can have dumplings (*mandu*; 만두), rice cake (*ddeok*; 떡) or processed cheese thrown in. Those travelling in the sticky Korean summer will find it hard to throw back a bowl of hot, spicy soup; a better choice may be **naengmyeon** (냉면), bowls of grey buckwheat noodles served with a boiled egg and vegetable slices in a spicy paste or an ice-cold spicy soup; it'll set you back around W5000, though more like double that at the best establishments.

Soups and broths

The names of **soup** dishes usually end with -*tang* (탕) or -*guk* (국), though special mention must be made of the spicy **jjigae** broths (찌개). These are bargain meals that cost W4500 and up, and come with rice and a range of vegetable side dishes; the red-pepper broth contains chopped-up vegetables, as well as a choice of tofu (*sundubu*; 순두부), tuna, soybean paste (*doenjang*; 된장) or *kimchi*.

Barbecued meat

Barbecued meat is one of Korea's signature foods, and a whole lot of fun – for carnivores, at least. Here, you get to play chef with a plate of raw meat commonly placed on a grill over charcoal, and a pair of scissors to slice it all up. As excess fat drips off the meat onto the briquettes it releases the occasional tongue of flame, which lends a genuine air of excitement to the meal. Two of the most popular meat dishes are *galbi* and *samgyeopsal*, which are almost always cooked by the diners

---

TOP 10 DINING SPOTS
Balwoo Buddhist temple food, Seoul (p.101).
Korea House Royal banquets, Seoul (p.102).
Bukcheong Sundae Noodle sausages and a ferry trip, Sokcho (p.149).
Dosol Maeul Pancakes and rice beer in a traditional wooden abode, Gyeongju (p.186).
Jagalchi fish market Busan (p.206).
Hwangsolchon Some of Korea's best barbecued meat, Gwangju (p.240).
Gomanaru Feasts of flowers and leaves, Gongju (p.266).
Daecheon beach The best place in Korea for a shellfish barbecue (p.271).
Haechon Eat cutlassfish *bibimbap* with a prime view of Sunrise Peak, Seongsan (p.296).
North Korea Anywhere and anything, for sheer excitement value (p.334).

FAST-FOOD CHAINS

Such is the pace at which Koreans live their lives that many find it impossible to spare time for a leisurely meal, so it should come as no surprise that their city streets are packed with **fast-food outlets**. Korean fast food is something of a misnomer: fast it may well be, but in general the local offerings are far healthier than their Western equivalents – you could eat them every day and never get fat. One slight problem for travellers is that few of these cheap places are used to dealing with foreigners, so don't expect English-language menus or service; you'll find a menu reader on p.378. Below is a selection of the outlets you're most likely to come across in cities across the nation.

Gimbap Cheonguk (김밥천국) In Korean street-space terms, this ubiquitous orange-fronted franchise is rivalled only by internet bars and the more prominent convenience store chains. The concept is pretty miraculous – almost all basic Korean meals are served here for around W5000 per dish, and despite the variety on offer you'll usually be eating within minutes of sitting down. They also sell *gimbap* from W1500, and these can be made to go: perfect if you're off on a hike.

Isaac Toast (이삭토스트) Toast, but not as you know it. The Korean variety is made on a huge hotplate – first your perfectly square bread will be fried and smeared with kiwi jam, then joined by perfect squares of spam and/or fried egg (or even a burger, for those to whom the word "cholesterol" means nothing), and the whole lot injected with two sauces, one spicy and one brown. No, it's not healthy, but it makes a tasty breakfast; prices start at around W2000.

Jaws (죠스) This chain has been a gigantic hit of late, selling rounds of street-eats *twigim* (see opposite) and *ddeokbokki* (see below) for less than the street stands, and at a much higher level of quality. W2500 will be enough for a plate of crispy *twigim*; ask to have it smothered with spicy *ddeokbokki* sauce.

Kim Ga Ne (김家네) A slightly more upmarket version of *Gimbap Cheonguk* (see above), serving more or less the same things with a few snazzy "fusion" additions. Most branches have their menu on the walls in pictorial form, handy if you don't speak Korean. Dishes W4000–8000.

Paris Baguette (파리바게뜨) & **Tous Les Jours** (뚜레쥬르) A pair of near-identical bakery chains, whose offerings may satisfy if you need a breakfast devoid of spice or rice; many branches are also able to whip up a passable coffee. Baked goods start at around W1500, but note that even the savoury-looking ones are usually extremely sugary. You'll find branches all over the place; harder to spot is *Paris Croissant*, a slightly more upmarket version.

Yu Ga Ne (유가네) This chain serves tasty barbecued meat, cooked at your table by an apron-wearing attendant. Unlike most barbecue joints, there are dishes for those dining alone, such as the delectable *dak-galbi beokkeumbap*, which is something like a chicken kebab fried up with rice. W10,000 should be enough to get a bellyful.

themselves in the centre of the table. **Galbi** is rib-meat, most often beef (*so-galbi*; 소갈비) but sometimes pork (*dwaeji-galbi*; 돼지갈비). **Samgyeopsal** (삼겹살) consists of strips of rather fatty pork belly. Prices vary but figure on around W13,000 per portion for beef and a little less for pork; a minimum of two diners is usually required.

In dedicated *galbi* restaurants the dish is usually eaten sitting on the floor, but many cheaper places have outdoor tables. In all cases, you'll be served free (and replenishable) side dishes, which may include pulses, tofu, leek, potato and tiny fish. A boiling bowl of egg broth and a tray of leaves are also usually thrown in for the group to share – barbecued meat is not a meal to eat on your own – and each person is given a bowl of chopped-up greens and a pot of salted sesame oil.

In Confucian Korea, it's common for the "lowest" adult member of the party – usually the youngest female – to cook and dish out the meat. To eat it, first place a leaf or two from the tray onto your left hand, then with your chopsticks add a piece of meat, and a smudge of soybean paste; roll the leaf around to make a ball, and you're ready to go. Lastly, meat is traditionally washed down with a bottle or three of *soju* – Korea's answer to vodka (see p.40).

Snack food

Though the most common variety of Korean **snack food** is *gimbap* there are many more options available. One is a dish called **ddeokbokki** (떡볶이), a mix of rice cake and processed fish boiled up in a highly spicy red-pepper sauce; this typically costs around W2000 per portion, and is

ROYAL CUISINE

Being such an important part of daily Korean life, it's inevitable that food should wend its way into traditional events. The hundredth day of a child's life is marked with a feast of colourful rice cake, while a simpler variety is served in a soup (*ddeokguk*) to celebrate Lunar New Year. More interesting by far, however, is **royal court cuisine**: a remnant of the Joseon dynasty, which ruled over the Korean peninsula from 1392 to 1910, this was once served to Korean rulers and associated nobility. The exact ingredients and styles vary and go by several different names, but usually rice, soup and a charcoal-fired casserole form the centre of the banquets, and are then surrounded by an array of perfectly prepared dishes; twelve was once the royal number of dishes and banned to the peasant class, but now anyone can indulge as long as they have the money. The aim of the combination is to harmonize culinary opposites such as spicy and mild, solid and liquid, rough and smooth; a balance of colour and texture is thereby achieved – the Yin–Yang principle in edible form.

Some of the best places to try this kind of food are *Korea House* (see p.102) and *Balwoo* in Seoul (see p.101).

doled out in bowls by street vendors and small roadside booths. The same places usually serve **twigim** (튀김), which are flash-fried pieces of squid, potato, seaweed-covered noodle-roll or stuffed chilli pepper, to name but a few ingredients. The price varies but is usually around W3000 for six pieces – choose from the display, and they'll be refried in front of you. You can have the resulting dish smothered in *ddeokbokki* sauce for no extra charge – delicious.

Convenience stores are usually good places to grab some food, as all sell sandwiches, rolls and triangles of *gimbap*, and instant noodles; boiling water will always be available for the latter, as well as a bench or table to eat it from, an activity that will mark you as an honorary Korean. A less appealing practice, but one that will endear you to Koreans more than anything else can, is the eating of **beonddegi** (번데기) – boiled silkworm larvae.

Desserts

You'll find **ice cream** in any convenience store, where prices can be as low as W500; if you want to keep your selection as Korean as possible, go for green tea, melon, or red-bean-paste flavours. An even more distinctively local variety, available from specialist snack bars, is *patbingsu* (팥빙수), a strange concoction of fruit, cream, shaved ice and red-bean paste – most Korean meals are for sharing, so it's inevitable that a dessert made for sharing is super-popular around the land. Also keep an eye out in colder months for a **hoddeok** (호떡) stand – these press out little fried pancakes of rice-mix filled with brown sugar and cinnamon for just W1000 per piece, and are extremely popular with foreigners.

Seafood, markets and mountain food

Some Korean eating places exude an essence little changed for decades. Raw fish stalls around the coast, city-centre marketplaces and mountain restaurants are your best options for that traditional feeling.

Korean **seafood** is a bit of a maze for most foreigners, and much more expensive than other meals, though it's worth persevering. Some is served raw, while other dishes are boiled up in a spicy soup. Jagalchi market in Busan deserves a special mention (see p.206), but in small coastal villages – particularly on the islands of the West and South seas – there's little other industry to speak of; battered fishing flotillas yo-yo in and out with the tide, and you may be able to buy fish literally straight off the boat. This may seem as fresh as seafood can possibly be, but baby octopus is often served live (*sannakji*; 산낙지), its severed tentacles still squirming as they head down your throat. Be warned: several people die each year when their prey decides to make a last futile stab at survival with its suckers, so you may wish to wait until it has stopped moving, or at least kill the nerves with a few powerful bites. A far simpler choice is *hoe deop-bap* (회덮밥), a widely available dish similar to *bibimbap*, but with sliced raw fish in place of egg and meat. A halfway house in excitement terms is *jogae-gui* (조개구이), a shellfish barbecue – the unfortunate creatures are grilled in front of you, and W35,000 will buy enough of them to fill two people.

Korean **markets** offer similar opportunities for culinary exploration. Here you're also likely to spot seafood on sale, along with fruits, vegetables, grilled or boiled meats and an assortment of snacks. Many

DOG MEAT

Korea's consumption of **dog meat** (*gae-gogi*; 개고기) became global knowledge when the country hosted the 1988 Olympics, at which time the government kowtowed to Western mores and attempted to sweep the issue under the carpet.

Today, eating dog meat amounts to a shameful national secret. Foreigners looking for it on the menu or in their hamburgers are likely to be relieved, as it's almost nowhere to be seen. Should the issue be raised, even with a Korean you know well, they'll probably laugh and tell you that they don't eat dog, and that the practice only takes place behind closed doors, if at all.

That said, and though it's true that few young people consume dog, the soup *yeongyangtang*, for one, is still popular with older Koreans due to its purported health-giving properties, and can be hunted down in specialist restaurants.

Any fears of Koreans chowing down on an Alsatian or Border Collie should be quelled; almost all dog meat comes from a scraggly mongrel breed colloquially known as the *ddong-gae* (똥개), or "shit-dog", an animal named for its tendency to eat whatever it finds on the floor. Even so, the poor conditions that the animals are often kept in, and the continuing – and occasionally verified – stories of dogs being clubbed to death to tenderize the meat, are good reasons to avoid this kind of meal. For those who wish to know, it's a slightly stringy meat somewhere between duck and beef in texture, and is generally agreed to taste better than it smells.

options have been detailed under "Snack food" (see p.38), but one favourite almost unique to the market is *sundae* (순대), a kind of sausage made with intestinal lining and noodles (see box, p.100). Sokcho on the Gangwon coast is the best place to sample this (see p.149).

Korea's wonderful **national parks** feature some splendid eating opportunities located around the main entrances. One of the most popular hiker dishes is *sanchae bibimbap* (산채 비빔밥), a variety of the Korean staple made with roots, shoots and vegetables from the surrounding countryside – knowing that everything is sourced locally somehow makes the dish taste better. Most popular, though, are *pajeon* (파전); locals may refer to these as "Korean pizza", but they're more similar to a savoury pancake. They usually contain strips of spring onion and seafood (*haemul*; 해물) *pajeon*, though other varieties are available; it's usually washed down with a bowl or three of *dongdongju*, a milky rice wine.

International cuisine

While many visitors fall head over heels for Korean food, it's not to everybody's taste, and after a while the near-permanent spicy tang of red-pepper paste can wear down even the most tolerant taste buds. One problem concerns **breakfast**, which, to most Koreans, is simply another time window for the intake of *kimchi* and rice. This is too heavy for many Westerners, but though a fry-up or smörgåsbord will be hard to find outside the major hotels, you may find some solace in the buns, cakes and pastries of major bakery chains such as *Tous Les Jours* and *Paris*

Baguette (see box, p.38), or the mayonnaise-heavy sandwiches of the convenience stores.

International food is getting easier to come by in Korea, though only Seoul can be said to have a truly cosmopolitan range. **American-style fast food**, however, can be found pretty much everywhere – *McDonald's* and *Burger King* are joined by *Lotteria*, a local chain, and there are also a great number of fried-chicken joints scattered around. Traditional **Japanese food** has made serious inroads into the Korean scene, and the obligatory red lanterns of *izakaya*-style bar-restaurants are especially easy to spot in student areas. **Italian food** has long been popular with Koreans, who have added their own twists to pizzas and pasta – almost every single meal will be served with a small tub of pickled gherkin, an addition that locals assume to be de rigueur in the restaurants of Napoli or Palermo. **Chinese restaurants** are equally numerous, though unfortunately they're no more authentic than their counterparts in Western countries, even in the many cases where the restaurateurs themselves are Chinese. One recommendation, however, is *beokkeumbap* – fried rice mixed with cubes of ham and vegetable, topped with a fried egg and black bean sauce, and served with deliciously spicy seafood broth; the whole thing will cost about W5000, and is, therefore, a great way to fill up on the cheap.

Drink

A sweet potato wine named **soju** (소주) is the national drink – a cheap, clear Korean version of vodka that you'll either love or hate (or love, then hate the next morning) – but there's a pleasing variety of grog to choose from. The country also has a wealth of excellent tea on offer, though coffee is increasingly winning the urban caffeine battles.

Bars and hofs

Though the imbibing of *soju* is de rigueur at restaurants of an evening, most people do their serious drinking in bars and "*hofs*". There are a quite incredible number of both in the cities, though the majority can be surprisingly empty, even at weekends – you may wonder how most of them stay in business. **Hofs**, pronounced more like "hop" (호프), are bright, booth-filled places serving **beer** (*maekju*; 맥주) by the bucketload. The main beers are Cass, OB and Hite; prices are more or less the same for each, starting at about W2500 for a 500cc glass. Quite fascinating are the three- or five-litre plastic jugs of draught beer (*saeng-maekju*; 생맥주), which often come billowing dry ice and illuminated with flashing lights. The downside of such places is that customers are pretty much obliged to eat as

well as drink; you'll be given free snacks, but customers are expected to order something from the menu.

Bars are almost invariably dark, neon-strewn dens; unlike in *hofs*, customers are not usually expected to eat and tend to take roost in an extensive cocktail menu; beer will still be available, in draught or bottled form. Each city has one or more main "going-out" district, with the most raucous to be found outside the rear entrances of the **universities** (which maintain a veneer of respectability by keeping their main entrances free of such revelry). Most cities have at least one resident **expat bar**; these are usually the best places for foreigners to meet fellow *waeguk-in* (foreigners) or new Korean friends. Often surrounded with tables and chairs for customer use, convenience stores are equally great places to meet new mates, and actually the best hunting grounds for local drinks. They also sell bottles of foreign **wine** for W7000 and up, though special mention must be made of a local variety named Jinro House Wine: this curiously pink liquid, which may or may not be derived from grapes, costs

GET DRUNK THE LOCAL WAY

Though Koreans largely favour beer and imported drinks, the country has more than a few superb **local hooches**, many of which go down very well indeed with the few foreigners lucky enough to learn about them.

Baekseju (백세주) A nutty, whisky-coloured concoction, about the same strength as wine. Its name means "one-hundred-year alcohol", on account of healthy ingredients including ginseng and medicinal herbs. Surely the tastiest path towards becoming a centenarian, *baekseju* is available at all convenience stores (W4500) and many barbecue houses (W7000 or so).

Bokbunjaju (복분자주) Made with black raspberries, this sweet, fruity drink is somewhat similar to sugary, low-grade port. It's available at all convenience stores (W6500), though those off on a mountain late in late summer may be lucky enough to try some freshly made: it's sold by farmers at makeshift stalls.

Dongdongju (동동주) Very similar to *makgeolli* (see p.42), *dongdongju* is a little heavier taste-wise, and since it can only be served fresh you'll have to head to a specialist place for a try. The restaurants most likely to have *dongdongju* are those also serving savoury pancakes known as *pajeon*; these establishments are usually rustic affairs decked out with Korean bric-a-brac, and serving *dongdongju* in large bowls (W8000). A word of warning: many foreigners have "hit the wall" on their first dabble, suddenly finding themselves floored by this deceptively quaffable drink.

Maehwasu (매화수) Similar to *baekseju* in colour, strength and price, this is made with the blossom of the *maesil*, a type of Korean plum, and some bottles come with said fruit steeping inside.

Makgeolli (막걸리) Milky rice beer that's usually around 6 percent alcohol by volume (see box, p.42).

Soju (소주) The national drink, for better or worse. Locals are fond of referring to it as "Korean vodka", but it's only half the strength – a good thing too, as it's usually fired down in staccato shots, preferably over barbecued meat. It's traditionally made with sweet potato, but these days most companies use cheap chemical concoctions: the resultant taste puts many foreigners off, but some find themselves near-addicted within days of arrival. Expect to pay W1300 from a convenience store, W3000 at a restaurant.

about W2000 per bottle and can only be described as "comedy wine" as it tends to give people the giggles.

The local drinking scene has recently been shaken up by sudden increases in demand for two particular alcoholic drinks. First of all came the **makgeolli** craze: for decades young Koreans pooh-poohed this delicious rice beer (see box below), but it has been given a new lease of life, and is now sold at mini-markets and convenience stores across the country; Seoul even has a bunch of chic bar-restaurants dedicated to the stuff. More recently, the "regular" beer scene has been stirred by the arrival of **smaller-scale breweries**; though the ripples are still slowly emanating from Seoul's Itaewon district, a whole generation of Koreans is now experiencing craft ale for the first time.

Tea and coffee

Tea is big business in Korea. Unfortunately, most of the drinking takes place at home or work, though Insadong in Seoul has dozens of interesting tearooms (see p.105), and there are some gems outside national parks and in Jeonju's *hanok* district (see p.248). Green tea is by far the most popular, though if you find your way to a specialist tearoom,

---

KOREAN TEA VARIETIES

Daechu-cha 대추차 Jujube tea
Gukhwa-cha 국"차 Chrysanthemum tea
Gyepi-cha 계피차 Cinnamon tea
Ggulsam cha 꿀삼차 Honey ginseng tea
Insam-cha 인삼차 Ginseng tea
Ma-cha 마차 Wild herb tea
Maesil-cha 매실차 Plum tea
Nok-cha 녹차 Green tea
Omija-cha 오미자차 Five Flavours tea
Saenggang-cha 생∞차 Ginger tea
Yak-cha 약차 Medicinal herb tea
Yuja-cha 유자차 Citron tea
Yulmu-cha 율무차 "Job's Tears" tea

---

do take the opportunity to try something more special (see the box above for suggestions).

Korea is now a bona fide coffee nation. **Café culture** has found its way into the lives of Korean youth, and even in smaller towns you shouldn't have to look too far to find somewhere to sate your caffeine cravings. In addition to coffee, modern cafés usually serve delicious **green tea latte**, with some of the more adventurous throwing in ginseng or sweet potato varieties for good measure. Though

---

MAKGEOLLI

The milky-coloured rice beer known as **makgeolli** (막걸리) has become increasingly hip in recent years. It's somewhat similar to real ale, in that the drink is still "living" when you drink it – the best will last no longer than a week, even while refrigerated. The following are just some of the varieties available around the country:

Sobaeksan Geomeunkong (소백산 검은콩) Made in Danyang (see p.277), this creamy number is the best of Korea's many black-bean *makgeolli* brands.

Baedari (배다리) Pleasantly sour brew from Ilsan (a satellite city west of Seoul), and a one-time favourite of ex-dictator Park Chung-hee – it was once delivered in caseloads to the Blue House (see p.68).

Busan Geumjeongsan (부산 금정산) Too sour for some, invigoratingly so and slightly appley to others, this hails from Busan but is actually easier to hunt down in the *mak*-bars of Seoul (see p.106).

Jeju Makgeolli (제주 막걸리) Jeju Island (see p.282) has some cloyingly disgusting varieties, but this pink-labelled one, made with "friendly" bacteria, is a real winner.

Boeun Daechu (보은 대추) You'll have to be in the Songnisan mountains (see p.275) to have any chance of finding this delicious *makgeolli*, made with local jujube dates.

Gongju Albam (공주 알밤) Found all over Gongju (see p.262), and even Seoul these days, this chestnut *makgeolli* is a good one for beginners to sample.

Jangsu (장수) Purists scoff at this sweet, fizzy brand, which has cornered much of the Seoul market, but the truth is that it's still pretty tasty – not to mention very easy to find in the capital's convenience stores.

Hongsam Jujo (홍삼 주조) One of the most notable of Jeonju's many brands (see box, p.250), and made with red ginseng.

Jipyeong (지평) A fresh-tasting, easy-to-quaff brand, which has since 1925 been made in Jipyeong – a village east of Seoul – in a giant *hanok* (traditional wooden house).

Dosan (도산) Smooth brew that's only really available in Tongyeong (see p.210) – grab a bottle and drink it outside, next to the town's cute little harbour.

certainly not for purists, worth mentioning are the cans and cartons of coffee on sale in convenience stores, and the three-in-one instant mixes that pop up all over the place, including most motel rooms.

The media

Korean media has come a long way since bursting out of the dictatorial straitjacket of the 1970s and 1980s, but most of it is only accessible to those fluent in Korean.

Newspapers, magazines and the web

The two big English-language **newspapers** are the *Korea Times* (Ⓦkoreatimes.co.kr) and *Korea Herald* (Ⓦkoreaherald.com), near-identical dailies with near-identical addictions to news agency output and dull business statistics. That said, both have decent listings sections in their weekend editions, which detail events around the country, as well as the goings-on in Seoul's restaurant, film and club scenes. For Korean news translated into English, try the websites of *Yonhap News* (Ⓦenglish.yonhapnews.co.kr), or *Dong-a Ilbo* (Ⓦenglish.donga.com); the *Chosun Ilbo* (Ⓦenglish.chosun.com) has a translated version too, but it's rather conservative in nature.

The *International Herald Tribune* is pretty easy to track down in top hotels, with copies containing the eight-page *Joongang Daily* (Ⓦkoreajoongangdaily.joins.com), an interesting local news supplement. You should also be able to hunt down the previous week's *Time* or *Economist* in most Korean cities – try the larger bookstores, or the book section of a large department store. Lastly, Seoul has its own clutch of useful websites and magazines (see p.317), some of which also cover destinations elsewhere in Korea.

Television

Korean **television** is a gaudy feast of madcap game shows and soppy period dramas, and there are few more accessible windows into the true nature of local society. **Arirang** (Ⓦarirang.co.kr) is a 24hr English-language television network based in Seoul, which promotes the country with occasionally interesting (but often propaganda-like) documentaries, and has regular news bulletins. Arirang TV is free-to-air throughout much of the world, and though not free in Korea itself, it comes as part of most cable packages.

Festivals

On even a short trip around the country you're more than likely to stumble across a special event of some sort. Many are religious in nature, with Buddhist celebrations supplemented by Confucian and even animist events. Most festivals are concentrated around spring and autumn, but there are many spread throughout the year. If you're heading to one, don't be shy – the locals love to see foreigners joining in with traditional Korean events, and those who dare to get stuck in may finish the day with a whole troupe of new friends.

Though there are some crackers on the calendar, it must be said that a fair number of **Korean festivals** are brazenly commercial, making no bones about being held to "promote the salted seafood industry", for example. Other festivals can be rather odd, including those dedicated to agricultural utensils, clean peppers and the "Joy of Rolled Laver" – you'll easily be able to spot the duds. The most interesting events are highlighted below, though bear in mind that celebrations for two of the big national festivals – **Seollal**, the Lunar New Year, and a Korean version of Thanksgiving named **Chuseok** – are family affairs that generally take place behind closed doors. There are also festivals specific to Seoul (see box, p.110) and Busan (see box, p.206).

APRIL–JUNE

Cherry blossom festivals Usually early April. Heralding the arrival of spring, soft blossom wafts through the air across the country, a cue for all good Koreans to lay down blankets at parks or riverbanks, barbecue some meat and throw back the *soju*.

Jeonju International Film Festival Ⓦjiff.or.kr. Last week of April. Smaller and more underground than the biggie in Busan, JIFF focuses on the arty, independent side of the movie industry (see p.244).

Buddha's Birthday Late May. A public holiday during which temples across the land are adorned with colourful paper lanterns; there's an even more vibrant night parade in Seoul.

International Mime Festival Ⓦmimefestival.com. May. Held in the Gangwonese capital of Chuncheon, this foreigner-friendly event is a showcase of soundless talent (see p.141).

Dano Usually June. A shamanist festival held on the fifth day of the fifth lunar month, featuring circus acts, *ssireum* wrestling, mask dramas and a whole lot more. The city of Gangneung (see p.153) is host to the biggest displays.

JULY–AUGUST

Boryeong Mud Festival Ⓦmudfestival.or.kr. Late July. This annual expat favourite pulls mud-happy hordes to Daecheon beach (see p.269) for all kinds of muck-related fun.

International Puppet Festival Aug. Puppets and their masters come from around the world to flaunt their skills in Chuncheon (see p.140), a city in Gangwon province.

Firefly Festival Aug. Glow worms are the tiny stars of the show at this modest night-time event, which takes place over a weekend near Muju (see p.251). One unexpected treat is the chance to don a firefly costume.

SEPTEMBER–NOVEMBER

Gwangju Biennale ⓦ gwangjubiennale.org. Sept–Nov. A wide-ranging, two-month-long festival of contemporary art, the biennale usually takes place on alternate autumns, though it has also been held in spring.

Andong Mask Dance Festival ⓦ maskdance.com. Late Sept or early Oct. Legend has it that if a person fails to attend a mask festival in their lifetime, they cannot get into heaven, so if you're in Korea in the autumn you might as well have a crack at salvation by participating in one of the country's most popular events – a week of anonymous dancing, performed by the best troupes in the land (see p.171).

Pusan International Film Festival ⓦ piff.org. Usually Oct. One of Asia's biggest such events, PIFF draws in big-shots and hangers-on for a week of cinematic fun (see p.201).

Baekje Festival ⓦ baekje.org. Early Oct. This annual event commemorating the Baekje dynasty is held each year in the old Baekje capitals of Gongju (see p.262) and Buyeo (see p.267).

Kimchi Festival Late Oct. In Gwangju. You'll be able to see, smell and taste dozens of varieties of the spicy stuff, and there's even a *kimchi*-making contest for foreigners keen to show off.

Pepero Day Nov 11. A crass marketing ploy, but amusing nonetheless – like Pocky, their Japanese cousins, Pepero are thin sticks of chocolate-coated biscuit, and on the date when it looks as if four of them are standing together, millions of Koreans say "I love you" by giving a box to their sweethearts, friends, parents or pets.

Sports and outdoor activities

The 1988 Seoul Olympics did much to thrust Korea into the international spotlight, a trick repeated with the even more successful 2002 FIFA World Cup, an event co-hosted with Japan. But sport here is less about watching than doing, a fact evident in the well-trodden trails of the national parks, and the svelte proportions of the average Korean.

Hiking

The most popular activity in Korea is **hiking**, which is the national pastime owing to the country's abundance of mountains and national parks. There are no fewer than seventeen **national parks** on the mainland – their names all end with the suffix "-san", which means mountain or mountains – and these are supplemented by an even greater number of lesser parks, mountains and hills. English-language **maps** (W1000) are available at all park offices, trails are well marked with dual-language signs, and each national park has a cluster of accommodation and restaurants outside its main entrance. Some are mini-towns bursting with neon signs and karaoke rooms, which dilutes the experience somewhat, but a Korean hike is not complete unless it's finished off with a good **meal**: *pajeon* is the most popular

POPULAR HIKES

Day-trips from the city With so much of the country covered by mountains, it's possible to see any Korean city from the vantage point of its surrounding peaks. Even Seoul has a national park. Bukhansan (see p.82) is the world's most visited, though it occasionally offers surprising serenity.

Multi-day hikes Only a couple of parks have shelters where you can stay the night. Jirisan (see p.213) is the largest in the country, and features a three-day, 26km-long spine route. Seoraksan (see p.149) is not quite as expansive, but is considered the most beautiful in the country, with great clumps of rock peeking out from the pines like giant skulls.

Scaling peaks South Korea's highest peak is on Jeju Island. The 1950m-high extinct volcanic cone of Hallasan (see p.310) dominates the island, but is surprisingly easy to climb, as long as Jeju's fickle weather agrees. The highest mountain on the whole peninsula is Paekdusan (2744m) on the Chinese-North Korean border (see p.339); its sumptuously blue crater lake, ringed by jagged peaks, is a font of myth and legend.

Getting away from it all Hiking is so popular in Korea that some trails resemble supermarket queues, but there are a few splendid ways to get away from it all. Taebaeksan (see p.162) has long been a shamanist place of worship, while the small park of Wolchulsan (see p.233) sees few visitors dash across the vertigo-inducing bridge that connects two of its peaks. Though popular on account of its enormous bronze Buddha, Songnisan (see p.275) has a tiny, secluded guesthouse; when the sun goes down, you'll be alone with nature, a trickling stream and a bowl of creamy *dongdongju*.

post-hike dish, a kind of savoury pancake made with mountain vegetables, while the creamy rice wine *dongdongju* (see box, p.41) is the drink of choice. Deceptively mild, it can pack a punch, especially the next morning.

Despite the wealth of choice available, many of Korea's trails contrive to be packed to the gills, especially during **holidays** and warm **weekends**, when the parks are full with locals enjoying a day out. Many families bring along sizeable picnics to enjoy on their way to the peaks, and lone travellers may be invited to join in – Koreans hate to see people on their own.

Spectator sports

The two most popular spectator sports in the country are **football** and **baseball**. Koreans tend to follow one or the other, though football has been in the ascendancy of late, particularly with females and the younger generations. Those looking for something authentically Korean should try to hunt down a *ssireum* wrestling tournament.

Football

Soccer, or *chuk-gu* (축구), became the most popular sport in the country following its co-hosting of the World Cup in 2002. The ten gleaming new *gyeonggi-jang* built for the tournament were swiftly moved into by teams from the national K-League (see below), but the high attendances that the tournament spawned dropped sharply as spectators realized that their local boys weren't really better than Argentina – rows of empty seats mean that you'll always be able to get a ticket at the door, with prices generally W10,000–20,000.

The championship trophy usually sits in or around Seoul: Suwon, Seongnam and FC Seoul have achieved domestic and international success, though Pohang and Jeonbuk have also won titles recently. Suwon and Daejeon are said to have the rowdiest fans. Other teams are listed below, though note that most teams operate as American-style "franchises" that can move lock, stock and barrel to more profitable locations at the drop of a hat. A few locals have escaped the K-League for more lucrative pastures, and Koreans are immensely proud of their sporting diaspora.

K-LEAGUE TEAMS

Busan I'Park Asiad Main Stadium, Busan
Daejeon Citizen World Cup Stadium, Daejeon
FC Seoul World Cup Stadium, Seoul
Gwangju FC Guus Hiddink Stadium, Gwangju
Incheon United Incheon Football Stadium, Incheon
Jeju United FC World Cup Stadium, Seogwipo
Jeonbuk Motors World Cup Stadium, Jeonju
Jeonnam Dragons Gwangyang Stadium, Gwangyang
Pohang Steelers Steel Yard, Pohang
Seongnam FC Tancheon Sports Complex, Seongnam
Suwon Bluewings World Cup Stadium, Suwon
Ulsan FC Munsu Cup Stadium, Ulsan

Baseball

Until 2002, **baseball** (*yagu*; 야구) was the spectator sport of choice. Though its popularity has waned, you'll see a lot of games on Korean television, or you can attend a professional game at one of the *yagu-jang* listed below; seasons run from April to October, with a break at the height of summer. Though the fielding, in particular, isn't quite up to the level that American fans will be used to (and neither is the ballpark atmosphere), several Korean players have made their way into the Major League, including pitchers Kim Byung-hyun and Park Chan-ho. Since the turn of the century, the Unicorns, Lions and Wyverns have ruled the roost, though the Giants also deserve a mention thanks to their noisy support. Bear in mind that the team names listed below are subject to regular change, thanks to the franchise system.

KOREAN BASEBALL TEAMS

Doosan Bears Jamsil Baseball Stadium, Seoul
Hanhwa Eagles Baseball Stadium, Daejeon
Kia Tigers Champions Field, Gwangju
KT Wiz KT Wiz Park, Suwon
LG Twins Jamsil Baseball Stadium, Seoul
Lotte Giants Sajik Baseball Stadium, Busan
NC Dinos Masan Baseball Stadium, Changwon
Nexen Heroes Mokdong Baseball Stadium, Seoul
Samsung Lions Baseball Stadium, Daegu
SK Wyverns Munhak Baseball Stadium, Incheon

Ssireum

Though inevitably compared to *sumo*, this Korean form of wrestling (씨름) bears more resemblance to Mongolian styles – the wrestlers are chunky, rather than gargantuan, and they rely on grabs and throws, rather than slaps and pushes. As with *sumo*, the object of the wrestlers is to force their opponents to the floor, but in **ssireum** the fights start with both fighters interlocked. The sport is markedly less popular than its Japanese counterpart; few Koreans will be able to point you in the right direction if you wish to see a tournament, and even if you hunt one down the atmosphere will usually be low-key. The best place to catch a fight will be as part of a traditional festival, notably the early summer Dano in Gangneung (see p.153).

Participatory sports

In addition to being a nation of compulsive hikers, all Koreans are taught at school to exercise as a matter of course. Martial arts are among the nation's most famed exports, but Western activities such as golf and skiing have caught on in recent decades.

Martial arts

Most Korean martial arts are variations of those that originated in China or Japan. **Taekwondo** (태권도) is the best known – developed in Tang-dynasty China, it was given a Korean twist during the Three Kingdoms period, going on to become one of the country's most famed exports, and an Olympic sport to boot. The predominantly kick-based style is taught at schools, and forms the backbone of compulsory military service for the nation's men; it's possible to take classes around the country, though easiest in Seoul (see p.112). There are dozens of less common local styles to choose from. These include *hapkido* (합기도), better known in the West as *aikido*, its Japanese counterpart; and *geomdo* (검도), a form in which participants get to bonk each other with wooden poles and likewise known to the world as *kendo*.

Golf

The success of professional Korean golfers, mainly females such as LPGA champ Park Se-ri, has tempted many into taking up the game. Over a hundred **courses** dot the country, mainly surrounding Seoul or on Jeju Island; most are members-only clubs, however, and those that aren't are pretty pricey – the fact that Korean golfers often go to Japan to save money says it all. If you come in with clubs, don't forget to **declare** them on arrival at the airport. Tourist offices will have information about nearby courses, though the average traveller will have to stick to the **driving ranges** dotted around the cities – scan the urban horizon for tower blocks topped by a large green net.

Skiing

With sub-zero winters and mountainous terrain, it's hardly surprising that **skiing** is big business in Korea – and a sport that's likely on the rise, since the country will play host to the 2018 Winter Olympics

(see p.157). Non-Olympians looking to ski or snowboard in Korea should have few problems – there are a number of resorts, mainly in the northern provinces of Gyeonggi and Gangwon (see p.114 & p.136); most of these have ample accommodation facilities, though prices soar in the ski season (usually Dec–Feb). Clothes and ski equipment are available for hire, and many resorts have English-speaking instructors; **prices** vary from place to place, but expect lift passes to cost around W65,000 per day, with ski or snowboard rental another W40,000 on top of that.

Culture and etiquette

You may have mastered the art of the polite bow, worked out how to use the tricky steel chopsticks, and learnt a few words of the Korean language, but beware, you may upset new friends by accepting gifts with your hand in the wrong place. While even seasoned expats receive heartfelt congratulations for getting the easy bits right (some are even surprised when foreigners are able to use Korean money), there are still innumerable ways to offend the locals, and unfortunately it's the things that are hardest to guess that are most likely to see you come a cropper.

Korea is often said to be the world's most **Confucian** nation, such values having been instilled for over a thousand years across several dynasties (see p.357). Elements of Confucianism still linger on today – it's still basically true that anyone older, richer or more important than you (or just male as opposed to female) is simply "better" and deserving of more respect, a fact that becomes sorely clear to many working in Korea. Perhaps most evident to foreigners will be what amounts to a national obsession with **age** – you're likely to be asked how old you are soon after your first meeting with any Korean, and any similarity of birth years is likely to be greeted with a genuine whoop of delight (note that Koreans count years differently from Westerners – children are already 1 when they're born, and gain another digit at Lunar New Year, meaning that those born on December 31 are already two years old the very next day). Women have traditionally been treated as inferior to men, and are expected to ditch their job as soon as they give birth to their first child; however, recent years have shown a marked shift towards gender equality, with males more forgiving in the home and females more assertive in the workplace.

Foreigners are largely exempt from the code of conduct that would be required of both parties following their knowledge of age, employment and background, and little is expected of them in such terms, but this does have its drawbacks – in such an ethnically homogenous society, those that aren't Korean will always remain "outsiders", even if they speak the language fluently or have actually spent their whole lives in the country. Meanwhile, foreigners with Korean blood will be expected to behave as a local would, even if they can't speak a word of the language.

Conduct

The East Asian concept of "face" is very important in Korea, and known here as **gibun** (기분); the main goal is to avoid the **embarrassment** of self or others. Great lengths are taken to smooth out awkward situations, and foreigners getting unnecessarily angry are unlikely to invoke much sympathy. The traditional Korean retort to an uncomfortable question or incident is an embarrassed smile; remember that they're not laughing at you, merely trying to show empathy or move the topic onto safer ground. Foreigners may also see Koreans as disrespectful: nobody's going to thank you for holding open a door, and you're unlikely to get an apology if bumped into. **Dressing well** has long been important, but though pretty much anything goes for local girls these days, foreign women may be assumed to be brazen hussies (or Russian prostitutes) if they wear revealing clothing.

Meeting and greeting

Foreigners will see Koreans **bowing** all the time, even during telephone conversations. Though doing likewise will do much to endear you to locals, don't go overboard – a full, right-angled bow would only be appropriate for meeting royalty (and the monarchy ended in 1910). Generally, a short bow with eyes closed and the head directed downwards will do just fine, but it's best to observe the Koreans themselves, and the action will become quite natural after a short time. **Attracting attention** is also done differently here – you beckon with fingers fluttering beneath a downward-facing palm. Koreans are great lovers of **business cards**, which are exchanged in all meetings that have even a

whiff of commerce about them. The humble rectangles garner far greater respect than they do in the West, and folding or stuffing one into a pocket or wallet is a huge faux pas – accept your card with profuse thanks, leave it on the table for the duration of the meeting and file it away with respect (a card-holder is an essential purchase for anyone here on business). Also note that it's seen as incredibly rude to write someone's name in red ink – this colour is reserved for names of those who have died, a practice that most Koreans seem to think goes on all around the world.

If you're lucky enough to be invited to a Korean home, try to bring a **gift** – fruit, chocolates and flowers go down well. The offering is likely to be refused at first, and probably on the second attempt too – persevere and it will eventually be accepted with thanks. The manner of receiving is also important – the receiving hand should be held from underneath by the non-receiving one, the distance up or down the arm dependent on exactly how polite you want to be. This will only come with experience and will not be expected of most foreigners, but you will be expected to take your **shoes off** once inside the house or apartment, so try to ensure that your socks are clean and hole-free.

Dining

There are innumerable codes of conduct when it comes to dining, although Koreans will usually guide foreigners through the various dos and don'ts. Koreans will tolerate anything viewed as a "mistake" on the part of the foreigner, and offer great encouragement to those who are at least attempting to get things right. This can sometimes go a little too far – you're likely to be praised for your chopstick-handling abilities however long you've been around, and it's almost impossible to avoid the Korean Catch-22: locals love to ask foreigners questions during a meal, but anyone stopping to answer will likely fail to keep pace with the fast-eating Koreans, who will then assume that your dish is not disappearing quickly because you don't like it.

Chopsticks

Many rules surround the use of **chopsticks** – don't use these to point or to pick your teeth, and try not to spear food with them unless your skills are really poor. It's also bad form, as natural as it may seem, to leave your chopsticks in the bowl: this is said to resemble incense sticks used after a death, but to most Koreans it just looks wrong. Just leave the sticks balanced on the rim of the bowl.

Table manners

Many Korean meals are group affairs, and this has given rise to a number of rules surrounding who **serves the food** from the communal trays to the individual ones – it's usually the youngest woman at the table. Foreign women finding themselves in this position will be able to mop up a great deal of respect by performing the duty, though as there are particular ways to serve each kind of food, it's probably best to watch first. The **serving of drinks** is a little less formal, though again the minutiae of recommended conduct could fill a small book – basically, you should never refill your own cup or glass, and should endeavour to keep topped up those belonging to others. The position of the hands is important – watch to see how the Koreans are doing it (both the pourer and the recipient), and you'll be increasing your "face" value in no time.

One big no-no is to **blow your nose** during the meal – preposterously unfair, given the spice level of pretty much every Korean dish. Should you need to do so, make your excuses and head to the toilets. It's also proper form to wait for the **head of the table** – the one who is paying, in other words – to sit down first, as well as to allow them to be the first to stand at the end of the meal. The latter can be quite tricky, as many Korean restaurants are sit-on-the-floor affairs that play havoc on the knees and backs of foreigners unaccustomed to the practice.

Paying the bill

Korea's Confucian legacy can often be a great boon to foreigners, as it has long been customary for hosts (usually "betters") to **pay** – as with the rest of the local workforce, many English teachers get taken out for regular slap-up meals by their bosses, and don't have to pay a penny. Koreans also tend to make a big show of trying to pay, with the bill passing rapidly from hand to hand until the right person coughs up. Nowadays things are changing slowly – "going Dutch" is increasingly common where it would once have been unthinkable.

Travel essentials

Costs

Some people come to Korea expecting it to be a budget destination on a par with the Southeast Asian countries, while others arrive with expectations of Japanese-style prices. The latter is closer to the truth – those staying at five-star hotels and eating at Western-style restaurants will spend almost as much as they would in other developed countries, though there are numerous ways for budget travellers to make their trip a cheap one. Your biggest outlay is likely to be **accommodation** – Seoul has some grand places to stay for W400,000 and up, though most cities have dedicated tourist hotels for around W100,000, and decent mid-range options for W70,000 or so. Though they're not to everyone's taste, motels usually make acceptable places to stay; thet cost around W30,000 (or often double that in Seoul). The capital has a few backpacker hostels with dorms for around W20,000, while real scrimpers can stay at a *jjimjilbang* (see p.35).

Because the country is small, **transport** is unlikely to make too much of a dent in your wallet – even a high-speed KTX train from Seoul in the northwest to Busan in the southeast won't set you back much more than W50,000, and you can cut that in half by taking a slower service. Inner-city transport is also good value, with most journeys costing just over W1000, and **admission charges** to temples, museums and the like are similarly unlikely to cause your wallet discomfort.

By staying in motels or guesthouses and eating at reasonably cheap restaurants, you should be able to survive easily on a daily budget of W40,000, or even half this if seriously pushed. After you've added in transport costs and a few entry tickets, a realistic daily figure may be W60,000.

Tipping plays almost no part in Korean transactions – try not to leave unwanted change in the hands of a cashier, lest they feel forced to abandon their duties and chase you down the street with it. Exceptions are tourist hotels, most of which tack a 10 percent service charge onto the room bill; these are also among the few places in the country to omit **tax** – levied at 10 percent – from their quoted prices.

Climate

Korea is a land of extremes in many senses, and its weather is no exception. Temperatures can rise to over 35ºC in the **summer** (broadly June–Sept), when it's also incredibly humid – more than half of Korea's annual **rainfall** comes down in the summer monsoons. **Winters** (Nov–March), on the other hand, can be surprisingly chilly for a country at the same latitude as Iraq, Cyprus and California, with the mercury occasionally plummeting to -20ºC. **Spring** and **autumn** are very pleasant times to visit, though some years, blink and you'll miss them.

AVERAGE MONTHLY TEMPERATURES AND RAINFALL

	Jan	Feb	Mar	Apr	May	Jun	Jul	Aug	Sep	Oct	Nov	Dec
BUSAN												
Max/Min(°C)	6/-2	7/-1	12/3	17/8	21/13	24/17	27/22	29/23	26/18	21/12	15/6	9/1
Max/Min (°F)	43/28	45/30	54/38	63/47	70/55	75/63	81/72	84/73	79/64	70/54	59/43	48/34
Rainfall (mm)	43	36	69	140	132	201	295	130	173	74	41	31
JEJU CITY												
Max/Min (°C)	10/5	12/6	15/8	19/10	23/14	26/18	28/23	29/24	27/20	23/14	17/8	13/6
Max/Min (°F)	50/41	54/43	59/46	66/50	73/57	79/64	82/73	84/75	81/68	73/57	63/46	55/43
Rainfall (mm)	84	89	94	176	171	205	356	243	184	95	93	82
PYONGYANG												
Max/Min (°C)	-3/-13	1/-10	7/-4	16/3	22/9	26/15	29/20	29/20	24/14	18/6	9/-2	0/-10
Max/Min (°F)	27/7	34/14	45/25	61/37	72/48	79/59	84/68	84/68	75/57	64/43	48/28	32/14
Rainfall (mm)	15	11	25	46	67	76	237	228	112	45	41	21
SEOUL												
Max/Min (°C)	0/-9	3/-7	8/-2	17/5	22/11	27/16	29/21	31/22	26/15	19/7	11/0	3/-7
Max/Min (°F)	32/16	37/19	46/28	63/41	72/52	81/61	84/70	88/72	79/59	66/45	52/32	37/19
Rainfall (mm)	31	20	38	76	81	130	376	267	119	41	46	25

Crime and personal safety

Korea is a country in which you're far more likely to see someone running towards you with a dropped wallet than away with a stolen one – tales abound about travellers who have left a valuable possession on a restaurant table or park bench and returned hours later to find it in the same place. Though you'd be very unlucky to fall victim to a crime, it's prudent to take a few simple precautions. The country has a poor **road safety** record, the statistics heightened by the number of vehicles that use pavements as shortcuts or parking spaces. Caution should also be exercised around any **street fights** that you may have the misfortune to come across – since Korean men practise taekwondo to a fairly high level during their compulsory national service, Korea is not a great place to get caught in a scuffle. These days many local women avoid taking taxis alone in the evening; you'd be extremely unlucky to have something untoward happen, but it may be prudent to keep a phone in your hand as a deterrent.

Electricity

The electrical **current** runs at 220v, 60Hz throughout the country, and requires European-style plugs with two round pins, though some older buildings, including many *yeogwan* and *yeoinsuk*, may still take flat-pinned plugs at 110v.

Entry requirements

At the time of writing, citizens of almost any Western nation can enter Korea **visa-free** with an onward ticket, though the duration of the permit varies. Most West European nationals qualify for a visa exemption of three months or ninety days (there *is* a difference), as do citizens of the USA, New Zealand and Australia; Portuguese are allowed sixty days, South Africans just thirty, and Canadians a full six months. If you need more than this, apply before entering Korea.

Overstaying your visa will result in a large fine (up to W500,000 per day), with exceptions only being made in emergencies such as illness or loss of passport. Getting a new passport is time-consuming and troublesome, though the process will be simplified if your passport has been registered with your embassy in Seoul, or if you can prove your existence with a birth certificate or copy of your old passport.

Work visas

Work visas, valid for one year and extendable for at least one more, can be applied for before or after entering Korea. Applications can take up to a month to be processed by Korean embassies, but once inside the country it can take as little as a week. Your **employer** will do all the hard work with the authorities, then provide you with a visa confirmation slip; the visa must be picked up outside Korea (the nearest consulate is in Fukuoka, Japan; visas here can be issued on the day of application). Visas with the same employer can be extended without leaving Korea. An **alien card** must be applied for at the local immigration office within ninety days of arrival – again, this is usually taken care of by the employer. Work visas are forfeited on leaving Korea, though re-entry visas can be applied for at your provincial immigration office. Citizens of seventeen countries – including Americans, Australians, British, Canadians and New Zealanders – can apply for a **working holiday** visa at their local South Korean embassy, as long as they're aged between 18 and 30.

SOUTH KOREAN EMBASSIES AND CONSULATES ABROAD

Australia 113 Empire Circuit, Yarralumla, ACT 2600 ☎ 02 6270 4100, Ⓦ aus-act.mofa.go.kr.

Canada 150 Boteler St, Ottawa, Ontario K1N 5A6 ☎ 613/244-5010, Ⓦ can-ottawa.mofa.go.kr.

China No 3, 4th Avenue East, Sanlitun, Chaoyang District, Beijing 100600 ☎ 10 6532 0290.

Ireland 20 Clyde Rd, Ballsbridge, Dublin 4 ☎ 01 660 8800, Ⓦ irl.mofa.go.kr.

Japan 1-2-5 Minami-Azabu, 1-chome, Minato-ku, Tokyo 106 ☎ 03 3452 7611, Ⓦ jpn-tokyo.mofa.go.kr.

New Zealand 11th Floor, ASB Bank Tower, 2 Hunter St, Wellington ☎ 04/473 9073, Ⓦ nzl-wellington.mofa.go.kr.

Singapore 47 Scotts Rd #08-00 Goldbell Towers, Singapore 228233 ☎ 6256 1188, Ⓦ www.koreaembassy.org.sg.

South Africa Green Park Estates, Building 3, 27 George Storrar Drive, Groenkloof, Pretoria ☎ 012 460 2508.

UK 60 Buckingham Gate, London SW1E 6AJ ☎ 020 7227 5500, Ⓦ gbr.mofa.go.kr.

US 2450 Massachusetts Ave NW, Washington, DC 20008 ☎ 202 939 5600, Ⓦ usa.mofa.go.kr.

Gay and lesbian travellers

Despite Goryeo-era evidence suggesting that undisguised homosexuality was common in Royal and Buddhist circles, the **gay scene** in today's Korea forms a small, alienated section of society. Thankfully, a spate of high-profile comings-out have countered the prevailing local belief that Korean homosexuality simply does not exist, and fewer and fewer regard it as a "foreign disease" that instantly gives people AIDS.

Confucian attitudes, together with the lack of a substantial gay scene, have been the bane of many a queer expat's life in the country. For Korean homosexuals, the problems are more serious – although the law makes no explicit reference to the legality of sexual intercourse between adults of the same sex, this is less a tacit nod of consent than a

refusal of officialdom to discuss such matters, and gay activities may be punishable as sexual harassment, or even, shockingly, "mutual rape" if it takes place in the military. In the early 1990s, the first few gay and lesbian websites were cracked down on by a government that, during the course of the subsequent appeal, made it clear that human rights did not fully apply to homosexuals – all the more reason for the "different people" (*iban-in*), already fearful of losing their jobs, friends and family, to lock themselves firmly in the closet.

Korean society is, however, becoming more liberal. With more and more high-profile homosexuals coming out, a critical mass has been reached, and younger generations are markedly less prejudiced on – and more willing to discuss – the pink issue. Gay clubs, bars and saunas, while still generally low-key outside "Homo Hill" in Seoul's Itaewon district (see p.109 for more on gay Seoul), can be found in every major city, and lobbyists have been making inroads into the Korean parliament. The **Korean Queer Culture Festival** – still the only pride event in the country – takes place over a fortnight in early June at locations across Seoul (see box, p.110).

GAY INFORMATION SOURCES

Chingusai Ⓦ chingusai.net. Loosely meaning "Among Friends", *Chingusai*'s trailblazing magazine is available at many gay bars in the capital. Mainly in Korean, but with some English-language information.

Travel Gay Asia Ⓦ travelgayasia.com. Pan-Asian site featuring listings of bars, clubs and saunas, in the case of Korea mainly focused on Seoul and Busan.

Utopia Asia Ⓦ utopia-asia.com. Useful information about bars, clubs and saunas, including a fair few non-Seoul spots.

Health

South Korea is pretty high in the world rankings as far as **healthcare** goes, and there are no compulsory vaccinations or diseases worth getting too worried about. Hospitals are clean and well staffed, and most doctors can speak English, so the main health concerns for foreign travellers are likely to be financial – without adequate insurance cover, a large bill may rub salt into your healing wounds if you end up in hospital (see opposite).

Though no **vaccinations** are legally required, get medical advice ahead of your trip, particularly regarding hepatitis A and B, typhoid and Japanese B encephalitis (which are all rare in Korea but it's better to err on the side of caution), and make sure that you're up to date with the usual boosters. It's also wise to bring along any medicines that you might need, especially for drugs that need to be prescribed – bring a copy of your prescription, as well as the generic name of the drug in question, as brand names may vary from country to country.

Despite the swarms of mosquitoes that blanket the country in warmer months, **malaria** is not prevalent in Korea. However, infected mosquitoes breed in the DMZ, so those planning to hang around the rural north of the Gyeonggi or Gangwon provinces should take extra precautions to prevent getting bitten. All travellers should get up-to-date malarial advice from their GP before arriving in Korea, and wherever you are in the country during the monsoon season in late summer, it's also a good idea to slap on some repellent before going out.

Drinking Korean **tap water** is a bad idea, and with free drinking fountains in every restaurant, hotel, supermarket, police station and department store in the country, there really should be no need. Water is also sold at train and bus stations – around W700 for a small bottle. Restaurant food will almost always be prepared and cooked adequately, and all necessary precautions taken with raw fish.

In an **emergency**, you should first try to ask a local to call for an ambulance. Should you need to do so yourself, the number is ☎119, though it's possible that no English-speaker will be available to take your call. Alternatively, try the tourist information line on ☎1330 (see p.54). If you're in a major city and the problem isn't life-threatening, the local tourist office should be able to point you towards the most suitable doctor or **hospital**. Once there, you may find it surprisingly hard to get information about what's wrong with you. As in much of East Asia, patients are expected to trust doctors to do their jobs properly, and any sign that this trust is not in place results in a loss of face for the practitioner.

For minor complaints or medical advice, there are **pharmacies** all over the place, usually distinguished by the Korean character "yak" (약) at the entrance, though English-speakers are few and far between. Travellers can also visit a practitioner of oriental medicine, who uses acupuncture and pressure-point massage, among other techniques, to combat the problems that Western medicine cannot reach. If you have Korean friends, ask around for a personal recommendation in order to find a reputable practitioner.

Insurance

The price of hospital treatment in Korea can be quite high so it's advisable to take out a decent **travel insurance** policy before you go. Bear in mind that most policies exclude "dangerous activities"; this term may well cover activities as seemingly benign as hiking or skiing. Keep the emergency number of your insurance company handy in the event of an accident and, as in any country, if you have anything stolen make sure to obtain a copy of the police report, as you will need this to make a claim.

Internet

You should have no problem getting online in South Korea, possibly the most connected nation on the planet. **Wi-fi** access is becoming ever more common, with many cafés allowing customers to use their connection for free. *Tom N' Toms* and *Hollys* are generally the best chains for this (though the coffee at the former is pretty poor). You may also be able to get online at your accommodation, though ironically the cheaper places are better: most modern motels have free-to-use terminals inside the rooms, while hotels generally charge extortionate rates of over W20,000 per day.

If wi-fi fails, **PC rooms** (PC 방; pronounced "pishi-bang") are everywhere. Though declining in number with each passing year, there should always be one within walking distance – just look for the letters "PC" in Roman characters. These cafés charge around W1500 per hour, with a one-hour minimum charge.

Laundry

Almost all tourist hotels provide a **laundry** service, and some of the Seoul backpacker hostels will wash your smalls for free, but with public laundries so thin on the ground those staying elsewhere may have to resort to a spot of DIY cleaning. All motels have 24-hour hot water, as well as soap, body lotion and/or shampoo in the bathrooms, and in the winter clothes dry in no time on the heated *ondol* floors. Summer is a different story, with the humidity making it very hard to dry clothes in a hurry.

Mail

The Korean postal system is cheap and trustworthy, and there are **post offices** in even the smallest town. Most are open Monday to Friday from 9am to 6pm; all should be able to handle international mail, and the larger ones offer free internet access. There's a relative dearth of **postcards** for sale, though if you do track some down you'll find that postal rates are cheap, at around W400 per card. Letters will cost a little more, though as with **parcels** the tariff will vary depending on their destination – the largest box you can send (20kg) will cost about W150,000 to mail to the UK or USA, though this price drops to about W50,000 if you post via **surface mail**, a process that can take up to three months. All post offices have the necessary boxes for sale, and will even do your packing for a small fee. Alternatively, international courier chains such as UPS and FedEx can also ship from Korea.

Maps

Free maps – many of which are available in English – can be picked up at any tourist office or higher-end hotel, as well as most travel terminals. The main drawback with them is that distances and exact street patterns are hard to gauge, though it's a complaint the powers-that-be are slowly taking on board. Excellent **national park** maps, drawn to scale, cost W1000 from the ticket booths.

Money

The **Korean currency** is the won (W), which comes in notes of W1000, W5000, W10,000 and W50,000, and coins of W10, W50, W100 and W500. At the time of writing the **exchange rate** was approximately W1700 to £1, W1250 to €1, and W1100 to US$1.

ATMs are everywhere in Korea, not only in banks (은행; *eunhaeng*) but 24-hour convenience stores such as *7-Eleven* or *GS25*. Most machines are capable of dealing with foreign cards, and those that do are usually able to switch to English-language mode; note that you may have to try a few machines. Smaller towns may not have such facilities – stock up on cash in larger cities.

Foreign **credit cards** are being accepted in more and more hotels, restaurants and shops. It shouldn't be too hard to **exchange** foreign notes for Korean cash; banks are all over the place, and the only likely problem when dealing in dollars, pounds or euros is time – some places simply won't have exchanged money before, forcing staff to consult the procedure manual.

Opening hours and public holidays

Korea is one of the world's truest 24-hour societies – **opening hours** are such that almost everything you need is likely to be available when you require it. Most shops and almost all restaurants are open daily, often until late, as are tourist information offices. A quite incredible number of establishments are open 24/7, including convenience stores, saunas, internet cafés and some of the busier shops and restaurants. Post offices (Mon–Fri 9am–6pm) and banks (Mon–Fri 9.30am–4pm) keep more sensible hours.

Until recently, the country was one of the few in the world to have a **six-day working week**; though this has been officially altered to five, the changes haven't filtered through to all workers, and Korea's place at the top of the world's "average hours worked per year" table has not been affected. The number of **national holidays** has fallen, however, in an attempt to make up the slack, and as most of the country's population are forced to take their holiday at the same times, there can be chaos on the roads and rails. Three of the biggest holidays – Lunar New Year, Buddha's birthday and *Chuseok* – are based on the lunar calendar, and have no fixed dates (see box opposite, for further details on national holidays and festivals).

Phones

Getting hold of a **mobile phone** while you're in the country is easy – there are 24-hour **rental booths** at Incheon Airport. Using your own phone is more problematic, but you'll be able to rent a data-only SIM at the same places, or simply switch on

KOREAN PUBLIC HOLIDAYS

Sinjeong (New Year's Day) Jan 1. Seoul celebrates New Year in much the same fashion as Western countries, with huge crowds gathering around City Hall.

Seollal (Lunar New Year) Usually early Feb. One of the most important holidays on the calendar, Lunar New Year sees Koreans flock to their home towns for a three-day holiday of relaxed celebration, and many businesses close up.

Independence Movement Day March 1.

Children's Day May 5. Koreans make an even bigger fuss over their kids than usual on this national holiday – expect parks, zoos and amusement parks to be jam-packed.

Memorial Day June 6. Little more than a day off for most Koreans, this day honours those who fell in battle.

Constitution Day July 17.

Independence Day Aug 15. The country becomes a sea of Korean flags on this holiday celebrating the end of Japanese rule in 1945.

Chuseok Late Sept or early Oct. One of the biggest events in the Korean calendar is this three-day national holiday, similar to Thanksgiving; families head to their home towns to venerate their ancestors in low-key ceremonies, and eat a special crescent-shaped rice cake.

National Foundation Day Oct 3. Celebrates the 2333 BC birth of Dangun, the legendary founder of the Korean nation. Shamanist celebrations take place at shrines around Seoul, with the most important on Inwangsan mountain.

Christmas Day Dec 25. Every evening looks like Christmas in neon-drenched Seoul, but on this occasion Santa Haraboji (Grandpa Santa) finally arrives.

roaming. If you're going to be in Korea for a while, you may care to buy a **secondhand** mobile phone; the best places to look are shopping districts, electrical stores or underground malls. After purchase you'll need to register with a major service provider – KT and SK Telecom are two of the biggest chains, and so ubiquitous that the nearest store is likely to be within walking distance. Registration is free, though you'll need a Korean ID of some sort (bring a Korean friend along if you're not legally employed in the country); you can top up pay-as-you-go accounts in increments of W10,000.

Despite the prevalence of mobile phones, you'll still see **payphones** on every major street; many of these ageing units only take coins, meaning that you'll have to pump in change at a furious pace to avoid the deafening squawks that signal the end of your call time. Pre-paid travel cards (see box, p.95) work with some machines.

Korea's **international dialling code** is ☎82. When dialling from abroad, omit the initial zero from the area codes. Korean area codes are given throughout the guide.

Photography

Photography is a national obsession in Korea. If you want a personal shot, few locals will mind being photographed, though of course it's polite to ask first. One serious no-no is to go snap-happy on a tour of the DMZ (see p.129) – this can, and has, landed tourists in trouble. You may also see temple-keepers and monks poised at the ready to admonish would-be photographers of sacrosanct areas.

Studying in Korea

Korea has long been a popular place for the study of **martial arts**, while the country's ever-stronger ties with global business are also prompting many to gain a competitive advantage by studying the Korean language.

Language

Courses at the institutes run by many of the larger **universities** vary in terms of price, study time, skill level and accommodation. Most of the year-long courses are in Seoul and start in March – apply in good time. There's a good list at ⓦenglish.visitkorea .or.kr, while information on study visas and how to apply for them can be found on the Ministry of Education's website (ⓦstudyinkorea.go.kr). There are **private institutes** dotted around Seoul and other major cities – ⓦenglish.seoul.go.kr has a list of safe recommendations in the capital, while other official city websites are the best places to look for institutes elsewhere.

If you're working in Korea, you may not have time for intensive study; if so, it's worth looking into the **government-funded courses** run by a few major cities, some of which are so cheap that their price is barely an issue. Many people opt for an even higher degree of informality and take language lessons from friends or colleagues, but with so few English speakers around, just living in Korea can be all the practice you need.

Martial arts classes

Finding classes for the most popular styles (including **taekwondo**, *hapkido* and *geomdo*) isn't hard, but very few classes cater for foreigners – it's best to go hunting on the expat circuit. Those looking for something more advanced should seek advice from their home country's own *taekwondo* federation.

Buddhist teachings

Many **temples** offer teaching and templestay programmes for around W50,000 per night – a wonderful opportunity to see the "Land of Morning Calm" at its most serene (as long as you can stand the early mornings). Some temples are able to provide English-language instruction, and some not – see ⓦ eng.templestay.com for more details.

Teaching English in Korea

Uncomplicated entry requirements, low tax and decent pay cheques make Korea one of the most popular stops on the **English-teaching** circuit. Demand for native speakers is high and still growing; the cost of living, though rising, is still below that in most English-speaking countries; English-teaching qualifications are far from essential (though they certainly help), and all that is usually required is a degree certificate, and a copy of your passport – many people have been taken on by a Korean school without so much as a telephone interview.

To land a full-time job from outside Korea you'll have to go **online**, and it's still the best option if you're already in Korea. Popular sites include Dave's ESL Café (ⓦ eslcafe.com) and HiTeacher (ⓦ hiteacher .com), though a thorough web search will yield more.

Most language schools are reputable; you can typically expect them to organize **free accommodation**, and to do the legwork with your **visa** application. Some countries operate Working Holiday visa schemes with Korea, but others will need a full working visa to be legally employed; those unable to collect this in their home country are usually given a plane ticket and directions for a quick visa-run to Japan (the closest embassy is in Fukuoka).

Most new entrants start off by teaching kids at a **language school** (학원; *hagwon*). There are a whole bunch of pan-national chains, with YBM and Pagoda among the two biggest; like the smaller-fry operations, they pay around W2,500,000 per month in Seoul, and a little less outside the capital. After a year or two, many teachers make their way to a **university** teaching post; pay is usually lower and responsibilities higher than at a *hagwon*, though the holiday allowances (as much as five months per year, as opposed to less than two weeks per year in a *hagwon*) are hard to resist. Most teachers give their bank balance a nudge in the right direction by offering **private lessons** on the side – an illegal practice, but largely tolerated unless you start organizing them for others.

One of the most regular *hagwon*-related complaints is the **long hours** many teachers have to work – figure on up to thirty per week. This may include Saturdays, or be spread quite liberally across the day from 9am to 9pm – try to find jobs with "no split shift" if possible. Questionable **school policies** also come in for stick; for example, teachers are often expected to be present at the school for show, even if they have no lessons on.

With the number of teaching jobs on offer, it's quite possible to hand-pick a city or province of your choice. Seoul is an obvious target and the easiest place from which to escape into Western pleasures if necessary, though note that a hefty proportion of positions listed as being in the capital are actually in uninteresting satellite cities such as Bundang, Anyang or Ilsan, all a long journey from central Seoul – try to find the nearest subway station to your prospective position on a map if possible. Those who head to provincial cities such as Daejeon, Mokpo or Busan generally seem to have a better time of things, and emerge with a truer appreciation of the country, as well as better Korean language skills.

Time

The Korean peninsula shares a **time zone** with Japan: one hour ahead of China, nine hours ahead of Greenwich Mean Time, seven hours ahead of South Africa, fourteen hours ahead of Eastern Standard Time in the US or Montreal in Canada, and one hour behind Sydney. Daylight Saving hours are not observed, so though noon in London will be 9pm in Seoul for much of the year, the difference drops to eight hours during British Summer Time.

Tourist information

The Korean tourist authorities churn out a commendable number of English-language maps, pamphlets and books, most of which are handed out at **information booths** – you'll be able to find one in every city, usually outside the train or bus stations. Not all of these are staffed with an English-speaker, but you'll be able to get 24-hour assistance and advice on the dedicated **tourist information line** – dial ❶1330 and you'll be put through to helpful call-centre staff who speak a number of languages and can advise on transport, sights, accommodation, theatre ticket prices and much more. If calling from a mobile phone or abroad, you'll also need to put in a regional prefix – to reach Seoul, for example, dial ❶02 1330. The official **Korean tourist website** (ⓦenglish.visitkorea.or.kr) is quite useful, and most cities and provinces have sites of their own.

Travelling with children

Korea is a country with high standards of **health and hygiene**, low levels of crime and plenty to see and do – bringing children of any age should pose no special problems. **Changing facilities** are most common in Seoul – department stores are good places to head – though few restaurants have highchairs, and baby food labelled in English is almost nonexistent. A few hotels provide a **baby-sitting service**, though those in need can ask their concierge for a newspaper with baby-sitter adverts. Every city has cinemas, theme parks and a zoo or two to keep children amused; Everland (see p.127)

and Seoul Land (see p.92) are the two most popular escapes from Seoul, while there are a number of interesting museums in the capital itself. Note that some of the restaurants listed in this guide – especially those serving *galbi*, a self-barbecued meat – have hotplates or charcoal in the centre of the table, which poses an obvious danger to little hands, and in a country where it's perfectly normal for cars to drive on the pavements, you may want to exercise a little more caution than normal when walking around town.

Travellers with disabilities

Despite its First World status, Korea can be filed under "developing countries" as far as **disabled accessibility** is concerned, and with rushing traffic and crowded streets, it's never going to be the easiest destination to get around. Until recently, very little attention was paid to those with disabilities, but things are changing. Streets are being made more wheelchair-friendly, and many subway and train stations have been fitted with lifts. Almost all motels and tourist hotels have these, too, though occasionally you'll come across an entrance that hasn't been built with wheelchairs in mind. Some museums and tourist attractions will be able to provide a helper if necessary, but wherever you are, Koreans are likely to jump at the chance to help travellers in obvious need of assistance.

Seoul

CHEONGGYECHEON

1

Seoul

An intoxicating cocktail of high-rise buildings and people-thronged streets, all ringing with commerce, the Korean capital, Seoul (서울), is a veritable assault on the senses. Even small streets find themselves alive with frenzied activity by day and searing neon after sunset, while eardrums are set pounding by clamouring shop assistants and the night-time thump of a thousand karaoke rooms. Restaurants serving Korea's delectably spicy national dishes lure you in with their amazing aromas and tastes while doing minimal damage to your figure (or wallet), and for tactile bliss, the hot pools and ice rooms of the ubiquitous *jjimjilbang* bathhouses have no equal. The city's open-all-hours culture gives it an almost unmatched vitality, and the temptation to throw yourself in at the deep end is almost impossible to resist.

With over twenty million souls packed sardine-like into a metropolitan area smaller than Luxembourg, this is one of the most densely populated places on the planet, but for all its nonstop consumption, Seoul is also a place of considerable tradition and history. **Joseon-dynasty palaces**, displayed like medals in the centre of the city, proclaim its status as a seat of regal power from as far back as 1392; the tiled roofs of wooden *hanok* houses gently make their way, fish-scale-like towards the ash-coloured granite crags of **Bukhansan**, the world's most-visited national park; and the ancient songs and dances of farmhands and court performers are still clashed out in a whirligig of sound and colour along the street of Insadonggil. A city with a hyper-efficient transport system, a negligible crime rate, locals eager to please foreign guests and an almost astonishing wealth of locally produced modern art: it's little wonder that so many visitors come away impressed.

Top of most tourists' agendas are the half-a-dozen sumptuous **palaces** dating from the late fourteenth century that surround the city centre; these include **Gyeongbokgung** and **Changdeokgung**, together with the nearby ancestral shrine of **Jongmyo**. Situated in the middle is **Insadong**; by far the most popular part of the city with tourists, its warren of tight streets is littered with traditional restaurants, quaint tearooms, art galleries and trinket shops, and makes for a great wander. **Samcheongdong** and **Bukchon Hanok Village** are two areas offering similar delights, though with fewer tourists. The amount of art on display in all three areas can come as quite a surprise – contemporary Korean work receives a fraction of the international press devoted to

CHANGING OF THE GUARD, GYEONGBOKGUNG

Highlights

❶ Royal palaces Five beautiful palaces remain from Seoul's time as capital of the Joseon dynasty, each with its own merits; most visitors find Gyeongbokgung and Changdeokgung the most charming. **See p.65**

❷ Bukchon Hanok Village Despite its central location, this area remains markedly traditional and filled with wooden *hanok* housing. **See p.68**

❸ Insadonggil There's enough to fill a day on Seoul's most popular street – tearooms, galleries and traditional restaurants crammed into a network of alleys. **See p.69**

❹ Namsan at sunset Make sure you're at the top of Seoul's mini-mountain for sunset and the spectacular city's transition from grey to neon. **See p.75**

❺ Gwangjang Market A delectable slice of Koreana, this market is a highly atmospheric place in which to get a handle on some of the country's earthier drinks and dishes. **See p.77**

❻ Hanok guesthouses Stay a night in a *hanok* – a wooden building kept warm in the winter by underfloor fires – an authentically Korean experience. **See p.97**

❼ Nightlife Seoul's nightlife gets better and better, and is best soaked up in the throbbing university area of Hongdae. **See p.106**

HIGHLIGHTS ARE MARKED ON THE MAP ON PP.60–61

1

art from Japan or China, but is just as creative. Also offering a modern-day fusion of Korea old and new are the colossal **markets** of **Dongdaemun** and **Namdaemun**, in whose sprawling reaches you'll find anything from pig intestines to clip-on ties. The more modern facets of the city can be seen in the shoppers' paradise of **Myeongdong** or achingly fashionable **Apgujeong**, while the number of American soldiers hanging out in cosmopolitan **Itaewon** hint at Seoul's proximity to North Korea – it's even possible to take a day-trip to the border.

To get a sense of what makes Seoul so unique, however, you'll need to do more than tick off the sights. To truly appreciate the subtle facets of this distinctive society, take a

SEOUL

HIGHLIGHTS
1. Royal palaces
2. Bukchon Hanok Village
3. Insadonggil
4. Namsan at sunset
5. Gwangjang Market
6. Hanok guesthouses
7. Nightlife

leap of faith into the local cuisine, follow the Korean lead on a wild night (and early morning) out, and spend a decent amount of time simply walking the streets.

Brief history

Contrary to the expectations of many a visitor, Seoul possesses a long and interesting past; after first rising to prominence at the beginning of the **Three Kingdoms** period, it was then ruled over by almost every major power in Korean history. In 18 AD, then named Wiryeseong, it became the first capital of the **Baekje** kingdom (see box, p.264); the exact location is believed to be a site just east of present-day Seoul, but this was to

1

change several times. The kings and clans were forced far south to Gongju in 475, having been squeezed out by the rival **Goguryeo** kingdom; less than a century later, the city completed a Three Kingdoms clean-sweep when King Jinheung expanded the domain of his **Silla** kingdom (see box, p.180) far to the north, absorbing Seoul – then known as Hanseong – on the way. By 668, Silla forces held control of the whole peninsula, but having chosen Gyeongju as their capital, Seoul faded into the background. In the tenth century, Silla was usurped by the nascent **Goryeo** kingdom – they chose Kaesong, in modern-day North Korea, as the seat of their power, though Seoul was close enough to become an important trading hub, and soon earned yet another name, Namgyeong, meaning "Southern Capital".

The Joseon dynasty

It was not until the end of the Goryeo dynasty that Seoul really came into its own. In 1392, the "Hermit Kingdom" of **Joseon** kicked off over five centuries of power; after running the rule over a few prospective candidates, **King Taejo** – the inaugurator of the dynasty – chose Seoul as his new capital, impressed by its auspicious location. He immediately set about reorganizing the city with a series of major projects (see box below). Exactly two hundred years after its birth, Joseon was invaded by **Japanese** forces from 1592 to 1598 under the control of warlord Hideyoshi; Seoul was pillaged in the course of the battles, and many of its most beautiful buildings lay in ruins. Though the country survived this particular struggle, mainly thanks to the heroic Admiral Yi (see box, p.224), the Japanese proved more obdurate on their return in the late nineteenth century.

Under Japanese occupation

After making tame inroads with a series of trade treaties, an escalating series of events – including the assassination of Queen Min in Gyeongbokgung (see box, p.66) – culminated in Japan's outright **annexation** of the peninsula in 1910, which lasted until the end of World War II, and closed the long chapters of Korean regal rule. During this time, Japan tried its best to erase any sense of Korean nationality; part of this was a drive to wipe out the Korean language, which earned Seoul yet another name – **Keijo**, which roughly translates as "Walled-off Capital". The city was to suffer greater indignity when its beloved palaces were modified in an attempt to make them "more Japanese"; a few of these alterations are still visible today.

To the present day

After the Japanese were defeated in World War II, peninsular infighting and global shifts in power and ideology resulted in the **Korean War** (1950–53). Seoul's position in the centre of the peninsula, as well as its obvious importance as the long-time Korean capital, meant that it changed hands four times, coming under North Korean control

---

BUILDING A CAPITAL

Rarely can a capital have been built so quickly. On the inauguration of his Joseon kingdom in 1392, the ambitious **King Taejo** immediately set his minions to work on a truly incredible number of gigantic projects. Even more astonishing is the fact that many of them can still be seen today, albeit in reproduction form, since few original structures survived the Japanese occupation and Korean War.

Gyeongbokgung Seoul's first palace, completed in 1394 (see p.65).
Changdeokgung Seoul's second palace, built in 1395 (see p.69).
Jongmyo The ancestral shrines, built in 1394 (see p.71).
Namdaemun The city's south gate; construction started in 1395 (see p.78).
City walls Built in stages from 1396.
Dongdaemun The east gate, built in 1396 (see p.77).

SEOUL ORIENTATION

Seoul is colossal, its metropolitan area stretching far and wide in a confusion of concrete and cleaved in two by the **Han**, a wide river crossed by many bridges. But despite its size, a very definite city centre – just small enough to be traversed by foot – has been in place north of the Han River since the late fourteenth century, and bounded by the five **grand palaces**. Sitting in the middle of these is **Insadong**, Seoul's tourist hub. A short walk north are **Samcheongdong** and **Bukchon Hanok Village**, two quirky zones that offer similar pleasures – though less touristed – to Insadong. This whole area is hemmed in to the north by the muscular granite peaks of **Bukhansan**, a wonderful backdrop to **Gyeongbokgung** and **Changdeokgung**, the most northerly – and popular – of the five palaces.

South of Insadong are the busy parallel roads of Jongno and Euljiro, two of Seoul's most important thoroughfares. These sit either side of **Cheonggyecheon**, a recently gentrified stream that lies beneath street level. A walk east along this stream will bring you to **Dongdaemun**, once the eastern gate to the city, but now a traffic-heavy focal point of the colossal 24-hour market that blankets the area. Walking west instead to Cheonggyecheon's "source" – the point at which the subterranean stream becomes open-air – will land you near **City Hall**; surrounded by skyscrapers, it's flanked on one side by **Deoksugung** – another of the five palaces – and on the other by a maze of five-star hotels. These segue into **Myeongdong**, the busiest shopping area in the country, packed with clothes stores and restaurants. Just west of Myeongdong is **Namdaemun** – a market almost as big as Dongdaemun, and similarly named after a city gate – while heading south will bring you to the slopes of **Namsan**, Seoul's very own mountain, which affords fantastic views of the city centre and beyond.

South of Namsan is **Itaewon**, long the hub of foreign activity in the city; a curious mix of the sleazy and the cosmopolitan, it's home to some of Seoul's best restaurants, bars and clubs, but also most of its brothels. However, even Itaewon's nightlife is nothing compared with that found in happening **Hongdae**. This is a university area west of central Seoul, and possesses by far the most rocking nightlife in the country, a neon-drenched maze of hip-hop clubs, live music venues and trendy subterranean bars.

A number of important city districts lie south of the Han River. Starting in the west is the islet of **Yeouido**, Seoul's main centre of business and politics, and a rather uninteresting place. Further east are **Gangnam**, a shop- and restaurant-filled south-bank alternative to Myeongdong, and ultra-trendy **Apgujeong**, filled with boutiques and some of the best restaurants in the city. The **Coex Mall**, a gigantic underground shopping complex, is also in the south, as is the **Jamsil** area – home to **Lotte World**, one of the country's most popular theme parks – and **Olympic Park**, where Seoul's Summer Games were held in 1988.

twice before being wrested back. Seoul finally ended up under South Korean control, though most of the city lay in ruins. Despite – or perhaps, because of – all these setbacks, there has been no stopping it since then. The economic reforms inaugurated by president **Park Chung-hee** in the 1970s brought it global attention as a financial dynamo, and Seoul's population has ballooned to over ten million, more than double this if the whole metropolitan area is taken into account. The city has also played host to some of the world's largest events: the Summer Olympics in 1988, part of football's World Cup in 2002, and the G20 Summit in 2010.

Gyeongbokgung and around

Seoul is one of the world's largest urban agglomerations, racing out for mile after mile in every direction, and swallowing up whole cities well beyond its own official limits. As such, it's hard to imagine that the Korean capital was once a much smaller place, bounded by fortress walls erected shortly after the nascent Joseon dynasty chose it as their seat of power in 1392. The palace of **Gyeongbokgung** was erected during these fledgling years, and centuries down the line its environs are still the seat of national

1

GYEONGBOKGUNG AND AROUND

0   200
metres

● CAFÉS & TEAROOMS
Café Yung   2
Cha-teul   3
Second Best Place
in Seoul   1

● RESTAURANTS
Blacksmith Pizza   4
Cheonjin Poja   5
Tosokchon   6

● SHOPS
Ccomaque   2
Kwang Ju Yo   3
Yido Pottery   1

■ NIGHTLIFE
Dugahun   1
Jeon Daegamdaek   3
Sanchez   2

■ ACCOMMODATION
Bukchon Maru   1
Haemil Guesthouse   5
Hide & Seek Guesthouse   4
Rakkojae   2
Sopoong Guesthouse   3

power – as well as the area of most interest to foreign visitors. To the east is **Changdeokgung**, a little more refined than Gyeongbokgung, and the only one of Seoul's five palaces to have been added to UNESCO's World Heritage list.

While the palaces are the main draw, there's much more to see in the area. Abutting Gyeongbokgung to the northeast is the neighbourhood of **Samcheongdong**, a trendy, laidback area filled with cafés, galleries, wine bars and clothing boutiques. Across a small ridge, hilly **Bukchon Hanok Village** provides the traditional counterpoint – you'll find plenty of tearooms and traditional culture among the splendidly tiled rooftops of its wooden buildings.

One popular **day-trip** itinerary is to start the morning at Gyeongbokgung and take in the on-site museums before heading to Samcheongdong for a meal and a cup of coffee; energy thus restored, you can head across hilly Bukchon towards the palace of Changdeokgung, then perhaps down into Insadong (see p.69) for dinner.

Gyeongbokgung

경복궁 • Daily except Tues: March–Oct 9am–6pm; Nov–Feb 9am–5pm • Free English-language tours 11am, 1.30pm & 3.30pm • Changing of the guard Wed–Mon 10am, 1pm & 3pm • W3000, or on W10,000 combination ticket with Changdeokgung (see p.69), Changgyeonggung (see p.78), Deoksugung (see p.74) and Jongmyo shrine (see p.71) • ⓦ royalpalace.go.kr • Gyeongbokgung subway (line 3)

The glorious palace of **Gyeongbokgung** is, with good reason, the most popular tourist sight in the city, and a focal point of the country as a whole. The place is absorbing, and the chance to stroll the dusty paths between its delicate tile-roofed buildings is one of the most enjoyable experiences Seoul has to offer. Gyeongbokgung was ground zero for Seoul's emergence as a place of power, having been built to house the royal family of the embryonic **Joseon dynasty**, shortly after they transferred their capital here in 1392. The complex has witnessed fires, repeated destruction and even a royal assassination (see box, p.66, and p.349), but careful reconstruction means that the regal atmosphere of old is still palpable, aided no end by the suitably majestic crags of Bugaksan to the north. A large historical complex with excellent on-site **museums**, it

WHICH PALACE?

Seoul has five **palaces** (and one "unofficial" palace) to choose from, and while they're all great, you may not have the time, energy or patience to traipse around all of them. The following is a short summary of their merits. Note that a **combination ticket** (W10,000) is available to the four palaces that charge admission – Gyeongbokgung, Changdeokgung (including the Secret Garden), Changgyeonggung and Deoksugung – as well as Jongmyo shrine (see p.71). Available at all venues, these tickets are valid for a month from first usage; note that certain venues are closed on Mondays or Tuesdays.

Gyeongbokgung (above) The oldest and most historically important of the palaces, this attracts the greatest number of visitors and boasts a splendid mountain backdrop, as well as two great museums.

Changdeokgung (p.69) Perhaps best viewed as the connoisseurs' choice, this has been listed as World Heritage on account of its superb architecture and charming garden.

Unhyeongung (p.71) Never used as a regal residence and thus not an official palace, this is rarely busy and well worth tracking down if you're in the Insadong area.

Gyeonghuigung (p.73) Viewed by Seoulites as the runt of the palace litter, this is the one to pick if you'd like to be away from the crowds – it's still a charming and beautiful place, and handily located next to the city's museum of history.

Deoksugung (p.74) Used as a palace in the early twentieth century, when Korea was opening up to the wider world, Deoksugung's grounds contain some incongruous European-style structures, one of which now functions as one of the city's best art museums.

Changgyeonggung (p.78) More natural in feel than the other palaces, Changgyeonggung has some delightful grassy areas – and a particularly intriguing history, involving Japanese desecration and a royal murder.

1

THE SECRET HISTORY OF SEOUL'S GRANDEST PALACE

Gyeongbokgung's construction was ordered by **King Taejo** in 1394, and the "Palace of Shining Happiness" held the regal throne for over two hundred years. At its peak, the palace housed over four hundred buildings within its vaguely rectangular perimeter walls, but most were burned down during the **Japanese invasions** in the 1590s. Though few Koreans will admit to it, the invaders were not directly to blame – the arsonists were actually a group of local slaves, angered by their living and working conditions. The palace was only rebuilt following the coronation of child-king **Gojong** in 1863, but the Japanese were to invade again shortly afterwards, forcibly opening up Korea to foreign trade, and slowly ratcheting up their standing on the peninsula.

In 1895 **Empress Myeongseong**, one of Gojong's wives and an obstacle to the Japanese – who refer to her as "Queen Min" – was assassinated in the Gyeongbokgung grounds, a shady tale told in countless movies and soap operas, and a precursor to the full-scale **Japanese annexation** of Korea in 1910. During the occupation, which ended with World War II in 1945, the Japanese used Gyeongbokgung for police interrogation and torture, and made numerous changes to the building in an apparent effort to destroy Korean pride. The front gate, Gwanghwamun, was moved to the east of the complex, destroying the north–south geometric principles followed during the palace's creation, while a Japanese command post was built in the sacred first courtyard in a shape identical to the Japanese written character for "sun" (日). One interesting suggestion – and one certainly not beyond the scope of Japanese thinking at that time – is that Bukhansan mountain to the north resembled the character for "big" (大) and City Hall to the south that of "root" (本), thereby emblazoning Seoul's most prominent points with the three characters that made up the name of the Empire of the Rising Sun (大日本).

can easily eat up the best part of a day. Try to time your visit to coincide with the colourful **changing of the guard** ceremonies.

The palace

Most visitors will start their tour at **Gwanghwamun** (광화문), the palace's southern gate. Entering through the first courtyard you'll see **Geunjeongjeon** (근정전), the palace's former throne room, looming ahead. Despite being the largest wooden structure in the country, this two-level construction remains surprisingly graceful, the corners of its gently sloping roof home to lines of tiny guardian figurines. The central path leading up to the building was once used only by the king, but the best views of its interior are actually from the sides – from here you'll see the golden dragons on the hall ceiling, as well as the throne itself, backed by its traditional folding screen.

After Geunjeongjeon you can take one of a number of routes around the complex. To the east of the throne room are the buildings that once housed **crown princes**, deliberately placed here to give these regal pups the day's first light, while behind is **Gangnyeongjeon** (강녕전), the former living quarters of the king and queen, furnished with replica furniture. Also worth seeking out is **Jagyeongjeon** (자경전), a building backed by a beautiful stone wall, and chimneys decorated with animal figures.

West of the throne room is **Gyeonghoeru** (경회루), a colossal pavilion looking out over a tranquil **lotus pond** that was a favourite with artists in regal times, and remains so today. The pond was used both for leisure and as a ready source of water for the fires that regularly broke out around the palace (an unfortunate by-product of heating buildings with burning wood or charcoal under the floor), while the pavilion itself was once a place for banquets and civil service examinations.

North of the throne room, and right at the back of the complex, are a few buildings constructed in 1888 during the rule of King Gojong to house books and works of art. These structures were designed in the Chinese style that was the height of fashion at the time, and are markedly different from any other structures around the palace.

1

The National Folk Museum

국립민속박물관 • Daily except Tues: March, April, Sept & Oct 9am–6pm; May–Aug 9am–6pm, Sat & Sun until 7pm; Nov–Feb 9am–5pm • Entry free with palace ticket • Ⓦ nfm.go.kr

On the east side of the palace complex is the **National Folk Museum**, a traditionally styled, multi-tier structure that fits in nicely with the palatial buildings. Despite its size, there's only one level, but this is stuffed with dioramas and explanations of Korean ways of life long since gone, from fishing and farming practices to examples of clothing worn during the Three Kingdoms era.

The National Palace Museum

국립고궁박물관 • Tues–Fri 9am–6pm, Sat & Sun 9am–7pm • Free English-language tours 11am & 2.30pm • Free • Ⓦ gogung.go.kr

At the far southwest of the palace grounds is the **National Palace Museum**. The star of the show here is a **folding screen** which would have once been placed behind the imperial throne, and features the sun, moon and five peaks painted onto a dark blue background, symbolically positioning the seated kings at the nexus of heaven and earth. It's a glorious, deep piece of art that deserves to be better known. Other items in the fascinating display include a jade book belonging to King Taejo, paraphernalia relating to ancestral rites, and some of the wooden dragons taken from the temple eaves, whose size and detail can be better appreciated when seen up close. Equally meticulous is a map of the heavens engraved onto a stone slab in 1395.

Samcheongdong

삼청동

The youthful district of **Samcheongdong** is crammed with restaurants, cafés and galleries, most of which have a more contemporary appearance than their counterparts in Insadong. The area's charming main drag, Samcheongdonggil (삼청동길), heads off from Gyeongbokgung's northeastern corner – it's a mere five-minute walk from the palace's eastern exit. On the way between the two, be sure to pop into at least one of the excellent galleries on **Samcheongno**, a road running along the east flank of the palace (see box below).

National Museum of Modern and Contemporary Art

국립미술관 • Tues, Thurs, Fri & Sun 10am–6pm, Wed & Sat 10am–9pm • W4000 • Ⓦ mmca.go.kr • Anguk subway (line 3); shuttle buses (4 daily) run to their other location in Gwacheon

Opened in late 2013, this third wing of the **National Museum of Modern and Contemporary Art** (see p.74 and p.93 for the others) was erected to house the Japanese

---

THE SAMCHEONGNO ART STRETCH

Perhaps Korea's most important road in artistic terms, **Samcheongno** sports a number of lauded **galleries**, all free to browse around, as well as the new National Museum of Modern and Contemporary Art (see above). Anguk station (line 3) is best for the whole lot.

Arario Seoul Ⓦ ararioseoul.com. This large venue lends itself to sculpture work or large paintings, and the offerings are always from renowned artists. With a sister gallery in Shanghai, the Arario is often a great place to check out the latest work from the increasingly interesting art scene over the West (Yellow) Sea. Tues–Sun 11am–7pm.

Gallery Hyundai Ⓦ galleryhyundai.com. This large gallery possesses the most esteemed collection in the area; in existence since the 1960s, it's Korea's longest-running commercial gallery. The focus has long been on artists born before 1930, but times are changing and there's an ever-increasing emphasis on newer trends. Tues–Sun 10am–6pm.

Kukje Gallery Ⓦ kukjegallery.com. The Kukje is one of the most important players in the area, actively promoting Korean artists abroad, and hauling a wide, well-selected range of exhibits into its own space. It's surrounded by excellent cafés and restaurants, too. Mon–Sat 10am–6pm, Sun 10am–5pm.

1

Defence Security Command during the occupation period. Despite this weighty history, the art on display is not just modern in nature, but on the very edge of contemporary. There's no permanent display, but each and every exhibition (there's usually a new one every two weeks) is highly creative, revolving around the open-air Madang Gallery, Seoul's own equivalent to the Turbine Hall in London's Tate Modern.

Cheongwadae

청와대 • Guided tours Tues–Sat at 10am, 11am, 2pm & 3pm • Free but must be booked at least three weeks in advance at ⓦ english. president.go.kr; remember to bring your passport • Gyeongbokgung or Anguk subway (both line 3)

What the White House is to Washington, **Cheongwadae** is to Seoul. Sitting directly behind Gyeongbokgung and surrounded by mountains, this official presidential residence is named the "Blue House" on account of the colour of its roof tiles. In Joseon times, blue roofs were reserved for kings, but the office of the president is the nearest modern-day equivalent to regal rule. The road that borders the palace is open for public access, but don't venture too close to the entrance as it's understandably a high-security area. In 1968, a group of 31 North Korean soldiers were apprehended here during an attempt to assassinate then-President Park Chung-hee; while you're unlikely to be accused of doing the same, if you loiter or stray too close you may well be questioned.

Bukchon Hanok Village

북촌 한옥 마을

A few of Samcheongdong's cafés and galleries spill over into **Bukchon Hanok Village**, an area characterized by the prevalence of traditional wooden **hanok buildings**. These once covered the whole country, but most were torn down during Korea's economic revolution and replaced with row upon row of fifteen-storey blocks. The city council spared this area the wrecking ball, and as a result there's some delightful walking to be done among its quiet lanes, where tiny restaurants, tearooms and comic-book shops line the streets, and children play games on mini arcade machines, creating a pleasant air of indifference hard to find in the capital; a few of the buildings have even been converted into guesthouses (see box, p.97). Many Bukchon visitors make a beeline to **Bukchon Hanok Ilgil** (북촌 한옥 1길), a steep lane with a particularly good view of the *hanok* abodes.

SEOUL'S QUIRKY MUSEUMS

Samcheongdong and Bukchon are home to countless **tiny museums**, and while none are exactly must-sees, it can be worth popping into one or two on your way around the area – especially if the weather is inclement.

Chicken Art Museum (닭문화관; Tues–Sun 10am–6pm; W5000). Impressionism, Art Deco, Bauhaus… chicken art. Focusing solely on the last of these, this is one of Korea's more peculiar museums, and has proven highly popular with international visitors. The greatest surprise is finding out how many countries have produced artists obsessed with the humble chicken.

Gahoe Museum (가회 박물관; Tues–Sun 10am–6pm; W3000). Housed in one of the area's many wooden *hanok* abodes, the folk art here is suitably traditional. The friendly curators also offer regular hands-on craft programmes.

Owl Art & Craft Museum (부엉이 박물관; Tues–Sun 10am–7pm; W5000). The result of its founder's quirky (and slightly scary) obsession, this small museum is stuffed to the gills with anything and everything pertaining to owls. There's a small tearoom-cum-café in which you can purchase strigiform trinkets of your very own.

World Jewellery Museum (세계장신구박물관; Tues–Sun 11am–5.30pm; W5000). With a name that's as coldly descriptive as they come, it may come as a surprise that this museum is the most rewarding in the area, with the pieces on display offering great subtlety and variety.

Changdeokgung

창덕궁 • Tues–Sun: Feb–Oct 9am–6pm; Nov–Jan 9am–5.30pm • English-language palace tours 10.30am & 2.30pm • Secret Garden by tour only, usually on the hour 10am–4pm • Palace W3000, Secret Garden W5000, or on W10,000 combination ticket with Gyeongbokgung (see p.65), Changgyeonggung (see p.78), Deoksugung (see p.74) and Jongmyo shrine (see p.71) • Ⓦ eng.cdg .go.kr • Anguk subway (line 3)

Sumptuous **Changdeokgung** is, for many, the pick of Seoul's palaces, with immaculate paintwork and carpentry augmenting a palpable sense of history; home to royalty as recently as 1910, this is the best-preserved palace in the city. Its construction was completed in 1412, under the reign of King Taejong. Like Gyeongbokgung, it suffered heavy damage during the **Japanese invasions** of the 1590s; Gyeongbokgung was left to fester, but Changdeokgung was rebuilt and in 1618 usurped its older brother as the seat of the **royal family**, an honour it held until 1872. In its later years, the palace became a symbol of Korea's opening up to the rest of the world: King Heonjong (who ruled 1834–49) added distinctively Chinese-style buildings to the complex, and his eventual successor King Sunjong (ruled 1907–10) was fond of driving Western cars around the grounds. Sunjong was, indeed, the last of Korea's long line of kings; Japanese annexation brought an end to his short rule, but he was allowed to live in Changdeokgung until his death in 1926.

The palace

The huge gate of **Donhwamun** is the first structure you'll come across – dating from 1609, this is the oldest extant palace gate in Seoul. Next is Changdeokgung's suitably impressive **throne room**, which is without doubt the most regal-looking of any Seoul palace – light from outside is filtered through paper doors and windows, bathing in a dim glow the elaborate wooden-beam structure, as well as the throne and its folding-screen backdrop. Beyond here, you'll pass a number of buildings pertaining to the various kings who occupied the palace, some of which still have the original furniture inside; one building even contains King Sunjong's old Daimler and Cadillac, which look more than a little incongruous in their palatial setting. Further on you'll come to **Nakseonjae**, built during the reign of King Heonjong; Qing-style latticed doors and arched pavilion reveal his taste for foreign cultures, and the colours of the bare wood are ignited with shades of gold and honey during sunset.

The Secret Garden

The palace's undoubted highlight is **Huwon** (후원), usually referred to in Seoul's tourist literature as the "Secret Garden". Approached via a suitably mysterious path, the garden is concealed by an arch of leaves. In the centre is a **lotus pond**, one of Seoul's most photographed sights, and alive with colourful flowers in late June or early July. A small building overlooking the pond served as a library and study room in imperial times, and the tiny gates blocking the entrance path were used as an interesting checking mechanism by the king – needing to crouch to pass through, he'd be reminded of his duty to be humble.

Insadong

인사동

The undisputed hub of Korea's tourist scene, **Insadong** is a city district whose tight lattice of streets is full to the brim with art galleries (see box, p.71), shops (see p.112), tearooms (see p.106) and traditional restaurants (see p.100) – you could quite happily spend most of the day here. The appeal of the area lies in simply strolling around and taking it all in, but there are a fair few bona fide sights around, too. At the southern end of **Insadonggil**, a pedestrianized road which courses through Insadong, is tiny **Tapgol Park**, home to an ancient pagoda. East of Insadonggil are two regal sights: the

1

INSADONG

RESTAURANTS
Abiko	15
Ahndamiro	9
Balwoo	7
Bärlin	2
Bukchon Sonmandu	13
Doodaemunjip	3
Gogung	5
Gwangjujip	11
Meokgeorichon	14
Nwijo	1
Potala	16

ACCOMMODATION
Banana Backpackers	3
Doulos	9
Fraser Suites	7
Hostel Korea 11th	2
Insa Hostel	4
Noble	1
Seven Street	10
Sheel	8
Somerset Palace	5
Sunbee	6

SHOPS
Bandi & Luni	5
Lee Geon Maan	4
Myung Sin Dang	2
Ssamiziegil	1
Tongin	3

CAFÉS & TEAROOMS
Bizeun	12
Coffee Bean & Tea Leaf	10
Dawon	4
O'Sulloc	6
Su Yo Il	8

NIGHTLIFE
Barcode	2
Baekseju Maeul	3
Brew 3.14	1

lesser-known palace of **Unhyeongung**; and **Jongmyo**, a shrine where ancient ancestral ceremonies are still performed. Heading west instead will bring you to **Jogyesa**, Seoul's most-visited temple. Running along the southern edge of Insadong is **Cheonggyecheon**, a gentrified stream which forms a below-street-level paradise for pedestrians and joggers.

Tapgol Park

탑골공원 • Daily 9am–6pm • Free • Jonggak subway (line 1)

Insadonggil finishes at small **Tapgol Park**, a small patch of land containing as much concrete as it does grass. It is, however, a place famed to Koreans as the venue for 1919's declaration of independence against Japanese rule (see p.349). It's also home to a huge, stunning Joseon-era **stone pagoda**, which sits resplendent at the park's northern end; grandly titled official "National Treasure Number Two", the pagoda has actually been the de facto number one since the burning down of Sungnyemun (see box, p.78), but sadly the beauty of its ancient design has been hugely diluted by the ugly glass box placed around it for protection.

INSADONG ART GALLERIES

All of these **galleries** are on or around **Insadonggil**, and can be reached via several subway stations: Jonggak (line 1), Jongno 3-ga (lines 1, 3 & 5) or Anguk (line 3). Admission is free unless otherwise stated.

Insa Art Centre This interesting building's seven floors of exhibitions could keep you busy for some time – the acres of wall space display a wide range of modern styles. Those spending a while in Seoul can return for further helpings, as the place is stripped every week to make room for new works. Admission is free, unless there's a special exhibition on. Usually open 10am–7pm; closes early Tues and opens late Wed to install new exhibitions.

Insa Gallery ⓦ insagallery.net. This three-floored gallery's collection features some of the most interesting Korean artists of recent times. Its exploration of modern themes and styles is renowned in this competitive neighbourhood, and the twice-monthly change-around system keeps things fresh. Daily 10am–6.30pm; free.

Kyungin Museum of Fine Art Exhibitions are rarely poor at this long-time local favourite, whose tradition-with-a-twist style reflects a desire to fuse the conventional with the contemporary. Its four rooms are pleasant and spacious, and are centred around a leafy traditional courtyard that's also home to *Dawon*, a decent tearoom (see p.106). Daily 10am–6pm.

Sun Art Center ⓦ sungallery.co.kr. Spoken about in hushed tones by curators at other Insadong galleries, this houses probably the most renowned collection in the area. It mainly consists of early twentieth-century paintings, and shows that modern art in Korea goes back way before the country's growth into an economic power – look for pieces by Kim Sou, who had a Rubens-like obsession with flesh, or the floral works of Kim Chong Hak. Tues–Sun 10am–6pm.

Toto Is it a gallery, a museum or a shop? Regardless, Toto is filled with toy planes, trains and automobiles, as well as toy action figures of characters who wear their underpants on the outside. Some pieces are rare, but there are cheaper ones to take away as quirky souvenirs. W1000 admission. Daily 10am–6pm.

Unhyeongung

운현궁 • Tues–Sun 9am–7pm • Free • Anguk subway (line 3)

Having never been an official royal residence, the tiny palace of **Unhyeongung** doesn't qualify as one of Seoul's "big five" palaces; accordingly, it's less showy than the others, but the relative pancity of tourists makes it a pleasant place to visit – the bare wood and paper doors would provide the perfect setting for a Japanese *anime*. Though he never lived here, King Gojong married the ill-fated Princess Myeongseong in Unhyeongung, and it was also the centre of neo-Confucian thought during the Joseon period, which sought to base civil progress on merit rather than lineage (see p.172 for information on Yi Toegye, one of the main instigators).

Jongmyo

종묘 • Mon, Wed–Fri & Sun guided tours only (English-language tours 10am, noon, 2pm & 4pm); Sat open access 9am–6pm • W1000, or on W10,000 combination ticket with Gyeongbokgung (see p.65), Changdeokgung (see p.69), Changgyeonggung (see p.78) and Deoksugung (see p.74) • Jongno 3-ga subway (lines 1, 3 & 5)

Along with the palace of Gyeongbokgung, the construction of **Jongmyo shrine** was on King Taejo's manifesto as he kicked off the Joseon dynasty in 1392. He decreed that dead kings and queens would be honoured here in true Confucian style, with a series of ancestral rites. These ceremonies were performed five times a year, once each season, with an extra one on the winter solstice, when the ruling king would pay his respects to those who died before him by bowing profusely, and explaining pertinent national issues to their **spirit tablets**. These wooden blocks, in which deceased royalty were believed to reside, are still stored in large wooden buildings that were said to be the biggest in Asia at the time of their construction. Jeongjeon was the first, but such was the length of the Joseon dynasty that another building – Yeongnyeongjeon – had to be added.

For most of the week the shrine is only accessible on **guided tours**, which remove the joy of simply wandering around the wooded complex – **go on Saturday** if at all possible,

1

which is the one day on which you'll be given free rein. Whether on a tour or not, note that the buildings themselves remain locked, though the courtyards are open – take the opportunity to walk on the raised paths that were once reserved for kings. The one exception to this is on the first Sunday in May, which is the day of **Jongmyo Daeje** (see box, p.110), a long, solemn ceremony followed by traditional court dances – an absolute must-see.

Jogyesa

조계사 • Tues–Sun 9am–6pm • Free • W10,000 • Jonggak station (line 1)

Near the north end of Insadonggil, on the west side, is **Jogyesa**, the only major temple in the centre of Seoul. Created in 1910 and hemmed in by large buildings, it has neither history nor beauty to its credit, but for visitors with little time in the country it may represent the only chance to see a Korean temple of such size. The best times to visit are on Buddha's birthday (see p.43) and the Lotus Lantern festival.

Cheonggyecheon

청계천 • 24hr • Free • Accessible from many stations, including Gwanghwamun (line 5) and Jonggak (line 1)

Until recently, **Cheonggyecheon** was a mucky stream running under an elevated highway, but in 2003 the Mayor of Seoul decided to ditch the road and beautify the creek – this controversial project saw heads rolling on corruption charges, grumbles from local businesses and protests from environmentalists, but since completion in 2005 it has been looked upon as a resounding success. Both the stream and the walkways that flank it are below street level, and on descending you'll notice that Seoul's ceaseless cacophony has been diluted and largely replaced by the sound of rushing water.

Cheonggyecheon starts just southeast of Gwanghwamun Plaza, at a point marked by a curious piece of **modern art** designed to resemble a snail (many locals prefer to call it a turd). Heading east, you'll pass a series of features, including fountains, sculpture and stepping stones; it's around 3km from the start to Dongdaemun market (see p.77), though the paths continue on for a whopping 7km beyond, joining the Hangang near Oksu station – a stretch used almost exclusively by local joggers, cyclists and power-walkers.

Gwanghwamun and City Hall

Looking north from Gwanghwamun, the main gate of Gyeongbokgung palace, you can see little but cascading palace roofs, and the mountains beyond. Turn south instead, and the contrast is almost unbelievably stark – looming up behind **Gwanghwamun Plaza** are the ranked masses of high-rise blocks that announce Seoul's main **business district**, its walkways teeming with black-suited businessfolk and their civil servant brethren racing in and out of the grand new **City Hall**. However, there's more tourist interest than you might expect in this *balli-balli* (Korean for "quickly, quickly!") area, including two palaces, a few major **museums** and **art galleries**, some fine examples of colonial architecture, and **Jeongdonggil**, one of Seoul's most charming roads, lined with ginkgo trees and popular with couples.

National Museum of Korean Contemporary History

대한민국 역사박물관 • Tues, Thurs, Fri & Sun 9am–6pm, Wed & Sat 9am–9pm • Free • ⊕ much.go.kr • Gyeongbokgung subway (line 3)

A relatively new addition to the area, opened in 2012, the **National Museum of Korean Contemporary History** focuses on Korean goings-on post-1876. With Japanese occupation and the Korean War forming part of that period, they've plenty of material to be going on with; of particular note are a spellbinding series of photographs from the occupation and war periods, as well as a recreated "street" from the time. The on-site café on the upper level has a grand view of Gyeongbokgung.

Gyeonghuigung

경희궁 • Tues–Sun 9am–6pm • Free • Gwanghwamun subway (line 5)

Humble **Gyeonghuigung** is the most anonymous and least visited of Seoul's Five Grand Palaces – even locals may struggle to point you towards it – but its simplicity tends to strike a chord with those who choose to track it down. Gyeonghuigung was built in 1616, and became a royal palace by default when Changdeokgung (see p.69) was burned down in 1624. Though a little forlorn, it's a pretty place nonetheless, and may be the palace for you if crowds, false-bearded guards in faux period clothing and the necessity of avoiding camera sightlines aren't to your liking. Unlike other palaces, you'll be able to enter the throne room – bare except for the throne, but worth a look – before scrambling up to the halls of the upper level, which have a visually pleasing backdrop of grass and rock.

1

Seoul Museum of History

서울 역사박물관 • Tues–Fri 9am–10pm, Sat & Sun 10am–7pm • Free; around W12,000 for big-name special exhibitions •
Gwanghwamun subway (line 5)

Adjacent to Gyeonghuigung is the **Museum of History**, whose **permanent exhibition**
on the third floor focuses on Joseon-era Seoul. Here you'll find lacquered boxes
with mother-of-pearl inlay, porcelain bowls and vases thrown in gentle shapes, and
silk gowns with embroidered leaves and dragons. Another room popular with
visitors features a gigantic photographic image of Seoul covering its entire floor
space. Certain halls play host to **rotating exhibitions**, which usually justify the
extra charge.

Seoul Museum of Art

서울시립미술관 • Tues–Fri 10am–9pm, Sat & Sun 10am–6pm • Admission price varies by exhibition; figure on W15,000 for major
ones • ⓦ sema.seoul.go.kr • City Hall subway (lines 1 & 2)

The large, modern **Seoul Museum of Art**, otherwise known as SeMA, sits just off
Jeongdonggil. More gallery than museum, it's well worth popping in for a look at what
are invariably high-quality exhibitions of art from around the world – Picasso, Monet,
Van Gogh and Renoir have all found temporary homes here. In addition, there are
always free secondary exhibitions to peruse, most commonly the work of local (or at
least Asian) artists. On exiting the museum look out for a strange piece of art across the
road – a black metal statue of a man perpetually hammering, a mute reminder to folk
from the nearby business district that life's not all about work.

Deoksugung

덕수궁 • Tues–Sun 9am–9pm • English-language tours Tues–Fri 10.30am, plus either Sat or Sun at 1.40pm • Changing of the
guard 11am, 2pm & 3.30pm • W1000, or on W10,000 combination ticket with Gyeongbokgung (see p.65), Changdeokgung (see p.69),
Changgyeonggung (see p.78) and Jongmyo shrine (see p.71) • ⓦ deoksugung.go.kr • City Hall subway (lines 1 & 2)

Located in the very centre of Seoul's business district, it's no surprise that the palace of
Deoksugung receives plenty of visitors, a volume amplified by the compound's
relatively small size. This was the last palace of Seoul's big five to be built, and it
became the country's seat of power almost by default in 1592 when the Japanese
destroyed Gyeongbokgung (see p.65); its reign was short, however, since only two
kings lived here before the seat of power was transferred to a newly rebuilt
Changdeokgung (see p.69). Deoksugung then became the de facto royal residence
again in 1895; **King Gojong** fled here after the murder of his wife, and declared the
short-lived **Empire of Korea** here before ceding control to Japan.

The **palace** is entered through **Daehanmun** (대한문), a gate on the eastern side of the
complex – this goes against the tenets of *feng shui*, which usually result in south-facing
palace entrances. Most visitors then make a beeline to the main hall, **Junghwajeon**
(중화전), whose ceiling sports a pair of immaculate carved dragons. Be sure to check
out **Jeonggwanheon** (정관헌), a pavilion used for **coffee-drinking** by King Gojong,
who developed something of a taste for said beverage here.

National Museum of Modern and Contemporary Art

국립미술관 • Tues, Thurs, Fri & Sun 10am–7pm, Wed & Sat 10am–9pm • Admission price varies by exhibition; usually
W3000–10,000 • ⓦ mmca.go.kr

Deoksugung contains a couple of **Western-style buildings**, dating back to when the
"Hermit Kingdom" of the Joseon dynasty was being forcibly opened up to trade. At
the end of a gorgeous rose garden is **Seokjojeon** (석조전), designed by an English
architect and built by the Japanese in 1910; the first Western-style building in the
country, it was actually used as the royal home for a short time. It now houses a
wing of the **National Museum of Modern and Contemporary Art** (see p.67 and p.93

for the others), whose exhibits are usually quality works from local artists, more often than not blending elements of traditional Korean styles with those of the modern day.

Myeongdong and Dongdaemun

To Koreans, and a whole generation of travellers from other Asian countries, the words **Myeongdong** and **Dongdaemun** mean one thing and one thing alone: **shopping**. Many visitors from China, Japan, Thailand and Taiwan pin their Korean travel plans on these two areas alone, and never venture beyond their wider perimeter – a pity, for sure, but testament to the zone's ever-increasing international reputation. Myeongdong's tightly packed web of streets features literally hundreds of shops selling clothing, cosmetics and street snacks, while Dongdaemun is the marketplace equivalent, and of more interest to those buying fabric or knock-off handbags. However, it's not all about consumption – **Myeongdong Cathedral** is up there with Korea's prettiest Christian places of worship, while just to the south rises **Namsan**, Seoul's own mini-mountain.

Myeongdong Cathedral

명동성당 • Weekday Mass 6.30am & 6pm; English-language Mass Sun 9am • Free • Euljiro 1-ga subway (line 2)

The hub of Korea's large – and growing – **Catholic** community, **Myeongdong Cathedral** stands proudly over the shopping area. Designed in Gothic style by **French missionaries**, the elegant lines of its red-brick exterior are a breath of fresh air in the business district's maze of concrete cuboids. It was completed in 1898 at the bequest of King Gojong, who desired to make up for persecutions witnessed under his predecessors: the site on which the cathedral stands had previously been home to a Catholic faith community, many of whom were executed during the **purges** of 1866 (see p.359).

Namsangol Hanok Village

남산골 • Daily: April–Oct 9am–9pm; Nov–March 9am–8pm • Free • Chungmuro subway (lines 3 & 4)

On your way up to Namsan, you may care to stop by at **Namsangol**, a small recreated **folk village** of *hanok* housing. The area is pretty and quite photogenic; there are usually a few traditional games for kids (and the young at heart) to play, and occasional displays of dance and music. The buildings back onto a pleasing park, which makes as good an entry point as any for Namsan itself.

Namsan

남산 • Cable car daily 10am–11pm • W6000 one-way, W8000 return • Dedicated buses every 15–20min: #2 from Chungmuro, #3 from Seoul station and Itaewon, #5 from Myeongdong and Chungmuro

South of Myeongdong station the roads rise up, eventually coming to a stop at the feet of **Namsan**, a 265m-high peak in the centre of Seoul. Though it may be hard to believe today, Namsan once marked the natural boundary of a city that has long since swelled over the edges and across the river – some restored sections of the old city wall can still be seen on the mountain, as can the remains of **fire beacons** that once formed part of an ingenious pan-national communication system. Most visitors reach the top by **cable car**, but don't be fooled into thinking you'll be whisked up without a bead of sweat, since the base is an uphill slog south of Myeongdong subway station; you can chalk much of it off by taking a nearby lift. Alternatively, just walk up from Myeongdong, Seoul station or Itaewon.

1

MYEONGDONG AND DONGDAEMUN

● SHOP
Gwangjang Market   1

■ ACCOMMODATION
Ibis Ambassador   2
Metro   1
Royal   3
The Shilla   4

■ NIGHTLIFE
Neurin Maeul   1
Pierre's Bar   2

● RESTAURANTS
Bulgogi Brothers   7
Din Tai Fung   6
Gostiniy Dvor   4
Gwangjang Market   1
Korea House   9
Mongmyeok Sanbang   10
N Grill   11
Pierre Gagnaire à
  Seoul   8
Taj   3
Woo Rae Oak   2

● CAFÉS & TEAROOMS
Cat Café   8
Mongmyeok Sanbang   10

1

N Seoul Tower

서울타워 • Viewing platform Mon–Fri 10am–11pm, Sat & Sun 10am–midnight • W9000 • ⓦ nseoultower.net

N Seoul Tower sits proudly on Namsan's crown and is the most recent incarnation of Seoul Tower, whose name was clearly not trendy enough to pass the consultancy test that followed the redesigning of its interior in 2005. The five levels of the upper section are now home to a **viewing platform**, and assorted **cafés and restaurants**. For many, the free views from the tower's base are good enough, and coming here to see the **sunset** is recommended – the grey mass of daytime Seoul turns in no time into a pulsating neon spectacle.

Dongdaemun

동대문

Dongdaemun's famed market area (see box below) was named after a gigantic **ornamental gate** that still stands here – *dong* means "east", *dae* means "great" and *mun* "gate". Originally built in 1396, this was once the eastern entrance to a much smaller Seoul; its counterpart, way to the southwest, was Namdaemun, which was savaged by fire in 2008 (see box, p.78). Dongsaemun was yet another of the structures built by the incredibly ambitious **King Taejo** in the 1390s (see box, p.62), at the dawn of his Joseon dynasty; fires and warfare have taken their inevitable toll, and the present structure is of a mere 1869 vintage.

Dongdaemun Design Plaza (DDP)

동대문 디자인 플라자 • Complex daily 24hr • Most exhibitions around W8000 • Museum daily 9am–6pm • Free • ⓦ ddp.or.kr • Dongdaemun History & Culture Park subway station (lines 2, 4 & 5)

The newest and most notable sight in the Dongdaemun area is the **Dongdaemun Design Plaza**, a collection of futuristic buildings and grassy walking areas. Opened in 2014 and colloquially referred to as the "DDP", this gargantuan city project was designed by Iraq-born architect **Zaha Hadid**, who won the tender with a design said to echo plumes of smoke – it was then altered slightly to its present shape, which is far

---

DONGDAEMUN AND NAMDAEMUN: MARKET MADNESS

Between them, the colossal markets of **Dongdaemun** (동대문 시장) and **Namdaemun** (남대문 시장) could quite conceivably feed, and maybe even clothe, the world. Both are deservedly high on most visitors' list of sights to tick off in Seoul.

Dongdaemun market is the largest in the country, spread out, open-air and indoors, in various locations around the prettified Cheonggyecheon creek (see p.72). It would be impossible to list the whole range of things on sale here – you'll find yourself walking past anything from herbs to *hanbok* or paper lanterns to knock-off clothing, usually on sale for reasonable prices. Though each section of the market has its own opening and closing time, the complex as a whole simply never closes, so at least part of it will be open whenever you decide to come. Night-time is when the market is at its most atmospheric, with clothes stores pumping out music into the street at ear-splitting volume, and the air filled with the smell of freshly made food sizzling at streetside stalls. Though some of the dishes on offer are utterly unrecognizable to many foreign visitors, it pays to be adventurous. One segment particularly popular with foreigners is **Gwangjang market** (광장 시장), a particularly salty offshoot of Dongdaemun to the northwest, and one of Seoul's most idiosyncratic places to eat in the evening – just look for something tasty and point. During the day, it's also the best place in Seoul to buy **secondhand clothes** (see p.113).

Smaller and more compact than Dongdaemun, where you'll find essentially the same goods, is Namdaemun market, which stretches out between City Hall and Seoul station. It's best accessed through Hoehyeon subway station (exits five or six), while Dongdaemun market's spine road runs between Dongdaemun and Dongdaemun Stadium stations.

1

THE DEATH OF NATIONAL TREASURE NUMBER ONE

Namdaemun, Seoul's "Great South Gate", was built in 1398 by **King Taejo** as a means of glorifying and protecting his embryonic kingdom. This was by no means the only major project to come out of Taejo's first years of rule (see box, p.62), but random fires, Japanese invasions and civil war rubbed out the rest over the following centuries. Namdaemun, also known as Sungnyemun, was feted as the country's official "**National Treasure Number One**" on account of its age, beauty and importance. It was the sole survivor from the Taejo era, which made things all the more harrowing when after six centuries standing proudly over Seoul, it was destroyed in a matter of minutes by a lone **arsonist**, Chae Jong-gi. Chae had noticed that Namdaemun was guarded by nothing but a single set of motion sensors – not the best way to protect one of the oldest wooden structures in the land. Early in the morning on February 10, 2008, he mounted the gate armed with a few bottles of paint thinner – hours later, images of weeping Seoulites were being beamed around the world, all bemoaning the loss of their smouldering city icon. However, Korea's incendiary history means that it has substantial experience of reconstructing its treasures, and **renovation** of Namdaemun was completed in 2013.

more proximate to a high-heeled shoe. The reason for this change was the discovery of thousands of **dynastic relics** found in the earth; construction was delayed for over a year, and a small **museum** added to display some of the bounty. Elsewhere, bar a café or two and a couple of gallery and **exhibition spaces**, the complex seems a little overlarge and underused.

Northern Seoul

North of Gyeongbokgung, Seoul appears to come to a rather abrupt end, with lofty mountains rearing up immediately behind the palace. The city did, indeed, once peter out here, but the "economic miracle" of the 1970s saw its population mushroom, and consequently Seoul's urban sprawl pushed around the mountainsides. Development was, however, not as rampant as in other parts of the city, and Seoul's **northern quarters** maintain a relatively secluded air. Northwest of Changdeokgung is the buzzing student district of **Daehangno**, a long-time favourite with visiting backpackers. Better for sightseeing is **Seongbukdong**, just north of Daehangno; here you'll find a secluded temple, plus the enchanting *Suyeon Sanbang* tearoom (see p.106), possibly the best in the city.

Seongbukdong lies on the eastern slopes of **Bugaksan**, a mountain whose trails provide some superb views of Seoul. On its western side is **Buamdong**, a quiet, hilly area becoming increasingly popular thanks to assorted clothing boutiques and swanky restaurants and a couple of superb galleries.

Finally, there are the peaks of **Bukhansan**, feted as the most-visited national park in the world, and possessing a range of historical sites and excellent hiking paths.

Changgyeonggung

창경궁 • Daily except Tues 9am–5pm; free tours 11.30am & 4pm • W1000, or on W10,000 combination ticket with Gyeongbokgung (see p.65), Changdeokgung (see p.69), Deoksugung (see p.74) and Jongmyo shrine (see p.71) • 15min walk from Hyehwa subway (line 4), 30min walk from Insadong, or bus #150 or #171 from Anguk station

Separated from Changdeokgung (see p.69) by a perimeter wall, **Changgyeonggung** tends to split visitors into two camps – those who marvel at its history and the relatively natural beauty of grounds far greener than Seoul's other palaces, and those who feel that there's a little less to see. **King Sejong** built Changgyeonggung in 1418 as a resting place for his father, the recently abdicated King Taejong. In its heyday the palace had a far greater number of buildings than are visible today, but these were to suffer badly from fires and the damage inflicted during the Japanese invasions. Almost the whole of the complex burned down in the Japanese attacks of 1592, and then again during a devastating inferno in 1830, while in 1762 the palace witnessed the murder of a crown prince by his father (see box below).

When the Japanese returned in 1907, they turned much of the palace into Korea's first **amusement park**, which included a botanical garden and zoo, as well as a museum; the red brick exterior and pointed steel roof were very much in keeping with the Japanese style of the time, and pictures of this era can still be seen around the palace entrance. Almost all of the Japanese-built features were tolerated by the local government for well over half a century, until almost everything was finally ripped down in 1983, though the **botanical garden** still remains today (access on palace ticket).

THE MURDER OF CROWN PRINCE SADO

In 1762, a sinister event occurred in the grounds of Changgyeonggung, one whose story is, for some reason, omitted from the information boards that dot the palace grounds – a **royal murder**. A young prince named **Sado** was heir to the throne of **King Yeongjo**, but occasionally abused his position of power, as evidenced by the apparently groundless murder of several servants. Fearing dire consequences if the nation's power were placed into his son's hands, Yeongjo escorted Sado to Seonninmun, a gate on the eastern side of the palace, and ordered him to climb into a rice casket; his son obeyed, was locked in, and starved to death. Sado's wife, Hyegyong, held the secret until after Yeongjo's death in 1776, at which point she spilled the beans in a book named *Hanjungnok* (published in English as *The Memoirs of Lady Hyegyong*). Sado's son **Jeongjo** became king on the death of Yeongjo, and built Hwaseong fortress in Suwon (see p.126) to house his father's remains. Jeongjo went on to become one of Korea's most respected rulers.

1

The palace

Considering its turbulent history, the palace is a markedly relaxed place to wander around. The buildings themselves are nowhere near as polished as those in the Gyeongbok or Changdeok palaces, though some feel that they look more authentic as a result; the history of each structure is chronicled on information boards. Be sure to look for **Myeongjeongjeon** (명정전), the oldest main hall of any of Seoul's palaces – it was built in 1616, and somehow escaped the fires that followed. From here, a number of lovely, herb-scented paths wind their way to a pond at the north of the complex. Near the pond are a couple of dedicated **herb gardens**, while also visible are the white-painted lattices of the Japanese-built **botanical garden**.

Gilsangsa

길상사 • Daily 24hr • Free • Templestay (W50,000) available on third Sat of month • ⓦ kilsangsa.info • Hansung University subway (line 4), then shuttle bus (see site for details) or 20min walk

Way uphill in the Seongbukdong area is the wonderful **Zen temple** of **Gilsangsa**. This was once one of Seoul's most famous *gisaeng* (similar to the Japanese geisha) houses of entertainment, but was converted into a Seon (the Korean word for Zen) temple in 1997; it now makes one of the most convenient places for visitors to Seoul to experience a **templestay**, though it's only possible on one weekend each month. Gilsangsa's colouration is notably bland compared to most Korean temples, and as a result it looks its best under a thin blanket of winter snow; this is also the best time to take advantage of the little tearoom on the complex.

Buamdong

부암동

Hidden from central Seoul by the mountain of Bugaksan, **Buamdong** is one of the capital's quaintest and calmest corners. Recent years have seen its fame propelled by modern Korea's number-one cultural catalyst, the television drama: ever since the picturesque café *Sanmotungi* (see p.104) was used as a set in hit drama *The Coffee Prince*, young Seoulites have been heading to the area in ever greater numbers. Despite this, Buamdong retains a tranquillity that's almost impossible to find in other parts of Seoul, as well as a smattering of galleries and excellent places to eat and drink.

Whanki Museum

환기 미술관 • Tues–Sun 10am-6pm • W7000 • ⓦ whankimuseum.org • Bus #1020 from Gwanghwamun subway, or a 20min walk from Gyeongbokgung subway

The little-visited **Whanki Museum** is a shrine of sorts to the unfortunately monikered (to english-speakers) Kim Whanki, one of Korea's first modern artists. In the 1940s, Kim proved a conduit between east and west, mopping up ideas from the Paris avant-garde movement while disseminating Asian techniques to a curious Europe. You may have to ask around to get to it – it's located down a small slope from the main road.

Bugaksan

북악산 • Hiking route open daily 9am–5pm; last entry 3pm • Free • Bring passport to register at entrance • West entrance in Buamdong; east entrance at Waryong Park, a taxi ride or 25min walk from Anguk station

Rising up directly behind the palace of Gyeongbokgung (see p.65) is **Bugaksan**, one of the most significant mountains in Seoul. It provides some of the most glorious possible views of the capital, but for decades only soldiers were able to take them in, the mountain trails having been rendered off limits thanks to the rather important building nestling on its southern slopes – Cheongwadae, official home of the country's president (see p.68).

FROM TOP INSADONG (P.69); GANGNAM (P.89) >

1

These protective measures were not without foundation: in 1968 Bugaksan was the scene of an **assassination attempt**, when a squad of North Korean commandos descended from the mountain with the intention of assassinating then-president **Park Chung-hee**. Near the mountain's eastern entrance, beside the gate of **Sukjeongmun**, a tree riddled with bullet holes is evidence of the shootout that occurred when the would-be assassins were sprung. You can now follow in their dubious footsteps, since the mountain was finally reopened to the public in 2006. Understandably, there's still a substantial military presence here, and those wishing to hike in the area must **register** with officials on arrival.

The **hiking route** across Bugaksan is 3.8km long, and though it gets rather steep at times almost everyone will be able to get up and down in one piece. On the way you'll see remnants of Seoul's fortress wall, which once circled what was then a much smaller city.

Bukhansan National Park

북한산 국립공원

Few major cities can claim to have a national park right on their doorstep, but looming over central Seoul, and forming a natural northern boundary to the city, are the peaks of **BUKHANSAN NATIONAL PARK** – spears and spines of off-white granite that burst out of the undulating pine forests. While an undeniably beautiful place, its popularity means that trails are often very busy indeed – especially so on warm weekends – and some can be as crowded as shopping mall aisles, hikers literally having to queue up to reach the peaks.

The national park can be split into north and south areas. The southern section – **Bukhansan** proper – overlooks Seoul and is home to the fortress ruins, while 10km to the north is **Dobongsan**, a similar maze of stony peaks and hiking trails. Both offer good day-trip routes which are easy enough to be tackled by most visitors, but still enough of a challenge to provide a good work-out. Maps are available at all entrances, and larger signboard versions can be seen at various points en route. Most local hikers choose to wear proper boots, but unless it's rainy a sturdy pair of trainers should suffice.

Southern Bukhansan

Gupabal station (line 3), then bus #704 to park entrance (10min)

The southern half of Bukhansan is best accessed through **Sanseong**, an entry point on the western side of the park. It's around two hours from the entrance to **Baekundae** (백운대; 837m), the highest peak in the park, though note that the masses tramping through Bukhansan have resulted in routes being closed off in rotation to allow them time to regenerate – bilingual signs will point the way. Around ten minutes into your walk you'll find yourself at **Daeseomun** (대서문), one of the main gates of the fortress wall. From here, it's a long slog up to Baekundae; once you've reached **Yaksuam** (약수암), a lofty hermitage, you're almost there (and will doubtless be grateful for the presence of spring-water drinking fountains). As you continue on, the route becomes more precipitous, necessitating the use of steel stairways and fences. Having finally scaled the peak itself, you'll be able to kick off your boots awhile and enjoy the wonderful, panoramic views.

Northern Bukhansan

Mangwolsa and Dobongsan subway (both line 1), then an uphill walk

The scenery in the **Dobongsan** area is much the same as around Baekundae to the south – trees, intriguing rock formations and wonderful views at every turn – though the hiking options are less numerous. Most choose to scale the main peak (740m) on a C-shaped route that curls uphill and down between **Mangwolsa** and **Dobongsan** subway stations. Most hikers start at the latter, but whichever way you go, it takes just over two hours up to the gathering of peaks at the top; like Baeundae to the south of

BUKHANSAN NATIONAL PARK

the park, the upper reaches of the trail are patches of bare rock, and you'll be grateful for the steel ropes on which you can haul yourself up or down. Coming back down, you can take a rest at **Mangwolsa** (망월사), a small but rather beautiful temple originally built here in 639, before heading back into Seoul.

Western Seoul

Western Seoul is best known for the huge university area which spreads north from the Hangang. It should come as no surprise to learn that this is the most important nightlife area in the country, with the action going on all through the night – streets here are stuffed to the gills with bars, nightclubs, karaoke rooms and cheap

1

restaurants. The area's most famous component, **Hongdae**, is also a pleasantly artsy place by day.

Closer to the city centre is the **Seodaemun** district, an unprepossessing area that's host to two great sights: an eponymous **prison** that hosted immunerable atrocities during the Japanese occupation; and **Inwangsan**, a small mountain with a spider's web of fantastic walking trails. The **Hangang** river (see box opposite) separates Hongdae from **Yeouido**, an island that's one of Korea's most important business districts, and home to the city's largest fish market.

Seodaemun Prison

서대문 형무소 역사관 • Tues–Sun 9.30am–6pm • W3000 • Dongnimmun subway (line 3)

The occupied Korea of 1910–45 saw umpteen prisons built across the land to house thousands of activists and those otherwise opposed to Japanese rule. **Seodaemun Prison** was by far the most notorious, and the red-brick wings of its main barracks have now been reopened as a "history hall". Photos of the prison during occupation fill the rooms and corridors, together with written material from the period, and some televised documentaries. Few of these exhibits are in English, but the eerie vibe of the buildings themselves needs no translation, from the tiny vertical booths used for "coffin" torture to the lonely outpost where executions were conducted.

One piece of information not conveyed on any signboards, in any language, is the fact that the prison was not only used by the Japanese. Though independent, South Korea only became democratic in the late 1980s, and until then the prison was used to hold political activists and other enemies of the state. It was finally closed in 1987, immediately after the first fully democratic elections. Also absent is any information on

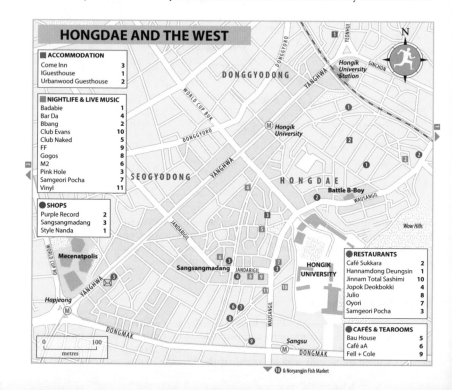

HONGDAE AND THE WEST

ACCOMMODATION

Come Inn	3
IGuesthouse	1
Urbanwood Guesthouse	2

NIGHTLIFE & LIVE MUSIC

Badabie	1
Bar Da	4
Bbang	2
Club Evans	10
Club Naked	5
FF	9
Gogos	8
M2	6
Pink Hole	3
Samgeori Pocha	7
Vinyl	11

SHOPS

Purple Record	2
Sangsangmadang	3
Style Nanda	1

RESTAURANTS

Café Sukkara	2
Hannamdong Deungsin	1
Jinnam Total Sashimi	10
Jopok Deokbokki	4
Julio	8
Oyori	7
Samgeori Pocha	3

CAFÉS & TEAROOMS

Bau House	5
Café aA	6
Fell + Cole	9

DONGGYODONG

Hongik University Station

SINCHON

YEONHUI

DONGGYODONG

Hongik University

WORLD CUP BUK

YANGHWA

SEOGYODONG

YANGHWA

HONGDAE

Battle B-Boy

WAUSANGIL

Wow Hills

Mecenatpolis

WORLD CUP RO

YANGHWA

Hapjeong

Sangsangmadang

JANDARIGIL

JANDARIGIL

HONGIK UNIVERSITY

WAUSANGIL

DONGMAK

Sangsu

DONGMAK

& Noryangjin Fish Market

0   100
metres

the role played by local collaborators during resistance, or on how independence was actually achieved: it was simply part of the package in Japan's surrender to the United States (see p.350).

Inwangsan

인왕산 • 24hr • Free • Dongnimmun subway (line 3)

Just north of Seodaemun Prison rise the craggy peaks of **Inwangsan**, which you may have noticed flanking the western side of Gyeongbokgung palace (see p.65). Here you'll find a number of **temples**, one of the longest sections of Seoul's old **fortress wall** and some **shamanist shrines**. One of these shrines, **Guksadang** (국사당), forms the main sight here; a boulder-surrounded prayer hall, it hosts at least three shamanist ceremonies known as *gut* (굿) each day, giving visitors a convenient opportunity to take in this surprisingly unheralded facet of Korea's religious make-up. The **peak** of Inwangsan itself (338m) lies a further 1km hike uphill from the shrine, and from here the massif's spider's web of routes continues further north.

Hongdae

홍대

Studenty **Hongdae** is one of the edgiest districts in the whole country, teeming with young and trendy people at almost every hour. The area only truly comes into its own after dark, its hundreds of bars and clubs buzzing with activity every night of the week (see p.107). During the daytime, it's fun to explore the streets lined with small shops selling stylish and secondhand clothing, and there are quirky cafés on every corner.

HANGING ALONG THE HANGANG

The banks of the **Hangang** are a hive of activity, and proof of Seoul's open-all-hours nature: at any time of day or night, you'll see locals riding their **bikes**, puffing and panting on **exercise equipment** or going for a run. However, the river and its banks also offer up a whole raft of other possibilities, the best of which are detailed below.

Coffee and cocktails Six bridges now have stylish cafés at their northern and southern ends, providing great views of the river and the teeming bridge traffic. They're a little tricky to get to, and are best approached by taxi; all are open daily from 10am to around 2am, making them equally good spots for an evening cocktail. The Dongjak and Hannam bridges are particularly recommended, since they provide great views of the Banpo bridge fountain shows (see below).

Cycling The Hangang is the most popular spot for cycling in Seoul, and a scoot along the grassy riverbanks constitutes one of the city's most pleasurable and picturesque activities. The main route runs for a whopping 21km between World Cup Stadium to the west and Olympic Park in the east (see p.92). Rental booths have been around for years.

Fountain shows Banpo bridge, located between the Seobinggo and Express Bus Terminal subway stations, plays host to eye-catching, ten-minute-long fountain shows from April to October. Jets of water burst from the bridge at noon, 2pm, 4pm, 8pm and 9pm (with more shows on weekends); the night-time shows are particularly recommended, since the fountains are illuminated in eye-catching colours.

Picnicking On balmy summer evenings in Seoul, the Hangang's banks are packed solid with happy troupes of locals barbecuing meat, throwing back beer and supping *soju* on mats known as *dotjari* (돗자리). These mats, and disposable barbecue sets, are sold for a pittance at most convenience stores close to the river – simply pop into a local butcher for some meat. This being Korea, simply ambling along the river looking curious may nab you an invite to a *dotjari* party.

Swimming Seven open-air swimming pools have opened up along the Hangang, with those on Yeouido easiest to reach for foreign visitors. All are open 9am–8pm from June to August, and entry costs W5000; note that they may be closed during bad weather.

1

Hongdae university itself specializes in the **arts**, a fact that'll be most evident in **Nolita Park** (놀이터 공원) – actually a triangular wedge of ground with almost no greenery – which plays host to anything and everything from punk-rock bands to choreographed street dance. On weekends there's an interesting **flea market** at which local students sell handmade jewellery and other trinkets.

Yeouido island

South of Hondae is **Yeouido island**, which is important to locals on account of it being Korea's centre of politics – it's home to the National Assembly – and one of Seoul's main business hubs.

63 Building

63 빌딩 • Sky Art observation deck daily 10am–11pm • W13,000 • Seaworld daily 10am–10pm • W19,000 • Wax Museum daily 10am–10pm • W15,000 • ⓦ 63.co.kr • Yeouinaru (line 5) or Yeouido subway (lines 5 & 9)

Poking up from the eastern corner of Yeouido island is the **63 Building**, one of the largest and most notable of Seoul's innumerable towers. A distinctive golden monolith 249m in height, it was the tallest structure in Asia when completed in 1985. The sixtieth-floor **observation deck** provides predictably good views of Seoul, and is actually at the top of the building, the other three floors from the building's name being basement levels. Down in the basement you'll find the **Seaworld** aquarium, and a **Wax Museum**.

The Full Gospel Church

순복음 교회 • Services most days; check website for details • ⓦ english.fgtv.com • National Assembly subway (line 9)

Yeouido is also home to the almost sinfully ugly **Full Gospel Church**, by some measures the largest church on earth – it has a membership exceeding one million. Obviously, not all of them pop along for prayers at the same time, but to meet the needs of Seoul's huge Protestant population there are no fewer than seven separate Sunday services, translated into sixteen languages. On occasion half of the congregation ends up in tears, as Korean pastors have a habit of ratcheting up the rhetoric.

A BANGING GOOD TIME

University areas are a good place to get a grip on the "**bang**" culture that pervades modern Korean life. The term is a suffix meaning "room", and is attached to all sorts of places where locals – and occasional foreigners – like to have fun. Below are a few of the most popular:

DVD-bang Imagine a small room with wipe-clean sofas, tissue paper on hand and a large television for movies – if it sounds a little sleazy, you'd be absolutely right. Though people do occasionally come to appreciate plot, cinematography or Oscar-winning performances, these places are more often used by couples looking for a cheap bit of privacy – going in by yourself, or with a person of the same sex, would draw some baffled looks. Figure on around W11,000 per movie.

Jjimjilbang Popular with families, teenagers and the occasional budget-minded traveller, these steam rooms have sauna rooms, a range of hot and cold pools, and often services from massage treatments to internet booths. Though they might sound dodgy, the reality is somewhat tamer; most are open all night, making them an incredibly cheap way to get a night's sleep – prices tend to be around W6000 (see p.35 for more information).

Noraebang These "singing rooms", found all over the country, are wildly popular with people of all ages; if you have Korean friends, they're bound to invite you, as *noraebang* are usually *sam-cha* in a Korean night out – the "third step" after a meal and drinks. You don't sing in front of a crowd, but in a small room with your friends, where you'll find sofas, a TV, books full of songs to choose from and a couple of maracas or tambourines to play. Foreigners are usually intimidated at first, but after a few drinks it can be tough to get the microphone out of people's hands. Figure on around W20,000 per hour between the group.

Noryangjin fish market

노량진 • Daily 24hr • Auctions 4–6am • Noryangjin subway (lines 1 & 9)

Dongdaemun (see p.77) and Namdaemun (see p.77) may be the city's best-known markets, but for **seafood** there's only one winner: **Noryangjin**, which remains well off the radar for most foreign visitors. During the evening the place is particularly picturesque – under strings of bright lights, you can wander around whole soggy acres of shells, seaworms, spider crabs and other salty fare. Prime time is early morning, when noisy **fish auctions** are held.

Seonyudo

선유도 • Daily 24hr • Free • Seonyudo subway (line 9), or walkable from Hongdae and Hapjeong on Seonyugyo bridge

A tiny island just west of Yeouido, **Seonyudo** was once the site of a gargantuan water treatment plant; gentrified in 2009, it has begun a new lease of life as a strolling and picnicking place. It has since become extremely popular, especially on weekends, when you'll see Seoulites arriving in their hundreds for a spot of cycling, rollerblading, or a family meal; stay until evening time to see **Seonyugyo** – a bridge that links Seonyudo to the north and south banks of the Hangang – lit up in pretty colours.

Itaewon

이태원

One of Seoul's most famed quarters, **Itaewon** is something of an enigma. It has, for years, been popular with American soldiers, thanks to the major military base situated nearby. Expat businessmen and visiting foreigners have followed suit, and until English teachers started pouring into Korea by the planeload it was one of the only places in the country in which you could buy "Western" items such as leather jackets, deodorant, tampons or Hershey's Kisses. While it remains a great place to shop for cheap tailored suits and shoes, Itaewon's popularity also made it a byword for transactions of a more sexual nature – **hostess bars** sprung up all over the place, particularly south of the *Hamilton*, a hotel that marks the centre of the area, on the affectionately named "**Hooker Hill**".

Times are changing, however. Most Western goods are available in cities across the country, and the gradual withdrawal of American troops has coincided with the opening of an ever more cosmopolitan array of **restaurants** (see p.103) and **bars** (see p.108), possibly the hippest in the city. The area is also heaving with clubbers on weekends, and from Hooker Hill also sprouts "**Homo Hill**", Seoul's only real gay area (see p.109 for more on the scene).

Leeum Museum of Art

리움미술관 • Tues–Sun 10.30am–6pm • W10,000, plus W7000 for special exhibitions • Ⓦ leeum.samsungfoundation.org • Hangangjin subway (line 6), or an easy walk from Itaewon

The excellent **Leeum Museum of Art** is not so much a museum as one of the most esteemed galleries in the country. It's split into several halls, each with a distinctive and original design; one, built in black concrete, was designed by acclaimed Dutch architect Rem Koolhaas. The museum hosts the occasional special exhibition of world-famous artists, including such luminaries as Mark Rothko and Damien Hirst.

War Memorial of Korea

전쟁기념관 • Tues–Sun 9.30am–5.30pm • Free • Ⓦ warmemo.or.kr • Samgakji subway (lines 4 & 6), or 10min walk from Itaewon

To the west of central Itaewon is the **War Memorial Museum**, a huge venue that charts

1

CENTRAL ITAEWON

N

ITAEWON 19GA

HANNAMDONG

ITAEWON 19

ITAEWON

ITAEWON

Itaewon

Itaewon Tourist
Information Center

BOGWANG 59

ITAEWON 2GA GIL

GOGWANG

0   100
metres

RESTAURANTS	
Copacabana	3
Gecko's Garden	2
Happy Home	8
Le Saigon	9
Le Saint-Ex	4
Menya Sandaime	6
Petra Palace	5
The Wolfhound	7
Zelen	1

ITAEWON

DUTEOPBAWIGIL

Namsan

CAFÉS	
Millimeter Milligram	11
Passion 5	10

HANGANGNO

Hyochang
Park

Sookmyung
Women's
University

HDENAMUGIL

Leeum
Museum
of Art

N

BACKBEOMNO

War Memorial
of Korea

ITAEWON

South
African
Embassy

Yongsan
Electronics
Market

Namyeong

YONGHORO

ITAEWONGIL

SEE ABOVE

Noksapyeong

Itaewon

HANNAMDONG

Samgakji

YONGSANDONG

BANPORO

CGV

HANGANGNO

Hannam

HANNAM BRIDGE

Yongsan
Station

Sinyongsan

BOGWANGDONGGIL

National
Museum
of Korea

SONGBINGGODONG

Ichon

SEOBINGGORO

SEOBINGGODONG

DUMUGAESGIL

ICHONDONG

ICHONDONGGIL

Seobinggo

Hangang River

0   750
metres

HANGANG
BRIDGE

GANGBYEON EXPRESSWAY

Nodeulseom
Island

DONGJAK BRIDGE

BANPO BRIDGE

Floating
Islands

NIGHTLIFE	
All That Jazz	1
B1	6
BricX	4
Bungalow	3
Craftworks Taphouse	11
Gecko's Terrace	7
Hollywood Grill	5
Prost	2
The Wolfhound	8
Queen	9
Why Not?	10

SHOPS	
Hahn's Custom Tailoring	4
Hamilton Shirts	2
Millimeter Milligram	3
Royal Antiques	6
What the Book	1
Yongsan Electronics Market	5

ACCOMMODATION	
D'Oro	2
Grand Hyatt	4
Hamilton	3
IP Boutique	1

OLYMPIC EXPRESSWAY

the history of Korean warfare from ancient stones and arrows to more modern machinery. The museum's park-like periphery is riddled with B-52 bombers and other flying machines; with some, you'll be able to clamber up ladders to cockpit windows for a look inside. Before entering the main building itself, look for the names written on the outer wall: these are the names of every known member of Allied forces who died in the **Korean War**, and the list seems to go on forever. This is particularly heart-wrenching when you consider the fact that a far greater number of people, unmarked here, died on the Chinese and North Korean side – in total, the war claimed over two million souls. After all this, the main hall itself is a little disappointing, but you'll find plenty of exhibits and video displays relaying information about the Korean War.

National Museum of Korea

국립 중앙 박물관 • Tues, Thurs & Fri 9am–6pm, Wed & Sat 9am–9pm, Sun 9am–7pm • Free • Ⓦ museum.go.kr • Ichon subway
(line 4 & Jungang line)

1

The huge **National Museum of Korea** is a Seoul must-see for anyone interested in
history. It houses over eleven thousand artefacts, including an incredible 94
official National Treasures, but only a fraction of these will be on show at
any one time. Among the many rooms on the ground level are exhibitions
from the **Three Kingdoms** period, which showcase the incredible skill of
the artisans during that time – gold, silver and bronze have been cast into
ornate shapes, the highlight being a fifth-century crown and belt set that once
belonged to a Silla king. Move up a floor and the focus shifts to paintings,
calligraphy and wooden art, and there's usually a colossal **Buddhist scroll** or two,
over 10m high; some were hung behind the Buddha statue in temples' main halls,
while others were used for such purposes as praying for rain. The museum owns
quite a few, but due to the fragility of the material, they're put on a rota system and
displays are changed regularly.

The uppermost floor contains countless metal sculptures and a beautiful
assortment of pots – some of these are over a thousand years old, though look as if
they were made yesterday. From this floor you'll also get the best view of the
museum's pride and joy, a ten-storey stone **pagoda** that sits in the main museum
hall on the ground level and stretches almost all the way to the top floor. It's in
remarkable condition for something that was taken apart by the Japanese in 1907,
hauled overseas then all the way back some years later; from on high, you'll be able
to appreciate more fully its true size, and the difficulties this must have posed for
the people who built it.

Southern Seoul

Meaning "South of the River", **Gangnam** (강남) is the name for a huge swathe of land
south of the Hangang, and an all-encompassing term for several distinct city districts.
Before Seoul outgrew its boundaries and spread over most of the northwest of the
country, the city's southern perimeter ran through Namsan, north of the river – and,
accordingly, the capital's historical sights become sparser on the south side of the Han
river. Still, to appreciate just how life ticks along in this fine city you'd do well to spend
some time here.

Bongeunsa is the most enchanting temple in Southern Seoul, while just down the
road, are the **royal tombs** in **Samneung Park**, the grassy resting place of a few dynastic
kings and queens. In terms of modern-day attractions, there's **Coex**, a large
underground shopping mall, and **Lotte World**, a colossal theme park. However,
southern Seoul is perhaps best viewed as a window into modern Korean society – the
teeming streets surrounding Gangnam station are pulsating with neon and noise, and
loomed over by innumerable tower blocks rising into the heavens. In addition, the
restaurants, cafés and **boutique shops** of the classy **Apgujeong** district are without
doubt the costliest and most exclusive in the land.

Samsung d'light

삼성 딜라이트 • Daily 10am–7pm • Free • Gangnam subway (line 2)

The Gangnam station area has precious little in the way of sights. The single exception
is **Samsung**, a showroom of sorts for electronic goodies produced by Samsung, Korea's
largest company. It's the place to come if you want a sneak preview of the gadgets that
will be racing around the world in the near future.

1

SOUTHERN SEOUL

APGUJEONG

N

Galleria Department Store

Ⓜ Apgujeong Rodeo

SEOLLEUNGNO
SEOLLEUNGNO 152
SEOLLEUNGNO 157

HAKDONG INTERSECTION

APGUJEONGNO
APGUJEONGNO 48

DOSANDAERO

Dosan Park

Ⓜ Apgujeong

EONJURO

DOSANDAERO
DOSANDAERO INTERSECTION
DOSANDAERO 152
DOSANDAERO 153

EONJURO 160
NONHYEONG 164
NONHYEONG 164

NONHYEONRO

0 _____ 250
metres

Ⓜ Cheonho

CHEONHODAERO

OLYMPIC EXPRESSWAY

OLYMPICRO

GANGDONGDAERO

Olympic Swimming Pool

Gymnastic Arena

Olympic Park

Tennis Court

Ⓜ Bangi

Convention Center

Ⓜ Gangdong-gu Office

Velodrome

SOMA

Olympic Museum

Mongchontoseong

Jamsillaru

Jamsilnaru Ⓜ

Jamsil Ⓜ

SONGPADAERO

GANGBYEON EXPRESSWAY

GANGDONGDAERO

GUUI

Ⓜ Guui

GANGBYEON EXPRESSWAY

Ⓜ Gangbyeon

Hangang River

Lotte World

Ⓜ Sincheon

JAMSIL

OLYMPIC EXPRESSWAY

Ⓜ Konkuk Univ.

Ⓜ Ttukseom Resort

JAVANG

Ⓜ Jayang

DONGBU ARTERIAL RD

Olympic Stadium

Jamsil Arena Ⓜ

Sports Complex

Jamsil Baseball Stadium

BUNDANG EXPRESSWAY

Ⓜ Daecheong

Daemosan Ipgu

IRWONDONG

Hangnyeoul

YANGJAEDAERO

Bongeunsa

Coex Mall

Aquarium

Samseong-jungang Ⓜ

Samseong Ⓜ

SAMNEUNG

YEONGDONGDAERO

HAKDONG

HAKDONGNO

Cheongdam

APGUJEONGNO

Samneung Park

Seolleung Ⓜ

TEHERANNO

YEOKSAMNO

Hanti Ⓜ

Daechi Ⓜ

Dogok Ⓜ

Guryong Ⓜ

SEOLLEUNGNO Ⓜ

GAEPODONG

Ⓜ Apgujeong

Ⓜ Apgujeong Rodeo

APGUJEONG

Dosan Park

SEE INSET

Ⓜ Gangnam-gu Office

SEOLLEUNGNO

Seonjeong-neung Ⓜ

Samneung-jungang

Eonju Ⓜ

EONJURO

YEOKSAMDONG

Ⓜ Yeoksam

TEHERANNO

Ⓜ Maebong

GANGNAM

Ⓜ Yangjae

Ⓜ Hak-dong

HAKDONGNO

Ⓜ Nonhyeon

GANGNAMDAERO

Ⓜ Sinsa

Ⓜ Sinnonhyeon

Samsung d'light

Ⓜ Gangnam

GANGNAMDAERO

GYEONGBU EXPRESSWAY

Ⓜ Nambu Bus Terminal

SEOCHODONG

Ⓜ Seocho

TEHERANNO

Ⓜ Bangbae

HYOREYONGRO

Ⓜ Hydreyeongro

NAMBU RINGWAY

Seoul Arts Center

0 _____ 800
metres

■ ACCOMMODATION

Grand Parnas	3
Jelly	7
Park Hyatt	4
Richmond	5
Ritz-Carlton	6
Sheraton Grande	1
W Seoul	2

● RESTAURANTS

Bloom & Gouté	2
Lee's Gimbap	5
Melting Shop	7
Pasha	4
Seventy Four	6
Sushi Chohi	8
Tutto Bene	1

● CAFÉS & TEAROOMS

Café Madang	9
The Lounge	3

■ NIGHTLIFE

Ax	2
Octagon	3
Woo Bar	1

● SHOPS

Coex Mall	2
Lee Young Hee	3
Techno Mart	1

Samneung Park

삼릉공원 • Tues–Sun 6am–4.30pm • W1000 • Seolleung subway (line 2)

During the Three Kingdoms period and beyond, deceased Korean royalty were buried in highly distinctive **grass mounds**. While these are more numerous elsewhere in Korea – notably the former Silla capital Gyeongju way down in the southeast of the country (see p.178), or the Baekje capitals of Gongju (see p.262) and Buyeo (see p.267) – closer to the capital, Seoul has a few of its own. The easiest to reach are in **Samneung Park**, which is within walking distance of Gangnam station.

The park's name means "Three Mounds". One was for **King Seongjong** (ruled 1469–94), an esteemed leader who invited political opponents to have a say in national government. Two of his sons went on to rule: **Yeonsangun** (ruled 1494–1506) undid much of his father's hard work in a system of revenge-driven purges, and was overthrown to leave his half-brother **Jungjong** (ruled 1506–44) in control. Jungjong's mound can also be found in the park, as can one created to house one of Seongjong's wives. For all the history, it's the prettiness of the park itself that appeals to many visitors, a green refuge from grey Seoul crisscrossed by gorgeous tree-shaded **pathways**.

Coex Mall

코엑스 • Tues–Sun 9.30am–10pm • Samseong subway (line 2)

Within walking distance of Gangnam, the **Coex** complex is a huge assortment of shopping, dining and office space. Inclement weather sees Seoulites heading here in droves – its large underground **mall** area is one of the only sizeable covered spaces in the whole city. Also part of the complex are a couple of five-star hotels (see p.99), and a good **aquarium**.

Coex Aquarium

코엑스 아쿠아리엄 • Daily 10am–8pm • W22,000 • ⓦ coexaqua.com

The **Coex Aquarium** has been designed with rare flair – this must be the only aquarium in the world to use toilets as goldfish tanks, though mercifully there are normal facilities for public use. Sharks, manta rays and colourful shoals of smaller fish are on display.

Bongeunsa

봉은사 • 24hr • Free • Samseong subway (line 2)

Sitting directly across from the north face of COEX is **Bongeunsa**, the most appealing major Buddhist temple in Seoul. Despite an incongruous location amid a plethora of skyscrapers, this is a fairly decent rendition of a Korean temple; like Jogyesa, its uglier sibling to the north of the river (see p.72), it's affiliated to the **Jogye sect**, the largest Buddhist denomination in Korea. There has been a temple here since the late eighth century, but assorted fires and invasions mean that all of its buildings are of fairly recent vintage; still, it's worth peeking at its gorgeous main hall and clutch of small yet appealing outer buildings.

Apgujeong

압구정

Seoulites refer to **Apgujeong** as "Korea's Beverly Hills", and the comparison is not far off the mark – if Louis Vuitton bags are your thing, look no further. Clothing boutiques, chic restaurants and European-style outdoor cafés line streets frequented by a disproportionate number of Seoul's young and beautiful, but note that their good looks may not be entirely natural – this is also Korea's plastic surgery capital, and clinics

1

are ubiquitous. Though there are no real sights as such, Apgujeong is one of the most interesting places in Korea to sit down with a skinny latte and people-watch.

The best cafés (see p.105) and restaurants (see p.104) huddle in a pleasantly relaxed, leafy area outside the main entrance to **Dosan Park** (도산 공원). Heading further north, past the clothes shops and plastic surgeons, you'll eventually come out onto **Apgujeongno**, the area's main road, which features the most exclusive clothes shops and department stores in Korea (see p.112).

Garosugil
가로수길 • Sinsa station (line 3)

West of Dosan Park, though actually far closer to Sinsa station, is **Garosugil**, a particularly trendy street studded with hip cafés and sharp designer boutiques. Its name literally means "tree-lined street", bestowed on account of the roadside lines of gorgeous ginkgo trees, whose spectacular golden foliage makes this a superb place to stroll in Seoul's all-too-short autumn.

Lotte World
롯데월드 • Daily 9.30am–11pm • Lotte World Adventure W46,000 (W26,000 after 4pm, W17,000 after 7pm); Lotte Water Park W35,000 (W30,000 after 2pm) • ⓦ lotteworld.com • Jamsil subway (line 2 & 8)

This local version of Disneyland is incredibly popular – the **Lotte World** complex receives over five million visitors per year, and it's hard to find a Korean child, or even an adult, who hasn't been here at some point. While it may not be quite what some are looking for on their visit to "The Land of Morning Calm", Lotte World can be a lot of fun, particularly for those travelling with children. It comprises two theme parks: the indoor section is known as **Lotte World Adventure**, and this is connected by monorail to **Lotte Water Park**, an outdoor section located in the middle of a lake, and also home to a spa. Also within the complex are a bowling alley, an overpriced ice rink and a large swimming pool.

Olympic Park
올림픽공원 • Daily 24hr • Free • Mongcheontoseong (line 8) or Olympic Park subway (line 5)

Built for the **1988 Summer Olympics**, this large **park** remains a popular picnicking place for Seoul families, and hosts a regular roster of small-scale municipal festivals; you're likely to see one if you turn up on a weekend. It's a very large place, around 2km square, and it's possible to **rent bikes** (W3000 per hour) at the two main entrances. The **Olympic Stadium** itself is actually a few subway stops to the west (immediately north of Sports Complex station), and can usually still be entered during the day for a nose around.

Seoul Grand Park and around
서울대공원 • Park daily 9.30am–9pm • ⓦ grandpark.seoul.go.kr • Zoo daily 9am–6pm • W3000, dolphin shows W1500 • Seoul Land daily 9am–6pm, later in peak season • Entry W20,000, day-pass for rides W36,000 • ⓦ eng.seoulland.co.kr • Seoul Grand Park subway (line 4)

Seven subway stops south of the Hangang on line 4 is **Seoul Grand Park**, one of the largest expanses of greenery in Seoul, and one of the best places to take children for a fun day out. The highlight of the park is its **zoo**, home to a diverse variety of animals from around the world, and, thankfully, several leagues above par for such venues in Asia. It puts on special dolphin shows at least four times per day, as well as other animal performances.

Elsewhere in the park is **Seoul Land** (서울랜드), a large amusement park with an abundance of roller coasters and spinning rides – around forty of them, at the last count. Like Lotte World, this is one of the most popular draws in the country for domestic tourists – they average almost three million visitors each year, and it's hard to find a Korean who hasn't been at least once.

National Museum of Contemporary Art

국립미술관 • March–Oct Mon–Fri 10am–6pm, Sat & Sun 10am–9pm; Nov–Feb Tues–Fri 10am–5pm, Sat & Sun 10am–8pm • Admission usually W3000–10,000 • ⓦ mmca.go.kr • Seoul Grand Park subway (line 4)

Nestled into the Seoul Grand Park area is the **National Museum of Contemporary Art**, an excellent collection of works by some of the biggest movers and shakers in the Korean modern art scene. It's affiliated to the facility of the same name in central Seoul (see p.67 & p.74), though here the focus is on visual arts rather than paintings and sculpture – architecture, design and craft all get a look-in here.

ARRIVAL AND DEPARTURE   SEOUL

Korea has one of the best public transport systems in the whole world, and it should come as no surprise to learn that Seoul is extremely well connected to the rest of the country. However, given the choice, it's often best to leave or arrive **by train** – the stations are far more central than the bus terminals, which are rather confusing entities to boot, while trains themselves are more impervious to the traffic that occasionally snarls up the capital's access roads.

BY PLANE

INCHEON INTERNATIONAL AIRPORT

The vast majority of international planes to Korea touch down at Incheon International Airport (인천 공항), which sits in curvy, chrome-and-glass splendour on an island about 50km west of central Seoul. The capital is the first and last Korean city that most foreign visitors see, and the main options linking it with the airport are bus, train and taxi. Buses race all around the country from the airport – if you're headed elsewhere, there's usually no need to transit in Seoul.

To Seoul by bus There are umpteen services to the capital (45min–1hr 30min; W10,000–15,000) – check at the airport's many information desks to find the one most appropriate for you.

To Seoul by train The AREX train (ⓦ english.arex.or.kr) heads to Seoul station several times an hour (56min; W4000), via Gimpo Airport and Hongdae; most services are subway-like in nature, though once an hour a more comfy train makes a direct run to Seoul station (43min; W8500). Built in 2008, the system was poorly designed, and cars and buses easily beat the trains for pace – it's due for an overhaul.

To Seoul by taxi It's not all that expensive to go by taxi, especially if you're in a group; figure on W65,000–110,000 depending upon the time of day and your Seoul departure or arrival point, and don't be afraid to haggle. Black "deluxe" taxis are more expensive, and not worth the extra money.

GIMPO AIRPORT

Most domestic services run from Gimpo (김포 공항), another airport sitting about halfway from the capital to Incheon.

Onward transport to Seoul From Gimpo, plenty of bus services head into Seoul (around W7000; ask at information booths for the most appropriate one), while it's also a stop on the AREX train line to Seoul station (25min), via Hongdae. A taxi into town from Gimpo will be W30,000–50,000, depending on your destination and the time of day.

Destinations Busan (every 30min; 1hr); Gwangju (7 daily; 50min); Jeju City (every 15min; 1hr 5min); Jinju (3 daily; 55min); Mokpo (1 daily; 55min); Yeosu (8 daily; 55min).

INFORMATION

Airlines Aeroflot ☎ 02 569 3271; Air Canada ☎ 02 3788 0100; Air China ☎ 02 774 6886; Air France ☎ 02 3483 1033; All Nippon Airways ☎ 02 2096 5500; American Airlines ☎ 02 3483 3909; Asiana Airlines ☎ 02 2669 8000; Japan Airlines ☎ 02 3788 5770; KLM ☎ 02 2011 5500; Korean Air ☎ 1588 2001; Qantas ☎ 02 777 6871; United Airlines ☎ 02 751 0300.

Airport information The information line for both Incheon Airport (ⓦ airport.kr) and Gimpo Airport (ⓦ airport.co.kr) is ☎ 02 1577 2600, and there are excellent info-booths at both airports.

BY TRAIN

There are three major train stations in Seoul, all of them large and modern. The two big ones are Seoul station (서울역) and Yongsan (용산역) station, both in the city centre on subway lines 1 & 4; the line south splits in Daejeon, with services from Seoul station heading on southeast to Busan, and those from Yongsan heading southwest to Mokpo – be sure to go to the right station. From both stations, you'll have a choice of train classes, which vary in speed and price (see p.30 for more information). Seoul's third station is Cheongnyangni (청량리역), a short way to the east on subway line 1; this is the terminus of slow lines from Gangwon and Gyeongsang. The trains between the major cities listed below are the fastest, most direct services.

Destinations (Cheongnyangni station) Andong (7 daily; 3hr 20min); Busan (Haeundae station; 2 daily; 7hr); Chuncheon (hourly; 1hr); Danyang (9 daily; 2hr); Jeongdongjin (6 daily; 5hr 30min).

Destinations (Seoul station) Busan (every 10–30min; 2hr 45min); Cheonan (every 10–40min; 50min); Daegu (every 10–30min; 1hr 50min); Daejeon (every 10–30min; 1hr); Suwon (every 20–40min; 30min).

Destinations (Yongsan station) Cheonan (every 15–40min; 1hr); Daecheon (hourly; 2hr 30min); Daejeon (Seodaejeon station; every 10–30min; 1hr); Gwangju (hourly; 3hr); Jeonju (hourly; 2hr 15min); Mokpo (hourly; 3hr 20min); Suwon (every 20–40min; 30min).

1

BY BUS

When travelling to or from other Korean cities by bus, you have a choice of Seoul terminals: most buses head to either the express bus terminal (고속 버스 터미널) on the south side of the river (subway lines 3, 7 & 9), or Dong-Seoul terminal (동서울 버스 터미널) to the east of town on line 2 (Gangbyeon station). There's also the smaller Nambu terminal (남부 버스 터미널), a few stations south of the express terminal on line 3. To find out which one is best for you, ask at a tourist information office, or call the foreigners' helpline on ☎ 1330 (with area code if calling from a mobile phone).

EXPRESS BUS TERMINAL

This mammoth venue has connections to most destinations around the country, but is badly signed and made up of three different terminals: in general, the Gyeongbu side serves areas to the southeast of Seoul, and the Honam building across the way serves the southwest, while a smaller terminal has buses to more local destinations in Gyeonggi province.

Destinations (Gyeongbu section) Busan (every 30min; 4hr 15min); Cheonan (every 10min; 1hr); Daegu (every 20min; 3hr 30min); Daejeon (every 15min; 2hr); Gongju (every 40min; 1hr 50min); Gyeongju (hourly; 3hr 45min); Pohang (every 20min; 4hr); Tongyeong (hourly; 4hr 10min).

Destinations (Honam section) Daecheon (hourly; 2hr 10min); Gwangju (every 10min; 3hr 30min); Jeonju (every 10min; 2hr 40min); Mokpo (every 45min; 4hr); Sokcho (every 30min; 2hr 30min); Wando (4 daily; 5hr); Yeosu (every 40min; 4hr 30min).

DONG-SEOUL TERMINAL

The equally huge Dong-Seoul terminal is the main launching point for intercity buses, but also hosts a bunch of express services.

Destinations (express section) Busan (11 daily; 4hr 20min); Daegu (every 30min; 3hr 40min); Daejeon (every 20min; 2hr); Gangneung (every 30min; 2hr 30min); Gwangju (every 20–30min; 4hr); Jeonju (every 30min; 2hr 50min); Jinju (5 daily; 3hr 50min); Samcheok (13 daily; 3hr).

Destinations (intercity section) include: Andong (every 20min; 2hr 50min); Busan (5 daily; 3hr 30min); Buyeo (8 daily; 2hr 30min); Cheonan (every 15min; 1hr 20min); Chuncheon (every 15min; 1hr 10min); Danyang (hourly; 2hr 30min); Gangneung (every 30min; 2hr 30min); Gongju (12 daily; 2hr 10min); Guinsa (12 daily; 3hr); Gyeongju (18 daily; 4hr); Haeundae (14 daily; 5hr 30min); Incheon (every 20min; 1hr 10min); Jeongdongjin (3 daily; 3hr 10min); Sokcho (every 20min; 2hr 20min); Songnisan (hourly; 3hr 30min); Taebaek (every 30min; 3hr 10min).

NAMBU TERMINAL

The smallest of Seoul's three main bus terminals is also the easiest to navigate, and hosts services to a seemingly random collection of destinations down south, including many of the same locations as the larger terminals.

Destinations Anmyeondo (12 daily; 3hr); Buyeo (every 30min; 2hr); Daecheon (3 daily; 2hr 50min); Gongju (every 50min; 1hr 30min); Jeonju (every 30min; 2hr 40min); Jinju (every 30min; 3hr 40min); Muju (5 daily; 2hr 30min); Songnisan (3 daily; 3hr 30min); Tongyeong (every 30min; 4hr 30min).

BY SUBWAY

So vast is Seoul's underground network that it's actually possible – and, in some cases, advisable – to reach some surrounding destinations by subway.

Incheon Just over an hour away from central Seoul at the western end of line 1, with ticket prices (W1900) much cheaper than buses heading the same way.

Suwon An hour away from central Seoul – slower than the trains, but cheaper (W1600). It's also connected to Seoul by line 1, though on a separate branch line to the one heading to Incheon – check the destination on the front of the train.

Cheonan Suwon-bound trains often head to Cheonan (two whole hours south of the capital) and beyond, though these are only for the most budget-conscious travellers.

GETTING AROUND

With Seoul's hectic streets making car hire almost tantamount to suicide, and bicycle riding even more so, it's lucky that the city is covered by a cheap, clean and highly comprehensive **public transport** system – the subway network is one of the best developed in the world, not least because of the sheer number of workers it has to speed from A to B. Buses dash around the city every which way, and even taxis are cheap enough to be viable for many routes. If you're staying in the city for more than a few days, invest in a **transport card** (see box opposite), which saves you not only money but also time waiting in ticket queues.

THE SUBWAY

With nine underground lines, eight light-rail lines and over three hundred stations, Seoul's subway system (⊛ smrt.co.kr) is one of the most comprehensive on Earth – in the area bounded by the circular 2 line, you'll never be more than a short walk or taxi ride from the nearest station, while line 1 runs for a whole third of the country's length, stretching well over 100km from Soyosan in the north to Sinchang in the south.

Fares Ticket prices are reasonable, starting at W1150 for rides of less than 10km; this will get you almost everywhere you need to go in the centre, though even for further-flung locations it's very rare for the price to rise above W2000. You'll get W100 off each trip when using a travel card (see box opposite).

Buying tickets Ticket purchase has become slightly trickier since station staff were laid off en masse in 2009;

TRANSPORT CARDS

T-money transport cards are sold for a refundable W3000 at all subway stations, and some street-level kiosks. After loading them with credit (easiest at machines in the subway station), you'll save W100 on each subway or bus journey, and any remaining balance can be refunded at the end of your stay. These cards make it possible to switch at no extra cost from bus to subway – or vice versa – should you need to. In addition, you can use them to pay **taxi fares**, make **phone calls** from most streetside booths, and even pay your bill at **convenience stores**.

Special **tourist cards** are also available (W10,000 for one day, up to W59,500 for one week), though you'd have to be doing an awful lot of travelling to make them value for money.

unless you've invested in a transport card (highly recommended; see box above), you'll have to buy a single-use card from a machine; though the operating system is a little curious, you should get there in the end. Bafflingly, each card requires a deposit of W500, retrievable from machines outside the turnstiles when you've completed your journey.

Maps The subway system itself is very user-friendly: network maps are conveniently located around the stations, which are easily navigable with multilingual signs. You'll find maps of the surrounding area on walls near the station exits, though be warned that north only faces upwards a quarter of the time, since each map is oriented to the direction that it happens to be facing.

Operating hours The subway runs from around 5.30am to midnight, and trains are extremely frequent, though some lines are packed to bursting point at rush hour; services finish slightly earlier on weekends.

BUSES

In comparison with the almost idiot-proof subway system, Seoul's bus network often proves too complicated for foreign guests – English-language signage is rare, and some of the route numbers would look more at home in a telephone directory (for instance, the #9009-1 to City Hall). Routes are given at almost every stop, though often in Korean only, or with only the main subway stations listed in English.

Bus types Buses are split into four coloured categories: blue buses travel long distances along major arterial roads; green buses are for shorter hops; red ones travel to the suburbs; and yellow (or sometimes small green) ones use tight loop routes.

Fares Tickets start at W1150 for blue and green buses, W1950 for red buses and W950 for yellow buses, increasing on longer journeys; cash is no longer accepted on most buses, so travel cards are the way to go (see box above).

Handily, a bus-plus-subway-plus-bus journey often counts as just one trip; beep out with your card when you exit the bus to take advantage of this.

TAXIS

As in every Korean city, Seoul's taxis are cheap and ubiquitous. You should never have to wait long for a cab, though when the subway starts to shut down at night, hawker cabs emerge, quoting far higher prices. Drivers do not expect tips, but it's also unlikely that they'll speak any English – having your destination written in *hangeul* is the easiest way to get the information across, though drivers are able to phone interpreters for no extra charge.

Fares A W3000 fare covers the first 2km, and goes up in W100 increments every 142m – given that bus and subway fares start at W1150, it often works out almost as cheap for groups of three or four to travel short distances by cab rather than public transport. Note that a twenty percent surcharge is added between midnight and 4am.

Mobeom cabs There are also deluxe *mobeom* cabs, which are black with yellow lights on top; these usually congregate around expensive hotels, charging W5000 for the first 3km and W200 for each additional 164m.

ON FOOT

Busy roads and noxious emissions mean that walking through Seoul is rarely pleasurable, though Insadonggil is closed to traffic on Sundays; the shopping district of Myeongdong and club-heavy Hongdae are so swamped with people that vehicles tend to avoid these areas; and there are innumerable malls and underground shopping arcades.

BY BIKE

Riding a bike is only really advisable on specially designed routes along the river (see p.85 for further details).

INFORMATION

Seoul is dotted with **information booths**, all of which dole out maps of the city, can advise on accommodation and help out with any transportation enquiries. Wherever you are in Korea, you can also make use of a supremely useful **dedicated foreigners' helpline** – just dial ☎ 1330 (with area code if calling from a mobile phone or abroad).

1

SEOUL ON THE WEB

10 Magazine ⓦ10mag.com. A fun publication with good listings sections for Seoul and other Korean cities.

Eloquence ⓦeloquence.co.kr. Stylish magazine that focuses on upper-class Seoul society.

Marmot's Hole ⓦrjkoehler.com. This personal blog of long-time expat Robert Koehler is full of interesting, extremely informative snippets about Seoul's culture and history.

Roboseyo ⓦroboseyo.blogspot.com. Expat blog that takes an often offbeat view of Seoul society.

Seoul ⓦmagazine.seoulselection.com. City-sponsored magazine that's usually much more interesting than its name may suggest.

Seoul Eats ⓦseouleats.com. Food blog with an admirable selection of restaurant reviews, though not updated as frequently as it once was.

The Seoul Times ⓦtheseoultimes.com. Though the news itself is stale to say the least, the site has good job listings and is a useful place to hunt for flatmates.

Visit Seoul ⓦvisitseoul.net. Much improved in recent years, this is the official tourist site of Seoul's city government.

Zen Kimchi ⓦzenkimchi.com. Another food blog, with a pleasingly user-friendly interface.

KTO Tourist Information Center Cheonggyecheonno ❶02 1330; map p.70. On the basement level of the Korea Tourist Organization's HQ, this is the largest and most info-packed tourist office in town. They're able to help with anything from accommodation to tours, and have handy pamphlets detailing sights nationwide. English spoken. Daily 9am–8pm.

Insadong Tourist Information Center Yulgongno, no phone; map p.70. Right at the north end of Insadonggil, and conveniently located for an array of surrounding sights, this small office can help with basic sightseeing queries. Daily 9am–6pm.

Itaewon Tourist Information Center Itaewon station ❶02 3785 0942; map p.88. Within Itaewon subway station itself, this small office can come in handy if you're looking for something local. Daily 9am–6pm.

Myeongdong Tourist Information Center Euljiro 2-ga 171 ❶02 778 0333; map p.76. The largest of Seoul city's own array of tourist offices, though also very helpful when trying to glean advice for destinations around the country. English-speakers always on hand. Daily 9am–8pm.

ACCOMMODATION

Those seeking high-quality **accommodation** have a wealth of places to choose from in Seoul, while at the lower end of the price spectrum are the city's ballooning number of **backpacker guesthouses**. There are five-stars around City Hall and Gangnam, upper-class venues around Myeongdong, some good mid-rangers in and around the tourist hive of Insadong, and hostel clusters in Hongdae and Daehangno. **Motels** form a cheap alternative to official tourist hotels, sometimes having rooms of comparable size and quality, and can be found all over the city. Lastly, Seoul city operates a decent site listing some of the more modern **boutique guesthouses** (ⓦstay.visitseoul.net).

GYEONGBOKGUNG AND AROUND

★**Bukchon Maru** 북촌 마루 Gyedong 2-164 ❶02 744 8571, ⓦbukchonmaru.com; Anguk subway; map p.64. Presided over by a delightful, English-speaking local couple, this is a homely affair, with granny whipping up breakfast, and guests encouraged to get to know each other. A lovely choice. **W90,000**

Haemil Guesthouse 해밀 게스트하우스 Gwonnongdong 152-2 ❶070 8950 1546, ⓦhaemilguesthouse.com; Anguk subway; map p.64. A touch more expensive than most *hanok* guesthouses in the area, though just about worth the extra expense on account of a wonderful location facing Jongmyo shrine (see p.71), and rooms decorated with even more attention to detail. **W115,000**

★**Hide & Seek Guesthouse** 하이덴식 게스트하우스 Tonguidong 35-68 ❶02 6925 5916, ⓦhidenseek.co.kr; Anguk subway; map p.64. Set in a building dating back to the Japanese occupation period, this is a truly charming place – the family who runs it make every effort to please, especially with their yummy breakfasts. Rooms are cosy, and there are sunloungers on the wide patio area, which is grand for an evening drink, too. **W60,000**

★**Rakkojae** 락고재 Gahoedong 218 ❶02 742 3410, ⓦrkj.co.kr; Anguk subway; map p.64. The most authentic of the *hanok* bunch, character-wise. Not only is this one an 1870s original, but the owners serve traditional

HANOK GUESTHOUSES

In **Bukchon Hanok Village**, a tranquil city sector north of Anguk subway station, lie some of Seoul's most interesting places to stay – here you can spend the night in traditional Korean housing known as **hanok** (한옥). These are wooden buildings with tiled roofs, set around a dirt courtyard – a style that once blanketed the nation, but is rarely seen in today's high-rise Korea. The generally bed-less rooms – you'll be sleeping Korean-style in a sandwich of blankets – are kept deliberately rustic and heated in the winter with the underfloor *ondol* system; most, however, provide modern indoor toilets and free wi-fi.

There are a few "proper" *hanok* **guesthouses** dotted around (see "Gyeongbokgung and around" reviews, below), as well as some charming **homestay** options bookable through the district authorities (ⓦhomestay.jongno.go.kr); the latter option will cost in the region of W50,000 per room.

food for dinner: it's a little like a Japanese *ryokan*. Studded with maple and pine trees, the courtyard is divine, featuring precious few concessions to the modern day; it's best appreciated at night, when soft light pours through the paper doors. W275,000

★**Sopoong Guesthouse** 소풍 게스트하우스 Gyedong 140-17 ⓣ010 8998 9159; Anguk subway; map p.64. A tiny place with only three rooms, this relatively recent addition to the Bukchon area's *hanok* list has proven a real winner with international guests. The owner will do everything possible to ensure that guests are happy – the breakfasts are particularly nice. W85,000

INSADONG AND AROUND

Banana Backpackers 바나나 배크패커스 Ikseondong 63 ⓣ02 3672 1972; Anguk subway; map p.70. One of the oldest hostels in the city, this is an easy walk from Insadonggil; it has free internet, laundry and cooking facilities, and a common area that's great for making new mates. There's bread and jam to tuck into in the morning, as well as free tea and coffee throughout the day. Dorm beds W23,000

★**Doulos** 돌로스 호텔 Gwansudong 112 ⓣ02 2266 2244, ⓦdouloshotel.com; Jongno 3-ga subway; map p.70. Excellent value, comfy rooms, friendly staff and a convenient location... this mid-range hotel ticks all the boxes, even if it's a little tricky to find: take a few steps south of Jongno and you should be able to make out its sign. Usually neat discounts if booking online. W120,000

★**Fraser Suites** 프레이저 스위츠 Insadong 4-gil 18 ⓣ02 6262 8888, ⓦseoul.frasershospitality.com; Jongno 3-ga subway; map p.70. The plushest serviced residence in Seoul, with rack rates starting at W7,000,000 per month for a single room. Also on site are a gym and swimming pool, as well as a rooftop driving range for golfers. The location, just off Insadonggil, is hard to beat. W330,000

Hostel Korea 11th 호스텔 코리아 11th Waryongdong 140 ⓣ070 4705 1900, ⓦcdg. hostelkorea.com; Anguk subway; map p.70. High-rise

hostel just down the road from the palace of Changdeokgung (see p.69). It's a trendy place with a café-like lobby area, and is often full on account of its popularity with tourists from other Asian countries. Dorm beds W26,000

Insa Hostel 인사 호스텔 Insadong 14-gil 48 ⓣ02 714 0644, ⓦinsahostel.co.kr; Anguk subway; map p.70. Hostel in the very thick of the Insadong action. Though it could occasionally benefit from more attentive service, the rooms are fine. Dorm beds W26,000

Noble 노블 관광 호텔 Yulgongno 6-gil 13-3 ⓣ02 742 4025, ⓦnoblehotel.co.kr; Anguk subway; map p.70. One of the least seedy options in this convenient, highly atmospheric area – it's a hotel, rather than a motel, and rooms are not rentable by the hour. Some are rather small, but they're quiet and kept at the right temperature. W60,000

Seven Street 세븐스트리트 호텔 Cheonggyecheonno 117 ⓣ02 2260 6300; Jongno 3-ga subway; map p.70. One of precious few hotels overlooking the Cheonggyecheon creek (see p.72), this place has passed through several owners of late – at the time of writing, the *Sutton Hotel* signs were still in place. Only twin rooms face the stream, and these are the hotel's best picks in any case. Book online for discounts. W185,000

Sheel 쉘 모텔 Gwansudong 137 ⓣ02 2278 9993; Jongno 3-ga subway; map p.70. Something of a "high-end" love motel, filling its rooms with all sorts of interesting quirks. Lace curtains billow from the ceilings, projectors fill whole walls with computer or televisual output, and some bathrooms are decked out in the style of a sauna; there's free coffee and popcorn at reception. You can usually cut the price in half if checking in after 9pm. W100,000

Somerset Palace 서머세트 팰리스 Yulgongno 2-gil 7 ⓣ02 6730 8888, ⓦsomersetpalace.co.kr; Anguk subway; map p.70. Venue of choice for long-term expats, thanks to impeccable service and wonderful on-site facilities. Some rooms have views of Gyeongbokgung (see p.65), though you'll be paying a premium; rack rates start at W4,600,000 per month. W380,000

1

Sunbee 호텔 썬비 Gwanhundong 198-11 ☎02 730 3451, ⓦhotelsunbee.com; Anguk subway; map p.70. Tucked into a side street near Insadonggil, this hotel has benefitted from a recent renovation, and remains good value despite the doubling of prices. Professional staff will lead your way from the fancy lobby, which features a pleasant café; the rooms themselves can be quite large, and some have views of Inwangsan (see p.85). W100,000

GWANGHWAMUN AND CITY HALL

The Plaza 더 플라자 Sogongno 119 ☎02 771 2200, ⓦhoteltheplaza.com; City Hall subway; map p.73. Directly facing City Hall and adjacent to Deoksugung: you could hardly wish for a more central location. In addition, a thorough overhaul in 2010 made its interior one of the most attractive in the city, with immaculate rooms and superb on-site restaurants – even the corridors exude a sleek beauty. Try to grab a room on one of the north-facing upper floors for some wonderfully Manhattanesque views. W360,000

★Westin Chosun 웨스틴 조선 Sogongno 106 ☎02 771 0500, ⓦechosunhotel.com; City Hall subway; map p.73. Serious effort has been put into making this the most appealing hotel in central Seoul – an energetic group of knowledgeable staff preside over rooms that eschew the typical Korean concrete blockiness for splashes of lime, plush carpets and curved sofas. Even the bathrooms are graced with modern art, and a free mobile phone will be yours for the duration of your stay. Prices often fall to W250,000 off season. W420,000

MYEONGDONG AND DONGDAEMUN

Ibis Ambassador 이비스 앰배서더 Namdaemunno 78 ☎02 3454 1101, ⓦibishotel.com; Euljiro 1-ga subway; map p.76. Mid-range hotel right in the centre of Myeongdong, with clean and presentable rooms. Staff make a concerted effort, and are particularly adept at dispensing advice to those fresh off the plane: handy, since the airport bus stops right outside. W240,000

★Metro 메트로 호텔 Myeongdong 2-gil 14 ☎02 752 1112, ⓦmetrohotel.co.kr; Euljiro 1-ga subway; map p.76. A modern, squeaky-clean hotel away from the bustling Myeongdong main roads, where the staff are friendly, and breakfast is included. Rooms are fresh and have free wi-fi, though views are generally poor – ask to see a few rooms. W140,000

Royal 로얄 호텔 Myeongdong 1-ga 6 ☎02 756 1112, ⓦseoulroyal.co.kr; Euljiro 3-ga subway; map p.76. Golden hues and comfy beds make rooms rather appealing at this towering hotel, which rises near the cathedral at the centre of Myeongdong's sprawling shopping district. Rooms are cosy, the grill and buffet bars on the 21st floor are great places to eat, and there are free shuttle buses to and from the airport. W220,000

★The Shilla 더 신라 Donghoro 249 ☎02 2233 3131, ⓦshilla.net; Dongguk University subway; map p.76. Tucked away in a quiet area on the eastern access road to Namsan, this hotel is characterized by the traditional style of its rooms and exterior. The lobby and restaurants are a luscious shade of brown, as if they've been dunked in tea, though the common areas can often be a little busy – this is one of Seoul's most popular conference venues. The rooms themselves are five-star quality, if a little overpriced, and feature genuine Joseon-era antiques. W480,000

NORTHERN SEOUL

Fully Guesthouse 풀리 게스트하우스 Myeongnuyn 3-ga 5 ☎010 3266 4721; Hyehwa subway; map p.79. A little bit of a trek from central Daehangno, but worth the extra effort – this is the most welcoming of the area's many hostels. The English-speaking owner encourages guests to bond, and often leads pub crawls himself. In addition, it's one of the cheapest hostels in Seoul, with a further W2000 knocked off the price on weekdays. Dorm beds W17,000

Golden Pond 골든 폰드 Changgyeonggungno 240-15 ☎02 741 5621, ⓦgoldenpond.co.kr; Hyehwa subway; map p.79. Highly popular with Western backpackers and those seeking work in Seoul, this is the cleanest and most secure guesthouse in the area. Set around a *hanok*-style building, it's small and very often full. Dorm beds W20,000

WESTERN SEOUL

★Come Inn 컴인 Seogyodong 358-91 ☎070 8958 7279, ⓦcomeinnkorea.com; Hongik University subway; map p.84. A winner for its dorms and private rooms alike, this guesthouse draws a real mixed bag of travellers – most emerge feeling as though they've been staying at a local's home, such is the welcome. The place is spick and span, while seems a little odd when the country's biggest nightlife area lies just outside. Dorm beds W15,000, doubles W58,000

iGuesthouse 아이 게스트하우스 Donggyodong 10-14 ☎070 8779 6161, ⓦseouliguesthouse.com; Hongik University subway; map p.84. While Apple Corp probably wouldn't be too happy about the name, guests usually come away more than satisfied with this hostel, which is the best of a glut in this residential part of Hongdae. Dorms are more spacious and better-appointed than most of the competition, and staff keep abreast of the area's goings-on. Dorm beds W20,000

★Urbanwood Guesthouse 어번우드 게스트하우스 Seogyodong 333-30 ☎010 8320 0833, ⓦurbanwood.co.kr; Hongik University subway; map p.84. Run by an affable, English-speaking local who whips up a mean cup of coffee in the morning, this is the most pleasant of the Hongdae area's many new boutique-style operations, its few rooms decorated along seasonal colour schemes; only the triple room, though, is en suite. The rooftop is a grand place for evening drinks. W80,000

ITAEWON

D'Oro 호텔 디오로 Itaewondong 124-3 ☎02 749 6525; Itaewon subway; map p.88. Highly recommended mid-range establishment just uphill from Itaewon's main drag, and rare value for money in a notoriously poor area for accommodation. Free wi-fi and minibar, and standards of service more akin to a hotel. W90,000

Grand Hyatt 그랜드 하야트 Sowollo 322 ☎02 797 1234, ⓦseoul.grand.hyatt.com; Noksapyeong subway; map p.88. A favourite of visiting dignitaries, this is one of Seoul's top hotels in more ways than one – perched on a hill overlooking Itaewon, almost every room has a fantastic view through floor-to-ceiling windows. There's a fitness centre, an ice rink and squash courts, as well as indoor and outdoor swimming pools. W390,000

Hamilton 해밀톤 호텔 Itaewondong 119-25 ☎02 794 0171, ⓦhamilton.co.kr; Itaewon subway; map p.88. More of an Itaewon landmark than a decent place to stay, but countless foreigners make this their Seoul home in any case. Rooms are a wee bit dated, but staff are professional, and guests can make use of an outdoor pool in warmer months. W145,000

IP Boutique IP부티크 Hannamdong 737-32 ☎02 3702 8000, ⓦipboutiquehotel.com; Itaewon subway; map p.88. Korea's first genuine stab at the boutique hotel concept, though sadly a little flawed. Rooms have all been individually decorated, with different colour schemes for each floor, and are mercifully a lot better than the nightmarish lobby – something like a giant handbag with a few swing-chairs and medieval statues. W260,000

SOUTHERN SEOUL

Grand Parnas 그랜드 파르나스 Teheranno 521 ☎02 555-5656, ⓦihg.com; Samseong subway; map p.90. Designed with exceptional attention to detail, this *Intercontinental* hotel belies its age with regular overhauls. Rooms are fresh and tastefully decorated in pleasing tones, with modern furniture. Some great restaurants can be found on the lower floors, and guests have access to a gym and indoor swimming pool. W450,000

★**Jelly** 젤리 호텔 Yeoksamdong 648-7 ☎02 553 4737, ⓦjellyhotel.co.kr; Yeoksam subway; map p.90. A hip and extremely interesting love hotel that has achieved cult status with young Seoulites, some of whom come to couple up (a "rest" is half the price of a night's stay), others to party with a group of friends. The hotel is possibly home to the most idiosyncratic rooms in the city – some contain pool tables, jacuzzis or karaoke systems, making them popular with young groups wanting a night out. W100,000

★**Park Hyatt** 파크 하야트 Teheranno 606 ☎02 2016 1234, ⓦseoul.park.hyatt.com; Samseong subway; map p.90. First things first: this is Seoul's best hotel. Designed in its entirety by Japanese firm Super Potato, its class will already be evident by the time you've entered the lobby, which is actually on the top floor. Rooms employ an almost Zen-like use of space, and the hewed-granite bathrooms were voted "Asia's best place to be naked" by *Time* magazine. Staff are experts at making themselves available only when needed, and those on a repeat visit will find their preferred room temperature, TV channels and light level all ready and waiting. Bliss. W520,000

Richmond 호텔 리치몬드 Yeoksamdong 605-17 ☎02 562 2151, ⓦhotel-richmond.co.kr; Sinnonhyeon subway; map p.90. A fantastic lower-budget option in an area whose establishments usually pride themselves on valet parking and other five-star facilities. Rooms come with free internet access and large TVs, and the more expensive ones are at least as big as those in the nearby *Ritz*. W65,000

Ritz-Carlton 리츠 칼튼 Bongeunsaro 120 ☎02 3451 8000, ⓦritzcarltonseoul.com; Sinnonhyeon subway; map p.90. Service here is as professional as you'd expect from the chain, and no effort has been spared to make this one of Seoul's top hotels. The on-site bakery and restaurants are excellent (including a leafy outdoor area for warmer months), and though the rooms aren't terribly spacious, there are wonderful views from those that face north. W430,000

Sheraton Grande 쉐라튼 그란드 Walkerhillo 177 ☎02 455 5000, ⓦsheratonwalkerhill.co.kr; Gwangnaru subway; map p.90. With scented, plush-carpeted corridors and muted-tone rooms, this immaculately designed establishment is one of the best hotels in the land – a pity about the inconvenient location. There are some wonderful restaurants within the complex, which also features the most expensive rooms in the country – up to a colossal W15,000,000 per night. W480,000

★**W Seoul** W서울 Walkerhillo 177 ☎02 465 2222, ⓦstarwoodhotels.com; Gwangnaru subway; map p.90. The *W* is the most distinctive hotel in Korea. With artfully designed furniture in the rooms, neon gym rings in the elevators, sharp-suited staff and a loungey beat pulsing through the lobby, every inch of it is achingly trendy – not to everyone's tastes, though it's particularly popular with Korean honeymooners. Rooms range in style – many have their own whirlpool and views over the river – while there's also a gym, a juice bar and a great swimming pool within the complex. On-site restaurants are excellent, as is the *Woo Bar* (see p.108), where the city's nouveaux riches come to slurp pricey cocktails. W520,000

1

EATING

Food in Seoul is cheap by international standards and invariably excellent, while the number of **restaurants** is nothing short of astonishing – there's almost one on every corner, and many more in between. Korean food has a well-deserved reputation as one of the spiciest around; those looking for something a little blander can stick to the ever-growing choice of restaurants serving global cuisine, or breakfast at one of the many **bakeries** strewn around the city. If you do get stuck, head for one of Seoul's seemingly infinite number of **convenience stores**. For something even more authentic, head to one of Seoul's many **markets**, those at Dongdaemun and Namdaemun being the most popular. Also note that the consumption of food and drink have long been entwined in Korea; many **bars** (including some of those listed from p.106) serve meals every bit as good as you'd find in a restaurant.

RESTAURANTS

Many parts of Seoul have their own particular culinary flavour. Most popular with tourists are the streets around Insadonggil, where restaurants serve traditional Korean food in a suitably fitting atmosphere. At the other end of the scale is Itaewon, where local restaurants are outnumbered by those serving Indian, Japanese, Thai or Italian food, among others. Student areas such as Hongdae, Sinchon and Daehangno are filled with cheap restaurants, and the establishments of trendy Apgujeong cater to the fashionistas.

GYEONGBOKGUNG AND AROUND

★**Blacksmith Pizza** 대장장이 화덕 피자집 Gahoedong 62-1 ☏ 02 765 4298; Anguk subway; map p.64. Regularly deemed the "best pizzas in Seoul" by expats, this restaurant is run by real, genuine blacksmiths, who crafted the metalwork you'll see around the place; their pizzas (W16,000 and up) are just as lovingly prepared, and the place

is usually rammed to the gills. Daily noon–10pm.

Cheonjin Poja 천진포자 Yulgongno 1-gil ☏ 02 3210 1122; Anguk subway; map p.64. Almost permanently packed, this small, steamy restaurant is so popular that you may have to wait outside while the Chinese chef doles out portion after portion of his famed Tianjin dumplings (W6000) to hungry diners. Daily 10am–10pm.

★**Tosokchon** 토속촌 Chebudong 85-1 85 ☏ 02 737 7444; Gyeongbokgung subway; map p.64. The grandest and most famous place in town for *samgyetang* (삼계탕), a delicious soup comprising chicken stuffed with ginseng, jujube and other healthful ingredients (W15,000). Fame and size aside, the food really does taste fantastic – be prepared to queue. Daily 11.30am–11.30pm.

INSADONG AND JONGNO

★**Abiko** 아비코 Gwancheoldong 13-12 ☏ 02 730 3236; Jongno 3-ga subway; map p.70. Perhaps the

---

CULINARY CURIOSITIES

While even "regular" Korean food may be utterly alien to most visitors, there are a few edibles that deserve special attention; you'll find some of the following at restaurants, but street stalls and markets are the best places to go hunting.

Beonddegi (번데기) In colder months, stalls selling this local delicacy – silkworm larvae – set up on pavements and riverbanks across the whole country. The smell of these mites boiled up in a broth is so disgusting that it may well breach international law. The treat is also served as a bar snack in many *hofs*, bursting in the mouth to release a grimy juice – perfect drinking-game material.

Dak-pal (닭발) So you've learnt the word for "chicken" in Korean (*dak*), spotted it on the menu and ordered a dish. Unfortunately, with this particular meal the suffix means "foot", and that's just what you get – dozens of sauced-up chicken feet on a plate, with not an ounce of meat in sight.

Gaegogi (개고기) This is dog meat, but let it be known that – contrary to the expectations of many a traveller – it rarely features on Korean menus: you're not going to get it on your plate unless you go to a dedicated restaurant. It's usually served in a soup: *yeongyangtang* and *bosintang* are its most common incarnations.

Sannakji (산낙지) Octopus tentacles served still wriggling on the plate – every year, people die of suffocation when their still-wriggling prey makes a last bid for freedom, but as long as you don't throw down your tiny octopod whole (as many Korean guys do, in an effort to impress) you should be okay.

Sundae (순대) Don't let the romanization fool you – this is nothing whatsoever to do with ice cream. In Korea, it's actually a sausage made with intestinal lining, and stuffed with clear noodles. Head to the nearest market to try some.

spiciest food in Seoul, and it's not even Korean – *donkkaseu*, (돈까스) from Japan, is a breaded pork cutlet, often served with curry, on rice. There are five levels of spice here – see if you can handle the hottest one. Various toppings and additions available; it'll work out at around W11,000 per head, all in. Daily 11am–9.30pm.

Ahndamiro 안다미로 Gwanhundong 15-2 ☎02 730 5777; Anguk subway; map p.70. There's something rather romantic about this Italian restaurant, tucked into an Insadong side alley. It's a great date spot, and if you're worried about paying for two then rock up before 3pm for the W10,000 pasta or pizza lunch specials – a bargain. Daily 10.30am–midnight.

★**Balwoo** 발우 Ujeonggungno 56 ☎02 2031 2081, Ⓦbaru.or.kr; Anguk subway; map p.70. Overlooking Jogyesa temple (see p.72), this is quite simply one of the best places to eat in Seoul, particularly for vegetarians. The huge set meals are consummately prepared approximations of Buddhist temple food, and the balance of colour, texture, shape and taste is beyond reproach. Mung-bean pancakes, acorn jelly, sweet pumpkin tofu and sticky rice with ginkgo nuts are among the dozens of items that may appear on your table. Sets go from W27,500; note that cheaper versions of the same dishes are sold on a lower floor. Reservations recommended. Daily: lunch 11.40am–1.20pm & 1.30–3pm; dinner 6–9pm.

Bärlin 바르린 Susongdong 85 ☎02 722 5622, Ⓦbaerlin.co.kr; Anguk subway; map p.70. Those hankering for a bit of bratwurst or sauerkraut should hunt down this upmarket German restaurant. Schnitzels can be made in three different styles (all around W27,000), the raw beef tartare on rye is delectable (W25,000) and there's even herring on the menu – extremely rare in Korea. Daily 11.30am–11.30pm.

Bukchon Sonmandu 북촌 손만두 Insadong 3-gil 6 ☎02 735 1238; Jonggak subway; map p.70. Cheap, tasty Insadong eats – this dumpling restaurant always has several different batches on the go, with portions selectable from a picture menu for W3000–4500. Good noodles, too. Daily 11.30am–11.30pm.

Doodaemunjip 두대문집 Gwanhundong 64 ☎02 737 0538; Anguk subway; map p.70. Tucked into the Insadong alleys, this is perhaps the most attractive of the area's many traditional restaurants, with chandeliers lending elegance to the scene. Their lunch sets are super cheap (W6000–8000), and there's plenty of Korean booze to enjoy of an evening. Daily 10.30am–10pm.

Gogung 고궁 Gwanhundong 38 ☎02 736 3211; Anguk subway; map p.70. On the basement floor of the Ssamziegil complex, the decor here is accordingly quirky, with walls festooned with threads and tie-dye. The food is traditional Korean – best is the Jeonju *bibimbap* (W11,000), a tasty southwestern take on the Korean staple. Daily 10.30am–8.30pm.

★**Gwangjujip** 광주집 Donguidong 43 ☎02 764 3574; Jongno 3-ga subway; map p.70. You can get barbecued meat all across the city, but the little three-way junction just north of Jongno 3-ga subway exit 6 is perhaps the most atmospheric in town – dozens and dozens of diners munch away outside every single night, eating from what look like overturned oil drums. This little venue usually has the best meat – W11,000 for a 200g portion of succulent beef. Daily 3pm–midnight.

★**Meokgeorichon** 먹거리촌 Insadong; Jonggak subway; map p.70. Not a restaurant, but a whole clutch of ramshackle stands operating illegally (look at the floor: this is technically a car park) in what looks like an aircraft hangar. Tremendously atmospheric, this is one of Seoul's most enjoyable places to eat and drink – some menus are now in English, and you'll pay W10,000–15,000 per head to fill up. Daily 6pm–midnight.

Nwijo 뉘조 Gyeongundong 84-13 ☎02 730 9301; Anguk subway; map p.70. Charmingly low-key restaurant in which chefs create rounds of lovingly prepared traditional cuisine. Come before 4pm and you can take advantage of the great-value lunch meals (W18,000); dinner sets are W27,500 and up. Daily 10.30am–10pm.

Potala 포탈라 Gwancheoldong 35-2 ☎02 318 0094; Jongno 3-ga subway; map p.70. Run by a Nepali–Korean couple and centred on a functional Tibetan prayer wheel, this charmingly decorated basement restaurant serves Himalayan specialities (W15,000 for most curries, W9000 for Tibetan *momo* dumplings). Highly recommended is the *samosa chat* – three large samosas served with chopped green onion, chickpeas, curry sauce and sour cream (W11,000). Daily 10am–10pm.

GWANGHWAMUN AND CITY HALL

The Place 더 플레이스 Sinmunanno 103 ☎02 722 1300; Gwanghwamun subway; map p.73. Swanky Western-oriented place popular with staff from the local banks and embassies. Pasta meals go from W16,000, while waffles and cakes are available for dessert, and there are plenty of coffee styles to choose from. Daily 8.30am–10pm.

MYEONGDONG AND DONGDAEMUN

Bulgogi Brothers 불고기 브라더스 Myeongdong 1-ga 7-1 ☎02 319 3351; Myeongdong subway; map p.76. The barbecuing of raw meat at your table is a quintessential Korean experience, but new arrivals can find it hard to jump straight in at the deep end. This elegant venue is the easiest place to learn the ropes, and the meat is always of exceptional quality. Around W30,000 per person, including side dishes and drinks. Daily 11am–10pm.

Din Tai Fung 딘타이펑 Myeongdong 1-ga 59-1 ☎02 3789 2778; Euljiro 1-ga subway; map p.76. The Seoul outlet of a Taiwanese chain, which is still milking a decades-old magazine review, but still makes darn good dumplings.

1

It's W6500 for a round of their famed *xiaolongbao*, or try the shimp and wonton noodles (W10,000). Daily 11am–10pm.

★ **Gostiniy Dvor** 가스티니드보르 Daehoro 34-gil 22 ☎ 02 2275 7501; Dongdaemun History & Culture Park subway; map p.76. Still the best restaurant in Dongdaemun's curious little Russiatown. Its owners are Uzbek but the food is typical Russian, including meaty mains (W10,000), filling soups (W6000) and delicious salads (W5000). The total lack of any sort of Korean atmosphere (and Koreans) can come as quite a surprise if you've been in Seoul a while, and the Russian beer (W5000) goes down nicely. Daily noon–2am.

★ **Gwangjang Market** 광장시장 Off Jongno; Jongno 5-ga subway; map p.76. If you haven't had a meal at Gwangjang (see p.77), you haven't really been to Seoul. It's a beguiling place with all manner of indoor and outdoor places to eat; best is a *bindaeddeok* (mung-bean pancake) 빈대떡) in the central crossroads, though at lunchtime track down the alley selling raw beef tartare (*yukhoe*; 육회). Daily noon–2am.

Korea House 한국의 집 Toegyero 10 ☎ 02 2266 9101, ⓦ koreahouse.or.kr; Chungmuro subway; map p.76. Modelled on the court cuisine enjoyed by the kings of the Joseon dynasty, dinner sets here go for W68,000 and up (small lunch sets from W18,000), and are made up of at least thirteen separate components, usually including broiled eel, ginseng in honey, grilled sliced beef and a royal hotpot. For W50,000 extra you'll be able to enjoy a performance of traditional song and dance after dinner. Reservations recommended. Daily: lunch noon–2pm; dinner 5.30–6.30pm & 7.30–8.30pm.

★ **Mongmyeok Sanbang** 목멱산방 Namsan ☎ 02 318 4790; Myeongdong subway; map p.76. On the Namsan walking track, a short walk uphill from the lower cable car terminus, this traditionally styled venue is one of the most enchanting places to eat in Seoul (and also a great place for tea; see p.106). They sell three types of *bibimbap*: normal (W8000), with *bulgogi* beef on top (W9000) or with raw beef (W11,000), and it's beautifully presented. Eat outside, under the maple trees. Daily 11.30am–9pm.

N Grill N 그릴 Namsan ☎ 02 3455 9298, ⓦ nseoultower. net; map p.76. Expensive steakhouse perched atop the N Seoul Tower (see p.77). You won't get much change from W100,000 per person, but the steaks are top-class, and there are few better views of Seoul. Daily 11am–11pm.

Pierre Gagnaire à Seoul 피에르간예르 Euljiro 30 ☎ 02 317 7181, ⓦ pierregagnaire.co.kr; Euljiro 1-ga subway; map p.76. Molecular gastronomy hits Seoul: the unique creations of Michelin-starred French megachef Pierre Gagnaire are tickling tastebuds atop the *Lotte Hotel*. The menu has a discernable Korean twist, with ingredients such as ginger, sesame leaves and "five-flavoured" *omija* berries letting off little flavour bombs in certain dishes. Lunch menu W85,000, dinner W170,000 and up;

reservations essential. Daily noon–3pm & 5–11pm.

Taj 타지 Myeongdong 1-ga 1-3 ☎ 02 776 0677; Euljiro 1-ga subway; map p.76. One of the best and most attractive Indian restaurants in Seoul, just downhill from Myeongdong Cathedral (see p.75). Curries start at W17,000 and dinner sets are around double that, though on weekdays noon–3pm there are bargain lunch deals for just W11,000. Daily noon–3pm & 6–10pm.

★ **Woo Rae Oak** 우래옥 Jugyodong 118 ☎ 02 2265 0151; Euljiro 4-ga subway; map p.76. This meat house and its elegant, hotel-lobby-like atrium have been here since 1946 – only one year less than Korea itself. The customer base seems to have changed little in decades, and the sight of septuagenarians munching away in their Sunday best is rather charming. Most are here for the meat (W25,000 or so per head), though they also serve superb *naengmyeon* (W12,000), cold buckwheat noodles similar to Japanese *soba*. Daily 11am–10.30pm.

NORTHERN SEOUL

Bongchu Jjimdak 봉추찜닭 Myeongnyun 4-ga 80-1 ☎ 02 745 6981; Hyehwa subway; map p.79. *Jjimdak* is a southeast Korean dish in which chicken and veggies are marinated in a soy-like sauce, and served with glass noodles – the tantalizing aroma will hit you as soon as you open the restaurant door. W20,000 for a two-person portion. Daily 11.30am–11.30pm.

Ggochiwa Chingudeul 꼬치와 친구들 Myeongnyun 2-ga ☎ 02 747 3020; Hyehwa subway; map p.79. With a name roughly meaning "skewered friends", this little shack sells divine chicken sticks for W1700 – just one reason why it's popular with students from the local university. Tues–Sun noon–midnight.

★ **Jaha Sonmandoo** 자하 손만두 Buamdong 245-2 ☎ 02 379 2648; Gyeongbokgung subway; map p.79. Dumplings known as *mandu* are a cheap Korean staple, but unlike the regular processed fare, the handmade versions on offer here (from W8000) are delectable, filled with chunks of quality beef, radish, shiitake mushrooms and the like. The setting is just as pleasant, a minimalist space with mountain views. Daily noon–10pm.

Saemaeul Sikdang 새마을 식당 Myeongnyun 4-ga 90 ☎ 02 3672 7004; Hyehwa subway; map p.79. So what if it's a chain restaurant – this pleasingly noisy venue still doles out the best-value barbecue meat in the wider Hyehwa area. Try the wafer-thin *yeoltan bulgogi* beef (열탄 불고기; W7000 per portion), and throw it down with some soybean broth (된장찌개; W5000). Daily 11.30am–midnight.

WESTERN SEOUL

Café Sukkara 카페 수까라 Seogyodong 327-9 ☎ 02 334 5919; Hongik University subway; map p.84. Not so much a café as a delightful light-food restaurant, in which

1

vegan pumpkin pudding, chickpea salad, wholewheat spaghetti and the like are whipped up in the (very) open kitchen. Mains from W9000; wash them down with homemade ginger ale (W6000) or black shandygaff (W7500). Tues–Sun 11am–3pm & 6–11pm.

Hannamdong Deungsin 한남동 등신 Eoulmadangno 145 ☎02 3144 0264; Hongik University subway; map p.84. At the time of writing, cheesy *deung-galbi* (등갈비; barbecued pork ribs) was Korea's trendiest foodstuff, and a fad likely here to stay. This Hongdae joint is a great place to get a handle on it; W14,000 will buy you a portion, plus the gloves you'll need to eat it. Daily noon–2am.

Jinnam Total Sashimi 진남 회집 Noryangjin Market ☎02 815 2732; Noryangjin subway; map p.84. The most reliable restaurant in fascinating Noryangjin Market (see p.87), with a range of good seafood. Most dishes are for groups, but the *hoedeopbap* (회덮밥; sashimi on rice; W10,000) will please all. Daily 10am–10.30pm.

Jopok Deokbokki 조폭떡볶이 Seogyodong 407-1 ☎02 337 9933; Sangsu subway; map p.84. A dish of rice cakes in spicy sauce, *deokbokki* (떡볶이) is available at street stands all across the city, though this small sit-down restaurant is by far the most famous venue, since its staff are rumoured to be connected to the local mafia (*jopok*). Fact or fib, the food's pretty good, especially if you have a few refried treats (*twigim*; 튀김) thrown on top: just point at what you'd like. Most dishes W3000. Daily 11am–6am.

Julio 후리오 Seogyodong 678 ☎02 3141 5324; Sangsu subway; map p.84. Stylish restaurant selling Mexican staples such as tacos and burritos from W8500 – consider trying one of their Korean fusion specials, such as fried *kimchi carnitas* (W11,500). Kitchen daily noon–9.40pm.

★**Oyori** 오요리 Seogyodong 409-10 ☎02 332 5525; Sangsu subway; map p.84. One has to admire the thinking behind this restaurant, which not only gives employment to single mothers from other Asian countries, but uses the profit to send their children to kindergarten. The various nationalities working here take it in turns to enrich the menu, which contains Malaysian stir-fries, Japanese noodles, Burmese curry and Russian desserts (around W15,000 for mains). Benevolence aside, the food is excellent, and the setting surprisingly stylish thanks to connections with a local art society. Daily 11.30am–11pm.

Samgeori Pocha 삼거리포차 Seogyodong; Sangsu subway; map p.84. Nights out in Hongdae usually end late, meaning that this rustic raw-fish restaurant can be heaving with drunken students at 6am: it's an integral part of the nightlife scene, and one of the most atmospheric places to be of a weekend. Having a bit of *soju* for Dutch courage makes it easier to handle the house speciality, *sannakji* (W15,000, feeds two) – chopped-up baby octopus

that, while not exactly alive, is so fresh that it's still writhing on your plate when served. Daily 6pm–late.

ITAEWON

Copacabana 코파카바나 Itaewondong 119-9 ☎02 796 1660; Itaewon subway; map p.88. Anyone who's been to a Brazilian *churrascaria* will know exactly what to expect here – W29,000 buys as much grilled meat and salad as you can eat. Daily 11.30am–10pm.

Gecko's Garden 게코스 가든 Itaewondong 116-6 ☎02 790 0540x; Itaewon subway; map p.88. Not to be confused with *Gecko's Terrace*, an expat bar just down the way (see p.108), this rambling restaurant is fenced off from Itaewon by a line of trees, and feels a world removed from smoky Seoul. The silver bistro tables impart a vaguely European air to the courtyard, and the menu follows suit with pastas and risottos (from W17,000); in the evenings, chefs will grill your choice of meat on an open barbecue. Daily noon–3.30pm & 5pm–1am.

Happy Home 해피홈 Itaewondong 64-15 ☎02 797 3185; Itaewon subway; map p.88. Itaewon isn't all English-teachers and soldiers – there's a sizeable Nigerian population here too, and a fair few restaurants catering to them. This is the best by far, a welcoming venue serving grilled plantains, black-eyed peas and beef-and-fish soups to eat with your *fufu* ("grinded" cassava). It's around W10,000 per dish, though ask first since prices are not on the menu. Daily noon–midnight.

Le Saigon 레사이곤 Itaewondong 74-33 ☎02 792 0336; Itaewon subway; map p.88. Vietnamese restaurant whose decor is pleasingly authentic, even if the food doesn't always hit the mark. If you want something beyond the inevitable *pho* noodles, try *banh mi* baguettes (W7000), or vermicelli salads with charbrilled pork (W8000). Daily 11.30am–9.30pm.

Le Saint-Ex 레손텍스 Itaewondong 119-28 ☎02 795 2465; Itaewon subway; map p.88. Check out the blackboard for the daily specials at this French bistro; expect grilled pork ribs, home-made sausage or something similar from the lunch sets (W25,000). Teasingly set out on the counter, the desserts are hard to resist, and there's a good wine list. Mon–Fri noon–3pm & 6pm–2am, Sat & Sun noon–2am.

★**Menya Sandaime** 멘야 산다이메 Itaewonno 206 ☎02 790 4129; Itaewon subway; map p.88. Ramen joint serving noodles that are almost, *almost* as good as you'd find across the pond in Japan. Bowls go from W7000, though in summertime consider the delicious *tsukemen* (W8000), in which you dip noodles into a spicy soup; their *gyoza* dumplings (W3000) always go down well. Daily 10am–10pm.

Petra Palace 페트라 팰리스 Itaewondong 197 ☎02 749 9329; Itaewon subway; map p.88. Small, Jordanian-run place serving delicious falafel wraps

1

(W5000), which are just the treat if you're pacing around Itaewon. Daily 10am–10pm.

The Wolfhound 울프하운드 Itaewondong 128-6 ☎ 02 749 7971, ⊛ wolfhoundpub.com; Itaewon subway; map p.88. Irish-style drinking hole notable for an authentic selection of pub grub, including burgers, fish & chips and shepherd's pie. Best, however, are the fried breakfasts, which cost from W11,900 including a tea or coffee, and slide down quite nicely. Kitchen daily noon–11pm.

Zelen 제렌 Itaewonno 27-gil 52 ☎ 02 749 0600; Itaewon subway; map p.88. Bulgarian cuisine is one of the culinary world's best kept secrets, taking hearty meat and veg dishes from the Slavic lands to the west, and fusing them with kebabs and breads from the Turkic east. Meals here (around W22,000) are well prepared; best may be the gigantic "couple" *shashlik* kebab. Daily 11am–3pm & 6–11pm.

SOUTHERN SEOUL

Bloom & Gouté 블룸 앤 구떼 Apgujeongno 10-gil 35-1 ☎ 02 545 6659; Apgujeong subway; map p.90. A great two-level brunch spot off the Garosugil shopping street. Eggs Benedict stands out (W15,000), or try quiche, salads or lasagne, or a range of organic teas. Daily 11am–11pm.

Lee's Gimbap 리스 김밥 Sinsadong 610 ☎ 02 548 5552; Apgujeong subway; map p.90. Korean staple foods are being trendified, one after another, so it was only a matter of time before the humble *gimbap* rice-tube received the treatment. Fillings here include Edam or Gouda cheese, shiitake mushrooms and paprika – ooh la la. Around W4000 a tube, takeaway only. Mon–Fri 9am–9pm, Sat 7.30am–8pm.

Melting Shop 멜팅 샵 Apgujeongno 46-gil 55 ☎ 02 544 4256; Anguk subway; map p.90. Apgujeong probably has the full set of international comestibles now, after the addition of this dreamily pretty "retro ricotta bar". The ricotta itself sells for W12,000, pasta dishes for double that and crab bisque for W13,000. A place to impress, especially if you can score the seats overlooking Dosan Park. Daily 11.30am–3pm & 5pm–midnight.

Pasha 파샤 Seochodong 1317-31 ☎ 02 593 8484; Gangnam subway; map p.90. Style and substance mix perfectly at this Turkish kebab house, whose attractive interior sets it apart from its dowdier counterparts in Itaewon. The meals (generally W15,000) are filling, with the familiar *döner* and *köfte* dishes supplemented by more unusual fish meals. *Pide* – a kind of Turkish pizza – is best washed down with some sour *ayran* yoghurt. Daily 11.30am–11.30pm.

Seventy Four 카페74 Cheongdamdong 83-20 ☎ 02 542 7412; Apgujeong subway; map p.90. This swanky venue serves up excellent brunches and light meals (from W20,000). Come early to grab a window seat, and watch bag-laden shoppers trooping up and down one of the most fashionable streets in the country. Daily 10am–1am.

★Sushi Chohi 수시 초히 Sinsadong ☎ 02 545 8422; Apgujeong subway; map p.90. Sushi fans will be in their element at this pine-lined restaurant, overlooking Dosan Park. Absolutely no concessions are made regarding the fish or its preparation: the blades and chopping boards used cost upwards of $1000 each, while each fish is selected from the best possible place, whether it be southwestern Korea or northern Japan. The head chef speaks English, and if you're seated at the main bar he will be happy to discourse on the merits of each creature as he performs his magic upon them. Sets from W50,000. Daily 11am–10pm.

Tutto Bene 투또베네 Cheongdamdong 118-9 ☎ 02 546 1489; Cheongdam subway; map p.90. The setting of this Italian restaurant is utterly gorgeous, its Orient Express-like wooden panelling offset by amber and honey-yellow lighting, and the scent of freshly cut flowers mingling with the creations of the chef. Pasta dishes are most popular (W25,000 and up), but don't overlook the seafood menu – sourced from remote islands off Korea's west coast, the oysters are superb. Daily noon–midnight.

CAFÉS

Seoul's café society has come a long way since the turn of the millennium – good coffee is available on almost every corner, at almost any hour. There are a number of major chains knocking around; *Hollys* has the best wi-fi access. Far more interesting for the visitor are the thousands of privately run ventures, which reach heights of quirky individuality around Hongdae and Samcheongdong; some effectively count as dessert cafés, focusing more on sweeties or baked goods than drinks.

GYEONGBOKGUNG AND AROUND

★Café Yung 카페융 Palpandong 27-2 ☎ 02 736 7652; Anguk subway; map p.64. Set in a traditional *hanok*, this is a Samcheongdong dessert café par excellence, a quaint place comparing favourably with the more pretentious competition on the main drag. Pride of place goes to the delectable *hoddeok* (호떡; W5000), a sweet

---

SEOUL EATING: TOP 10

Best pizza *Blacksmith Pizza* (p.100)
Best naengmyeon *Woo Rae Oak* (p.102)
Best atmosphere *Meokgeorichon* (p.101)
Best barbecued meat *Gwangjujip* (p.101)
Best concept *Oyori* (p.103)
Best dumplings *Jaha Sonmandoo* (p.102)
Best veggie food *Balwoo* (p.101)
Best bibimbap *Mongmyeok Sanbang* (p.102)
Best Samgyetang *Tosokchon* (p.100)
Best for Korean dessert *Second Best Place in Seoul* (p.105)

pancake stuffed with seeds and brown sugar, and served with berries. The persimmon yoghurt (W6500) is also worth mentioning, and the coffee's good. Daily noon–10pm.

★**Second Best Place in Seoul** 서울에서 두번째 로잘하는집 Samcheongdong 122; Anguk subway; map p.64. A rarity on cosmopolitan and fast-changing Samcheongdonggil – not only has it been here for decades, but it also serves traditional fare. The menu is short and sweet, with an assortment of Korean teas and snacks. Best is the *patjuk* (W5500), something like a viscous red-bean fondue containing all manner of ingredients from cinnamon to chestnut chunks. Daily 10am–9pm.

INSADONG

Bizeun 비즌 Insadonggil 16 ☎02 738 1245; Jonggak subway; map p.70. Waffles and ice cream are the regular snacks in Korean cafés, but here you'll be able to chow down on something more traditional: sweet rice cakes, known as *ddeok* (떡), which come in a wonderful kaleidoscope of colours, with flavours running the gamut from pumpkin to black sesame. Daily 8.30am–10pm.

O'Sulloc 오설록 Insadonggil 45-1 ☎02 732 6427; Anguk subway; map p.70. O'Sulloc is Korea's largest producer of green tea, but don't let that fool you into thinking that people come to their flagship tearoom to drink the stuff. Instead, this is a café and dessert bar *par excellence*, since the precious leaves have been blended into tiramisu, ice cream, lattes and chocolates (W5000–8000). Daily 9am–10pm.

MYEONGDONG AND DONGDAEMUN

Cat Café 고양이 다락방 Myeongdong 2-ga 51-14 ☎02 318 3123; Myeongdong subway; map p.76. Yes, that's right – a café filled with cats. It's hugely popular with visitors from China, who race up to this sixth-floor venue to take gazillions of pictures with the furry felines – great fun. W8000 entry gets you a free hot drink. Daily 1–10pm.

NORTHERN SEOUL

Sanmotungi 산모퉁이 Buamdong 97-5 ☎02 391 4737; map p.79. Made famous by its use as a set in Korean drama *The Coffee Prince*, this remote coffee house is worth a visit for the fresh air and mountain views on offer from its upper level. Coffees W7000. Daily 11am–10pm.

WESTERN SEOUL

Bau House 바우하우스 Seogyodong 394-44 ☎02 334 5152; Hapjeong subway; map p.84. Koreans are more famed abroad for eating dogs than owning them, but this café should show where the balance lies these days. Over a dozen cuddly pooches are on hand to greet customers, who are encouraged to bring their own dogs along. The coffee's good too (from W6000), but in such a bizarre atmosphere you may barely notice the taste. Daily 1.30–11.30pm.

Café aA 카페aA Seogyodong 408-11 ☎02 3143 7312; Sangsu subway; map p.84. Several things set this place apart from the regular Korean café: the huge, church-like front door; a ceiling at least three times higher than the national average; the bespectacled, artsy clientele; and a range of chairs imported from Europe. The upstairs floor functions as a sort of furniture museum, featuring examples from luminaries such as Jean Prouvé and Salvador Dali. Art aside, the coffee here is excellent (around W5000), as are the various cakes. Daily noon–2am.

★**Fell + Cole** 펠앤콜 Seopyongdaero 8-gil 7 ☎010 8895 1434; Sangsu subway; map p.84. Divine ice cream in a tidy little hidey-hole, secreted away in the alleys behind Sangsu station. Flavours change by the day, but expect the likes of carrot cake, fig mascarpone and caramel sweet potato. Daily noon–10pm.

ITAEWON

Millimeter   Milligram   밀리미터밀리그램 Itaewonno 240 ☎02 3210 1601; Hangangjin subway; map p.88. Also known as MMMG, Millimeter Milligram are a local design team producing arty stationery, postcards and other such items. This is the best place to buy their products – even the cool cup your coffee's served in will be available for sale. Daily 10am–10pm.

Passion 5 파션5 Hannamdong 729-74 ☎02 2071 9505; Hangangjin subway; map p.88. Part bakery, part dessert café, part brunch spot, this stylish place is also the headquarters of the *Paris Baguette* chain. Their baked goods are delectable (from W2000), and the ice creams superb; head on upstairs for Eggs Benedict and coffee. Daily 7.30am–10pm.

SOUTHERN SEOUL

★**Café Madang** 카페 마당 Sinsadong 630-26 ☎02 546 3643; Apgujeong subway; map p.90. The Hermès flagship store has a café discreetly tucked away on the basement level, and W11,000 will be enough to get you coffee. All cutlery, cups and glasses – plus the tables and chairs – are Hermès originals, and a fair proportion of the customers are local celebrities. There's no cheaper way to buy your way into high society, but dress smartly. Daily 10am–9pm.

The Lounge 더 라운지 Teheranno 606 ☎02 2016 1205; Samseong subway; map p.90. Sitting atop the *Park Hyatt* (see p.99) alongside the infinity pool of the hotel's fitness centre, this is a superb place for a coffee or light snack. Better still are a range of smoothies designed by David Beckham's nutritionist, Patricia Teixeira – well worth the W16,000 splurge. Daily 9am–midnight.

TEAROOMS

Insadonggil and its surrounding alleyways are studded with tearooms, typically decorated in a traditional style and therefore much in keeping with the area. The teas are high-quality products made with natural ingredients

1

(see box, p.42 for some varieties), and often come with traditional Korean sweets.

★**Cha-teul** 차마시는뜰 Bukchonno 11-gil 26 ☎02 722 7006; Anguk subway; map p.64. Utterly gorgeous *hanok* tearoom with a splendid range of fine brews, including unusual local varieties such as mistletoe and pine mushroom, and some imported from China. It's right next to a decaying brick smokestack – an easy landmark to spot. Teas go from W5500. Daily 10am–1pm.

Dawon 다원 Gwanhundong 30-1 ☎02 730 6305; Anguk subway; map p.70. Located in the grounds of the Kyungin Museum of Fine Art (see p.71), in warm weather you can sit outside in the courtyard, while inside you'll find traditionally styled rooms where guests are encouraged to add their musings to the graffiti-filled walls. Teas from W6000 are on the menu, alongside information about their purported health benefits. Daily 10am–11pm.

★**Mongmyeok Sanbang** 목멱산방 Minsokjaryo 11 ☎02 746 1736; Myeongdong subway; map p.76. This secluded Namsan restaurant (see p.102) also makes a great spot for tea, with most brews costing around W5000. Daily 11am–10.30pm.

★**Suyeon Sanbang** 수연산방 Seongbukdong 248 ☎02 764 1736; Hansung University subway; map p.79. Though a little out of the way and hard to find, this secluded *hanok* tearoom is highly recommended for those looking for a piece of old-world Seoul. Built in the 1930s, it exudes the charm of a bygone age, turning down the volume button of modern Seoul to leave only the sounds of bird chatter and running water. Teas cost around W10,000, desserts a little more. Daily 11.30am–10pm.

Su Yo Il 수요일 Gwanhundong 23 ☎02 8723 0191; Anguk subway; map p.70. Fancy tearoom with a few tables overlooking Insadonggil – a fine place for people-watching. Teas cost W7500, and many are served with floating flowers; in addition to the Korean options, they also offer Earl Grey, Darjeeling and other more familiar teas, as well as some fine desserts. Daily 10am–10.30pm.

NIGHTLIFE

Clubs pumping out techno, trance and hip-hop to wiggling masses; loungey subterranean lairs heavy with philosophical conversation; noisy joints serving up live jazz and rock; neon-tinged cocktail bars in the bowels of five-star hotels. After a lengthy gestation, Seoul's nightlife scene is finally wide open, and the drinkers themselves are becoming ever more liberal. As well as simple bars and clubs, there are some more local elements that can be factored into a night out: Korean friends are likely to drag you before long into a **noraebang** singing room to belt out your favourite songs amid a cacophony of castanets, while couples can end the night cuddled up at a **DVD-bang** (for both, see box, p.86). Summer sees most of the city's convenience stores surround themselves with plastic tables and chairs; a cheap and popular way to start a night out (see p.41 for a rundown on local hooch).

GYEONGBOKGUNG AND AROUND

Dugahun 두가헌 Sagandong 80 ☎02 3210 2100; Anguk subway; map p.64. A charmingly characteristic venue to fall into for a glass of wine, set as it is in a revamped *hanok* building. Their selection runs the gamut from under W70,000 to well over W1,000,000 per bottle, augmented by fine European cuisine from the kitchens. Some of the views disappoint, so choose your table carefully. Mon–Sat noon–4pm & 6pm–midnight, Sun noon–4pm.

★**Jeon Daegamdaek** 전대감댁 Angukdong 85

KNOW YOUR NEIGHBOURHOOD: GOING OUT IN SEOUL

Koreans love going out, whether it's with family, colleagues, social acquaintances or old study friends, making Seoul a truly 24-hour city – day and night, year-round, its streets are a thrilling merry-go-round of noise, which ramps up as evening approaches, and stays at a maximum until the early hours. Each area of Seoul has its own particular flavour, with **Hongdae** by far the busiest. Its streets are saturated with bars, clubs and restaurants, and full every day of the week from early evening on. Towards midnight the crowds are swelled further with Seoul's clubber population, who get on the last subway services of the day to Hongdae, party all night, then slink off home as dawn breaks. Almost as busy at the weekend is **Itaewon**, which has some of the best bars, clubs and restaurants in the capital. It has become trendified of late, and also functions as the most popular **gay** area in the whole country, with some excellent bars catering to Seoul's ever-growing pink community (see p.109 for details). Also worth mentioning are **Sinchon**, one subway stop from Hongdae and full of cheap yet interesting bars; studenty **Daehangno**, which is busy every evening (though most drift towards Hongdae as midnight approaches); and **Samcheongdong**, which has a few relaxing places to wine and dine in. South of the river, **Gangnam** has a couple of good clubs, and there are trendy bars aplenty in nearby **Apgujeong**.

📍 02 735 0723; Anguk subway; map p.64. An integral part of the newly trendy Seochon district, this bar-restaurant sells a great range of *makgeolli* for W4000–8000; one particular recommendation is the slightly sour Baedari brand (배다리), once beloved of dictatorial ex-president Park Chung-hee. This place is great for meals, too; most go for the eponymous savoury *jeon* (전; pancakes). If there's room, push back to the courtyard area at the back – a beautiful place to drink, with occasional glimpses of the Seoul night sky. Daily 11pm–midnight.

★**Sanchez** 산체스 Angukdong 85 📍 02 735 0723; Anguk subway; map p.64. One of the best new *makgeolli* dens in Seoul, with a fantastic range (W6000 or so per bottle) sourced from all over the country – there's no English-language signage or advice, but you basically can't go wrong. The food's great, too; try the super-tasty "America-style" *gamjajeon* (미국감자전; W15,000), which sees the regular local potato pancake covered with bacon and egg – you may never want the "normal" variety again. The only problem is a lack of table space – it's tiny and very popular, so you may well have to wait, or come back another day. Daily 6pm–2am.

INSADONG AND JONGNO

Baekseju Maeul 백세주마을 Gwancheoldong 256 📍 02 0000; Jonggak subway; map p.70. This presentable bar-restaurant prides itself on *baekseju* (see box, p.41), and serves local bar food – entire meals, in other words – to go with it. It's also one of the only places in town when you'll find *ihwaju* (이화주; W29,000); something like evaporated *makgeolli*, it's pleasantly gloopy. Daily 5pm–2am.

Brew 3.14 브루 3.14 Donnamunno 11-gil 39 📍 010 6706 7769; Anguk subway; map p.70. What a pleasant addition to the Anguk neighbourhood this little place has been – somewhere to send a craft beer down with a few slices of tasty pizza pie (from W8000). Daily 5pm–midnight.

MYEONGDONG AND DONGDAEMUN

Neurin Maeul 느린 마을 Suhadong 67 📍 02 6030 0999; Jonggak subway; map p.76. The Neurin Maeul *makgeolli* brand has spotted a gap in the market, and run

with it – they've dressed their tasty brew up to the nines as a boutique label, and are now selling it in myriad forms (including seasonal flavours) in this highly presentable restaurant-bar. You'll have to buy some food, but that's very good too. Daily 11.30am–11pm.

Pierre's Bar 피에르스바 Euljiro 30 📍 02 317 7183, ⓦ pierregagnaire.co.kr; Euljiro 1-ga subway; map p.76. Adjoining the superb *Pierre Gagnaire* restaurant (see p.102) at the top of the *Lotte Hotel*, this stylish bar is a firm favourite with international businessmen. Despite the modern yet opulent surroundings, and the sky-high food prices next door, drinks aren't *that* expensive – beer and spirits start at W13,000. Daily 6–11pm.

NORTHERN SEOUL

Dan Vie Myeongnyun 3-ga 154-2 📍 02 741 2550; Hyehwa subway; map p.79. Tucked into a basement just off Daehangno, this bar is a curious mix of decorative styles – some areas are cordoned off with dangling beads or shower curtains, others have space-station-style swivel chairs, and movies are projected onto the far wall. Daily 5pm–2am.

WESTERN SEOUL

Bar Da 바다 Seogyodong 365-5 📍 02 334 5572; Sangsu subway; map p.84. Getting to this bar is an adventure in itself – finding the entrance, crawling up the steep steps, then back outdoors to navigate what probably used to be a fire escape for the final leg to the top. Once you're there, it's wonderful, a broodingly dim, candle-studded hideaway for a nice drink. Daily 7pm–3am.

Club Naked 클럽 네이키드 Seogyodong 364-3 📍 010 8072 3461; Hongik University subway; map p.84. Hip-hop club that's not quite as packed or starchy as some of its neighbours, but still pretty darn busy on weekends. Drinks are cheap, too, and Thursday is Ladies' Night; entry usually W10,000 after 10pm on weekdays, and W20,000 on weekends. Daily 8pm–6am.

Gogos 고고스 Seogyodong 407-8 📍 02 337 8083; Sangsu subway; map p.84. Let's cut to the chase here – this is one of Hongdae's prime meat markets, with a good mix of Koreans and foreigners, cheap drinks, a fun vibe, and a W5000 entry fee. Tues–Thurs & Sun 8pm–2am, Fri & Sat 6pm–6am.

A REAL KOREAN NIGHT OUT

The "proper" Korean night out has long followed the same format, one that entwines food, drink and entertainment. The venue for stage one (*il-cha*) is the **restaurant**, where a **meal** is chased down with copious shots of *soju*. This is followed by stage two (*i-cha*), a visit to a **bar**; here beers are followed by snacks (usually large dishes intended for groups). Those still able to walk then continue to stage three (*sam-cha*), the **entertainment** component of the night, which usually involves a trip to a *noraebang* room for a sing-along (see box, p.86), and yet more drinks. Stages four, five and beyond certainly exist, but few participants have ever remembered them clearly.

1

M2 클럽 엠투 Seogyodong 367-11 ☎02 3143 7573; Sangsu subway; map p.84. Focusing on electronica, this is the area's largest nightclub; accordingly packed to the gills on weekends, it manages to rope in the occasional top international DJ. On weekends, you may be spending upwards of an hour waiting in line to get in. Entry W10,000–20,000. Tues–Thurs & Sun 9.30pm–5am, Fri & Sat 9.30pm–7am.

Samgeori Pocha 삼거리포차 Seogyodong; Sangsu subway; map p.84. Technically a restaurant (see p.103), this rustic-looking place is an integral part of Hongdae's nightlife – after a dance or a drink, Koreans love to eat (and drink a little more), so if you've made new friends you may well find yourself dragged along here, where raw fish and steaming broths are on the menu, and tables are littered with empty *soju* bottles. Daily 6pm–late.

★**Vinyl** 바이닐 Seogyodong 411-1 ☎02 322 4161; Sangsu subway; map p.84. Pick up takeaway cocktails from the window of this small bar, where you can get Pina Coladas and Sex on the Beach in what appear, at first glance, to be colostomy bags. Such ingenuity brings the price down – just W5000 for a cocktail. It's a great place to drink too, if you can find a seat free. Mon–Thurs & Sun 4pm–midnight, Fri & Sat 4pm–2am.

ITAEWON

B1 비원 Itaewondong 119-7 ☎02 749 6164; Itaewon subway; map p.88. Underground club with a decent sound system, and usually DJs that know how to make the most of it – a mix of house, techno, electronic and more. With lounge areas and snazzy decoration, it's far classier than most dance venues in the area – at the beginning of the night, at least. W10,000-20,000 in on weekends. Daily 7pm–4am.

BricX 브릭스 Itaewondong 119-10 ☎02 3785 1555; Itaewon subway; map p.88. This candlelit underground lair is a popular place to take a date, with its reasonably priced cocktails and excellent food – try the falafel. The seating areas are highly attractive, featuring curtains, oriental silk pillows and the like. Daily 6.30pm–3am.

Bungalow 번갈로 Itaewondong 112-3 ☎02 793 2344; Itaewon subway; map p.88. There are drinking options aplenty in this loungey, multilevel bar – sup sangria on the swing-seats, drink martinis in the sand pit, have a romantic glass of wine on a candlelit table or kick back with a beer on the outdoor terrace. The cocktails, however, are best avoided. Daily 4.30pm–3am.

★**Craftworks Taphouse** 크라브워크스 Noksapyeongdaero 238 ☎02 749 2537; Noksapyeong subway; map p.88. One of the main drivers behind the recent surge in local demand for craft beer. Their signature brews are all named after Korean mountains, including Geumgang Dark Ale, Halla Golden Ale, Seorak Oatmeal Stout and the Jirisan Moon Bear IPA; their popularity is such that they're starting to pop up in cities all over the country. Daily 11am–1am.

Gecko's Terrace 게코스 테러스 Itaewondong 178 ☎02 749 9425; Itaewon subway; map p.88. Unlike most Itaewon bars, this gets busy every day of the week. A lively mix of Koreans and foreigners, it's popular with people who don't feel like dancing, and those filling up on cheap beer before a night on the tiles – local draught beer is just W3000, and pints of Guinness reasonable for Korea at W8000. Mon–Thurs & Sun 11am–1am, Fri & Sat 11am–3am.

Hollywood Grill 할리우드 그릴 Itaewondong 123-33 ☎02 749 1659; Itaewon subway; map p.88. American-style bar-restaurant showing Premier League football, Major League baseball or any other sport coverage in demand from Seoul's expat community. At quieter times, it's a pleasant place for a game of pool or darts, while during major sporting events you'll be lucky to find standing room. If you're hungry, try one of their pizzas – some of the best in Seoul. Daily noon–2am.

Prost 프로스트 Itaewondong 116-1 ☎02 796 6854; Itaewon subway; map p.88. This multi-floor drinking venue behind the *Hamilton Hotel* has been full to bursting almost every night since it first opened. Sassy staff, a global range of beers (including some of their own), and a bunch of people to rub shoulders with – whether you like it or not. Daily 11.30am–2am.

The Wolfhound 울프하운드 Itaewondong 128-6 ☎02 749 7971, ⊛wolfhoundpub.com; Itaewon subway; map p.88. If you're feeling homesick, this Irish-style pub isn't a bad choice – they've a bunch of good beer, and it's also a fine place to eat (see p.104). Daily noon–2am.

SOUTHERN SEOUL

★**Octagon** 오크타곤 Nonhyeondong 175-2, ⊛cluboctagon.co.kr ☎02 516 8847; Hakdong subway; map p.90. Seoul's most popular club at the time of writing, this EDM venue has state-of-the-art light and sound systems (and even a gourmet chef), and regularly hauls in superstar DJs from across the globe. Entry is W30,000 on weekend evenings, and you'll have to be dressed up. Thurs–Sat 10pm–7am.

Woo Bar 우바 Walkerhillo 177 ☎02 2022 0333; Gwangnaru subway; map p.90. Located in the entrance lobby of the futuristic *W Hotel* (see p.99), this bar is almost a rite of passage for young Seoulites with a bit of cash to flash. Simply breathing ultra-trendiness, it's not for everyone, but if egg-shaped chairs, UV-lit sofas and space-helmet-like DJ booths sound appealing, this is the place to head. Daily 10am–2am.

GAY AND LESBIAN SEOUL

Seoul's burgeoning **gay nightlife** scene has come on in leaps and bounds since 2000, when star actor **Hong Seok-cheon** came out of the closet – the first Korean celebrity to do so. He has since opened up a whole raft of gay-friendly bars and restaurants in **Itaewon**, which remains the best gay area for foreigners; the best are listed below. Seoul does have other **gay zones**; the area around Jongno 3-ga station has long been home to underground gay bars, though few venues are foreigner-friendly. Additionally, the university district of **Sinchon** is popular with the local **lesbian** community, many of whom congregate of an evening in "Triangle Park", a patch of concrete near exit 1 of Sinchon subway station (take the first right).

Barcode 바코드 Myodong 41-1 ☎02 3672 0940; Jongno 3-ga subway; map p.70. The Jongno district has umpteen gay bars, but most of these are essentially off limits to foreigners. This is a neat exception to the rule, a fun place with English-speaking staff, and a bearish, 30-something clientele. Daily 7.30pm–3am.

Coffee Bean & Tea Leaf 커피빈 앤 티리브 Nagwondong 272; Jongno 3-ga subway; map p.70. Young gay fellas congregate throughout the day – but most clamorously on weekend evenings – at this café, located at the bottom of the *Fraser Suites* (see p.97). Daily 10am–9pm.

Pink Hole 핀크홀 Seogyodong 124-2 ☎02 712 1792; Hapjeong subway; map p.84. There are plenty of lesbian establishments in the wider Hongdae area, but this is one of the only options for those who feel like a dance – a pity, then, that they seem to put on the same pop playlist every night. Usually W10,000, including two free drinks. Daily 9pm–2am.

Queen 퀸 Itaewondong 136-42 ☎010 9039 2583; Itaewon subway; map p.88. Attractive "Homo Hill" venue with inviting staff and highly comfortable chairs. On warm weekend evenings, even these can't stop the crowd – usually quite a mixed bag in terms of race and persuasion – spilling out onto the street for a dance. Tues–Sun 6pm–4am.

★**Why Not?** 와이 낫? Itaewondong 137-4 ☎02 795 8193; Itaewon subway; map p.88. Now, this is a trip. Here you're likely to see dozens of young locals performing expertly choreographed K-pop dances – some of these guys are seriously talented. Other nights have drag shows, or more "regular" house music. Cover W10,000, includes a free drink. Daily 8pm–3am.

ENTERTAINMENT

There's no real excuse for being bored in Seoul. The city has a jaw-dropping amount going on almost every single day of the year, anything from **traditional dance** performances to **classical music** or **live jazz**; in addition, Hongdae functions as a breeding ground for local **rock** acts. The big bookstores (see p.112) have ticket booths, or get a Korean friend to help you book online at ⊛ticketlink.co.kr.

CINEMA

Korean cinema has become the subject of growing worldwide attention and acclaim, but because almost no films are screened with English-language subtitles, it's probably best to hunt them down in your home country. Wherever you find yourself in Seoul, you won't be too far from the nearest cinema. CVG and Megabox are the two major cinema chains; foreign films are shown in their original language with Korean subtitles.

★**CGV** Yongsan Station complex ☎1544 1122; Yongsan subway; map p.88. The Yongsan branch of Korea's biggest cinema chain shows some Korean films with English subtitles, as well as all of the latest blockbusters from abroad. Some films are shown in "4D", with wind machines, vibrating chairs and choreographed scents making you feel part of the show. There's also a "Gold Class" theatre, designed to resemble the first-class section on a plane, and seating just forty. Lastly, screens have cushy "couple" seats at the back, for snuggling up with that special someone. Tickets W8000; 4D W21,000; Gold Class W30,000.

Cinematheque 시네마테크 Nagwondong 284-6 ☎02 741 9782; Jongno 3-ga subway; map p.70. Also going under the name of "Seoul Art Cinema", the cinema here has a rolling calendar of themed events, some of which are based around foreign films; pop by and pick up a pamphlet. Tickets around W8000.

Mirospace 미로스페이스 Sinmunno 2-ga 1-153 ☎02 3210 3358; Seodaemun subway; map p.73. Interesting hundred-seat venue showing arty films, usually from abroad. For once, there's no popcorn on offer, and after the movie customers can glide into the sleek adjoining bar. Tickets W8000.

Sangsangmadang 상상마당 Eoulmadangno 65 ☎02 330 6243; Sangsu subway; map p.84. The basement of this arts complex has some arty English-language screenings, of which around half are from abroad. Interestingly, they try to show films whose themes match what's on show in the second-floor gallery. Tickets W8000.

THEATRE AND PERFORMANCE ARTS

Seoul's wide array of traditional performances and musicals are particularly popular with foreign travellers.

Battle B-Boy 배틀 비보이 Hongdae B-Boy Theater, Wausanno 121 ☎02 323 5233, ⊛sjbboys.com; Hongdae subway; map p.84. One way to get into the

1

SEOUL FESTIVALS

As long as you're not in Seoul during the long, cold winter, you'll almost certainly be able to catch a **festival** of some kind. In addition to national festivals (see p.43) and the traditional parades and **street performances** taking place on **Insadonggil** (usually every Thursday, Friday and Saturday), there are a whole host of events. A selection is detailed below.

Seoul Fashion Week March & Oct ⓦseoulfashionweek.org. Since it started in 2000, this has become Asia's largest fashion event, functioning as a great showcase for Seoul's up-and-coming designers.

International Women's Film Festival Late April ⓦwffis.or.kr. A week-long succession of films that "see the world through women's eyes" (even if some were created by men).

Jongmyo Daeje First Sun of May. Korean kings performed their ancestral rites at the Jongmyo shrine for hundreds of years, a tradition that's been carried forward to this day; the event is necessarily sober but very interesting, and is followed by traditional court dances.

Seoul International Cartoon & Animation Festival Late May ⓦsicaf.or.kr. Koreans young and old are major cartoon addicts, but while most of the national fix is sated by Japanese fare, there's still a lot of local talent: *The Simpsons*, *Family Guy* and *Spongebob Squarepants* are among the shows inked and lined here.

Korean Queer Culture Festival June ⓦwww.kqcf.org. Not exactly an event trumpeted by the local tourist authorities – in fact, not so long ago the police were still trying to ban it – this is a great way to see Korea crawling out of its Confucian shell. A fortnight-long programme includes a film festival, art exhibitions and the obligatory street parade.

Jisan Valley and Pentaport Rock Festivals July/Aug ⓦvalleyrockfestival.com & ⓦpentaportrock.com. Two competing European-style music festivals (think tents, mud and portaloos) which manage to rope in major international acts, though admittedly ones usually on the wane in their homelands. Both events stretch across three alcohol-fuelled nights.

Seoul Fringe Festival Aug ⓦseoulfringefestival.net. This fortnight-long platform for all things alternative is very popular with local students, and its semi-international nature means that it appeals to overseas visitors too. Hongdae is usually the best place to be.

Seoul Performing Arts Festival Sept/ Oct ⓦspaf.or.kr. This increasingly acclaimed event has seen performances from as far afield as Latvia and Israel, though its main aim is to showcase Korean talent. It takes place in various locations around Seoul over a three-week period.

Seoul Drum Festival Early Oct. The crashes and bangs of all things percussive ring out at this annual event, which takes place in the Gwanghwamun area.

Hi Seoul Festival Oct ⓦhiseoulfest.org. With everything from choreographed firework displays and tea ceremonies to men walking across the Han River by tightrope, this ten-day-long celebration of the coming of summer also incorporates the Seoul World DJ festival. There's simply no better time to be in the city.

B-Boy breakdancing still enthralling the nation, this long-running stage concept gets a refreshing every couple of years, and has some pretty incredible routines. W55,000. Performances Wed–Fri 8pm, Sat 6pm, Sun 4pm.

Chongdong Theatre 정동극장 Jeongdonggil 43 ☎02 751 1500, ⓦchongdong.com; City Hall subway; map p.73. "Miso" (W40,000), an 80min traditional show of song and dance, has extremely popular with foreign visitors for many a year; "Giparang" (W30,000) is newer, and tells a love story from the Silla dynasty. Miso performances: Tues–Sun 4pm & 8pm; Giparang performances Tues–Sun 7.30pm.

Jump 점프 Cinecore Theater, Jeongdong 22 ☎02 722 3995, ⓦhijump.co.kr; Jongno 3-ga subway; map p.73. Ever wondered what a family entirely made up of martial arts experts would be like? Experience all of the inevitable jumps and kicks in this entertaining musical. W40,000.

Performances Mon 8pm, Tues–Sat 4pm & 8pm, Sun 3pm & 6pm.

Korea House 한국의집 Toegyero 10 ☎02 2266 9101, ⓦkoreahouse.or.kr; Chungmuro subway; map p.76. Highly polished traditional performances from some of the top artistes in the country, combined with some of Seoul's best food (see p.102): this is one of the city's most popular nights out. The wonderful shows (W50,000) include fan dances, *pansori* opera and the long-ribboned hats of the "farmers' dance". Performances daily 6.30pm & 8.30pm.

Namsan Gugakdang 남산 국악당 Toegyero 34-gil 28 ☎02 2261 0500; Chungmuro subway; map p.76. Those looking for a traditional Korean performance should make this their first port of call. Part of the Namsangol complex (see p.75), its shows revolve around *gugak*, an ancient style of Korean music, but the savvy curators bring a pleasant variety to the offerings with regular thematic events of song, music, dance or a combination of the three. Ticket prices vary but are usually in the region of W30,000.

Nanta 난타 Myeongdong 2-ga 50-14 **☎** 02 739 8288, ⓦ nanta.co.kr; City Hall subway; map p.76. This madcap kitchen-based musical has gone down a storm since opening up in 1997 (making it Korea's longest-running show), with song, circus tricks and all sorts of utensil drumming mixed with a nice line in audience participation. W40,000. Performances daily 2pm, 5pm & 8pm.

Sejong Centre 세종 문화 회관 Sejongdaero 175 **☎** 02 399 1114, ⓦ sejongpac.or.kr; Gwanghwamun subway; map p.73. Gigantic venue offering a truly diverse array of music: everything from traditional Korean *gugak* to concertos from world-famous pianists. There'll be something going on every night of the week; check the website for details.

LIVE MUSIC

There's a decent little indie scene centred around Hongdae (check out ⓦ koreagigguide.com for listings). In addition, there are a few venues at which you can hear more highbrow offerings such as jazz or classical music.

All That Jazz 올 댓 재즈 Itaewondong 112-4 **☎** 02 795 5701, ⓦ allthatjazz.kr; Itaewon subway; map p.88. An Itaewon institution, this has been roping in jazz lovers for donkey's years. The atmosphere is fun, rather than stuffy, and audience interaction is commonplace. Tickets usually W5000. Performances Mon–Thurs 8.30pm, Fri & Sat 6.30pm, 8.30pm & 11.30pm, Sun 6.30pm & 8.30pm.

Ax 악스 Gwangjangdong 319-33 **☎** 02 457 5114; Gwangnaru subway; map p.90. Just like the *Ax* in Tokyo,

this is where many international bands come to roost during their time in Seoul – there's room for 2000 spectators here. Ticket prices vary.

Badabie 바다비 Donggyodong 182-5 **☎** 02 4454 2343; Sinchon subway; map p.84. A short walk from central Hongdae, this showcases the talents of bands from the local universities and beyond – an eclectic mix of rock, punk, folk and more. It costs up to W15,000 to get in; bring your own drinks. Wed–Sun 7pm–midnight.

Bbang 빵 Seogyodong 327-18 **☎** 010 8910 1089; Hongik University subway; map p.84. A good place to get a handle on local talent, this relaxed venue has been going, in a few different locations, since the mid-1990s. There are usually a few bands on most nights; entry is usually W15,000. Wed–Sun 6.30–11pm.

Club Evans 클럽 에반스 Seogyodong 407-3 **☎** 02 337 8361; Sangsu subway; map p.84. Hongdae's most popular jazz venue by a mile, this place is small enough to generate some decent acoustics, but large enough to create a good atmosphere. The acts are usually of more than acceptable quality, and the experience surprisingly refined for this nightclub-filled street. Tickets usually W5000–7000. Daily 7pm–midnight.

FF 클럽FF Seogyodong 407-8 **☎** 010 9025 3407; Sangsu subway; map p.84. You're in for some good ol' rock at this highly popular venue. A great many of the bands are foreign, bringing their pals then staying on for the DJ sets afterwards. A great place to make new friends. Entry W10,000–15,000. Tues–Thurs & Sun 8–11pm, Fri & Sat 6pm–6am.

SPORTS AND ACTIVITIES

Seoul has a small but pleasing range of ways to keep **sport** nuts entertained, as well as simple **exercise equipment** on almost every mountainside, as well as in parks, and dotting the banks of the Hangang and other waterways. The local **spectator sport** scene is also worth diving into.

BASEBALL

Pro baseball Seoul has three main professional teams. The two biggest are the LG Twins and the Doosan Bears, long-time rivals who both play in Jamsil Baseball Stadium (Sports Complex subway); the Nexen Heroes are a newer team playing west of Yeouido in Mokdong (Omokgyo subway). Games take place most days from April to October, and tickets can cost as little as W5000.

Batting cages Avid players can get some practice at a number of batting nets dotted around the city, particularly in student areas; these cost just W1000 for a minute's worth of balls. One is marked on the Insadong map (see p.70).

FOOTBALL

K-League Those wanting to watch some professional K-League action can catch FC Seoul at the World Cup Stadium (ⓦ fcseoul.com; tickets from W10,000), with games taking place on weekends from March to October.

Seongnam and Suwon, two of the most dominant Korean teams of recent times, also play near Seoul; the atmosphere at all grounds is fun but they can be on the empty side, unless you're lucky enough to be around for a major international game (ⓦ fifa.com).

ICE-SKATING

Outdoor rinks Those visiting in winter will be able to skate outdoors at various points in the city: Seoul Plaza and Gwanghwamun Plaza (see p.72) often turn into gigantic ice rinks for the season (usually Dec–Feb; daily 10am–10pm; W1000), though skaters are turfed off every 15min or so for surfacing.

Indoor rinks There's a year-round rink in Lotte World (see p.92), which charges W15,000 for entry and skate rental (daily 10am–9.30pm); far cheaper is the Olympic-size rink at Korea National University (daily 2–6pm; W5000), which is within walking distance of Korea University subway station.

1

SWIMMING

Outdoor pools In summer months (generally June–Aug), a number of outdoor pools open up around the Hangang; most convenient for visitors are those on the western side of Yeouido park (daily 9am–6pm; W5000). The *Hamilton Hotel* (see p.99) also opens its rooftop pool during the summer months (daily 9am–6pm; W22,000).

TAEKWONDO

Namsangol Hanok Village ⓦ taekwonseoul.com; Chungmuro subway (lines 3 & 4). This is the best place to head to watch taekwondo, or have a go yourself. They put on free performances every day except Tuesday, and in summertime often run hands-on programmes (see website for details). Tourist information offices (see p.96) can also organize longer programmes: figure on around W50,000 per day.

SHOPPING

Shopaholics will be quite at home in Seoul: the city has everything from trendy to traditional, markets to malls. High on the itinerary of many tourists are the colossal markets of **Dongdaemun** and **Namdaemun** (see p.77). There are **department stores** all over the city; the bustling streets of **Myeongdong** host department stores from the biggest nationwide chains – Migliore, Shinsaegae, Lotte and Galleria – and there are also luxury examples in Apgujeong. Perhaps more interesting are the city's **boutiques**; these are most numerous (and expensive) around Apgujeong, though there are cheaper versions of the same in Hongdae and Samcheongdong. Itaewon is also worth a mention for its excellent **tailored suits**. The best place to head for anything vaguely arty is **Insadonggil** and its side streets, which have numerous **craft** shops selling paints, brushes, calligraphy ink and handmade paper. There are also a few shops selling **antiques** here, and more of the same in Itaewon.

ARTS, CRAFTS AND ANTIQUES

★**Kwang Ju Yo** 광주요 Gahoedong 203 ☎02 741 4801, ⓦ kwangjuyo.com; Anguk subway; map p.64. Korea has been at the forefront of world pottery for centuries, and this conveniently located store is one of the best places to go shopping for it. Celadon bowls and porcelain vases are among the items on offer, and they also sell Andong *soju* (a particularly potent form of the national drink, at 41 percent ABV) in elaborate jars: perfect souvenirs. Daily 10am–9pm.

Millimeter Milligram 밀리미터밀리그람 Itaewonno 240 ☎02 549 1520, ⓦ mmmg.net; Hangangjin subway; map p.88. Seoul-based design team making cutesy cups, cutlery, stationery and the like. They have a few branches around the city, but their flagship store is the best, set into a lovely café (see p.105). Daily 11am–9pm.

Myung Sin Dang 명신당 Insadonggil 34 ☎02 736 2466; Anguk subway; map p.70. The most renowned of Insadong's many art supplies shops, focusing solely on the humble paintbrush – there are hundreds of styles on offer here, including some made with baby hair. Daily 10am–6pm.

★**Royal Antiques** 로얄 엔틱 Bogwangdong 137-2 ☎02 794 9976, ⓦ royal-antique.com; Itaewon subway; map p.88. This remains the best place to head if you're hunting for a genuine Joseon-era piece of furniture. The owners are friendly and can speak English. Tues–Sun 10am–6pm.

Sangsangmadang 상상마당 Eoulmadangno 65 ☎02 330 6243; Sangsu subway; map p.84. Hongdae was once more famed for its art than its bars; this arty complex features a gallery, café and cinema, while the ground floor sells small lifestyle goods designed by local students. Daily 9am–9pm.

★**Ssamiziegil** 쌈지길 Gwanhundong 38; Anguk subway; map p.70. A wonderfully designed building

whose spiral walkway plays host to countless small shops selling traditional clothing, handmade paper, jewellery and the like. There's also a rooftop market on weekends, selling all manner of quirky arts and crafts. Daily 10.30am–9pm.

Tongin 통인 가게 Insadonggil 32 ☎02 733 4867, ⓦ tonginstore.com; Anguk subway; map p.70. Colonial structure with whole floors full of antique cases, cupboards, medicinal racks and other furniture, much of it in a distinctively oriental style. Daily 10am–8pm.

★**Yido Pottery** 이도 포터리 Changdeokgunggil 191 ☎02 722 0756, ⓦ yido.kr; Anguk subway; map p.64. Just up the road from *Kwang Ju Yo* (see above), this pottery store is perhaps even more interesting. Here you'll find tea sets, plates and other great offerings from some of the country's top talents; many of them learned their craft at Hongdae. Daily 10am–7pm.

BOOKS AND MUSIC

Bandi & Luni 반디 앤 루니 Jongno Tower B2, Jongno 2-ga 6 ☎02 2198 3000; Jonggak subway; map p.70. Large underground bookshop in the second basement level of Jongno Tower; they've a fairly sizeable dedicated English-language section. Daily 9.30am–10pm.

Kyobo Books 교보 문고 Kyobo Building B1, Jongno 1 ☎1544 1900; Gwanghwamun subway; map p.73. Taking up the basement level of the huge Kyobo building, this is the country's largest bookshop, and fantastic for foreign-language books. There's also a branch in Gangnam, just south of Sinnonhyeon station. Daily 9.30am–10pm.

Purple Record 퍼플 레코드 Seogyodong 343-5 ☎02 336 3023; Sangsu subway; map p.84. The best selection of foreign independent music in Korea, and a happy hunting ground for the works of local artists; a thoroughly pleasant place to hang out and sift through records. Daily 10am–11pm.

★ **What the Book** 오 오 오 Itaewon 1-dong ☎ 02 797 2342, ⓦ whatthebook.com; Noksapyeong subway; map p.88. Dedicated foreign-language bookshop that's extremely popular with expats. They've an extensive secondhand selection, and the country's best range of guidebooks. Daily 10am–9pm.

CAMERAS AND ELECTRONIC EQUIPMENT

Techno Mart 테크노 마트 Cheongparo 125; Gangbyeon subway; map p.90. Out near the Dongseoul bus terminal in eastern Seoul, this is a gigantic place stocking all manner of electronic goods. Daily 10am–7pm.

Yongsan Electronics Market 용산 전자 상가 Cheongparo 125; Yongsan subway; map p.88. This multilevel giant rises up alongside the Yongsan train station. Many staff speak a little English, and it's a grand place just to look around, even if you're not buying. It's a bit more expensive than Techno Mart. Daily 10am–7.30pm.

CLOTHING

Ccomaque 꼬마 Bukchonno 5-gil 25 ☎ 02 722 1547, ⓦ ccomaque.com; Anguk subway; map p.64. Skirts and dresses featuring cute, cartoonish designs based around purportedly Korean motifs, including animals such as deer, turtles and cranes, and natural elements such as clouds and pine trees. Daily 10am–8pm.

Gwangjang Market 광장시장; Jongno 5-ga subway; map p.76. Though most famed for its culinary offerings, this sprawling market has a truly excellent secondhand section, with all manner of zany shirts, coats and jackets imported from abroad. It's a little hard to find: hunt down the staircase on the western side of the market, and head

for the second floor. Mon–Sat 9am–6pm.

★ **Hahn's Custom Tailoring** 한스 양복 Itaewondong 34-16 ☎ 02 793 0830, ⓔ hanstailor@hotmail.com; Itaewon subway; map p.88. Get a perfectly tailored suit for around US$500. Affable owner Hahn speaks excellent English, and will be pleased to discuss the particular style you're after; his tailors also make good shirts. Daily 10am–9pm.

Hamilton Shirts 해밀튼 셔츠 Hannam 2-dong 736-9 ☎ 02 798 5693, ⓦ hs76.com; Itaewon subway; map p.88. Tailored shirts at lower prices than you'd pay for factory-made on your local high street: most shirts go for around W45,000. The quality is amazingly high for the price. Daily 10am–9.30pm.

★ **Lee Geon Maan** 이건만 Insadonggil 29 ☎ 02 733 8265, ⓦ leegeonmaan.com; Anguk subway; map p.70. Well-located store selling ties for men and handbags for women. Their unique selling point is an innovative use of *hangeul*, the Korean text conspicuous by its absence on Korean clothing. Daily 10.30am–8pm.

★ **Lee Young Hee** 오 오 오 Sinasdong 665-5 ☎ 02 544 0630, ⓦ leeyounghee.co.kr; Apgujeong subway; map p.90. Korea's traditional clothing, *hanbok* (한복), is okay to wear for a photoshoot, but since it looks a little ridiculous on foreigners, few of them would actually go out and buy the stuff. This store sells striking contemporary takes on the style, and counts Hillary Clinton as a customer at their New York branch. Daily 11am–6.30pm.

Style Nanda 스타일 난다 Wausanno 29-gil 23 ☎ 02 333 9215; Hongik University subway; map p.84. From humble beginnings as an online retailer of secondhand clothing, this has become one of Korea's most famous youth labels – this three-storey flagship store has single-handedly raised rent prices in the area. Daily 11am–11pm.

DIRECTORY

Banks and exchange Banks will exchange foreign currency or travellers' cheques, while some have a "Global ATM" that can be used with cards from around the world. If you have a debit card it may be easier to head to a convenience store such as 7-Eleven or GS25.

Embassies Australia ☎ 02 2003 0100; Canada ☎ 02 3783 6000; China ☎ 02 738 1038; Ireland ☎ 02 774 6455; New Zealand ☎ 02 3701 7700; Russia ☎ 02 318 2116; South Africa ☎ 02 792 4855; UK ☎ 02 3210 5500; US ☎ 02 397 4114.

Emergencies Call the tourist information line (☎ 1330) for the fastest possible foreign-language advice in emergencies. Staff at the top hotels will also be willing to provide assistance, even to non-guests. Emergency numbers are ☎ 112 for the police, ☎ 1339 for ambulance, and ☎ 119 for the fire brigade.

Hospitals and clinics To find an English-speaking doctor, or a clinic suited to your needs, call the Seoul Help Center's medical line on ☎ 02 2075 4180.

Immigration There are immigration offices

(ⓦ immigration.go.kr) at both Incheon and Gimpo airports, as well as one just off Jongno (☎ 02 731 1799).

Left luggage Most subway, train and bus stations have storage lockers costing from W1000 for a few hours, though these are too small to accommodate suitcases or large backpacks. Some hotels offer left luggage facilities, and a couple of guesthouses are willing to put your bags somewhere safe while you travel around the country.

Lost property There's a national lost property hotline (☎ 02 2299 1282), but since staff are unlikely to speak English it may be best to go through the tourist information line (☎ 1330). There are also lost property offices in City Hall and Chungmuro subway stations, as well as the main train stations.

Post offices There's a post office in every neighbourhood, all of which can handle international mail – just ask for the nearest *ucheguk* (usually Mon–Fri 9am–5pm). The main office on Jongno Road is open until 8pm on weekdays, 6pm on weekends (☎ 02 3703 9011).

Gyeonggi

FARMERS' DANCE, KOREAN FOLK VILLAGE

Gyeonggi

If you meet a Korean who claims to live in Seoul, there's a fifty-fifty chance that they actually mean Gyeonggi (경기), a province encircling the capital and bristling with high-rise hives for many of its worker bees. Gyeonggi has an urban mass of over 25 million people – around half of the country's population, and one of the world's most densely populated areas. Seoul functions as the province's beating heart, yet while most of its satellite cities are commuter-filled nonentities, there's still plenty to see here for those willing to put in the miles: a giant fortress from the days of dynasty; the country's biggest Chinatown; more islands than you could count; and – most excitingly of all – the chance to tiptoe across the border to the forbidden North.

Of the province's cities, **Incheon** to the west of the capital and **Suwon** to the south merit a visit. Suwon's main draw is its UNESCO-listed fortress, while Incheon was the first city in the country to be opened up to international trade, and remains Korea's most important link with the outside world thanks to its international airport and ferry terminals.

A residue of traditional Korean life can be found off the mainland in the **islands** of the West Sea – better known internationally as the Yellow Sea – from whose shores fishermen roll in and out with the tide as they have for generations. Some of the more notable isles are **Yeongjongdo**, home of Korea's main international airport and a rather scruffy place; **Deokjeokdo**, a laidback and refreshingly unspoilt retreat from Seoul; and **Ganghwado**, an island within spitting distance of the North Korean border (not that you're allowed even to see North Korea from its army-controlled shores, let alone spit at it).

Those who want to catch a glimpse of the neighbours should head to **Panmunjeom**, a village inside the **Demilitarized Zone** that separates North and South Korea. With security so tight, access is understandably subject to the conditions of the time, but most should be lucky enough to take a step across the world's most fortified border to what is technically **North Korean territory**. Alternatively, you can make do with a view of the empty "Propaganda Village" on the opposite side of the DMZ, or a scramble through tunnels built by the North in readiness for an assault on Seoul.

Incheon

인천

Almost every international visitor to Korea gets to see some of **INCHEON**. Korea's third most populous city, it's home to the main airport and receives all ferries from China, though most new arrivals head straight to Seoul as soon as they set foot on Korean territory. However, in view of its colourful recent history, it's worth at least a day-trip from the capital. This was where Korea's "Hermit Kingdom" finally crawled out of self-imposed isolation in the late nineteenth century and opened itself up to international trade, spurred

Highlights

❶ Incheon Climb Jayu Park to gaze out over the Lego-like jumble of container ships surrounding the city, before trotting down the hill into Korea's largest Chinatown. **See p.118**

❷ West Sea islands Clean air, homely villages and a thriving fishing industry are what make a visit to the islands worthwhile; all this and only a day-trip from Seoul. **See p.122**

❸ Suwon Scramble up a UNESCO-listed fortress wall, visit a nearby folk village or join what may be the world's only toilet tour. **See p.125**

❹ Yangsu-ri Seoul's best sunsets can be found way out east of the centre, on this charming island surrounded by mountains. **See p.129**

❺ The DMZ Walk through a tunnel under the world's most heavily fortified border, or take a couple of steps into official North Korean territory in the eerie Joint Security Area. **See p.129**

❻ Paju With its fun Book City and arts complex, Paju is more than just the average Seoul satellite-suburb. **See p.134**

HIGHLIGHTS ARE MARKED ON THE MAP ON P.118

2

on by the Japanese following similar events in their own country (the Meiji Restoration). Incheon was also the landing site for **Douglas MacArthur** and his troops in a manoeuvre that turned the tide of the Korean War (see box, p.120). However, despite its obvious importance to Korea past and present, there's a palpable absence of civic pride, possibly due to the fact that Incheon is inextricably connected to the huge Seoul metropolis – the buildings simply don't stop on their long march from the capital.

Incheon's various sights can easily be visited from Seoul, which is just an hour away by subway. The most interesting part is **Jung-gu**, where you can wander around the country's only official Chinatown, a small but appealing area where you can rub shoulders with the Russian sailors and Filipino merchants who – after the Chinese – make up most of Incheon's sizeable foreign contingent. Jung-gu sits below **Jayu Park**, where a statue of MacArthur gazes out over the sea. The only other area of note is **Songdo New Town**, an area being built on land reclaimed from the sea. Lastly, Incheon is also a jumping-off point for ferries to a number of islands in the **West Sea** (see p.122).

Jung-gu

중구 • Incheon subway (line 1)

Jung-gu district lies way out on the western fringe of Incheon, but forms the centre of the city's tourist appeal. On exiting the gate at Incheon station, you'll immediately be confronted by the city's gentrified **Chinatown**; sitting across the main road and demarcated by the requisite oriental gate, it's a pleasant and surprisingly quiet area to walk around with a belly full of Chinese food. Uphill roads lead northeast to **Jayu Park**, which topples down to the south into a quiet but cosmopolitan part of town, where many Japanese lived during the colonial era.

Jayu Park

자유 공원 · 24hr · Free

Within easy walking distance of the subway station, **Jayu Park** is most notable for its statue of **General Douglas MacArthur**, staring proudly out over the seas that he conquered during the Korean War (see box, p.120). Also in the park is the Korean–American **Centennial Monument**, made up of eight black triangular shards that stretch up towards each other but never quite touch – feel free to make your own comparisons with the relationship between the two countries. Views from certain parts of the park expose Incheon's port, a colourful maze of

cranes and container ships that provide a vivid reminder of the city's trade links with its neighbours across the seas.

The Street of Culture and History

역사문화의 거리 · 24hr · Free

South of Jayu Park, Incheon has tried to evoke its colonial past on the slightly bizarre **Street of Culture and History**; the new wooden fronts added to the buildings are the only discernable things that constitute such a grand title, though they look decidedly pretty. Most of the businesses that received a face-lift were simple shops such as confectioners, laundries and electrical stores; many are still going, though they're now being augmented by bars, arty cafés and such like.

The former Japanese banks

Both daily 9am–6pm · W1500 combined ticket

One block south of the odd Street of Culture and History is a road more genuinely cultural and historic. Here you'll find a few distinctive **Japanese colonial buildings** which are surprisingly Western in appearance (that being the Japanese architectural fashion of the time). Three of the buildings were originally banks, of which two have now been turned into small **museums**. The former **58th Bank of Japan** offers interesting photo and video displays of life in colonial times, while the former **1st Bank** down the road has a less interesting display of documents, flags jung-gu. Sitting in a small outdoor display area between the two, you'll find some fascinating pictures taken here in the 1890s, on what was then a quiet, dusty road almost entirely devoid of traffic, peopled with white-robed gents in horsehair hats – images of a Korea long gone.

Incheon Art Platform

인천 아트 프래트폼 · ⓦ inartplatform.kr

It's usually worth popping by to see what's going on in and around **Incheon Art Platform**, a rambling culture and arts centre sprawled across several buildings just south of the former Japanese banks. There's nothing like a permanent exhibition here, since it's more a hub for artistic creativity than a place for displays, but there'll always be at least an outdoor installation to get your teeth into.

2

GENERAL MACARTHUR AND THE INCHEON LANDINGS

"We drew up a list of every natural and geographic handicap... Incheon had 'em all."

Commander Arlie G. Capps

On the morning of September 15, 1950, the most daring move of the **Korean War** was made, an event that was to alter the course of the conflict entirely, and is now seen as one of the greatest military manoeuvres in history. At this point the Allied forces had been pushed by the North Korean People's Army into a small corner of the peninsula around Busan, but **General Douglas MacArthur** was convinced that a single decisive movement behind enemy lines could be enough to turn the tide.

MacArthur wanted to attempt an amphibious landing on the Incheon coast, but his plan was greeted with scepticism by many of his colleagues – both the South Korean and American armies were severely under-equipped (the latter only just recovering from the tolls of World War II), Incheon was heavily fortified, and its natural island-peppered defences and fast tides made it an even more dangerous choice.

The People's Army had simply not anticipated an attack on this scale in this area, reasoning that if one were to happen, it would take place at a more sensible location further down the coast. However, the plan went ahead and the Allied forces performed **successful landings** at Wolmido island and two other Incheon beaches, during which time North Korean forces were shelled heavily to quell any counterattacks. The city was taken with relative ease. MacArthur had correctly deduced that a poor movement of supplies was his enemy's Achilles heel – landing behind enemy lines gave Allied forces a chance to cut the supply line to KPA forces further south, and Seoul was duly retaken on September 25.

Despite the Incheon victory and its consequences, MacArthur is not viewed by Koreans – or, indeed, the world in general – in an entirely positive light, feelings exacerbated by the continued American military presence in the country. While many in Korea venerate the General as a hero, repeated demonstrations have called for the **tearing down** of his statue in Jayu Park, denouncing him as a "war criminal who massacred civilians during the Korean War", and whose statue "greatly injures the dignity of the Korean people". Documents obtained after his eventual dismissal from the Army suggest that he would even have been willing to bring nuclear weapons into play – on December 24, 1950, he requested the shipment of 38 atomic bombs to Korea, intending to string them "across the neck of Manchuria". Douglas MacArthur remains a controversial character, even in death.

Wolmido

월미도 • Ferry cruises daily at noon, 2pm, 4pm & 6pm (1hr 20min; W15,000) • Bus #2, #15, #23 or #45 from Incheon subway, or a cheap taxi ride

Famed across the land as the place where the tides turned the tide of the Korean war, the island of **Wolmido** – 1km from Jung-gu and connected to the mainland by road – is now renowned for some pretty sorry-looking funfair rides and a musical fountain. It's possible to embark on a **ferry cruise** here, though, and there are umpteen restaurants in which to wolf down a round of super-fresh seafood. You may also notice a monorail heading here from Incheon station – stalled for years at the time of writing, it may eventually enter service in 2016.

Songdo New Town

송도 • Central Park station (Incheon subway line 1), or a W12,000 taxi ride from Incheon subway

Built on a man-made island just south of central Incheon, **Songdo New Town** is essentially a gigantic, $40bn experiment in modern-day urban living. This symphony of chrome and glass was created with an ambitious green, eco-friendly manifesto – "City of the Future", "High-Tech Utopia" and "The World's Smartest City" were phrases bandied about by government bureaucrats. More than half of its buildings were in place at the time of writing, making use of fancy underground waste-disposal systems, super-fast internet connections and other unexcitingly incremental improvements on modern life. It's all a bit dull, and more than a little creepy in feel, but the difference with "regular" Korean cities is quite striking. At the time of writing Songdo was home to South Korea's tallest building, the **Northeast Asia Trade Tower** (305m); proposals for another tower twice that height were still being batted around after years of delays.

ARRIVAL AND INFORMATION
INCHEON

By plane Importantly, there's no need to hit central Incheon itself to get to and from the international airport, which is actually on an island west of the city proper and connected to the mainland by bridge: there are dedicated airport bus connections from Seoul and all over the country. Several limousine bus routes connect the airport with central Incheon, or take city bus #306 to Incheon subway station.

By subway Despite the city's size, there's no train station: it's best to take subway line 1 from Seoul (1hr), though be sure that your train is bound for Incheon, as the line splits when leaving the capital.

By ferry Ferries from China dock at one of two terminals (see p.28 for details on these services). Terminal 2 is the closer to the city centre, and is best accessed by taxi (W4000 from Incheon or Dong-Incheon subway stations). Terminal 1 is further out; a taxi will be less than W10,000, or buses #28 and #24 head the same way from Incheon and

Dong-Incheon stations respectively. Right next to Terminal 1 is the Yeonan terminal, which caters for domestic ferries to almost all of the accessible islands in the West Sea (see details in the relevant island accounts).

By bus Incheon bus terminal is located next to a subway station of the same name on Incheon line 1, six stops south of Bupyeong, where it meets Seoul's own line 1.

Destinations Andong (frequent; 4hr 10min); Busan (11 daily; 4hr 30min); Chuncheon (frequent; 2hr); Daegu (13 daily; 4hr 30min); Daejeon (frequent; 2hr 45min); Gangneung (hourly; 3hr 30min); Gwangju (every 30min; 4hr); Jeonju (hourly; 3hr 10min); Mokpo (15 daily; 4hr 30min); Seoul (frequent; 1hr 10min); Sokcho (10 daily; 3hr 50min).

Tourist information The helpful booth outside Incheon subway station (daily 9am–6pm; ☎ 032 773 2225) usually has an English-speaker; further offices can be found in the ferry terminals.

ACCOMMODATION

Incheon's proximity to Seoul means that most people choose to visit on a **day-trip**, but it's quite possible to spend a night here. There are a number of **motels** in and around Incheon and Dong-Incheon subway stations, as well as in Chinatown itself.

Atti 아띠 호텔 Songhak 1-dong 9-6 ☎ 032 772 5233, ⓦ attihotel.com. This little gem is tucked away in a quiet area behind the Jung-gu district office, near *Tochon* restaurant (see p.122). Recent renovations have seen it become a little too trendy – the big bugbears here are the glass partitions that make the bathrooms a little too visible. However, the surrounding area is highly pleasant, making it easy to put big-city bustle out of mind. W60,000

Harbor Park 하버파크 호텔 Jemullyangno 217 ☎ 032 770 9500, ⓦ harborparkhotel.com. Value-for-money option in Jung-gu, with excellent service

standards and great sea views. Unfortunately, standard rooms can be extremely small, so try to check a few if possible; suites, on the other hand, are generously sized. W125,000

Paradise 향만성 Jemullyangno 257 ☎ 032 762 5181, ⓦ incheon.paradisehotel.co.kr. Though service can be a little ropey at times, and the crane-filled views may not appeal to some, this is the best hotel in the area. Despite being just a stone's throw from Incheon subway station, the hotel entrance is uphill and hard to reach, so you may prefer to take a taxi. W250,000

EATING AND DRINKING

Rarely for a Korean city, and perhaps uniquely for a Korean port, Incheon isn't renowned for its food, though the presence of a large and thriving **Chinatown** is a boon to visitors. Don't expect the food to be terribly authentic, since Koreans have their own take on Chinese cuisine (see box, p.122).

RESTAURANTS

Fog City 포그시티 Jungangdong 1-ga 19-1 ☎ 032 766 9024. Steakhouse-cum-café which certainly stands out in the wider Chinatown area. The coffee's pretty poor, but the pizzas are fine (W16,000), as is the clam chowder (W6000). Pride of place, however, goes to their excellent home-made sourdough bread, or a weird-but-tasty variety made with

makgeolli. Tues–Sun 11am–10pm.

Gonghwachun 공화춘 Chinatown-no 43 ☎ 032 765 0571. This is where Korea's *jjajangmyeon* fad started – it has been served here since the 1890s. W5000 will buy you a bowl, or you could try the sautéed shredded beef with green pepper (W20,000), and finish off your meal with fried, honey-dipped rice balls. Daily 11am–11pm.

2

CHINESE FOOD, KOREAN-STYLE

Korea's biggest **Chinatown** can be found in Incheon, and there are some decent restaurants hereabouts (see p.121 and below for a couple). However, even at these, the food is not exactly what you'd expect to find across the West Sea – even though the majority of the restaurateurs are Chinese, Korean visitors usually order precisely the same dishes as they would at any Chinese restaurant across the land. When with the Romans, do as the Romans do: the **top choices** here, and available at every single restaurant, are sweet-and-sour pork (탕수육; *tangsuyuk*), fried rice topped with a fried egg and black-bean paste (볶음밥; *beokkeumbap*), spicy seafood broth (짬뽕; *jjambbong*), and the undisputed number one, *jjajangmyeon* (자장면), noodles topped with black-bean paste.

Mandabok 만다복 Bukseongdong 2-ga 9-11 ☏ 032 773 3838. There are various Chinese dishes on offer at this vaunted, impressively authentic Chinatown institution, whose innards are resplendent with cheesy golden wallpaper. The shark fin, scallop and abalone dishes are pricey and made for small groups, though single diners and won-pinchers can rejoice with the rice staples, such as the shredded chilli pork (W7000). Daily 10am–10pm.

★**Tochon** 토촌 Songhakdong 1-ga 10 ☏ 032 464 5511. A wonderfully rustic multi-floor warren, with a ground level surrounded on three sides by interconnected fish tanks. Try the *ddeok-galbi* (Korean burgers; see box, p.241) for W20,000, filling *jeongsik* (set meals) from W20,000, or a *meonggae bibimbap*. Daily 10am–10pm.

BARS

Bboya 뽀야 Jungangdong 3-ga 1-8 ☏ 032 762 8800. Many bars in Korea decorate themselves with beer bottle tops, but here the concept is taken to its logical extreme – both interior and exterior alike are smothered with them. Despite the busy decor, it's a relaxing place to drink. Daily 7pm–1am.

The West Sea islands

Gyeonggi's perforated western coast topples into the **West Sea** in an expanse of mud flats – the **tidal range** here is said to be the second biggest in the world after the Bay of Fundy in eastern Canada, though this is challenged by Britain's Bristol Channel. Whoever the silver medallist, the retreat of the tides is fantastic news for hunters of clams and other sea fare; it does, however, mean that beaches are in short supply. Fear not, Korean land rises again across the waves in the form of dozens of **islands**, almost all of which have remained pleasantly green and unspoilt; some also have excellent **beaches**. Life here is predominantly fishing-based and dawdles by at a snail's pace – a world away from Seoul and its environs, despite a few being close enough to be visited on a day-trip. Quite a number of these islands have next to no traffic, making them ideal places for a ride if you can find a bike to bring along.

Up the Gyeonggi coast from Incheon is **Ganghwado**, an island whose **dolmens** betray its ancient history. Just to the west is delightfully quiet **Seongmodo**, home to an enchanting temple. Ganghwado is connected to the mainland by bus, but there are other islands that can take hours to reach by ferry; two of these are **Deokjeokdo** and **Baengnyeongdo**, both beautiful and sufficiently far away from "regular" Korea to provide perfect escapes for those in need of a break. Swarms of less-visited islands are also there for the taking, if you're in an adventurous mood. The suffix **-do** (도) means "island" in Korean; accordingly, you may see signs for "Deokjeok Island" and so on.

Ganghwado

강화도 • Bus #3000 (every 15–20min; 1hr 40min) from Sinchon subway in Seoul (line 2); walk directly up from exit 1

Unlike most West Sea islands, **GANGHWADO** is close enough to the mainland to be connected by road – buses run regularly from Seoul to **Ganghwa-eup** (강화읍), the ugly main settlement; from here local buses dash to destinations across the island, though the place is so small that journeys rarely take more than thirty minutes. While this

2

> ## THE YELLOW SEA
>
> The West Sea is far better known abroad as the "**Yellow Sea**", a reference to the vast quantity of silt deposited into it by the Yellow River, which flows from the Chinese desert. Be warned that few Koreans will take kindly to this term, even though it's the accepted international name; there's nowhere near the intensity of debate that the East Sea/Sea of Japan on the other side of the country has inspired (see box, p.158), but those who want to stay on the better side of their Korean friends should refer to the body of water off the Gyeonggi coast as the "**West Sea**", or even better, the Korean name, **Seohae** (서해).

accessibility means that Ganghwado lacks the beauty of some of its more distant cousins, there's plenty to see. One look at a map should make clear the strategic importance of the island, which not only sits at the mouth of Seoul's main river, the Han, but whose northern flank is within a frisbee throw of the **North Korean border**. Would-be adventurers should note that this area is chock-full of military installations, and closed to the public.

Before the latest conflict, this unfortunate isle saw **battles** with Mongol, Manchu, French, American and Japanese forces, among others (see p.348). However, Ganghwado's foremost sights date from further back than even the earliest of these confrontations – a clutch of **dolmens** scattered around the northern part of the island date from the first century BC and are now on UNESCO's World Heritage list.

Goindol

고인돌 • 24hr • Free • From Ganghwa-eup, take one of the buses bound for Changhu-ri, which depart every hour or so, and make sure that the driver knows where you want to go

Misty remnants from bygone millennia, Ganghwa's **dolmens** are overground burial chambers consisting of flat capstones supported by three or more vertical megaliths. The Korean peninsula contains more than 30,000 of these ancient tombs – almost half of the world's total – and Ganghwado has one of the highest concentrations in the country. Most can only be reached by car or bike, though one, **Goindol**, is situated near a main road and accessible by bus. Goindol is a granite tomb sitting unobtrusively in a field, as it has for centuries: a stone skeleton long divested of its original earth covering, with a large 5m by 7m capstone.

Hajeom

하점

The countryside surrounding Goindol is extremely beautiful, and you can combine a visit to the dolmen with a delightful walk. One of the best places to head to is the village of **Hajeom**, not far to the west, where the roofs of some houses have been traditionally decorated with distinctive patterns. From the hills above Hajeom it's possible to view the North Korean bank of the Hangang, though sadly the propaganda that the North used to boom across the border from giant speakers can no longer be heard. Visual propaganda still remains, however, in the form of giant slogans best seen from the small mountain of **Bongcheonsan** (봉천산), a forty-minute walk north of Hajeon – the message visible across the border translates as "Yankees go home", a request that would doubtless be more effective were it not written in Korean.

Jeondeungsa

전등사 • Daily 8am–6pm • W3000, or free out of hours • From Ganghwa-eup, take one of the half-hourly buses bound for Onsu-ri; the #3100 also runs here from Sinchon in Seoul

In the south of the island is **Jeondeungsa**, a pretty temple dating from the fourth century – when Buddhism was just taking root on the peninsula – making it one of the oldest temples in the country. It was also the venue for the creation of the famed Tripitaka Koreana, eighty-thousand-plus blocks of carved Buddhist doctrine which

2

now reside in Haeinsa temple near Daegu (see p.177). These days, due in part to its proximity to Seoul, it's a highly popular place to **templestay** (see p.35).

Gwangseongbo

광성보 • Daily 9am–6pm • W1000 • From Ganghwa-eup, buses run down the coast every hour or so

Studding Ganghwado's east coast are three **fortresses**, best seen by making use of the bicycle lanes that run alongside the main road, though buses also follow the same route. **Gwangseongbo** is the northernmost and most interesting of the three, and dates from the mid-seventeenth century; its strategic importance will be obvious to all visitors, as it peers out over the channel that separates Ganghwado from the mainland.

Oepo

외포 • Buses (hourly; 25min) from Ganghwa-eup; some come straight through from Sinchon

Small and delightfully old-fashioned, the settlement of **OEPO** (pronounced "Way-paw") on the island's western coast is a little like stepping into the Korea of the 1970s, before the country's "economic miracle" mopped up old traditions by the bucketload. There are no particular sights, so wandering around to soak up the atmosphere is the order of the day. There's an appealing little fish market near the dock, and restaurants all around it.

Seongmodo

석모도 • Ferries (every 30min; 10min) run from Oepo on Ganghwado; the last one back is at 8.30pm

Ferries run from Oepo's tiny terminal to **SEONGMODO**, across the water from Ganghwado; ornithophobes should note that large flocks of seagulls tend to circumnavigate the vessel for the entire journey, waiting to catch thrown crisps (and highly proficient at doing so). Buses meet the ferries and make the fifteen-minute journey to **Bomunsa** (보문사), a charming temple that constitutes the island's main sight. The complex is a five-minute uphill pant from the bus stop, and has a small tearoom at its entrance; many choose to give their legs an extra workout by taking the mountain path behind the temple, which leads to a clutch of small grottoes that function as **Buddhist shrines** and boast wonderful sea views. Ferries back to Ganghwado dry up early, but this is a wonderfully peaceful place to be stranded – there are **restaurants** and simple **accommodation** around both the temple and ferry terminal, as well as **bicycle hire** immediately off the ferry ramp for those with the muscle to pump up and down the island's hilly roads.

Deokjeokdo

덕적도 • Two fast ferries (1hr) run from Incheon's Yeonan pier, departing at 9.30am & 2.30pm; slower ferries (1 daily; 2hr 30min) leave at 8am from the same terminal

Possibly the prettiest and most tranquil of the West Sea isles, **DEOKJEOKDO** feels a world away from Seoul, though it's quite possible to visit from the capital on a day-trip. There's little in the way of sightseeing, and not much to do, but that's just the point – the island has a couple of stunning beaches and some gorgeous mountain trails, and makes a refreshing break from the hustle and bustle of the mainland. Around the ferry berth are a few shops, restaurants and *minbak*, while a bus meets the ferries and makes its way round to **Seopori beach** (서포리 해수욕장) on the other, quieter side of the island – also home to a few *minbak*. Most who stay here for a day or two spend their time chatting to locals, lazing or throwing back beers on the beach, going fishing or taking the easy climb up to the island's main peak.

Some adventurous souls make their way to **Soyado** (소야도), an island facing the ferry berth, and only a few minutes away if you can flag down a fishing boat. There's even less to do here than on Seongmodo, though there are a couple of motels and *minbak* if you look hard enough, and you can rest assured you'll be one of very few foreigners to have overnighted on the island.

Baengnyeongdo

백령도 • Ferries (3 daily; 4hr 30min; W57,400) run from Incheon's Yeonan pier, departing at 8am, 8.50am and 1pm; return sailings are at 8am, 1pm and 1.50pm

A tortuous ferry-ride from Incheon is **BAENGNYEONGDO**, almost tickling the North Korean coastline and as such home to many military installations. In 2010 the **Cheonan**, a South Korean naval vessel, sank just off the island in suspicious circumstances, seriously damaging relations between the two Koreas (see p.354). Baengnyeongdo literally means "White Wing Island", due to its apparent resemblance to an ibis taking flight, and although the reality is somewhat different you will find yourself gawping at Baengnyeongdo's spectacular **rock formations**, best seen from one of the tour boats that regularly depart the port. Some of the most popular are off Dumujin, to the west of the island, while at Sagot beach the stone cliffs plunge diagonally into the sea.

The tranquil nature of these islands is sometimes diluted by swarms of summer visitors – it's best to visit on weekdays, or outside the warmest months. Given the island's distance from Incheon, and the occasional military problems, you should organize accommodation at a tourist information office before heading out.

Suwon and around

수원

All but swallowed up by Seoul, **SUWON** is a city with an identity crisis. Despite a million-strong population, and an impressive history – best embodied by the **UNESCO-listed fortress** at its centre – it has had to resort to unconventional means to distance itself culturally from the capital, the best example being the dozens of individually commissioned **public toilets** that pepper the city (see box, p.126). Suwon, in fact, came close to usurping Seoul as Korea's seat of power following the construction of its fortress in the final years of the eighteenth century, but though the move was doomed to failure, Suwon grew in importance in a way that remains visible to this day – from the higher parts of the fortress wall, it's evident that this once-small settlement burst through its stone confines, eventually creating the noisy hotchpotch of buildings that now forms one of Korea's largest cities.

An hour away from central Seoul, Suwon is certainly an easy **day-trip** from the capital, though those who choose to stay will benefit from cheaper accommodation, and a wholesomely provincial experience. East of the centre lie **Everland** and the **Korean Folk Village**, two sites ideal for anyone travelling with children, though just as easily accessible from Seoul.

2

MR TOILET

Bar its fortress, central Suwon carries precious little sightseeing potential, though one interesting facet is what may be the world's greatest concentration of public toilets – they all have names, and some are even marked on tourist maps. This concept was the brainchild of **Sim Jae-deok**, a man referred to, especially by himself, as "**Mr Toilet**". Apparently afflicted by something of a cloacal obsession (best evidenced by his house, custom-built to resemble a giant loo), Sim claims to have been born in a public restroom, but transcended these humble beginnings to become mayor of Suwon and a member of the national assembly. He then went on to create, and declare himself head of, the *other* WTO – the **World Toilet Organization**. Undoubtedly spurred on by his team's debatable findings that the average human being spends three years of their life on the toilet, Sim desired to improve his home city's facilities for the World Cup in 2002, commissioning dozens of individually designed public toilets. Armed with the relevant pamphlet from the tourist office, it's even possible to fashion some kind of **toilet tour**. Features may include skylights, mountain views or piped classical music, though such refinement is sadly sullied, as it is all over Korea, by the baskets of used toilet paper discarded throne-side.

Hwaseong fortress

화성 • Daily 9am–6pm • W1000, or free out of hours; ticket also includes Hwaseong Haenggung (see below); archery W2000 for 10 arrows • ⓦ swcf.or.kr • Buses #2-2, #11 and any beginning with #13, #16 or #50 from train station; #36 from bus terminal

Central Suwon has but one notable sight – **Hwaseong fortress**, whose gigantic walls wend their way around the city centre. Completed in 1796, the complex was built on the orders of **King Jeongjo**, one of the Joseon dynasty's most famous rulers, in order to house the remains of his father, **Prince Sado**. Sado never became king, and met an early end in Seoul's Changgyeonggung Palace at the hands of his own father, King Yeongjo (see p.79); it may have been the gravity of the situation that spurred Jeongjo's attempts to move the capital away from Seoul.

The fortress

Towering almost 10m high for the bulk of its course, the **fortress wall** rises and falls in a 5.7km-long stretch, most of which is walkable, the various peaks and troughs marked by sentry posts and ornate entrance gates. From the higher vantage points you'll be able to soak up **superb views** of the city, but while there's also plenty to see from the wall itself, the interior is disappointing: other fortresses around the country – notably those at Gongju (see p.263) and Buyeo (see p.267) – have green, tranquil grounds with little inside save for trees, squirrels, pagodas and meandering paths, but Hwaseong's has had concrete poured into it, and is now a cityscape filled with restaurants, honking traffic and ropey motels. Even on the wall itself, it's hard to escape the noise, which is often punctuated by screaming aircraft from the nearby military base.

Most visitors start their wall walk at **Paldalmun** (팔달문), a gate at the lower end of the fortress, exuding a well-preserved magnificence now diluted by its position in the middle of a traffic-filled roundabout. From here a steep path leads uphill to Seonammun, the western gate. At various points you may be able to practice your **archery** skills.

Hwaseong Haenggung

화성행궁 • Daily 9am–6pm; martial arts displays Tues–Sun 11am; traditional dance and music performances April–Nov Sat & Sun 2pm • Entry included in W1000 fortress ticket (see above)

In the centre of the area bounded by the fortress walls is **Hwaseong Haenggung**, once a government office, then a palace, and now a fine place to amble around; its pink walls are punctuated by the green lattice frames of windows and doors, which overlook dirt courtyards from where you can admire the fortress wall that looms above. There's a daily **martial arts display**, and occasional performances of traditional **dance and music**.

Korean Folk Village

한국 민속촌 • Generally daily 9.30am–6pm; farmers' dance 11am & 2pm; tightrope walk 11.30am & 2.30pm, wedding ceremony 12pm & 4pm • W15,000 • ⓦ koreanfolk.co.kr • Free shuttle buses (30min) from Suwon station at 10.30am, 12.30pm & 2.30pm (returning at 2pm, 3.30pm & 4.30pm), or take regular city bus #10-5 or #37 (50min). From Seoul take bus #5001-1 or #1560 from Gangnam station (50min), or #5500 from Jonggak station (1hr 20min)

This recreation of a traditional **Korean Folk Village** has become one of the most popular day-trips for foreign visitors to Seoul, its thatch-roofed houses and dirt paths evoking the sights, sounds and some of the more pleasant smells of a bygone time, when farming was the mainstay of the country. Its proximity to the capital makes this village by far the most visited of the many such facilities dotted around the country, which tends to diminish the authenticity of the experience. Nevertheless, the riverbank setting and its old-fashioned buildings are impressive, though the emphasis is squarely on performance – **shows** of tightrope walking and horseriding take place regularly throughout the day. **Traditional wedding ceremonies** provide a glimpse into Confucian society, with painstaking attention to detail including gifts of live chickens wrapped up in cloth like Egyptian mummies. Don't miss the **farmers' dance**, in which costumed performers prance around in highly distinctive ribbon-topped hats amid a cacophony of drums and crashes – quintessential Korea.

2

Everland

에버랜드 • Daily, usually 9.30am–9pm • W46,000, W38,000 after 3pm, W20,000 after 5pm; discount and combination tickets often available on website • ⓦ everland.com • Bus from Suwon train station (depart on the half-hour; around 1hr). From Seoul, bus #5700 from the Dong-Seoul bus terminal via Jamsil subway station (1hr 10min), or #5002 from Gangnam subway station, via Yangjae (45min); more expensive daily shuttles (50min; W12,000) run at 9am from Hongdae, 9.30am from City Hall & 9.40am from Jongno 3-ga (returning at 6pm & 9pm); or take the Everline, a spur running from the Bundang line (around 2hr in total)

Everland is a colossal theme park that ranks as one of the most popular domestic tourist attractions in the country – male or female, young or old, it's hard to find a *hangukin* (Korean person) who hasn't taken this modern-day rite of passage. Most are here for the fairground rides, and the park has all that a roller-coaster connoisseur could possibly wish for. Other attractions include a **zoo** (which features a safari zone that can be toured by bus, jeep or even at night), a speedway track, a golf course, and the surprisingly good **Hoam Museum**, which contains a few excellent examples of Buddhist art, and some interesting French sculpture in an outdoor garden.

Caribbean Bay

캐리비언 베이 • Daily, usually 9.30am–6pm; outdoor section June–Aug only • W35,000, W30,000 after 2.30pm; discount and combination tickets often available on website • ⓦ everland.com

The most popular part of the theme park is **Caribbean Bay**, with an indoor zone that's open year-round containing several pools, a sauna and a short river that you can float down on a tube, as well as massage machines and relaxation capsules. The **outdoor section** with its man-made beach is what really draws the summer crowds. It's no longer just the beach that's artificial – despite a fairly innocent beginning, when it was marketed squarely at family groups, this has become one of the most popular places for Korea's silicon crowd to show off their new curves. Off the beach, facilities include a water bobsleigh, which drops you the height of a ten-floor building in just ten seconds, and an artificial surfing facility.

ARRIVAL AND INFORMATION   SUWON

By train and subway Suwon's main train station is a convenient place to arrive, and just about within walking distance of the fortress. It handles both national rail and Seoul subway trains (line 1; though note that this splits south of Seoul). If you're coming from the capital it's faster and far more comfortable to go by train (30min) rather than subway (1hr), though it's more expensive and may well end up taking you longer, once transfers at Seoul or Yongsan stations have been factored in.

Destinations Busan (every 10–30min; 2hr 50min); Daejeon (every 10–30min; 1hr); Daegu (every 10–30min; 2hr); Gwangju (hourly; 3hr 30min); Jeonju (10 daily; 2hr

2

30min); Seoul (frequent; 30min–1hr).

By bus Buses run from several parts of Suwon to several parts of Seoul – ask at your accommodation if you think that this may benefit you. Otherwise, Suwon's main bus terminal handles services to destinations all across the country.

Destinations Busan (7 daily; 5hr); Daegu (14 daily; 3hr 30min); Daejeon (8 daily; 1hr 30min); Gwangju (frequent; 3hr 30min); Jeonju (12 daily; 2hr 40min); Mokpo (7 daily;

4hr 30min); Sokcho (8 daily; 4hr 30min).

Transport cards If you have a Seoul transport card (see box, p.95), you can also use it for buses or subway trains in Suwon.

Tourist information The main information office was in the process of being moved at the time of writing, though nobody knew where to – it'll eventually land somewhere in or around the train station. Alternatively, there's a small office visible from Hwaseong Haenggung.

ACCOMMODATION

Despite the fact that **accommodation** in Suwon is markedly cheaper than similar places up the road in Seoul, most travellers visit on **day-trips** from the capital. There are troops of motels in the area bounded by the fortress wall, but you'd do well to disregard all images that staying inside a UNESCO-listed sight may bring to mind, as it's one of the seediest parts of the city. True budget-seekers can make use of an excellent *jjimjilbang* just off Rodeo Street (W7000).

Central 센터럴 호텔 Gyodong 1-2 ☎031 246 0011, ⓦ suwoncentral.com. In an excellent location for the fortress, as the name suggests, and not too run-down for a Korean tourist hotel. Rooms are reasonably good value and have cable TV; a small breakfast is also thrown in for free, but the bar-filled street outside can get noisy at night. __W77,000__

Hwaseong Guesthouse 화성 게스트하우스 Jeongjoro 801-gil 11 ☎031 245 6226, ⓦ hsguesthouse. com. Central Suwon's first hostel, and it's a decent enough effort, if a little sterile – also note that the dorms have no a/c, which can be troublesome in summer (winter's fine thanks to underfloor heating). The big plus here is the location, smack bang in the centre of the fortress area.

Dorm beds __W18,000__, doubles __W30,000__

Moon Motel 문 모텔 Jungdong 39-1 ☎031 246 2285. The best of the love motels in the Paldalmun area – the galloping horses on top are just about visible from the gate itself. Rooms are large, comfortable, clean and quiet, and that's all you really need in this type of place. __W30,000__

★**Ramada Plaza** 라마다프라자 Jungbudaero 150 ☎031 230 0001, ⓦ ramadaplazasuwon.com. Suwon's best hotel, though in an uninteresting corner of the city, attracts well-heeled visitors – primarily Europeans on business – and offers all the comfort you'd expect of the chain. Some of the suites are truly stunning, and even standard rooms have been designed with care. __W220,000__

EATING AND DRINKING

Suwon is famous for a local variety of *galbi*, whereby the regular meat dish is given a salty seasoning. You will more than likely find something appealing on **Rodeo Street**; the city's youth flocks here in the evening to take advantage of the copious cheap restaurants, and eating segues into **drinking** as the evening goes on.

RESTAURANTS

Bonsuwon Galbi 본수원 갈비 Uman 2-dong 103-1 ☎031 211 8434. Around the back of *Hotel Central* (and therefore a little out of the way for those not staying there) is what may well be the best *galbi* restaurant in the city. The succulent meat doesn't come cheap (at least W25,000 per portion), but is worth it for the chance to try Suwon's local take on Korea's most pyromaniacal eating experience. Daily 11.30am–8.30pm.

Haenggungjeong 행궁정 Haenggungno 22-gil 17 ☎031 243 8020. Not far from the entrance to Haenggung (look uphill for the sign with three Korean characters in primary colours), this presentable restaurant is primarily another meat place, but also serves tasty *bibimbap* (W7000) and *naengmyeon* (W7000). Daily 11am–10pm.

Yechon 예촌 Namchangdong 132-1 ☎031 254 9190. It's retro to the max at this little hidey-hole near Paldalmun, a folk-styled establishment serving savoury

pancakes known as *jeon* (전) in many different styles (from W10,000), as well as superb *makgeolli* from Jeonju, a city in the southwest of the country. Tues–Sun 3.30pm–midnight.

★**Yeonpo Galbi** 연포 갈비 Buksudong 25-4 ☎031 255 1337. In a quiet area just inside the fortress wall lies the best restaurant in the area. The *galbi* meat is rather expensive (W33,000 and up), but cheaper noodle dishes are available, and those who arrive before 3pm can get a huge *jeongsik* (set meal) for W20,000, which includes several small fish and vegetable dishes. Daily 9am–9pm.

BARS

Big Chill 빅 칠 3F Jungdong 1-5 ☎010 7600 2574. The most popular bar in the central area, with a cast of expat regulars throwing down cheap beer (W3000) and cocktails (from W5000), often over a game of pool or darts. Mon, Tues & Fri–Sun 8pm–5am, Wed & Thurs 8pm–2am.

Yangsu-ri

양수리

Taking the subway east of Seoul, it seems like an eternity before the capital's mess of high-rises comes to an end. The train then plunges through a long tunnel and shoots over a wide river, emerging in **YANGSU-RI**, a tranquil village surrounded by mountains and water – it sits at the confluence of the Namhangang and Bukhangang, two rivers that combine to create the Hangang, which pours through Seoul. The village has long been famed as a spot for extramarital affairs – a fact made evident by a large number of seedy motels. However, in recent years its natural charm has also started to draw in an ever-increasing number of genuine couples, families, students and curious foreign visitors.

The focus of the area is a small **island**, one that's an easy walk from Yangsu station. Farmland takes up much of the interior, while a pleasant walking track skirts much of its perimeter – the stretch to the south of the island is particularly pleasant, and there are numerous photo opportunities at the very southern tip, which also makes a spectacular place to watch the sunset, if the weather agrees.

ARRIVAL AND GETTING AROUND   YANGSU-RI

By subway Yangsu is a stop on the Jungang line, which starts in Yongsan – the journey is around an hour. It's a 15min walk to the island from Yangsu station, though it's also possible to take a bus. It's also possible to access the island from Gukcheon, the station immediately west of Yangsu – from here, simply find the bridge, and walk across.

By bike Though it may be more than 35km from central Seoul, Yangsu-ri is becoming more and more popular as a bike trip from the capital, and is certainly within day-trip distance. You can also rent bikes at Yangsu-ri itself: there's a booth immediately outside Yangsu station, and another within visible distance of Gukcheon station. Cycling the island's perimeter is very pleasant, and the track even continues all the way down to Busan (see p.197).

ACCOMMODATION AND EATING

E-Motel E모텔 Yangsu-ri 552-1 ☎031 771 8676. Sitting just north of the village hub, this motel is more modern than many others on the island, and some of the higher rooms have views of the river and mountains – thankfully the windows are slightly larger than the letterboxes more typical of Korean motels. **W40,000**

★**Gelateria Panna** 빤나 Yangsu-ri 649-5 ☎031 775 4904. It's quite odd to think that Seoul's best ice cream should be found way out in Yangsu-ri, but it's true – the couple that run this tiny place lived in Milan for a decade, and during that time learned how to make some kick-ass gelato (W3500 for a cup). Their ice-cream roster changes daily (the ginger and vanilla are particularly tasty), and they also make a mean espresso. It's in the village, just south of the main road. Daily except Wed 11am–8pm.

Gongreungdong Myeolchiguksu 공릉동 멸치국수 Yangsu-ri 565-11 ☎031 772 1560. The cold, spicy noodles (비빔국수; W4500) at this simple sit-on-the-floor joint are just the treat after a summer walk; there are warmer noodle broths available too, and portions are huge. It's on the main road heading across the island, near the bridge on the western side. Daily except Wed 11am–8pm.

Green Hill 그린힐 호텔 Yongdam-ni ☎031 772 5752. Don't fancy the Yangsu love motel experience? Then this is pretty much your only choice – and even here, at the one hotel in town, there are sex toy vending machines in many of the rooms. It's south of Yangsu station, on the way to the island. **W70,000**

The Demilitarized Zone

"The visit to the Joint Security Area at Panmunjeom will entail entry into a hostile area, and possible injury or death as a direct result of enemy action."

Disclaimer from form issued to visitors by United Nations Command

As the tour bus crawls out of Seoul and heads slowly north through the traffic, the seemingly endless urban jungle slowly diminishes in size before disappearing altogether. You're now well on the way to a place where the mists of the Cold War

2

still linger on, and one that could still be ground zero for the World War III – the **DEMILITARIZED ZONE**. More commonly referred to as "the DMZ", this no-man's-land is a 4km-wide buffer zone that came into being at the end of the Korean War in 1953. It sketches an unbroken spiky line across the peninsula from coast to coast, separating the two Koreas and their diametrically opposed ideologies. Although it sounds forbidding, it's actually possible to enter this zone, and take a few tentative steps into North Korean territory – thousands of civilians do so every month, though only as part of a **tightly controlled tour**. It's even home to two small communities, **Freedom Village** and **Propaganda Village** (see box, p.133). Elsewhere are a few platforms from which the curious can stare across the border, and a **tunnel** built by the North, which you can enter.

While most visitors content themselves with a packaged DMZ tour, there are more adventurous options available. The city of **Paju**, just southwest of Panmunjeom, has a few sights not at all related to North Korea – a small **arts village**, and a **publishing town** whose buildings are among the most adventurously designed in the land.

Brief history

For the first year of the **Korean War** (1950–53), the tide of control yo-yoed back and forth across the peninsula (see p.350 for more details). Then in June 1951, General Ridgeway of the United Nations Command got word that the Korean People's Army (KPA) would "not be averse to" armistice talks. These talks took place in the city of Kaesong, now a major North Korean city (see p.336), but were soon shifted south to **Panmunjeom**, a tiny farming village that suddenly found itself the subject of international attention.

Ceasefire talks went ahead for two long years and often degenerated into venomous verbal battles littered with expletives. One of the most contentious issues was the repatriation of prisoners of war, and a breakthrough came in April 1953, when terms were agreed; exchanges took place on a bridge over the River Sachon, now referred to as the **Bridge of No Return**. "Operation Little Switch" came first, seeing the transfer of sick and injured prisoners (notably, six thousand returned to the North, while only a tenth of that number walked the other way); "Operation Big Switch" took place shortly afterwards, when the soldiers on both sides were asked to make a final choice over their preferred destination.

Though no **peace treaty** was ever signed, representatives of the KPA, the United Nations Command (UNC) and the Chinese Peoples' Liberation Army put their names to an **armistice** on July 27, 1953; South Korean delegates refused to do so. The room where the signing took place was built specially for the occasion, and cobbled together at lightning speed by KPA personnel; it now forms part of most tours to North Korea (see p.315).

After the armistice

An uneasy truce has prevailed since the end of the war – the longest military deadlock in history – and the DMZ is now something of a natural haven filled with flora and fauna that's been left to regenerate and breed in relative isolation. However, there have been regular spats along the way. In the early 1960s a small number of disaffected American soldiers **defected** to the North, after somehow managing to make it across the DMZ alive (see p.363), while in 1968 the crew of the captured USS *Pueblo* (see opposite) walked south over the Bridge of No Return after protracted negotiations. The most serious confrontation took place in 1976, when two American soldiers were killed in the **Axe Murder Incident** (see box opposite), and in 1984, a young tour leader from the Soviet Union fled North Korea across the border triggering a short gun battle that left three soldiers dead.

THE AXE MURDER INCIDENT

Relations between the two Koreas took a sharp nose dive in 1976, when two American soldiers were killed by a pack of **axe-wielding North Koreans**. The cause of the trouble was a **poplar tree** which stood next to the Bridge of No Return: a UNC outpost stood next to the bridge, but its direct line of sight to the next Allied checkpoint was blocked by the leaves of the tree, so on August 18 a five-man American detail was dispatched to perform some trimming. Although the mission had apparently been agreed in advance with the North, sixteen soldiers from the KPA turned up and demanded that the trimming stop. Met with refusal, they launched a swift attack on the UNC troops using the axes the team had been using to prune the tree. The attack lasted less than a minute, but claimed the life of First Lieutenant Mark Barrett, as well as Captain Bonifas (who was apparently killed instantly with a single karate chop to the neck). North Korea denied responsibility for the incident, claiming that the initial attack had come from the Americans.

Three days later, the US launched **Operation Paul Bunyan**, a show of force that must go down as the largest tree-trimming exercise in history. A convoy of 24 UNC vehicles streamed towards the plant, carrying more than 800 men, some trained in taekwondo, and all armed to the teeth. These were backed up by attack helicopters, fighter planes and B-52 bombers, while an aircraft carrier had also been stationed just off the Korean shore. This carefully managed operation drew no response from the KPA, and the tree was successfully cut down.

Panmunjeom

판문점

There's nowhere in the world quite like the **Joint Security Area** ("the JSA"), a settlement squatting in the middle of Earth's most heavily fortified frontier, and the only place in DMZ territory where visitors are permitted. Visits here will create a curious dichotomy of feelings: on one hand, you'll be in what was once memorably described by Bill Clinton as "the scariest place on Earth", but as well as soldiers, barbed wire and brutalist buildings you'll see trees, hear birdsong and smell fresh air. The village of **PANMUNJEOM** itself is actually in North Korean territory, and has dwindled to almost nothing since it became the venue for armistice talks in 1951. But such is the force of the name that you'll see it on promotional material for most **DMZ tours** that run to the area; these tours are, in fact, the only way to get in.

The Joint Security Area

Situated just over an hour from Seoul is **Camp Bonifas**, an American army base just outside the DMZ. Here you'll meet your guides – usually young infantry recruits whose sense of humour makes it easy to overlook the seriousness of the situation – and be given a briefing session reminding you of the various dos and don'ts. Back on the bus look out for the white-marked stones pushed into the wire fence – these are detection devices that will fall out should anyone try to climb over. On both sides of the road you'll see hilltop points from where UNC forces keep a constant lookout across the border for any military build-up that would precede a large-scale attack.

Once inside the **JSA** itself, keep your fingers crossed that you'll be allowed to enter one of the three **meeting rooms** at the very centre of the complex, which offer some serious travel kudos – the chance to step into North Korea. The official Line of Control runs through the very centre of these cabins, the corners of which are guarded by South Korean soldiers, who are sometimes joined by their Northern counterparts, the enemy soldiers almost eyeball to eyeball. Note the microphones on the table inside the room – anything you say can be picked up by North Korean personnel. The rooms are closed to visitors when meetings are scheduled, which is just as well since some of them have descended into farce. One such fiasco occurred when members of one side – it's not clear which – brought a bigger flag than usual to a meeting. The others followed suit with an even larger banner, and the childish

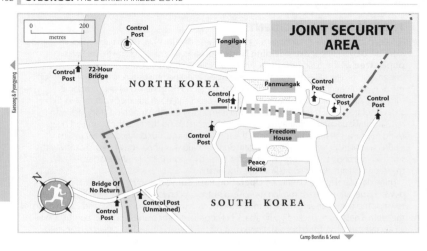

process continued until the flags were simply too large to take into the room; at this point, both sides agreed on a standard flag size.

From an outdoor **lookout point** near the cabins you can soak up views of the North, including the huge flag and shell-like buildings of **"Propaganda Village"** (see box opposite). You may also be able to make out the jamming towers North Korea uses to keep out unwanted imperialist signals – check the reception on your phone. Closer to the lookout point, and actually within JSA territory, is the **Bridge of No Return**, the venue for POW exchange at the end of the Korean War (and also for James Bond in *Die Another Day* – though for obvious reasons it was filmed elsewhere).

On arriving back at Camp Bonifas you'll usually have time to pop into a gift shop, stocked with "I did the DMZ" T-shirts and a nice line in North Korean blueberry wine. Also in the area is a golf course once named by *Sports Illustrated* as the most dangerous on Earth, but there's only one hole (a par three, for the record) and you won't be allowed to use it.

TOURS

PANMUNJEOM AND THE JOINT SECURITY AREA

Almost all **tours** to the DMZ start and finish in Seoul, and there are a great number of outfits competing for your money. We've listed a couple of recommended operators below, but you'll find pamphlets from other operators in your hotel lobby; most speak enough English to accept reservations by telephone. Note that some operators are much cheaper than others – these probably won't be heading to **the JSA**, the most interesting place in the DMZ (around W77,000 with most operators), so do check to see if it's on the schedule. Most tours also include lunch.

Panmunjom Travel Center ☎02 771 5593, ⓦ koreadmztour.com. Offers the regular tour, plus a session with a North Korean defector willing to answer questions about life on the other side. Runs from the *Lotte Hotel*, near Euljiro 1-ga subway (line 2). W77,000

★**USO** ☎02 6383 2570, ⓦ koridoor.co.kr. Run in conjunction with the American military, these are still the best tours to go for, and include a 20min presentation by a US soldier in Camp Bonifas. Book at least four days in advance. Runs from Camp Kim near Namyeong subway (line 1). $80

INFORMATION

Note that each tour comes with a number of **restrictions**, most imposed by the United Nations Command. Be warned that schedules can change in an instant, and remember that you'll be entering an extremely dangerous area – this is no place for fooling around or wandering off by yourself.

Paperwork For all tours to the DMZ you'll need to bring your passport along. Citizens of certain countries are not allowed into DMZ territory, including those from most nations in the Middle East, some in Africa, and

"FREEDOM VILLAGE" AND "PROPAGANDA VILLAGE"

The DMZ is actually home to two small settlements, one on each side of the Line of Control. With the southern village rich and tidy and its northern counterpart empty and sinister, both can be viewed as a microcosm of the countries they belong to.

The southern village – referred to as **"Freedom Village"** by the US military, but actually called **Daeseongdong** – is a small farming community, but one out of limits to all but those living or working here. These are among the richest farmers in Korea: they pay no rent or tax, and DMZ produce fetches big bucks at markets around the country. Technically, residents have to spend 240 days of the year at home, but most commute here from their condos in Seoul to "punch in", and get hired hands to do the dirty work; if they're staying, they must be back in town by nightfall, and have their doors and windows locked and bolted by midnight. Women are allowed to marry into this tight society, but men are not; those who choose to raise their children here also benefit from a school that at the last count had eleven teachers and only eight students.

North of the Line of Control lies an odd collection of empty buildings referred to by American soldiers as **"Propaganda Village"**. The purpose of its creation appears to have been to show citizens in the South the communist paradise that they're missing – a few dozen "villagers" arrive every morning by bus, spend the day taking part in wholesome activities and letting their children play games, then leave again in the evening. With the aid of binoculars, you'll be able to see that none of the buildings actually has any windows; lights turned on in the evening also seem to suggest that they're devoid of floors. Above the village flies a huge **North Korean flag**, one so large that it required a fifty-man detail to hoist, until the recent installation of a motor. It sits atop a 160m-high pole, the eventual victor in a bizarre game played out over a number of years by the two Koreas, each hell-bent on having the loftier flag. See p.131 for details of yet another flag-centred battle.

communist territories such as Vietnam, Hong Kong and mainland China.

Dress code An official dress code applies (no flip-flops, ripped jeans, "clothing deemed faddish" or "shorts that expose the buttocks"), but in reality most things are OK.

Photography In certain areas photography is not allowed – you'll be told when to put your camera away.

The Third Tunnel of Aggression

제3땅굴

In 1974, a South Korean army patrol unit discovered a tunnel that had been burrowed under the DMZ in apparent preparation for a military attack from the North; tip-offs from North Korean defectors and some strategic drilling soon led to the discovery of another two, and a fourth was found in 1990. North Korea has denied responsibility, claiming them to be coal mines (though they are strangely devoid of coal), but to be on the safe side the border area is now monitored from coast to coast by soldiers equipped with drills and sensors.

The third tunnel, now bombastically referred to as the **Third Tunnel of Aggression**, is the closest to Seoul, a city that would have been just a day's march away if the North's plan had succeeded. The tunnel is only accessible as part of a **tour** – either those covering the wider DMZ (see opposite), or shorter trips from Imjingang (see box, p.134). Many visitors emerge from the depths underwhelmed – it is, after all, only a tunnel, even if you get to walk under **DMZ territory** up to the Line of Control that marks the actual border. On busy days it can become uncomfortably crowded – not a place for the claustrophobic.

Dorasan observatory and station

도라전망대 • Observatory Tues–Sun 10am–5pm • Free • Light-rail from Seoul station to Dorasan station, at the end of the Gyeongui line; or "DMZ Train" from Seoul station (departs Seoul 8.30am & 1.15pm, returns 12.10pm & 5.30pm; Tues–Fri W8700, Sat & Sun W8900)

South of the Third Tunnel is **Dorasan observatory**, from which visitors are able to stare

2

RAIL TOURS FROM IMJINGANG

The Third Tunnel of Aggression (see p.133) and Dorasan observatory and station (see p.133 & below) are accessible on many DMZ tours (see p.132), but are also lassooed together on **tours** starting at **Imjinjang** station: tours run regularly from 9.10am to 3pm, and last about three hours (W8700).

Imjingang station sits one stop from the end of the Gyeongui line, which starts in Yongsan and goes via Hongik University (around 1hr). Alternatively, take the new "**DMZ Train**" service, a slightly cheesy affair with game-playing staff, gaudily decorated carriages and barbed wire souvenirs for sale. It leaves Seoul station at 8.30am & 1.15pm, returning from Dorasan station at 12.10pm & 5.30pm (Tues–Fri W8700, Sat & Sun W8900). You'll still need a ticket for the tours, though these are sold at a discounted price.

at the North through binoculars – W500 is a cheap price to satisfy a bit of curiosity. The observatory forms part of many DMZ **tour** schedules (see p.132), but unlike the Joint Security Area you can also visit independently.

Dorasan station lies at the end of the Gyeonghui light-rail line. This line continues to China, via Pyongyang: as one sign says, "it's not the last station from the South, but the first station towards the North". A gleaming, modern station was built at Dorasan in early 2007, and in May of that year the first train in decades rumbled up the track to Kaesong in North Korea (another going in the opposite direction on the east-coast line), while regular freight services got going that December. Such connections were soon cut, but there remains hope that this track will one day handle KTX services from Seoul to Pyongyang; in the meantime, there's a wall map showing which parts of the world Seoul will be connected to should the line ever see regular service, as well as a much-photographed sign pointing the way to Pyongyang.

Paju and around

파주

South of Imjingang is the Seoul satellite city of **PAJU**, which contains some of the most interesting sights in the border area; for once, some of these do not revolve solely around North Korea. There's **Paju Book City**, a publisher-heavy area actually more notable for its architecture than anything literary; **Heyri Art Valley**, a twee little artistic commune; and finally something pertaining to the North at **Odusan observatory**.

Paju Book City

파주 출판도시 문화재단 • ⓦ pajubookcity.org • Bus #200 (every 30min; 1hr) from Hapjeong subway (lines 2 & 6)

Quirky **Paju Book City** is ostensibly a publishing district. Many publishers were encouraged to move here from central Seoul (though a whole glut of small-fry printing houses remain in the fascinating alleyways around Euljiro) and most of the major companies based here have **bookstores** on their ground levels. However, the main attraction for visitors is the area's excellent **modern architecture** – quite a rarity in this land of sterile high-rises. There's no focus as such, but strolling the quiet streets is rather pleasurable, and there are a bunch of great little book cafés dotted around – none truly stand out but you can't really lose, so just walk into the first one you see.

| **ACCOMMODATION** | **PAJU BOOK CITY** |

★ **Jijihyang** 지지향 Munpal-li 524-3 ☎ 031 955 0090. A great boutique hotel sitting near the streamside in the book village – both the complex in general and the rooms themselves are quite exquisite, and they don't cost a fortune. <u>W125,000</u>

SHOPPING

Bomulseom 보물섬 Munpal-li 524-3 ☎031 955 0077. More tempting than the area's many major book stores is this one, selling discounted books of the used variety. It's attached to *Jijihyang* hotel (see opposite), and usually has hundreds of English-language books in store, as well as thousands of Korean ones. Mon–Sat 11am–6pm, Sun 1–6pm.

Heyri Art Valley

헤이리 문화예술마을 • ⓦ heyri.net • Bus #200 (every 30min; 45min) from Hapjeong subway (lines 2 & 6)

Seven kilometres to the north of Paju Book City, similar architectural delights are on offer at **Heyri Art Valley**. This artists' village is home to dozens of small **galleries**, and its countryside air is making it an increasingly popular day-trip for young, arty Seoulites here to shop for paintings or quirky souvenirs, or drain a latte in one of several cafés. However, such mass-market appeal means that the complex in general is more twee than edgy.

Odusan observatory

오두산 통일전망대 • Daily 9am–5pm • W3000 • Bus #20 (every 50min; 45min) from Daehwa subway (lines 3), or a short taxi-ride from Heyri

Sitting atop a hill just 1km west of Heyri is **Odusan observatory**, where you'll be able to peer across the border through binoculars – the difference between the lush, busy South and the barren North is quite striking. When inter-Korean relations are good, the observatory sells alcoholic drinks from North Korea – don't hold your breath.

2

Gangwon

TEMPLE ROOF, SEORAKSAN

Gangwon

For Koreans, Gangwon (강원) exerts a magnetic pull. Enclosed by Gyeonggi to the west, Gyeongsang to the south, North Korea and the East Sea, it's a lush, green land blessed with beaches, lakes and muscular peaks. A lofty range of mountains scores its eastern flank, mopping up national and provincial parks along the way, and ensuring that Gangwon remains the most natural and least populated part of the country: despite being Korea's second-largest province, it has a smaller population than many of its cities. This isn't to say that Gangwon is an undiscovered paradise – those in the know will direct you here, rather than to the more obvious tourist draw of Jeju Island. In summer, the east-coast beaches and national parks are teeming with visitors, while skiers work their way around several resorts in the winter. Regardless of where you head, however, you're never likely to be far from a rushing blue river, a mountainside village, or lofty trees and peaks that recede into the distance – regular Korea can feel a world away.

Chuncheon is Gangwon's capital and major city, but though it's an agreeable enough place, and unhurried enough to allow for some pleasant bike riding, most people aren't visiting the province to sate urban pleasures. There are four **national parks** in Gangwon, each differing in topography and popularity; the acknowledged champion of them is **Seoraksan**, which contains some of Korea's highest peaks. It sits alongside the city of **Sokcho**, a simple but highly enjoyable place with some of the best places to eat in the land. Gangwon's eastern shore sketches a fairly straight line from the North Korean border to the Gyeongsang provinces, so you're never far away from a perfect sunrise. Head down the coast and you'll come to **Gangneung**, home to a wonderful Confucian shrine; **Jeongdongjin** beach, the nation's favourite sunrise spot and home to a fascinating clifftop hotel; **Samcheok**, a dull city whose periphery includes Penis Park and one of the world's largest caves; and **Odaesan National Park**, similar to Seoraksan but much less touristed.

Brief history
Despite its natural attractions, Gangwon hasn't always been a paragon of serenity. Its historical boundaries actually extend far into North Korea, but since the end of the Korean War the province has been divided by the twin perimeters of the **Demilitarized Zone**. During the war, the mountainous terrain that for so long preserved Gangwon's tranquillity became a curse, with ferocious battles fought for strategically important peaks. Even today, the tension is palpable – much of the region's coast is fenced off to protect against attacks from the North, and even some of the most popular beaches are fringed with barbed wire and military installations – from the end of the Korean War

Highlights

❶ Abai Island, Sokcho Getting to this tiny island is half the fun – pull yourself across the water from Sokcho on a specially customized winch-ferry, before tucking into the tasty blood sausage the island's famed for. **See p.146**

❷ Seoraksan National Park With its tall pines and naked rock, Koreans are in near-unanimous agreement that this is the most beautiful national park in the country. **See p.149**

❸ Gyeongpo beach The number one beach in the province, and perhaps the most popular nationwide after Busan's Haeundae. **See p.154**

❹ Jeongdongjin An American warship and a North Korean submarine lie side by side near this small village, just begging to be clambered around. **See p.158**

❺ Penis Park Overlooking the coast south of Samcheok, this may well be the weirdest park in Korea. **See p.161**

❻ Hwanseongul Explore 1.6km of subterranean passageways in one of the world's largest caves, hidden in the countryside west of Samcheok. **See p.162**

HIGHLIGHTS ARE MARKED ON THE MAP ON P.140

until the signing of the armistice in 1953, all land above the 38th Parallel (which hits the coast at a point roughly halfway between Sokcho and Gangneung) came under **North Korean control**, and was eventually exchanged for an area almost equal in size north of Seoul. Tunnels under the DMZ were found in the 1970s, and a spy-filled North Korean submarine crashed on the Gangwon coast in 1996 (see box, p.159); the latter can still be seen, next to an old American warship, near the small village of **Jeongdongjin** (see p.158).

Chuncheon and around

춘천

Despite its status as Gangwon's capital city, **CHUNCHEON** remains small and relatively relaxed; in fact, it's the country's smallest provincial capital. Mountain-fringed and surrounded by artificial **lakes**, its fresh air comes as a welcome change for anyone who's been cooped up in a larger city. Its most popular sight, the island of **Jungdo** (중도), is now off limits as it transforms into the world's latest **Legoland** – due for completion in 2017, it'll see visits to Chuncheon go through the roof. Otherwise, Chuncheon's periphery is perhaps more popular than the city itself, with hordes of youngsters flocking to nearby **Gangchon** and **Nami Island** for some rural fun. Back in town there are a few good **bicycle** tracks, though for many the city's main draw is the chance to sample *dak-galbi*, a famed local chicken dish (see box, p.142).

CYCLING CHUNCHEON

Chuncheon is flanked to its west by the **Bukhangang** (북한강), a river which eventually forms part of the Hangang in Seoul. Much of the riverbank has been given a cycle-friendly pimping, and peddling along these paths constitutes the best thing to do in a city of few actual sights. The best place to **rent a bike** (W3000 per hour or W10,000 per day) is on the west side of town, next to the Ethiopian Veterans' Memorial Hall (에티오피아 참전 기념관), a building that looks somewhat like a half-submerged Russian church; it's best to take a taxi here. From the Memorial Hall, a **cycleway** runs along the lake-like river. Head **north** and you'll soon be upon a small war memorial; the path joins a road but does continue much further (you'll have to cross a bridge, then bank to the left). Heading **south**, you'll race through a park then hug a hillside on a newly built wooden path; you'll soon arrive at the dock, once the ferry gateway to Jungdo. Again, the path goes much further – even as far as Seoul.

Each August, performers from Korea and abroad take part in a delightful **puppet festival** (ⓦccpt.or.kr); most events take place at the Puppet Theatre, to the north of the city centre. Other popular annual events include a **mime festival** (ⓦmimefestival.com), which takes place in May at venues across town.

ARRIVAL AND INFORMATION   CHUNCHEON

By subway Chuncheon is the terminus of the Gyeongchun line from Seoul (1hr 15min). The good news is that you can use Seoul travel cards to get here. There are two stations in town; Namchuncheon, the south station, is actually a little closer to the centre than Chuncheon main station. To get anywhere in town it's advisable to take a taxi (almost always less than W5000), as bus routes are too confusing and irregular for most travellers.

By bus Buses run from the capital's Dongseoul terminal, and cities across Korea.
Destinations Busan (hourly; 5hr); Daegu (5 daily; 3hr 30min); Gangneung (1–2 hourly; 2hr 30min); Samcheok (hourly; 4hr); Seoul (every 15min; 1hr 20min); Sokcho (10 daily; 2hr); Taebaek (1 daily; 5hr 40min).
Tourist information There's a small information booth inside the bus terminal, which is fine for maps but little else.

ACCOMMODATION

There's a line of reasonable, fairly new **motels** across the main road and downhill from the bus station; older places are dotted around the city's shopping district. As is often the way in provincial Korea, there's little real quality at the top end of the scale.

Grand Motel 그랜드 모텡 Okcheondong 39-6 ☎033 243 5021. The motel of choice for foreign backpackers can feel like a youth hostel at times, with helpful staff able to advise on the area. They even offer a free pick-up from the tourist office or bus station, but you won't be allowed to leave without signing the guestbook. The rooms are fine, and it's near Chuncheon's main shopping area. <u>W40,000</u>
Jagalseom Nakksiteo 자갈섬 낚시터 Sports Town 223-gil 73 ☎033 253 9221. The "floating guesthouses" that featured in Kim Ki-duk chiller *The Isle* (see p.362) were no mere movie sets – there are a bunch of such places in Gangwon province, mostly catering to fishermen who want a bit of peace and quiet. This one is the most accessible of the lot, on the lakefront a short taxi ride from central Chuncheon, and facing the mountains; rooms have futon bedding only and are extremely basic, though they do have outhouse-like toilet facilities. You'll be taken to your

lake-hut by boat, and then you're stuck for the night – all quite romantic, really. <u>W70,000</u>
Sangsangmadang 상상마당 Sportstown 399-gil 25 ☎033 818 4200, ⓦsangsangmadang.com. Affiliated to the eponymous arts complex in Seoul (see p.112), this building is chock-full of gallery space, to which they've added three floors' worth of bedrooms, which are every bit as quirkily designed as you might expect. The attached café, *Dancing Caffeine* (see p.142), is pretty good too. <u>W80,000</u>
Sejong 세종 호텔 Bonguidong 15-3 ☎033 252 1191, ⓦchuncheonsejong.co.kr. Overlooking central Chuncheon, and a slightly exerting pant uphill if you're walking rather than catching a cab, this is the top hotel in town, in more ways than one. It's a comfortable enough place with an on-site restaurant and decent-sized rooms, though poor value if you have to pay full rack rate. <u>W130,000</u>

EATING AND DRINKING

Galbi is the word in Chuncheon; **dak-galbi**, to be precise (see box, p.142), and the shopping area in the city centre has a whole street of restaurants (Dakgalbi Golmok; 닭갈비골목) where you can sample this speciality. Another local favourite

DAK-GALBI

You may have sampled regular *galbi*, whereby you cook (or to be more precise, set fire to) meat at your own table. **Dak-galbi** (닭갈비) is a little different – it's made with chicken meat, rather than beef or pork, and is grilled in a wide pan so there's no visible flame action for regular *galbi* arsonists to enjoy. You'll find this dish pretty much anywhere in Korea, but for some reason Chuncheon gets the glory. Imagine throwing a **raw chicken kebab** into a hot metal tray to boil up with a load of veggies and sesame leaves – you get to do this at your table for around W8000 per portion. You usually need at least two people for a meal, and once you're nearly finished it's common to throw some **rice or noodles** into the pan for a stomach-expanding second course. These days it's even more obligatory to chuck some **cheese** in too – a trend that has swept over Korea in recent years. Once you go cheesy, you never go back.

is the bargain *makguksu* (막국수) – cold buckwheat noodles with soup and hot-pepper paste. There's only really one place to head for a **drink**, and that's the area around **Gangwon University** (강원대); expats and locals alike often plan their night over a beer in front of the GS25 convenience store.

Dancing Caffeine 댄싱카펜 Samcheondong 223-2 ☎033 243 4757. The nicest café in the city is actually outside the centre, on the bike route heading south along the Bukhangang (see box, p.141), and connected to the *Sangsangmadang* guesthouse/arts complex (see p.141). There are great river and mountain vistas from the outdoor tables, and a sophisticated vibe inside. Coffees cost from W5500, or go for a gelato (W7500). Daily 10am–11pm.

Ddung's Bob Burger 뚱스밥버거 Hyojadong 15-4 ☎033 244 8283. The "bob" in the name is actually *bap*, or rice – yep, what we have here is Korean staple food served inside rice rather than bread buns. Fusion burger options include spicy chicken, breaded pork cutlet and a fair few veggie options too; they start at a bargain W1500. Daily 10am–10pm.

Gumi Dakgalbi 구미 닭갈비 Dakgalbi Golmok

☎033 252 9653. One of the smaller restaurants on Dakgalbi Street, this place stands out simply because it's the most willing to serve single portions of the good stuff (W9000); when you near the end of your meal, ask for some rice (볶음밥; *bokkeumbap*) to throw in for a crispy second course. Daily 9am–4am.

Sheriff 셰리프 3F Hyojadong 632-15 ☎033 256 9909. This bar has been a mainstay of the Gangwon University scene for years – head up the appropriately creaky stairs for some cheap beer and a game of darts. Daily 6pm–4am.

Spoon 스푼 Hyoja 3-dong 20-14 ☎033 251 8563. Stylish restaurant with mood music, latticed wood frames and tatami mats to sit on. Japanese-style *shabu-shabu* (thinly sliced beef, boiled in broth; from W9000 per portion) is the main dish here; come before 3pm and you can make use of a free salad bar. Daily 10.30am–10.30pm.

Gangchon

강천 • Three stops before Chuncheon (20min) on the Gyeongchun line from Seoul (every 30min; 55min)

Chuncheon's surrounding area is alluringly green and undulating, and well worth delving into. One of the most accessible places is the small town of **GANGCHON**, a pretty and (usually) tranquil place just west of Chuncheon. Although it has a national reputation as a student "MT" centre par excellence – **Membership Training** is a somewhat non-studious exercise that usually involves lots of drinking, singing and buzzing about on quad bikes – such revelry tends to confine itself to student holidays, and at other times it's a far more relaxing place to stay than Chuncheon for those who want a taste of inland Gangwon.

Gugok Waterfall

구곡폭포 • Daily 8am–7pm • W1600 • Bus #50 from Gangchon

The major sight in Gangchon is **Gugok-pokpo**, a tumbling waterfall surrounded by hills and trails that make for a rewarding few hours of exploration. It's 5km away from Gangchon down a highly picturesque valley studded with tiny houses.

FROM TOP JEONGDONGJIN (P.158); HWANSEONGUL (P.162) >

The village has enough **motels** and **restaurants** to cater for the students during their holidays, and an excess for the rest of the year. Cheaper and more rural *minbak* accommodation can be found in the valley linking the town with Gugok-pokpo.

Good-Time Motel 굿타임 모텔 Gangchon-ni
☎ 033 261 4720. Despite the all-too-honest name, this is a relatively comfortable place to stay in this party-fuelled area. Rooms are large and clean with big TVs. W40,000

Lorellai 로렐라이 Gangchon-ni ☎ 033 262 6688. Up on the way to the waterfall, this is a pleasant cabin-style tearoom and restaurant. It's probably best used for tea – it'll cost around W5000 for a delectable Korean brew. Daily 9am–7pm.

Nami Island

남이섬 • Train to Gapyeong from Seoul (every 30min; 40min) or Chuncheon (every 30min; 20min), then a taxi (W5000)

Further downstream from Gangchon is tiny **Nami Island**, which has achieved international fame for being the scene of the main characters' first date and kiss on the hugely successful *Winter Sonata* soap opera (see box below). The programme was most successful in Japan, and the island is often packed with Nipponese tourists, mostly middle-aged and female. Soap hysteria aside, you're likely to enjoy the island, which has plenty of paths lined with ginkgo and chestnut trees, maples and white birches that make for a beautiful walk; you might even encounter the occasional **ostrich**.

Cheongpyeongsa

청평사 • 24hr • W2000 • Bus #11 or #12 (40min; W1200) to Soyang Dam from Chuncheon train station, then ferry (15min; W5000) from along the road; the temple is a 30min walk from the dock

The gorgeous, man-made **Soyang Lake** (소양호) lies just east of Chuncheon, hemmed in at its western end by the huge **Soyang dam** (소양댐). Ferries leave from the dam for **Cheongpyeongsa**, a majestic temple that, until fairly recently, was only accessible by boat; ferries remain the easiest way of getting here. The temple's appeal lies not in

---

WINTER SONATA

Korean drama has recently enjoyed enormous popularity across Asia, with snow-filled **Winter Sonata** the biggest success to date. The story runs as follows: a boisterous girl named **Yujin** meets withdrawn **Junsang** on a bus. Despite being total opposites they fall in love and Yujin lends her gloves to her new man, who promises to give them back on New Year's Eve. He doesn't turn up, and Yujin hears that he died in a car accident on the way. Fast forward ten years to Yujin's engagement ceremony, when she thinks that she sees Junsang – now, for some reason, choosing to wear pink lipstick – through the crowd. She later finds out that it isn't Junsang but **Min-hyung**, a successful American architect. Yujin ends up working at the same company, and one further car crash later it transpires that unbeknown to Yujin not only is the man Junsang after all, but that he's Yujin's half-brother. As the pair part ways, Yujin hands him the blueprints for a beautiful house she'd designed as a farewell present. Of course, they're not related after all, and when Yujin returns to Korea from France three years later she finds out that Junsang is in fact the half-brother of her erstwhile fiancé. She then happens across the house that she once handed Junsang in blueprint form, finds him inside – now blind, just to heighten the tragedy – and they fall in love once more.

Junsang got hearts racing all over Asia, and **Bae Yong-jun**, the actor who played him, is now an international superstar whose face is plastered across all kinds of merchandise – just look at the socks on sale in Seoul's Myeongdong district. Nowhere was he more successful than in Japan, where he is now revered as *Yon-sama*, a title roughly equivalent to an English knighthood. Junsang also helped the stereotypically strong-but-sensitive Korean male replace the martial arts hero as Asia's role model, and Korean men now enjoy considerable demand from females across the continent.

superb architecture or historical importance (though it's over a thousand years old, it was razed to the ground and rebuilt several times), but in the watery approach. Unfortunately, the secret is out, and the temple is now fronted by restaurants, snack stalls and *minbak* of a small tourist village.

Sokcho and around

속초

Most foreign visitors to **SOKCHO**, South Korea's northernmost city, wind up here by default – **Seoraksan**, the country's most popular national park, raises its granite fingers within visible range to the west (see p.149). However, this ugly yet appealing place certainly has merit of its own, lent a briny vibrancy by the local fishing industry. Fishing boats dock in Cheongcho Lake, around which Sokcho curls in a C-shape – loosely tied together in a very literal sense by the steel cables along which tiny ferry-platforms winch their way to **Abai Island**. This is the place to head for the city's culinary speciality – *sundae*, a sort of noodle-filled blood sausage. The harbourfront makes for a lovely walk at night – near the middle of the "C" you'll find a pier with some free-to-use binoculars at the end.

Bar Abai Island and the local **beach**, sights in Sokcho are thin on the ground, but there are some good day-trips on offer around the city: on the way north towards the

SOKCHO

0 — 500 metres

Yeongnangho Lake

YEONGRANGDONG

Golf Course

Intercity Bus Terminal

Old Ferry Terminal

City Hall

JUNGAGDONG

Abai Ferry

EAST SEA

MISIRO

Cheongcho Lake

Expo Park

E-Mart

Express Bus Terminal

Sokcho Beach

CHEONGHODONG

JOYANGDONG

■ ACCOMMODATION	
Donggyeong Motel	1
Eastern	4
Esher House	8
James Blue Hostel	3
Motel Rocustel	6
Sunsea	5
The Class 300	7
The House Hostel	2

● EATING	
Bistro Son	4
Bubdaero	5
Bukcheong Sundae	3
Bulyaseong	6
Jungang Market	1
Narutbae Sikdang	2
Yeongrangjeong Garden	7

Seoraksan, Naksansa & Yangyang Airport ▽

barbed wire of the DMZ is **Hwajinpo lagoon**, while heading south will bring you to **Naksan Beach** and its resident temple.

Abai Island

아바이 마을 • Daily 24hr • Free • Ferries run 24hr (W200 one-way)

Connected to the mainland by road and winch-ferry, tiny **Abai Island** is the most brackish part of this salty city. Seemingly transported here from a bygone era, Abai's warren of tight lanes is well worth a wander; it's also famed for the peculiar local speciality food, *sundae* (see box, p.100). The island is connected on its southern side to the express bus terminal road by an unnecessarily large bridge, and to the City Hall area by an incredibly cute **ferry service**. Little more than a platform attached to steel cables, it runs day and night along a winch line, the two operators using what look like giant tuning forks to haul the ferry across. These days the pilots are in the habit of encouraging tourists to do the fork-hauling themselves, a truly unique experience that may well be the cheapest thrill you can get in Korea.

Yeongnangho

영랑호 • Bus #1 or #1-1 from Sokcho's main road

A twenty-minute walk north of the intercity bus terminal will bring you to **Yeongnangho**, a tranquil lake set away from Sokcho's brine and bustle. From its eastern shore, you can see Ulsanbawi – Seoraksan's distinctive spiny rock ridge – reflected in the water. It's a great area for a **bike ride** – the nearest rental outlets are in the city centre (see opposite).

Sokcho beach

속초 해수욕장

South of the city centre, and within walking distance of the express bus terminal, is **Sokcho beach**; this small stretch of sand can get extremely busy in the summer, when you can rent out rubber rings or take a banana boat ride. At all times of year, you'll be able to dine on great seafood in the slew of **fish restaurants** (see p.148).

Hwajinpo Lagoon

화진포 • Bus #1 or #1-1 from Sokcho (W5200); get off at Chodo (초도) stop, from which the lagoon is a short walk

As you travel north of Sokcho by road, tensions emanating from the area's proximity to North Korea become more and more apparent. Huge chunks of concrete sit suspended at the roadsides, ready to be dropped to block the path of any North Korean military vehicles that might one day come thundering along. Those with their own vehicle will be able to go all the way along to **Goseong unification observatory** at the border, but perhaps even more interesting is **Hwajinpo**, a stupendously beautiful **lagoon** en route. This was once used as a holiday escape by the Korean great and good – **summer villas** belonging to former Korean leaders can be visited on the same ticket. It's possible to walk between both villas mentioned here, but neither is particularly interesting; the beauty of the lagoon, however, makes a visit worthwhile, as does its sandy beach – white sands cordoned off by barbed wire and traps for North Korean frogmen (don't go swimming too far, if you're allowed in the water at all).

Summer House of Kim Il-sung

김일성 별장 • Daily 9am–5pm • Combined ticket with Syngman Rhee villa W3000

Kim Il-sung (North Korea's creator, "Great Leader" and still the country's president despite his death in 1994; see p.324) had a holiday home of sorts just south of

Hwajinpo beach before the area was given to the South after the Korean War. This building was destroyed, but a replica has been built in its place, and now contains a mildly interesting collection of photographs; two particular displays are titled "Ceaseless provocations and atrocities by North Korea" and "Nothing has changed at all" – hardly in the spirit of reconciliation. Head up onto the rooftop for a grand view of the beach.

Summer House of Syngman Rhee

이승만 별장 • Daily 9am–5pm • Combined ticket with Kim Il-sung villa W3000

Syngman Rhee, president of South Korea from 1948 to 1960, also had a villa at Hwajinpo. Protests forced Rhee to flee to Hawaii in 1960, at which point his deputy, **Lee Ki-boong** (who also had a villa in this area) killed himself, shortly after shooting his parents.

Hwajinpo Aquarium

화잔포해양박물관 • Daily 9am–6pm • W5000

Korea often tries to soften up areas connected to the forbidden North with something more jovial – anything to take people's minds off the reality of what's going on over the border. In the case of Hwajinpo it's an **aquarium**, located to the north of the lagoon. It's not bad, and focuses more on local marine life than other Korean aquariums do.

Naksansa

낙산사 • Daily 24hr • Free • Bus #9 or #9-1 from Sokcho

Twelve kilometres south of Sokcho is **Naksansa**, a temple situated on the shore; it's highly photogenic, as you'd expect of a sea-facing temple – it's worth noting that this combination is almost unique on the Korean peninsula. A walk to the elegant white Goddess of Mercy statue at the top of the complex affords great views of the sea to the east and Seoraksan National Park to the west, with the gleaming teeth of Ulsanbawi particularly evident from here. The temple is breezy and open, with plenty of nooks and crannies to explore, particularly around the rocky shore area.

Just south of the temple is **Naksan beach** (낙산 해수욕장), by far the longest on this stretch of coast. Almost unbearably popular in the summer, it is, accordingly, surrounded by hundreds of **motels** and seafood restaurants. If you fancy staying on, note that rates in the area go up and down with the temperature, but motels get newer and cheaper as you move away from the beach and main access road.

ARRIVAL AND DEPARTURE   SOKCHO

By plane The local airport is at Yangyang, down the coast. After a long period of charter-only use, it has started fielding a few scheduled flights to Busan (up to 2 daily; 1hr 10min) and Gwangju (3 weekly; 1hr 30min).

By bus To the north of the city is the intercity bus terminal, from which plenty of local buses trundle through the city centre to the express bus terminal in the south. Buses #7

and #7-1, from either terminal, continue on to Seoraksan National Park (see p.149).

Destinations Busan (10 daily; 6hr); Chuncheon (frequent; 2hr 10min); Daegu (10 daily; 4hr 30min); Gangneung (frequent; 1hr 10min); Samcheok (9 daily; 2hr 45min); Seoul (frequent; 2hr 30min).

GETTING AROUND

By bus Sokcho's C-shaped main road is ploughed by umpteen local bus routes – you can board almost any number to get between the two main bus terminals.

Bike rental Bikes can be rented next to the waterfront Expo Park for W6000 per hour.

INFORMATION

Tourist information Info-booths are located outside both bus terminals, but at the time of writing these were among the least helpful in the country. Both can give you maps, but for assistance it may be better to call tourist enquiries (☎033 1330).

Hiking equipment Those planning to hit one of the neighbouring national parks should track down one of numerous hiking stores on the main road of the city centre, including North Face, Korean clone Red Face, and clone-of-a-clone Black Face. Alternatively, try Treksta, opposite City Hall.

Post office The main branch (Mon–Fri 9am–6pm) is located near the intercity bus terminal, just a short walk from City Hall.

ACCOMMODATION

Many places to stay in Sokcho were built in the 1970s, during the first big burst of domestic tourism, and today they're looking rather drab. **Motels** can be found around both bus terminals and pretty much anywhere along the lakefront in between; pickings are best down south, around the express terminal, which has the bonus of a beach down the road. Seoraksan National Park (see p.149) and Naksan beach (see p.147) have plenty of options too.

Donggyeong Motel 동경모텔 Dongmyeongdong 261-42 ☎033 631 6444. Right next to the intercity bus terminal, this is where the tourist office usually points budget travellers – rooms are great for the price and the owners amiable. W25,000

Eastern 이스턴 관광 호텔 Cheongchohoballo 319 ☎033 638 8637. Despite the soulless lobby and earthy surrounding area, this hotel has the comfiest rooms in central Sokcho (not a massive claim). Rooms are stylishly decorated and have wooden floors, with views of the city's port from the hotel's top levels. Ask about discounts off season, when it can become quite a bargain. W120,000

Esher House 에쉐르 하우스 Daepodong ☎010 6370 6147. Located south of Sokcho beach, this is a boutiquey, cottage-like affair whose balcony offers great views of the sea. The English-speaking owner makes every effort to please, and the breakfasts are excellent. W90,000

James Blue Hostel 제임스블루 호스텔 Dongmyeongdong ☎033 637 2789, ⓦhostel-jamesblue .com. New hostel option which seems to attract a fair few party-seekers – the lobby is also a bar, which should be a giveaway. Dorms are relatively spacious, and the common area good for hanging out. Dorm beds W20,000, doubles W40,000

Motel Rocustel 모텔 로커스텔 Joyangdong 1418-3 ☎033 633 4959. You can't miss this pink jalopy of a building behind the express bus terminal. It's too brash for some, but has nice rooms with a bit of thought put into their design. Prices are a little high in peak season. W40,000

Sunsea 해바다팬션 Joyangdong 1450-56 ☎033 638 7373. North of the beach are a few simple guesthouses facing the sea. This is the best of the bunch, with a French-speaking manager and decent en-suite rooms – though they're overpriced, as all on this stretch are. W50,000

The Class 300 더클래스300 Donghaedaero 3915 ☎033 630 0900, ⓦtheclass300.com. A new higher-end option, rising up south of the express terminal, with good sea views. Rooms are large, attractive and well-equipped, though there's no breakfast or tourist assistance, and the price tag is a little steep. W240,000

★**The House Hostel** 더하우스 호스텔 Dongmyeongdong ☎033 633 3477, ⓦthehouse-hostel.com. This extremely amiable hostel has comfy rooms, and a homely atmosphere that makes meeting new friends almost inevitable; the free bike rental is also a nice touch. It's a short walk from the intercity terminal – head downhill, turn the corner and keep an eye out to your right. Dorm beds W18,000, doubles W45,000

EATING

Like the accommodation, **restaurants** in Sokcho have a general air of decay about them; nonetheless, there are some decent places to eat. **Sundae** (순대) is the local speciality, but be warned that it has nothing to do with ice cream. It's actually a kind of sausage with various odds and ends stuffed into intestinal lining; like haggis, most people find the dish somehow tastes better than the sum of its parts. Though *sundae* is available all over Korea – mainly in markets – the squid variety (오징어 순대; *ojingeo sundae*) is an Abai speciality, and the island is the best and most atmospheric place in Sokcho to eat all varieties of the dish.

Bistro Son 비스트로손 Cheonghodong 910 ☎010 3777 5524. A grand place for coffee, if only because the circus show of the winch-ferries is unfolding right outside – a wonderful spot to sit and gather your thoughts in the morning. Daily 9am–11pm.

★**Bubdaero** 법대로 Cheongchohoballo 60 ☎033 636 9777. All you can eat for W6500 – if that doesn't tempt you, you're not hungry enough. Despite the low price and the canteen atmosphere, the (largely veggie-based) food is actually pretty good – just the treat for hungry hikers.

Daily 10am–9pm.

★**Bukcheong Sundae** 북청 식당 Cheonghodong 874-9 ☎033 632 7243. If you really fancy getting into the local groove and chowing down on *abai sundae*, this friendly Abai Island restaurant is the best place to head. Go for the *modeum sundae* set (W10,000 per head) and you'll get the blood sausage, another version stuffed inside a squid, a small *bibimbap*, a broth, soy-marinated shrimp, salad, and more. For the full works, wash it down with some local corn *makgeolli*. Some of Gangwon's best-value food. Daily 8.30am–9pm.

Bulyaseong 불야성 Jeonjeokbi-ap ☎033 636 1346. Off the north end of Sokcho beach, this tent-like venue is a great place for shellfish barbecue (조개구이; W40,000, feeds two) under a permanent Christmas of twinkly lights. Daily 1–10pm.

Jungang Market 중앙 시장 Jungangdong. The food arcade of this atmospheric market is a good place to track down one of the town's culinary specialities: fried, spiced chicken known as *dakgangjeong* (닭강정). It's sold cold from W3000 for a small pack, and makes great hiking fodder for those heading to Seoraksan. Other items worth sniffing out are shrimp tempura and red-bean pancakes. Daily 7am–2pm.

★**Narutbae Sikdang** 나룻배 식당 Jeonjeokbi-ap ☎033 636 1346. *Saengseon-gui* (생선수이; grilled fish) dishes in Korea usually revolve around just the one grilled fish. In this unassuming Abai Island restaurant, there are no fewer than seven different fishes served at once – a veritable feast for W12,000 per person (minimum two). Daily 8am–10pm.

Yeongrangjeong Garden 영랑정 가든 Joyangdong 1509-1 ☎033 636 4149. Food in this mushroom-like building near Expo Park is expensive, but locals swear it's the best in town. The English-language menu has a list of succulent beef to barbecue from W29,000 per person, or there are cheaper noodle dishes. Daily 10am–10pm.

Seoraksan National Park

설악산 국립 공원 • Open 24hr, in theory • W3500 fee levied at some park entrances • ⓦ english.knps.or.kr

Koreans gush about **SEORAKSAN NATIONAL PARK**, and with good reason. The nation's northernmost park, it contains some of the tallest peaks in the country, with mist-fringed bluffs of exposed crag that could have come straight from a Chinese painting. The name gains ambiguity in translation, but roughly translates as "Snow-cragged Mountains"; these bony peaks are pretty enough on a cloudy day, but in good weather they're set alight by the sun, bathed in spectacular hues during its rising and setting. Seoraksan is one of the highest parks in the country and, as a result, usually the first to display the reds, yellows and oranges of autumn.

The park stretches around 40km from east to west and about the same from north to south, with the wide area crisscrossed with myriad **hiking trails**: the routes mentioned here are by no means exhaustive. Also bear in mind that some are closed off from time to time in rotation in order to protect the land: in peak season there can be literally queues of hikers stomping along the more popular routes, and this pressure takes its toll. The park offers several two-day hikes heading around **Daecheonbong**, its highest peak, but the focal point is undoubtedly **Ulsanbawi**, a beautiful spine of jagged rock to the north which resembles a stegosaur spine, the fossilized jaw of a giant crocodile, or a thousand other things depending on your angle, the time of day, and the weather.

Seoraksan can be roughly split into three main areas: **Outer Seorak**, the most accessible part of the park from Sokcho, is where most of the action takes place; **South Seorak** looms above the small spa town of Osaek; while to the west are the less crowded peaks of **Inner Seorak**.

Outer Seorak

외설악 • Bus #7 or #7-1 from Sokcho main road (frequent; 30min) • Cable car W9000 return

It's a very short trip from Sokcho to **Seorakdong** (설악동), the main **Outer Seorak** (*oe-seorak*) entrance – the transition from the beaches and seafood restaurants of the coast to the peaks and pine lodges of the mountains can be surprisingly swift, but on warm weekends and holidays the access road can be blanketed by one huge traffic jam. Just beyond the Seorakdong entrance is the entry terminal of a **cable car**, which whisks you

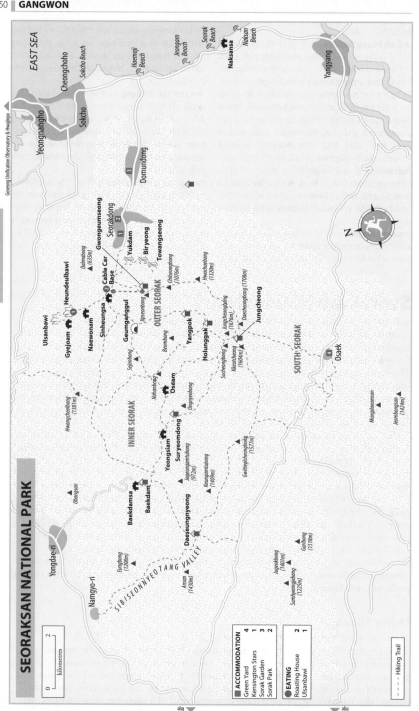

SEORAKSAN NATIONAL PARK

EAST SEA

Goseong Unification Observatory & Hwajinpo

Yeongnangho
Sokcho
Cheongchoho
Sokcho Beach
Haemaji Beach
Jeongam Beach
Seorak Beach
Naksan Beach
Naksansa
Yangyang
Domundong

Gwongeumseong
Seorakdong
Dalmabong (635m)
Cable Car Base
Yukdam
Biryeong
Towangseong
Heundeulbawi
Sinheungsa
Geumganggul
Jipseonbong
OUTER SEORAK
Chiceonbong (1076m)
Hwachaebong (1320m)
Daecheongbong (1708m)
Jungcheong
Ulsanbawi
Gyejeom
Naewonam
Seojinbong
Beombong
Yangpok
Jungcheongbong (1676m)
Socheongbong
Keuricheong (1604m)
Holunggak
SOUTH SEORAK
Osaek
Mangdaeamsan
Nahantaegak
Oseam
Ongnyedong
Jeombongsan (1424m)
INNER SEORAK
Hwangcheolbong (1381m)
Yeongsiam
Suryeomdong
Jogeungamtubong (972m)
Keungtubong (1409m)
Gwiteojicheongbong (1527m)
Obongan
Baekdamsa
Baekdam
Deseungnyeong
SIBISEONNYEOTANG VALLEY
Yongdae-ri
Namgyo-ri
Eungbong (1208m)
Ansan (1430m)
Samhyeongjebong (1225m)
Jugeokbong (1401m)
Gurbong (1518m)

Inje
Inje

N

0   2
kilometres

ACCOMMODATION
Green Yard   4
Kensington Stars   1
Sorak Garden   3
Sorak Park   2

EATING
Roasting House   2
Ulsanbawi   1

- - - - Hiking Trail

up to the top of a nearby peak for some great views. Three easy and rewarding two-hour **round-trip hikes** head off the base of the cable car lead; everything is signposted in Korean and English, though it's prudent to nab a **map** from the park entrance.

The Heundeulbawi trail

Seoraksan's most popular (ie easy) trail heads north from the Seorakdong entrance to Heundeulbawi. On the way you'll pass **Sinheungsa**, a modest temple-with-a-view founded in the seventh century but rebuilt several times since; this is home to a large bronze Buddha and some wonderfully detailed "Heavenly Kings", four painted guardians that watch over the temple. The trail then continues up to Gyejoam, a **cave hermitage** chiselled from the rock – this has for centuries been a place of meditation, but given the popularity of the trail you'll have to arrive very early to get any sense of serenity – from where it's a short distance to **Heundeulbawi** (흔들바위; literally "the rocking rock"), a sixteen-ton boulder, which, despite its size, can be (and is, frequently) rocked to and fro by groups of people. Many visitors choose to stop here for a picnic, and there's also a small snack bar – it's hard to resist the sweet-smelling waffles on sale, though tea made from local fruits is a healthier option for those wishing to head beyond the rock, where the path becomes much steeper.

An hour up this trail, which consists of metal stairways, vertigo-inducing bridge passes and more than eight hundred steps, is the summit of **Ulsanbawi** (울산바위), a highly distinctive 873m-high granite crag thrusting out of the surrounding pine trees. Legend has it that the large rock formation was once a living being that came from Ulsan, a city in southeast Korea. It heard one day that a new mountain range was being put together – the Geumgang mountains in present-day North Korea – which were to be the most beautiful on the whole peninsula. Finding on arrival that there was no more room for gargantuan masses of rock, Ulsanbawi headed back home, but fell asleep in the Seorak mountains and never woke up.

The Towangseong trail

From the cable car base, a second popular hike heads southeast through a tight ravine, taking in a few **waterfalls** on the way – Yukdam, Biryeong and Towangseong. **Yukdam** is less a waterfall than a collection of tumbling cascades; hence its name, which means "Six Pools". The **Biryeong** fall further on is far taller, toppling almost forty metres down a cliff face. Almost an hour into the ravine, most hikers turn back here, but though it looks like the end of the line the last waterfall, **Towangseong**, is a further twenty-minute hike away.

The Geumganggul trail

A third walk – arguably the most pleasant in the whole park – heads west from Sinheungsa to the lofty cave of **Geumganggul** (금강굴). Just over half an hour's walk from the cable car, this grotto sits almost halfway up one of the many spires of rock that line the valley; it was created as a place of meditation, though the height of the cave and the commanding views it provides make it hard to truly relax.

Daecheongbong

The park's highest peak, **Daecheongbong** (대청봉; 1708m), is an otherworldly confusion of rock that constitutes the third-highest mountain in the country. It's a tough all-day hike from Geumganggul cave, or there's a well-signed route from the top of the cable car that cuts out some of the upward climb. Either way, you'll probably need to spend the night at one of several **shelters** (see box, p.152 for details).

South Seorak

남설악 • Buses from Sokcho intercity terminal to Osaek (every 30min; 1hr)

The **South Seorak** section sits pretty at the southern border of the national park, and boasts superlative views of the mountains beyond. The focus here is **OSAEK** (오색), a small village famed for the **hot spring waters** that course beneath its rolling hills. From here, it's possible to make an attempt on Daechongbong, which is just within day-hike territory – four hours up, three down. Osaek itself actually means "five colours", though this was a reference to the flowers fed by the nutritious springs, rather than the waters themselves. The subterranean bounty can be imbibed at several points in the village – the taste something close to an infusion made from flat lemonade and copper – or bathed in at the communal washrooms of numerous *yeogwan*, many of whose facilities are open to non-guests.

Inner Seorak

내설악 • Buses from Sokcho intercity terminal to Yongdae-ri (6 daily; 1hr); Baekdamsa is a 90min walk, or 15min on a shuttle bus

If you want a quiet hike, **Inner Seorak** (*nae-seorak*), is the place for you. Further away from Sokcho than the Outer Seorak range, there is less to see here, and it receives a fraction of the visitors. Inner Seorak is still accessible from Sokcho; a good target is **Baekdamsa** (pancake 백담사), a temple with a curious history in the northwestern side of the park. Baekdamsa started life much further west in the seventh century, but a series of unexplained fires led to several changes of location, until the monks finally settled in Seoraksan surrounded by water – Baekdamsa actually means "The Temple of a Hundred Pools".

From Baekdamsa, there are a number of **hiking** options – one day-long trail heads to Seorakdong in the east of the park, while others converge on Daecheongbong. One of the most pleasant trails is a ridge route that runs from **Daeseungnyeong**, a peak lying around four hours' hike south of Baekdamsa – unless you're starting extremely early, you may have to stay the night at a park shelter.

ACCOMMODATION   **SEORAKSAN NATIONAL PARK**

The bulk of Seoraksan's accommodation is situated a downhill walk from the **Seorakdong** entrance on the east of the park; there are a few classy hotels near the park gates, and a clutch of much cheaper motels around twenty minutes' walk back down the access road. It's also possible to stay at **Osaek**, the spa village at the southern end of the park; most of the *yeogwan* here pump hot spring water into the bedrooms, and some have communal hot spring baths that can be used by non-guests (W5000–10,000). Note that all around the park, **prices** from June to October tend to be far higher than at other times of year, especially on weekends.

SEORAKDONG

★**Kensington Stars** 켄싱튼 스타스 호텔 ☎033 635 4001, ⓦwww.kensington.co.kr. A favourite of visiting dignitaries, the *Kensington* has a genuinely English feel to it, with London buses parked up outside, suits of armour in the faux library and mahogany everywhere. Built in 1971, it's

managed to keep itself on form, with excellent rooms; hefty discounts can be enjoyed off season, plus slightly smaller ones if you give breakfast a miss. W210,000

Sorak Garden 설악가든 리조텔 ☎033 636 7156. This revamped motel lies, as the name suggests, in a leafy setting just off the main road in Seorakdong's main motel

---

MOUNTAIN SHELTERS AND CAMPING IN SEORAKSAN

If your hiking schedule necessitates an overnight stay in the mountains, you'll need to hunt down one of several basic **shelters**. These make for an atmospheric stay, and cost from W5000 to W7000 per night (an extra W1000 for blankets). While you're unlikely to be kicked out on a wet evening, to guarantee a place you'll have to book ahead on Korea's national park website (ⓦknps .or.kr) or reserve through the Seoraksan park office (☎033 636 7700). Unfortunately, you'll have to select the specific shelter in advance, which is a pain for those whose hike takes them longer than expected; most popular are the **Yangpok** and **Jungcheong** shelters, which generally allow for the most leeway. Sleeping at the peaks themselves is not allowed, though some intrepid hikers do so in their sleeping bags, waking sodden with dew in the midst of empty trails and wonderful views – just make sure you're well hidden. Rudimentary **camping facilities** are also available from W1000 per tent at Seorakdong and Jangsudae. Book ahead in summer or on weekends in the autumn, when the leaves are turning and the trails are at their busiest.

area. Rooms are simple, lino-floored and have TVs; there's also a cheap restaurant in the lobby. **W50,000**

Sorak Park 설악 파크 ☎033 636 7711, ⓦhotelsorakpark.co.kr. Views of Seoraksan's peaks are particularly good from the balconies of this scrupulously clean hotel; from some rooms, you'll be able to see the sea at the same time. There are a few excellent restaurants, and free shuttle buses to Yangyang airport. **W235,000**

OSAEK

★**Green Yard** 그린야드 호텔 ☎033 670 1000, ⓦgreenyardhotel.com. This huge, leisure-centre-like hotel just leaps out of nowhere in the calm, green Osaek area. Rooms are a bit old-fashioned, but staying here can be rather pleasant – the presence of an on-site spa certainly helps. **W180,000**

EATING AND DRINKING

The **Seorakdong** entrance has plenty of small restaurants, snack-stands and cafés, though few places are genuinely special. The places mentioned here are both on the hike towards Heundeulbawi. Like every other national park in the land, the done thing is to scoff down a *pajeon* (pancake) post-hike.

Roasting House 커피볶는 하늘. Just before you hit Sinheungsa (see p.151), you'll walk past this traditionally styled café, which roasts its own beans amid the trees, and serves quality hand-drip coffee from W7000 (cheaper Italian styles are available too). They're proud of their handmade cookies, though they only rustle up a single batch in the morning – get them on your way up, since they'll be gone by the time you get back down. Daily

8.30am–6pm; sometimes closed in winter.

Ulsanbawi 울산바위집. From the outdoor tables of this simple place near Heundeulbawi (see p.151), the Ulsanbawi massif is clearly visible, and rather spectacular. Several kinds of *jeon* are available from W18,000, and served with the local speciality, *dotorimuk* (a near-tasteless jelly made with acorn); you can have the latter served with rice and soup for W8000. Daily 9am–sunset; often closed in winter.

Gangneung

강릉

With regard to size and numbers, **GANGNEUNG** is a big player in Gangwon terms – it's the biggest city on the northeastern coast and, like its provincial buddies Sokcho and Donghae, is spread thinly over a large area. Despite its relaxed atmosphere, staying overnight in Gangneung is not really recommended; nearby Jeongdongjin (see p.158) is a far better option. That said, Gangneung makes a good base for hikers or temple-hunters heading to charming **Odaesan National Park** (see p.155), and has a couple of sights of its own, including excellent **beaches**. If you're here in winter, you'll be able to make use of the superb **skiing** facilities at nearby **Alpensia** and **Yongpyeong** (see p.157); like those two resorts, Gangneung will play a role at the **2018 Winter Olympics**, where it's set to host the ice hockey, curling and skating events.

Ojukheon

오죽헌 • Daily 8am–6pm • W3000 • Bus #202 from train station or bus terminals (tell the driver where you want to go, as it can be a little hard to know when to get off), or a W4500 taxi ride

Gangneung's main sight is **Ojukheon**, a network of floral paths and traditional buildings, and the birthplace of **Lee Yulgok**, also known as Yi-Yi, a member of the

---

THE DANO FESTIVAL

The best time to be in Gangneung is around the fifth day of the fifth lunar moon, usually in June, when the riverside **Dano festival** is held. Events take place all over the country on this auspicious date, but Gangneung sees by far the biggest celebration – the five-day event has commemorated the "Double Fifth" with dancing and shamanist rituals for over four hundred years. Even hard-working Koreans, including students, sometimes get a day or two off for this. The festival provides your best opportunity to see **ssireum**, a Korean version of wrestling often compared to sumo, but far more similar to the Mongolian practice.

3

YI-YI: STAR OF THE W5000 NOTE

Lee Yulgok (1536–84), more commonly known by his pen name **Yi-Yi**, is one of the most prominent Confucian scholars in Korea's history, and once lived in the **Ojukheon** complex in Gangneung. A member of the country's *yangban* elite, he was apparently able to write with Chinese characters at the age of 3, and was composing poetry by the time he was 7 years old, much of it on pavilions surrounding the glassy lake at Gyeongpoho just down the road. At 19 he was taken to the hills to be educated in Buddhist doctrine, but abandoned this study to excel in **political circles**, rising through the ranks to hold several important posts, including Minister of Personnel and War. At one point, he advised the King to prepare an army of 100,000 to repel a potential **Japanese invasion** – the advice was ignored, and a huge attack came in 1592, just after Yi-Yi's death. His face is on one side of the **W5000 note**, while on the other is the famed "Insects and Plants" painting by his mother, **Sin Saimdang** (1504–51), who was a well-known poet and artist; you'll find her on the **W50,000 note**. Her selection, interestingly, managed to ruffle feathers with traditionalists and liberals alike – Confucian-thinking men were aghast that a woman should be on the front of Korea's most valuable note, while feminists were similarly distraught that this role model of "inferior" Confucian-era womanhood should be chosen ahead of more progressive women.

---

yangban – Korea's Confucian elite – and one of its most famous scholars (see box above). The complex is quite large, and much of it is paved, but there's a pleasant green picnic area surrounded by tall pines, as well as a patch of rare black bamboo to stroll through. Ojukheon is especially popular in the autumn, when its trees burst into a riot of flame. Rice fields surround the complex, which is a little set back from the main road and now near-surrounded by artsy cafés, and a couple of uninteresting galleries.

Chamsori Edison Gramophone Museum

참소리 축음기 에디슨 박물관 • Daily 9am–5.30pm • W7000 • Bus #202 from train station or bus terminals, or a W7000 taxi ride from the centre

East of Ojukheon is **Gyeongpoho** (경포호), a lake overlooked by an ornate pavilion, and the slightly bizarre **Chamsori Edison Gramophone Museum**, which claims to be the largest gramophone museum in the world. The pavilion is a short walk back up towards Ojukheon; in this area you'll also be able to rent a bike for a pace around the lake.

Gyeongpo beach

경포 해수욕장 • Bus #202 from train station or bus terminals, or a W6000 taxi ride from the centre

The lake of Gyeongpoho almost tickles a near-eponymous beach – **Gyeongpo**, a long stretch of white sand that's one of the most popular beaches in the province; there is all kinds of water-based fun to be had in the summer, when it can be heaving with people. Well-informed locals prefer **Anmok beach** (안목 해수욕장), a more relaxed stretch of sand further south, which rarely fills up; you can walk between the two beaches, though those venturing too close to the military installations will get barked at by soldiers.

ARRIVAL AND INFORMATION   GANGNEUNG

By train Gangneung is on Korea's rail network, but at the time of writing its small station was closed in preparation for the 2018 Winter Olympics; the new KTX line from Seoul should be finished in 2017, until which time the closest rail access will be at Jeongdongjin (see p.158).

By bus The express and intercity terminals are joined at the hip in the west of the city. Bus #202-1 will take you to the train station, though this only leaves every half-hour – it's far easier to take a taxi (W3000).

Destinations Busan (10 daily; from 5hr); Chuncheon (1–2 hourly; 2hr 30min); Samcheok (hourly; 1hr); Seoul (every 30min; 2hr 40min); Sokcho (every 20–30min; 1hr 10min); Taebaek (hourly; 2hr 30min).

Tourist information There's a helpful office between the bus terminals (daily 9am–6pm; ☎033 640 5121).

ACCOMMODATION

Spread-out Gangneung isn't terribly attractive – little Jeongdongjin (see p.158), a seaside village just down the coast, is a far more pleasant place to stay. In Gangneung itself, half a dozen **motels** line the area behind the bus terminal, though it's a particularly horrible area – best head into town, or to the glut of motels near **Gyeongpo beach**.

Herren Haus 헤렌 하우스호텔 Gyeongsodong 287-21 ☎033 651 4000. One of a bunch of hotels overlooking Anmok beach, this one stands out for its artistically decorated rooms, some with grand sea views. Rack rates almost halve on weekdays. <u>W130,000</u>
Hong C 홍시 호텔 Okcheondong 273 ☎033 641 8100, ⓦhongchotel.kr. The most comfortable place to stay in the centre, with rooms that are small but rather attractive – forget about the rack rates, which you can usually cut in two. Breakfast is cooked up by the hotel chef, and comes as quite a treat. <u>W180,000</u>

★**Hyusim Pension** 휴심 펜션 Jeodonggolgil 21 ☎033 642 5075. It's almost like staying in the countryside at this log-cabin-style pension, which is tucked into the fields behind the Gramophone Museum. Rooms are just as earthy in fashion but rather comfy, and the place has proven so popular with young Korean travellers that they were building a huge annexe at the time of writing. <u>W70,000</u>
Sharp Motel #모텔 Okcheondong 329-7 ☎033 645 9692. Stylish motel in the centre, and slightly less seedy than its neighbours; you can see its neon hash sign from the train station area. <u>W40,000</u>

3

EATING AND DRINKING

There really isn't much of culinary interest in the city centre, but the **beach areas** have plenty of great seafood restaurants. The area around Anmok beach is absolutely riddled with cafés – youngsters come from far afield to drain a coffee here. None of them stand out, though several have good sea views from their balconies – take your pick.

Gyeongpo Beach Hoetjip 경포비치 횟집 Gangmundong 304-5 ☎033 644 2243. Gangneung is famed for its *sundubu* (tofu), said to be particularly soft here on account of the local sea water used (don't ask how this works). The city has an area dedicated to the stuff, though it's ugly and out of the way – better to have precisely the same meal here, overlooking the sea. This Gyeongpo beach restaurant is a good choice; it's lined with pine and has a second-floor veranda. *Sundubu jjigae* (broth) will cost you W7000. Daily 24hr.
Taksabal 탁사발 Geumhakdong 20-3 ☎033 645 4001. The city centre can be a bit dull, even on weekend evenings, but this second-floor joint is usually rocking – pick *pajeon* (pancakes; from W13,000) or other Korea pub grub from the picture menu, and wash down with one of several breeds of *makgeolli* rice beer. Daily 5pm–midnight.

Odaesan National Park

오대산국립공원 • Open 24hr, in theory; hiking prohibited from sunset until 2hr before sunrise • W3000 • ⓦ english.knps.or.kr

A short ride to the west of Gangneung is **ODAESAN NATIONAL PARK**, markedly smooth and gentle compared with its jagged Gangwonese neighbours. A maze of tumbling waterfalls, bare peaks and thickly forested slopes, full of colour in the autumn, it's nevertheless relatively empty for a Korean national park as hikers tend to be sucked into the Seoraksan range a short way to the north.

Odaesan has **two main entrance points**: one in the pretty **Sogeumgang** area (소금강; "Little Geumgang"), named after the spectacular range just over the border in North Korea to the north of the park; and a south gate reached via the small town of **Jinbu** (진부). The south of the park contains more of historical interest, since it contains

HIKING ODAESAN

A **hiking** trail leads from the temple of Sangwonsa to **Birobong**, the highest peak in the park at 1563m. Although the ascent can be made in less than two hours, it's steep and not an easy walk. Those who get to the top can continue along a ridge trail to **Sangwangbong**, or even attempt a U-shaped day-hike to **Dongdaesan** via Durobong – this walk is particularly tough on the legs. A waterfall-strewn day-hike heads up through Sogeumgang via Noinbong to Odaesan's **spine road**; unfortunately, this twisty thoroughfare sees no public transport, limiting onward movement from the park to hitchhiking or a lengthy walk.

two sumptuous **temples** – Woljeongsa and Sangwonsa, both of which have little tearooms in which to rest. Throughout the park there are innumerable shrines, some of which are quite remote and receive next to no visitors – just the treat for adventurous hikers.

Woljeongsa

월정사 • Daily 24hr • W3000

Woljeongsa dates from 645, and contains an impressive octagonal nine-storey pagoda from the early Goryeo dynasty, adorned with wind chimes and striking a perfect balance with the thick fir trees surrounding the complex. It faces an ornate, and rare, kneeling Buddha. The complex as a whole addresses function rather than beauty, though in the main hall are two elaborate Buddhist paintings – most interesting is the one on the left, which features some hellish scenes of torture.

Sangwonsa

상원사 • Daily 24hr • Free

Ten kilometres through the pine trees from Woljeongsa is **Sangwonsa**, a complex containing what is believed to be Korea's oldest bronze bell, which dates from 725. Sangwonsa's appeal is its magical setting, facing a mountain ridge swathed with a largely deciduous wall of trees; in a country where pine green reigns supreme, the blaze of colour that these create in the autumn is rather welcome.

ARRIVAL AND DEPARTURE   ODAESAN NATIONAL PARK

By bus The Sogeumgang entrance is easiest to get to, with regular direct buses heading from Gangneung bus terminal (40min). To the south gate, you'll have to change in Jinbu (진부; 1–2 hourly; 45min from Gangneung), from where onward connections to the park are infrequent – there's one every hour or so, and some only go as far as Woljeongsa.

ACCOMMODATION

There's a pleasantly low-key **minbak** area downhill from both park entrances, with rooms in traditional houses going from W30,000. There's also a **campsite** between Woljeongsa and Sangwonsa; it costs up to W6000 per tent in July and August and is free for the rest of the year (though the showering facilities will be unavailable).

Kensington Flora 켄싱튼 플로라 ☎ 033 330 5000, ⓦ www.kensingtonflorahotel.co.kr. Downhill from the south entrance, this bank of high-rises constitutes the most luxuriant accommodation in or around the park. There's an outdoor swimming pool on site, as well as a pub and restaurant. **W120,000**

Pyeongchang

평창

At the time of writing, **PYEONGCHANG** county – the hub of which is around 30km southwest of Gangneung – was preparing to be thrust into the limelight as the host of

KIM YUNA

Forget the Korean football stars plying their trade in Europe, or the pitchers breaking records in the United States – glamorous figure skater **Kim Yuna** is, without doubt, Korea's top sporting star of all time. She started skating at the age of 5, and won the 2009 World Championship while still in her teens; the 2010 Winter Olympics gold came shortly after that, her riveting dance to a James Bond medley blowing away the already-stellar performance of Japanese hope Mao Asada with a world record. "Queen Yuna" retired with a clutch of medals in 2014, having made the podium in every single event that she competed in, and will serve as an ambassador for the 2018 Games.

the **2018 Winter Olympics**. It was awarded the Games in 2011, after narrow failures in the two previous rounds of voting – it lost out to Vancouver for the 2010 Games, and the Russian resort of Sochi for 2014. Third time lucky, then, and a full set of major sporting festivals for Korea after its hosting of the football World Cup in 2002 and Summer Games in 2012 – only France, Germany, Italy, Japan and the USA can make a similar boast. As is par for the course with such major events, expect wholesale changes to the area's accommodation, transport and culinary scene before the Games actually get under way (see ⓦpyeongchang2018.com for more information). The main ski resorts in Pyeongchang are **Yongpyeong** and **Alpensia**; if you're looking for smaller, less crowded ski resorts, head to **Phoenix Park** and **Hyundae Sungwoo**, further down the Yeongdong highway, in the direction of Wonju.

Yongpyeong Ski Resort

용평 • Range of passes available for around W50,000; ski/board rental for around W25,000; see website for full details • ⓦ yongpyong.co.kr

Also known as **Dragon Valley**, **YONGPYEONG** is Korea's largest ski resort, though it has been largely ignored for Olympic activities – it's only pencilled in to host the alpine skiing. The resort has all kinds of activities from snowboarding to sledding available in the winter, and a mammoth **31 slopes** to choose from, accessed on fifteen ski lifts and gondolas.

3

Alpensia Ski Resort

알펜시아 • Range of passes available for around W50,000; ski/board rental for around W25,000; see website for full details • ⓦ alpensiaresort.co.kr

A newer and (for now) smaller resort than Yongpyeong, the **ALPENSIA** resort is set to host the opening ceremony of the 2018 Games, and much of its sporting activity – though financial problems may mean that some of these events are shifted elsewhere. Still, it's an excellent ski resort, with six slopes and counting, as well as a dedicated run for snowboarders.

ARRIVAL AND DEPARTURE   PYEONGCHANG

By bus There are direct shuttle buses to the main ski resorts from far afield – even Seoul (daily departures from several stops; 2hr 30min) and Incheon Airport (5 daily; 3hr). Otherwise you may have to head to Hoenggye (횡계), a nearby town; this receives buses from Seoul (every 30min; 2hr 30min) and Gangneung (every 20min; 30min), as well as some other Gangwon destinations. From Hoenggye there are free shuttle buses during the ski season; at other times you can take a local bus.

ACCOMMODATION AND EATING

There are deluxe **accommodation** options at both resorts, though Yongpyeong also has several *yeogwan* and a youth hostel. During ski season this will all be booked out – at such times you may have to stay down the road in **Hoenggye**, where there are motels aplenty. For food, there's a small mall's worth of **cafés** and fast-food **restaurants** near the *Dragon Valley* complex; you'll find a bowling alley and lively bar in the basement of the same building.

YONGPYEONG

Dragon Valley 드래곤 밸리 호텔 Yongpyeong ❶033 335 5757, ⓦwww.kensingtonflorahotel.co.kr. The area's top dog for many years is now being upstaged somewhat by the Alpensia options, but still makes a great place to stay. Rooms are warm and cosy, which is just what you need in such a place, and if you don't fancy shelling out for meals at its restaurants, there are cheaper options just a walk away. Ask about discounts. **W300,000**

Yongpyeong Youth Hostel 용평 유스호스텔 Yongpyeong ❶033 335 5757. Immediately opposite the *Dragon Valley* hotel (who can handle bookings, bless them) is this spartan youth hostel, which is by far the cheapest place to stay in the vicinity of the slopes. As with all official Korean hostels, it's an otherwise dull place usually filled with families, teens and tweens. Open Nov–March & July–Aug. Dorm beds **W18,000**

ALPENSIA

★**Holiday Inn** 홀리데이 인 Alpensia ☎ 033 335 5757, ⓦ ihg.com. The chain has a couple of good, fresh options in the Alpensia resort area – both make great places to stay, and have fancy rooms boasting plush carpets and huge beds – perfect to wind down in after a hard day. W180,000

HOENGGYE

Daegwanryoung 대관령 호텔 Daegwallyeongno 90 ☎ 033 336 3301. Good option near the bus terminal in Hoenggye, featuring six floors' worth of cheap, clean rooms, plus an unintentionally retro sky lounge for coffee or evening drinks, and a sauna on the first floor. W50,000

Jeongdongjin

정동진

For those bored with temples, war museums and national parks, the area around **JEONGDONGJIN** has some rather more unusual attractions to float your boat, if you'll pardon the pun. Near this small, windswept coastal village lie two retired nautical vessels: an **American warship** from the Korean War, and an equally authentic **North Korean submarine**. From Gangneung, trains make the short trip down the coast, much of which is cordoned off with barbed wire, before stopping at what is apparently the world's closest train station to the sea. A short stretch of sand separates the track from the water, and it's here that Korean couples flock to hold hands and watch the sunrise – the area was featured in *Sandglass*, a romantic Korean soap opera (truly a truism, since all Korean soap operas are romantic).

Sun Cruise Hotel

썬크루즈 호텔 • 24hr • W5000, free to guests; entry price taken off bill in hotel bar or café • ⓦ english.esuncruise.com

There's not too much to see in the town itself, but the **Sun Cruise Hotel** is as much a tourist attraction as a place to stay. Designed to look like a boat, you really can't miss it – just look for the ship hanging precariously from a cliff. Although its souvenir shop is only on the ninth floor, the combined height of hotel and cliff means that you're a whopping 165m above sea level, and as you walk out of the shop onto the **viewing platform**, it's tempting to let your mind soar and imagine that you're up on the deck of an impossibly large ship. One floor up is a revolving bar-cum-café, which makes a great place to while away some time (see p.160).

Sandglass Park

모래시계 공원 • Museum daily 9am–6pm • W6000 • Rail-bikes on the hour: Mon–Fri 9am–5pm, Sat & Sun noon–5pm • W20,000 for two-seater, W30,000 for four-seater

Look out for the **giant egg-timer** near the beach – couples gather to watch it being turned over each New Year. The egg-timer forms the centrepiece of **Sandglass Park**,

---

VICTIMS OF NAUTICAL NOMENCLATURE

The **victim mentality** drilled into Korean students during their history lessons is such that any perceived slant against the nation, no matter how slight, can turn into a serious issue that has the whole country boiling with rage. Anger is further magnified should the insult come from Korea's one-time colonial masters, the **Japanese** – witness the case of the waters east of the Korean mainland, generally known across the world as the "Sea of Japan". Koreans insist that this name is a symbol of Japan's imperial past, and youth hostel wall maps around the world have had the name crossed out by *kimchi*-chomping Korean travellers and replaced with "**East Sea**". Korean diplomats raised enough of a stink to take the issue to the United Nations, which tentatively sided with the Japanese, but left the topic open for further discussion. Although both terms have been used for centuries, neither is strictly correct – Korea controls a large portion of the waters, yet the sea lies plainly to Japan's west – so while this storm in a teacup continues to rage on, feel free to send your own suggestions of compromise to the UN: "Sea of Peaceful Diplomatic Negotiations", perhaps?

ESPIONAGE IN THE EAST SEA

Those who deem the Cold War long finished should cast their minds back to September 1996. On the fourteenth, a submarine containing 26 **North Korean spies** arrived at Amin, on South Korea's Gangwon coast. Three disembarked, and made it back to the submarine after completing their surveillance mission on the Air Force base near Gangneung, but the waves were particularly strong that day and the sub came a cropper on the rocks. Eleven non-military crew members were killed by the soldiers, lest they leaked classified information to the South, and important documents were incinerated inside the vessel – the ceiling of the cabin in question is still charred with burnt North Korean spy material. The remaining fifteen soldiers attempted to return to the North overland, with their Southern counterparts understandably keen to stop them; the mission continued for 49 days, during which seventeen South Korean soldiers and civilians lost their lives. Thirteen of the spies were killed, one was captured, and the whereabouts of the last remains a mystery.

3

a small expanse also featuring the **Time Museum**, an uninteresting look at the concept of time spread over seven disused train carriages. From here you can hop onto a customized **rail-bike** and zip along to the train station on a 5.2km course, which takes around an hour to complete (or just forty minutes if you set the machine to automatic, which rather takes the fun out of the whole thing).

Haslla Art World

하슬라 아트월드 • W haslla.kr • Taxi from Jeongdongjin (around W4000)

Around 2km north of Jeongdongjin is **Haslla Art World**, a superbly designed **contemporary art** complex ranged up a verdant hillside off the coast. There are a few indoor halls, one of which features what may well be the world's only **Cow Dung Art Gallery** – note that only a few of the sculpted dollops are real. However, the bulk of the installations lie outdoors: witness the metal spiders clambering up the hillside, or the much-photographed pair of adjoining chairs (again, Jeongdongjin is highly popular with couples) peering over the sea. The on-site "Sea Café" is an equally great place from which to watch the sunset, but perhaps best of all is the chance to stay in the wonderful **hotel** (see p.160).

Tongil Park

통일 공원 • Daily: March–Oct 9am–6pm; Nov–Feb 9am–5pm • W3000 • Bus #111, #112 or #113 from Gangneung or Jeongdongjin (every 30min or so)

Jeongdongjin's resident warship and sub are permanently moored next to each other at **Tongil Park**, 4km north of the village on the coast. The ship saw action, having served in the Korean War, but the **submarine** has an even more interesting tale to tell, having made a dramatic final voyage (see box above). It's hard to imagine that this small metal tube could hold a crew of thirty, as even with nobody else on board it's tough enough to navigate without bumping your head; faced with just one dark, cramped corridor, you're unlikely to be inside for long. By comparison, the US-made **warship** is 120m long, and it can take an hour or so to hunt down every nook and cranny; in the bridge you can play with the chunky steering equipment, twiddle knobs, check dials and shoot imaginary torpedoes at your enemies. Though the ship is on dry land, nearby military installations and the waves crashing below can make it easy to let your imagination go wild, and if your karma is in credit there'll be fighter jets from the local Air Force base roaring overhead.

ARRIVAL AND DEPARTURE   JEONGDONGJIN

By train Jeongdongjin is best reached by train, and its station is right next to the beach – the closest station in the world to the sea, according to local authorities. The journey from Seoul (Cheongnyangni station; 7 daily; 5hr 30min) does take forever though; in addition, Gangwon's coastal line operates a frustratingly infrequent service, so it pays to find out times in advance. One relatively new introduction is the "Sea Train", a special service connecting Jeongdongjin

and Samcheok (2 daily; 1hr 20min; W15,000); taking its lead from similar trains in Japan, its zanily decorated interior features swivel seats aimed at large, sea-facing windows.

By bus From Gangneung, bus #109 (40min) runs from the bus terminal direct to the *Sun Cruise* hotel, and #111, #112 and #113 from various stops around the city to central Jeongdongjin, passing Tongil Park on the way (30min).

ACCOMMODATION

Jeongdongjin trades on the romance dollar, with amorous couples arriving to hold hands and watch the sunset year round, so there are plenty of rooms to choose from – New Year and summer weekends are the only times you should have to book ahead.

Full House Motel 풀하우스 모텔 Jeongdongjin-ni 310-2 ☎ 033 644 5880. The pick of the roadside motels near the train station, with en-suite facilities and pleasantly decorated rooms; make sure to get one with a sea view. There's also a little veranda up on the roof. **W45,000**

★**Haslla Museum** 하슬라 호텔 Yulgongno 1441 ☎ 033 644 9411, ⓦ haslla.kr. Forming part of the Haslla Art World complex just to the north of town (see p.159), this is without doubt the most distinctive hotel on the east coast. Each room has been individually, artistically designed; floor-to-ceiling windows provide wonderful sea views, and some rooms have their beds tucked away in gigantic wooden bowls – more comfortable than it may sound. Rack rates are high,

though you can usually knock a fair chunk from this, and almost half on weekdays. **W300,000**

Hyanggi 향기 호텔 Heonhwaro 982-6 ☎ 033 642 7512. Sitting in a prime location at the south end of the beach, this is a decent place to stay if you can nab a sea-facing berth, but rooms are a little stuffy and rather overpriced. **W80,000**

★**Sun Cruise** 썬크루즈 호텔 Jeongdongjin-ni 50-1 ☎ 033 610 7000, ⓦ english.esuncruise.com. You can't miss this place, perched as it is atop a cliff south of the station, and basically a tourist attraction in its own right (see p.158). It can be surprisingly cheap off season (down to W70,000 for a double), and, mercifully, the nautical theme isn't carried through into its plain rooms. A good place to go wild with a bunch of friends. **W130,000**

EATING AND DRINKING

Jeongdongjin has no shortage of **restaurants**, and it should come as no surprise that most (but by no means all) places focus on fish. Perhaps most fun for foreign visitors will be the chance to enjoy a **shellfish barbecue** (조개구이; *jogae gui*), which should cost from W40,000 for two people.

Café Sun 카페 썬 Jeongdongjin-ni 328-3 ☎ 033 644 5466. Pleasant café overlooking the sea, selling a range of coffees from around the world (W5000 and up), and cocktails of an evening. It opens up at crazy o'clock in order to sate the needs of couples itching to see the sunrise, but in need of caffeine and some warmth. Daily 4am–8pm.

★**Jeonmangdae Hoetjip** 전망대 횟집 Jeongdongjin-ni 2-6 ☎ 033 644 5406. Just back from the *Hyanggi* hotel, this is the most friendly and reliable place for a shellfish barbie (W40,000 for two), which comes with various tasty side dishes. Alternatively, go for *hoedeopbap* (sashimi on rice; W12,000), or *hamulgalguksu* (spicy

seafood and noodle soup; W10,000 per head, minimum two). Daily 10am–11pm.

Sseon Hansik 썬한식 Jeongdongjin-ni 296-7 ☎ 033 644 5460. This European-style white cottage, sitting off the main road near the train station, deserves a mention for its *sundubu* (순두부), a local speciality made from tofu in a spicy sauce (W20,000 for two people). Opens early to nab sunrise-seekers. Daily 3.30am–9pm.

Sun Cruise 썬크루즈 호텔 Jeongdongjin-ni 50-1 ☎ 033 610 7000. Come to the revolving café-bar atop the famous hotel (see above) for a coffee (around W8000) or something stronger (cocktails W9000). Daily 24hr.

Samcheok and around

삼척

A typically ugly Gangwon coastal city, **SAMCHEOK** is nevertheless a good base for a range of interesting sights, including **Penis Park**, several secluded **beaches** and the gigantic cave of **Hwanseongul**. All of these are some way away, and there's little to see in the city itself, though the **port area** to the east is worth a stroll. Here, it's common to see acres of squid hung out like laundry to dry in the sun, and there are more fish restaurants than you can count. The **city centre** itself is bound by a rough quadrilateral of roads which are home to plenty of chain restaurants and high-street clothing stores; much of the area in between is taken up by an appealingly grimy market.

Samcheok beach

A few kilometres north of the centre is **Samcheok beach**, which attracts a young crowd in the summer; like many other beaches in the province, much of it is cordoned off with **barbed wire**. This makes it a rather interesting place to sunbathe; the wire is in place to prevent amphibious North Korean landings such as the one that occurred up the coast in Jeongdongjin in 1996 (see box, p.159); also look out at night for the large spotlights used to keep an eye on the seas.

ARRIVAL AND INFORMATION   SAMCHEOK

By bus Samcheok is best approached by bus, as the train station is some distance from the centre and in any case carries a sparse service. The city's two bus terminals – express and intercity – lie almost side by side on the southern flank of town.
Destinations Busan (10 daily; 5hr); Chuncheon (10 daily;

4hr); Gangneung (hourly; 1hr); Gyeongju (hourly; 5hr); Seoul (8 daily; 4hr 30min); Sokcho (9 daily; 3hr); Taebaek (hourly; 1hr 10min).
Tourist information Helpful staff at the booth outside the express bus terminal are able to advise on accommodation and the ever-changing vagaries of local transport.

ACCOMMODATION AND EATING

There are plenty of cheap sleeps in town, but for a more old-time coastal Gangwon atmosphere, adventurous travellers could do worse than head to the cheap guesthouses sprinkled around the **port area** east of town, an area whose restaurants and shops are almost entirely dedicated to fish, and which has something of an end-of-the-world atmosphere. **Samcheok beach** is also a pleasant place to stay, though prices at its various motels rise in summer.

★**Moon Motel** 문 모 텔 Jeongsangdong 432-63 ❶ 033 572 4436. Set in a quiet part of town between the bus terminal and the river, this motel has clean, comfy rooms that are remarkably stylish for a Korean motel. **W40,000**
Palace 팰리스관광호텔 Jeonghadong ❶ 033 575 7000. Way out of town on the coast, Samcheok's luxury

option has several large restaurants and banquet halls; the cavernous rooms are linoleum-floored, making it feel a little like a well-tended Korean apartment. You can halve the rate in off season, or by even more if you don't require a sea view. **W180,000**

Penis Park

해신당 공원 • Daily 9am–6pm • W3000 • Bus #24 from Samcheok bus terminal (hourly; 40min)
South of Samcheok near Yonghwa beach is the rather curious **Penis Park**, whose paths are lined with **penis sculptures** of metal, stone and wood – one is lined with nails,

---

BEACHES SOUTH OF SAMCHEOK

The Gangwon coast continues on south of Samcheok, squeezing numerous **beaches** into a fairly short stretch along the way, although continued development of the coastal roads and the resulting increase in traffic means that in addition to the one in Samcheok only two beaches are actually worth visiting – **Maengbang** and **Yonghwa**. The former is one of the largest in the area and its calm waters make it good for swimming. Surrounded by pine trees, it's usually quite peaceful as it's a twenty-minute walk from the nearest bus stop and *minbak* village. The beach at Yonghwa is smaller – only 200m in length – and much closer to the road, but equally attractive.

several are carved into people-like shapes and one metal ithyphallus is mounted on cannon wheels. While it may seem bizarre, the park owes its existence to one of the area's most intriguing **folk tales**, the story of a young bride-to-be who died by the shore in a violent storm. After this, her angry spirit chased the fish from the seas, depriving locals of their major source of income and sustenance. The only way around this, apparently, was to placate the newly dead's soul with carved wooden phalluses, which were driven into the beach – spirit thus satisfied, the fish returned in record numbers.

The main building's **folk exhibition** can be safely ignored, and is interesting only for a small display showing how local squid are lured to their deaths, and an almost comically bad simulation of a boat ride. It gets better in the **sculpture zone**, which has replicas of ancient pornographic statuary from Asia and beyond – don't leave until you've checked out the Greek god's horny pose. Various **trails** make for a pleasant walk around the park – though one often made brisk by the seaside winds – with views of the sea crashing on to the crags below. You can go all the way down to the pebbly shore, which is certainly not safe for swimming thanks to the often fierce East Sea waves. A few *minbak* and stalls selling grilled fish from as little as W1000 can be found around the park's southern end.

Hwanseongul

환선굴 • Daily: March–Oct 8am–5.30pm; Nov–Feb 8am–4.30pm • W4000; monorail W4000 one-way, W7000 return • Bus from Samcheok bus terminal (6 daily, last useful bus 2.20pm; 45min); last bus back 7.30pm

Though Korea contains a fair number of navigable caves, **Hwanseongul**, hiding away under a sumptuous range of hills west of Samcheok, is the one that can most justly be described as "cavernous" – it's one of the **largest caves in Asia**, over 6km long and featuring umpteen rooms and some subterranean water features. Hwanseongul's largest chamber measures 100m by 30m, its dimensions, shading and vaguely creepy atmosphere bringing to mind a Gothic cathedral. Only 1.6km of the cave is open to the public, most of which is traversed by platforms and staircases; be sure to bring suitable shoes and an extra layer of clothing, as it's damp and not very warm down there – it'll take at least an hour to navigate the passageways if you want to see everything. Also bear in mind that the cave entrance is a rather steep half-hour trek from the ticket office, next to which are some examples of *gulpi*, the area's traditional wooden mountain housing; you can chalk some of this off on a short but steep **monorail** track, though the walk is beautiful, particularly in the autumn.

EATING AND DRINKING   HWANSEONGUL

Daemiri Golpijip 대미리 골페집 ☎033 541 7288. Heading up from the entrance to the cave, you'll spot three little restaurants. The first sells *gamja-jeon* (potato pancake) for W5000, the second for W4000, and the third for W3000 – a bargain, since it can be more like W15,000 in Seoul. The middle restaurant is best; it's set in a mocked-up version of a *gulpi*, and heated with a wooden stove in colder months – it looks like a good kick would bring the whole place crashing down. They're also proud of their acorn-jelly salad here (W5000). Daily 9am–5pm.

Taebaeksan Provincial Park

태백산 도립 공원 • Daily 24hr • W2000 • Bus from Taebaek bus or train stations (every 30–45min; 30min), or around W20,000 by taxi

A thoroughly enjoyable maze of hiking trails, and especially beautiful in the winter months, **TAEBAEKSAN PROVINCIAL PARK** lies around 40km southwest of Samcheok. Trails in the park are well signposted, but for peace of mind you can buy a map at the entrance. This is already 870m above sea level, and from here a pair of easy two-hour routes run to the twin peaks of **Munsubong** (1517m) and **Cheonjedan** (1561m), two of the highest in Korea. These are of particular importance to **shamanists**, as

Taebaeksan is viewed as Korea's "motherly mountain" – ancient Korean kings were said to perform rituals here, and at the summits it's still common to see offerings left behind by hikers in honour of **Dangun**, the legendary founder of Korea (see box, p.343). Cheonjedan plays host to a shamanist ceremony every year on October 3 – "National Foundation Day" in Korea, and a public holiday – as does the Dangun hall near the entrance.

A rather less spiritual **coal museum** (daily 9am–6pm; W2000) sprawls out just below the park entrance; the Taebaeksan area was once the heart of Korea's coal industry, and this museum charts its gradual decline. The top floor shows some interesting pictures in a coal of village life, and there are a couple of surprise simulations in store too.

The park's main entrance lies a half-hour bus (or taxi) ride from the small, sedate city of **TAEBAEK** (태백) one of the most typical of the Gangwonese interior. Surrounded by mountains and with little large-scale commerce to speak of, its elevation means the air is clean and fresh, and the climate is usually a little colder here than on the coast. It's mainly used as a transit point for the national park.

ARRIVAL AND INFORMATION

By train Trains run from Jeongdongjin (6 daily; 1hr 30min) and Seoul (6 daily; 5hr 30min) to Taebaek train station. From here you'll need to take an onward bus or taxi to the park.
By bus Taebaek's bus terminal is by the train station at the northern end of town.
Destinations Andong (5 daily; 3hr); Busan (5 daily; 4hr

TAEBAEKSAN NATIONAL PARK

3

30min); Gangneung (hourly; 2hr 30min); Samcheok (hourly; 1hr 10min); Seoul (hourly; 3hr 30min).
Tourist information There's an information booth (daily 9am–5pm; ☎ 033 550 2081) by the train and bus stations in Taebaek, and a smaller version of the same at the entrance to the park.

ACCOMMODATION AND EATING

There is a range of cheap sleeps near **Taeaek**'s train and bus stations; for decent food, though, you'll have to make your way into the city centre – walk down from the train station and turn right at the main road. The park itself makes a much prettier place to stay. A two-storey parade of buildings near the **park entrance** houses restaurants on the ground floor and *minbak* accommodation above. Nearby motels offer greater comfort. Further downhill is a bunch of newer, homelier *minbak*, all charging around W25,000 per room.

TAEBAEK
Aegis Motel 이지스 모텔 Hwangjidong 88 ☎ 033 553 9980. You can't really miss this place, with its white frame towering over the train station. Rooms here are large and clean, though as the train line has some early morning services, it may not be ideal for light sleepers. **W40,000**

PARK ENTRANCE
Ujin Motel 우진 모텔. This basic guesthouse across the stream from the park entrance is, restaurant, which is attached, allows you to eat in little private huts. **W25,000**

Gyeongsang

ULLEUNGDO

Gyeongsang

A land of mountains and majesty, folklore and heroes, the southeastern Gyeongsang provinces (경상) are home to some of the most wonderful sights that Korea has to offer. In terms of its history, Gyeongsang was the base of the Silla kingdom that ruled for nearly a thousand years; though this came to an end a similar timespan ago, a horde of jewellery, regal tombs and wonderful temples provide present-day evidence of past wonders. Next, tradition: in Gyeongsang's richly traditional hinterland you may see beasts ploughing the fields, villages of thatch-roofed houses or even ancestral rites being performed. Then there are more contemporary aces in the pack, with the south-coast city of Busan rivalling Seoul for Korea's best nightlife. Finally, there are natural attractions in abundance: a bunch of great beaches, a slew of scraggly islands and all the seafood you could wish for.

Though the Korean capital was transferred to Seoul following the collapse of the Silla dynasty, Gyeongsang has continued to exert influence on the running of the country. Since independence and the end of Japanese occupation, the majority of Korea's leaders have been Gyeongsang-born, with the resulting distribution of wealth and power making the area the country's most populated, and industrial, outside Greater Seoul.

Covering one-fifth of the country, the largely rural province of **Gyeonbuk** (경북; "North Gyeongsang") is South Korea's largest. Here, age-old tradition lingers on to a degree unmatched anywhere else in Korea, with sights strewn around the area providing a chronological view into more than two thousand years of history. Wonderful **Gyeongju** was capital of the **Silla empire** from 57 BC to 935 AD, and is now a repository to the resulting treasures. The main sights here are the **regal tombs**, small hillocks that held the city's kings, queens and nobles; **Bulguksa**, one of the country's most revered temples; and **Namsan**, a holy mountain crisscrossed with paths, and studded with relics of Silla times. Traces of the **Joseon dynasty**, which ruled the peninsula from 1392 until its annexation by the Japanese in 1910, are evident in a number of Confucian academies and traditional villages; both of these can also be found around **Andong**, a small, peaceful city that's becoming ever more popular with foreigners. The years immediately preceding Korea's mass industrialization in the 1980s can be savoured on the scenic island of **Ulleungdo**, where fishing and farming traditions exist unadulterated by factory smoke or sky-high apartment blocks. Meanwhile, the saccharine delights of present-day Korea

JIRISAN NATIONAL PARK

Highlights

❶ Folk villages Savour a taste of Korean life long forgotten at Hahoe Folk Village near Andong, and at Yangdong, an equally gorgeous version near Gyeongju. **See p.171 & p.192**

❷ Confucian academies Two stunning Joseon-dynasty academies can be found in the Gyeongsang countryside – Dosan Seowon and Oksan Seowon. **p.172 & p.190**

❸ Gyeongju Once the Silla kingdom's capital and now Korea's most laidback city, Gyeongju has enough sights to fill at least a week. See p.178

❹ The Underwater Tomb of King Munmu Take an easy but enjoyable day-trip east of

Gyeongju to two remote temples, before finishing at this unique coastal tomb. **See p.189**

❺ Ulleungdo This island's isolation out in the East Sea makes it the perfect place to see traditional life first-hand, or kick back and relax for a few days. **See p.193**

❻ Busan This smaller, more characterful version of Seoul has many sights including the Jagalchi Fish Market and Haeundae, the country's most popular beach. **See p.197**

❼ Jirisan National Park Korea's largest national park – with its own resident population of bears – has umpteen lofty trails, including a three-day hike across the ridge. **See p.213**

HIGHLIGHTS ARE MARKED ON THE MAP ON P.168

can be savoured in **Daegu**, the largest city in the region, and a fun place to hole up for a couple of days.

Korea's most southeastern province, **Gyeongnam** (경남; "South Gyeongsang"), is as closely connected to the sea as its northern neighbour, Gyeongbuk, is to the land. The southern coast splinters off into an assortment of cliffs, peninsulas and **islands**, many of the latter preserved as the **Hallyeo Haesang National Park**. Here you can head by ferry to minute specks of land where life goes on as it has for decades, free of the smoke, noise and neon often hard to escape on the mainland. This greenery is

GYEONGSANG

N

Chungju

SOBAEKSAN
NATIONAL PARK

Uljin

WORAKSAN
NATIONAL PARK

GYEONGBUK

45

35 Dosan
Seowon
1

Hupo

SONGNISAN
NATIONAL
PARK

Hahoe Folk
Village
2

Andong

55

EAST SEA
(SEA OF JAPAN)

Ulleungdo
5

JUWANGSAN
NATIONAL
PARK

1

Gimcheon

PALGONGSAN
PROVINCIAL
PARK

Oksan
Seowon
2

Pohang

Yangdong
Folk Village
1

GAYASAN
NATIONAL PARK

1

Daegu

Gyeongju
3

Gampo

Haeinsa

DAEGU

4

12

Underwater
Tomb of
King Munmu

55

JIRISAN
NATIONAL
PARK

35

3

7

Tongdosa

ULSAN

Ulsan

Gimhae

1

10

BUSAN

Jinju

10

Masan

Changwon
104

10

6

Busan

Goseong

Samcheonpo

Gohyeon

Jangseungpo

Namhae

Tongyeong

Geojedo

Yeosu

Saryangdo

Haegeumgang

Japan

0   20
kilometres

HIGHLIGHTS

1 Folk villages

2 Confucian academies

3 Gyeongju

4 The Underwater Tomb
  of King Munmu

5 Ulleungdo

6 Busan

7 Jirisan National Park

Jeju Island

••••••• High speed rail

not just confined to the province's shoreline – **Jirisan**, to the west, is the largest national park in the country. It's a real favourite among hikers, and not just for its size, or its beauty – a chain of **shelters** runs across the park's central spine, making multi-day hikes a possibility. Despite all this, Gyeongnam is no natural paradise. Nearly eight million people live in the area, making it the most densely populated part of the country outside Greater Seoul. Here lies Korea's second city, **Busan**, a fantastic place with good beaches, excellent nightlife, and a friendly, earthy nature.

Andong and around

안동

To walk around the unhurried streets of little **ANDONG**, you'd never guess that this is one of the most popular draws in the region for foreign travellers. It's true that there's little going on in the centre, but there are some truly magical sights in the highly picturesque countryside surrounding the city. **Dosan Seowon** to the north is a stunning Confucian academy dating from Joseon times, while to the west is **Hahoe Folk Village**, a rustic approximation of traditional Korean life that's a mainstay of present-day Korean tourist pamphlets. A similar folk village can be found nearer the centre, next to a rather absorbing **folklore museum**.

Folk village

민속 마을 • 24hr • Free • Bus #3 from train station – get off immediately after crossing the river

Just outside the main body of the city lies a small **folk village**. With its buildings mere models, rather than functioning abodes, this is basically a heavily diluted version of the terrific folk village at Hahoe (see p.171), but it's worth a quick nose around, especially if the bus schedules from Andong to Hahoe or Dosan Seowon have left you with an hour or two to spare. If you have more time, you can stop at one of the **restaurants** at the top of the complex (see p.170). After seeing the village, it's possible to cross the river on a zigzagging pedestrian bridge then catch the bus back to Andong from the other side of the road.

Folk museum

민속 박물관 • Daily 9am–6pm • W1000

Don't leave the folk village without seeing the **Folk museum** near the entrance to the complex, which is chock-full of interesting information about local culture and practices – including why Korean women traditionally give birth facing the south or east; it's altogether more explanatory and less obsessed with cold, hard facts than most Korean museums. Look out for dioramas portraying village games – some of which still go on in the countryside on occasion – and some fascinating collections of clothing and headwear; if you're in luck, you may even walk out with a free scroll of calligraphy from an on-site artist.

Soju museum

소주 박물관 • Mon–Sat 9am–5.30pm • Free • ⓦ andongsoju.net • A taxi from central Andong should cost less than W5000

Soju, of which Andong is home to a particularly strong variety, is the grog that oils Korea's wheels, and the town has a whole **museum** dedicated to the stuff, a couple of kilometres to the south of town. Unfortunately, it isn't too interesting, but you're welcome to buy a bottle of the local variety that, at about 45 percent alcohol by volume, is nearly twice as strong as any other.

4

ANDONG

Dosan Seowon

Hahoe Folk Village, bus terminal

Ungbu Park

TOEGYERO

FOOD STREET

YEDINSUK ST

HWARANGNO

Bus Stop for
Hahoe Folk Village

Andong Station

HWARANGNO

JEBIWON-RO

Bus Stop for
Dosan Seowon

CHUKJEJANG-GIL

0   300
metres

Nakdong River

Soju Museum

Andong Folk Village & Folk Museum

N

■ BAR	
Hulk Bar	1

■ ACCOMMODATION	
Andong	1
Andong Park	2
Peter Pan Guesthouse	3

● RESTAURANTS & TEAROOMS	
Andong Gan Godeungeo	4
Andong Gwan	2
Jaerim Galbi	3
Punggyeong Sori	1

ARRIVAL AND INFORMATION   ANDONG

By train Andong's train station is in the very thick of things, and within a ten-minute walk of all the accommodation and eating options listed below.
Destinations Busan (Haeundae station; 3 daily; 3hr 30min); Danyang (7 daily; 1hr 15min); Gyeongju (3 daily; 2hr); Seoul (Cheongnyangni station; 7 daily; 3hr 20min).
By bus The new bus station is inconveniently located around 6km to the west of the town centre – bus #11 (20min; W1200) connects it to the train station. If you're heading to Hahoe Folk Village and not the town centre,

take bus #46 instead, and you'll save a lot of time.
Destinations Busan (frequent; 2hr 30min); Daegu (frequent; 1hr); Daejeon (14 daily; 2hr 10min); Gyeongju (8 daily; 2–4hr); Pohang (hourly; 2hr); Seoul (frequent; 3hr); Sokcho (2 daily; 4hr); Taebaek (3 daily; 3hr 30min).
Tourist information There's an excellent information office (daily 9am–6pm; ☎ 054 852 6800) outside the train station; staff are helpful and informative, especially with regard to finding a place to stay or eat, and there's usually an English-speaker on hand.

ACCOMMODATION

Andong's **accommodation** simply hasn't caught up with its increasing popularity as a tourist destination – if you're after any form of **luxury** you're advised to stay in Gyeongju and visit Andong on a tour or day-trip. Less picky souls should be able to find an acceptable place within walking distance of the train station, or even out in Hahoe Folk Village (see opposite); the tourist office will ring ahead to book a room if required. Lastly, if you're on a bare-bones budget, there's a street filled with *yeoinsuk* (around W15,000) just north of the train station.

★**Andong** 안동 호텔 Samsandong 103-3 ☎ 054 858 1166. The best-value motel in the area features flash rooms with great showers; some also have nice paintings. It may be worth paying extra for the more expensive deluxe rooms, which are huge. A café and noodle restaurant are attached to the base. **W40,000**
Andong Park 안동 파크 호텔 Gyeongdongno 707 ☎ 054 853 1501. The only official hotel in town, though it's pretty poor, despite recent renovations; rooms look for all

the world like those you'd find in a motel, though prices remain low. No English spoken, though service is friendly. **W50,000**
Peter Pan Guesthouse 피터팬 게스트하우스 Anheungdong 312-2 ☎ 010 3124 8277. Bare-bones hostel, whose excellent location and homely vibe just about outweigh the negatives, such as the fact that there's only one toilet, and few locks to speak of. Dorm beds **W20,000**

EATING AND DRINKING

A dedicated **food street** starts just opposite the train station – look for the gate with the mask – though the best restaurants are to be found away from this road. One interesting place to eat is the folk village east of the centre (see p.169), where a rustic bunch of restaurants is primarily occupied with the making and selling of *jeon* (fried savoury pancakes). The tourist booth outside the train station is an excellent source of information – they even have a cursory **restaurant map** for visiting foreigners.

★**Andong Gan Godeungeo** 안동 간고등어 Gyeongdongno 625 ☎054 858 1118. An easy walk from the station, here you can dine on salted mackerel, an Andong speciality. Ask for the *jeongsik* (정식) – a belly-filling set course featuring salted mackerel plus an array of side dishes, yours for just W8000. Daily 9am–8pm.

Andong Gwan 안동관 Samsandong 102-1 ☎054 854 9933. The most luxurious place to order a portion of *jjimdak* (찜닭; steamed chicken in soy broth), an Andong speciality (W25,000; feeds two or three). There are also cheaper staples on the English-language menu. Daily 9am–9pm.

Hulk Bar 홀크 바 Samsandong 132-2. Perhaps the most distinctive bar in the centre, with a picture of the Hulk on the outside, and inside a variety of cheap beers available to take straight from refrigerators. Daily 6pm–1am.

Jaerim Galbi 재림 갈비 Unheungdong 171-6 ☎054 857 6352. The best joint in town, and very popular with foreign tourists. Unlike most such restaurants, they're just about willing to cater for single diners – put on your biggest smile. Pork *galbi* is W9000 per portion, with marinated *bulgogi* a little more. The best meat, *hanu galbi*, costs a whacking W22,000 per portion, but is absolutely delicious. Daily 10am–10pm.

Punggyeong Sori 풍경소리 Samsandong 104-4 ☎054 843 3004. Small, quaint tearoom located above an oriental medicine clinic – two of Korea's best smells in one building. Teas W5000–7000. Daily 1–10pm.

Hahoe Folk Village

하회 마을 • Officially daily 9am–7pm, though open 24hr • W2000, free outside official visiting hours • Ⓦ hahoe.or.kr

Korea has made many efforts to keep alive its pastoral traditions in the face of rapid economic growth; one particularly interesting example is its preserved **folk villages**. While some – such as the one near central Andong (see p.169) – exist purely for show, others are functioning communities where life dawdles on at an intentionally slow pace, the residents surviving on a curious mix of home-grown vegetables, government subsidy and tourist-generated income. Now under World Heritage protection, **Hahoe Folk Village** is one of the best and most popular in the country, a charming mesh of over a hundred **traditional countryside houses** nestling in the gentle embrace of an idle river. This charming mix of mud walls, thatched roofs and dusty trails is no mere tourist construct, but a village with a history stretching back centuries, and you'll be able to eat up at least a couple of hours exploring the paths, inspecting the buildings and relaxing by the river. The village's past is told on information boards outside the most important structures – seek out the Yangjin residence, for example, the oldest in the village, and built in a blend of Goryeo- and Joseon-era styles.

The village can sometimes get a little busy with visitors, but it's easy to escape and find space – try the riverside at the far end of the village, past the church. Even better, stay on to experience the village at night, when the vast majority of visitors have gone home – misty early morning walks can be rather wonderful, too. If you're around in October, you'll be able to catch Hahoe's absorbing **mask dance festival** (Ⓦ maskdance.com).

4

ARRIVAL AND DEPARTURE   HAHOE FOLK VILLAGE

By bus Bus #46 runs to the village from Andong (8 daily; 40min). Day-trippers will be dropped off 2km from the complex and asked to buy a ticket to the village; bus #46 continues merrily on into the village with genuine residents aboard, while visitors will have to take one of the regular shuttle buses (included with ticket price), even if they're staying the night.

ACCOMMODATION AND EATING

Temptingly, there are a number of *minbak* at which you can **stay the night** in Hahoe, costing about W50,000 for a spartan room, and heated in colder months with the underfloor *ondol* system. The tourist information office in Andong (see opposite) will be happy to book you into one of these guesthouses; all serve light meals, which is handy since there are **no restaurants** in the village; there are, however, a couple of simple **grocery stores**.

Rakkojae 락고재 Hahoe-ri 695 ☎054 857 3410. The one upper-class option in Hahoe is this small yet extremely atmospheric complex, affiliated to a similar establishment of the same name in Seoul (see p.96), and equipped with its own *jjimjilbang*. You'll be able to eat breakfast just outside your room, overlooking the courtyard – quite a wonderful experience on misty mornings – and *samgyetang* (chicken soup) is available for W20,000 in the evenings if you book in advance. __W180,000__

TOEGYE, NEO-CONFUCIANIST

Poet, scholar, all-round good guy and bearded star of the thousand-won note, **Toegye** (퇴계; 1501–70) is one of Korea's most revered historical characters. Born Yi Hwang, but better known by his pen name (pronounced Twegg-yeah), he exerted a major influence on the politics and social structure of his time. The country was then ruled by the **Joseon dynasty**, one of the most staunchly **Confucian** societies the world has ever known – each person was born with a predefined limit as to what they could aspire to in life, forever restricted by their genetics. The aristocracy oversaw a caste-like system that dictated what clothes people could wear, who they could marry, and what position they could hold, among other things.

Toegye was lucky enough to be born into privileged society. He excelled in his studies from a young age, and eventually passed the notoriously difficult governmental exams necessary for advancement to the higher official posts. Once there, he refused to rest on his laurels – he hunted down those he thought to be corrupt, and as a reward for his integrity was **exiled**, several times, from the capital. However, his intelligence made him a force to be reckoned with, and he set about introducing **neo-Confucian thought**, much of it borrowed from the Song dynasty in China; he advocated, for example, advancement based on achievement rather than heredity. After his death, the Confucian academy **Dosan Seowon** was built in his honour; it retains the contemplative spirit of the time, and of Toegye himself.

Dosan Seowon

도산 서원 • Daily: March–Oct 9am–6pm; Nov–Feb 9am–5pm • W1500 • Ⓦ dosanseowon.com • Bus #67 from Andong (5 daily; 50min)

Dosan Seowon is a Confucian academy, surrounded by some of the most gorgeous countryside that the area can offer – on the bus journey here from Andong, you'll find yourself winding your way past rice paddies and some pleasantly unspoilt countryside, before ducking down to the academy's entrance. From here it's a short walk to the complex itself; the wide **valley** to your right is simply stunning, the sound of rushing water from the stream occasionally augmented by the splutter of a faraway tractor.

The academy was established in 1574, in honour of Yi Hwang, a well-respected Confucian scholar also known as **Toegye** (see box above). It no longer functions as a place of study, but a refurbishment in the 1970s helped re-establish the tranquillity of its original *raison d'être*: this was a highly important study place during the Joseon era, and the only one outside Seoul, for those who wished to pass the notoriously hard tests necessary for governmental officials.

Opposite the main entrance, you may notice a little man-made hill topped by a **traditional-style shelter**; the stele underneath once marked an important spot for the government exams, with the original location somewhere towards the bottom of the lake that you pass on the bus in. As you enter the complex, you'll see, beyond the flower gardens and up the steps, two libraries whose nameplates are said to have been carved by Toegye himself; the buildings were built on stilts to keep humidity to a minimum. Further on are structures that were used as living quarters, the main lecture hall, and a shrine to Toegye, though this last one is usually closed off. Passing back down under a cloak of maple – which flames roaring red in late autumn – you'll find an **exhibition hall** detailing the great man's life and times, as well as an astrolabe for measuring the movements of celestial bodies.

Daegu and around

대구

DAEGU is Korea's **fourth-largest city** by population, and a major centre of business. The core of town is effectively one large shopping mall, the department stores supplemented by a lattice of streets devoted to particular products. Herbal Medicine Street is the best known, as the city has for centuries been a centre of **herbal medicine**, but you could also head to Steamed Rib Meat Street or Rice Cake Street if you're hungry, Shoe Street or Sock Street if your feet need clothing, or Washing Machine Appliance Street if, well, your washing machine needs maintenance. Daegu is also one of the few places in Korea where you'll notice a substantial American military presence – the city's nightclubs are often prowled by grinding grunts from the surrounding army bases.

It has to be said that Daegu as a city is not particularly attractive. There are few notable sights in the centre, but it's a pleasant place to shop, or to catch up on your **partying** if you've been trawling the Gyeongsang countryside. There are also a few surprisingly rustic restaurants and tearooms to hunt down in the city core; several alleyways in **Jingolmok**, which spreads out around the famed Herbal Medicine Market, have been given a gentle gentrification in recent years, and make for pleasant strolling. Head a little further afield **Palgongsan** and you'll find a wonderful park to the north of town, while **Haeinsa**, one of Korea's best-known temples, is just a short bus ride to the west.

Herbal Medicine Market

한약 시장 • Exhibition hall Mon–Sat 9am–5pm, Sun 10am–5pm • Free

Daegu's **Herbal Medicine Market** first got going in the 1650s. Such places used to be found all over the country but only a few now remain, and today almost half of the country's buying and selling of medicinal herbage is undertaken on these streets – don't expect to see a physical market as such, more a prevalence of stores selling everything from fruits to roots, bark to bugs and lizard tails to deer antlers, with practitioners able to whip up combinations of weird and wonderful ingredients for a range of ailments. On the main street is the **Yangnyeongsi Exhibition Hall**, a mildly diverting display of medicinal ingredients and how they're used, though very little information is in English.

4

The churches

Near the Herbal Medicine Market you'll be able to spot the spire of **Je-il Church** (제일 교회), a red-brick building that constitutes Daegu's first Christian place of worship, having been founded by Presbyterian missionaries in 1898 (the present building, though, only dates to 1933). Just around the corner is the more Gothic-style **Gyesan Cathedral** (계산 성당).

Dalseong Park

달성 공원 • Daily 5am–9pm • Free

Forming a western boundary to the specialist shopping street area is **Dalseong Park**, created on the site of what was apparently the oldest fortress in Korea. Nowadays it functions as a zoo of sorts, though in keeping with many such places across Asia the animals look a little forlorn.

Apsan Park

앞산 공원 • Daily 24hr • Free; cable car W7000 return • Bus #300, #410 or #750 from Daegu train station

Daegu's only other notable stretch of greenery is **Apsan Park**, around 6km to the south of the city centre. It's more of a mountain than a park, and there are some good trails to tackle; you'll find plenty of temples and pavilions, and a small exhibition on the Korean War. You can also walk or take a cable car to a ridge that provides wonderful views of Daegu's sprawl.

4

ARRIVAL AND DEPARTURE | DAEGU

By plane The city's international airport is a short bus or taxi ride east from Dongdaegu train station, and has connections to Jeju (13 daily; 1hr) and Seoul (2 daily; 1hr), as well as flights to China and Thailand.

By train Daegu station stares straight down at the main downtown area, and as such is the best place in which to arrive. For high-speed KTX services you'll have to head to Dongdaegu station, three stops to the east by subway.

Destinations (Daegu station) Busan (1–2 hourly; 1hr 20min); Daejeon (1–3 hourly; 1hr 45min); Pohang (2 daily; 1hr 45min); Seoul (1–3 hourly; 3hr 45min).

Destinations (Dongdaegu station) Busan (every 10–20min; 50min); Daejeon (every 10–20min; 50min); Gyeongju (hourly; 1hr 10min); Seoul (every 10–20min; 2hr).

By bus Arriving by bus can be a little confusing since there are several terminals across the city, though only a few of these are likely to be used by tourists. The Bukbu terminal and Seodaegu express terminal are frustratingly far (9km) to the northwest of the centre, as is the Seobu terminal to the southwest. The Dongbu terminal is marginally more central, but best is the Dongdaegu express (고속; *gosok*)

terminal, whose several buildings connect with trains and the subway system – to get here from other Korean cities you should head to their own *gosok* terminal.

Destinations (Express terminal) Andong (9 daily; 1hr 20min); Busan (every 50min; 1hr 40min); Daejeon (frequent; 2hr 20min); Gwangju (every 40min; 3hr 20min); Gyeongju (frequent; 50min); Incheon (10 daily; 4hr 30min); Jeonju (every 1hr 20min; 3hr 30min); Jinju (hourly; 2hr 10min); Seoul (frequent; 3hr 50min); Sokcho (3 daily; 4hr).

Destinations (Dongbu terminal) Gangneung (frequent; 5hr); Gyeongju (frequent; 50min); Pohang (frequent; 1hr 20min); Samcheok (11 daily; 6hr 30min); Sokcho (8 daily; 7hr).

Destinations (Seobu terminal) Busan (8 daily; 1hr 50min); Gyeongju (19 daily; 1hr 10min); Haeinsa (frequent; 1hr 30min); Jinju (frequent; 1hr 40min); Pohang (frequent; 1hr 30min); Tongyeong (frequent; 2hr 40min); Yeosu (7 daily; 4hr).

Destinations (Bukbu terminal) Andong (frequent; 1hr 30min); Gangneung (9 daily; 4hr); Guinsa (1 daily; 4hr); Muju (3 daily; 3hr 30min).

GETTING AROUND AND INFORMATION

By subway Daegu's two train stations are connected to the city's two-line subway system, which is cheap (W1200 per ride) and efficient.

By bus As with all Korean cities, Daegu's local bus network is comprehensive, though likely to bewilder foreign tourists. It's W1200 per ride.

Travel card If you're staying in the city for more than a couple of days you could use the Daegyong travel card (W2000), which gives slight discounts and avoids the need to rummage for change.

Tourist information Both train stations have information booths, with English-speakers most likely at Dongdaegu (daily 9am–7pm; 📞 053 939 0080).

THE DAEGU SUBWAY FIRE

On February 18, 2003, a calamitous event took place under Daegu's downtown streets, one that was to have a heavy impact on the Korean psyche, and a terrible comedown after the spectacular success of the previous year's World Cup. The simple facts – around two hundred killed in a **subway fire** – do not even begin to tell the story, with failings before, during and after the event bringing about a national sense of shame, and a level of introspection previously unseen in a country accustomed to looking abroad for excuses.

A few months before the fire, a man named **Kim Dae-han** had suffered a stroke that left him partially paralysed. Ostracized by his family and friends, and losing his sanity, he decided to take his frustrations out on society. During a Tuesday morning rush hour, he wandered into a subway train armed with gasoline-filled containers, which caught fire as the train pulled into Jungangno station. The fire spread rapidly through the carriages, owing to the lack of any fire-extinguishing apparatus on board; both the seats and the flooring produced toxic smoke as they burned. Kim managed to escape, along with many passengers from his train, but the poor safety procedures on the line meant that the driver arriving in the opposite direction was not informed of the problem, and pulled in to a plume of thick, toxic smoke. At this point the fire detection system kicked in and shut off power on the line, leaving both trains stranded. The driver of the second train told passengers to remain seated while he attempted to contact the station manager, and when finally put through was told to leave the train immediately. He duly scurried upstairs, but in his haste had removed the train's key, shutting off power to the doors, and effectively sealing the remaining passengers inside – death on a large scale was inevitable. The total count has never been fully established, as some bodies were burnt beyond all recognition.

The families of the victims, and the country as a whole, needed someone to blame. The arsonist was sentenced to life in prison, avoiding the death penalty on the grounds of mental instability; he died in jail soon afterwards. The incident raised some serious questions, primarily about **safety** being compromised by a thirst for profit, and the treatment of the **disabled** in Korean society – a baptism of fire for incoming president Roh Moo-hyun. Safety on Daegu's subway has since been significantly improved, and facilities for the disabled have improved across Korea. At least some good may be coming out of one of Korea's biggest modern-day disasters.

4

ACCOMMODATION

The information booths outside the train stations will be able to help you find a room. There are a few good **hotels**, **motels** aplenty can be found near both terminals, and there are some cheaper **yeogwan** within staggering distance of the nightlife area around Jungangno subway station. For those on a real budget, or just in need of a good scrub, there's *Greenvill*, a decent **jjimjilbang** (W8000) outside Banwoldang subway station, and another right outside Daegu station.

Canel Motel 카넬 모텔 Namseongno 10-2 ☎053 252 4466. Near the western end of Herbal Medicine Street, and therefore also within walking distance of downtown, this motel (whose name is supposed to be "Chanel") will suffice for anyone on a tight budget. **W40,000**

Danim Backpackers 다님 배크패커스 Jongno 2-ga 84-2 ☎010 6428 9766. Newish hostel with two venues: the larger main branch is dull with slightly clueless staff, but this more central one functions more like a homestay, and though rough around the edges can be good fun. It's up on the third (and fourth) floor; keep your eyes peeled for the sign. Dorm beds **W20,000**

Inter-Burgo 인터부르고 Manchondong 300 ☎053 602 7114, ⓦhotel.inter-burgo.com. Though it may look like a leisure centre from outside, this is billed as Daegu's top hotel. It's overpriced and in an uninteresting part of town, though mercifully a short taxi ride from the airport or the train station. Book online, or at the tourist office outside Dongdaegu station, for big discounts. **W275,000**

Pan 판 Gyeongsangangyeonggil 43-5 ☎053 252 7529. Something a bit different: an Italian restaurant (see p.176) that also allows guests to stay in its pleasing *hanok*-style rooms. The dorms are poor value, though the private rooms offer comfort and a romantic ambience. Dorm beds **W30,000**, rooms **W60,000**

The Style 더 스타일 Seongnae 3-dong 53-3 ☎053 214 6116. The best of Daegu's new mini-glut of hostel-like guesthouses, with two almost entirely pine-lined floors of capsule-style dorm beds and tiny private rooms (shared bathrooms only). Service is amiable, and there's a café on the ground level. Dorm beds **W23,000**, rooms **W50,000**

EATING

There's a good, cheap **restaurant** around every corner in Daegu, and the rising number of expats means that the choice is becoming ever more cosmopolitan; Indian restaurants are becoming particularly popular. **Coffee** and morning snacks are far easier to hunt down in the Jungangno downtown area, as are Western joints such as *TGI Friday's*.

Bongsan Jjim-galbi 봉산찜갈비 Dongindong 1-ga 332-3 ☎053 425 4203. Daegu has a number of dedicated shopping streets, so it should come as no surprise that there's one dedicated to the city speciality – *galbi-jjim* (갈비찜), steamed rib meat, which goes down particularly well with a few shots of *soju*. *Bongsan Jjim-galbi* is the oldest and most famous establishment hereabouts, having doled out the dish since the 1960s. You'll pay W15,000 per portion (minimum two). Daily 9am–10pm.

★**Mido** 미도 Jongno 2-ga 75. Fancy a trip back in time? This tearoom seems to have been plucked straight from the Korean 1970s, with only its staff and customers showing any signs of ageing. The sight of a foreigner walking in will likely cause quite a stir; a *hanbok*-clad lady will be guiding you to a silk cushion-covered couchette in no time, offering tea from W2000, and some ginger to dunk in sugar and munch. A fantastic place. Daily 9am–10pm.

Pan 판 Gyeongsangangyeonggil 43-5 ☎053 252 7529. This charming restaurant is set beside one of central Daegu's few traditional-style houses, though oddly the food served here is Italian – pizzas and pasta from W13,000. If you can track it down (you may have to ask directions), you'll find that the atmosphere can be quite romantic, and it's even possible to stay the night (see p.175). Daily 11am–midnight.

★**Sogadam** 소가담 Daemyeong 9-dong 487-6 ☎053 721 6112. Now, here's a good idea. This restaurant serves up some interesting takes on the humble pork cutlet (돈까스; *donkkaseu*) in a sleek, industrial-chic space. Try it chopped up in a salad, with balsamic vinegar and bread, or smothered with chilli – all variations cost W8900. Daily 10am–10pm.

Songjeong Hanjeongsik 송정한정식 Jongno 2-ga 78 ☎053 425 2221. On the same cute road as *Danim Backpackers* and *Mido* tearoom, this place offers earthy delights in a *hanok*-style setting – think sliding paper doors, yellow lino floors and a pleasantly leafy exterior. Their food's great, too – plump for one of the W6000 lunch specials, which give you a choice of mackerel (고등어), *kimchi* broth (김치찌개) or soybean broth (된장찌개) as a centrepiece. Daily 10am–10pm.

DRINKING

The downtown area has innumerable places to **drink**, though most are fairly generic. The focus is Rodeo Street, which holds all of the city's most popular **clubs** and lures local expats (and plenty of American soldiers) at weekends to dance until dawn.

Club Frog 클럽 프로그 Samdeokdong 1-ga 8-8 ☎010 8533 1828. There isn't much to choose between the several clubs tightly jammed into this area, but this hip-hop venue has stood the test of time, and remains enduringly popular despite verging on the cheesy. Daily 8pm–late.

Jaengi 쟁이 Dongsungno 3-ga 8-8 ☎010 8594 5011. The coolest bar in town by far, presided over by a local chap who barely speaks, and illuminated with candles and precious little else. Cocktails go for a bargain W5000, and there's usually live music at 9pm on Saturdays. Daily 6pm–2am.

Palgongsan Provincial Park
팔공산 도립공원

Just 20km north of Daegu, the land rises and folds, creating a peak-lined ridge and a series of valleys now studded with temples, hermitages and the odd carved Buddha. This area, **PALGONGSAN PROVINCIAL PARK**, is an ideal setting for a day of relaxed hiking.

Donghwasa
동화사 Bus #401 from Dongdaegu station in Daegu (1hr)

Dating way back to 493, **Donghwasa** is the park's most famous temple, though a little over-hyped by the local authorities. Visitors are most likely to be impressed by a seated Buddha thought to date from the eighth century, and the gloriously intricate interior of the main hall. More modern is the mammoth **Tongil Buddha**, which stands next to some similarly outsized stone pagodas and lanterns. These uninspired creations were placed here in the hope that the two Koreas will one day become one – *tongil* means "reunification" – and though the religion-lite powers that be in Pyongyang are unlikely to approve of the Buddha, they're sure to be impressed by a liberal use of concrete rarely seen outside Communist societies.

Gatbawi

갓바위

Gatbawi, another carved Buddha, occupies a lofty and far more natural setting, providing a view that's not quite top-of-the-world, but at least high enough to present Daegu in all its apartment-block-filled glory. Situated up near the peak of Gwanbong (850m), it's around an hour's walk from the tourist village below Donghwasa, at the bottom of the trail. Many people make the journey on the 1st or 15th of the month to make a wish, as it is claimed that the Buddha will hear one from every visitor on these occasions.

Yeombulbong and Yeombulam

Cable car W3500 one-way, W5500 return

Beyond Gatbawi, a few hours should be enough to bring you to **Yeombulbong** (1121m), from where you can drop down the trail back to Donghwasa, stopping at **Yeombulam**, a hermitage on route. You could even take the **cable car** to or from an observation point near the hermitage – this runs from the tourist village beneath Donghwasa.

4

Haeinsa

해인사 Daily 8.30am–6pm • W3000 • ⓦ haeinsa.or.kr • Bus from Daegu's Seobu terminal (every 20min; 1hr)

A bus ride away from Daegu, the secluded temple of **Haeinsa** (해인사) is part of Korea's holy trinity of "Jewel Temples" – the other two are Tongdosa (see p.192) and Songgwangsa (see p.227), which represent the Buddha and Buddhist community respectively, while Haeinsa symbolizes the religion's teachings, or *dharma*. These doctrines have been carved onto more than eighty thousand wooden blocks, known as the **Tripitaka Koreana** (see box below), and remain visible through the vertical wooden rungs of the buildings that house them. Still in use today, Haeinsa's various buildings are pleasant enough; its location, however, is nothing short of spectacular: the path leading up to the main entrance, lined on both sides with colossal trees, is worth the trip alone, while the complex backs onto **Gayasan National Park** (가야산 국립 공원). Fame and beauty conspire to make the complex uncomfortably crowded at times, but few venture off the beaten track to enjoy the surrounding area. This is a shame, as a few

---

THE TRIPITAKA KOREANA

One of the most famous sights in the land, the eighty-thousand-plus wooden blocks of Buddhist doctrine known as the **Tripitaka Koreana** were first carved out in the eleventh century, over a 76-year period, in an attempt to curry the favour of the Buddha in a time of perpetual war. Though the originals were destroyed by rampaging Mongol hordes in the thirteenth century, the present set were carved shortly after that, and once again every possible measure was taken to please the Buddha. The best wood in the area was tracked down then soaked for three years in sea water before being cut to shape and boiled. The slabs then spent another three years being sheltered from sun and rain but exposed to wind, until they were finally ready for carving. Incredibly, not a single mistake has yet been found in over **fifty million** Chinese characters, a fact that led other countries to base their own Tripitaka on the Korean version. The blocks represent a superb feat of craft, patience and devotion, and their outer spines blocks are still visible today at Haeinsa temple; and the set has been added to UNESCO's World Heritage list.

hermitages can be found on the opposite side of the stream, and innumerable paths snake their way through the trees to peaks, farmland and secluded villages.

ACCOMMODATION   HAEINSA

There are plenty of **places to stay** in the winding streets that surround the small bus terminal. Haeinsa itself is a grand place for at which to take a templestay programme (ⓦ eng.templestay.com; W40,000) – you'll have to be up early, but dawn at the temple is simply magical.

Haeinsa Tourist Hotel 해인사 관광 호텔 Chi-in-ni 13-45 ☎ 053 933 2000. The best rooms in the area are on high at this tourist hotel, though it possesses the stained carpeting and slight chemical odour typical of official Korean tourist accommodation. The views, however, can be stunning, particularly on misty mornings. **W87,000**

Sanjangbyeoljang Yeogwan 산장별장 여관 Chi-in-ni 10 ☎ 053 932 7245. More interesting than Haeinsa's official accommodation, this *yeogwan* features spartan rooms in a traditional-style building in keeping with its natural surroundings. **W25,000**

Gyeongju
경주

Travellers seeking to delve headfirst into Korea's rich and storied history should make little **GYEONGJU** their primary target – here you can walk among kings from a dynasty long expired and view the treasures accumulated during a millennium of imperial rule. If this sounds a little like Kyoto, you'd be half right – unlike Japan's more illustrious ancient capital, Gyeongju remains decidedly semi-rural in nature, and a little rougher around the edges. Strangely, much of its present charm is all down to a bit of good, old-fashioned dictatorship: in the 1970s and 1980s, authoritarian President **Park Chung-hee** managed to ensure that Korea's most traditional city stayed that way at a time when rapid economic progress was turning the country upside down. He introduced height restrictions on structures built anywhere near historical remains, and passed a bill requiring many new constructions to sport a traditional Korean-style roof. The rules have, sadly, not always been followed, but the contrast with regular urban Korea remains quite striking.

Gyeongju's **city centre** is surprisingly mucky for a place of such dynastic repute. During harvest months, many of its streetsides are lined with old *chonnyeo* (a slang term for country ladies) hawking fruit, vegetables and all manner of roots and shoots – this gives a palpably bucolic twist to goings-on in one of Korea's foremost tourist centres. Chief among Gyeongju's sights are the Silla-dynasty **royal tombs**, rounded grassy hills that you'll see all over the town's periphery (see box, p.181); in **Tumuli Park** it's even possible to enter one for a peek at the ornate way in which royalty were once buried. To the east of the centre there's **Anapji Pond**, a delightful place for an evening stroll under the stars, and the **National Museum**, which is filled with assorted trinkets and fascinating gold paraphernalia from Silla times.

South of the city centre, and accessible by bicycle, is the small mountain of **Namsan**, centrepoint of a wonderful park filled with trails and carved Buddha images. Many more sights can be found in the countryside around Gyeongju; see the "Around Gyeongju" section, p.187, for a few possibilities.

Brief history

The most interesting period of Gyeongju's lengthy history was during its near-millennium as capital of the **Silla kingdom** (see box, p.180). After so long as Korea's glamourpuss, the degree to which Gyeongju faded into the background is quite surprising – having relinquished its mantle of power, the city lived on for a while as a regional capital, but then fell into a **steep decline**. The Mongols rampaged through the city in the fourteenth century, the Japanese invasions a couple of hundred years later stripped away another few layers of beauty, and from a peak of over a million, Gyeongju's population fell to next to nothing.

Ironically, centuries after carrying countless spoils of war across the sea after their successful invasion, it was the Japanese who reopened Gyeongju's treasure chest of history, during their occupation of the country in the early twentieth century. In went the diggers, and out came hundreds of thousands of relics, so that, even today, much visible evidence of the dynasty still remains around the city. Not all of this is above ground – excavations continue, and new discoveries are made every year.

Tumuli Park

대릉원 • Daily 8.30am–9pm • W2000

Gyeongju is often described by the Korean tourist board as an open-air museum, thanks to its large number of grassy regal, burial mounds. The tombs in question are known as **Tumuli**, which are prolific and impossible to miss. Right in the centre of town, the walled-off **Tumuli Park** contains over two dozen tombs. It's hard to imagine that this was until quite recently a functioning – though quiet – part of town, but in the 1970s the buildings were removed and the area beautified, creating a path- and tree-filled park that's wonderful for a stroll.

Cheonmachong

Entrances are located at the east and north of the complex, but its most famous hump sits to the far west. Here lies **Cheonmachong** (천마총), the only tomb in Korea that you can actually enter. Its former inhabitant is not known for sure, but is believed to be a sixth- or seventh-century king whose many horse-related implements gave rise to the name – Cheonmachong means "Heavenly Horse Tomb". Excavated in 1973, it yielded over twelve thousand artefacts, which was the largest single haul in the country, and although many went to Gyeongju's National Museum, a few decorate the inner walls of the tomb. There's also a full-scale mock-up of how the inhabitant was buried.

THE SILLA DYNASTY

In 69 BC a young Herod was learning how to talk, Julius Caesar was busying himself in Gaul and Spartacus was leading slave revolts against Rome. Legend has it that at this time, a strange light shone down from the East Asian sky onto a **horse** of pure white. The beast was sheltering an egg, from which hatched **Hyeokgeose**, who went on to be appointed king by local chiefs at the tender age of 13. He inaugurated the **Silla dynasty** (sometimes spelt "Shilla", and pronounced that way), which was to go through no fewer than 56 monarchs before collapsing in 935, leaving behind a rich legacy still visible today in the form of jewellery, pottery and temples. Many of the regal burial mounds can still be seen in and around **Gyeongju**, the Silla seat of power.

Though it was initially no more than a powerful city-state, successive leaders gradually expanded the Silla boundaries, consuming the smaller **Gaya kingdom** to the south and becoming a fully fledged member of the **Three Kingdoms** that jostled for power on the Korean peninsula – Goguryeo in the north, Baekje to the west, and Silla in the east. Silla's **art and craft** flourished, Buddhism was adopted as the state religion, and as early as the sixth century a detailed social system was put into use – the *golpuljedo*, or "bone-rank system" – with lineage and status dictating what clothes people wore, who they could marry and where they could live, and placing strict limits on what they could achieve.

Perversely, given their geographical positions on the "wrong" sides of the peninsula, Baekje was allied to the Japanese and Silla to the Chinese Tang dynasty, and it was Chinese help that enabled Silla's **King Muyeol** to subjugate Baekje in 660 (see box, p.264). Muyeol died the year after, but his son, **King Munmu**, promptly went one better, defeating Goguryeo in 668 to bring about a first-ever unified rule of the Korean peninsula. The resulting increase in power drove the state forward, though abuse of this new wealth was inevitable; pressure from the people, and an increase in the power of the nobility, gradually started to undermine the power of the kings from the late eighth century. Gyeongju was sacked in 927, and eight years later **King Gyeongsun** – by that time little more than a figurehead – finally handed over the reigns of power to **King Taejo**, bringing almost a millennium of Silla rule to a close, and kicking off the Goryeo dynasty.

Tomb of King Michu

Elsewhere in the complex is the large **tomb of King Michu**, who reigned from 262 to 284 and fought many battles to protect his empire from the neighbouring Baekje dynasty. According to legend, he even dispatched a ghost army from beyond the grave when his successor was losing one particular bout of fisticuffs; these phantoms disappeared during the resulting celebrations, leaving behind only the bamboo leaves that had infested the cavities of the enemy dead. For this reason, the tomb is often referred to as the "Tomb of the Bamboo Chief". One other tomb of note is the double-humped **Hwangnam Daechong**, which was almost certainly the resting place of a king and queen.

Noseo-ri and Nodong-ni

노서리 and 노동리 • Daily 24hr • Free

Across the main road from Tumuli Park, the tumuli continue, though less abundantly, into the city's main shopping district. Split by a road into two sections known as **Noseo-ri** and **Nodong-ni**, these areas are not walled off, and are free to enter at any time of the day or night. Here lie some colossal mounds, as big as those you'll find in Tumuli Park – one, known as Bonghwangdae, is 22m high, with a 250m circumference. Although you're not allowed to climb onto the tombs, a faint path heading up this largest hump indicates that some find the temptation too great to ignore, and you'll usually find a couple of people seated here after the sun has gone down. Opposite, in Noseo-ri, is a monument dedicated to **Prince Gustav Adolf VI** of Sweden, who participated in the excavations here in 1926 before inheriting his country's throne.

GYEONGJU'S SILLA TOMBS

Every culture has its own solutions for what to do with the deceased. Tibetan corpses are often left on a mountainside for vultures to carry away, certain Filipino societies place the departed in a coffin and pack it into a cliff, while the Yanomami of the Amazon rainforest choose to cremate their dead then eat the ashes with banana paste. Koreans have long preferred burial – a slightly more prosaic journey to the afterlife, for sure – and those who have travelled around the country a while will doubtless have seen the little green bumps that dot hills and mountains in the country's rural areas. Larger versions used to be a matter of course for Korean royalty.

Literally hundreds of **tombs** from the **Silla dynasty** can be found all over Gyeongju and its surrounding area. However, the identities of few of the tombs' occupants are known for sure – there were only 56 Silla kings, so it's clear that many were created for lesser royals, military leaders and other prominent members of society. Equally mysterious are the **interiors**, as the super-simple green parabolas give almost no hints as to their construction; however, a look inside **Cheonmacheong** in Tumuli Park should provide a few hints. Layers of gravel and stone make up the base of the tomb, with a wooden chamber placed in the centre to house the deceased – unlike a pharaoh, he or she would not have supervised the construction, but as in Egypt they would have been buried with some of their favourite belongings. The chamber was then covered with large, rounded stones (these would eventually crush the chamber, after sufficient putrefaction of the wood), which in turn was covered with clay and dirt, and sown with grass.

Given the riches inside, surprisingly few of the tombs were plundered for their treasures – while such an endeavour would be long and rather conspicuous, that didn't stop thievery elsewhere in the country. Over the past century, many tombs have been carefully excavated, yielding thousands of artefacts, many of which are now on display in Gyeongju's National Museum (see p.182).

Wolseong Park

월성 공원 • Daily 24hr • Free • Grasshopper bus every 30min (W3000)

A short walk southeast of Tumuli Park will bring you to the pretty patch of greenery called **Wolseong Park**, in and around which are some of the city's most popular sights. The paths that run through the park are pedestrianized, but you can also take a short horse-and-carriage ride around the area – you'll see them lined up opposite the main entrance to Tumuli Park – or tour the area in a kid-friendly grasshopper bus.

Cheomseongdae observatory

첨성대 • Daily 9am–10pm • Free

There are plenty of tombs around, though most Koreans make an eastward beeline to have their picture taken next to **Cheomseongdae**, an astronomical observation tower dating from the seventh century. Looking a little like a rook from a giant chessboard, its simplicity conceals a surprising depth of design: the twelve stones that make up the base represent either the months of the year or the signs of the Chinese zodiac, while the 27 circular layers were a nod to Queen Seondeok, ruler during the tower's construction and the 27th ruler of the Silla dynasty. Added to the two square levels on top and the base, this equals thirty, which is the number of days in a lunar month, while the total number of blocks equals the number of days in a year. Even more amazingly, the various gaps and points on the structure are said to correspond to the movements of certain celestial bodies.

Anapji Pond

안압지 • Daily 9am–10pm • W2000

Down the northern fringe and across the road from Cheomseongdae is **Anapji**, a pond and pleasure garden constructed in 674 by **King Munmu** (see opposite). Numerous battles in the preceding decade had led to a first-ever unification of the Korean peninsula, after which Munmu built what was – and still remains – a tranquil, tree-filled area around a **lotus pond** whose shape roughly mirrored that of his kingdom. In an interesting twist of fate, this was where the empire also came to an end, being the scene of King Gyeongsun's handover of power to King Taejo, founder of the Goryeo dynasty. In the following centuries, the area fell into disrepair until 1975, when it received its first modern makeover. When the pond was dredged it revealed a few relics from Silla times. That few then grew to hundreds, then thousands – much of the bounty, including a whole barge, now sits in the National Museum just down the road. The pond and gardens themselves are pleasantly illuminated at night – a great time to come for a walk among the bamboo.

Gyeongju National Museum

경주 국립 박물관 • Tues–Fri 9am–6pm, Sat & Sun 9am–9pm (7pm in Jan & Feb) • Free • ⓦ gyeongju.museum.go.kr

On the southern perimeter of Wolseong Park, **Gyeongju National Museum** is a repository of riches from the surrounding area, and with the exception of Seoul's National Museum (see p.89), it's quite possibly the best in the country. The rooms run in chronological order from locally sourced stone tools and ancient pottery to modern times, via the Bronze Age. But it's the **Silla** bling that most are here to see. Beautifully crafted earrings, pendants and other paraphernalia in gold, silver and bronze were cast into spectacular shapes, often adorned with tiny golden discs or leaves. You'll also find pottery, golden antlers and some uncomfortable-looking spiked bronze shoes, but the undisputed star of the show, hidden away in its own private room, is a glorious golden sixth-century crown, intricately sculpted and boasting an array of dangling bean-shaped jades.

Bomun Lake

보문호 • Musical performances May & June Sat & Sun 8.30pm; July–Oct daily except Wed 8.30pm • Free • Bus #10 or #18 from Gyeongju

Travel a few kilometres east of Wolseong Park, and on the bus route towards Bulguksa temple (see p.188), and you'll come to **Bomun Lake**. Surrounded by five-star hotels, this tranquil expanse has become the Gyeongju venue of choice for the well-heeled; largely devoid of the historical sights found elsewhere in the city, it's still a good place to head for a bit of easy fun. You can hire swan-shaped pedalos – the doyens of Korea's artificial waterways – and bikes for the cycle-trails around the lake, or have fun in a cheesy **amusement park**. There are also regular cultural and **musical performances** at the Bomun Outdoor Performance Theater just down from the *Commodore Hotel*. A number of **golf courses** can be found around the lake, ranging in size from 9 to 36 holes.

Namsan

남산 • Buses #500 to #508 run down the western flank of Namsan; #10 and #11 can be used for some sights on the eastern side

Central Gyeongju's ragtag assortment of buildings fades to the south, turning from urban to rural. Mercifully, development of this area is unlikely, as the city is hemmed in on its southern flank by **Namsan**, a small, park-like mountain area packed with trails

---

THE EMILLE BELL

Outside Gyeongju National Museum lies the **Emille Bell**, a veritable beast dating from 771. Known to Koreans as the Bell of King Seongdeok – in whose memory it was created – this is the largest existing bell in the country, and one of the biggest in the world; though estimates of its weight vary, even the smallest – nineteen tons – makes it a whopper by any standard. Legend surrounding the bell says that when it was first cast it failed to ring, only doing so once its constituent metal was melted back down and mixed with the body of a young girl. Her death-cry "Emille" (which rhymes with "simile") was a word for mother in the Silla dialect, and can apparently still be heard in the ring of the bell.

and sights. New discoveries of ancient relics are made regularly, but even if you don't find yourself unearthing a piece of Silla jewellery, this is another of the city's must-sees. Roads run along the park's perimeter, giving access to a wealth of sights on both sides, while the interior is strewn with carved Buddhas and offers some fantastic hikes. Namsan is best tackled either by **bicycle** around its pleasantly traffic-free perimeter (see box below), or with a pair of hiking boots through its interior.

Oreung

오릉 • Daily: March–Oct 9am–6pm; Nov–Feb 9am–5pm • W1000

The first sight that you'll come to on Namsan's western flank is **Oreung**, which means "five tombs". The grassy area just inside the perimeter wall is popular with picnicking families in the summer, but if you make your way through the pines along one of the park's lovely paths you'll soon come to the tomb of Hyeokgeose (ruled 57 BC to 4 AD), the **first king** of the Silla dynasty. Little else is known about him, but a history this long deserves to be acknowledged with a little perspective: Hyeokgeose was born in 69 BC, the same year as Cleopatra – Hyeokgeose's hump has been around for a seriously long time. Nearby mounds contain three of his immediate successors – Namhae, Yuri and Pasa were the second, third and fifth Silla monarchs respectively – as well as Hyeokgeose's wife, **Alyeong**, who was apparently born as a dragon in a nearby well, and therefore suitably auspicious. The well can still be seen; just follow the signs. Hyeokgeose himself trumped his future wife's spectacular birth by hatching from an egg laid by a phantom horse; his birthplace is outside the park, just down the road at **Najeong**, but the site is badly neglected in comparison.

Poseokjeong

포석정 • Daily 9am–6pm • W1000

Heading south and across the main road from Oreung you'll soon come across **Poseokjeong**, an uninteresting site, but one that's hugely popular with Korean tourists. Here once lay a villa in which Silla kings held regular banquets, but with the buildings long gone, you may wonder what all the fuss is about. The draw is actually a 6m-long water canal set within a loose perimeter of rocks – don't step inside – which was once used for royal **drinking games**: one member of the party would reel off a line of poetry, choose another guest to supply a suitable second line, and float a cup of wine down the watercourse. If the drink reached the challenger before he could think of a line, he had to drain the cup.

Just across the way, and signposted from the Poseokjeong car park, is the **Tomb of King Jima**, who was the sixth Silla king, but now finds himself isolated among the trees. The neighbouring village of **Poseok** remains charming, and is worth a nose around. It's

---

TOURING NAMSAN BY BIKE

For those with the inclination, and as long as the weather agrees, a **bike tour** around Namsan is one of the most enjoyable ways to spend a day in Gyeongju. To reach the mountain, come out of Tumuli Park's eastern entrance and turn right at the main road; the tombs of Wolseong Park should be on your left, and a few tourist shops and restaurants to your right. Turn left at the T-junction and head over the bridge. When you reach the end of the road turn left to get to Namsan's eastern flank, or right for the west. For the **west side**, turn left after the golden Buddha and you'll be at the northeast corner of **Oreung**; the entrance is down the main road on the south side. After seeing the sights on the western flank, you can avoid the main road back by using the farming track running parallel to the road. On Namsan's **east side** a patchwork of fields provides more opportunities to get away from the main roads than on the west, and you can use your own initiative to hug Namsan's skirt of trees.

There are numerous places to **hire bikes** in Gyeongju (see p.185), but the most convenient for Namsan is the outlet in the car park outside the main entrance to Tumuli Park.

also home to some good, cheap **restaurants**, which is handy if you've been in the Namsan area for a while.

Baeri Samjon-seokbul

배리 삼존 석불 · 24hr · Free

Further south down either the road or the footpath from Posekjeong you'll find a couple of tiny temples housing a standing Buddha trio known as **Baeri Samjon-seokbul**, which are said to date back to the early seventh century. This is a pretty area, and the starting point for a number of paths into Namsan's interior.

Samneung

삼릉 · 24hr · Free

Continuing south from Baeri Samjon-seokbul you come to **Samneung**, a small, pretty complex containing three tombs. Here lies Adalla, the eighth Silla king (ruled 154–184 AD), next to Sindeok and Gyeongmyeong, the 53rd and 54th leaders, who ruled for just a few years each in the early tenth century as the empire struggled to its close.

The eastern flank and the interior

A number of carved Buddhas were placed on Namsan's **eastern side** so that they may face the rising sun, though you'll need to trek a short way into the park to see them – the tourist office have detailed **maps** of the area, and some guesthouses create their own. One of the first you'll reach on your way from Gyeongju is also the most accessible – follow signs for **Woljeongsa** temple – but the one uphill behind **Borisa** (보리사), the largest functioning temple on Namsan, is more interesting; it dates from the eighth century and is backed by richly detailed stonework. A path from here leads all the way to a viewing platform on the top of the mountain, after which you'll have a choice between heading west to Poseokjeon (see p.183), or south to the ruin-surrounded peak of **Geumosan**.

West of the centre

The sights **west of Gyeongju** are quite scattered, making exploration a little tricky. For those not yet weary of dead Silla kings, a few **tomb complexes** lie a couple of kilometres beyond the River Hyeongsan, which tickles the western flank of the city. The closest two are accessible by bike (see opposite for rental information).

Tomb of General Kim Yu-sin

김유신묘 · Daily 9am–6pm · W1000

A right turn after the Hyeongsan bridge near Gyeongju will take you in the direction of the **tomb of General Kim Yu-sin**. Records in the *Samguk Sagi* (see p.190) state that in between his birth in 595 and his death in 673, he led the battles that defeated the Baekje and Goguryeo kingdoms, paving the way for Silla rule over the whole peninsula. The road leading here is quieter than those heading elsewhere from the bridge, but unfortunately for walkers and cyclists there are no real side routes to make use of.

Tomb of King Muyeol

무열왕릉 · Daily 9am–6pm · W1000

The **tomb of King Muyeol** – who defeated the rival Baekje kingdom in 660, and essentially unified the Korean peninsula for the first time – lies just south of the Hyeongsan bridge, though as the road leading south of the bridge is both a little too narrow and a little too busy for comfortable walking or cycling, it's best to head through the fields. Turn left down the bumpy riverside track immediately after the bridge, then down the first decent road that falls off to the right, and under the railway bridge. The tomb itself is quite delightful, perhaps on account of the fact that you're likely to have it more or less to yourself.

Geumcheok

금척 • 24hr • Free

Several kilometres down the main road leading west from the Hyeongsan bridge is the beguiling **Geumcheok** collection of tomb-mounds. Legend has it that Hyeokgeose, the first Silla king, once owned a golden stick (*geum-cheok*) that could restore the dead to life. However, the village got so overcrowded with Silla-dynasty undead that the townsfolk decided to bury the rod in a mound – forty decoy mounds were also raised in the area, and to this day nobody knows which one houses the stick.

ARRIVAL AND DEPARTURE   GYEONGJU

By train Gyeongju's small train station is on the east of the city centre, within easy walking distance of most accommodation and a number of central sights. The new Singyeongju high-speed station sits 10km to the west; from here, buses #50, #70 and #700 make their way to the bus terminal in town.

Destinations (Gyeongju station) Andong (2 daily; 2hr); Busan (Haeundae station; 10 daily; 1hr 30min); Danyang (3 daily; 2hr 20min); Daegu (10 daily; 1hr 20min); Pohang (6 daily; 40min).

Destinations (Singyeongju station) Busan (every 20–40min; 30min); Daejeon (every 20–40min; 1hr 15min); Seoul (every 20–40min; 2hr 15min).

By bus Gyeongju's main bus terminals – express and intercity – sit side by side on the west of the city centre. It's an easy walk to most accommodation and the central attractions.

Destinations Andong (12 daily; 3hr); Busan (frequent; 50min); Daegu (frequent; 50min); Daejeon (frequent; 2hr 40min); Gangneung (16 daily; 5hr 30min); Gwangju (2 daily; 3hr 30min); Incheon (every 50min; 5hr 30min); Jinju (6 daily; 2hr 30min); Seoul (frequent; 4hr 15min); Sokcho (2 daily; 8hr).

GETTING AROUND

On foot Central Gyeongju is small enough to walk around, while the number of landmarks dotted around town – and the fact that you can actually see them, without apartment blocks getting in the way – makes navigation easy in relation to other Korean cities.

By taxi Taxi rides between central locations shouldn't cost more than W5000, though many of the city's attractions are far-flung – ask at your accommodation about organizing a taxi for the day, which should work out somewhere in the region of W80,000–170,000, depending on precisely what you'd like to see.

By bicycle One excellent way of getting around – almost uniquely, for a Korean city – is by bike. Rental outlets can be found all over town, including outside the main entrance to Tumuli Park and opposite the bus terminal information booth. You'll need to hand over some form of ID for security (if unwilling to part with your passport, you may be able to use a library card or something similar), and a bike will be yours for around W10,000 per day, or W5000 for a few hours. Bikes are particularly good for touring Namsan (see box, p.183) or the wider Wolseong Park area (see p.181).

INFORMATION

Tourist information There are booths outside the train and bus stations (daily 9am–6pm; ☎054 772 9289), usually staffed by friendly English-speakers; they're eager to dole out pamphlets, and are adept at assisting with accommodation and travel queries.

Services Banks with exchange facilities include the Korea First Bank opposite the train station, and there are plenty of ATMs at 24hr convenience stores such as GS25 or 7-Eleven. The main post office is opposite the train station (Mon–Fri 9am–5pm; ☎054 740 0114).

ACCOMMODATION

For a city that trades so heavily on the tourist dollar, central Gyeongju's range of **accommodation** is a little poor. Its **five-stars** stand proud in a swanky collective around Bomun Lake, a short way east of the centre (see p.182); rack rates can fall by up to fifty percent at quieter times of the year, but rooms are on the small side and lack character. Cheaper **motels** can be found together with some lower-end hotels near the bus terminals, though prices tend to be higher here than elsewhere in Korea. There are a fair few backpacker-oriented hostels and **guesthouses**, which generally provide free internet and cooking facilities, and common rooms in which to hang out with fellow travellers.

CITY CENTRE

Cool Zzam 꿀잠 Gyerimno 106-gil 9 ☎054 8239 5006, ⓦcoolzaam.com; map p.179. Great little alpine cottage-like hostel, presided over by a friendly English-speaking lady. Two of the wood-ceilinged dorms have pleasant views out over a field, and there are some private bunk-bed rooms available. Dorm beds W23,000, rooms W50,000

Hanjinjang Yeogwan 한진관 여관 Wonhyoro 26-gil 21-14 ☎054 771 4097, ⓦhanjinkorea.wo.to; map p.179. Grubby, hostel-like place that ropes in a surprising number of ultra-budget backpackers. Standards of cleanliness are low and the rooms spartan as they come, but it's a decent place to meet people, especially when evenings are warm enough to allow for a spot of drinking on the roof terrace. Dorms W17,500

★**N Motel** 엔모텔 Noseodong 119-1 ☎054 777 4364; map p.179. Forget the cluster of motels spreading out from the bus terminal – this is the best one in town. Evidence includes big TVs in big rooms, free Dutch coffee whenever you ask, snazzily illuminated corridors – oh, and a location right next to some of the regal tombs that Gyeongju is famed for. Lovely! W40,000

★**Sarangchae** 사랑채 Hwangnamdong 238-1 ☎054 773 4868, ⓦkjstay.com; map p.179. Quite possibly the best guesthouse in the country, the *Sarangchae* offers friendly, informative management, free internet and cooking facilities and some friendly dogs along with a gorgeously traditional courtyard setting. Book ahead though, as there are only a few rooms; also note that they're usually closed in Dec. W40,000

The DY 더다이 Noseodong 170-1 ☎054 701 0090, ⓦhotelthedy.com; map p.179. Formerly the worn-down *Gyeongju Park*, the city centre's only official tourist hotel dragged itself into the modern day in 2013 with a fancy makeover – and a somewhat baffling name ("The Die?"). Rooms are a tiny bit overpriced now, but in those sporting a massage chair, you can buzz those cares away. Breakfast is optional at W19,000 per head, or you could nip to the *McDonald's* next door. W100,000

BOMUN LAKE

Bomun World 보문 월드 Cheongundong 1444-2 ☎054 772 0062, ⓦbomunworld.com; map p.188. For a change from Bomun's five-star hotels try this collection of intriguingly designed villas south of the lake – a 20min walk, more if you choose to head the long way across the fields. Some of the rooms are duplex in nature, and they're predictably popular with young couples. W70,000

Commodore 코모도 호텔 Bomunno 422 ☎054 745 7701, ⓦcommodorehotel.co.kr; map p.188. Rooms here are as tastefully designed as the lobby, with a choice of hill or lake views – the latter are best but marginally more expensive. There are a few good restaurants on site, as well as a lovely spa. W230,000

Concorde 콘코드 호텔 Bomunno 410 ☎054 745 7000, ⓦconcorde.co.kr; map p.188. A slightly cheaper alternative to its flashy neighbours, this hotel has benefitted from a refreshing makeover in 2014 – the swimming pool and sauna make nice additions. Rooms are rather good value for the location, and all come with balconies facing the lake. Service standards, however, remain pretty poor. W140,000

★**Hilton** 힐튼 Bomunno 484-7 ☎054 745 7788, ⓦhilton.com; map p.188. Possessing a slightly more international ambience than its neighbours, the *Hilton* has a swimming pool, gym, squash court and jogging track – and a Miró original in the lobby. Rooms are every bit as comfy as you'd expect for the price. W320,000

Hyundai 호텔 현대 Bomunno 338 ☎054 748 2233, ⓦwww.hyundaihotel.com; map p.188. This hotel probably offers the best lake views in the area, though rooms with a hill view are a little cheaper. Rooms are pleasing, with some nice touches and relatively large bathrooms, and service is very good; there are also Italian, Chinese, Korean and Japanese restaurants to choose from, as well as a coffee shop that serves delectable pecan pie. W310,000

BULGUKSA

Kolon 코오롱 호텔 Madong 111-1 ☎054 746 9001, ⓦkolonhotel.co.kr; map p.188. Despite the unfortunate name, this is a quality place to stay, out of town and just down the road from Bulguksa, in a tree-surrounded setting that includes a nine-hole golf course. Rooms are a little dated, but views over the course and trees are lovely. Rooms are cheaper at weekends. W180,000

EATING AND DRINKING

Gyeongju is not known for its food, and unfortunately there's little of interest in the centre – the best food is served in the **five-star hotels** that surround Bomun Lake. One interesting feature is the simply incredible number of small **bakeries** selling *gyeongju-bbang* (경주빵), small, sweet cakes that are eagerly snapped up by Japanese tourists seeking their *omiyage* (near-compulsory edible travel souvenirs).

RESTAURANTS
CITY CENTRE

★**Dosol Maeul** 도솔 마을 Hwangnamdong 71-2 ☎054 748 9232; map p.179. You can tuck into *pajeon* pancakes and quaff *dongdongju* – a milky Korean wine – by the bucket-load here, in traditional rooms set around an equally rustic courtyard. It's near the *Sarangchae* guesthouse (see above) and very similar in appearance. A great place to kick back after a day's sightseeing. Daily 10am–8pm.

Gisoya 기소야 Nodongdong 33-3 ☎054 746 6020;

GYEONGJU FESTIVALS

Throughout the year the city puts on many shows and events to please its guests. In warmer months, regular performances of traditional song and dance take place on **Bomun Lake** (see p.182) and around **Anapji Pond** (see p.181) at 8pm on Saturdays from April to October, but the biggest event by far is the three-day **Silla Cultural Festival**, in October, one of the best and most colourful in the land. On the menu are wrestling, archery, singing and dancing, and a parade in which a mock Silla king and queen are carried down the streets. Other events include the **Cherry Blossom Marathon**, held on the first Saturday of April, and a **Traditional Drink and Rice Cake Festival** in late March, while on December 31 the New Year's crowd heads to King Munmu's seaside tomb (see p.189) to ring in the change of digits and enjoy the first sunrise of the year.

map p.179. Facing some of the city centre regal tombs, this is a simple Japanese restaurant which gets the basics right. Try the *kimchi katsudon* (W7500), or a tempura *soba* set (W10,500). Tues–Sun 10am–3pm & 5–10pm.

Pipino Pizza 피피노 피자 Hwangseongdong 508-1 ☎054 773 0987; map p.179. While there are Western pizza chains in Gyeongju, *Pipino* offers a slightly more Korean experience, for W10,000 and up. Toppings include vegetarian, sweet potato, *bulgogi* or "super special". If you speak Korean, or can find someone willing to translate, you can call for free delivery – perfect on a rainy day. Daily 10am–10pm.

★**Sukyeong Sikdang** 숙영 식당 Hwangnamdong 13-5 ☎054 772 3369; map p.179. This sit-on-the-floor courtyard venue is, quite simply, the best restaurant in the Tumuli Park area, serving an array of dishes made with super-fresh ingredients. W9000 will buy you a *cheolboribap* set meal, which consists of soybean broth, *bibimbap* and a grilled fish surrounded by an armada of over a dozen side dishes. Not only that, but their home-made *dongdongju* (rice beer) costs just W5000 for a litre... and they'll be able to call you a taxi home. Daily except Tues 11am–9pm.

Yoseokgung 요석궁 Gyodong 19-4 ☎054 772 3347; maps p.179 & p.188. A fabulous place for fabulous food, set around a traditional courtyard in a quiet area facing Namsan. There's no English menu, but good traditional food is guaranteed – set meals go from W30,000 to W100,000 per head, though there's a two-person minimum. Daily 11.30am–9pm.

NAMSAN
Todam 토담 Poseok-ap ☎054 775 5222; map p.188.

Little thatch-roofed bungalow-restaurant just off Namsan's western flank, and almost directly opposite the Tomb of King Jima (see p.183). Here you can get a filling *dolsotbap* (돌솟밥; rice and several kinds of bean in a sizzling earthenware pot) for just W8000 – perfect if you're touring the mountain by bike. Daily 10am–8pm.

CAFÉS AND TEAROOMS
CITY CENTRE
★**Arisol** 아리솔 Bonghwangno 47 ☎054 771 7625; map p.179. Solace from Gyeongju's scruffy city centre can be found in this cute, hard-to-find tearoom, whose low wooden beams may pose problems for tall foreigners. The place is even better in summer, when sliding doors open onto a small garden. There are all sorts of odd teas available from W5000 to W8000 – if you've had your fill of "regular" Korean teas, try the mugwort or persimmon leaf. Daily 10.30am–8pm.

Doldamae 돌담애 Dongseongno 131-12 ☎054 748 4000; map p.179. On the same quiet road as the *Cool Zzam* hostel (see p.185), this *hanok*-style venue is the most attractive café in central Gyeongju. The coffee's okay too, and in summer you can enjoy it on the swings in the garden outside. Daily 10am–8pm.

NAMSAN
★**Jeontong Chatjip** 전통 찻집 Samneung; map p.188. A wonderful find for those touring Namsan by bike, this is the sweetest-looking countryside tearoom imaginable, presided over by a cheery lady who'll ply you with fruit and sweet treats. The teas are great, too, and cost from W5000. Daily 10.30am–6pm.

Around Gyeongju

An almost overwhelming number of sights litter the countryside around Gyeongju – those listed here make up just a fraction of the possibilities, so be sure to scour local maps and pamphlets for things that might be of particular interest to you. East of the city centre is **Bulguksa**, one of Korea's most famous temples; splendidly decorated, it's on the UNESCO World Heritage list, as is **Seokguram**, a grotto hovering above it on a mountain ridge. Apart from that geared towards these two sights, **transport** in this area is not always regular – you may need to spend some time waiting for buses, so if possible, try to get the latest timetable from one of Gyeongju's tourist offices. While hitchhiking is never totally safe and can't be wholeheartedly recommended, you'll rarely get a better chance than on the run east to the **Underwater Tomb of King Munmu**, where traffic on the road is light and everyone is heading to or from Gyeongju. On the way to see the king's watery grave, and easily combined as part of a day-trip, you'll pass a rural spur road leading to **Golgulsa** and **Girimsa**, two out-of-the-way temples inhabiting a wonderfully unspoilt valley. To the north of Gyeongju are **Oksan Seowon**, one of the country's best examples of a Joseon-era Confucian academy, and **Yangdong Folk Village**, a collection of traditional housing.

Bulguksa

불국사 • Daily 7am–6pm • W4000 • Bus #10 or #11 from Gyeongju

Sitting comfortably under the tree-lined wings of the surrounding mountains is **Bulguksa**, which was built in 528 during the reign of King Beop-heung, under whose leadership Buddhism was adopted as the Silla state religion. It was almost destroyed by the Japanese invasions in 1593 and, though it's hard to believe now, was left to rot until the 1970s, when dictatorial president Park Chung-hee ordered its reconstruction. It has subsequently been added to the UNESCO World Heritage list. As one of the most-visited temples in the country, it can be thronged with people, many of whom combine their visit with a picnic on and around the path leading from the bus stop to the ticket office.

The temple

Once through the gates, you'll follow a pretty path past a pond and over a bridge, before being confronted by the temple. Here, **two staircases** lead to the upper level; these are officially "four bridges" rather than two flights of steps, leading followers from the worldly realm to that of the Buddha. Both are listed as national treasures, so you're not actually allowed to ascend them. Having entered the main courtyard, you'll be confronted by two three-level **stone pagodas** from the Unified Silla period – one plain and one ornately decorated, representing Yin and Yang.

■ ACCOMMODATION	
Bomun World	5
Commodore	3
Concorde	2
Hilton	4
Hyundai	1
Kolon	6

THE GYEONGJU AREA

Oksan Seowon & Yangdong Folk Village

Pohang

Gyeongju

Bomun Lake

Deokdong Lake

GYEONGJU NATIONAL PARK

Girimsa

Tomb of General Kim Yu-sin

SEE "GYEONGJU" MAP

Geumcheok Mounds

Tomb of King Muyeol

Oreung Tombs

Woljeongsa

Najeong

Borisa

Golgulsa

Poseokjeong

Tomb of King Heongang

Tomb of King Jima

Baeri Samjon-Seokbul

Tomb of King Jeonggang

Bulguksa

Seokguram

Singyeongju Station

Samneung tombs

Tongiljeon

Geumosan

Namsan

Underwater Tomb of King Munmu

● RESTAURANTS & TEAROOMS	
Jeontong Chatjip	3
Todam	2
Yoseokgung	1

0   3
kilometres

Busan & Tongdosa

Oedong & Ulsan

From the courtyard, it's best to stroll aimlessly and appreciate the views. The whole complex has been elaborately painted, but the artistry is particularly impressive in **Daeungjeon**, the main hall behind the pagodas, whose eaves are decorated both inside and out with striking patterns. At the top of the complex, another hall – **Gwaneumjeon** – looks down over Bulguksa's pleasing array of roof tiles; the steep staircase down causes problems for Korean girls in high heels, but there are other ways back. Making your way across the rear of the complex you'll come to **Nahanjeon**, a hall surrounded by bamboo and a cloak of maple leaves. Behind this lie small towers of stacked stones; you're welcome – expected – to add your own. The **tearoom** beneath the nearby trinket shop provides a useful rest stop.

Seokguram grotto

석굴암 • Daily: March–Sept 6.30am–6pm; Oct–Feb 7am–5pm • W4000 • Bus #12 from Bulguksa (every 30min; last bus back 6.20pm)

After Bulguksa, a visit to the Buddhist grotto of **Seokguram** may feel a little anti-climactic. However, the views from its lofty position alone justify the trip up, especially at sunrise. The East Sea is visible on a good day, and it is said that the statue was built to provide spiritual protection to the country from the Japanese across these waters. Until fairly recently, access was only possible via a 3km mountain path from Bulguksa, but today most choose to take the bus instead. It is still possible to hike the mountain path, if only to appreciate how hard it must have been for the grotto's builders to transport the necessary blocks of granite to such a height; you can judge for yourself how far it is by looking up at the horizon from the Bulguksa bus stop – that's the Seokguram ticket booth on top.

Once past the ticket booth, a winding but easy ten-minute walk through the trees leads to the grotto itself; inside its keyhole-shaped chamber sits an image of the Sakyamuni Buddha, surrounded by art of a similarly high calibre. However, the chamber has been sealed off in order to protect it from both the elements and visitors, and unfortunately, this could and should have been done better. A pane of glass separates you from the art and its beauty, and an ugly little protective hut now stands in the way of the grotto. As a result, it's almost impossible to appreciate the elegance and attention to detail that many experts consider to be the finest example of Buddhist art in the country.

Golgulsa

골굴사 • 24hr • Free • Ⓦ golgulsa.com • Bus #100 or #150 from Gyeongju (every 30min; 45min); get off at the village of Andong-ni, from where it's just under 1km (10min) to the temple turn-off

Famed as a centre of *seonmudo* (선무도), a Zen-based martial art, the simple temple of **Golgulsa** sits above some delicious-looking countryside. The walk up from the spur road is already quite inspiring; the track heads past a teahouse before rising into the small complex, from where it becomes even steeper – the place is backed by a sixth-century Buddha, carved into a cliff navigable on some short but precipitous paths. Though now protected by a monstrous modern structure, a clamber up to the Buddha is essential for the picture-perfect **view** alone; there are barriers to stop you from going over the edge. Those of an even steelier disposition may like to stay at the temple for some **martial arts practice** (visit their website for more information).

Girimsa

기림사 • Daily 9am–6pm • W3000 • Bus #100 or #150 from Gyeongju (every 30min; 45min); get off at the village of Andong-ni, and follow directions for Golgulsa, from where Girimsa is a further 5km walk

The temple of **Girimsa** receives few visitors on account of its location, 5km north of Golgulsa along the spur road. There are sometimes direct buses from Gyeongju – ask at the tourist office – but it's quite possible to make the long (and beautiful) walk here from Golgulsa: allow at least an hour. The road sees little traffic, and the journey is its own reward, with farmland-backed views and the occasional man walking his pet bird of prey while the surrounding rice paddies reverberate to the sound of thousands of frogs. After such majestic countryside, the slightly drab grounds of the temple itself may come as something of a letdown, but it's a quiet place rarely overrun with visitors. Notable are a couple of statues of the Goddess of Mercy, and a centuries-old bodhi tree.

The Underwater Tomb of King Munmu

문무대왕 수중릉 • 24hr • Free • Bus #150 from Gyeongju (1hr); get off as soon as you hit the coast

Within wading distance of the coast east of Gyeongju is the **Underwater Tomb of King Munmu**. Though the name befits a good novel, and it's popular with Korean tourists, the actual signature of rocky crags may come as an anticlimax; it's worth the trip, however, not only to see the beauty of the surrounding countryside but also to feast on delicious fresh seafood.

The king's final resting place lies literally a stone's throw from the coast. In his lifetime, Munmu achieved the first unification of the Korean peninsula, reasoning that the power of his united forces would better repel any invasion from the Japanese. On his deathbed, and still clearly concerned by the Nipponese threat, he asked to have his ashes scattered on the offshore rocks, believing that he would then become a **sea dragon**, offering eternal protection to the country's coast. Just 1km inland you'll be able to make out two giant stone pagodas, 13m high, which mark the former site of **Gameunsa** (감은사), a temple built on the orders of Munmu's son, Sinmun, in order to provide his sea-dragon father an inland retreat along the now-dry canal.

You may be lucky enough to witness one of the banana-heavy **shamanist ceremonies** that occasionally take place on the beach, honouring spirits of the local seas. Lining the beach are several **fish restaurants**, and it's possible to spend the night at one of several local **minbak**.

Oksan Seowon

옥산 서원 • Daily 9am–8pm • Free • Bus #203 from Gyeongju (10 daily, 1hr)

After enjoying the Silla-era delights in and around Gyeongju, you can leap forward in time to the **Joseon dynasty** by making a trip 30km north of town to **Oksan Seowon**, a Confucian school and shrine established in 1572 under the rule of King Seonjo. During this period Confucianism was the primary system of belief, particularly for the *yangban* aristocracy. However, most such places were closed in the 1870s at a time of social upheaval, and many were destroyed, making Oksan one of the oldest in the country, and quite possibly the most enjoyable to visit (though tiny Dosan Seowon near Andong gives it a run for its money, see p.172). It was dedicated to **Yi Eon-jeok** (1491–1533), a Confucian poet, **scholar** and all-round theological handyman who, while not as revered as his contemporaries Yi-Yi (see box, p.224) or Toegye (see box, p.172), certainly exerted an influence on neo-Confucian thought.

Now restored, following years of neglect and the occasional fire, the complex still manages to create a gentle atmosphere in keeping with its original function as a place of study and reflection, helped by the stream bubbling away below, as well as the gorgeousness of the surrounding countryside and the surprisingly low number of visitors. It's also home to a copy of the **Samguk Sagi**, the only concise records of the Three Kingdoms period (albeit one that seems to be biased towards the Silla dynasty).

Just a short walk beyond Oksan Seowon is Yi Eon-jeok's former abode at **Dongnakdang**. Some of his descendants still live in the cramped compound, which appears be hiding under the skirt of a large tree, and is every bit as tranquil as the academy itself. Further ahead again are **Jonghyesa**, a temple famed for its curiously shaped pagoda, and **Dodeokam**, a tiny hermitage with a view balanced high up on the rocks. All are just about within walking distance of each other, though considering the rather poor bus connections from Gyeongju, it may be best to stay the night near Oksan Seowon – there's a motel and a few *minbak* around the academy, and a few places to eat.

Yangdong Folk Village

양동 민속 마을 • Officially open daily 9am–6pm, though in practice 24hr • W4000, free outside official visiting hours • Bus #200-208, #212 or #217 from Gyeongju (frequent; 40min), then a signposted 2km walk

Korea has a number of "**folk villages**", a product of Park Chung-hee's desire to keep alive rural traditions at a time when large-scale economic growth was smothering the nation in concrete. Usually they consist of a rural group of houses and associate buildings; some openly exist for show alone, while others are living, breathing communities whose denizens work the local fields, rewarded for their enforced deprivation in terms of urban amenities with governmental subsidy. **Yangdong Folk Village**, tucked into a countryside fold near the village of Angang-ni, is one of the best in the country, and home to some real history – one reason behind its World Heritage status, received in 2010. Dating from the 1400s, this was once a thriving community of **yangban**, the aristocracy that ruled the country during the Joseon dynasty. Yi Eon-jeok, the great Confucian scholar to whom Oksan Seowon (see p.190) was dedicated, was born here in 1491; his life and the academy's history are relayed on information boards. As you walk around, try to suspend belief and imagine yourself back in nineteenth-century Korea (though it probably smells much more pleasant now). Some buildings are permanently open, and you may even be lucky enough to be invited into a private house.

Tongdosa

통도사 • Daily 8.30am–5.30pm • W3000 • ⓦ tongdosa.or.kr • Regular buses from Gyeongju (bus #12, #63 or #67; every 10min; 1hr 30min) and Busan (every 20min; 1hr)

Well worth a visit if you are zooming between Gyeongju and Busan, **Tongdosa** is one of Korea's three "Jewel Temples" (the others being Songgwansa and Haeinsa; see p.227 and p.177), and as such one of the most heralded in the land. It's a truly captivating place, especially around sunset, when its various buildings fall into a darkness amplified by their setting, shoehorned into a tight valley. From the entrance, it's a twenty-minute walk to the temple itself, along a gorgeous path that's illuminated after sunset with picturesque stone lanterns.

Part of the local **Jogye** sect, Tongdosa has been in existence since the mid-seventh century – long enough to pick up a few interesting quirks. Firstly, the candle is said to have stayed alight this whole time; easier to verify with your own eyes is the fact that there's no Buddha in the main hall. Rather, the main subject of veneration is a hall housing **sani**, a crystal-like substance said to be created inside the bodies of pure monks. Of course, it's not on public display. Lastly, take a look at the drum and bell tower: you'll see two of all four instruments (wooden fish, brass gong, drum and bell), rather than the more usual one. Despite its age, only the Daeungjeon hall withstood the Japanese attacks of the 1590s. However, most other buildings have been reconstructed with consummate care, and look rather beautiful.

The semi-rural location may tempt you to stay the night, and you'll have no problems finding a motel; their neon signs start right outside the temple entrance.

Ulleungdo

울릉도

With island groups dotted all around Korea's southern and western coasts, you may feel tempted to forgo the three-hour ferry ride to a small turret of land between Korea and Japan, and head instead to a closer isle. However, this would be a mistake – **ULLEUNGDO**, covered in a rich, green cloak of trees and fringed with juniper, is refreshingly unspoilt and simply stunning. Its volcanic origin and the flora splashed around on its nutritious soils mark it out as a mini Jeju, but, while increasingly popular with Korean travellers, Ulleungdo's isolation has kept it largely free from the ravages of mass tourism. Its armies of middle-aged Korean tourists are here mainly due to its proximity to **Dokdo**, an even smaller speck of land claimed by both Korea and Japan, and a focus of nationalistic demonstrations (see box, p.194). With no chain stores or five-star hotels, and just one bumpy main road tracing a vague parallel to the coast, the only time that the island's pulse seems to quicken is in the half-hour window surrounding ferry arrivals, when *ajummas* race around trying to draw tourists back to their *minbak* accommodation.

Few islands in Korea can provide as spectacular an arrival as Ulleungdo's main settlement, **Dodong-ni**, whose port makes a sudden appearance in a sumptuous pirate-like cove hidden and encircled by precipitous mountains, and squeezed in on both sides by the valley walls. Ulleungdo's second main settlement, **Jeodong-ni**, lies just up the coast, and is slightly smaller, but relatively open and rather different in character. These two villages, both an untidy but undeniably appealing mishmash of *minbak* and fish restaurants, give guests a taste of Ulleungdo island is like. **Naribunji** is a farming area of tremendous beauty to the north of the island, whose flatness will come as a great surprise to those who've travelled the bumpy coastal road to get there. On the way, picturesque fishing settlements dot the coast, while there's some

4

DOKDO

Ninety kilometres east of Ulleungdo lies a remote, straggly bunch of rocks, a small archipelago that seems to be good for little bar fishing, fighting and assertions of national identity. **Dokdo** (독도) to the Koreans, **Takeshima** (竹島) to the Japanese, it is claimed by both nations, and like the East Sea/Sea of Japan dispute (see box, p.158), the issue is unlikely to be resolved any time soon. The problem centres on political rivalry resulting from Korea's Japanese occupation, which lasted from 1910 until the end of World War II – Koreans tend to take even the slightest whiff of neo-imperialism quite seriously.

In the decades following the war, a number of **armed confrontations** took place in and around the islands, but after things eventually died down Korea took the upper hand, and built a wharf, a lighthouse and a helicopter-landing pad, around which are stationed a couple of permanent residents. In 2004, Korea issued a set of stamps featuring the islands; Japan took this as a claim of ownership, and a couple of years later sent two ships to Dokdo on an unauthorized survey mission. After protracted talks, Japan agreed to suspend the survey, but shortly afterwards Korea sent in ships to do exactly the same thing.

Today, **right-wing elements** in Korea use Dokdo in promotional materials, and the islands have become the focal point of a new nationalist wave. A few of the biggest mobile telecom operators in the country recently built communications towers on the island (totally for show, given the puny local population) and flag-waving ferry-loads of Korean tourists regularly make the journey across from Pohang on the mainland.

It's quite possible for foreign travellers to do likewise, but few choose to take the **ferry tours** from Ulleungdo (March–Nov; 2 or 3 daily; W45,000). The only form of access, if you're even allowed to disembark, is a spiral staircase with one step for each day of the year; after panting your way to the top you'll come out at the island's one lofty "town" (population: 2). A half-hour later, you're on the boat back out again – without the bombastic fervour, it's not exactly a thrilling trip.

good **hiking** to be enjoyed around the rugged, volcanic peaks that rise up in the centre of the island, almost totally untouched by modern life.

Dodong-ni

도동리

Though still just a village in population terms, **DODONG-NI** is the largest settlement on Ulleungdo and its main port, and as a result houses most of the island's overnight guests. However, despite the visitor numbers, it has remained surprisingly true to its old ways. The atmospheric village sits in a tight valley up from the ferry terminal, its few roads all heading uphill past a looping parade of *minbak*, small shops and raw-fish restaurants. There are few sights as such, but many visitors find themselves heading to a **lighthouse** to the east of town, which can be reached on a number of routes; the most scenic is the half-hour walk around the jagged coast from the ferry terminal. You can walk a short way on the opposite side of the terminal, but all you'll find here – if you're lucky – are a couple of fish snack shacks.

Following any one of Dodong-ni's upward trails from the ferry terminal will bring you, after what may seem like a never-ending climb, to the island's main "coastal" road. Turn left from the village exit, then immediately right, and you'll find **Daewonsa** (대원사), a tiny temple that marks the beginning of most hikes into the interior (see box opposite).

Dokdo Museum

독도 박물관 • Museum daily 9am–6pm • Free • Cable car W7500 return

If you head uphill from the ferries and stick to the left, you'll eventually come across a sign pointing to the **Dokdo Museum**, which together with an adjacent historical museum forms part of a small park. The former is the most interesting, as it details the Korean claim on Dokdo, a tiny scrawl of rock east of Ulleungdo (see box above). Also in the park is a "healthy water" spring (the metallic taste presumably proof of some kind of goodness), while those who still have some energy after the climb can bounce off any remaining calories on the see-saw at the very top. The walk up is quite a slog, and most who make the climb are heading to the base of a **cable car**, ready to be whisked up a nearby peak to take in some wonderful views: on clear days, you may be able to see Dokdo across the seas.

Jeodong-ni

저동리

A short taxi ride – or a half-hour walk – away from Dodong-ni is **JEODONG-NI**. Open-plan and spread out along a harbour, rather than wedged into a valley, it's something like a flattened version of its neighbour; while Dodong hasn't exactly been ravaged by tourism, here you'll see far fewer visitors, fewer *minbak*, and therefore an atmosphere more in keeping with the general nature of the island. It's the kind of place where you can idle away a fair few hours doing nothing at all.

The **harbour** is a great place for a walk, and is full of fishing boats dangling dozens of high-wattage bulbs, used to lure squid to their doom. To its right-hand side is a ramshackle group of corrugated metal cabins hanging precariously from the hillside; from here there's a good view of the harbour, and the tall finger of stone that protrudes through its outer wall, called "**Candlestick Rock**", the village's defining landmark. You can take a stroll up to the rock, on the way to the harbour passing two **large concrete penguins** whose decidedly phallic appendages are used to load material onto waiting boats – if you can see one in action, it's likely to be the funniest moment of your stay.

4

Naribunji

나리분지 • Take the coastal road bus and get off at Cheonbu (천부), where a 4WD will be waiting to take passengers over the hill to Naribunji (W1000)

To the north of the island lies a geographic anomaly. **Naribunji** is literally the only flat space on Ulleungdo, a dreamy patchwork of fields entirely encircled by mountains; it's a fantastic place to base yourself and spend a day or two walking through fields, taking in the surrounding forest, or doing absolutely nothing. It's also a good start or finish point for a **hiking trip** up and over the mountain; you may notice cable-car wires heading up into the hills, but unfortunately this service is for the use of local military only.

ARRIVAL AND DEPARTURE   ULLEUNGDO

Due to the absence of an airport on the island, there's only one way to arrive – by **ferry**. At the time of writing, all services were using the port at the main settlement of Dodong-ni, but plans have long been afoot to make a larger terminal elsewhere on the island. Ferry schedules were also in a constant state of flux – double-check with any tourist office before heading out.

From Pohang Most travellers get here from Pohang (포항), a large but uninteresting city near Gyeongju on the mainland's eastern coast. Services leave each morning at 9.50am (3hr; W70,000), returning at 4pm. The terminal at Pohang is a short taxi journey from the train station or either bus terminal; fortunately, the ferry

HIKING ULLEUNGDO

Wherever you are on the island, you're likely to see the sea on one side, and a group of verdant peaks hovering over you on the other. These unspoilt, richly forested slopes offer some wonderful **hiking** opportunities, and fortunately the walk up to the main summit, **Seonginbong** (984m), and back can be done in one day. There are several paths into and around the interior, but the main access point is just north of Dodong-ni, near Daewonsa, a small temple. A spur-road just before the temple leads uphill to the right, marking the start of a clammy 4.1km walk to the top. From here, you can either turn back, or make your way further north to the opposite trailhead at Naribunji, 4.5km from the summit. Trails are well signposted, though as there's almost nothing en route, be sure to bring water and snacks.

bay is one of the quieter, more pleasant areas in a generally ugly city, and if you're unlikely to arrive in time for the ferry you can stay at one of several motels around the terminal. Alternatively, it's possible, with an early start, to wake up in Gyeongju and make it to Pohang in time to catch the ferry – be sure to arrive at the terminal before 9am. Note that the ferry has no windows on economy level, and will usually smell of *kimchi* – those likely to suffer sea-sickness should splurge the extra W20,000 for first class.

From Donghae A daily service (either 8.20am or 9am; 3hr; W60,500) leaves for Ulleungdo from the Mukho (묵호) terminal near Donghae (동해) in Gangwon province. It's the closest port to Seoul, and the earliest express buses (followed by a taxi ride) should have you at the port in time.

GETTING AROUND

By bus Getting around the island is harder than you might expect – the coastal road runs in a "U" rather than a circle, ending in the northeast of the island, and just seven daily buses (W1000–1500) bump their way around, making it impossible to use them for more than a couple of sights per day.

Tours More convenient than public transport are the daily bus tours (4hr; W20,000) that leave from the ferry terminal; there'll be a scramble for the sea-side seats. It's also possible to take one of the round-island ferry tours (2hr; W25,000) which run six times a day in the summer, and twice a day at other times. Lastly, it's also possible to take a taxi tour for around W120,000 for the day.

INFORMATION

Tourist information There's a small office just uphill from the ferry terminal – where the water stops, look to your left. Though you'll be lucky to find an English-speaker here, staff will be able to hunt down accommodation across the island, and arm you with the requisite maps and pamphlets. The island's website (⊛ ulleung.go.kr) is also worth a look.

Money One very important thing to consider on Ulleungdo is money – those with non-Korean bank cards won't have much luck here, though the island's few banks may be able to exchange foreign cash.

ACCOMMODATION

Korea's developers must have a fear of long ferry rides – Ulleungdo is almost entirely devoid of modern **accommodation**, bar one tourist hotel and a few overpriced motels in the main settlements, Dodong-ni and Jeodong-ni. Every building in Dodong-ni seems to have **minbak** rooms, and these can also be found in Jeodong-ni and other settlements. You won't need to go hunting for offers, as elderly women will scream them at you on your walk up from the ferry. A fair price for a room sleeping two is usually around W30,000 in off season and W70,000 in peak summer months; don't be afraid to see a couple, or to play the *ajummas* off against each other. Heading around the island, there are a few tiny settlements where it's possible to stay, but the best by far is **Naribunji** in the north: there's a campsite here, as well as a few *minbak*.

DODONG-NI

Seonginbong Motel 송인봉 모텔 Dodong-ni 26 ☎054 791 2078. Just up from the ferries on the right-hand side of the road you'll find best motel in the village, though the quality and accessibility mean that it's often packed with tour groups, and the price is accordingly a little high. **W50,000**

Ulleung Hotel 울릉 모텔 Dodong-ni 263-1 ☎054 791 6611. This is the one official tourist hotel in the village, but not too overpriced, especially when the off-peak discounts kick in, and some of the more expensive rooms are colossal. Walking up from the ferries, keep on the right-hand side, and you'll eventually see the hotel up some stairs to your right. There's a good restaurant on the ground floor, and another, the *Eddiang* (see opposite), underneath. **W90,000**

JEODONG-NI

★**Motel Jeil** 모텔 제일 Jeodong-ni 252 ☎054 791 2637. Set back from the seafront, next to a small park visible from the waterfront, this is the best of Jeondong-ni's motley selection of accommodation. Rooms are surprisingly large and well appointed, and some have pretty sea or mountain views; there's also an attached sauna, in which you can take a scrub for a few thousand won. **W45,000**

ELSEWHERE

Dae-a Resort 대아 리조트 Sadong-ni 302-1 ☎054 791 8800. The most comfortable place to stay on the island by far, with stylish (if surprisingly small) rooms and good sea views, but little going on around it. **W200,000**

Neulpureun Sanjang 대아 리조트 늘푸른 산장 Nari 49 ☎054 791 8181. A standout among the several *minbak* of the Naribunji area, doubling as a good restaurant. At least one of the family members can speak English, though she may have to translate by phone if away from the island. **W40,000**

EATING

There are plenty of **restaurants** in Dodong-ni and Jeodong-ni, mostly centred around creatures culled from the sea, though less fishy things are available – the island's most famous edible product is, in fact, **pumpkin taffy**. Note that most places shut early (ie, before 9pm). In good weather, a few **fish shacks** cling limpet-like to the cliffs near Dodong-ni's ferry terminal, and there's a more permanent upper-floor parade above the fish shack in Jeodong-ni; W30,000 per person should be enough for a belly full of fish. Those wanting something more Western can make use of small **bakeries** in both of the main villages.

99 Sikdang 99 식당 Dodong-ni 150-6 ☎054 791 9919. This friendly restaurant, in the very centre of Dodong-ni, has whipped up an army of fans following appearances on Korean TV. Prices have stayed low, and there's an English menu of sorts, including spicy fish soup (W20,000), steamed rice with mussels, and the house special – spicy grilled squid known as *ojingeo bulgogi*

(W15,000). All meals come with seasonal side dishes. Daily 8am–11pm.
Eddiang 에띠앙 Dodong-ni 262-5 ☎054 791 8484. Located under the *Ulleung Hotel*, this homely place offers reasonably priced spaghetti, steak and pizza for W15,000 or so – the perfect respite from the ubiquitous fish restaurants. Daily 10.30am–11pm.

Busan
부산

Tell any Korean that you're about to visit **BUSAN**, and just watch their face light up – if one were to run a national census asking where everyone would most like to live, Korea's second city is likely to wind up in first place. "Seoul by the sea", or so the saying goes, Busan is by turns brackish, glamorous, clumsy and charismatic, and prides itself on simply being different from the capital. It has beaches, for a start – **Haeundae** is by far the most popular in the land, and quite a sight with its attendant high-rise buildings and five-star hotels forming a modern-day amphitheatre of sorts. The connection to the sea is also evident at the city's other major draw – **Jagalchi**, the most renowned fish market in the country. Busan is also the world's fifth-largest container **port** – its salty fringes tumble away into a colourful, confetti-like jumble of corrugated containers. In the evenings, the setting sun throws these ships into cool silhouette on a sea of gold, and the youth come out to paint the town red.

Indeed, it could be said that the locals alone make this city worth a visit: more characterful than those from the capital, Busanites talk almost as fast as their city moves, spouting provincial slang in a distinctive staccato that many foreigners initially mistake for Japanese. In fact, some locals aren't actually Korean at all – head across the road from the train station and you'll find a fascinatingly seedy district populated by **Russians**, **Chinese** and **Filipinos**.

Brief history

Even before it became the whirring economic dynamo that it is today, Busan played a pivotal role in the country's history. Though it was once part of the short-lived **Gaya kingdom** swallowed whole by the Silla dynasty (see box, p.180), it was at that time little more than a collection of fishing villages. In the fifteenth century it benefitted from its proximity to Japan, when a trade treaty opened it up as a port to international trade – up until that point, most goods had been leaving the area as loot on pirate ships. This competitive advantage promptly swung around and hit Busan squarely in the face when the city was attacked by the Japanese in 1592; under the astute leadership of **Admiral Yi Sun-shin** (see box, p.224) damage was limited, but still devastating.

Outside Busan's largest museum (see p.201) is a stone "stele of anti-compromise", whose Chinese characters read "All countrymen are hereby warned that anyone who does not fight against the Western barbarians is committing an act of treachery". Little

BUSAN

Seobu Intercity Bus Terminal & Gimhae International Airport

Hopo
Geumgeok
Dongwon
Yulli
Hwanmyeong
Sujeong
Namsaanjeong Mandeok
Sukdeung
Deokcheon

Beomeosa
Geumjeong Sanseong

Heosimcheong
Cable Car

GEUMJEONG-GU
Busan National University
Pusan National University
Jangjeon-dong

Nopo-dong Busan Central Bus Terminal
Beomeosa
Namsan-dong
Dusil
Guseo-dong

Oncheonjang
Myeongnyun-dong
Seodong
DONGNAE-GU
Dongnae
Minam
Sajik
Suam Nakmin
Myeongjang
Chungnyeolsa

Banyeo Agricultural Market
Geumsa
Seokdae

Dong-Busan College
Youngsan University

Sajik Sports Complex
World Cup Stadium
Sport Complex
Geoje
Busan National University of Education
Yeonsan-dong

City Hall
Yangjeon
Busan Global Center
Baesan
Mulmangol
Mangmi

Spa Land Centum City
Centum City
Busan Museum of Modern Art
Haeundae
Jung-dong
Jangsan

SEOMYEON
Bujeon-dong
Seomyeon
Jeonpo
Suyeong
Millak
Dongbaek
HAEUNDAE
Haeundae Beach
SEE 'HAEUNDAE' MAP

Dongeui University
Bunam
Gaya
Gaegeum
Naengjeong
Beomil-dong
Munjeon
Geumnyeonsan
Gwangan
Gwangalli Beach
Diamond Bridge

NAM-GU
Jwacheon-dong
Munhyeon
Daeyeon
Namcheon
Kyungsung University

Beomnaegol
Jigegol
Motgol
Busan Museum
UN Memorial Cemetery

Busanjin
Choryang-dong

SEO-GU
Dongdaeshin-dong
Toseong-dong
Busan Station
Busan Train Station

Jagalchi
Seodoshin-dong
JUNG-GU
Jungang-dong
Ferry Terminals
Nampo-dong
Jagalchi Fish Market
SEE 'CENTRAL BUSAN' MAP

Yeongdo

Taejongdae Park
Pebble Beach

N

BARS & CLUBS
Basement	1
Club Fix	2
Guri Bar	3
Vinyl Underground	5
Yung Ggom	4

SUBWAY LINES
———	Line 1
———	Line 2
———	Line 3
———	Line 4

0   2
kilometres

RESTAURANTS
Hong Kong Banjeom	1
Johnson Family Rib	2

ACCOMMODATION
Kyungsung Hostel	2
Lotte Hotel	1

Jeju Island   Japan

BUSAN ORIENTATION

With buildings sprawling across the whole horizon, filling the gaps between the city's mountains and swamping some of the smaller hills entirely, Busan can be quite confusing for the first-time visitor. The de facto centre of the city, known as **Jung-gu**, is the area heading south from the train station down to Jagalchi Fish Market; on the way, you'll pass the ferry terminals, Busan Tower and Nampodong's maze of shops, cinemas, markets and restaurants. A short way north of the train station is trendy **Seomyeon**, a brand-name shopper's paradise, but also home to some of the earthiest restaurants, and excellent nightlife. A way east of here you'll find **Haeundae**, a fascinating beach area that's home to rich Koreans and five-star hotels, but still manages to retain much of its fishing village character.

did they know that Korea would eventually be consumed by its closest neighbour – the Japanese annexed the peninsula in 1910 – then fight a bloody civil war, only to be bailed out both times by said barbarians. Busan was at the forefront of the **Korean War**; indeed, for a time, the city and its surrounding area were the only places left under Allied control, the North Koreans having occupied the peninsula up to what was known as the **Pusan Perimeter** (Pusan being the correct romanization at the time). At this point, up to four million refugees from elsewhere on the peninsula crowded the city, before **General Douglas MacArthur** made a bold move at Incheon (see box, p.120) to reverse the tide of the war.

4

Downtown

The city's **downtown** spreads south from the train station to Jagalchi Fish Market. This area, often referred to as **Jung-gu**, is dripping with character but rather run-down. Head across the main road from Busan train station and you'll come to **Shanghai Street**, a pedestrianized "Chinatown" road filled with restaurants, and marked with the oriental gates you'll find in all such areas. This joins **Texas Street**, which has yet more places to eat – predominantly Russian and Filipino – but it's not all about the food. This area rivals Haeundae for the title of most cosmopolitan part of the city, though it has an entirely different air: whereas Haeundae draws in beach bums and the convention crowd, here you may find yourself rubbing shoulders with Russian sailors, American soldiers, Filipino restaurateurs and lost tourists, and it makes a great place to people-watch.

Busan Modern History Museum

부산 근대 역사관 • Tues–Sun 9am–6pm • Free • ⓦ modern.busan.go.kr • Jungang subway (line 1)

A relative newcomer to the city's roster of sights is the **Busan Modern History Museum**, set inside a building that dates back to the Japanese colonial period. Attractive on the outside, its innards are interesting too, charting the more recent episodes of Busan's history, including the opening of its port (with a recreated shopping street from the time), the havoc caused during wartime, and the effects of the economic boom.

Busan Tower

부산 타워 • Daily 8am–10pm • W4000 • Nampo subway (line 1)

Rising over Nampodong is **Busan Tower**, a structure affording **excellent views** of the city's boat-filled surroundings. This long-standing city landmark is now crying out for renovation, though the viewing levels at the top have been turned into a café of sorts. The tower is the crowning glory of **Yongdusan Park** (용두산 공원), a popular area for walkers. The top of the park is already high enough for good views – take an early

CENTRAL BUSAN

ACCOMMODATION
Blueboat Hostel	4
Commodore	2
Hwangeum Motel	3
Toyoko Inn	1

CAFÉS & RESTAURANTS
Amby's	1
Jagalchi Market	6
Mr Choi Sushi	3
O'Sulloc	4
Wonhyangjae	2
Yugane	5

BAR
Three Monkeys	1

morning walk to the top, buy some instant *ramyeon* from the convenience store and watch the sun break through the mist.

Jagalchi Fish Market

자갈치 시장 • Daily 8am–10pm • Free • Jagalchi subway (line 1)

Every single person in Korea knows about **Jagalchi**, the largest and most popular **fish market** in the country. Wonderfully atmospheric, it's been used as a set in numerous movies and dramas. Mid-October is the best time to visit, when the **Jagalchi festival** offers a rare shot at hands-on fish preparation and a whole slew of freebies to munch. If you're just here on a regular day, you'll see that it's more a place in which to consume than simply somewhere to look around (see p.206 for some advice).

Yeongdo

영도 • Bus #88 from Seomyeon via the train station and ferry terminals, or #30 from Nampodong

Facing Jagalchi Fish Market in downtown Busan is **Yeongdo** – technically an island, though the double-bridge connection to downtown Busan makes it feel more like a peninsula. There's not much to see here, but a walk around **Taejongdae** (태종대), a pretty park at the far end of the island, is worthwhile. From the main entrance, regular train-shaped shuttle buses run to **Pebble beach**, a rocky outcrop at the very end of the island, but as roads are otherwise empty it makes an appealing walk, particularly in the evenings, when the sun sets over the mainland peninsula west of Yeongdo.

Nam-gu
남구

Nam-gu, a district splayed out between Busan station and Haeundae, holds a couple of sights relating to the city's fascinating history: the city's main **museum**, and a **cemetery** where many of the Allied forces who died in the Korean War were laid to rest. Also in the area are **Kyungsung University**, famed for its nightlife; and **Gwangalli beach**, a smaller, less interesting version of Haeundae.

Busan Museum
부산 박물관 • Daily 9am–8pm • Free • Daeyeon subway (line 2); bus #68 from Seomyeon, #139 from Haeundae or #134 from Busan station

A short walk south of Daeyeon subway station, **Busan Museum** charts the local area's history and its remains from the Neolithic era to the present day; exhibits include a **gilt-bronze crown** once worn by a Silla king, and a **standing Bodhisattva** of similar age and material. More recent history is generally presented in diorama form, with one of the more compelling displays showing Busan station in the 1920s; the building has, of course, changed somewhat. Unfortunately, the more modern part of the exhibit leaves a rather bad taste in the mouth, stemming from the sad inevitability of the museum's choice to focus on the Japanese occupation rather than the Korean War. There's just a single wall commemorating the tens of thousands of foreign troops who died here when Korean fought Korean – a pattern repeated all over the country, in classrooms as well as museums, but particularly galling here since many of the fallen are lying just outside in the **UN Memorial Cemetery**.

The UN Memorial Cemetery
UN기념 공원 • Daily 9am–6pm • Free • Daeyeon subway (line 2); bus #68 from Seomyeon, #139 from Haeundae or #134 from Busan station

Adjacent to the museum grounds lies the **UN Memorial Cemetery**, where you'll find over two thousand dead soldiers from Britain, Turkey, Canada, Australia, the Netherlands, France, the USA, New Zealand, South Africa and Norway; many more, of course, were never found, and those from Belgium, Ethiopia, Colombia, Thailand, Greece, India and the Philippines, as well as the vast majority of Americans, were repatriated. A photographic exhibition on site provides a small, mute tribute, and the grounds are welcoming and pretty. At 2pm on every second Saturday (the second and fourth of the month), there are moving ceremonies featuring marching bands and rifle salutes.

4

Gwangalli beach
광안리 해수욕장 • Gwangan subway (line 2)

At 1.4km in length, **Gwangalli beach** is a shorter, marginally less popular version of Haeundae; locals still arrive here in droves, as do students from the nearby university. Its most famous feature is actually located off the coast – the Gwangan suspension bridge, usually referred to as the **Diamond Bridge**, which is certainly quite dazzling when the sun has gone down.

Haeundae
해운대

On the eastern side of Busan, and about 25 minutes away from downtown by subway, is **Haeundae**, without a doubt the most popular **beach** in Korea. Whether it's the best or not is open to question – in the summer it draws in families, teens and bronzed beach bums by the bucketload, though at only 2km in length, space here is tighter than a Brazilian's Speedos, while the sand gradually becomes a composite of cigarette butts, firework ash and other debris. Like it or not, it's an interesting place – Haeundae is not just the name of the beach, but also its surrounding area, one that attracts all sorts throughout the year. The **Pusan Film Festival**, one of the biggest in Asia, rolls into town each October with a cast of directors, actors, wannabes and

HAEUNDAE

Museum of Modern Art

(S) *Jungdong*

Haeundae Train Station

Megabox Cinema

(S) *Haeundae*

HAEUNDAEBYEONNO

HAEUNDAERO

GUNAMNO

Grand Hotel

Busan Aquarium

Haeundae Beach

Dongbaek Park

0   500
metres

■ BARS & CLUBS

Club Tao	2
Sharky's	1
Thursday Party	3

■ ACCOMMODATION

Ace Motel	2
Paradise	4
Popcorn Hostel	1
Seacloud	3
Sunset	5
The Westin Chosun	6

● CAFÉS & RESTAURANTS

Namaste	4
Obanjang	3
OPS	1
Pojangmacha Chon	5
Sharky's	2

hangers-on; hungry Koreans come to chow down on **raw fish** and throw back a few bottles of *soju* from the comfort of a plastic chair; affluent expats, trendy locals and the international convention crowd populate the many luxury apartments and **five-star hotels**; and youngsters come from all over the country to spend a starry night on the beach. If you catch it at the right time, Haeundae can be quite magical.

The **beach** itself is good for swimming; tubes and boats are also available to rent, and the purchase of puny, multi-round fireworks is near compulsory. At the end of the beach, past a clutch of raw-fish stalls and behind the *Westin Chosun*, there's **Dongbaek Park**, a pleasant place for a stroll, skate or bike ride.

Busan Aquarium

부산 아쿠아리움 • Mon–Thurs 10am–8pm, Fri–Sun 9am–10pm • W24,000 • ⓦ busanaquarium.com • Haeundae subway (line 2)

Sitting pretty on the beach is **Busan Aquarium**, where three million litres of water host up to thirty thousand fish. Penguins and crocodiles are also on the complex, and there's a touch pool for the kids. There's an underwater tunnel for those who want to see fish from below, or you can pay an extra W5000 to ride a glass-bottomed boat and see them from above instead.

Busan Museum of Art

부산 시립 미술관 • Tues–Sun 10am–8pm • Free • ⓦ art.busan.go.kr • Museum of Art subway (line 2)

One subway stop away from Haeundae is the **Busan Museum of Art**, an excellent gallery that keeps its exhibitions fresh and interesting – no mean feat considering the fact that they're arrayed in umpteen halls across two main levels. Displays often seem to reference the sea, sometimes in a manner that feels a little forced.

Spa Land Centum City
스파랜드 센텀시티 • Daily 6am–midnight; no children under 12 allowed • Mon–Fri W12,000, Sat & Sun W14,000 • ⓦ shinsegae
.com • Centum City subway (line 2)
Built on the site of Busan's former airport (many locals wish that the new one was half
as convenient), **Centum City** is the city's latest urban mega-development, bankrolled by
the good folks at Shinsegae Corporation. The mall areas are typically bland, but it's
certainly worth swinging by the **Spa Land** section – the largest bathing facility in a
country absolutely full of them. Size is not the only difference, since the whole place
has been designed with a rare attention to detail – the outdoor footbaths are
particularly lovely, though the themed steam rooms look a bit cheesy.

Northern Busan
Most of the foreigners you'll see around Busan's **northern fringes** are international
students, or teachers, from Pusan National University. However, there are a few tourist
sights hereabouts – and, for once, they've nothing to do with water or the sea. Busan's
foremost temple, **Beomeosa**, can be found here, as well as a splendid **fortress**.

Beomeosa
범어사 • Daily 24hr • Free • ⓦ beomeo.kr • Beomeosa subway (line 1), then a 3km uphill walk or bus #90 (every 15min)
A half-hour subway ride to the north of central Busan is where you'll find one of the
best sights in the city. The temple of **Beomeosa**, dating from 678, occupies a
spectacular setting high above town and is a popular choice for foreigners looking to
templestay (see p.35). Despite the age of the complex, most of its buildings were built
much later, the result of the occasional fire or destruction during the Japanese invasion.
The first main gate, Iljumun, dates from 1781 and continues to carry its age well, the
eaves radiating rich colour from its four pillars. Ascending past a patch of bamboo,
you'll pass through four bearded guardians to the main concourse, and Daeungjeon,
the main hall and scene of fervent morning prayer. In the courtyard there's a three-
storey stone pagoda dating from the ninth century.

4

However, the main appeal of the place lies not in its buildings, but in its
mountainous setting. The forested slopes are impressive, and there's a surprising
preponderance of deciduous trees for a Korean mountain area – a beautiful sight in the
autumn. On the complex itself, smaller trees and shrubs lend their own spindly
nuances to an enchanting scene.

Geumjeong Sanseong
금정산성 • Daily 9am–6pm • Oncheonchang subway (line 1), then bus #203 or cable car (starts within walking distance of
station; W5000 return)
Looming above Beomeosa is **Geumjeong Sanseong**, a mountaintop fortress that's
popular with Busanese hikers at weekends, the sheer numbers of whom mean that it's
best by far to visit during the week. It was built in the early eighteenth century, far too
late to provide protection from the Japanese invasions of the 1590s, or the repeat
attacks of the following century. Though it fell into disrepair, much of the wall still
stands, as do the main gates. It's quite a walk up from Beomeosa, or a **cable car** can do
most of the work for you.

ARRIVAL AND DEPARTURE   BUSAN
Busan's unwieldy size means that the best way to arrive largely depends on exactly where you want to go. In general, most
prefer train to bus as the train station is right in the centre of the city, whereas the two main bus terminals are on the fringes.

By plane Gimhae Airport lies in a flat estuary area around
15km west of the city centre. There are an extraordinary
number of flights to Jeju (every 20min; 50min) and Seoul

(every 30min; 55min), as well as services to Japan,
Thailand, China, Vietnam, Taiwan, the Philippines and
Cambodia. The airport has its own dedicated spur-line on

the subway system, but the limousine buses are faster if you want to get across the city to Haeundae. In addition, there are direct buses to the airport from most of the main cities in the Gyeongsang region.

By train Busan station forms the terminus of the Gyeongbu railway line, which starts in Seoul and hurtles through Daejeon and Daegu en route. The fantastic slow line from Seoul (see "Itineraries", pp.24-25) also finishes in Busan, just after it hits Haeundae station, out east by the beach. The station area is quite absorbing, and connected to the rest of the city by subway.

Destinations (Busan station) Daegu (every 10–30min; 45min); Daejeon (every 10–30min; 1hr 40min); Gyeongju (Singyeongju station; hourly; 25min); Seoul (every 10–30min; 2hr 45min).

Destinations (Haeundae station) Andong (3 daily; 3hr 30min); Danyang (2 daily; 5hr); Gyeongju (10 daily; 1hr 30min); Seoul (Cheongnyangni station; 2 daily; 7hr).

By bus Arriving in Busan by bus is not really recommended, unless you're heading somewhere specific near either of the two main terminals. The so-called "central terminal" is way to the north (Nogodan subway, line 1), and is actually made up of two separate stations – one express and one intercity, with the latter often referred to as the Dongbu

terminal. The Seobu terminal is way out west (Sasang subway, line 2).

Destinations (Central bus terminal) Andong (frequent; 3hr); Chuncheon (14 daily; 6hr); Daegu (frequent; 1hr 20min); Daejeon (frequent; 3hr 10min); Gangneung (10 daily; 5hr); Gwangju (frequent; 3hr 40min); Gyeongju (frequent; 50min); Incheon (11 daily; 4hr 30min); Jeonju (12 daily; 3hr 20min); Jinju (frequent; 2hr); Pohang (every 10min; 1hr 30min); Seoul (frequent; 4hr 30min); Sokcho (12 daily; 7hr); Yeosu (13 daily; 3hr 20min).

Destinations (Seobu bus terminal) Gwangju (frequent; 3hr 30min); Jinju (frequent; 1hr 30min); Mokpo (7 daily; 5hr 40min); Ssanggyesa (3 daily; 2hr); Tongyeong (frequent; 2hr); Wando (5 daily; 6hr 40min).

By ferry The most spectacular way to arrive into Busan is by sea, though, sadly, domestic connections have been curtailed of late. The city has two ferry terminals (one international, one domestic), both near Jungangdong subway station in the centre of town, just minutes from each other by foot. All international ferries head to Japan (see p.28), with the Fukuoka connection especially popular with *hagwon* teachers on visa runs; there are other ferries to Shimonoseki. The only domestic connections are to Jeju Island (7pm daily except Sun; 11hr; W47,000).

GETTING AROUND

By subway Busan's subway system now boasts three lines, with a light-rail spur heading to Gimhae airport. The city is divided into two sections (vaguely inner and outer); tickets cost W1300 for one section, W1500 for two.

By bus As with every Korean city, the bus system is comprehensive and convenient, but often incomprehensible for foreign travellers. Fares start at W1200.

By taxi Taxis start at W3000, but given Busan's size fares can stack up quickly.

INFORMATION

Tourist information For a city of such size, and with so many foreign visitors, Busan has a surprisingly poor network of information offices. The most useful one is in Busan train station (☎051 441 6565): you're unlikely to find any English-speakers at the offices in Haeundae and Seomyeon. Five-star hotels can come in very handy, but if you need some English-language information in a hurry,

it's best to call ☎1330 (add an area code if using a mobile phone – Busan's is ☎051).

Expat services The Busan Global Center (☎051 668 7900, ⓦbfia.or.kr) near Yangjeong subway (line 1) can come in handy for expats living in Busan – they run Korean classes, host lectures, help with banking, offer counselling and more.

ACCOMMODATION

Busan has plenty of choice at the top end of the accommodation range. The five-stars are almost all in **Haeundae**, the beach district to the east of the centre; it's by far the most interesting place to stay, but the motels here can get expensive on weekends and during summer, and cheaper places are disappearing. Elsewhere, there are cheap motels all over the city; if you want to go out at night you're best basing yourself in **Seomyeon** or around the **university** drinking areas (see p.207), whereas sightseers should head for the cheap areas around the **train station** or **ferry terminal**. There are now a few **hostels** kicking around, while those who want to save even more cash can get a night's sleep for less than W10,000 in a **jjimjilbang** (see p.35); two of the most convenient are *Vesta*, east of the main hotel district in Haeundae, and *Nokju* in central Seomyeon.

DOWNTOWN

★**Blueboat Hostel** 블루보트 호스텔 Donggwangdong 2-ga 10-4 ☎010 8511 9049, ⓦblueboat-hostel.com; Nampo subway (line 1);

map p.200. A tremendous new choice in the Nampodong neighbourhood, and possibly the most elegant hostel in the land – snazzy lighting in the huge common area and even, in what may be a world hostel first, a "powder room" for the ladies. The dorm rooms are fine, but the twins are poky for the price; all rates get cut a bit out of season. They've another venue out near Haeundae (check the site for details), but it's not quite as nice. Dorm beds W29,000, twins W72,000

Commodore 코모도 호텔 Jungguro 151 ☎051 466 9101; Busan station subway (line 1); map p.200. Visible from the port, this distinctive fusion of skyscraper and temple has acceptable rooms, and lies a short taxi ride from the main train station. The sliding windows are a nice feature, even more so given the views – Busan's crane-filled port on one side, and what passes for a Korean version of Naples on the other. However, many guests find the place as a whole a little overblown. W180,000

Hwangeum Motel 환금 모텔 Jungangdong 79-1 ☎051 463 3851; Jungangdong subway (line 1); map p.200. The pick of a dirt-cheap bunch in the appealingly rustic area near the ferry terminal, with acceptable en-suite rooms, a rambling layout and likeable owners. Take exit 17 from the station and turn left – it's just under the staircase. W25,000

★**Toyoko Inn** 토오코 인 Jungangdaero 196-gil 12 ☎051 466 1045, ⓦtoyoko-inn.com; Busan station subway (line 1); map p.200. Japan's biggest business hotel chain has arrived in Busan, conveniently landing just a few steps from the train station. If you've stayed at a *Toyoko* before you'll know what to expect – small but perfectly clean rooms, near-total silence, free bathrobe and slippers, and a decent breakfast... like a little trip to the Land of the Rising Sun. W70,000

HAEUNDAE

Ace Motel 에이스 모텔 Udong 544-9 ☎051 742 4777; Haeundae subway (line 2); map p.202. Motel prices in Haeundae have gone through the roof of late, but this place is usually pretty easy to haggle down to something respectable – all the more surprising when you consider that its colourful rooms are some of the most striking in the area. W90,000

Paradise 파라다이스 호텔 Jungdong 1408-5 ☎051 749 2111, ⓦparadisehotel.co.kr; Haeundae subway (line 2); map p.202. With widescreen TVs in the rooms, stylish lighting in the corridors and W8,000,000 suites, the *Paradise* has been carefully designed in a refreshingly modern style. It's a busy place with all manner of bars and restaurants, and there's even a boutique mall; the pine-fringed outdoor pool stays open year-round and has views over the beach – an absolute must. Try to stay in the newer main building, and book online for the best deals. W480,000

★**Popcorn Hostel** 팝콘 호스텔 11F Haeundaehaebyeonno 321 ☎1644 9540, ⓦpopcorn-hostel.com; Haeundae subway (line 2); map p.202. The best of the small glut of new Haeundae hostels, set way up on top of a high-rise building – there are stunning sea views from some rooms. The staff are great, the whole place looks chic, and you can run to the beach *sans* flip-flops. Dorm beds W25,000, private rooms W70,000

Seacloud 씨클라우드 호텔 Haeundaehaebyeonno 287 ☎051 933 1000, ⓦseacloudhotel.com; Haeundae subway (line 2); map p.202. Benefitting from a relaxed ambience hard to come by in Haeundae's other big hitters, this smart-but-friendly business-oriented hotel is home to a healthy number of long-term guests. There are substantial discounts in colder months, while in summer an outdoor pool opens up. W360,000

Sunset 선셋 비지니스 호텔 Jungdong 1391-66 ☎051 730 9900, ⓦsunsethotel.co.kr; Haeundae subway (line 2); map p.202. Stylish, hotel-like rooms with good views from certain parts of the building; the only thing lacking is good service. Prices often drop nearer W100,000 during the week; book online for discounts. W200,000

★**The Westin Chosun** 웨스틴 초선 호텔 Dongbaengno 61 ☎051 749 7428, ⓦwestin.com; Haeundae subway (line 2); map p.202. This Haeundae landmark provides great views of the beach, which comes to an abrupt end here. Though perfectly acceptable, rooms are surprisingly drab compared with the sleek lobby area, which includes an oh-so-trendy beach-facing bar, as well as an Irish "pub" that pulls a mean Guinness. Reserve through the website for the cheapest deals. W390,000

OTHER AREAS

Kyungsung Hostel 경성 호스텔 Daeyeondong 58-35 ☎010 9221 1014, ⓦkyunqsunghostel.com; Kyungsung University subway (line 2); map p.198. Bare-bones hostel with cheap prices and a great location: in a student party zone near Haeundae, and also within walking distance of a beach. Check-in can be a little confusing, since most of the rooms are in a completely different building to the reception, which doubles as a good bar. Dorms W15,000

Lotte Hotel 롯데 호텔 Gayadaero 772 ☎051 810 1000, ⓦlottehotelbusan.com; Seomyeon subway (lines 1 & 2); map p.198. Located in trendy Seomyeon, the small rooms and mall-like atmosphere found here are typical of the chain, which caters almost exclusively to shopaholics from Korea and other East Asian countries. The place is huge – as is the attached shopping mall. W545,000

EATING

Busan's cosmopolitan nature is reflected in its culinary options. One of the most interesting eating areas is opposite the train station – no five-star paradise, but rather a motley crew of snack bars catering to sailors and assorted night-crawlers. Here, "**Shanghai Street**" provides a wealth of safe but relatively expensive **Chinese** restaurants, before merging effortlessly into "**Texas Street**", home to a lower-key choice of outlets; despite the American name, the most appealing food here lies in the cheap, cheerful **Filipino** snack-halls. The area running from the station to Jagalchi Fish Market is uninspired, though Korean staples are easy to track down, while the student areas (see "Nightlife", opposite) are predictably cheap – take your pick from innumerable **meat houses** or *izakaya*-style **Japanese** restaurant-bars. If you're looking for something a little classier, head to one of the five-star hotels around **Haeundae** beach.

RESTAURANTS

DOWNTOWN

Amby's 암비스 Choryang 2-dong 486-1 ☎051 467 6206; map p.200; Busan station subway (line 1). The pick of the train station area's many Filipino restaurants, serving tasty (if smallish) Penoy dishes such as *adobo* chicken (W13,000), and *tocilog* (marinated pork; W6000). They also offer a selection of Russian staples – the borscht (W5000) is a winner. Daily 24hr.

★Jagalchi Market 자갈치 시장 Nampodong; Jagalchi subway (line 1); map p.200. One of Busan's foremost attractions (see p.200), this huge market can be utterly confusing for the average non-Korean (see p.39 for some advice on local seafood). Many of the outlets in the large indoor market have picture menus, or you could simple point at what you fancy (figure on at least W30,000 per head for a mixed platter). Easier on brain, palate and wallet are the fried slabs of tuna (참치; *chamchi*) served at the outdoor stalls (W5000 for four). Daily 8am–10pm.

Mr Choi Sushi 초이 초밥 Gwangbungno 73-1 ☎051 242 0331; Nampo subway (line 1); map p.200. Jagalchi can be intimidating for first-timers, who may prefer the comforting familiarity of Japanese-style sushi. This place is pretty good, with its W10,000 lunch sets particularly good value. Daily noon–3pm & 5–10pm.

Wonhyangjae 원향재 Choryangdong 561 ☎051 468 5220; Busan station subway (line 1); map p.200. This Chinese restaurant is one of several good options on "Shanghai Street". Meals are fairly pricey by Korean standards – figure on at least W15,000 per head – though simple rice and noodle dishes are delicious and cheap. Daily 11am–10pm.

Yugane 유가네 Nampodong 3-ga; map p.200. If you don't fancy raw fish, you could do worse than heading to this large, fresh hall, full to the brim in the evenings with the young, hungry and budget-conscious. Staff will do the necessary chopping and mixing on your table – meat and fried rice are yours for around W5500, or chicken *galbi* for W8000, and unlike most places that serve the latter, single diners are welcome. There are branches around the city, including one in Seomyeon. Daily 11am–11pm.

HAEUNDAE

★Namaste 나마스테 Udong 626-4 ☎051 746 1946; Haeundae subway (line 2); map p.202. Underground restaurant serving delectable Indian food. All of the main curry styles are on the menu (W12,000–15,000 per portion); the tandoori dishes are particularly recommended, as is the rare chance to try ginseng lassi. Daily noon–midnight.

Obanjang 오반장 Udong 542-11 626-4 ☎051 747 8085; Haeundae subway (line 2); map p.202. The most popular meat-joint on the strip, at the time of writing – especially the fairy-light-studded outdoor section. Meat portions cost around W9000 but are a little small, so you may have to order more than one per head. Daily noon–1am.

Pojangmacha Chon 포장마차촌 Udong; Haeundae subway (line 2); map p.202. A quintessential Korean

BUSAN FESTIVALS

Busan hosts an incredible number of **festivals**, and many of them are a little bit comical in nature – you may care to visit one dedicated to anchovy-rubbing or egg-rolling, for example.

Pusan International Film Festival (ⓦ piff.org). The most popular festival in town, PIFF takes place over a week or so each October. One of the biggest such events in Asia, it draws the cream of the continent's talent, and has recently expanded its scope to please non-mainstreamers too. Most of the action takes place around Nampodong and Haeundae, with the latter a great place to star-spot – you could even find yourself pitching ideas to a director over *soju*.

Busan Biennale (ⓦ busanbiennale.org). Interesting festival of contemporary art which takes place on even-numbered years, though in seemingly random months.

International Rock Festival (ⓦ rockfestival.co.kr). Busan's major music event takes place in early August on Dadaepo beach.

Polar Bear Swim Contest This competition sees participants splash through the cold Haeundae waters each January.

Mass-Media Cutting-Edge Marine Fireworks Festival. Worth mentioning for the name alone, this event sees things go bang over Gwangalli beach each November.

dining experience – raw fish and assorted seafood served up by an equally salty *ajumma*. Look for the tarpaulin-covered stands sheltering tanks of fish, and prepare your stomach – some of your prey may still be moving. Happily, all stalls now have English-language menus; everything seems to cost W20,000 per portion. Daily 6pm–midnight.

Sharky's 샤키스 Udong 1305 626-4 ☎ 010 4038 2907; Haeundae subway (line 2); map p.202. Primarily a bar (see p.208), but the great food on offer may drag you back the morning after – tempting hangover-busters include *huevos rancheros* (W13,000), beef *chimichangas* (W14,000) and a range of burgers. Mon–Thurs & Sun 6–11pm, Fri & Sat 6pm–1am.

SEOMYEON

Hong Kong Banjeom 홍콩반점 Bujeon 2-ga 502-25 ☎ 051 805 0410; Seomyeon subway (lines 1 & 2); map p.198. Cheap, delicious Korean takes on Chinese food – don't expect too many marks for authenticity. W4000 will buy you many of the dishes here, including black-bean noodles (짜장면), spicy squid soup (짬뽕) or fried dumplings (쿤만두). Daily 10am–10pm.

Johnson Family Rib 존슨네 치즈 등갈비 Gayadaero 784-gil 48 ☎ 1666 5848; Seomyeon subway (lines 1 & 2);

map p.198. At the time of writing, Korea's "in" dish was a cheesy take on *deung-galbi* (등-갈비) – the regular *galbi* (barbecued pork ribs), but served with the meat still on the bone, and a whole lot of mozzarella. This convivial place is the most popular of many such eateries serving the dish in the Seomyeon area – it's W13,000 per portion for the regular dish, and W9000 for the chicken option. Daily 11am–midnight.

CAFÉS AND TEAROOMS
DOWNTOWN

O'Sulloc 오설록 Gwangbongno 70 ☎ 051 246 5285; Nampo subway (line 1); map p.200. Korea's green-tea phenomenon shows no sights of abating, and this Jeju Island tea company (see p.200) has opened a café-like tearoom in Busan. Most people aren't here for the tea but for the green-tea lattes, tiramisu and *patbingsu* (a dessert made with red bean and shaved ice). Daily 8am–10pm.

HAEUNDAE

OPS Jung 1-dong 1394-82 ☎ 051 747 6886; Haeundae subway (line 2); map p.202. Heralded local bakery chain with branches across the city. This one in Haeundae is perhaps the most conveniently located, and great for coffee – don't leave without trying the delectable *pains au chocolats* (W2300). Daily 8am–11pm.

NIGHTLIFE

Busan has an excellent and varied **nightlife scene** – a single evening can see you sipping *soju* over raw fish at sunset, rubbing shoulders with Russian sailors near the train station, throwing back beer with students in one of the university areas, then dancing all night at a beachside hip-hop club. See the box below for some advice on which neighbourhood to pick.

DOWNTOWN

Three Monkeys 쓰리 먼키스 Gwanbongno ☎ 051 245 2160; Nampo subway (line 1); map p.200. Microbrewery named after the range of ales it sells – there are now actually four monkeys on offer for W7000 each, namely red, white and black, plus a "green" pilsner. Free nachos and garlic chips. Daily 5pm–2am.

HAEUNDAE

Club Tao 클럽타오 Jung 1-dong 1124-6 ☎ 1544 8030; Haeundae subway (line 2); map p.202. The owners describe this as a "bistro and beach" club – they do indeed offer good dining, as well as a wide spectrum of music including electro, house, funk and R&B. Entry W15,000 or so; more on party nights. Daily 9.30pm–6.30am.

BUSAN NIGHTLIFE: WHICH NEIGHBOURHOOD?

Busan's nightlife scene is spread in uneven clumps across various parts of the city – to avoid spending a small fortune on taxi fares, it's best to simply pick an area and hunker down for the night. The two main student areas – **Busan National University** to the north, and **Kyungsung University** west of Haeundae – are among the most interesting places to go out, and certainly the cheapest. Weekdays can be tame, but on weekends the partying is on until the wee hours. The same can be said for the two beach areas – **Haeundae** and **Gwangalli** – which cater to a more upmarket crowd, and throw a couple of clubs and cocktail bars into the mix; there's also the option of buying some cans at a convenience store and drinking on the beach. Central Busan is markedly less interesting: **Seomyeon** has a few clubs, though these can be full of soldiers, with fights breaking out on a regular basis, while the bars around **Busan station** tend to be populated with Russian prostitutes and men in the market for them.

Sharky's 샤키스 Udong 1305 626-4 ☎ 010 4038 2907; Haeundae subway (line 2); map p.202. This bar is perhaps better for its food (see p.207), but it has a range of real ale and it's a pleasant place to be most nights. Mon–Thurs & Sun 6–11pm, Fri & Sat 6pm–1am.

Thursday Party 썰스데이 파티 Udong 524-5 ☎ 051 746 1010; Haeundae subway (line 2); map p.202. You'll find branches of this Busanese bar chain all over the city; cheap beer and clever choices of location mean that most of them are busy every night. The Haeundae branch, in the oddly named Palé de CZ complex, is a particularly fun place to be on weekends. Daily 3pm–2am.

OTHER AREAS

★**Basement** 베이스먼트 Busandaehangno 62; Pusan National University subway (line 1); map p.198. This underground lair has, for many a year, been by far the most popular bar in the Busan National University area. Drinks are cheap, staff are super-friendly, and there are regular theme and live music nights. Tues–Sun 7pm–2am.

Club Fix 클럽픽스 Bujeon 2-dong 186-1; Seomyeon subway (lines 1 & 2); map p.198. Busan's "in" club at the time of writing, this place pulses out a mix of electro and progressive house against a photogenic backdrop. Strict dress code; W10,000–20,000 entry. Daily 10pm–6am.

★**Guri Bar** 구리빠 Bujeonno 66-gil; Seomyeon subway (lines 1 & 2); map p.198. You'll find bar-restaurants known as *pojangmacha* all over Korea – tarp-covered shacks selling seafood and cheap booze. This one's been pimped up, and now functions as a weird little outdoor bar – grab a cocktail (W7000) and get chatting to whoever's sitting next to you. Daily 7pm–late.

Vinyl Underground 바이늘 언더그라운드 Suyeongno 322-gil ☎ 010 9239 9792; Kyungsung University subway (line 2); map p.198. Vibrant, stylish, student-friendly bar which hosts occasional movie nights, live music and other events – look out for the Warholesque banana out front. Daily 8pm–late, often weekends only.

Yung Ggom 융꿈 Beomil 1-dong 1313-12 ☎ 051 646 5924; Beomil subway (line 1); map p.198. A cab ride from the main train station, this is Busan's oddest bar for sure – it's set in a cave used during the war era. Head to the back and the air will become awfully clammy – the cave goes further, but you can't. Unfortunately, they've got rid of the cheap eats you used to be able to throw back with the superb *dongdongju* (rice beer; W6000); you're now obliged to buy something costly between the group, with the cheapest item on the menu being the barbecued shrimp (W25,000). It's still worth it, at least once, for the atmosphere. Daily 11.30am–11pm.

DIRECTORY

Bookshops Nampo Bookstore, across the main road from the Jagalchi Fish Market, has a good selection of books covering Korean language and culture, as well as the usual Rowlings and Grishams.

Cinemas Four large multiscreens stand almost eyeball-to-eyeball on PIFF Square in Nampodong. When PIFF rolls into town in October there are also showings at the big cinemas in Haeundae.

Embassies and consulates China, 1418 Uidong ☎ 051 743 7984; Japan, 1147-11 Choryangdong ☎ 051 465 5101; Russia, 10F Korea Exchange Bank BD, 89-1 Jungangdong 4-ga ☎ 051 441 1104.

Hospitals Pusan National University Hospital, 10 1-ga,

Amidong (☎ 051 254 0171), is most likely to offer English-language help, or try the more central Maryknoll Hospital, 4-ga Daecheongdong (☎ 051 465 8801).

Post The largest post office is just south of Jungangdong subway station on the main road (Mon–Fri 9am–8pm, Sat 9am–6pm), but there are smaller branches in every city suburb.

Sport Despite being the country's second-largest city, Busan's sporting teams usually fail to make waves in their national leagues. Busan I'Park is the city's football team, and plays in red-and-white-quartered shirts at the Asiad Stadium. The Lotte Giants are one of the best-known baseball teams in Korea, and you can catch them (and their manically noisy supporters) at the Sajik Baseball Stadium.

Geojedo

거제도

Connected to the mainland by giant bridges, **GEOJEDO** is Korea's second-largest island; measuring 40km by 25km, it's a craggy paradox of stone and steel. Here can be found large tracks of forest and some of the most impressive **coastal scenery** in the land, but while the island is famed for its natural vistas, parts of it have been shattered by industry – around a third of the world's container ships are built here in the two mammoth **shipyards** that now define the island, and provide much of its employment. The island's biggest town and main travel hub is **Gohyeon** (고현), tucked in to the north and sheltered from the South Sea. Other sights include **Haegeumgang**, where a simply gorgeous rock formation – quite possibly

the most beautiful on the whole Korean coast – rises from the sea just
offshore, and **Oedo**, a tiny, flower-covered island that's incredibly popular with
Korean tourists.

Prisoner of War Camp Museum

포로수용소 유적공원 • Daily 9am–6pm • W3000 • The museum is just about within walking distance of Gohyeon bus terminal, but
poorly signed – a taxi won't cost more than a few thousand won

During the Korean War, Geojedo was the base of one of the Allied forces' main
prisoner of war camps, which kept Chinese and North Korean captives almost
as far as possible from the wavering line of control. The largest of several such bases
was in Gohyeon, where the freshly spruced-up **Prisoner of War Camp Museum**
recreates part of the original camp. Despite being diorama-heavy, the open-air
display is surprisingly diverting for a Korean historical exhibition, right from the
introductory escalator-based greeting from Mao, MacArthur, Kim and their
cardboard comrades. Simulated gunfire, explosions and revolutionary music crackle
around the squat buildings and dirt tracks, much of which are cordoned off by
barbed wire, but the effect is spoilt somewhat – in Korean fashion – by the new
flyover swooping above the complex. There's little information in English, but some
of the exhibits speak for themselves – keep an eye out for the video footage of what
life was like in the camp.

Haegeumgang

4

해금강 • Various buses run from Gohyeon

The Geumgang Mountains in North Korea are rightly revered as the most beautiful
on the peninsula, a Chinese painting come to life, where tree-fringed scoops of
sculpted rock rise through the mist. Similar sights – far smaller, but infinitely
more accessible – are on offer at **Haegeumgang** off the south coast of Geojedo
(*hae* means sea), where the precipitous crags lift their skinny fists like antennas
through the waters rather than the North Korean hinterland. Topped with a
sprinkling of camellia and highly photogenic, Haegeumgang can also be seen from
dry land – a network of trails web out from a nearby village, heading to a viewing
point that's perfect for a picnic, but becomes yet more majestic under the light of
the moon.

Oedo

외도 • Daily 9am–6pm • W8000 • Ferries (10 daily; 3hr round-trip including 90min on island; W25,000 on weekdays, W27,000 on
weekends) run from Jangsuengpo, accessible by bus from Gohyeon

The brainchild of a couple of botanists from Seoul, the islet of **Oedo** (pronounced
"way-dough", and now rechristened "Oedo Botania"), has been almost entirely
covered with flowers, and is now one of the most popular sights in the country
for **Korean tourists**, pulling in a couple of million each year. Though the flowers
are beautiful, it's one of those experiences that appeals to Koreans far more than
it does to foreign visitors, and the island's tight paths can get uncomfortably
crowded – don't dare to go against the current. Also note that you're only allowed
on the island for a specified time – your ticket will say which vessel you have to
return on.

ARRIVAL AND DEPARTURE   GEOJEDO

By bus Thanks to the mammoth bridges linking the island
to Tongyeong and Busan, Geojedo is easily accessible by
bus from many mainland destinations. Gohyeon has by far
the best connections, including Busan (every 30min; 1hr
30min), Jinju (every 30min; 2hr 30min), and Tongyeong
(every 30min; 40min).

Tongyeong

통영

Straddling the neck of the Geosong peninsula, affable **TONGYEONG** occupies a special place in Korean hearts as the base from which **Admiral Yi Sun-shin** orchestrated some of his greatest victories against the invading Japanese (see box, p.224). The town is now a laidback place concentrating as much on its present as its past, with enough diversions to keep visitors occupied for a day, after which you may care to head off to the emerald confetti of islands that surround it (see box below). Tongyeong's four-sided **harbour** – known as Ganguan – forms the focal point of the city, and is where you'll be able to see, and taste, the city's pride and joy – **chungmu gimbap** (see opposite). The **promenade** lining its western flank can be a relaxing place to drink on warm evenings; its north bank forms the base of a small hill, with a maze of houses, tiny lanes and drainage channels snaking their way to the top.

Tongyeong is the proud host of a genuinely international summer **music festival**, a feast of modern and classical tunes. And those who prefer muscles to music, Korea's number one **triathlon** sees competitors splash, dash and cycle through the city each June.

Sebyeonggwan

세병관 • Daily 9am–6pm • W3000

A steep five-minute walk from the harbour brings you to **Sebyeonggwan**, a huge single-floor house built in 1605 as the headquarters of the Admiralty, and one of the oldest wooden structures in the country. Its lack of walls, windows or doors makes it almost unrecognizable as a house, but in the summer the giant roof, balanced on top of fifty carved wooden columns, provides welcome shade for *gimbap*-munching tourists.

Nammangsan

남망산 • Sculpture park daily 24hr • Free

East of the harbour, Nammangsan hill is home to an excellent international **modern sculpture park** and a statue of Lee Sun-shin (see above). The bearded

---

ISLANDS OF THE SOUTH SEA

An almost innumerable number of islands radiate out into the South Sea like emerald stepping stones. Much of this area is protected as the **Hallyeo Haesang National Park** (한려 해상 국립 공원) and, as do other island groups around the country, it offers a look into the heart of traditional Korean life. Here ports and villages have changed little for generations, and remain places inextricably connected to their surrounding waters, where the busy urban realities of modern Korea are little more than memory.

Mainland Tongyeong is the area's main transport hub, and from here you can hop to dozens of islands by ferry. **Mireukdo** (미륵도) is immediately opposite the ferry terminal, but is built up and a little too industrial, and in any case connected to Tongyeong by bridge. Just 20km to the west of Tongyeong, the twin-peaked island of **Saryangdo** (사량도) is far more serene, and popular with young travellers in the summer on account of some good beaches; at these times, many choose to camp under the stars, but there are *minbak* available. **Hansando** (한산도) is even closer to Tongyeong, and was once home to Admiral Yi's main naval base; nowadays it's best known for **Jeseungdang**, a large shrine. Just off its northeastern flank is the relaxed island of **Bijindo** (비진도), whose long, east-facing beach is a wonderful place to watch the sunrise over a smattering of small islets. Further afield, **Yeonhwado** (연화도) is home to a remote temple, as well as the *Yongmeori* – needles of rock protruding from the eastern cape. These are just a few possibilities – allow yourself a few days, armed with a map of the area, and forget about the mainland for a while. Many of the islands have simple *minbak* accommodation, but as banking facilities are all but nonexistent it's essential to bring the necessary funds along from the mainland.

Admiral Yi stands with his back to the art, fixing a patriotic gaze at the island-peppered scene of his victories.

ARRIVAL AND INFORMATION   TONGYEONG

By ferry Tongyeong is a local ferry hub, with regular services heading to the surrounding islands in all seasons (see box opposite). Most popular are trips to the twin peaks of Saryangdo (8 daily; 40min), and to Jeseungdang (8 daily; 30min).

By bus The bus station, inconveniently hidden in the northern suburbs, offers regular services to most cities in Korea, including half-hourly connections to Busan and Daegu.

Destinations Busan (every 30min; 2hr); Daegu (every 30min; 2hr 40min); Daejeon (frequent; 2hr 40min); Geojedo (frequent; 40min); Gwangju (3 daily; 2hr 30min); Haegeumgang (2 daily; 1hr 30min); Jinju (frequent; 1hr 30min); Seoul (frequent; 4hr 10min).

Tourist information There are small booths on the harbour and at the bus station, though neither are much use.

ACCOMMODATION AND EATING

There's **accommodation** all over the city, but by far the most pleasant place to stay is the harbour, where there's a clutch of cheap motels and *yeogwan*, as well as an acceptable *jjimjilbang*. For **food**, there's only one recommendation – get your teeth around the city's famed **chungmu gimbap** (충무 김밥). These are small rice rolls with radish *kimchi* and chillied squid, and though available in specialist *gimbap* restaurants across the land they taste infinitely better here – you'll find plenty of tiny outlets on the western side of the harbour. Also try to hunt down a bottle of **Dosan** (도산), the delicious local *makgeolli* (rice wine), from any convenience store – best enjoyed by the harbour, on a picnic mat.

Myeongga 명가 Jungang Sijang Ipgu ☎055 644 0072. The town's best restaurant for *chungmu gimbap* (see above), according to a straw poll of in-the-know locals. It'll cost you a mere W4000 for the town speciality. Daily 7.30am–9.30pm.

Napoli Motel 나폴리 모텔 Baro-ap ☎055 646 0202. Standing out like a sore thumb over the harbour, this motel is one of the tallest buildings around, and a little overpriced,

but nice enough. It's attached to a café boasting good views out over the harbour – great for breakfast. W50,000

Popcorn Hostel 나폴리 모텔 Dongmunno 31 ☎1644 9540. Together with Yeosu (see p.223), Tongyeong is perhaps the most random place in the country to boast a hostel. It's a good one, too, with a bar that's up there with the best in town, serving cocktails and draught Hoegaarden. Dorm beds W14,000, four-person private rooms W64,000

Jinju

진주

A small city typical of Korea's southern coast, **JINJU** is worth dropping into on account of its superb **fortress** alone. This was the scene of one of the most famous suicides in Korean history (see box below), but such dark days are behind Jinju, and today you can walk for hours along pretty paths, gaze over the river from traditional pavilions and pop into the odd temple.

THE JAPANESE ATTACKS ON JINJU

Jinju's fortress received its first serious test in October of 1592, during the first attacks of what was to be a prolonged Japanese invasion. Like Admiral Yi along the coast in Yeosu (see p.223), **General Kim Si-min** held the fort despite being heavily outnumbered, with records claiming that 30,000 Japanese soldiers were seen off by just 3800 local troops. The following June, the Japanese returned in greater numbers, with up to 100,000 soldiers eager to obliterate the shame of their previous defeat, and it is estimated that 70,000 Koreans were killed during a week-long siege. Every tragedy needs a hero – or, in this case, a heroine – and this time a local girl named **Nongae**, one of several girls selected to "entertain" the Japanese top dogs after their victory, stepped into the breach. After using her charms to lure Japanese general Keyamura to what should have been a suspiciously lofty position on the riverside cliff, she jumped to her death, bringing the general down with her. A **festival** commemorating Nongae's patriotic valour takes place in the fortress each May, while General Kim's memory lives on in statue form at the centre of the fortress.

The beauty of Jinju is that all you need is within easy walking distance – the fortress is close to the intercity bus terminal, and surrounded by places to stay and eat. Unlike most towns in the region, the city is famed for its food, and a clutch of excellent **eel restaurants** can be found outside the fortress entrance. Jinju even has its own take on *bibimbap* – a popular dish across the nation, but prepared here with consummate attention. The city also makes a good base for nearby national park of **Jirisan** (see p.213), one of the most popular in the country.

Jinjuseong

진주성 • Daily 9am–6pm • W1000

The focal point of the city, and its best sight by far, is the walled-off riverside fortress of **Jinjuseong**, which can easily eat up hours of your time. Constructed in 1379 to protect the city from Japanese invasions, it did its job in 1592 during the first attacks of what was to be a prolonged war (see box, p.211). Just in from the entrance you'll find **Chokseongnu**, a beautiful pavilion facing the river; if you're lucky, you may find it full of old men in white, chatting and playing *baduk*. From here, a network of pretty, tree-lined trails forms a spider-web across the complex, with something to see at every turn. One of the most impressive sights is little **Hoguksa**, a temple at the opposite end – small and unheralded, but highly atmospheric. The compact central square is surrounded by an immaculately balanced amphitheatre of palms, bamboo and other foliage, with this leafy cocktail especially pleasing when augmented by the drones and wooden clacks of morning prayer. There's also a large **museum** on site, which has been built in an unnecessarily modern style, at odds with its surroundings. However, it is good on history, with an inevitable focus on the 1592 Japanese invasions, several battles from which are depicted on folding screens.

ARRIVAL AND DEPARTURE   JINJU

By plane Sacheon Airport is 20km away, and rather quiet at the best of times – the only flights are to Jeju (2 weekly; 45min) and Seoul (2 daily; 1hr).

By train The train line passing through Jinju sees precious few services – a pity, since the station's quite nice. The only one foreign travellers may be interested in is the long haul to Mokpo (1 daily; 5hr); this goes via Suncheon (for Jogyesan Provincial Park; 5 daily; 1hr 20min), where you

can also change for Yeosu. From the train station, it'll cost W7000 to the fortress area by taxi; a couple of bus routes head that way too.

By bus Most of Jinju's visitors arrive by bus. The express terminal is to the south of town, past the train station, but the intercity terminal is well located in the thick of things, just north of the Nam River and within walking distance of the fortress.

JINJU FESTIVALS

The suicide of Nongae, who became a posthumous hero during the Japanese invasions (see box, p.211), is commemorated by an annual weekend festival at the end of May. The river comes alive during an annual **lantern festival** at the beginning of October; this usually coincides with one of Korea's only **bullfighting** events, though you may be cheered to hear that the bulls fight each other, and don't die in front of a baying crowd.

Destinations Busan (frequent; 1hr 30min); Daegu (frequent; 2hr); Daejeon (hourly; 2hr); Daewonsa (hourly; 1hr 10min); Gwangju (2 daily; 2hr 30min); Haeinsa (3 daily; 2hr 20min); Seoul (every 30min; 3hr 35min); Suncheon (15 daily; 1hr 30min); Tongyeong (frequent; 1hr 30min); Yeosu (3 daily; 2hr 20min).

ACCOMMODATION

While there are **places to stay** all over the city, there's little point in basing yourself anywhere other than the strip running from the bus station to the fortress, which is dotted with a simply incredible number of cheap motels and *yeogwan*.

Dongbang 동방호텔 Nongaegil 103 ☎ 055 743 0131. Better than the average Korean tourist hotel, though this really isn't saying much, and rooms are overpriced. The river-facing location, however, is a plus, though it'll cost you W20,000 more. W145,000
Songjuk-jang 송죽장 Jeongmun-ap. A cheap, interesting place run by a gaggle of *ajummas*, opposite the main entrance of the fort and down a side street. Rooms have their own toilet, which means that they're fine for the price. W25,000
Sumnus Motel 솜누스 모텔 Jangdaedong 107-27 ☎ 055 748 7457. Located facing the river, this is one of the nicest motels around. Its best rooms feature computers, TV and a balcony. W50,000

EATING

Jinju's **food** is good, even by Korean standards. **Jeollanese** influence has clearly crept across the provincial border – meals are often served with a copious array of **side dishes**, and there's even a local version of that Jeonju favourite, the *bibimbap*, though surprisingly few Jinjuites will be able to point you to a restaurant serving this delectable dish. It's eel, instead, which is the local speciality – there are a parade of near-identical restaurants serving it just downhill from the fortress entrance.

Cheonhwang 천황 Daeandong 4-1 ☎ 055 741 2646. It takes a fair bit of hunting to find this super-cute shack-restaurant, one of the only places in town still serving Jinju *bibimbap* (W9000) – as it has done since 1927. With metal chair frames, blue cushioning and wooden tables, it's almost like eating lunch back at school. Daily 10am–10.30pm.
Gangnaru 강나루 Dongseongdong 16-15 ☎ 055 746 9235. The most strikingly decorated of the city's eel restaurants, with a whole zoo's worth of stuffed animals lining the walls. Choose between river (W20,000) or sea eel (W26,000), or just have a bowl of *naengmyeon* noodles (W6000). Daily 10am–10.30pm.
Zio Ricco 지오 릿초 Dongseongdong 3-19 ☎ 055 741 7776. This surprisingly attractive Italian restaurant is a *kimchi*-free refuge, with its proximity to the bus station and fortress making it a good choice for tourists. Pasta forms the bulk of the menu (from W12,000), and is inevitably served with the sweet pickles that Koreans must assume to be a regular side dish in Italy; pizzas from the wood oven go from W15,000. Daily 10am–11pm.

4

Jirisan National Park

지리산국립공원 • Daily 24hr • Free, though small fees may be levied at or near certain entrances • ⓦ english.knps.or.kr

Korea's largest national park, **JIRISAN**, pulls in hikers from all over the country, attracted by the dozen peaks measuring over 1000m in height, which include Cheonwangbong, the South Korean mainland's highest. It has also found fame for its **resident bear population**; a park camera spotted an Asiatic Black Bear wandering around in 2002, almost two decades after the last confirmed Korean sighting. The bear group was located and placed under protection, and continue to breed successfully. Although you're extremely unlikely to see them, it lends the park's various twists and turns an extra dash of excitement – nowhere else in Korea will you be fretting over the sound of a broken twig.

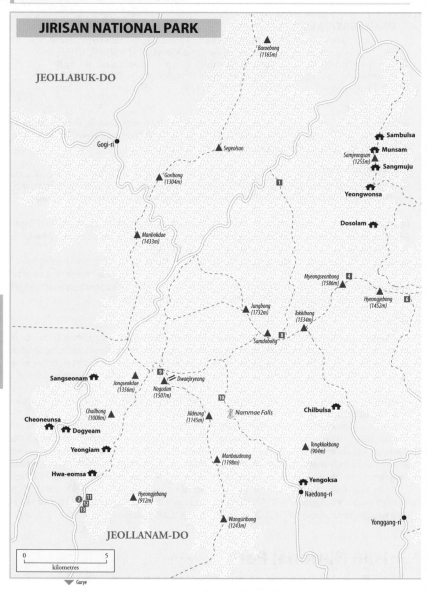

JIRISAN NATIONAL PARK

JEOLLABUK-DO

Baraebong (1165m)

Gogi-ri

Segeolsan

Sambulsa
Munsam
Samjeongsan (1255m)
Sangmuju

Goribong (1304m)

1

Yeongwonsa

Dosolam

Manbokdae (1433m)

Myeongseonbong (1586m) 4

Hyeongjebong (1452m) 6

4

Jungbong (1732m)

Tokkibong (1534m)

8

Samdobong

Sangseonam

Jongseokdae (1356m)

9
Dwaejiryeong

Nogodan (1507m)

10

Jildeung (1145m)

Nammae Falls

Chilbulsa

Cheoneunsa

Chailbong (1008m)

Dogyeam

Yeongiam

Tongkkokbong (904m)

Hwa-eomsa

Manbaudeung (1198m)

Yengoksa
Naedong-ri

2
11
12
13

Hyeongjebong (912m)

Wangsiribong (1243m)

Yonggang-ri

JEOLLANAM-DO

0 ————— 5
kilometres

Gurye

Jirisan is one of the only national parks in the country with an organized system of overnight **shelters** – there are few more atmospheric places to fall asleep in this corner of Korea. This makes **multi-day hikes** an exciting possibility; one popular route heads across the main spine of the park from east to west, and takes three days to walk (see box, p.216). It's impossible to detail all of the possible hikes and sights in the park, better instead to arm yourself with the **park map** (available at park entrances and nearby tourist offices for W1000) and find your own lofty piece of paradise.

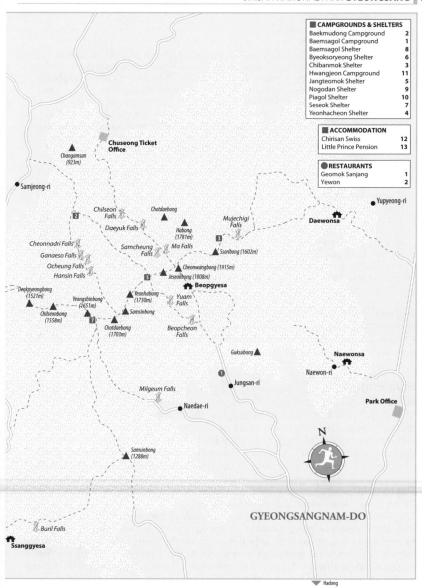

The park actually sprawls across three provinces, with its most popular access point – the temple of **Hwa-eomsa** – on the west of the park, and actually located across the provincial border in Jeonnam. The eastern side of Jirisan, in Gyeongnam province, lacks such a focal point – there are dozens of entrances, but though none are particularly popular or easy to get to, this usually makes for a quieter visit than you'd get at other national parks. One of the most popular trails is up from **Ssanggyesa** (쌍계사), a beautifully located temple at the south of the park. There's little of historical note here, bar a stone tablet apparently dating from 887, but the surroundings are

HIKING JIRISAN

Jirisan has literally hundreds of potential hiking iterations, which can make things a little confusing. Mercifully, a few are particularly popular. The biggest is the **26km-long trail** heading along the east–west main spine of the park. The hike connects **Nogodan** (1507m) in the west – best accessed from Hwa-eomsa (see below for details) – and **Cheonwangbong** (1915m) in the east, the highest peak on the South Korean mainland and the second highest in the country. There are large peaks all the way along this central ridge, from which numerous picturesque valleys drop down to the fields and foothills below. The trail takes most people three days to walk, with a couple of overnight stays at the **shelters** sprinkled along the way; there are eight of these on the spine, costing from W5000 to W7000 per person, and all are marked on the map. The westernmost shelter, at **Nogodan**, is very often full due to its proximity to a bus stop: to guarantee a place at any of the shelters you're asked to reserve a berth in advance through Korea's national park website (ⓦ english.knps.or.kr). This can prove frustrating, as it's hard to tell where you will run out of daylight or energy on your hike, but reserving beds at Samdobong and Seseok should give you enough leeway whether you're heading east or west.

Numerous valleys head up to the park's main spine, and most make for excellent day-hikes. One of the most popular runs from **Jungsan-ni** (중산리), a village connected to Jinju by bus, up to the principal peak of Cheonwangbong and back again, though many choose to continue north and emerge out of the park at Chuseong, down a valley lined with small waterfalls. Others start at the temples of Daewonsa and Ssanggyesa, which are a little far away from the spine for a day-trip, so you'd have to overnight at a shelter.

delightful, particularly in the early morning before the sun has risen beyond Jirisan's muscular peaks; it may also be Korea's noisiest temple in terms of birdlife. **Daewonsa** (대원사) is another pretty temple, this one on the park's eastern fringe, and it also has trails leading up to the peaks.

Hwa-eomsa

화엄사

Even if you're not up for a hike, the temple of **Hwa-eomsa**, locked in Jirisan's muscular embrace a short distance inside the park, is a highly worthy detour. An early morning visit is recommended, as you'll avoid any school groups and, hopefully, be able to see the sun rise over the peaks. A couple of hours' hike north of here is **Nogodan peak**, where you can begin the 26km-long multi-day hike across the park (see box above).

The temple

Daily 7am–7.30pm • Free • 1km walk from bus stop outside the park entrance

The **temple guardians** at the entrance to the temple of **Hwa-eomsa** are worth a look – the three regular bulgy-eyed fellows are joined by a serene buck-toothed figure strumming an instrument with huge fingers. Inside the complex are two **pagodas**; the western one is the more interesting, carved in Silla times with Buddhist figures that remain visible to this day. Nearby is a **stone lantern** that is – if you believe the Korean tourist authorities – the largest such sculpture in the world, an oversized beast emblazoned with cloud and lotus motifs, stretching over 6m from the ground. Subtler in its approach is the neighbouring stone pagoda, its main block balanced on the heads of four smug-looking lions. You'll see that some of the buildings around the complex are painted while some remain bare; attempts were made at repainting the whole lot, but these were quashed by a lack of funds and the deteriorating wood.

On your way around the temple, be sure to track down **Gakhwangjeon** (각황전), a particularly appealing hall. Looking all the better for its lack of renovation, its largely bare wooden structure forms a delicious contrast with the huge pictures that hang inside – a rhapsody in red. If you're after solitude, head behind the heart of the complex to **Gu-am** (구암); this hermitage is not as old or pretty as the buildings in the main complex, but filled as it is with vegetable plots, birdsong and mossy paths, and almost no signs of modern life, it's quite enchanting.

Nogodan peak

노고단 • Infrequent buses from the Hwa-eomsa bus stop run roughly every hour 7am–6pm – check at the small information centre near the bus stop

From Hwa-eomsa you can hike up to **Nogodan peak** (1507m; around 3hr), or save time and energy by taking a connecting bus most of the way up. If you do take the bus, the remaining distance to the top is an easy walk of an hour or so – leave enough time if catching the last bus down.

ARRIVAL AND DEPARTURE   JIRISAN NATIONAL PARK

There are dozens of places to start an assault on the Jirisan peaks, but the temples of **Hwa-eomsa** (in the west of the park) and **Ssanggyesa** (in the south of the park) are usually the easiest to get to.

To Hwa-eomsa Direct buses run to Hwa-eomsa from the major Jeollanese cities of Gwangju (every 20min; 1hr 30min) and Yeosu (hourly; 2hr), as well as from Busan in Gyeongsang province. From other cities, you'll have to change at the small town of Gurye (구례), from where there are bus connections to the temple (every 20min–1hr; 15min).

To Ssangyesa Infrequent direct buses head to Ssanggyesa from Jinju, though these pass through Hadong (하동), a small town nearer the park that you may be able to get to directly from other cities.

To Jungsan-ni Buses run to the village of Jungsan-ni from Jinju (hourly; 45min), but the park entrance is a frustratingly long (20min) uphill walk from the bus stop.

ACCOMMODATION AND EATING

In addition to the park shelters (see box opposite), there are **places to stay** and **eat** outside both of the main park entrances, as well as a smattering of campsites. **Hwa-eomsa** has the most extensive accommodation possibilities. Alternatively, the **Ssanggyesa** entrance, bucolic and open-plan, has *minbak* and restaurants spread over a wide area. There's also a clutch of *minbak* at the **Jungsan** park entrance, though the isolation of the place makes for a rather lonely stay. Lastly, Hwa-eomsa offers a **templestay** programme for W30,000 (see p.35). If you're on a multi-day hike you may be able to buy basic **provisions** in some park shelters, but while water is easier to find, it's advisable to bring your own food.

HWA-EOMSA
Chirisan Swiss 지리산 스위스 호텔 Hwangjeon-ni 61 ☎061 783 0700. The only deluxe accommodation in the area, though the rooms are a little on the "cosy" side, and the mattresses could be softer. Make sure to ask about discounts off season. W80,000
Little Prince Pension 페티프랑스 펜션 Hwangjeon-ni 521-4 ☎061 783 4700. The best of a string of similar places in the area, this vaguely log-cabin-like pension has big rooms, including some duplexes. The terrace at the back sometimes hosts *soju*-fuelled night-time feasts over the fire. W60,000

Yewon 예원 Hwangjeon-ni 546 ☎061 782 9917. The Hwa-eomsa area's best restaurant serves *sanchae jeongsik* (산채 정식), colossal, utterly delicious set meals of roots, shoots and mountain vegetables for just W10,000. Daily 10am–8pm.

JUNGSAN-NI
Geomok Sanjang 거목산장 Jungsan-ni 785 ☎055 973 9415. If you're entering or exiting Jirisan via Jungsan-ni, track down this little place, where a friendly man with his own unique English dialect serves some pretty good *pajeon* pancakes – just the treat after a long hike. Daily 9am–9pm.

4

Jeolla

TAPSA TEMPLE, MAISAN PROVINCIAL PARK

5

Jeolla

If you're after top-notch food, craggy coastlines, vistas of undulating green fields, and islands on which no foreigner has ever set foot, go no further. Jeju Island has its rock formations and palm trees, and Gangwon-do pulls in nature lovers by the truckload, but it's in the Jeolla provinces (전라) where you'll find the essence of Korea at its most potent – a somewhat ironic contention since the Jeollanese have long played the role of the renegade. Here, the national inferiority complex that many foreigners diagnose in the Korean psyche is compounded by a regional one: this is the most put-upon part of a much put-upon country. Although the differences between Jeolla and the rest of the country are being diluted daily, they're still strong enough to help make it the most distinctive and absorbing part of the mainland.

The Korean coast dissolves into thousands of **islands**, the majority of which lie sprinkled like confetti in Jeollanese waters. Some such as Hongdo and Geomundo are popular holiday resorts, while others lie in wave-smashed obscurity, their inhabitants hauling their living from the sea and preserving a lifestyle little changed in decades. The few foreign visitors who make it this far find that the best way to enjoy the area is to pick a ferry at random, and simply go with the flow.

Jeollanese cuisine is the envy of the nation – pride of place on the regional menu goes to *Jeonju bibimbap*, a local take on one of Korea's favourite dishes (see box, p.249). Jeolla's culinary reputation arises from its status as one of Korea's main food-producing areas, with shimmering emerald rice paddies vying for space in and around the national parks. The **Jeollanese people** themselves are also pretty special – fiercely proud of their homeland, with a devotion born from decades of social and economic repression. Speaking a dialect sometimes incomprehensible to other Koreans, they revel in their outsider status, and make a credible claim to be the friendliest people in the country.

Most of the islands trace a protective arc around **Jeonnam** (전남), a province whose name translates as "South Jeolla". On the map, this region bears a strong resemblance to Greece, and the similarities don't end there; the region is littered with ports and a constellation of islands, their surrounding waters bursting with seafood. Low-rise buildings snake up from the shores to the hills, and some towns are seemingly populated entirely with salty old pensioners. **Yeosu** and **Mokpo** are relatively small, unhurried cities exuding a worn, brackish charm; it's worth breaking the journey between the two to see **Jogyesan**, a provincial park home to two gorgeous temples, and the tea plantation at **Boseong**. Further inland is the

Highlights

❶ Hyangiram A tiny hermitage hanging onto cliffs south of Yeosu, and the best place in the country in which to see in the New Year. **See p.225**

❷ Mokpo This characterful seaside city is the best jumping-off point for excursions to the emerald isles of the West Sea. **See p.230**

❸ Naejangsan National Park The circular mountain ridge within this national park looks stunning in autumn, and is the best place in the land to enjoy the season. **See p.241**

❹ Byeonsanbando Look out across the sea from the peaks of this peninsular national park, then descend to the coast at low tide to see some terrific cliff formations. **See p.243**

❺ Jeonju's hanok village There are all sorts of traditional sights and activities to pursue in this wonderful area of *hanok* housing. **See p.244**

❻ Jeollanese food Jeollanese cuisine offers the best ingredients and more side dishes than you'll find elsewhere; it's best exemplified by Jeonju's take on *bibimbap*. **See p.249**

❼ Tapsa This cute temple, nestling in between the "horse-ear" peaks of Maisan Provincial Park, is surrounded by gravity-defying towers of hand-stacked rock. **See p.250**

HIGHLIGHTS ARE MARKED ON THE MAP ON P.222

5

region's capital and largest city, **Gwangju**, a young, trendy metropolis with a reputation for art and political activism.

The same can be said for likeable **Jeonju**, capital of **Jeonbuk** (전북; "North Jeolla") province to the north and one of the most inviting cities in the land; its **hanok district** of traditional buildings is a particular highlight. Green and gorgeous, Jeonbuk is also home to four excellent **national parks**, where most of the province's visitors head. Just east of Jeonju, the arresting "horse-ear" mountains of **Maisan Provincial Park** accentuate the appeal of Tapsa, a glorious temple that sits in between its distinctive twin peaks.

JEOLLA

HIGHLIGHTS
1. Hyangiram
2. Mokpo
3. Naejangsan National Park
4. Byeonsanbando
5. Jeonju's hanok village
6. Jeollanese food
7. Tapsa

Brief history

Jeolla's gripe with the rest of the country is largely political. Despite its status as the **birthplace** of the Joseon dynasty that ruled Korea from 1392 until its annexation by the Japanese in 1910, most of the country's leaders since independence in 1945 have hailed from the southeastern Gyeongsang provinces. Seeking to undermine their Jeollanese opposition, the central government deliberately withheld funding for the region, leaving its cities in relative decay while the country as a whole reaped the benefits of the "economic miracle". Political discord reached its nadir in 1980, when the city of Gwangju was the unfortunate location of a **massacre** which left hundreds of civilians dead (see box, p.238). National democratic reform was gradually fostered in the following years, culminating in the election of Jeolla native and eventual Nobel Peace Prize laureate **Kim Dae-jung**. Kim attempted to claw his home province's living standards up to scratch with a series of big-money projects, notably in the form of highway connections to the rest of the country once so conspicuous by their absence. Despite these advances, with the exception of Gwangju and Jeonju, Jeolla's urban centres are still among the poorest places in Korea.

Yeosu and around

여수

Charming in an offbeat way, **YEOSU** is by far the most appealing city on Jeonnam's south coast, with more than enough here to eat up a whole day of sightseeing. It's beautifully set in a ring of emerald islands, so the wonderful views over the South Sea alone would justify a trip down the narrow peninsula. In 2012 Yeosu played host to an international **Expo**, which brought in visitors en masse, but it has since seen part of town morph into the regular post-event white elephant.

Yeosu sprawls on for quite a distance, but for casual visitors the main area of interest is the "old" **downtown** (the new one is out west in the Hakdong area), a surprisingly quiet area abutting the city's harbour. Here, many content themselves by wandering around the several **fish markets**, though there are a few interesting, unassuming sights within walking distance of each other, including **Odongdo**, a bamboo-and-pine island popular with families, and a replica of Admiral Yi's famed **turtle ship**. Beyond the city limits are the black-sand beach of **Manseongni**, and **Hyangiram**, a magical hermitage at the end of the Yeosu peninsula.

5

ADMIRAL YI, CONQUEROR OF THE SEAS

"…it seems, in truth, no exaggeration to assert that from first to last he never made a mistake, for his work was so complete under each variety of circumstances as to defy criticism."

Admiral George Alexander Ballard, The Influence of the Sea on the Political History of Japan

Were he not born during the Joseon dynasty, a period in which a nervous Korea largely shielded itself from the outside world, it is likely that **Admiral Yi Sun-shin** (이순신; 1545–98) would today be ranked alongside Napoleon and Horatio Nelson as one of the greatest generals of all time. A Korean national hero, you'll see his face on the W100 coin, and **statues** of the great man dot the country's shores. The two most pertinent are at Yeosu, where he was headquartered, and Tongyeong (then known as Chungmu; see p.210), the site of his most famous victory.

Yi Sun-shin was both a beneficiary and a victim of circumstance. A year after his first major posting as Naval Commander of Jeolla in 1591, there began a six-year wave of **Japanese invasions**. Although the Nipponese were setting their sights on an eventual assault on China, Korea had the misfortune to be in the way and loyal to the Chinese emperor, and 150,000 troops laid siege to the country. Admiral Yi achieved a string of well-orchestrated victories, spearheaded by his famed **turtle ships**, vessels topped with iron spikes that were adept at navigating the island-dotted waters with ease.

Despite his triumphs, the admiral fell victim to a Japanese spy and the workings of the Korean political system. A double agent persuaded a high-ranking Korean general that the Japanese would attack in a suspiciously treacherous area; seeing through the plan, Admiral Yi refused the general's orders, and as a result was stripped of his duties and sent to Seoul for torture. His successor, Won Gyeun, was far less successful, and within months had been killed by the Japanese after managing to lose the whole Korean fleet, bar twelve warships. Yi was hastily **reinstated**, and after hunting down the remaining ships managed to repel a Japanese armada ten times more numerous. Peppering the enemy's vessels with cannonballs and flaming arrows, Yi waited for the tide to change and rammed the tightly packed enemy ships into one another. Heroic to the last, Yi was killed by a stray bullet as the Japanese retreated from what was to be the final battle of the war, apparently using his final gasps to insist that his death be kept secret until victory had been assured.

Jinnamgwan

진남관 • Pavilion daily 9am–6pm • Free • Museum Tues–Sun 9am–6pm • Free

In the very centre of town, and just ten minutes' walk northeast of the ferry terminal, is **Jinnamgwan**, a pavilion once used as a guesthouse by the Korean navy. The site had previously been a command post of national hero **Admiral Yi** (see box above), but a guesthouse was built here in 1599, a year after his death, and replaced by the current structure in 1718. At 54m long and 14m high it's the country's largest single-storey wooden structure. In front of the guesthouse is a stone man – initially one of a group of seven – that was used as a decoy in the 1592–98 Japanese invasions. Just below the pavilion is a small **museum** detailing the area's maritime fisticuffs, while crossing the footbridge over the main road will lead you to a quiet residential area with numerous specimens of street art.

Admiral Yi Square

이순신 광장 • Turtle ship daily 8am–8pm • Free

Just downhill from Jinnamgwan and abutting the port area is a statue of **Admiral Yi Sun Shin**, the town hero (and quite possibly the national one too – see box above). The statue was plonked here during prettification of the surrounding area before the Expo came to town in 2012. Admiral Yi appears to be surfing one of the **turtle ships** for which he's famed; you'll be able to spot a larger replica just a few paces away – a small, rounded vessel with a wooden dragon head at the front. Such boats spearheaded the battles against the Japanese in the sixteenth century, and were so-called for their iron roofs covered with spiked metal, which made them tough to attack from the top. The interior of the ship can be prowled around, though it contains little bar a few dioramas and a modern-day regiment of mannequins. There's a similar turtle ship to the south, just across the Dolsando bridge.

Odongdo

오동도 • Daily 9am–6pm • Free • Bus #333 from bus terminal or train station

Yet another statue of Admiral Yi stands to the east of the city centre, on a hill overlooking the small island of **Odongdo**. Essentially a botanical garden famed for its camellia trees, it's crisscrossed by a deliciously scented network of pine- and bamboo-lined paths, and has become a popular picnicking destination for local families. A 700m-long causeway connects it to the mainland, and if you don't feel like walking you can hop on the bus – resembling a train – for a small fee. The island's paths snake up to a lighthouse, the view from which gives a far clearer rendition of Yeosu's surroundings than can be had from Jinnamgwan in the city centre. In the summer, kids love to cool off in the fountain by the docks on the northern shore – the water show comes on every twenty minutes or so.

A number of **boat tours** operate from Odongdo – operators are unlikely to speak English, so these are best arranged through the tourist information centre outside the main entrance to Odongdo; routes include cruises across the harbour to Dolsan Bridge, and a longer haul to Hyangiram (see below) and back.

Expo Park

엑스포 공원 • Daily 10am–8pm, sometimes later in summer • Free • Sky Tower daily 10am–8pm • W2000 • Aqua Planet daily 10am–7pm • W25,000

You have to hand it to international Expos – they take years to prepare, are out-of-date by the time they come around and almost invariably become a waste of space once the circus leaves town. The zone created for **Expo 2012**, right next to the train station, is no exception, with few people generally present to watch the fountain shows put on through the day. The two redeeming features are the **Sky Tower**, from whose viewing deck you can gaze on Yeosu over a coffee; and **Aqua Planet**, a highly pleasing (once you've got over the ticket price) **aquarium** filled with all manner of marine life, including penguins, seals, otters, belugas and umpteen species of fish.

Manseongni

만성리 • Bus #7 from train station or bus terminal

Around 4km north up the coast from Yeosu's train station, you'll find *minbak* and raw fish restaurants aplenty at **Manseongni**, which is revered as the only **black-sand** beach on the Korean mainland – in truth, this volcanic material is actually rather grey in appearance. Mid-April is said to be the time of year when the beach "opens its eyes", and people flock to bury themselves in the allegedly nutritious sand, an experience somewhat akin to being a cigarette butt for the day.

Hyangiram

향일암 • Daily pre-dawn to 8pm • W2000 • Bus #113 from central Yeosu, or #111 from central Yeosu, Yeosu station and Odongdo (all W1200; around 50min)

Clinging to the cliffs at the southeastern end of Dolsando is the magical hermitage of **Hyangiram**, an eastward-facing favourite of sunrise seekers and a popular place to ring in the New Year. Behind Hyangiram is a collection of angular boulders which – according to local monks – resembles an oriental folding screen, and is soaked with

5

ISLANDS AROUND YEOSU

South of Yeosu, the mainland soon melts into a host of **islands**, many of which lie under the protective umbrella of **Dadohae Haesang National Park** (다도해 해상 국립 공원). Many can be accessed from Yeosu's ferry terminal (see below), and as with Jeolla's other island archipelagos, these are best explored with no set plan; you'll find simple *minbak* accommodation on all islands. **Dolsando** (돌산도), connected to the mainland by road, is the most visited and most famed for **Hyangiram**, a hermitage dangling over the crashing seas (see p.225). Further south are **Geumodo** (금오도), a rural island fringed by rugged cliffs and rock faces, and **Geomundo** (거문도), far from Yeosu – and briefly occupied by Britain during the 1880s, during an ill-planned stab at colonizing Korea's southern coast – but now an increasingly popular holiday destination. From Geomundo you can take a tour boat around the assorted spires of rock that make up **Baekdo** (백도), a protected archipelago containing a number of impressive formations. There are a couple of daily **ferries** from Yeosu to both Geomundo (2hr 30min) and Geumodo (1hr 10min).

camellia blossom in the spring. The area outside the hermitage makes a lovely place to stay; there are plenty of motels and restaurants to choose from – though none really stand out – and you'll only need to book ahead if you're going for New Year.

ARRIVAL AND INFORMATION   YEOSU

By plane The cute little airport lies around 20km to the north – take a bus from the city's main bus terminal – and has flights to and from Seoul (8 daily; 55min) and Jeju Island (2 weekly; 45min).

By train Trains arriving into Yeosu squeeze down a narrow isthmus, which opens out as it hits the city; the station's located adjacent to the new Expo Park. KTX high-speed trains arrive here too, though note that they won't have been on high-speed tracks since Daejeon; additionally, if you want to get to or from Jinju or Gwangju by train, you'll have to change at Suncheon. It's possible to walk into the old town from the station, though taxis are cheap (around W5000).

Destinations Jeonju (every 30min; 1hr 20min); Seoul (Yongsan station; hourly; 3hr 40min); Suncheon (hourly; 20min).

By bus The bus station is located frustratingly far to the north

of town – just about walkable, though it's not fun, so take one of the many bus routes (W1200), or hop into a cab (around W7000).

Destinations Busan (hourly; 3hr 40min); Gwangju (frequent; 2hr); Jeonju (11 daily; 3hr); Mokpo (every 40min; 2hr 40min); Seoul (frequent; 5hr).

By ferry Yeosu's ferry terminal hasn't been all that busy since ferries to Jeju dried up, but there are still services to the islands making up Dadohae Haesang National Park (see box above). The most popular are Geomundo (2 daily; 2hr 30min) and Geumodo (2 daily; 1hr 10min).

Tourist information The best booth in the city is just outside the train station exit (☎061 690 2588), and is usually staffed with at least one English-speaker. There's also a tiny one at the entrance to Odongdo.

ACCOMMODATION

Yeosu's old **downtown** is the best place to stay, though in addition to the places listed below there are options in the new downtown of Hakdong, out to the west. **Prices** are a cut above the national norm – motels here tend to charge W50,000, though poke around the old downtown and you'll also find some seedy, bare-bones *yeoinsuk* for around W25,000.

Flying Pig B&B 플라잉피그 Gonghwabuk 3-gil 7 ☎061 666 5533. A hop, skip and jump from the train station, this B&B is a thoroughly pleasant place to stay, right down to the English-ish breakfast fried up for you in the morning. Rooms are lovely, though it really is bed and breakfast only – bring your own toiletries and towels. **W70,000**

Motel T 모텔 T Gyodong 534 ☎061 665 5757. Perhaps the best value in the downtown motel area (though still a rip-off), this place scores points on account of having renovated its rooms, as well as the common areas, before the Expo rolled into town. A couple of bonus points, too, for the free can of beer waiting for you in the fridge. **W50,000**

MVL Odongdoro 111 ☎061 660 5800. Built for the Expo, this is far and away the fanciest place in central Yeosu – even the standard rooms are pretty plush. It's a big boy, so aim for as high a floor as possible – and, of course, for a sea view too. The fifth-floor sauna is quite gorgeous, though guests have to pay W18,000 for its use. **W190,000**

Yeosu Guesthouse 여수 게스트하우스 Dongmunno 16 ☎061 666 5533. Under the same management as the *Flying Pig*, Yeosu's first hostel is a fine little place, its simple, gender-segregated dorms – two of which have views of Jinnamgwan – augmented by a café-like common area. It's all under the stewardship of a friendly, informative, English-speaking owner. Dorm beds **W19,000**

EATING AND DRINKING

Yeosu's **restaurants** are surprisingly poor by Jeolla standards. If you're feeling brave, and have a decent command of Korean seafood menus, you will find that the market running along the **Yeondeungcheon canal** from the ferry terminal is a grand place to eat – try the **samhap** (a broiling mess of squid, scallops and pork belly; W30,000 for 3–4 people), a local dish served at most places hereabouts. Yeosu's marketplaces are the most atmospheric places to **drink** in the downtown area, which basically has no nightlife. Alternatively, head to the waterfront at night with a bottle of beer or Yeosu Makgeolli (a particularly delicious brand, available from all convenience stores and mini-marts for W1300). For a "proper" night out, you'll have to head out west to Hakdong (학동), though it's over half an hour away by bus, and expensive to reach by taxi.

Bukchon Sikdang 북촌 식당 Gyodongnam 1-gil 5-8 ☎061 662 5260. Sit-on-the-floor venue that's a real favourite with locals and domestic tourists, who come to gollop down raw tonguefish (서대회; W10,000), grilled cutlassfish (갈치구이; W10,000) or spicy eel soup (장어탕; W9000). Daily 10am–10pm.

Nokwon Galbi 녹원 갈비 Gonghwadong 595 ☎061 665 8729. Out near the Expo Park entrance, this is the cheeriest barbecue joint in town – its outdoor area is a delight on sunny days or warm evenings. Portions of meat go from W11,000; try the pork galbi (돼지 갈비). Daily 11.30am–9pm.

Jogyesan Provincial Park

조계산 국립 공원

The small but pretty **JOGYESAN PROVINCIAL PARK** is flanked by two splendid temples, **Seonamsa** and **Songgwangsa**. If you get up early enough, it's possible to see both temples in a single day, taking either the four-hour hiking trail that runs between them, or one of the buses that heads the long way around the park. The park and its temples are accessible by bus from **SUNCHEON** (순천), an otherwise uninteresting city that's easy to get to by bus, and occasionally train, from elsewhere in the area.

Seonamsa

선남사 • Daily sunrise–sunset • W2000

Seonamsa, on the park's eastern side, is the closer temple of the two to Suncheon. On the way in from the ticket booth you'll pass **Seungsongyo**, an old rock bridge whose semicircular lower arch makes a full disc when reflected in the river below: slide down to the water to get the best view.

There has been a temple at Seonamsa since 861 – the dawn of the Unified Silla period – but having fallen victim to fire several times, the present buildings are considerably more modern. Its **entrance gate** is ageing gracefully, though the dragon heads are a more recent addition – the original smaller, stealthier-looking ones can be found in the small museum inside. Notably, the temple eschews the usual four heavenly guardians at the entrance, relying instead on the surrounding mountains for protection – they look particularly imposing on a rainy day. The **main hall** in the central courtyard is also unconventional, with its blocked central entrance symbolically allowing only Buddhist knowledge through, and not even accessible to high-ranking monks – this is said to represent the egalitarian principles of the temple. The hall was apparently built without nails, and at the back contains a long coffin-like box which holds a large picture of the Buddha that was once unfurled during times of drought, to bring rain to the crops. Around the complex are a number of small **paths**, one leading to a pair of majestic stone turtles; the one on the right-hand side is crowned by an almost Moorish clutch of twisting dragons.

Songgwangsa

송광사 • Daily 9am–6pm • Free • ⓦ songgwangsa.org

To the west of the park is **Songgwangsa**, viewed by Koreans as one of the most important temples in the country, and one of the "**Three Jewels**" of Korean Buddhism – the others

5

are Tongdosa (see p.192) and Haeinsa (see p.177). Large, well maintained and often full of devotees, it may disappoint those who've already appreciated the earthier delights of Seonamsa. The temple is accessed on a peculiar bridge-cum-pavilion, beyond which can be found the four guardians that were conspicuously absent at Seonamsa. Within the complex is **Seungbojeon**, a hall filled with 1250 individually sculpted figurines, the painstaking attention to detail echoed in the paintwork of the main hall; colourful and highly intricate patterns spread like a rash down the pillars, surrounding a trio of Buddha statues representing the past, present and future. Unfortunately, the Hall of National Teachers is closed to the public – perhaps to protect its gold-fringed ceiling.

ARRIVAL AND DEPARTURE — JOGYESAN PROVINCIAL PARK

By train Suncheon is the closest train station; there are trains from here to Jeonju (hourly; 1hr 30min), Jinju (5 daily; 1hr 30min), and Yeosu (hourly; 35min).

By bus From central Suncheon, bus #1 runs to Seonamsa (7 daily; 1hr) and bus #111 to Songgwangsa (7 daily; 1hr); if travelling between the two you'll save a lot of time by transferring at Seopyeong-maeul, a small village where

the bus routes split. Also note that there are occasional buses to Songgwangsa from Gwangju.

Tours In the past, tour buses to the temples have run from Suncheon; these had been discontinued at the time of writing, though it's worth enquiring to find out whether they've started again.

ACCOMMODATION AND EATING

There are low-key **accommodation** and **restaurant** facilities at both entrances to the park. If you need to overnight in Suncheon, head for the district of **Yeonhyangdong** (연향동), which has plenty of motels and restaurants.

Saejogye Sanjang 새조계산장 Seonamsa ☎ 061 751 9200. The main selling point of this simple guesthouse is that it's marginally more comfortable than the many *minbak* sitting outside the Seonamsa temple entrance. **W30,000**

Suncheon Sikdang 순천 식당 Seonamsa. This basic

restaurant deserves a special mention, if only for the charming way in which its name has been spelled out in Korean characters. As in many Korean rural areas, *sanchae bibimbap* (산채 비빔밥; W7000) is a favoured dish, and is made with local ingredients. Opening hours vary.

Boseong

보성

The town of **BOSEONG** is famed for the **tea plantations** that surround it; visitors flock here during warmer months to take pictures of the thousands of tea trees that line the slopes. They may not be as busy or as verdant as those in, for example, Sri Lanka or Laos, but they're still a magnificent sight, particularly when sepia-tinged on early summer evenings. **Green tea** (녹차; *nok-cha*) rode the crest of the "healthy living" wave that swept the country in the early 2000s, and by the Boseong fields you can imbibe the leaf in more ways than you could ever have imagined.

Daehan Dawon

대한 다원 • Daily: March–Oct 5am–8pm; Nov–Feb 8am–6pm • W2000 • Bus to Boseong from Gwangju (1hr 30min) or Suncheon (1hr 20min), then another bus to Yulpo, and get off at the tea plantation (every 30min; 10–15min)

Daehan Dawon is the area's main tea plantation. Pluckers comb the well-manicured rows at all times of year, though spring (April–June) is the main harvest season, and if you're lucky you may be able to see the day's take being processed in the on-site factory. A couple of on-site **restaurants** serve up green tea chicken cutlet, green tea *bibimbap* and green tea with seafood on rice, as well as a variety of dishes featuring pork from pigs raised on a green tea diet. There's also a **café** serving *nok-cha* ice cream and snacks – if you've never tried a *nok-cha* latte, you'll never get a better opportunity (though, admittedly, it's on sale at pretty much every café up to the North Korean border).

Further up the same road are a few less-visited plantations that can be entered for free, one of which stretches down to a cute village by the water's edge.

Wando

완도

Dangling off Korea's southwestern tip is a motley bunch of more than a hundred islands. The hub of this group is **WANDO**, also the most popular owing to its connections to the mainland by bus and Jeju Island by sea. It's barely worth coming here if you're not planning to take a ferry elsewhere, but Wando does have a few diversions in its own right, and a journey away from **Wando-eup** (완도읍), the main town, will give you a glimpse of Jeolla's pleasing rural underbelly. Regular buses run from Wando-eup to **Gugyedeung** (구계등), a small, rocky beach in the coastal village of Jeongdo-ri, and to **Cheonghaejin** (청해진), a stone park looking over a tiny islet which, despite its unassuming pastoral mix of farms and mud walls, was once important enough to send trade ships to China.

ARRIVAL AND INFORMATION   WANDO-EUP

By bus Wando-eup's petite-size bus terminal has buses to plenty of Jeolla destinations, including Gwangju (frequent; 2hr 40min) and Mokpo (every 50min; 2hr); there are also buses to Seoul (4 daily; 6hr).

By ferry The ferry terminal is a 15min walk from the bus station, and very easy to find – hit the seafront and follow it along to the right. There are three daily services to Jeju, though the price and duration of these journeys varies substantially (1hr 40min–5hr). There are also services to

several islands around Wando (see box below), including Cheongsando (1 daily; 50min); ferries to Bogildo (11 daily; 40min) actually leave from the Hwaheungpo port, which is around W10,000 away by taxi, or a 20min bus ride.

Banks There are a few Nonghyeop Bank branches around town, and ATMs in the bus station and most convenience stores, though there are regular reports of all failing to work with foreign cards – it's prudent to bring as much money as you'll need.

ACCOMMODATION AND EATING

Most of the action in Wando-eup is centred around the bus station, but the area around the main ferry terminal makes a quieter and more pleasant **place to stay**. There are plenty of **restaurants** serving both raw and cooked food in the town centre, as well as a fish market next to the ferry terminal.

Jeonsama 전사마 Gaepo-ri 1273-13 ☎061 555 0838. A simple place on the main road between the bus and ferry terminals, this restaurant is the target of most Korean visitors to Wando, thanks to multiple appearances on TV – they're all here for the superb *Jeonbuk bulgogi* (전북 불고기; W13,000), a beef-and-abalone dish which tastes even better when *kimchi* is added to the already odd-sounding mix. Daily 10am–10pm.

Naju Yeoinsuk 나주 여인숙 Jangbogodaero 333-gil 4-1 ☎061 554 3884. Very close to the ferry terminal

in a building painted a fetching aquamarine, this *yeoinsuk* has the cheapest rooms around – all mats-on-the-floor affairs, though most of them are, surprisingly, en suite. **W15,000**

Tower Motel 타워 모텔 Jangbogodaero 302-1 ☎010 3646 6978. Relatively new motel near to the ferry terminal, boasting loudly decorated rooms – try to nab one with a view of the sea and the fish market (the smell from the latter, mercifully, doesn't reach the motel). **W40,000**

ISLANDS AROUND WANDO

There are so many islands around Wando that you'll be quite spoilt for choice, with even the tiniest inhabited ones served by ferry from Wando-eup; many form part of **Dadohae Haesang National Park** (다도해 해상 국립 공원). **Maps** of the islands are available from the ferry terminal, where almost all services depart, with a few leaving from a small pier just to the north. At the time of writing, **Cheongsando** (청산도) was the island most visited by local tourists, mainly due to the fact that it was the location of *Spring Waltz*, a popular drama series. Naturally, spring is the busiest time of year here – and quite beautiful, with the island's fields bursting with flowers. More beautiful is pine-clad **Bogildo** (보길도), a well-kept secret accessible via a ferry terminal on the west of Wando – free hourly shuttle-buses make the pretty twenty-minute journey from Wando-eup's bus terminal. In the centre of tadpole-shaped Bogildo is a lake, while the island's craggy tail, stretching east, has a couple of popular beaches.

5

Mokpo

목포

If you've been travelling around Korea for a while, you may well notice that **MOKPO** is, to put it bluntly, a little different. This charmingly ramshackle city is not just the end of the road, but the end of the rail line too; indeed, Mokpo gives the impression that it would happily be an island if it could. For decades, it was the hotbed of **opposition** support to the entities ruling Korea; for much of the 1970s and 1980s, central funding was deliberately cut in an attempt to marginalize the city, which was once among the most populous and powerful in the land. Much of the city remains run-down, and Mokpo is probably the **poorest** urban centre in the country. Koreans often say that taxi drivers are a good indicator of the wealth of the cities – here cabbies have a habit of beeping at pedestrians in the hope that they want a lift, and then occasionally swinging around for a second go.

Though it'll be a while before Mokpo's salty charms are eroded, things are changing. After being starved of funding for decades, the balance is now being redressed – witness the huge new **museums** out east, or the new town of **Hadang**, built on land reclaimed from the sea a little further on. There's also a permanent Christmas of neon lights festooned around the **city centre**, though they impart a sort of dreary melancholy to this dying area. However, Mokpo's main travel draw remains the same as it ever was – this is the jumping-off point for literally hundreds of **islands**, which start ganging up in the seas just to the west (see box, p.234). Heading inland in the other direction is Korea's smallest national park, **Wolchulsan** (see p.233), an easy day-trip from the city.

Yudalsan

유달산 • Daily 8am–6pm • Free

Many of the mind-boggling number of islands surrounding Mokpo are visible from the peaks of **Yudalsan**, a small hill-park within walking distance of the city centre and train station. It's a popular place, with troupes of hikers stomping their way up a maze of trails, past manicured gardens and a sculpture park, towards

5

FORMULA 1 COMES TO MOKPO

In 2010, the **Formula 1** circus finally came to Korea, with the inaugural Grand Prix taking place at a brand-new track just east of Mokpo. The first hosting of this event was fraught with problems: the track was only given its safety certificate days before the race, spectator enclosures were hastily put together, and there were only three acceptable hotels in the whole of Mokpo. Most fans, and even some VIPs, were forced to stay at **love hotels** – one BBC journalist returned to her room to find that it had been used in her absence (a used contraceptive on the floor providing the evidence).

Race day itself was also memorable for the wrong reasons. **Traffic jams** resulting from poor access to the track meant that thousands of spectators arrived late – and in some cases, not at all. **Rain** didn't help matters, with the newly built track stubbornly refusing to drain; concerns about driver safety led to the race being delayed for over an hour, and at one point the embarrassing possibility of cancelling the event entirely was raised. In the end, the clouds parted, and after several notable drivers had spun off the slippery track Spanish driver **Fernando Alonso** emerged victorious.

Some, inevitably, questioned the wisdom of hosting a Grand Prix in an out-of-the-way corner of a country with little track record in motor sports – the simple truth was that Jeonnam province had made the most generous offer to the F1 powers. The race ran until 2013, before being dropped from the calendar. It could resurface any year now, but few Koreans, bar those with financial interests at heart, could care less.

Ildeung-bawi, the park's main peak. After the slog to the top – a twenty-minute climb of 228m – you'll be rewarded with a **spectacular view**: a sea filled to the horizon with a swarm of emerald islands, some large enough to be inhabited, others just specks of rock. Similar views can be had from Yudalsan's second-highest peak, **Ideung-bawi**, just along the ridge past a large, precariously balanced boulder. Between the peaks, a trail runs west to a small **beach**, though the water here is not suitable for swimming.

Mokpo Modern History Museum

목포 자연사 박물관 • Tues–Sun 9am–6pm • W2000

Backing onto Yudalsan's foothills is the **Mokpo Modern History Museum**, housed in the former Japanese consulate. The building dates back to 1900 – made of red brick and with its wooden window frames painted baby-blue, it's probably the most beautiful in the city. The exhibits aren't as interesting as the architecture, but there are some fantastic photos of Mokpo in colonial times.

Dancing Fountain

목포 음악 춤분수 • Daily 8.40pm, Fri & Sat also 9.20pm • Free

Mokpo's newest attraction is the **Dancing Fountain** in Hadang (the new city centre, about 8km east of the old one), which puts on twenty-minute-long shows each evening. The jets spurt up to 70m from a "floating" platform on the ocean (yet another world first, according to the local tourist authorities, even though it isn't), and the overall effect is pretty spectacular.

National Maritime Museum

국립 해양 유물 전시관 • Tues–Fri 9am–6pm, Sat & Sun 9am–7pm • Free • Bus #15 from bus terminal or train station, but better approached by taxi (W5000 from the train station)

The most popular of Mokpo's cluster of modern museums is the **Maritime Museum**, around 3km east of the train station. Its prime exhibits are the remains of a ship sunk near Wando in the eleventh century – the oldest such find in the country. Preserved

5

from looting by its sunken location, celadon bowls and other relics scavenged from the vessel are on display, alongside a mock-up of how the ship may have once looked.

Natural History Museum

자연사 박물관 • Tues–Fri 9am–6pm, Sat & Sun 9am–7pm • W3000 • Bus #15 from bus terminal or train station, but better approached by taxi (W5000 from the train station)

Along the road from the Maritime Museum – and marginally more compelling – is the **Natural History Museum**, home to an artily arranged butterfly exhibit, as well as a collection of dinosaur skeletons that is sure to perk up any sleepy youngster. Accessible on the same ticket, the building next door contains rather more highbrow sights, including calligraphy and paintings from **Sochi**, a famed nineteenth-century artist from the local area. Sochi was a protégé of Chusa, one of the country's most revered calligraphers (see p.306). More works from this talented duo and their contemporaries are on display, as are modern works by Oh Sung-oo, a Korean impressionist who painted modern takes of oriental clichés.

ARRIVAL AND INFORMATION
MOKPO

By plane The closest airport to Mokpo is Muan, 20km to the north; there are a few flights to China, though the only domestic services are to Jeju (1–2 daily; 45min).

By train Mokpo is not the easiest Korean city in which to get your bearings. The most logical way to arrive is by train, as the main station is right next to a busy shopping area in the centre of the city.

Destinations Boseong (1 daily; 2hr 20min); Gwangju (Seongjeong station; 1–2 hourly; 35min); Jinju (3 daily; 4hr 35min); Seoul (Yongsan station; 1–2 hourly; 3hr 30min).

By bus Buses terminate some way to the north: taxis cost just W5000 to the centre, or there are several city bus routes (15min; W900). The most useful of these is #1, which passes both the bus and the train stations on its way to the ferry terminal.

Destinations Busan (9 daily; 4hr 20min); Gwangju

(frequent; 1hr 30min); Jeonju (frequent; 2hr 30min); Jindo (frequent; 1hr 10min); Seoul (frequent; 5hr); Wando (7 daily; 2hr); Yeosu (every 40min; 3hr).

By ferry Mokpo's huge terminal sits on the city's southern shore, a lavishly funded structure standing incongruously in an area of apparent decay, and as such one of the most telling symbols of modern Mokpo. There are services to and from many islands in the West Sea, including Heuksando (4 daily; 1hr 45min) and Hongdo (2 daily; 2hr 15min). Those to and from Jeju Island (2 daily; 3hr 10min–4hr 30min) use the inappropriately named "International" terminal a short way around the coast.

Tourist information Although things should improve as the city grows, tourist information has never been one of Mokpo's strong points; there's a near-useless booth in the train station, and a small info-hut outside the Natural History Museum.

ACCOMMODATION

Despite the city's new-found wealth, there are few options at the **top end** of the accommodation range, though a few places are springing up in Hadang, the "new" downtown out east. Further down the price scale, there are dozens of fairly decent **motels** by the train station, as well as some cheap – and seedy – *yeogwan*.

★ **Daeyang Park Motel** 대양 파크 모텔 Honamdong 12-43 ☎ 061 243 4540. One of the better options in the station area, this motel boasts stairwells and some corridors lit up with ultraviolet lights, stars and planets. After this NASA-friendly introduction the rooms are almost disappointingly plain – clean, with big TVs, internet-ready computers and free toiletries. <u>W35,000</u>

Marina Bay 마리나 베이 Bogwandong 3-7 ☎ 061 247 9900, ⊛ marinabayhotel.co.kr. The only actual hotel in the train station area, with its main selling point being large, well-appointed rooms, and the views from them. Prices drop by W20,000 or so on weekdays. <u>W100,000</u>

Shangria Beach Hotel 샹그리아 비치 호텔 Pyeonghwaro 79 ☎ 061 285 0100. Large hotel by the water in the new Hadang district, a taxi ride east of central Mokpo. Rooms are large and well kitted out, and though the prices can be a little high (off-season discounts notwithstanding) it's Mokpo's only decent option in this price range. <u>W130,000</u>

Shinan Beach Hotel 신안 비치 호텔 Heanno 2 ☎ 061 243 3399, ⊛ shinanbeachhotel.com. Cut off from the city centre by the mountains and with views of the sea, this was for decades Mokpo's only tourist hotel. Nowadays its stylings feel more than a little dated. <u>W88,000</u>

EATING, DRINKING AND NIGHTLIFE

You can't walk for five minutes in downtown Mokpo without passing a dozen **restaurants** serving cheap, delicious food – the area west of the train station is packed with all kinds of options, including cheap-as-chips snack bars, pizzerias and stacks of cafés. **Hadang** is the best place to head for a night out.

Café Brick Lane 카페 브리크 레인 Jukdong 14-5 ☎061 244 2556. Quite an oddity in grimy central Mokpo, this café wouldn't look out of place in Seoul. As well as good coffee (W3500 and up), they serve ciabatta filled with squid ink, tomato and mozzarella, or honey and camembert (both W9500). Daily 10am–midnight.

★**Hongdo Hoetjip** 홍도 횟집 Jukgydong 465-142 ☎061 245 5614. The main road opposite the ferry terminal is alive with raw fish outlets, but this restaurant, out west and overlooking the sea, serves better food, for the same price, in a nicer location – try the *hoedeopbap* (sashimi on rice; W15,000), a round of sushi (W15,000) or a seafood platter (W50,000, feeds two or three). Daily 10am–10.30pm.

House Filled With Happiness Jungangdong 1-3 ☎061 245 5887. Housed in one of Mokpo's few extant colonial buildings (and just down the road from the Modern History Museum), this café is a delightful spot on a sunny day – classical music will be playing over your coffee (from W5500) or Korean tea (W9000). There are several

charmingly furnished rooms to choose from, though the garden is best if the weather agrees. Daily 11am–10pm.

Isaac Toast 이삭 토스트 Myeongnyundong ☎061 273 5566. Shack-restaurant across from the train station, selling Korean-style toast for W2000–3000, and tasty fruit shakes too. Mon–Sat 8am–9pm.

★**Namupo** 나무포 Jukdong 10-1 ☎061 243 8592. Head here for the juiciest *galbi* in town, right in the city centre to boot. There's a variety of meat styles on the illustrated, English-language menu, though the dish of choice is the spicy-sweet *yangnyeom galbi* (W18,000); alternatively, go for some pork *galbi* (W10,000), or a bowl of *naengmyeon* (W8000). Daily 8am–10pm.

Noeul 노을 Opposite Shinan Beach. A nice little place for a drink – coffee (from W4000) and yoghurt smoothies by day, and beer (W4000) and cocktails (W7000) at night. Blur the two by coming for sunset; after the sun has gone down, you'll be left with the twinkling bridge for company, and the fairy lights dotting a nearby island. Daily 10am–midnight.

Wolchulsan National Park

월출산국립공원 • Free • ⓦ english.knps.or.kr • Bus to Yeong-am from Mokpo (every 20min; 35min), then taxi to park

A short bus-ride east of Mokpo, **WOLCHULSAN NATIONAL PARK** is the smallest of Korea's national parks and one of its least visited – the lack of historic temples and its difficult access are a blessing in disguise. Set within the gorgeous Jeollanese countryside, Wolchulsan's jumble of maze-like rocks rises to more than 800m above sea level, casting jagged shadows over the rice paddies.

From the main entrance at **Cheonhwangsaji**, a short but steep hiking trail heads up for an hour or so to **Cheonhwangbong** (809m), the park's main peak. Along the way, you'll have to traverse the "Cloud Bridge", a steel structure slung between two peaks – not for sufferers of vertigo. Views from here, or the peak itself, are magnificent, and with an early enough start it's possible to make the tough hike to **Dogapsa** (도갑사), an uninteresting temple on the other side of the park, while heeding the "no shamanism" warning signs along the way. There's no public transport to or from the temple, but a forty-minute walk south – all downhill – will bring you to **Gurim** (구림), a small village outside the park, on the main road between Mokpo and Yeong-am, where you can pick up a taxi.

West Sea islands

The Korean peninsula has thousands of **islands** on its fringes, but the seas around Mokpo have by far the most concentrated number. Though many of these are merely bluffs of barnacled rock that yo-yo in and out of the West Sea with the tide, plenty are large enough to support fishing communities; they're all accessible by **ferry** from Mokpo. The quantity of islands here is, in fact, so vast that it's easier to trailblaze here than in some less-developed Asian countries – many of the islands' inhabitants have never seen a foreigner, and it's hard to find a more quintessentially Korean experience.

5

Much of the area is under the umbrella of **Dadohae Haesang National Park**, which stretches offshore from Mokpo to Yeosu. The most popular islands are actually the furthest away – **Hongdo**, which rises steeply from the West Sea, and neighbouring **Heuksando**, a miniature archipelago of more than a hundred islets of rock.

Heuksando

흑산도 • Ferry from Mokpo (4 daily; 1hr 45min; W34,300) or Hongdo (2 daily; 40min; W11,000)

More than 100km west of the mainland, **Heuksando** is not one island but a jagged collection of forested bumps; the main ones offer good hiking opportunities. On the main island (also called Heuksando), the westerly trails are highly recommended at sunset, when Hongdo is thrown into silhouette on the West Sea; most people head to the 227m-high peak of Sangnabong. Ferries usually dock at **YERI** (예리), a delightful little village on the main island, from where **boat tours** of the dramatic coast are available; three are available (all W22,000), though the best is #1, which loops around several rocky islets to the north.

Hongdo

홍도 • Ferry from Mokpo (2 daily; 2hr 15min; W42,000) or Heuksando (2 daily; 40min; W11,000) • Boat tours W15,000 (2hr 30min)

Another 25km further out from Heuksando is **Hongdo**, whose slightly peculiar rock colouration gave rise to its name, which means "Red Island". Those who make it this far are less likely to be interested in its pigment than its spectacular shape. Spanning around 6km from north to south, the island rises sheer from the waters of the West Sea to almost 380m above sea level. It may seem like a hikers' paradise, but much of the island is protected, and there's only one real **trail** – even on this, much of the ascent is on wooden steps. Indeed, the best views of the rock formations will be from a **tour boat** (2hr 30min; W15,000): these run from the tiny village where the ferry docks, one of only two on an island whose population barely exceeds five hundred; most trips go around the rocky spires of **Goyerido** (고예리도), a beautiful formation poking out of the sea just north of Hongdo. The village itself sprawls saddle-like from one pinched side of the island to the other; something like a part of Greece exiled to East Asia, it makes a marvellous place to stay, with the bunched-together buildings engendering a palpable sense of community.

ISLANDS AROUND MOKPO

There are dozens of islands surrounding Mokpo, though few are truly noteworthy – no matter, since the key to enjoying them is to pick up a map, select an island at random, and make your way there; if you stop somewhere nice along the way, stay there instead. The **islanders** are among the friendliest people in Korea – some travellers have found themselves stuck on an island with no restaurants or accommodation, only to be taken in by a local family. These islands are not cut out for tourism and possess very few facilities, particularly in terms of banking – so be sure to take along enough **money** for your stay. It's also a good idea to bring a **bike** and/or **hiking boots**, as the natural surroundings mean that you're bound to be spending a lot of time outdoors.

All of the islands hereabouts are accessible from the ferry terminal in central Mokpo (see p.232); service at the **tourist information** office here is hit-and-miss, but at the very least you'll be able to pick up a **map** (in Korean only) of the islands and an up-to-date **ferry schedule**. One of the most pleasing ferry circuits connects some of Mokpo's closest island neighbours – a round trip will take around two hours, and there are several ferries per day. On this circuit, the only island that sees any tourists whatsoever is **Oedaldo** (외달도), which has a decent range of accommodation and restaurants. Only a few kilometres from the mainland, though hidden by other islands, little **Dallido** (달리도; home to just 104 families) offers some of the best walking opportunities. Beyond these lie a pack of much **larger islands**, accessible on several ferry routes from Mokpo. Most of these have swimming-friendly beaches, and hills to climb.

THE SINKING OF THE SEWOL

Until recently, the island of **Jindo** was the up there with the most popular in the wider Mokpo area – famed for a curly-tailed local dog, a highly loyal breed now exported across the world, the island was also a huge draw in early March, when local tides would withdraw to reveal a 3km-long land bridge, a phenomenon referred to locally as "Moses' Miracle". However, no Koreans now desire to walk in the waters hereabouts – this is where the **Sewol ferry** sank on 16th April 2014, with truly catastrophic loss of life. Of the 476 people on board when the Jeju-bound ferry departed Incheon, only 172 survived – the vast majority of those who died were students from a high school in Ansan, just south of Seoul.

Following the event, and even during the brief window when hundreds were trapped beneath the waves, fingers were pointed in just about every direction. Questions were asked of the conduct and competence of the captain and crew, who escaped to safety after issuing a message telling passengers to remain in their bunks, despite the vessel listing heavily; it was actually one of the student victims who made the first emergency call to the coastguard, transcripts of whose communication with the crew paint a picture of confusion and incompetence. It later transpired that the ferry had made far too fast a turn, and was also travelling with double the cargo and half the ballast required by law, partially as a result of its being reconfigured to carry more goods and passengers.

The event also had substantial **political ramifications**, with the opposition exploiting the situation in order to heap pressure on President Park Geun-hye. Protests took place in Seoul for many months afterwards, during which time Park was lambasted by the general public for her failure to deal with the issue. The sad fact of the matter is that poor regulatory enforcement, poor stewardship and poor communications came together in a perfect storm – another national tragedy to add to Korea's ever-increasing list.

ACCOMMODATION AND EATING   WEST SEA ISLANDS

HEUKSANDO

There are several settlements around the Heuksando archipelago. Many visitors are whisked to distant, group-booked pensions on arrival, though it's actually best to stay in Yeri, the village surrounding the main ferry terminal – a highly pleasant place to sleep and eat. Yeri also boasts a karaoke salon, a billiards hall and a curious bar inside an old bus – great places in which to capture that frontier feeling.

Daejungsusan Sikdang 대중수산 식당 Yeri 176-11 ☎061 275 9367. The local delicacy is fermented skate (홍어) – a truly revolting dish that even makes most Koreans retch – but this place is one of the very few restaurants serving the non-fermented (and therefore non-stinky) variety; ask for *shing-shing hong-eo* (싱싱 홍어). The powdery dipping mix they give you is also very tasty. It'll set you back W50,000 for a skate which, together with free side dishes, will feed three. Daily 8am–9pm.

Hwanggeum Motel 황금 모텔 Yeri 180-37 ☎061 246 5372. A short walk along the harbour from the ferry terminal in Yeri, this motel is, amazingly, the only place in town with beds. Rooms are nothing special, but many have

harbour views, and they do the job. W30,000

HONGDO

The main village on Hongdo is full of motels, *yeogwan* and *minbak*, though if you're coming during the summer holidays, you are advised to book your accommodation prior to arrival through the tourist offices in Mokpo or Gwangju.

Palace 펠라스 호텔 Hongdo 1-gil 51-5 ☎061 246 2005. On the opposite side of the village from the ferry terminal (in other words, a ten-minute walk), this simple motel is the last building in town – some rooms boast unobstructed sea views, and unlike most places hereabouts, some have beds. You'll have to book in the fish restaurant on the ground floor, which also makes a great place to eat. W50,000

1004 Hotel 1004 호텔 Hongdo 1-gil 65-1 ☎061 246 3758. One of the few "hotels" (it's a guesthouse) offering sea views on the ferry terminal side of the island, with decent-enough rooms, a few of which have beds. The restaurant is pretty good (*hoe-deopbap* W15,000), and has a few outdoor tables on which to soak up the sunshine. W50,000

Gwangju

광주

The gleaming, busy face of "new Jeolla", **GWANGJU** is the region's most populous city by far. Once a centre of political activism, and arguably remaining so today, it's still

5

associated, for most Koreans, with the brutal **massacre** that took place here in 1980 (see box, p.238). The event devastated the city but highlighted the faults of the then-government, thereby ushering in a more democratic era. Other than a **cemetery** for those who perished in the struggle, on the city outskirts, there's little of note to see in Gwangju itself, except perhaps the shop-and-dine area in its centre. Largely pedestrianized, this is one of the busiest and best such zones in the country – not only the best place in which to sample Jeollanese cuisine but also a great spot to observe why Gwangjuites are deemed to be among the most fashionable folk on the peninsula. Also in this area is "**Art Street**", a warren of studios and the hub of Gwangju's dynamic **art scene** (see box opposite).

Apart from its art spaces, central Gwangju's only genuine tourist sights are the **museums** lying on the northern fringe of the city, around the Honam Expressway. Further afield, **Mudeungsan Park** forms a natural eastern border to the city. Most tourists base themselves around **Geumnamno** (금남로), the major downtown artery, near the May 18th Democratic Plaza in Gwangju's main shopping district.

National Museum

광주 박물관 • Tues–Fri 9am–6pm, Sat 9am–9pm, Sun 9am–7pm • Free • ⓦ gwangju.museum.go.kr • Bus #48 from train station or #95 from city centre

The **National Museum** is set in a typically oversized, quasi-traditional building, a grubby place despite its relative youth. The most interesting rooms are those devoted to **Yuan-dynasty ceramics** scavenged from a Chinese trading boat, which was sunk off the Jeolla coast in the fourteenth century on its way to Japan, and lay undiscovered

ON THE ART TRAIL IN GWANGJU

Outside Seoul, Gwangju is by far Korea's most artistically inclined city. Much of this can be ascribed to the fact that it's the largest city in Jeolla, which during the 1970s and 1980s was a hotbed of political activism (see p.223); the gruesome massacre of 1980 (see box, p.238) saw raw emotion splashed onto many a piece of canvas. Regional tensions have long since subsided, meaning that present-day Jeollanese have a little less to say, but it's still worth taking a stroll through some of the city's many galleries.

The best place to go hunting is a narrow road in the city centre, affectionately known as **Art Street**. This is a funky collection of shops and studios selling art materials and works by local artists. There are similar streets in other Korean cities, but this one is larger, much more accessible and forms an active part of the city's life. Traditional art styles remain dominant but they're complemented – and sometimes sent up – by a more contemporary set. A few arty cafés and restaurants can be found in or just off the road, though as this area is also Gwangju's centre of after-school education, the discussions you'll hear are more likely to be about pop than Picasso. Also nearby is the site of the huge **Asian Culture Complex**, an arts venue yet to be completed after huge delays. Elsewhere in the city, one of Gwangju's more interesting art exhibitions, showing the work of a calligrapher named **Uijae**, can be found at Mudeungsan Park.

Those visiting Gwangju in the autumn of even-numbered years will be able to attend the **Gwangju Biennale** (ⓦ gb.or.kr), the biggest and most important art festival in the land. Most of the action takes place at a huge dedicated hall north of the train station, and there's so much to see that even a full day is unlikely to be enough.

until 1975. Yuan-dynasty artisans were renowned across East Asia for their celadon pottery, and many of the pieces on display can be traced to **Jingdezhen**, China's most famous centre of ceramic production. Despite their centuries underwater, most pieces are in pretty good condition, a testament to the procedures of the time. Another section is devoted to items scavenged from a Korean wreck found nearby in 1983, though these pieces lack the gentle balance of their Middle Kingdom counterparts.

Gwangju Folk Museum

광주시립민속박물관 • Tues–Fri 9am–6pm, Sat 9am–9pm, Sun 9am–7pm • W500 • Bus #48 from train station or #95 from city centre

From the National Museum, a tunnel under the expressway leads to the less interesting **Gwangju Folk Museum**, a diorama-centric look at Jeollanese costumes and customs from as far back as the Three Kingdoms period. The first floor focuses on aspects of day-to-day life such as cooking and housing, while things get more esoteric on the second floor, with exhibitions on folk games and religion.

May 18th National Cemetery

국립 5.18 묘지 • Daily 8am–5pm • Free • Bus #518 from train station (40min)

One of Gwangju's most important sights, the **May 18th National Cemetery**, lies in rolling countryside around forty minutes north of the city centre by bus. This is the resting place of those killed in the **1980 massacre** (see box, p.238); the thousands of participants who survived also have the right to be buried here. Though Gwangju has many sights related to this event, some even forming part of a rather macabre tour detailed in the official tourist literature, this is the least morbid and most factual.

An overlarge oval of walkways and sculpture, the **visitor centre** is more of a testament to concrete than to the lives of the demonstrators, though it's worth a visit for the **photograph exhibition hall** – there are some astonishing pictures on display, and the tension of the time is painfully palpable. Be warned that many images are rather graphic, though the worst have mercifully been cordoned off into a section of their own. The cemetery itself is a badly signed five-minute walk away.

5

THE GWANGJU MASSACRE

"At 10.30 in the morning about a thousand Special Forces troops were brought in. They repeated the same actions as the day before, beating, stabbing and mutilating unarmed civilians, including children, young girls and aged grandmothers... Several sources tell of soldiers stabbing or cutting off the breasts of naked girls; one murdered student was found disembowelled, another with an X carved in his back... And so it continues, horror piled upon horror."

Simon Winchester, Korea

Away from the bustle of Gwangju, in what may at first appear to be a field of contorted tea trees, lie those who took part in a 1980 **uprising** against the government, an event which resulted in a brutal **massacre** of civilians. The number that died is still not known for sure, and was exaggerated by both parties involved at the time; the official line says just over two hundred, but some estimates put it at over two thousand. Comparisons with the **Tiananmen** massacre in China are inevitable, an event better known to the Western world despite what some historians argue may have been a similar death toll. While Beijing keeps a tight lid on its nasty secret, Koreans flock to Gwangju each May to pay tribute to those who died.

In an intricate web of corruption, apparent Communist plots and a presidential assassination, trouble had been brewing for some time before **General Chun Doo-hwan** staged a **military coup** in December 1979. Chun had been part of a team given the responsibility of investigating the assassination of President Kim Jae-kyu, but used the event as a springboard towards his own leadership of the country. On May 17, 1980, he declared martial law in order to quash **student protests** against his rule. Similar revolts had seen the back of a few previous Korean leaders (notably Syngman Rhee, the country's first president); fearing the same fate, Chun authorized a ruthless show of force that left many dead. Reprisal demonstrations started up across the city – the MBC television station was burnt down, with protestors aggrieved at being portrayed as Communist hooligans by the state-run operator. Hundreds of thousands of civilians grouped together, mimicking the tactics of previous protests on Jeju Island by attacking and seizing weapons from police stations. With transport connections to the city blocked, the government was able to retreat and pool its resources for the inevitable crackdown. This came on May 27, when troops attacked by land and air, retaking the city in less than two hours. After having the protest leaders executed, General Chun resigned from the Army in August, stepping shortly afterwards into presidential office. His leadership, though further tainted by continued erosions of civil rights, oversaw an economic boom; an export-hungry world remained relatively quiet on the matter.

Also sentenced to death, though eventually spared, was **Kim Dae-jung**. An opposition leader and fierce critic of the goings-on, he was charged with inciting the revolt, and spent much of the decade under house arrest. Chun, after seeing out his term in 1987, passed the country's leadership to his partner-in-crime during the massacre, **Roh Tae-woo**. Demonstrations soon flared up once more, though in an unexpectedly conciliatory response, Roh chose to release many political prisoners, including Kim Dae-jung. The murky world of Korean politics gradually became more transparent, culminating in charges of corruption and treason being levelled at Chun and Roh. Both were pardoned in 1997 by Kim Dae-jung, about to be elected president himself, in what was generally regarded as a gesture intended to draw a line under the troubles.

Mudeungsan

무등산 • Daily 8am–5pm • Free • Bus #49 from train station or #9 from the bus terminal

Mudeungsan is a pleasant park bordering Gwangju on its eastern side, and easily accessible by bus from the city centre. It's named after its principal peak, a three-headed massif rising 1186m above sea level. The slopes here are gradual, and paths are well-signed.

Uijae Gallery

의재 미술관 • By the entrance of Mudeungsan • Tues–Sun 9.30am–5pm • W2000

Near the entrance of Mudeungsan, the **Uijae Gallery** showcases the work of Ho Baeknyon (1891–1977), better known by his pen name **Uijae**. Uijae was an important painter-poet-calligrapher, and in uniting those fine arts was proabably one of the main catalysts behind Gwangju's dynamic art scene. His old house and tea plantation, as well as a **gallery** dedicated to his work, stand in close proximity. The most interesting piece on show in the museum is a ten-picture **folding screen**, whose images are said to represent the world's rainbow of personal characteristics: are you bamboo-, blossom- or orchid-like in temperament?

ARRIVAL AND DEPARTURE   GWANGJU

By plane Gwangju's little airport is just over 6km west of the centre, and you can actually walk there from some parts of town. The airport subway station sits 300m away from the terminal (a slightly confusing walk), while various bus routes run past the entrance; alternatively, a taxi to or from the centre should cost less than W15,000.
Destinations Jeju (12 daily; 45min); Seoul (7 daily; 50min); Yangyang (in Gangwon; 3 weekly; 1hr 30min).

By train The main station is very close to the city centre – you could walk, or a taxi will cost around W5000. Some high-speed trains from Seoul stop here, though more (all of those on their way to Mokpo) use Gwangju-Songjeong, a larger station just past the airport to the west, and on the city subway network.
Destinations (Gwangju station) Daejeon (hourly; 2hr); Mokpo (1 daily; 1hr 15min); Seoul (Yongsan station;

hourly; 2hr 50min).
Destinations (Gwangju-Songjeong station) Daejeon (hourly; 1hr 40min); Mokpo (1–3 hourly; 35min); Seoul (Yongsan station; 1–2 hourly; 2hr 45min).

By bus The city's express and intercity terminals sit side by side in a newish construction to the west of the centre.
Destinations Busan (every 30min; 3hr 40min); Chuncheon (4 daily; 5hr); Daegu (every 40min; 3hr 40min); Daejeon (every 20min; 2hr 50min); Gurye (every 30min; 1hr 30min); Gyeongju (2 daily; 3hr 30min); Incheon (hourly; 3hr 40min); Jeonju (every 30min; 1hr 40min); Jindo (every 40min; 2hr 50min); Jinju (3 daily; 2hr); Mokpo (every 30min; 1hr 30min); Naejangsan (5 daily; 1hr 30min); Seonunsan (8 daily; 1hr 40min); Seoul (every 5min; 3hr 55min); Sokcho (4 daily; 6hr); Wando (every 40min; 2hr 40min); Yeosu (frequent; 2hr).

GETTING AROUND

By subway A subway line (W1200 per ride) runs through the centre from east to west, but for some reason doesn't connect with the train station or bus terminal (both of

which are fairly central). Line #2 is in planning, but political infighting means that nobody yet knows where it will run.
By bus Bus journeys in the city cost W1200.

INFORMATION

Tourist information There are decent tourist information booths outside both train stations, and another on Geumnamno (daily 9am–6pm; ☎ 062 226 1050).
Gwangju International Center The Gwangju International Center on Geumnamno (☎ 062 226 2733, ☯ eng.gic.or.kr) is an excellent source of local information,

and has a selection of secondhand English-language books and films. The centre puts on Korean-language classes for expats, and also stocks the excellent monthly *Gwangju News* (☯ gwangjunewsgic.com) – one of the best expat magazines in the country, it's very useful for visitors, too.

ACCOMMODATION

Gwangju's **accommodation** is relatively poor by the standards of major Korean cities, and hasn't kept pace with the city's other advances. There are a couple of decent options at the higher end of the price range, and motels can be found in groups around the train and bus stations, as well as the city centre. The bus station area isn't a great option, as not only is it a convoluted walk from the station to the motels, but the establishments are even more brazenly "love"-based than elsewhere in the country – those around Geumnamno are far more appealing.

Geumsujang Hotel 금수장 Gyerim 1-dong 559-1 ☎ 062 525 2111. A ten-minute walk east of the train station, this is an old-fashioned tourist hotel whose large, well-appointed rooms become decent value when you've halved the price by booking online. The on-site restaurant serves gigantic traditional banquets (see p.240). W110,000
Hotel Palace 호텔 팰리스 Hwanggeumdong 13-160 ☎ 062 222 2525. Smallish, immaculate rooms in the centre of the city, and much better value than the more

expensive hotels in the area. The entrance is on the fourth floor, but the place is slightly hard to find in the middle of a bank of bars and restaurants. W50,000
Namdo Hostel 남도 호스텔 Naebangdong ☎ 010 6476 3255. Acceptable hostel stuck in an uninteresting area to the west of the centre, though easy to track down from Ssangchon subway station. Rooms are fine, though they're overpriced and can feel very cramped when there are plenty of guests. The manager, however, is a friendly

5

fellow who's very good for information. Dorm beds **W20,000**

★**Pharaoh Motel** 파라오 모텔 Bullodong 27-5 ☏062 223 7861. The newest motel option in the area at the time of writing, and no more expensive than its competition despite the large, fairly fancy-looking rooms. Negative points are that wi-fi doesn't quite reach to them all (if you need it, check immediately then ask to switch if it doesn't work), and noise can carry a bit from adjacent rooms. **W30,000**

★**Ramada Plaza** 라마다 프라자 Jipyeongdong 1238-3 ☏062 717 7000, ⍓ramadagwangju.com. Gwangju's top hotel by far, located in the Hadang "new town" area, and walkable from Sangmu subway station. The whole complex is superbly designed – if the swish lobby doesn't blow you away, then check out the stunning suites (particularly the "Spa Corner"). In addition, prices are very fair – the cheapest rooms often dip below W180,000. **W285,000**

EATING

The Jeollanese pride themselves on their **food**, and, as in other cities in the region, Gwangju cuisine is excellent – whisper this quietly, but it may actually be better than the more vaunted cuisine from Jeonju, up the road. The areas around the bus terminal and train stations can be largely avoided; there's enough to eat in the centre.

Cheongwon Momil 청원 모밀 Chungjangno 3-ga 31-7 ☏062 222 2210. Opposite the NC Wave department store, this little restaurant has been serving cheap noodles since 1960, making it almost Jurassic in Korean terms, though prices have doubled, and the quality gone down, since inclusion in the *Michelin* guide and multiple appearances on TV. The spicy buckwheat noodles (*bibim momil*; W6000) are still pretty good though. Daily 10.30am–8.30pm.

★**First Alleyway** 퍼스트 앨리웨이 Chungjangno Angil 5-2 ☏070 4127 8066. Gwangju could claim to be the world's best place for Korean food, but if you're in the mood for something different, this Canadian-run place is the place to come. They have yummy poutine (fries topped with gravy and cheese curds; W7000), pizzas (W12,000), fish and chips (W10,000), sandwiches (W12,000) and much more. It's also a good place for drinks (see below). Tues–Thurs 10am–10pm, Fri 10am–midnight, Sat noon–1am, Sun 11am–8pm.

Geumsujang 금수장 Gyerim 1-dong 559-1 ☏062 525 2111. Gigantic banquet meals known as *hanjeongsik* are a Gwangju speciality, but places serving these traditional feasts tend to be hard to get to. This is the exception,

located in the *Geumsujang Hotel* (see p.239); W100,000 will buy a set meal for two that could easily feed three. Daily 9am–10pm.

★**Hwangsolchon** 황솔촌 Honamdong 73-2 ☏062 222 4815. Twinned with *Moojinjoo* across the road (see below), this opulent-looking meat restaurant serves absolutely delicious pork *galbi* (W11,000) in a pleasant atmosphere – if you're lucky, they'll crack eggs into the run-off tray to make a tasty omelette. There are also some cheapies available on the menu, including *galbitang* (a beef broth; W6500), *naengmyeon* (W6000) and *bibimbap* served in a sizzling bowl (W6500). Daily 11.30am–midnight.

★**Moojinjoo** 무진주 Bullodong 1-4 ☏062 224 8074. Set on several stylish levels, this adventurously designed restaurant serves the most aesthetically pleasing meals in the city. They specialize in *jokbal* (족발; meat from pig hooves); their signature *modeum bossam* meal (모듬 보쌈; W31,000) revolves around the stuff and will feed two. Even better are their gut-busting lunch specials (served until 5pm; W8000), which are perhaps the best-value meals in the country – and heaven for veggies, once they've pushed the pork to one side. Daily 11.30am–midnight.

DRINKING

Gwangju's main drinking area is near **Sangmu**, a western suburb – a little bit off the radar for casual visitors, especially since there are plenty of places to drink in the centre. The busiest zone is in a knot of alleys just east of **Seoseongno**, centred on an odd piece of street architecture – young local chaps lie in wait under this, and try to chat up any girl that walks past. The city's unofficial number-one **makgeolli** brand is *Mudeungsan*, available from more or less every convenience store, though if you look around you may find a delectable *yuja* (유자) brand, made with honey and lemon.

First Alleyway 퍼스트 앨리웨이 Chungjangno Angil 5-2 ☏070 4127 8066. This super restaurant (see above) has a range of Craftworks beer on tap, great bar snacks and a pool table – no wonder it's constantly full of contented expats, plus a growing number of Korean fans. Tues–Thurs 10am–10pm, Fri 10am–midnight, Sat noon–1am, Sun 11am–8pm.

Speakeasy 스피크이지 Jungangno 160-gil 31-31.

Now a mainstay on the Gwangju bar scene, this is an expat teacher hive if ever there was one – everyone seems to know everyone, and Koreans are greatly outnumbered. It's fun, cheap (draught beer from W4000) and good for meeting people; it's hosted live music in the past, though the quiz nights (every 2nd Thurs) are now more notable. Thurs–Sun 7pm–late.

5

DDEOK-GALBI: THE KOREAN BURGER

Koreans love to simplify their food in order to help poor foreigners get their heads around it. You've got *mandu* (translated as "Korean dumplings"), *pajeon* ("Korean pizza", though it's actually nothing like pizza), *soju* ("Korean vodka", though again it's very different in taste) and much more, though for some reason *ddeok-galbi* (떡갈비) is never referred to as a **Korean burger** – even though this is precisely what it is. Served bun-less on a hotplate with rounds of side dishes, *ddeok-galbi* is available around the country, though Gwangju has achieved national renown for this delicious dish – despite the fact that there's absolutely nowhere to eat it in the centre of the city. The place to head to is a parade of near-identical restaurants near **Gwangju-Songjeong** train station; the dish costs W11,000 per portion at all of them, and is well worth the trek out.

SHOPPING

Bookshops The large bookshop in the bus terminal has a decent selection of English-language books and magazines, as well as an array of English-teaching materials. Alternatively, try the Gwangju International Center (see p.239), which usually has a secondhand selection.

Department stores Gwangju is awash with department stores, including NC Wave in the downtown area, and Shinsaegae near the bus terminal. The funky shops of Clothes Street can also be found near NC Wave.

DIRECTORY

Cinema Blockbusters are shown at the Lotte Cinema and Megabox, while the Gwangju International Center (see p.239) also puts on films from time to time.

Hospital Chonnam University hospital lies between the KT building and the river (☎ 062 220 6902).

Post office There's a post office in every district (usually Mon–Fri 9am–5pm). Those in the bus terminal and just

west of the May 18th Democratic Plaza are most convenient for visitors.

Spectator sports Gwangju Sangmu is the only military football team in Korea's top division, and plays at the World Cup Stadium to the south of the city. Players are sourced from men taking their two-year compulsory military service.

Naejangsan National Park

내장산 국립 공원 • W3000 • ⓦ english.knps.or.kr

NAEJANGSAN NATIONAL PARK is one of Korea's most popular parks, its circle of peaks flaring up like a gas ring in the autumn. Maple trees are the stars of the show in this annual incandescence, with squads of elm, ash and hornbeam adding their hues to the mix. The many trails and peaks across the park keep hikers happy year-round, though most visitors head to the amphitheatre-shaped mountain circle in the northeast, where the nearby tourist village has plenty of accommodation and places to eat. The area's topography allows for two **hiking routes**: a short temple loop around the interior, and a far more punishing circuit around the almost circular ridge.

The temple route

The **temple route** takes less than two hours to complete. A pleasant, maple-lined path takes you from the park entrance to **Naejangsa**, an unremarkable but pretty temple whose complex is dotted with informative English-language signs. Head further up the valley and you'll come to isolated **Wonjeogam**, a tiny hermitage home to a couple of monks and an abnormally large golden statue, before the trail swings back along the mountain face towards **Baengnyeonam**, another hermitage that marks the final sight on this route. Built in 632, the structure has been destroyed and rebuilt several times since then, and enjoys the most arresting setting of the three – bamboo stalks in a grove behind the main building point up towards the sheer rock crags of Naejangsan's main ridge, while in the other direction is the awesome view of a distant pavilion nestling beneath the peaks.

5

The ridge route

There are eight main peaks on the **ridge route**, and it's possible to scale them all on a calf-burning 13.8km day-hike, but most visitors content themselves with a shorter trip up and down – wherever you are on this circular route, you won't be far from a path heading back towards Naejangsa in the centre. From a point on the approach from the park entrance to Naejangsa (around 40min from the entrance) it's even possible to take a **cable car** (daily 9am–6pm; W4000 one-way, W7000 return) up to a restaurant that's within a short hike of the southern ridge and some great views.

ARRIVAL AND DEPARTURE

NAEJANGSAN NATIONAL PARK

By bus The park lies almost midway between Gwangju and Jeonju, and there are occasional direct buses from both cities (around 1hr 30min for either). Otherwise you'll have to transfer in Jeongeup (정읍), a small town well serviced by bus and train, and connected to Naejangsan by bus (1–2 hourly; 25min; W1400) or taxi (W12,000). Naejangsan's bus stop is outside a convenience store; it's a half-hour walk from here to the park entrance, and cheap shuttle buses also run through the day.

ACCOMMODATION AND EATING

Simple places to **sleep** and **eat** are clustered around Naejangsan bus stop. If you're looking for something more rustic, note that slightly uphill from the stop (in the opposite direction to the park entrance) is a small, friendly village of family homes, many of which lease out *minbak* rooms from W25,000 or so.

Hanok Hoegwan 하녹 회관 ☎063 538 9448. Located at the end of the long parade of restaurants heading from the bus stop towards the park entrance, this attractive venue serves good local dishes such as *sanchae bibimbap* (W9000), or filling set menus centred on mountain mushroom (버섯 백반; W12,000). Daily 8am–9pm.

Sarangbang Motel 사랑방 모텔 ☎063 538 8186. Standing out simply because it stands apart, this motel lies across the stream on the way to the park entrance. Rooms are simple, but it'll do. **W40,000**

Seonunsan Provincial Park

선운산 도립 공원 • Daily sunrise–sunset • Free • Bus from Jeonju (3 daily; 1hr 30min) or Gwangju (4 daily; 1hr 30min), though access to the park is usually via Gochang (고창), the closest town to Seonunsan and connected to it by regular bus (every 30min; 30min)

SEONUNSAN PROVINCIAL PARK has more than a few aces hidden up its leafy sleeves. It offers some of the country's best **rock-climbing** and a few enjoyable hikes; these may not be as well signed as others in Korea, but some may find this liberating. A streamside path, lined with stalls selling delicious mountain berry juice in the summer and autumn, heads straight from the main entrance to **Seonunsa** (선운사), a dusty collection of buildings, stupas and the like that appear to have been thrown together with little care. It's quite possibly the least satisfying temple complex in the province, and the small hermitages strewn around the park are of more interest.

Once past Seonunsa, you'll have a diverse range of **hiking trails** to choose from. Hikers should head for the hills; the peaks are puny by Korean standards, rarely reaching above 400m, but this makes for some easy day-hikes, and you may be rewarded with occasional views of the West Sea. For more hard-core thrills, continue further on the temple path, across the river; hidden a ten-minute hike behind a small restaurant is a spectacular **rock-climbing** course. This is a tough route and should not be attempted alone or without equipment (see ⓦkoreaontherocks.com for climb details, and to contact the few Koreans and expats au fait with holds, conglomerates and juggy overhangs). Back towards the park entrance, an underused side path heads along the temple wall and up a gorgeous valley lined with rows of tea trees and a few rustic dwellings.

A motley collection of hotels and motels lies outside the park entrance – you're better off **staying** elsewhere.

5

Byeonsanbando National Park

변산반도 국립 공원 • Daily 24hr • W3000 at Naesosa entrance • ⓦ english.knps.or.kr

In addition to the usual mix of peaks and temples found in Korea's parks, **BYEONSANBANDO NATIONAL PARK** throws in some wonderful sea views. It's spread around a small, rural **peninsula** on the west coast from which it takes its name – *bando* literally means "half-island". However, it's in the process of being hauled towards the mainland on its northern side with the aid of a 33km causeway, a development that will yield thousands of hectares of new farmland, but has caused one hell of a stink with Korean environmental groups.

Naesosa

내소사 • Daily 24hr • W2000

Off the charming southern side of the peninsula is the temple complex of **Naesosa**; this is more notable for its rural, mountain-backed setting than for any of its buildings, and is the most accessible place from which to start a hike. From the **entrance** – surrounded by persimmon trees, which shed their leaves at the slightest sniff of autumn, leaving behind naked baubles of bright-orange fruit – it's a short walk to the temple and its adjacent *minbak* village. The main temple building's exterior is almost entirely devoid of paint, while inside four dragons ascend to heaven, two headless, one gnawing a fish. From here, **hiking** routes head up to Gwaneumbong (425m).

Chaeseokgang

채석강 • Daily 9am–6pm • W1600

The unusual rock formations of **Chaeseokgang** sit at the western tip of the peninsula. You have to time it right to get the most out of the place – for much of the day it's just a bunch of pretty cliffs, but the surrender of the tide reveals page-like leaves of rock piled up like rusty banknotes, and teeming with crabs and other oceanic fauna.

5

By bus The park is accessible on a single daily bus from Jeonju; note that these head to the north of the peninsula first, then pass by Chaeseokgang (2hr) before wrapping around to Naesosa (2hr 40min). For Naesosa you'll save time

transferring in the town of Buan (부안), accessible on regular buses from Jeonju (1hr) and Seoul (3hr); from Buan, hourly buses to the park (55min) depart from a stop diagonally across from the bus terminal, or it's W25,000 by taxi.

ACCOMMODATION AND EATING

There are simple places to stay around both Chaeseokgang and the Naesosa entrance, though nothing truly stands out bar the **templestay** programmes (W40,000) run by the temple. Rooms are surprisingly comfy, and there's free wi-fi – useful if you can't drop off at the early hour you'll be put to bed. There are also plenty of fish **restaurants** around Chaeseokgang.

Neuti Namu 느티나무 ☎ 063 581 7773. Right next to the Naesosa ticket booth, this restaurant's outdoor tables have the nicest views of any in the area, looking over persimmon trees and into the park. The food's excellent,

and best washed down with a splendid choice of local *makgeolli*; their bellflower root set (더덕 정식; W20,000) comes with a dozen side dishes and can feed two. Daily 8am–end of custom.

Jeonju

전주

The small city of **JEONJU** is a place of considerable appeal; though finally starting to attract domestic tourists in the numbers it richly deserves, it remains largely off the radar of international visitors. This is ironic, since it's possibly the best place in the land in which to get a handle on **Korean customs**. Most visitors make a beeline for the city's splendid **hanok village** of traditional wooden housing, which contains more than enough for a full day of sightseeing, as well as being a good introduction to Korea's indigenous **arts and crafts**. In addition, spring sees Jeonju hosting JIFF (⦿ eng.jiff .or.kr), by far the most eclectic major **film festival** in the country.

However, it's **food** that Koreans most readily associate with Jeonju. Many of the differences are too subtle to be noticed by foreigners – and in the cheapest places, nonexistent – but you're likely to find a greater and more lovingly prepared number of *banchan* (반찬; side dishes) here, and a slightly greater emphasis on herbal seasoning than on the somewhat less cultivated tastebud-tinglers of salt and red-pepper paste. Particularly notable is the city's take on the tasty Korean staple, **bibimbap** (see box, p.249). The only downside is that Korean food just won't taste as good when you've moved on elsewhere.

Jeonju's ginkgo-lined streets help to create an ambience notably relaxed for a Korean city, but this disguises a hidden historical pedigree – this unassuming place marked the beginning of one of the longest lines of kings that the world has seen. It was here in the fourteenth century that the first kings of the **Joseon kingdom** were born, and the dynasty went on to rule Korea for over five centuries. Overlooked as the dynastic capital in favour of Seoul, today's Jeonju is not brimming with historical riches, but it has its charms, and is well worth a visit.

The hanok village

한옥 마을

Jeonju's main attraction is undoubtedly its splendid **hanok village**, a city-centre thatch of largely **traditional housing**. Highlights include a cathedral, an ancient shrine and a former Confucian academy, as well as museums for calligraphy, paper and wine. Almost all sights are free, and there's enough to keep you busy for a full day. The best way to enjoy it is simply to turn up and wander around – whether it be a museum, a traditional restaurant or a photogenic house, there's something to see around every corner. There are no opening times or entry fees to the area and it remains a functioning part of the city, one that's particularly beautiful at night when most of the tourists have gone.

The area has a distinct **north–south divide** – the north is far more polished and home to an ever-increasing number of bars and cafés, while the southern section is a pleasingly authentic and untouched slice of old Korea, with locals meandering up and down the narrow lanes as they have for decades. Musical **pansori** performances are frequent, and you may even be able to participate in traditional activities such as lantern-making or calligraphy. The best place to get your bearings is **Taejoro**, a road that bisects the *hanok* village from west to east; it has two **information offices** (see p.247) that can provide you with maps of the area.

Pungnammun
풍남문 • 24hr • Free
Most visitors start by heading to a sight just outside the village, across the main road that marks its western boundary. Here lies **Pungnammun**, an ornate city gate whose present structure dates from 1768, but was originally built in the late fourteenth century as part of Jeonju's city wall. Now surrounded by a circle of rather ugly modern buildings, it holds a gruesome secret – this is where the heads of martyred Christians were displayed after purges in 1801 (see p.359).

Gyeonggijeon
경기전 • Daily 9am–7pm • W1000
Taking up much of the *hanok* village's northern half, **Gyeonggijeon** is a park-like shrine area full of ornate buildings and beautiful trees – quite a sight in the autumn.

5

TRADITIONAL ARTS AND CRAFTS IN THE HANOK VILLAGE

Near the eastern end of Taejoro, the road bisecting the *hanok* **village**, you'll find the **Traditional Craftworks Exhibition Hall** (Tues–Sun: March–Oct 10am–7pm; Nov–Feb 10am–6pm; free), a traditionally styled wooden structure which holds crafts created by Jeonju artisans – a great place to hunt for souvenirs. If you're lucky you may get to see one of the traditional song and dance shows that are occasionally held just outside the complex – there's a list of performance times on the *hanok* **village** map. North of Taejoro, exhibits in the **Traditional Wine Museum** (Tues–Sun 9am–6pm; free) aren't terribly interesting, but the beauty of the *hanok* building – and the fact that free tipples are occasionally handed out – make it worth a quick peek. Of more interest is the **Korean Paper Institute** (Tues–Sun 9am–6pm; free), where beautiful examples of products made with handmade paper (한지; *hanji*) are on display, many available to buy; if you ask nicely, you may even be able to try your hand at making a kite or lantern. This is also possible at a number of **craft shops** dotted around the village (see p.250 for a few recommendations).

Artistic beauty of a different kind can be found a five-minute walk east along the streamside road, at the **Traditional Culture Center**, which puts on occasional *pansori* shows (see box opposite). The mournful singing and sparse drum-raps are well complemented by the old-fashioned beauty of the buildings, the performers are usually of an extremely high standard, and the shows are not over-long, making this an absolute must-see if you're in town at the right time – consult a tourist office for details.

It was built in 1410 to preserve a portrait of **King Taejo**, first leader of the famed Joseon dynasty and native of Jeonju, who had died two years previously after arguably the most productive reign in Korea's long regal history (see p.62). The portrait shows Taejo resplendent in an embroidered robe, against a pale yellow background, and sits proudly in a hall to the rear of the complex. It's surrounded by potraits of other members of his family, who were only officially made royals after Taejo's death, a move that gave posthumous legality to his bringing down of the Goryeo dynasty (see p.347).

Jeondong Cathedral

전동성당 • Services daily 5.30am, also 7am Tues & Thurs, 10am Wed & Fri, 4pm & 6pm Sat, and 4 more on Sun • Free

Almost directly opposite Gyeonggijeon, on the southern side of Taejoro, sits **Jeondong Cathedral**, looking almost European, with its brown brick walls and soaring spire. It was one of the first cathedrals to be built in Korea, and remains an active place of worship. The entrance is often open to view outside service times.

Gangam Calligraphy Museum

강암 서예관 • Daily 10am–5pm • Free

South of Taejoro, and overlooking the stream that marks the *hanok* village's southern boundary, is the **Gangam Calligraphy Museum**. Stored inside are wonderful examples of writing from some of Korea's best-known calligraphers – much of the work is that of Song Seongyong, a reputed maker of temple name-boards in dynastic times, though there are also pieces here from several former Korean presidents.

Jeonju Hyanggyo

전주 향교 • Opening hours vary • Free

Near the southeastern corner of the *hanok* village is **Jeonju Hyanggyo**, a former Confucian academy. Present here since 1603, and still housing a few of the original buildings, it sees surprisingly few visitors – a very good thing, as you'll appreciate more its contemplative *raison d'être*. Most notable are a number of large ginkgo trees, a couple of which – incredibly – actually predate the complex; with a majesty all of their own, these alone make a trip to this *hyanggyo* worthwhile.

5

PANSORI

Usually marketed to foreigners as "Korean opera", **pansori** (판소리) performances are a modern-day derivative of the country's shamanist past. Songs and incantations chanted to fend off evil spirits or ensure a good harvest slowly mutated over the years into ritualized presentations; the themes evolved, too, with tales of love and despair replacing requests to spirits unseen.

A good *pansori* may go on for hours, but each segment will be performed by a cast of just two – a female singer (소리꾼; *sorikkun*) and a male percussionist (고수; *gosu*). The *sorikkun* holds aloft a paper fan, which she folds, unfolds and waves about to emphasize lyrics or a change of scene. While the *gosu* drums out his minimalist finger taps on the *janggo*, he gives his singer words – or, more commonly, grunts – of encouragement known as *chuimsae*, to which the audience are expected to add their own. The most common are "*chalhanda!*" and "*olshi-gu!*", which are roughly equivalent to "you're doing good!" and "hm!", a grunt acknowledging appreciation, usually delivered with a refined nod. Just follow the Korean lead, and enjoy the show.

Southeast of the hanok village

A place for poets and contemplation, **Hanbyeokdang** (한벽당) is a pavilion dangling off a rock face across the road from the *hanok* village's southeast corner; one can only speculate on how beautiful the view must have been when this was built in 1404, before the main road arrived. From here continue south along the river, where the scene is further diluted by the overlarge (and uninteresting) Nature Ecological Museum – how ironic. Before long, however, you'll be rewarded with **Seungam Maeul** (승암 마을), a picturesque village whose paths snake between walls of rock and up the hill to the pine forest behind. The atmosphere here is something special, especially considering its proximity to the city centre; all the more surprising, then, that this little hamlet may have been the true **birthplace** of Joseon-era Korea – local rumours suggest that this was the source of the dynasty's first royals. Nowadays it's home to **Seungamsa** (승암사), a simple, deserted but intricately painted temple.

Martyrs Hill

It's possible to access **Martyrs Hill** behind the village via a path starting a little further down the river. The martyrs in question include Yi Hang-geom, killed in 1801 along with six of his family for his religious beliefs; his head was displayed on Pungnammun (see p.245) in the city centre in order to show the populace what happened to Catholics. A thirty-minute slog will take you to his tomb, from where you can follow a number of paths back to the city, many of which are studded with yet more delightfully secluded temples and hermitages.

ARRIVAL AND INFORMATION   JEONJU

By train Jeonju's train station, which is shaped something like a giant temple building, is on several bus routes that head towards the *hanok* village. However, it's far easier to take a cab (W7000).
Destinations Daejeon (1–2 hourly; 1hr); Seoul (Yongsan station; 1–2 hourly; 2hr); Suncheon (1–2 hourly; 1hr); Yeosu (1–2 hourly; 1hr 20min).
By bus Bus passengers are disgorged at one of two crusty terminals – one express, one intercity – in a messy area to the north of the city centre. Plenty of buses run into town from the main road a short walk to the east. However, it's far easier to go by taxi, which is unlikely to cost more than W5000.
Destinations Buan (every 10min; 1hr 20min); Busan

(11 daily; 3hr 35min); Daegu (hourly; 3hr 30min); Daejeon (every 20min; 1hr 20min); Gurye (frequent; 2hr); Gwangju (every 30min; 1hr 40min); Jeongeup (every 10min; 1hr); Jinan (frequent; 50min); Jinju (frequent; 3hr 30min); Mokpo (frequent; 3hr); Muju (frequent; 2hr 30min); Seoul (every 10min; 2hr 50min); Suncheon (11 daily; 2hr 20min); Yeosu (11 daily; 4hr).
Tourist information There are two information booths inside the *hanok* village (daily 9am–6pm; ☎063 288 0105); the most useful is near the Gyeonggijeon ticket booth. Whichever you head to, pick up one of the excellent free maps of the *hanok* village; these should also be available at the train station and bus terminals.

5

SLEEPING THE TRADITIONAL WAY IN JEONJU

Somewhat ironically, one of Jeonju's main draws for domestic tourists is the opportunity to sleep in traditional Korean houses. Known as **hanok** (한옥), these have long been dwindling in number across the country, and few urban areas feature them in any significant quantity – Seoul's Bukchon neighbourhood being an honourable exception (see p.68). For foreign tourists, the chance to stay in such a place is perhaps even more enticing; both demand and supply have been rising of late, with an ever-increasing number of houses in Jeonju's *hanok* village allowing guests to stay. These are traditional dwellings, so don't expect large rooms or too much comfort. The experience is unique, nonetheless, especially in winter when your feet are toasted by the *ondol* floors, many of which are heated from beneath by burning wood.

One minor drawback is that very few *hanok* owners hereabouts will speak any English – this certainly complicates things when trying to make a booking. The city's tourist information offices (see p.247) will help find you a suitable room on arrival, and they have options listed on their website (**W** tour-eng.jeonju.go.kr). Figure on paying around W60,000 for a room.

ACCOMMODATION

For a place with such tourist potential, Jeonju has a surprising dearth of quality accommodation. However, the city does provide a rare opportunity to stay at specially adapted **hanok** buildings – an opportunity not to be missed (see the box above for more). There's precious little point in basing yourself outside the *hanok* area, though there's a seedy motel cluster in the "downtown" area just west of the *hanok* village.

Hanok Spa 한옥 스파 Gyeongwondong 1-ga 126-18 **☎** 063 232 0015. This *jjimjilbang*, north of Gyeonggijeon, is the city's super-budget choice. It doesn't quite live up to the "*hanok*" component of its name, though there are a variety of pools to enjoy, with the waters hauled from 170m beneath the surface. W8000

★**Jeonju Guesthouse** 전주 게스트하우스 Gyeongwondong 2-ga 62 **☎** 063 286 8886, **W** koreabackpackers.net. Charming hostel, conveniently located just north of the *hanok* village. The English-speaking owner is a priceless source of local information, and although the bedrooms are a tiny bit stuffy the large common area is a great place to meet new friends. Dorms W19,000, twins W50,000

Le Win 르윈 Girindaero 85 **☎** 063 232 7000, **W** hotellewin.com. This is the only large hotel in the area, standing somewhat obtrusively over the *hanok* village. All rooms are carpeted and homely, but despite recent modifications they remain poor value for the price – make sure you get one with a westward view over the traditional area below. W137,000

★**Pinetree View** 황토 민박 Omokdaegil 42 **☎** 010 5685 0804, **W** pinetreeview.kr. This *hanok* guesthouse is larger and less homestay-like than most options in the village, though somehow contrives to be more charming – its setting in the less-developed southern half certainly helps. There's a rooftop viewing area, and a few secluded niches for night-time drinks around the complex. W65,000

Star Maru 별빛 마루 Gyeongwondong 2-ga 40-11 **☎** 063 231 7770. Converted from a motel, this little guesthouse is one of the only places offering dorm beds in the *hanok* village; the common area is large and welcoming, and there's free breakfast. It's also almost as close as you'll get to Gyeonggijeon shrine, and also within an easy walk of the shopping quarter. Dorms W19,000, twins W55,000

Yangsajae 양사재 Omokdaegil 40 **☎** 063 282 4959. Formerly home to a famed local poet, this is another of the *hanok* district's wooden dwellings, with *ondol*-heated rooms as pleasingly traditional as they are tiny. They're now also going for the "culture" experience, with a variety of teas to sample during your stay. W60,000

EATING AND DRINKING

Jeonju has a national reputation as a city of culinary excellence and visitors should not leave without trying the city's wonderful **bibimbap** (see box opposite). There exist a number of excellent **traditional restaurants** in the *hanok* village, together with some rustic **tearooms** and an ever-growing number of **cafés**. The *hanok* district isn't exactly a nightlife hotspot, though in good weather it would be a shame not to take advantage of the unique opportunities the *hanok* district provides for al-fresco drinking (see box, p.250). Further afield, there are countless places to **drink** or dance the night away in the **student zones** around Jeonju's various universities; the area outside Chonbuk National University is generally regarded as the best.

RESTAURANTS

★**Cheon Nyeon Nuri Bom** 천년누리봄 Gyeongwondong 2-ga 53-1 **☎** 063 288 8813. Just north of Gyeonggijeon, this is a thoroughly noble restaurant – the volunteer staff here are all female retirees. The food they whip up is great, too; try their super-cheap lunch sets (W6000), or drop by in the evening for the filling *makgeolli* sets (W20,000). Daily 11am–9pm.

Guksu Ggot 국수 꽃 Seongdang Jeongmun-ap ☎063 283 1949. Cutesy restaurant with a small selection of noodle bowls served amid twee decorations, and views of the Gyeonggijeon walls. No English spoken, though the picture menu will help you choose – everything's around W5000. Daily 8am–8pm.

★**Gyodong Seongalbi** 교동 선갈비 Taejoro 26-1 ☎063 288 2282. One of the most attractive restaurants in the *hanok* area also makes some of its tastiest food – succulent pieces of minced beef *galbi* brought to you on a sizzling hotplate (W11,000 per portion), and served with a selection of lovingly prepared side dishes (the mushrooms are particularly delectable). Gluttons can add rice or noodles to the mix. Mon–Fri 11am–9pm, Sat & Sun 10am–9pm.

Hangukjip 한국집 Jeondong 2-1 ☎063 284 2224. Decent Jeonju *bibimbap* (W11,000) served plain or in a sizzling-hot bowl, with a charming garden view. For an extra W2000 you can have raw beef (something like a tartare) thrown into the mix – highly recommended, especially since the side dishes usually lack a little oomph. Daily 10am–9pm.

Jongno Hoegwan 종로 회관 Jeondong 60-1 ☎063 283 4578. Not the most atmospheric restaurant serving up genuine Jeonju *bibimbap*, but the location next to Gyeonggijeon is pretty impressive, as is the dish itself. For W10,000 you get the meal and a mouthwatering array of side dishes – the mushrooms, in particular, are nothing short of heavenly. Daily 9am–9.30pm.

★**Omokdae Sarangchae** 오목대 사랑채 Gyodong 63-13 ☎063 232 8533. Traditional food is on offer at this extremely beautiful restaurant – sitting in the rear, near the fish pond, is particularly recommended in the evening, when the interior is bathed in a soft glow. It's

almost easy to forget about the food in such surrounds, but their speciality is *galbi tang* – beef bone served in a clear soup (W10,000). Daily 8am–10pm.

CAFÉS AND TEAROOMS

Café Tomorrow 카페 투모로 Girindaero 71-1 ☎063 288 6455. Not the best coffee in town, but certainly up there with the best views – nab a seat on the balcony and gaze down over the *hanok* district. Coffee and tea from W3500. Daily 10am–10pm.

★**Dahwawon** 다화원 Choemyeonghuigil 13, no phone. The *hanok* district has been getting ever more gentrified of late, and the tearooms that have lasted the course have been those kowtowing to youthful trends such as waffles or cream-filled *churros*. Hurrah, then, for the one which has kept it real – nothing but tasty, traditional tea (W5000), a couple of traditional snacks, and an utterly beguiling interior boasting views of tiled rooftops and maple leaves. Wonderful. Daily 8am–10pm.

★**Nampodong Chapssal Ssieot Hoddeok** 남포동 찹쌀 씨엇호떡 Jeondong 69-2 ☎010 9322 4492. The name of this little booth is as much of a mouthful as the gloopy sugar-and-rice pancakes on sale for just W1000 each – *hoddeok* (호떡; pronounced a little like "hot dog") are extremely popular winter snacks, and on a cold evening are hard to beat. Here they're also filled with seeds – a new fad that originated in Busan, though this is perhaps the finest version you'll find in all Korea. Daily 8am–10pm.

Seolbing 설빙 Pungnamdong 3-ga 36-15 ☎070 7799 8883. Part of a dessert café chain which has swept the nation of late, this one stands out for the 500-year-old ginkgo tree standing outside – there are a couple of tables under its penta-centenarian branches. Try a *bingsu* – a Korean dessert made with shaved ice and (usually) red beans. Daily 10am–10pm.

JEONJU BIBIMBAP

Jeonju's most famous dish is, without doubt, its **bibimbap** (전주 비빔밥). Regular *bibimbap* – a mixture of vegetables served on a bed of rice, with a fried egg and meat on top – is available across the country, but in Jeonju they've picked up the formula and run with it. Recipes vary from place to place, but the ingredients are always well chosen and may include anything from pine kernels to bluebell roots or fern bracken in addition to the usual leaves and bean sprouts. In addition, your meal will invariably be surrounded by up to twenty free **side dishes**, made with just as much care, and an even greater variety of ingredients. Beware, however, of restaurants that claim to serve authentic Jeonju *bibimbap* – many places, particularly around the train station and bus terminals, will simply give you a regular version of the dish (though genuinely made in Jeonju, and thereby circumnavigating Korea's already weak product description laws). One way to sort Jeonju wheat from Jeonju chaff is the price – for the real deal, you shouldn't be paying less than W8000, but even at double this price it's likely to be money well spent.

5

DRINKING AL-FRESCO

Korea is a great country for those who like drinking outdoors – cheap alcohol is available round the clock from ubiquitous convenience stores, and as long as you're not making a nuisance or on private property, **al-fresco drinking** is completely legal. Jeonju is perhaps the best Korean city in which to take advantage of these possibilities – in addition to the romance bequeathed by streets lined with wooden housing and studded with fairy lights, it's the best place in the land for the milky rice beer known as **makgeolli**. About 6 percent ABV, this is available for as little as W1000 from any convenience store or mini-mart, and there are dozens of local varieties to enjoy – notable brands include *Myeongga* (명가) and *Namwonssal* (남원쌀), though you could also try hunting down red ginseng-infused *Hongsam Jujo* (홍삼주조). Jeonju actually seems most proud of a drink named **moju** (모주): flavoured with ginseng, jujube, ginger, cinnamon and licorice, this tasty beverage is only 1.5 percent in strength, and usually W3000 for a tiny bottle. As for where to drink, a few recommendations include the grassy area behind the middle school east of Gyeonggijeon; a blue-and-green-lit footbath on the western side of Eunhaengno; and the hilltop behind the Traditional Craftworks Exhibition Hall.

SHOPPING

Doggom 도꼼 Taejoro 14-3 ☎063 221 1222. Many shops in the *hanok* district sell earthenware products, but those on offer here are clearly a class above. You can even try your hand at making a cup if you'll be in town long enough for it to get fired – one night should do. Daily 9am–7pm.

Hobak 호박 Eunhaengno 15 ☎010 2690 1793. Tiny shop selling jewellery in pleasing Korean styles – think jade and turquoise rings, and all manner of brooches and necklaces. Daily 10.30am–7pm.

Pi 파이 Pungnamdong 1-45 ☎010 6711 2662. Small

shop in the *hanok* village selling clothing dyed with persimmon. Both male and female wearables are on offer. Daily 9am–7pm.

Traditional Craftworks Exhibition Hall 전주 공예 풍전시관 Taejoro 15 ☎063 285 0002. Set in a large complex across several buildings, this is a grand place to hunt for souvenirs. Examples include silk goods such as pillowcases and shawls, a range of traditionally styled ties, masks, ceramics and fans made with *hanji* (handmade) paper. Daily 10am–7pm.

Maisan Provincial Park

마이산 도립 공원 • Daily 24hr • W3000 • Northern entrance: take a bus (2–4 hourly from Jeonju; 1hr) to the small town of Jinan (진안), and then either another bus (hourly) or a taxi (W12,000) to the park • Tapsa entrance: bus from Jinan (3 daily), or Jeonju (3 direct buses daily); Tapsa itself is a gentle 30min walk from the stop

Korea's pine-clad mountain ranges tend to look rather similar to each other. One exception is tiny **MAISAN PROVINCIAL PARK**, or "horse-ear mountains", so named after two of its peaks. From the **northern entrance** – where you'll find restaurants and a couple of places to stay – steep flights of energy-sapping stairs take you between the horses' ears and over the scalp, where you'll probably need a rest. Unfortunately it's not possible to climb the peaks, which remained closed for regeneration at the time of writing.

If you continue between the peaks, around a half-hour from the entrance you'll hit **Unsusa**, a dainty temple surrounded by flowers in warmer months. Another quick burst down the mountain is the highly popular temple of **Tapsa** (탑사), Maisan's real gem, which sits in a surreal clasp of stacked rock. Mildly Gaudíesque in appearance, the near-hundred-strong towers were the work of one monk, Yi Kap-myong (1860–1957), who apparently used no adhesive in their construction, even though some are over 10m high. Rather than head over the ridge again, you can pick up a bus from a stop another half-hour walk downhill from Tapsa, a pleasing stretch lined with little restaurants and snack-stands.

Deogyusan National Park

5

덕유산 국립 공원 • Daily 24hr • Free • Ⓦ english.knps.or.kr

Locked into the northeast of Jeonbuk province is **DEOGYUSAN NATIONAL PARK**, whose lofty yet gentle terrain rises up south of **Muju ski resort**, then spills down in an undulating series of valleys. Though it's most popular in the wintertime, the **warmer months** are actually a great time of year to visit, since accommodation prices plunge, and there's great hiking on hills that would otherwise be covered with snow and skiers.

Muju ski resort

무주 • Ⓦ mujuresort.com

Despite being one of the warmest and most southerly ski resorts in Korea, **MUJU** is one of the peninsula's most popular, and attracts hordes of skiers throughout the winter, a season artificially elongated with the aid of some hefty snow machines. Less bulky ski equipment is available for hire, and whether you're a ski veteran or an absolute beginner, you'll have more than twenty slopes to choose from. It's also possible to sled or go cross-country skiing, or take part in non-snow related activities from golf and paintball to bungee-jumping and bike rides.

Muji–Gucheondong hike

A popular hike – one that almost every summertime visitor to Deogyusan follows – links Muju ski resort with the main park entrance at Gucheondong. Though it's not especially taxing, much of the upward slog can be chalked off by **cable car** from the resort, which whisks passengers up the 1520m peak of Seolcheon-bong. From here it's a 6.2km hike back down to the ski area, or a longer, more beautiful one along a trail riddled with rocks, small waterfalls and pools to the Gucheondong park entrance.

ARRIVAL AND DEPARTURE   DEOGYUSAN NATIONAL PARK

By bus The national park and ski resort can both be reached on regular buses via Muju town itself. The 19km drive in is astonishingly beautiful, taking you through a typically relaxed slice of rural Jeolla. Buses continue past the resort on to Gucheondong, the main entrance to the national park; there are also free hourly shuttle buses linking this entrance with the ski resort.

Destinations (Muju) Daejeon (frequent; 1hr 30min); Gwangju (frequent; 3hr 40min); Jeonju (frequent; 2hr); Seoul (5 daily; 2hr 40min).

ACCOMMODATION AND EATING

It'll cost a pretty penny to stay in or next to the **ski resort** itself, where prices go through the roof during ski season. Things are much less expensive in the small motel district down the hill; few establishments are worthy of special mention, and it will always pay to shop around, but the best are on and around Baebang-gil, near the main road at the bottom. There are cheaper options in **Gucheondong**, a village-like area below the park entrance; the most pleasant places to stay are on the western side of the water. All of these areas also have restaurants aplenty, but most notable during wintertime is **Carnival Street**, a quasi-Austrian collection of **restaurants** and cafés below the *Tirol* – a refreshing change if you've been in Korea for a while.

Kookmin 국민 호텔 Muju resort 185 ☎ 063 320 7000. The cheapest accommodation in the resort area, this 400-room behemoth is actually quite a steal if you manage to factor in some off-season discounts. ₩80,000

Tirol 호텔 티롤 Muju resort ☎ 063 320 7200. Right next to the ski runs and resembling an Austrian cabin, this hotel is absurdly expensive during the peak winter season, and far from cheap at other times. It's a nice place, though, with well-appointed rooms that are piping hot, even in the depths of winter – the suites also come with four-poster beds. ₩380,000

Chungcheong

BEOPJUSA TEMPLE

Chungcheong

Of South Korea's principal regions, Chungcheong (충청) is the least visited by foreign travellers, most of whom choose to rush through it on buses and trains to Gyeongju or Busan in the southeast, or over it on planes to Jeju-do. But to do so is to bypass the heart of the country, a thrillingly rural mishmash of rice paddies, ginseng fields, national parks and unhurried islands. One less obvious Chungcheong attraction is the local populace – the Chungcheongese are noted throughout Korea for their relaxed nature. Here, you'll get less pressure at the markets, or perhaps even notice a delay of a second or two when the traffic lights change before being deafened by a cacophony of car horns. The region's main cities are noticeably laidback by Korean standards, and the Chungcheongese themselves, particularly those living in the countryside, speak at a markedly slower pace than other Koreans.

Today split into two provinces, Chungcheong was named in the fourteenth century by fusing the names of Chungju and Cheongju, then its two major cities – they're still around today, but of little interest to travellers (Cheongju did, however, produce the world's first book; see p.276). Administratively separate from the two Chungcheong provinces, and lying in between them, is **Daejeon**, the area's largest city and a fun place to sample some urban delights.

The westernmost of the two provinces is **Chungnam** (충남), whose name somewhat confusingly translates as "South Chungcheong". Its western edge is washed by the West Sea, and has a few good beaches – the strip of white sand in **Daecheon** is one of the busiest in the country, with the summer revelry hitting its zenith each July at an immensely popular **mud festival**. Off this coast are a number of accessible **islands** – tiny squads of rock stretch far beyond the horizon into the West Sea, and sustain fishing communities that provide a glimpse into pre-karaoke Korean life. Head inland instead and the pleasures take a turn for the traditional: the small cities of **Buyeo** and **Gongju** functioned as capitals of the **Baekje dynasty** (18 BC–660 AD; see box, p.264) just as the Roman Empire was collapsing, yet each still boasts a superb wealth of dynastic sights. Both are home to fortresses, regal tombs and museums filled with gleaming jewellery of the period, which went on to have a profound influence on Japanese craft. North of Gongju, and actually part of Seoul's sprawling subway network, is **Cheonan**, which is home to the country's largest, and possibly most revealing, museum.

To the east, the land becomes ever more mountainous as you enter the province of **Chungbuk** (충북; "North Chungcheong"). As Korea's only landlocked province, this could be said to represent the heart of the country, a predominantly rural patchwork of fields and peaks, with a handful of national parks within its borders. **Songnisan** is

GUINSA TEMPLE

Highlights

❶ **Gongju and Buyeo** Head to the former capitals of the Baekje dynasty to feast your eyes on their regal riches. **See p.262 & p.267**

❷ **Boryeong mud festival** Get dirty on the beach at the most enjoyable festival on the Korean calendar. **See p.269**

❸ **West Sea islands** Chungcheong boasts a number of tiny, beach-pocked isles, home to fishing communities and a relaxed way of life that's hard to find on the mainland. **See p.271**

❹ **Independence Hall of Korea** The nationalistic side of the Korean psyche is laid

bare at this huge testament to the country's survival of Japanese occupation. **See p.273**

❺ **Beopjusa temple** This striking temple features the world's tallest bronze Buddha, and is surrounded by the hiker-friendly peaks of Songnisan National Park. **See p.275**

❻ **Danyang** Take a midnight stroll, *makgeolli* in hand, along this tiny town's lakeside promenade. **See p.277**

❼ **Guinsa** Clamber around the snake-like alleyways of what may well be Korea's most distinctive temple. **See p.280**

HIGHLIGHTS ARE MARKED ON THE MAP ON P.256

CHUNGCHEONG

HIGHLIGHTS

1. Gongju and Buyeo
2. Boryeong mud festival
3. West Sea islands
4. Independence Hall of Korea
5. Beopjusa temple
6. Danyang
7. Guinsa

High speed rail

WEST SEA (YELLOW SEA)

0 kilometres 20

N

GANGWON

GYEONGGI

GYEONGBUK

CHUNGBUK

CHUNGNAM

DAEJEON

JEONBUK

SOBAEKSAN NATIONAL PARK
Birobong (1440m)
Guinsa
Danyang
Yeongju

WORAKSAN NATIONAL PARK
Yeongbong (1097m)

Jecheon
Chuncheon
Chungjuho
Suanbo
Chungju
Mungyeong
Sangju
Gimcheon
Yeongdong
Muju
Sancheong

SONGNISAN NATIONAL PARK
Cheonhwangbong (1053m)
Boeun

Cheongju

Jincheon
Independence Hall of Korea
Cheonan
Sejong City
Sintanjin
Daejeon

Osan
Suwon
Pyeongtaek
Asan
Geumsan

GYERYONGSAN NATIONAL PARK
Gongju
Magoksa
Nonsan
Iksan

Unjong
Haemi
Boryeong
Buyeo

TAEAN HAEAN NATIONAL PARK
Mallipo Beach
Taean
Anmyeondo
Anmyeon
Yeongmok
Wonsando
Daecheon Beach
Muchangpo

Janggeodo
Hodo
Sapsido
Nokdo
Oeyeondo

Geumgang River
Gunsan
Gimje
Jeonju

Seoul

> **SLOW TALK**
>
> When passing through rural Chungcheong, those who've been travelling around Korea for a while may notice something special about the way locals talk. The **pace of conversation** here is slower than in the rest of the land (particularly the staccato patois of Gyeongsang province), with some locals speaking in a drawl that can even have non-native students of the language rolling their eyes and looking at their watches in frustration. One folk tale, retold across the nation, describes a Chungcheongese town that was destroyed by a falling boulder: apparently it was spotted early enough, but locals were unable to elucidate their warnings in a speedy enough manner.

deservedly the most popular, and has a number of good day-hikes emanating from Beopjusa, a highly picturesque temple near the park's main entrance. **Sobaeksan** is less visited but just as appealing to hikers; it surrounds the lakeside resort town of **Danyang**, which makes a comfortable base for exploring the caves, fortresses and sprawling temple of **Guinsa** on the province's eastern flank.

Daejeon

대전

Every country has a city like **DAEJEON** – somewhere pleasant to go about daily life, but with little to offer the casual visitor. These, however, arrive in surprisingly high numbers, many using the city as a default stopover on the high-speed rail line from Seoul to Busan. There are far better places in which to break this journey, including on the lesser-used slow line through Danyang, Andong and Gyeongju (see "Itineraries", pp.24-25), but if you do choose to hole up in Daejeon you'll find decent nightlife and a few mildly diverting attractions. The most vaunted of the latter is **Yuseong**, a therapeutic hot-spring resort sitting near the **Gapcheon River** on the western flank of the city. On the opposite side of the river lies the pleasant **Hanbat Arboretum**, while the peak of **Gyejoksan**, on the city fringes, makes for a rewarding climb. Lastly, and perhaps most importantly, Daejeon is also a good jumping-off point for **Gyeryongsan**, a small but pretty national park to the west (see p.260).

Yuseong Spa

유성온천 • Most springs open daily 9am–6pm • Entry W6000–10,000 • Yuseong Spa subway

The **Yuseong** hot-spring district is revered across the land for its purportedly curative waters, which bubble up into the communal steam rooms of a series of middling hotels (see p.260); non-guests can usually use them for a small fee. Unfortunately, this is a heavily built-up – and, to be frank, rather ugly – slice of urban Korea. One recent attempt at partial prettification saw a small channel of spring water routed along the area's main stretch, which makes for a rather lovely footbath.

The Gapcheon

갑천 • Hanbat Arboretum Daily 9am–6pm, summer evenings until 9pm • Free • Daejeon Art Gallery Tues–Sun 10am–5pm • W2000

Wide as it may appear, the **Gapcheon** is too short to qualify as a river, and is thus, according to Korean officialdom, officially a stream. Its banks come alive in the summer with picnickers, and the park-like area immediately south of the pedestrianized Expo Bridge is a popular weekend hangout for local families. You can rent bikes (around W3000 per hour) from a booth just south of the bridge. In the park-like expanse to the south, you'll also find the peaceful **Hanbat Arboretum**, and the excellent **Daejeon Art Gallery**, which tends to focus on modern art.

6

Gyejoksan

계족산 • On a number of bus routes, including the #720 and #102 (every 10–15min)

One of the best ways in which to enjoy Daejeon is to look down on it from one of the several mountains encircling the city. Budding hikers are advised to make their way to **Gyejoksan**, a 429m-high peak rising cone-like from a plateau on the city's northeastern fringe. After a simple, invigorating climb of under two hours, you'll have fantastic views of Daejeon on one side, and a man-made lake to the other; signs point the way to secluded temples and hermitages, and you can also see a couple of sections of fortress wall from the Baekje era. A more recent addition is the "eco-walking" **Red Clay Trail**, which stretches for 14km and apparently constitutes the nation's first barefoot mountain path – you don't have to do the whole lot.

ARRIVAL AND DEPARTURE   DAEJEON

By train The city has two train stations: Daejeon station is right in the centre and sits on the Seoul–Busan line, while Seodaejeon station is a ₩4500 taxi ride away to the west, sitting on a line that splits off north of Daejeon for Gwangju and Mokpo. Both handle high-speed KTX services, though slower, cheaper trains are available too.
Destinations (Daejeon station) Busan (3–6 hourly; 1hr 40min); Cheonan (3–6 hourly; 20min); Dongdaegu (frequent; 48min); Seoul (frequent; 50min).
Destinations (Seodaejeon station) Cheonan (1–2 hourly;

20min); Daecheon (1 daily; 2hr 20min); Gwangju (frequent; 2hr); Jeonju (hourly; 1hr 10min); Seoul Yongsan (1–2 hourly; 50min).
By bus Daejeon has excellent bus connections to every major city in the country, though arrivals are often hampered by the city's incessant traffic – and the fact that there are four terminals to choose from. The two main ones are the express (고속; *gosok*) terminal and the intercity Dongbu (동부) terminal, which sit across the road from each other to the northeast of the city. Buses from most

THE CURE-ALL ROOT

For centuries, perhaps even millennia, the **ginseng root** has been used in Asia for its medicinal qualities, particularly its ability to retain or restore the body's **Yin–Yang** balance; for a time, it was valued more highly by weight than was gold. Even today, Korean ginseng is much sought after on the global market, due to the country's ideal climatic conditions; known locally as **insam** (인삼), much of it is grown in the Chungcheong provinces under slanted nets of black plastic. The roots take anything up to six years to mature, and suck up so much nutrition from the soil that, once harvested, no more ginseng can be planted in the same field for over a decade.

The **health benefits** of ginseng have been much debated in recent years, and most of the evidence in favour of the root is anecdotal rather than scientific. There are, nonetheless, hordes of admirers, and ginseng's stock rose further when it rode the crest of the "healthy living" wave that swept across Korea just after the turn of the millennium. Today, it's possible to get your fix in pills, capsules, jellies, chewing gum or boiled sweets, as well as the more traditional tea or by eating the root raw. As the purported benefits depend on the dosage and type of ginseng used (red or white), it's best to consult a practitioner of oriental medicines, but one safe – and delicious – dish is **samgyetang** (삼계탕), a tasty and extremely healthy soup made with a ginseng-stuffed chicken, available for around W8000 across the land. Or for a slightly quirky drink, try mixing a sachet of ginseng granules and a spoon of brown sugar into hot milk – your very own **ginseng latte**.

Chungcheong destinations arrive at the Seobu (서부) terminal to the south of the city, though you'll get to some faster from the tiny Yuseong (유성) terminal, in the eponymous hot-spring area to Daejeon's west.

Destinations (Dongbu terminal) Andong (16 daily; 2hr 40min); Cheongju (every 10min; 1hr); Gongju (frequent; 1hr 10min); Muju (frequent; 1hr); Songnisan (frequent; 1hr 40min).

Destinations (express terminal) Busan (hourly; 3hr

10min); Cheonan (frequent; 1hr); Daegu (every 30min; 2hr 20min); Gwangju (every 30min; 2hr 30min); Gyeongju (4 daily; 2hr 40min); Jeonju (every 20min; 1hr 20min); Seoul (frequent; 1hr 50min).

Destinations (Seobu terminal) Buyeo (every 20min; 1hr 20min); Daecheon (frequent; 1hr 50min); Gongju (frequent; 1hr).

Destinations (Yuseong terminal) Seoul (frequent; 2hr 20min); Gongju (frequent; 25min).

GETTING AROUND AND INFORMATION

By bus The city's size and levels of traffic can make getting around frustrating. The city bus network is comprehensive but complicated, with hundreds of routes – two of the most useful are #841, which connects Daejeon station to all three bus terminals, and #107, which runs from the express terminal via Yuseong to Gyeryongsan National Park (see p.260).

By subway Given the traffic, it's usually better to make use of the single subway line bisecting the city whenever possible; with plans for line 2 still not yet finalized, the network is not exactly all-encompassing, but it's good for

heading from Daejeon station to Yuseong, or the bars of Dunsandong. Tickets come in the form of cute plastic tokens, and cost W1300 a pop.

By taxi This is Korea – taxis are absolutely everywhere (the ones with their roof lights on are available), and a ride across town is unlikely to set you back more than W10,000.

Tourist information The tourist office on the upstairs departure level of the main train station (daily 9am–6pm; ☎042 221 1905) can help out with accommodation or bus routes. There's also a tourist information booth outside the express bus terminal.

ACCOMMODATION

Finding a **place to stay** shouldn't be too much trouble, though don't expect much in the centre. The higher-end lodgings are all way out west in **Yuseong** (see p.257), and many squat over **hot springs**, the mineral-heavy waters coursing up into bathrooms and communal steam rooms. The city centre's main **motel** areas are notoriously sleazy, particularly the one surrounding the bus terminals. Pickings are even slimmer in Eunhaengdong, the area west of the main train station.

CITY CENTRE

Bijou Motel 비쥬 모텔 24-1 Jeongdong ☎042 254 6603. Across the main road from the train station (to the right of the T-junction as seen from the exit), this is an

acceptable lower-end choice, with clean and cheerily decorated en-suite rooms. <u>W30,000</u>

Hillton 힐튼 1488-1 Dunsan 1-dong ☎042 471 5335. Circumnavigating copyright laws with an extra "L", this

6

A CAPITAL IDEA

Thrusting up from the very centre of Daejeon are the buildings of the **National Government Complex** – four large, sinister cuboids whose red lights blink in eerie non-unison at night. While there's nothing for the Ordinary Joe to see inside, these buildings represent the most visible examples of Korea's attempts to shift a bunch of government agencies from Seoul. As well as the generic decentralization-driven rationale propping up such plans around the globe, the North Korea issue was a prime factor in the decision to relocate – Seoul lies just 50km from the border of a country with which it remains at war. The initial plans were to move the capital entirely from Seoul, though these were watered down following the discovery that doing so would violate the national constitution. Busan will now get fisheries and maritime agencies; Chuncheon gets tourism; Ulsan will house those pertaining to labour and energy, and so on. The main focus, however, is now **Sejong City**, a new development currently taking shape just north of Daejeon; though many of the first squads of government bureaucrats are somewhat miffed about being sent "to live in the countryside", the city is expected to be home to over half a million by 2030.

place is the most amenable to bargaining of all the motels in the wider Dunsandong party area – useful indeed, since almost all establishments here are ridiculously overpriced. Your cash will buy a neat room with a comfy bed and far too many mirrors, plus all the motel regulars such as free toothpaste and power showers. **W40,000**

YUSEONG

Riviera 리베라 7 Oncheonno ☎042 823 2111, ⓦhotelriviera.co.kr. The plushest hotel in the city features Japanese and Chinese restaurants, as well as a stylish lounge bar, and is large enough to seem quiet most of the time. The rooms have been pleasantly decorated and have internet, though not all have bathtubs. **W240,000**

Yousung 유성 9 Oncheonno ☎042 820 0100, ⓦyousunghotel.com. Yuseong's grand old dame (its name, appropriately, using now-retired Romanization) is ticking over nicely. Its partly outdoor on-site spa is the big draw, if functional rather than attractive, and it's open to non-guests for W6000. The hotel rooms themselves are spacious and furnished with all mod cons; though the views aren't great, it still pays to plump for as high a floor as possible. **W220,000**

EATING AND DRINKING

Daejeon's culinary scene is decidedly unremarkable, but this being Korea, you should still eat well – you'll never have too far to go before stumbling across a perfectly acceptable noodle or barbecued-meat **restaurant**, while all the major cheapo chains (see box, p.38) are out in force here. For **drinking**, the old downtown area west of the train station is increasingly becoming a ghost town by night, with action having shifted to **Dunsandong**, near City Hall; there's also a nice little student scene in **Gungdong**, around Chungnam University.

Pungnyeon Samgyetang 풍년 삼계탕 Hongdodong 9-3 ☎042 632 5757. This is the best place in town to hunt down the healthy local favourite, *samgyetang* (삼계탕), a ginseng-infused chicken soup (W10,000); the roots used here come from nearby Geumsan, one of the world's most vaunted locations for the growing of ginseng (see box, p.259). This restaurant lies ten minutes' walk southwest of the bus terminals along Dongseoro, though several places closer to the buses serve the same dish. Daily 10am–10pm.

Skåne 스코네 Dunsandong 1425, ☎042 487 0100. Daejeon has its fair share of middling pasta and curry places, but for something completely different, head to this classy Swedish restaurant, sitting pretty on the sixth floor in the Dunsan area. Fairly authentic sets go from W21,000, or pick out à la carte items such as the meatballs (W18,000). The cakes also look unfairly tasty. Daily 10.30am–10pm.

Sulsul Dongdong 술술동동 Eunhaengdong 168-10, ☎042 255 6911. There's not too much to write home about in the old downtown area, but this rustic, pleasantly gloomy lair serves up good savoury pancakes known as *jeon* (전; see p.40) for around W10,000 per serving. They also have plenty of *makgeolli* rice beer to choose from – several serious brands, plus some more youth-focused fruity infusions. Daily 2pm–1am.

Gyeryongsan National Park

계룡산 국립 공원 • Daily from 2hr before sunrise to sunset • Free • ⓦenglish.knps.or.kr

Despite its comparatively puny size relative to its Korean brethren, **GYERYONGSAN NATIONAL PARK** (see map, pp.262–263) is a true delight, with herons flitting along the trickling streams, wild boar rifling through the woods and bizarre long-net stinkhorn mushrooms – like regular mushrooms, but with a yellow honeycombed veil – found on the forest floors. It is said to have the most *gi* (기; life-force) of any national park in Korea, one of several factors that haul in 1.4 million people per year, making it the most visited national park in the Chungcheong region. The main reasons for this are accessibility and manageability: it lies equidistant from Gongju to the west and Daejeon to the east, and easy day-hikes run up and over the central peaks, connecting **Gapsa** and **Donghaksa**, two temples flanking the park, and each more than a millennium old.

6

Gapsa

갑사 • Daily 5.30am–8pm • W2000

On the western side of the park, **Gapsa** is the larger and more enchanting of Gyeryongsan's pair of temples, its beauty enhanced further when surrounded by the fiery colours of autumn – maple and ginkgo trees make a near-complete ring around the complex, and if you're here at the right time you'll be treated to a joyous snowfall of yellow and red. It was established in 420, during the dawn of Korean Buddhism, though needless to say no extant structures are of anything approaching this vintage.

Donghaksa

동학사 • Daily 5.30am–8pm • W2000

On the other side of the park entirely, and connected to Gapsa with umpteen hiking trails (see box below), **Donghaksa** is best accessed from Daejeon and is said to look at its most beautiful in the spring. It has served as a college for Buddhist nuns since 724, and its various buildings exude an air of restraint; some have, sadly, been renovated without much care, though be sure to check out the fantastic carvings on the doors to its main hall.

ARRIVAL AND DEPARTURE   GYERYONGSAN NATIONAL PARK

To Gapsa There are regular buses to the Gapsa entrance on the park's west side from Gongju's local bus terminal (1–2 hourly; 30min); it's also accessible from Yuseong terminal in Daejeon (7 daily; 50min). To get there from Gongju's main bus terminal, it's fastest to grab the next bus heading to or through Gyeryong-myeon, then wait to pick up the aforementioned local service. Lastly, a taxi

from Gongju shouldn't set you back more than W30,000. **To Donghaksa** Bus #107 (every 15min) runs from Daejeon train station to the Donghaksa entrance on the park's east side, though it can take over an hour; you're best advised to head to the Yuseong terminal by subway, from where the same bus takes as little as 20min.

HIKING GYERYONGSAN

Although Gyeryongsan's temples are pretty, most visitors to the park are actually here for the **hike** between them – two main routes scale the ridge and both should have you up and down within four hours, including rests. Given the terrain, it's slightly easier to hike east to west if you have a choice; heading in this direction, most people choose to take the path that runs up the east side of Donghaksa, which takes in a couple of ornate stone pagodas on its way to Gapsa. Others take a faster but more challenging route leading west from the temple, which heads up the 816m-high peak of **Gwaneumbong**; these two routes are connected by a beautiful **ridge path** boasting particularly sumptuous views. Whichever way you go, routes are well signposted, though the tracks can get uncomfortably busy at weekends; a less crowded (and much tougher) day-hike runs from **Byeongsagol** ticket booth – on the road north of the main eastern entrance to the park – to Gwaneumbong, taking in at least seven peaks before finally dropping down to Gapsa.

6

ACCOMMODATION AND EATING

Most visitors to the park stay in nearby Gongju or Daejeon, but with time on your side a night in the park can come as a pleasant change of pace. The bulk of Gyeryongsan's **rooms** and **restaurants** are around the bus terminal below Donghaksa, but not all are of high quality; there's also a campsite here (from W5000 per head). The Gapsa end is prettier and more relaxed; below the temple are some very rural *minbak*, while on the other side of the car park is a sweet village of **traditional houses** with simple rooms for rent (W20,000 or so) – at night the cramped, yellow-lit alleyways create a scene redolent of a bygone era, and make for a truly atmospheric stay. Finally, note that both temples offer **templestay** programmes for W40,000 per head (see p.35 for more).

Donghak Sanjang 동학산장 Hakbong-ri 735-2 ☎ 042 825 4301, ⓦ dhsanjang.co.kr. What a difference a renovation can make: once a run-of-the-mill flophouse, this is now a spick-and-span pension with a stylish lobby and conference facilities. It's angled at families and groups, though there are a few rooms sleeping two – a bit plain, but with comfy beds and sleek bathrooms. <u>W70,000</u>
Sanullim 산울림 Jungjang-ri 28-10 ☎ 041 857 5206. On both sides of the park, local *ajummas* will go out of their way to lure you into their restaurants. There isn't much to choose between the various establishments, but the first one you come to on the approach to Gapsa is recommended, and has been so since the 1970s – look for the big water wheel outside. Dishes here include acorn jelly pancakes (도토리전; W8000), while the mountain-vegetable sets (된장백반; W8000) are excellent value. As with any national park restaurant worth its salt, there's plenty of *makgeolli* (rice beer) here too. Daily 8am–9pm.

Gongju and around

공주

Is this Korea's most underrated travel destination? Presided over by the large fortress of Gongsanseong, small, sleepy **GONGJU** is one of the most charming cities in the land, and deserving of a little more fame. It's also the best place in which to see relics from the **Baekje dynasty** that it ruled, as capital, in the fifth and sixth centuries (see box, p.264). **King Muryeong**, the city's most famous inhabitant, lay here undisturbed for over 1400 years, after which his tomb yielded thousands of pieces of jewellery that provided a hitherto unattainable insight into the splendid craft of the Baekje people. It's tempting to think that the city has changed little in the meantime – notably, it remains off the national rail network, the result of traditionalist lobbying in the 1970s. Largely devoid of bustle, clutter and chain stores, and with a number of wonderful sights, Gongju is worthy of at least a day of your time – and perhaps more if you want to explore **Magoksa** temple or other sights in the wider area, and take full advantage of some surprisingly good restaurants.

The **Baekje Cultural Festival** (ⓦwww.baekje.org) takes place each September and/or early October, with colourful parades and traditional performances in and around Gongju.

Gongsanseong

공산성 • Daily 9am–6pm, closes 1hr earlier Nov–March • Changing of the guard April–June, Sept & Oct daily 2pm • W1500

For centuries, Gongju's focal point has been the hilltop fortress of **Gongsanseong**, whose 2.6km-long **perimeter wall** was built from local mud in Baekje times, before receiving a stone upgrade in the seventeenth century. It's possible to walk the entire circumference of the wall, a flag-pocked, up-and-down course that occasionally affords splendid views of Gongju and its surrounding area. The grounds inside are worth a look too, inhabited by stripey squirrels and riddled with paths leading to a number of carefully painted **pavilions**. Of these, **Ssangsujeong** has the most interesting history: where the pavilion now stands, a Joseon-dynasty king named Injo (ruled 1623–49) once hid under a couple of trees during a peasant-led rebellion against his rule; when this was quashed, the trees were made government officials, though sadly they're no longer around to lend their leafy views to civil proceedings. Airy, green **Imnyugak**, painted with meticulous care, is the most beautiful pavilion; press on further west down a small path for great views of eastern Gongju.

Down by the river there's a small temple, a refuge to monks who fought the Japanese in 1592, and on summer weekends visitors have the opportunity to dress up as a Baekje warrior and shoot off a few arrows. Lastly, note that two of Gongju's best **restaurants** are a stone's throw from the fortress entrance (see p.266).

6

THE BAEKJE DYNASTY

The **Baekje dynasty** was one of Korea's famed **Three Kingdoms** – Goguryeo and Silla being the other two – and controlled much of southwestern Korea for almost seven hundred years. The *Samguk Sagi*, Korea's only real historical account of the peninsula in these times, claims that Baekje was a product of sibling rivalry – it was founded in 18 BC by **Onjo**, whose father had kick-started the Goguryeo dynasty less than twenty years beforehand, in present-day North Korea; seeing the reins of power passed on to his elder brother Yuri, Onjo promptly moved south and set up his own kingdom.

Strangely, given its position facing China on the western side of the Korean peninsula, Baekje was more closely allied with the kingdom of Wa in Japan – at least one Baekje king was born across the East Sea – and it became a conduit for art, religion and customs from the Asian mainland. This fact is perhaps best embodied by the **Baekje artefacts** displayed in the museums in Buyeo (see p.267) and Gongju (see p.262), which contain lacquer boxes, pottery and folding screens not dissimilar to the craftwork that Japan is now famed for. Unabashedly excessive, yet at the same time achieving an ornate simplicity, Baekje jewellery also attained an international reputation, and went on to exert an influence on the Japanese craft of jewellery-making.

Though the exact location of the first Baekje capitals is unclear, it's certain that Gongju and Buyeo were its last two seats of power. **Gongju**, then known as Ungjin, was **capital** from 475 to 538; during this period the aforementioned Three Kingdoms were jostling for power, and while Baekje leaders formed an uneasy alliance with their Silla counterparts the large fortress of Gongsanseong (see p.263) was built to protect the city from Goguryeo attacks. The capital was transferred to **Sabi** – present-day **Buyeo** – which also received a fortress-shaped upgrade (see p.267). However, it was here that the Baekje kingdom finally ground to a halt in 660, succumbing to the Silla forces that, following their crushing of Goguryeo shortly afterwards, went on to rule the whole peninsula.

Though local rebellions briefly brought Baekje back to power in the years leading up to the disintegration of Unified Silla, it was finally stamped out by the nascent Goryeo dynasty in 935. Despite the many centuries that have elapsed since, much evidence of Baekje times can still be seen today in the form of the regal **burial mounds** found in Gongju and Buyeo.

The tomb of King Muryeong

무령왕릉 • Daily 9am–6pm • W1500

Heading west over the creek from Gongsanseong, you'll eventually come to the **Tomb of King Muryeong**, one of many regal burial groups dotted around the country from the Three Kingdoms period, but the only Baekje mound whose occupant is known for sure. Muryeong, who ruled for the first quarter of the sixth century, was credited with strengthening his kingdom by improving relations with those in China and Japan; some accounts suggest that the design of Japanese jewellery was influenced by gifts that he sent across. His gentle green **burial mound** was discovered by accident in 1971 during a civic construction project – after one and a half millennia, Muryeong's tomb was the only one that hadn't been looted. All have now been sealed off for preservation – the fact that you can't peek inside is disappointing, but the sound of summer cicadas whirring in the trees, and the views of the rolling tomb mounds themselves, make for a pleasant stroll. A small **exhibition hall** contains replicas of Muryeong's tomb and the artefacts found within (the originals are in the Gongju National Museum – see opposite).

Gongju Hanok Village

공주 한옥 마을 • Daily 24hr • Free

A short walk from the regal tombs is **Gongju Hanok Village**, a fairly decent recreation of a Baekje-era village – though one complete with café, restaurants and a convenience store. Unlike its counterparts in Seoul (see p.68) and Jeonju (see p.244), this is a tourist construct rather than a functional part of the city; nevertheless, it makes good camera fodder, and you may find yourself tempted to sleep (see p.266) or eat in these unusual environs.

Gongju National Museum

공주 국립 박물관 · Tues–Sun 9am–6pm · Free · ⓦ gongju.museum.go.kr

To see the actual riches retrieved from Muryeong's tomb, head west to **Gongju National Museum**, set in a quiet wooded area by the turn of the river. Much of the museum is devoted to jewellery, and an impressive collection of Baekje bling reveals the dynasty's penchant for gold, silver and bronze. Artefacts such as elaborate golden earrings show an impressive attention to detail, but manage to be dignified and restrained in their use of shape and texture. The highlight is the king's flame-like **golden headwear**, once worn like rabbit ears on the royal scalp, and now one of the most important symbols not just of Gongju, but of the Baekje dynasty itself. Elsewhere in the museum exhibits of wood and clay show the dynasty's history of trade with Japan and China.

6

ARRIVAL AND INFORMATION
GONGJU

By bus There are direct buses to Gongju's intercity bus terminal from cities and towns across the Chungcheong provinces, as well as Seoul and other major Korean cities. From the terminal, it's a beautiful 15min walk to Gongsanseong, along the river and over the bridge. There's another small local bus terminal near the fortress, serving destinations around Gongju's periphery, including Magoksa and Gyeryongsan National Park.

Destinations Buyeo (frequent; 1hr); Cheonan (frequent; 1hr 10min); Daecheon (frequent; 1hr 40min); Daejeon (every 5min; 50min); Seoul (frequent; 1hr 20min).

Tourist information The main tourist information centre (daily 9am–6pm, closes 1hr earlier in winter; ☎041 856 7700) is under Gongsanseong, and usually has helpful, English-speaking staff.

ACCOMMODATION

Gongju's poor range of **accommodation** is no doubt the main reason why the city has failed to attract international tourists. **Motels** are centred in two areas: there is a bunch of new establishments to the west of the bus terminal (including a couple of cheesy replica "castles" north of the river), and a group of older cheapies south of the river across the road from Gongsanseong. The latter is a quainter and more atmospheric area, and slightly closer to the sights, but the newer places are far more comfortable.

6

Gangseojang 강서장 Geumseongdong 194-11 ☎041 855 1414. This red-brick, creekside *yeogwan* is the best option south of the river, and has decent-enough rooms; ask for the one with a computer terminal and free internet. <u>W25,000</u>

★**Hanok Gongju** 한옥 공주 Ungjindong 337 ☎041 840 8900. A splendidly pretty little faux hamlet of traditional wooden *hanok* housing, sitting in calm isolation between the tombs and museum. Though recently constructed, the buildings certainly feel real enough, and are heated from beneath by burning wood; they're spartan, for sure, but the location is relaxing, and the experience somewhat unique. <u>W50,000</u>

★**Hotel Kumgang** 호텔 금강 Singwandong 595-8 ☎041 852 1071. The only official "hotel" in town, though in reality it's basically a less-seedy-than-average motel with a few twins and triples. However, it has friendly staff, spacious bathrooms, internet-ready computer terminals in most rooms and a moderately priced bar-restaurant on the second floor, and should suffice for all but the fussiest travellers. <u>W50,000</u>

Top Motel 탑 모텔 Singwandong 605-15 ☎041 854 8338. Perhaps the easiest to haggle down of the motel troupe west of the bus terminal, though rooms here are shinily colourful and perfectly acceptable, if a little small – strong showers and free wi-fi round out the picture. <u>W30,000</u>

EATING AND DRINKING

Food in Gongju is almost uniformly excellent, yet this wonderfully enjoyable facet of the city remains surprisingly off the radar, even for Korean tourists. The local specialities are **duck meat** (오리고기; *ori-gogi*), **chestnuts** (밤; *bam*) and **ginseng** (인삼; *insam*), and you'll find your table festooned with even more **side dishes** than the national norm (which is already a lot). Criminally, however, almost no restaurants have a view over the river. The area around **Gongju University** (공주대), north of the main bus terminal, has some interesting places to **drink**. Convenience stores, as well as the restaurants listed below, sell bottles of **chestnut makgeolli** (밤 막걸리; W1800 in a shop, W5000 in a restaurant), a particularly creamy and delicious local take on the drink.

Geumganggwan 금강관 Ungjindong 337 ☎041 840 8900. The best and most rustic in feel of the restaurants which have popped up around the *Hanok Gongju* complex (see above), featuring suitably traditional platters of Korean food – there's no à la carte menu, but sets start at W18,000. Daily 10am–8pm.

★**Gomanaru** 고마나루 Geumseongdong 184-4 ☎041 857 9999. This unassuming restaurant is, quite simply, one of Korea's most enjoyable places to eat. Here W15,000 per head (minimum two) will buy a huge *ssam-bap* (쌈밥), which features a tableful of side dishes, and over a dozen kinds of leaves to eat them with; there are a few choices for the centrepiece of the meal, though the barbecued duck is highly recommended. An extra W5000 will see the whole shebang covered with edible flowers – absolute heaven. Daily 9am–10pm.

Iyagi Gage 이야기 가게 Singwandong 241-1 ☎011 451 3361. A little away from the most vibrant bit of the student zone, this is by far the most attractive drinking hole in the area, and commonly frequented by foreigners. Those who drop by regularly refer to it as the "Art Bar", since there's all sorts of arty paraphernalia dangling from the ceilings and strewn across the tables, and there's a modest range of beers and cocktails to enjoy. Daily 6pm–2am.

Nongga 농가 Geumseongdong 192-3 ☎041 854 8338. This restaurant may not look like much, but the food is cheap and super-tasty. Everything on the menu features chestnut in some way; you'll likely see the things being shelled by the charming local family who own the joint. W8000 will buy you a chestnut and seafood pancake (밤 해물 파전), or it's W7000 for a bowl of buckwheat and chestnut cold noodles (밤 냉면). Daily 10.30am–8.30pm, though often closes earlier.

Magoksa

마곡사 • Daily sunrise–sunset • W2000 • Bus #600 or #601 from Gongju bus terminal (45min), or bus #7 or #18 from Gongju local bus terminal (45min)

A beautiful bus ride through the countryside west of Gongju is **Magoksa**. The exact year of this temple's creation remains as mysterious as its remote, forested environs, but it's believed to date from the early 640s. It is now a principal temple of the **Jogye** order, the largest sect in Korean Buddhism. Although the most important buildings huddle together in a tight pack, rustic farmyard dwellings and auxiliary hermitages extend into nearby fields and forest, and can easily fill up a half-day of pleasant meandering if you're not temple-tired. The hushed vibe of the complex is the main attraction, though a few of the buildings are worthy of attention. **Yeongsanjeon** (영산전) is a hall of a thousand individually crafted figurines, and has a nameplate said to have been written by King Sejo (ruled 1455–68), a Joseon-dynasty monarch perhaps best famed for putting his brother to the sword. At the top of the complex, **Daeungbojeon** (대응보전) is a high point in more than one sense; the three golden statues in this main hall are backed by a large, highly detailed Buddhist painting, and look down on a sea of fish-scaled black roof tiles.

ACCOMMODATION AND EATING   MAGOKSA

Gareung Binga 가릉빈가 Unam-ri 712-4. Just down the hill from the main clutch of accommodation, this is a restaurant-cum-teahouse that serenades diners with traditional piped music. Most teas go for around W5000; this being Chungcheong, the ginseng tea (인삼차) is recommended. Daily 8am–6pm.

Magok Motel 마곡 모텔 Unam-ri 723-1 ☎041 841 0042. The best motel in the area, and actually pretty swanky considering the rural location – rooms and lobby alike are resplendent in gold and various shades of brown, and the quietness of the area means that you should be able to score a good sleep. W40,000

6

Buyeo

부여

Smaller and sleepier than Gongju, its Baekje buddy to the east, **BUYEO** is almost equally worthy of a visit. The Baekje seat of power was transferred here from Gongju in 538, and saw six kings come and go before the abrupt termination of the dynasty in 660, when General Gyebaek led his five thousand men into one last battle against a Silla-Chinese coalition ten times that size. Knowing that his resistance would prove futile, the general killed his wife and children before heading into combat, preferring to see them dead than condemn them to slavery. Legend has it that thousands of the town's women threw themselves off a riverside cliff when the battle had been lost, drowning both themselves and the Baekje dynasty. Today, this cliff and the large, verdant **fortress** surrounding it are the town's biggest draw, along with an excellent **museum**.

Buyeo's main street runs between two roundabouts – Boganso Rotary to the north, and Guncheon Rotary 1km to the south. You can orient yourself with the **statue of General Gyebaek**, which stands at the latter.

Busosan

부소산 • Daily: March–Oct 9am–6pm; Nov–Feb 9am–5pm • W2000 • Ferry rides W4000

Buyeo's centre is dominated by its large fortress. **Busosan** lacks the perimeter wall of Gongju's Gongsanseong, but with its position perched high over the Baengman river, plus a greater variety of trees and a thoroughly enjoyable network of trails, many visitors find this one even more beautiful. It also has history on its side, as this is where the great Baekje dynasty came to an end after almost seven centuries of rule.

On entering the fortress, you'll happen upon one of the many **pavilions** that dot the grounds, though the scattered nature of the trails means that it's neither easy nor advisable to see them all. **Yeonggillu** is nearest the entrance and has a particularly pleasant and natural setting; it's also where kings brought local nobility for regular sunrise meetings, presided over by a pair of snake-like wooden dragons that remain today. Paths wind up to Sajaru, the highest point in the fortress and originally built as a moon-viewing platform. The path continues on to the **clifftop of Nakhwa-am**; from here, it is said, three thousand wives and daughters jumped to their deaths after General Gyebaek's defeat by the Silla-Chinese coalition, choosing suicide over probable rape and servitude. This tragic act gave Nakhwa-am its name – **Falling Flowers Rock** – and has been the subject of countless TV epics.

Down by the river is **Goransa**, a small temple backed by a spring with a bit of a history (see box, p.268). The best way to finish a trip to the fortress is to take a **ferry**

6

> ## BUYEO'S ELIXIR OF YOUTH
>
> Tucked behind Goransa temple, which sits on the river side of the Busosan fortress complex, is a small **water spring** which once provided water to the Baekje kings on account of its purported health benefits – servants had to prove that they'd climbed all the way here by serving the water with a distinctive leaf that only grew on a nearby plant. The spring water is said to make you three years younger for every glass you drink – throw down enough and, presumably, you'll be prenatal in no time.

ride from a launch downhill from the spring. These sail a short way down the river to a **sculpture park**, though you'll have to wait for the vessel to fill up before departure, which can be annoyingly infrequent in winter.

Jeongnimsaji

정림사지 • Daily: March–Oct 7am–7pm; Nov–Feb 8am–5pm • W1000

Heading south of Busosan's main entrance, you might want to swing by **Jeongnimsaji**, a small but pretty site once home to a large temple. Several buildings here have been recreated, and you'll also find a five-storey stone pagoda – one of only three survivors from Baekje times – and a seated stone Buddha dating back to the Goryeo era.

Buyeo National Museum

부여 국립 박물관 • Tues–Fri 9am–6pm, Sat & Sun 9am–7pm • Free • ⓦ buyeo.museum.go.kr

As with other "national" museums in Korea, the **Buyeo National Museum** focuses exclusively on artefacts found in its local area; here there's an understandable emphasis on Baekje riches. Some rooms examine Buyeo's gradual shift from the Stone to the Bronze Age with a selection of pots and chopping implements, but inside a room devoted to Baekje treasures is the museum's pride and joy: a **bronze incense burner** that has become the town symbol. Elaborate animal figurines cover the outer shell of this 0.6m-high egg-shaped sculpture, which sits on a base of twisted dragons; it's considered one of the most beautiful Baekje articles ever discovered, displaying the dynasty's love of form, detail and restrained opulence.

Gungnamji

궁남지 • Daily 24hr • Free

A short walk south of General Gyebaek's statue is **Gungnamji**, a beautiful lotus pond with a pavilion at its centre, and surrounded by a circle of willow trees. Outside this weepy perimeter lie acres of lotus paddies, making this peaceful idyll feel as if it's in the middle of the countryside. There's a particularly good café (see opposite) just off the park area's north flank.

ARRIVAL AND INFORMATION   BUYEO

By bus Buses arrive at a tiny station in the centre of town; from here most major sights – as well as the majority of motels and restaurants – are within walking distance, though it's easy to hunt down a taxi if necessary.
Destinations Cheongju (10 daily; 1hr 40min); Daecheon (11 daily; 1hr); Daejeon (frequent; 1hr 30min); Gongju (frequent; 1hr); Seoul (frequent; 3hr 30min).
Tourist information Next to the fortress entrance is a tourist information office (daily 9am–6pm; ☎ 041 830 2523), where you'll usually find an English-speaker.

ACCOMMODATION

As long as you're not too fussy, **accommodation** is easy to find in Buyeo, and a higher-end resort finally opened up just outside the city in 2010. Try to avoid the area around the bus terminal, which contains some rather insalubrious places to stay.

Baekje Hotel 백제호텔 Ssangbong-ni 3 ☎041 835 0871. Inconveniently located a short taxi ride from the bus terminal, this is the only official tourist accommodation near central Buyeo. Rooms are a little drab and motel-like; unless you want to sleep on mats on the floor, go for the "foreign" ones. There's also a small café-bar on site. W88,000

★**Lotte Resort** 롯데 리조트 Baekjemunno 400 ☎041 939 1000, ⓦlottebuyeoresort.com. Superbly designed resort hotel, whose pleasing, twin-horseshoe-shaped exterior is best described as "neo-Baekje".

Although service is occasionally patchy, the place is good value if you can knock something off the rack rates. The presence of good restaurants is welcome in such a far-flung location – it's located a W8000 taxi ride from central Buyeo, next to Baekje Cultural Land. W270,000

Motel VIP 모텔VIP Dongnam-ri 701 ☎041 832 3700. Near Boganso Rotary, this has the best rooms in central Buyeo, though this admittedly isn't saying much. The place is spotless though, with mood lighting in the rooms and piped music in the corridors. W30,000

6

EATING

267 Brunch Café Seodongno 56 ☎041 835 0267. A nice little addition to bucolic Buyeo, this airy café has a great location overlooking lotus ponds, plus decent coffee, lots of herbal teas and munchables including bacon-and-cheese omelette (W7500) and burgers (W8500). Daily 10am–8pm.

Baekje-ui Jip 백제의집 Gwanbung-ni 119-3 ☎041 834 1212. On the main road just outside the Busosan entrance, this is the place to hunt down before or after a fortress visit. Here you can have a gigantic set meal of leaves, duck meat (or beef, though duck is a local speciality) and innumerable side dishes, for around W17,000 per person; solo diners may have to contend with the almost equally delectable *yeonipbap* (연잎밥; W8000), a

surprisingly large set whose main component is rice and other goodies wrapped in a lotus leaf. Daily 9am–9pm.

★**Minsokgwan** 민속관 Gugyo-ri 34-3 ☎041 835 2445. Fascinating, traditionally styled restaurant with a courtyard full of old Korea paraphernalia, and tables and chairs inside fashioned from tree trunks. The cold buckwheat noodles (*naengmyeon*; 냉면) are good for cooling off in the summer and a snip at W7000; alternatively, try the home-made *kimchi*-tofu mix (두부김치; W10,000). The restaurant is on the road heading from Busosan to the ferry dock; keep an eye out for a Chinese-language sign with a pair of stone turtles straining their necks towards it. Daily 10am–8pm.

Daecheon beach

대천 해수욕장

Long, wide and handsome, **DAECHEON BEACH** is by far the most popular on Korea's western coast, attracting a predominantly young crowd. In the summer this 3km-long stretch of white sand becomes a sea of people, having fun in the water by day, feasting

---

THE BORYEONG MUD FESTIVAL

English teachers and American soldiers across the land circle the **Boryeong mud festival** (ⓦmudfestival.or.kr) in their diaries, count down the days, then head back to their schools or barracks bleary-eyed after the festivities. For two July weekends, and the space in between them, the beach is a sea of mud-splattered foreigners and their Korean buddies. The stuff is everywhere, allowing participants to wrestle or slide around in it, throw it at their friends or smear it all over themselves, then take lots and lots of pictures – some will end up on TV, in newspapers or even on tourism posters. The focus of activities is a fenced-off area filled with inflatable slides, mud pools and the like (9.30am–12.30pm & 1.30–6pm; W10,000), though for many the event is simply a fine excuse to get smashed on the beach at night.

This is all loads of fun, though you'll have more if you heed a few words of warning. Firstly, it pays to book **transport** and **accommodation** well ahead – take trains rather than buses if at all possible, since the latter can get caught up in horrendous traffic jams. Secondly, if you're going with a group, figure out assembly points when you arrive – the mobile phone network gets strained during the festival, and it can prove almost impossible to meet your buddies. Thirdly, hard as it may be, try to resist the temptation to bare all on the beach – oddly, given that this festival is famed for its debauchery, Korean families are arriving in ever greater numbers, and drunk, skinny-dipping foreigners have often found themselves filmed by tut-tutting news reporters.

6

on the delicious local **shellfish** (see box opposite), then drinking and letting off fireworks until the early hours. In summer, visitors can rent banana boats, jet skis and large rubber tubes, or even a **quad bike** to ride up and down the prom; there's also a 600m-long **zip-wire** ride here (W18,000). The revelry reaches its crescendo each July with the **Boryeong mud festival**, a week-long event that seems to rope in, and sully, almost every expat in the country (see box, p.269). In addition, it's a short ferry trip from the mainland bustle to the **West Sea islands**, a sleepy crew strung out beyond the horizon (see opposite).

Mud House

머드 하우스 • Daily 8am–6pm • W6000; mud packs W20,000 for face, W30,000 for full-body

You don't have to visit Daecheon during festival time to get nice and mucky – at other times you can still sample the brown stuff at the **Mud House**, the most distinctive building on the beachfront. The ticket gets you entry to an on-site **sauna**, at which you can bathe in a **mud pool** or even paint yourself with the stuff; all manner of mud-based cosmetics are on sale at reception, including mud shampoo, soap and body cream.

ARRIVAL AND INFORMATION   DAECHEON BEACH

Daecheon beach is just 15km from the town of **Boryeong** (보령), and the two places have been known to trade names on occasion – hence the "Boryeong" Mud Festival. Coming from elsewhere in Korea you'll arrive either at Boryeong train station (known as Daecheon) or Boryeong bus station (this time Boryeong), and will then need to take onward transport to the beach. The train and bus stations are visible from each other.

By train to Boryeong Daecheon station sits on a relatively quiet track, with trains every hour or so to Seoul's Yongsan station (2hr 40min) or Jeonju (around 2hr, via Iksan).

By bus to Boryeong The bus terminal has regular services to Cheonan (2hr 40min), Daejeon (2hr 50min) and Seoul (2hr).

Boryeong to Daecheon beach and harbour Buses to the beach run from the train and bus stations every 20min or so (W1400); get off just after the bus makes a right at the

Legrand Beach hotel. Alternatively, the beach is less than W10,000 by taxi from either station. The bus route finishes at Daecheon harbour, at the northern end of the beach; you'll have to go here to take a ferry to one of the nearby islands (see p.273 for details).

Tourist information There's a small booth near the mud centre; staff can reserve accommodation both in Daecheon and on the offshore islands. There's usually an English-speaker present, but otherwise a map and some controlled mime should be enough to land you a booking.

ACCOMMODATION

Although there's very little at the top end of the scale, **motels** and **minbak** are everywhere, and even at the peak of summer you can usually find a bed without too much difficulty; prices can go through the roof on summer weekends and holidays, though with time, patience and a few words with the ubiquitous *ajummas*, you should find a room for W30,000. Travellers and locals alike often save money by cramming as many people as possible into a room, or staying out all night on the beach with a few drinks. Lastly, there's a small **campground** behind the mud centre (W10,000 per tent, W2000 per shower). The options listed below are all between the bus stop and the mud centre.

Motel Coconuts 모텔 코코너츠 Sinheukdong 2001 ☎ 041 934 6595. Family-run motel whose rooms have been decorated with occasionally eye-searing wallpaper and bed linens; they're all en suite, with decent showers and cable TV. W55,000

Mudrin 리조트 머드린 Sinheukdong 2270-2 ☎ 041 934 1111, ⓦ mudrin.com. The best of the several higher-end options to have opened on the beachfront in recent

years. The spick-and-span rooms all boast a sea view, and there's a café and convenience store in the lobby. W155,000

Pine Motel 파인 모텔 Sinheukdong 2001 ☎ 041 931 7172. Easy to spot on account of its distinctive oriental roof, this motel's rooms are wood-panelled and quite pleasing – almost like a traditional *hanok* abode. All have en-suite facilities. W40,000

EATING

Daecheon's culinary scene is simple – fish, fish and more fish. The seafront is lined with **seafood restaurants** displaying their still-alive goods in outdoor tanks; among the myriad options are eel, blue crabs and sea cucumbers, but

SHELLFISH BARBECUES

For the uninitiated, Korean seafood can be a little daunting: the prey is often both unfamiliar and alive; English-language menus are hard to find; and the vast majority of meals are for groups rather than single diners. However, it would be a huge pity to leave Daecheon without enjoying a **shellfish barbecue** (*jogae-gui*; 조개구이). The West Sea coast is famed for this bounty, and if you bear in mind a few tips the experience isn't too tricky at all.

First of all, choose a restaurant – any busy one will do. Secondly, set a price: it's usually W30,000 for two people, and another W15,000–20,000 for each additional person; single diners will eventually get lucky for W20,000 if they ask at enough places. The charcoal briquettes at your table will then be fired up, and you'll be presented with a huge round of shellfish, as well as free side dishes such as noodles, pancakes and cheesy corn. Pop the shells on the grill a bunch at a time; the closed ones are ready when they've opened up, while the already-open ones are good when they've been bubbling for a while. You'll also have been handed a tin-foil tray; squirt a bunch of pepper paste in from the bottle, and add the "juice" from the various shells as they cook. This makes a broth for the giant **kijogae** (키조개), the tastiest shellfish of all; when cooked, the critter effectively becomes a sort of seafood steak, and has to be chopped up with the scissors you'll have on your table. Throw the pieces into the tin-foil broth, boil them up a while, and enjoy – some of the tastiest food Korea has to offer.

6

most are here for the **shellfish barbecues** (see box above). Since all of these restaurants serve the same thing and none have English-language menus, it would be unfair to recommend any particular establishment – just go for a popular place. A more rustic patch of restaurants can be found near **Daecheon harbour**; these are quite atmospheric, especially in the evenings when the ramshackle buildings, bare hanging bulbs and coursing sea water may make you feel as though you've been shunted back in time a couple of decades. If seafood's not your bag, try to hunt down one of the **bakeries** or pork cutlet places; instant noodles, snacks and cheap booze are also available from umpteen **convenience stores**.

★**Hangsusan Market** 항수산 시장. Out by the harbour, Daecheon's fish market is one of the best in the country; it also makes a good place to eat, since whatever you buy on the ground floor can be cooked and served upstairs for a small fee. The grilled eel here (장어구이) is nothing short of divine – it'll cost around W25,000 for a small eel serving two, plus another W5000 to have it cooked. Daily 6am–7pm.

West Sea islands

From Daecheon harbour, a string of tiny islands stretches beyond the horizon into what Koreans term the **West Sea**, a body of water known internationally as the Yellow Sea (see box, p.123). From their distant shores, the mainland is either a lazy murmur on the horizon or altogether out of sight, making this a perfect place to kick back and take it easy. **Beaches** and **seafood** constitute the main draws, but it's also a joy to sample the unhurried island lifestyle that remains unaffected by the changes that swept through the mainland on its freewheeling course to First World status; these islands provide the truest remnants of pre-industrial Korean life. Fishing boats judder into the docks where the sailors gut and prepare their haul with startling efficiency; it's sometimes possible to buy fish directly from them. Restaurants on the islands are usually rickety, family-run affairs serving simple Korean staples.

There are two main **ferry circuits** heading out from Daecheon: the first is a loop taking in **Sapsido**, **Janggodo** and **Anmyeondo**; while the second hits **Hodo** and **Nokdo** before terminating at **Oeyeondo**, a full 53km out to sea. The ferries on the latter circuit are for foot passengers only, and the islands they visit are thus a fair bit quieter. Remember to bring enough money for your stay, as most of the isles lack **banks**; the majority have mini-markets, but these can be hard to find as they tend to double as family homes.

6

Sapsido

삽시도

Pronounced "sap-shi-doe", **Sapsido** is the most popular island in the whole area. Its shores are dotted with craggy rock formations, some with a hair-like covering of juniper or pine, while the island's interior is crisscrossed with networks of dirt tracks – it's possible to walk from one end to the other in under an hour. Depending on the tides, ferries will call at one of two ports: there are *minbak* aplenty around each, and both have decent beaches within walking distance, but make sure that you know which one to go to when you're leaving the island.

Janggodo

장고도

The name of little **Janggodo** derives from its contours, which are said to be similar to the Korea *janggo* drum. Home to some stupendous rock formations, it's popular with families and – thanks to some particularly good beaches – the trendier elements of the Korean beach set. Local buses wait at the northern terminal (there are two) to take passengers to the *minbak* area (it's a little far to walk).

Anmyeondo

안면도

The largest island in the group, and the only one connected to the mainland by road, **Anmyeondo** also constitutes the most accessible part of **Taean Haean National Park** (태안해안 국립 공원). White-sand beaches fill the coves that dot the island's west coast, many of them only accessible by footpath from a small road that skirts the shore between **Anmyeon** (안면), the main settlement and transport hub, and **Yeongmok** (영목), a port village at the southern cape that receives ferries from Daecheon and other West Sea islands. Buses connect the two, running approximately once an hour.

Hodo

호도

Hodo attracts beach-hunters without the fuss of similar places on the mainland. The island's best beach is a curl of white sand just a short walk from the ferry dock and is great for swimming. Around the terminal are plenty of *minbak* rooms – pretty much every dwelling in the village will accept visitors, though there are only around sixty on the whole island. Try to track down Mr Choi at *Gwangcheon Minbak* (광천 민박); he's the proud owner of the only land vehicle on Hodo (a beat-up 4WD) and can be persuaded to give free night-time rides through the forest or a splash across the mudflats if the tide is out – tremendous fun.

Nokdo

녹도

The smallest island hereabouts is **Nokdo**, which is home to some superb hill trails. Unlike on the other islands, the hillside town and its accommodation options are a fair walk from the ferry dock – everyone will be going the same way, so you should be able to hitch a lift without too much bother.

Oeyeondo

외연도

The ferries make their final stop at **Oeyeondo**, a weather-beaten family of thickly forested specks of land. Though the most remote of any of the islands surrounding Daecheon, Oeyeondo possesses the busiest and most built-up port area on the loop, with walking trails heading up to the island's twin peaks, as well as a tiny beach that's good for sunsets.

| **ARRIVAL AND DEPARTURE** | **WEST SEA ISLANDS** |

By ferry Ferries connect the islands in two main circuits, though with so few sailings, you won't be able to see more than one or two islands in a day. There are usually three daily sailings linking Daecheon to Sapsido, Janggodo and Anmyeondo. For the second circuit, there are two sailings daily from Daecheon (8.10am & 3pm; 40min to Hodo, 20min more to Nokdo and a further 30min to Oeyeondo); ferries return from Oeyeondo at 10am & 4.40pm.

By bus Anmyeondo is connected by bus to Seoul (4 daily; 3hr 30min).

6

ACCOMMODATION AND EATING

All islands have *minbak* and pension **accommodation**, though don't expect anything too fancy – the rooms will be small and bare, and in the *minbak* you'll probably have to sleep on a blanket on the floor. Prices start at W25,000 per night, and increase in summer; when the weather's warm you may need to book ahead, which is easier said than done since almost nobody on the islands speaks English. Your best bet is to arrange things through the Daecheon beach tourist office (see p.270), or even one of their counterparts in Seoul (see p.96). Eating can be tricky – the islands all have **shops** and **restaurants**, though they tend to close early and no menus will be in English. Your accommodation may be able to whip up a meal, though on the larger islands it's quite common for restaurants to pick up customers for free. If you don't like seafood you may have to stick to instant noodles.

Cheonan

천안

After years in the shadows, **CHEONAN** – an easy day-trip from the capital – is a city on the up: now connected to Seoul by subway and high-speed train, its population has boomed in recent years. The new **KTX line** has enabled commuters to work in Seoul while living in a cheaper, more manageable city, but despite the flashy new department stores and housing complexes, there's little here to detain travellers bar the superb **Arario Gallery** and the fascinating **Independence Hall of Korea**, which sits some way out of town.

The Arario Gallery

아라리오 갤러리 • Daily 11am–7pm • W3000 • ⓦ arariogallery.com

The only sight of note in central Cheonan is the excellent **Arario Gallery** next to the bus terminal, which is linked to the contemporary gallery in Seoul (see box, p.67). Outside the main entrance sits one of Damien Hirst's generic body-with-bits-exposed sculptures, alongside a tall tower of car axles that pokes fun at the city's ever-declining reputation as a mere transit hub; inside are two exhibition floors, both small but almost always brimming with high-quality modern art. The gallery has excellent connections to China, which means that it's often possible to catch glimpses of the burgeoning art scene across the West Sea.

Independence Hall of Korea

독립 기념관 • Tues–Sun: March–Oct 9.30am–5pm; Nov–Feb 9.30am–4pm • Free • ⓦ independence.or.kr • Bus #400 from train station or bus terminal (40min)

Set in a wooded area east of Cheonan, Korea's largest museum, the **Independence Hall of Korea**, is a concrete testament to the country's continued struggle for independence during its most troubled time, from 1910 to 1945, when it suffered the indignity of being **occupied by Japan**. Though this was a relatively short period, the effects were

6

JAPANESE OCCUPATION

If you've done any sightseeing in Korea, you'll no doubt have come across information boards telling you when, or how often, certain buildings were burnt down or destroyed by the Japanese. The two countries have been at loggerheads for centuries, but the 1910–45 **occupation period** caused most of the tension that can still be felt today. In this age of empire, Asian territory from Beijing to Borneo suffered systematic rape and torture at the hands of Japanese forces, but only Korea experienced a full-scale assault on its **national identity**. Koreans were forced to use Japanese names and money, books written in *hangeul* text were burnt and the Japanese language was taught in schools. These measures were merely the tip of the iceberg, and Japan's famed attention to detail meant that even the tall trees were chopped down: straight and strong, they were said to symbolize the Korean psyche, and they were replaced with willows which drifted with the wind in a manner more befitting the programme. The most contentious issue remains the use of over 100,000 "**comfort women**", who were forced into slave-like prostitution to sate the sexual needs of Japanese soldiers; Koreans never discuss this, but women from other occupied countries suffered the same fate too.

The **atomic bombs** that brought about the end of the World War II also finished off the occupation of Korea, which slid rapidly into civil war. This post-occupation preoccupation kept both factions too busy to demand compensation or apologies from Japan – they were, in fact, never to arrive. While some countries have bent over backwards to highlight wartime misdeeds, Japan has been notoriously stubborn in this regard – its prime ministers have regularly paid respects at **Yasukuni**, a shrine to those who died serving the empire, but notably also to at least a dozen Class A war criminals, and school textbooks have increasingly glossed over the atrocities. This has led to repeated and continuing protests; surviving comfort women, having still not been compensated, hold weekly **demonstrations** outside the Japanese Embassy in Seoul. Korea, for its part, has failed to debate successfully the role of **local collaborators** during the resistance, or to acknowledge fully in its own schoolbooks and museums the foreign influences that ended both the Japanese occupation and the Korean War.

devastating (see box above), and despite the Korean government's initial appeal for locals not to be "filled with bitterness or resentment", the popularity of the place and the size of its seven large exhibition halls – each of which would probably function quite well as individual museums – show that the wounds are still sore. Scarcely an opportunity is missed to insert a derogatory adjective against the Japanese people and policies of the time, but this combination of vitriol and history makes the place an absorbing visit.

Each hall highlights different aspects of the occupation, with the most important displays labelled in English. Many locals head straight for those detailing **Japanese brutality** during the colonial period; "Torture done by Japan", a life-size display featuring some unfortunate mannequins, is one of the most popular exhibits, but there are also numerous photographs. Should you tire of the unrelenting indignation, head to the "Hall of National Heritage", which is filled with less bombastic displays detailing traditional Korean life.

ARRIVAL AND INFORMATION

CHEONAN

By train Cheonan station is pretty central, a 20min walk or W3000 taxi ride from the centre. Trains from Seoul take an hour; high-speed services (30min) stop at Cheonan Asan station, three subway stops to the west – including transfers, it saves no time and costs more travelling this way. The same goes for trains south to Daejeon, which take 30min from Cheonan Asan or 1hr from the main station.
By subway One branch of Seoul's subway line 1 heads to Cheonan train station, though it takes two hours to get

here – not a comfortable ride.
By bus The city's two bus terminals sit almost side by side in the city centre: the express (고속) terminal is for Seoul alone (45min), while the intercity (시외) heads to other destinations including Daecheon (frequent; 2hr 40min), Daejeon (frequent; 1hr) and Gongju (frequent; 1hr 10min).
Tourist information There's a small information booth outside the train station (daily 9am–5pm; ☎041 550 2445), though it's not of much use.

Songnisan National Park

속리산 국립 공원 • Daily 2hr before sunrise to sunset • W4000 (usually only levied at Beopjusa entrance) • ⓦ english.knps.or.kr

The myriad trails of **SONGNISAN NATIONAL PARK** are a joy to hike, its paths winding uphill alongside gentle streams to heady 1000m-high peaks – just what you'd expect from an area whose name translates as "mountains far from the ordinary world". This is justly one of the most popular parks in Korea, with most visitors here to gawp at fantastically photogenic **Beopjusa**, a temple featuring a visually arresting **33m-high bronze Buddha**. The park's popularity is also due, in no small part, to its highly central location – geographically speaking, the peak of Birobong can credibly claim to be the very centre of the country, since a drop of rain falling here – depending on what face it lands on – will end up flowing down the Nakdong River to Busan in the south, running through Gongju on its way to the west coast, or pouring north into the Han River and exiting the mainland through Seoul.

Located just down from Beopjusa, Songnisan's main accommodation area is provincial in feel and highly pleasant – stay the night if you can. The main road is lined with gingko trees, which glow a shimmering yellow in autumn months, though even at these times they're a mere prelude to the leafy pyrotechnics on offer in the park itself.

Beopjusa

법주사 • Daily 6am–6pm • ⓦ beopjusa.org

Inside the park, a short, shaded path leads to Songnisan's main draw – the glorious temple of **Beopjusa**. Entirely surrounded by pine and peaks, its name means – somewhat tautologically – "the temple where Buddhist teachings reside", and indeed it has been an active place of worship and religious study since it was built in 653. Standing with his back to the west (the direction of his death), the huge bronze **Buddha statue** stands atop an underground hall housing hundreds of figurines, including a rather splendid golden **goddess of compassion**.

Back outside and facing the statue is **Palsangjeon** (팔상전), an unconventional five-storey building that, despite a rather squat appearance fostered by the shallow lattice windows, is also the tallest wooden structure in Korea. As with all Korean temple halls bearing this name, it contains eight painted murals depicting various stages from the life of the Buddha; however, this is likely to be the oldest such building in the land. Nearby are two elaborately decorated **stone lanterns**; two lions hold up the torch segment on one (though

0 ——— 1 kilometre

N

SANGO-RI

Myobong (874m)
Gwaneumbong (982m)
Munjangdae (1054m)
Seongbulsa
Bus Stop
Munsubong (1031m)
Jungsa-am
Bus Stop
Birobong (1008m)
Beopjusa
Sanghwanam
Cheonhwangbong (1058m)
Bus Stop

ⓘ Ticket Office

ACCOMMODATION
Birosanjang 1
Lake Hills 2
Songnisan Pension 3

EATING
Beopjusa Chatjip 1
Songni Tosokeum Sikdang 2

Bus Terminal

SONGNISAN NATIONAL PARK

▼ Boeun & Daejeon

6

HIKING SONGNISAN

Plenty of **hiking** opportunities lie beyond Beopjusa. The main target is the 1054m-high summit of **Munjangdae**, an easy three hours away from Beopjusa; locals often make a wish after their third visit to this peak. From Munjangdae, the peak of **Birobong** (1008m) is a short walk away, or an easy ninety-minute ridge trail will bring you to **Cheonhwangbong**, the park's highest peak (1058m); a further two-hour walk west will bring you back down to the main park entrance, or you can continue east towards Sango-ri in Gyongsang province.

the flames have long been extinguished), while the other is adorned with four carved devas and a statue of a bodhisattva. This deity incarnate once held an incense burner until he was consumed by fire, presumably reaching nirvana during his show of determination.

ARRIVAL AND DEPARTURE   SONGNISAN NATIONAL PARK

By bus There are direct bus connections to Songnisan from Cheongju (every 20min or so; 1hr 30min), as well as regular services from Daejeon (1hr 30min) and from the Dong-Seoul terminal in the capital. Buses stop just under 1km away from the park entrance itself, and their arrival is often delayed on summer and autumn weekends by the solid traffic running into the park.

ACCOMMODATION

There are plenty of simple places to stay in the village-like area between the bus terminal and Beopjusa, as well as plenty of restaurants and karaoke rooms. Beopjusa also runs **templestay** courses (W40,000), with English-language options available if you book ahead (see p.35).

★ **Birosanjang** 비로산장 Inside the park ☎ 010 5456 4782. Why don't all Korean national parks have something like this? This fascinating budget option lies inside the park itself, hanging over a trickling stream; chipmunks, frogs and colourful moths pop by for regular visits. On the down side, prices have gone up of late and they no longer serve food or alcohol (mercifully, there's a restaurant a little back down the path); criminally, they've also got rid of their guestbooks, which dated back to the 1970s and were notable for the chance to see the word "groovy" used with no sense of irony. However, while overpriced it may be, this could be the most atmospheric stay in all Korea. W50,000

Lake Hills 레익 힐즈 Sanae-ri 198 ☎ 043 542 5281, ⓦ lakehills.co.kr. Snuggled up to the park entrance, this is the most comfortable accommodation in the area. Prices pack a bit of a punch, but the rooms are just about worth it; note that "standard" ones are Korean-style sleep-on-the-floor affairs, though "deluxe" ones come with bed and cost no more. Away from weekends and the summer peak, you can probably chop the price in two. W150,000

Songnisan Pension 속리산 펜션 Sanae-ri 280-1 ☎ 043 544 3844. Best value of the motel clutch, with large, comfortable rooms, satellite TV and free wi-fi access. It's on a small alley parallel to the main road. W30,000

EATING

You know the drill by now – after a hike you're supposed to eat *pajeon* (a kind of savoury pancake), and sling it back with a pot of **makgeolli**; try to hunt down the local brand, a tasty number made with jujube (대추). Corn jelly (도토리묵; *dotorimuk*) and grilled bellflower root (더덕구이; *deodeok gui*) are the official **local specialities**, but you'll find all sorts of mountain cuisine on offer here; there are a few pancake places in the park itself.

JIKJI

To the west of Songnisan lies the city of **CHEONGJU** (청주), an uninteresting place with just one claim to fame: it witnessed the birth of **Jikji** (직지), the first-ever book produced with **movable metal type** rather than single-use page-blocks, and as such a direct ancestor of every newspaper, magazine or novel you've ever read. A guide to Seon Buddhism (better known as Zen in the West), *Jikji* was produced in 1377, thereby predating Germany's **Gutenberg Bible** by some 78 years. Initially two books were made, but one was destroyed in a fire. The remaining copy was taken to Paris as a form of compensation for the murder of French missionaries towards the end of the Joseon dynasty, and has now become Korea's equivalent of the Elgin Marbles – despite attempts at repatriation, it still lies in Paris at the Bibliothèque Nationale de France.

Beopjusa Chatjip 법주사 찻집 Inside the park. Located right next to the eponymous temple, this calm tearoom serves Korean infusions from around W6000 – try the jujube tea (대추차). Daily 10am–6pm.

★**Songni Tosokeum Sikdang** 속리토속음식당 Sanae-ri 261 ☎ 043 543 3917. Mighty fine place to eat on the main road. Their mainly veggie bellflower-root set meal (더덕정식; W15,000) comes with over twenty separate dishes and is absolutely huge, making good use of local mushrooms and herbs; there's usually a two-person minimum, but they'll feed single diners who ask nicely. Other choices include good savoury pancakes from W7000. Daily 8am–10pm.

6

Danyang and around

단양

With its rarified and almost resort-like air, the sleepy town of **DANYANG** has become extremely popular of late, especially with families and young couples. However, it remains pleasantly relaxing, since there's little of the noise and clutter found in other urban areas; life dawdles by at a snail's pace, which is quite appropriate, really, since **river snails** are a local delicacy. These are dredged from **Chungju Lake**, a river-like expanse that curls a C-shape around the town centre. Green, pine-covered outcrops rise up from the lake, making for a thoroughly enchanting backdrop. The area's loftiest peaks converge at **Sobaeksan**, a pretty national park easily accessible from Danyang; on its cusp is **Guinsa**, one of the most distinctive temples in the whole of the land, and perhaps the highlight of the whole area.

Danuri Aquarium

다누리 아쿠아움 • Daily: July & Aug 9am–9pm; Sept–June 9am–6pm • W8000

Danyang's newest sight is the large **Danuri Aquarium**, a slightly over-twee venue set in a building connected to the bus terminal. Over 16,000 fish call these tanks home; most are local varieties, though there are some interesting imports, such as the Amazon stingray.

Chungju Lake

충주호

Green-blue **Chungju Lake** is outstandingly beautiful, and impossible to miss if you're spending any time in the area. The lake is a man-made creation, having come into being after the building of a dam downstream in 1986. It swallowed what was once Danyang town centre, and many old buildings still lurk beneath the surface – few locals give these any mind today.

A **lakeside promenade** runs for a couple of kilometres from the bus terminal to the *Edelweiss Hotel*. It offers staggeringly beautiful views of the unspoilt mountain range, starting opposite the town centre, but for some reason the local authorities have chosen to spoil this natural beauty by putting up dozens of speakers along the route; it's hard to think of something less appropriate to the surroundings than Korean happy hardcore, but if you can tolerate the sonic bombardment you'll find it quite romantic, especially at night.

ONDAL

Anyone spending any time in Danyang is sure to catch occasional glimpses of **Ondal** (온달), the town mascot – you'll see him, and his huge eyebrows, on everything from restaurant signs to toilet doors. According to local legend, he was the town fool until wooing a **local princess** (perhaps using those eyebrows) to one of the town's caves for an underground tryst; after their subsequent marriage, Ondal became a soldier of such skill that he eventually found himself promoted to general, fighting fierce battles at the **fortress** up the hill. The extremely Korean moral of the story seems to be that anything is possible with a good woman at your side.

6

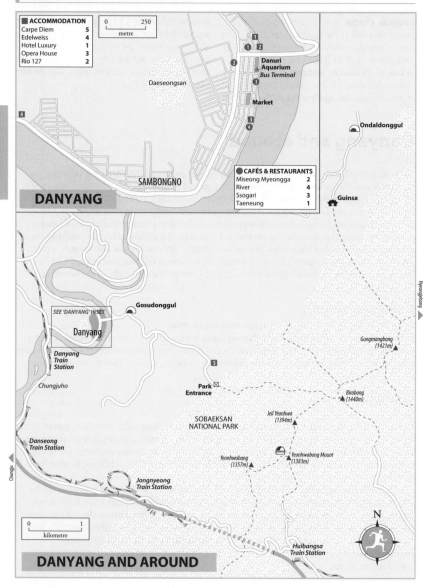

A little further afield, it's possible to take a **ferry** ride (50min; W12,000) for a view of the oddly shaped rocks and crags that pop out of the lake in and around Danyang; these depart from Janghoe downstream, accessible by bus (ask at the terminal) or taxi.

Gosudonggul

고수동굴 • Daily 9am–5pm • W5000, or W8000 for slightly longer route • 20min walk from Danyang, across the bridge

Within walking distance of the centre is **Gosudonggul**; dating back millennia, this

6

OUTDOOR ACTIVITIES IN DANYANG

There's one big reason why domestic tourism has blossomed in Danyang of late: **paragliding**. On any sunny weekend, you'll see dozens of tourists dropping to the ground like confetti from the Sobaeksan foothills. Several offices on the waterfront road will be able to get you (and your instructor) airborne for W100,000, including a transfer to the jumping point. The same companies offer **rafting trips** for W30,000 per person, and you can hire a two-person **all-terrain vehicle** for W40,000 per day.

1.7km-long grotto was discovered less than forty years ago. Underground, its honey-yellow stalagmites and stalactites ripple through the dim, damp tunnel, and are visible from metal walkways and staircases. Note, however, that the cave is a popular stopover with families out for a weekend drive through the countryside, and can become uncomfortably crowded: visit on a weekday, if possible.

ARRIVAL AND DEPARTURE   DANYANG

By train Danyang's station is inconveniently located a few kilometres west of the centre; it's a W7000 taxi ride into town, or a 40min walk along the lakeside trail.
Destinations Andong (7 daily; 1hr 20min); Busan (Haeundae; 2 daily; 4hr 40min); Gyeongju (3hr 30min); Seoul (9 daily; 2hr 10min).

By bus The bus terminal is more central than the train station, and can be found near the western end of the bridge crossing the lake.
Destinations Busan (1 daily; 5hr); Cheongju (frequent; 3hr 30min); Guinsa (13 daily; 40min); Seoul (frequent; 2hr 10min).

ACCOMMODATION

As with most of provincial Korea, there's next to nothing at the higher end of the **accommodation** scale. A few smart new motels have opened up around the bus station, though surprisingly few make use of the phenomenal lake view. Note that on weekends it can be hard to find a room; contrarily, on weekdays, you'll pay less than the prices stipulated here.

Edelweiss 단양 관광 호텔 Sanbongno 31 ☎043 423 7070, ⓦdanyanghotel.com. Away from the centre, and just across the river from the train station, this is an upmarket place with a sauna and the cushiest rooms in town. The prices are fair, though there's little of interest in the immediate area. W100,000
Hotel Luxury 호텔 럭셔리 Subyeonno 125 ☎043 421 9911. This is manifestly a love motel, not a hotel, as evidenced by the free condoms in the rooms. However, as far as love motels go it's a pretty good one, with large flatscreen TVs, excellent showers and a great deal of attention paid to decoration – take your pick from a dozen different room styles at the entrance. W70,000

Opera House 오페라 하우스 Subyeonno 67 ☎043 423 5751. Fronted by an impossible-to-miss frieze of naked Roman gods, this yeogwan is ideal for budget travellers. Its rooms are comfortable and en suite, and some have internet-ready computers. It may be a little seamy for some – there's a "nightclub" in the basement, though the soundproofing is good. W30,000
Rio 127 리오127 Subyeonno 127 ☎043 421 5600, ⓦrio127.com. Run by a friendly, English-speaking local (an excellent source of information), this is home to most of Danyang's backpackers. Rooms are a little poky for the price, but there are few better places to go for local information. W50,000

EATING

For such a small place, Danyang has some great places to eat, with many of the dishes revolving in some way around the **garlic** for which the town is famed (see box, p.280). Note, however, that most **restaurants** in Danyang shut up by 9pm.

Miseong Myeongga 미성명가 Byeolgong-ni 494 ☎043 421 9295. For a good sit-on-the-floor feed, head to this place, which specializes in sutbul dakgalbi (숯불닭갈비; W8000), a special sort of chicken galbi cooked on a grill, rather than the regular pan. Pay an extra W1000 and you can try the super-spicy version. Daily 10am–8pm.
River 리버 Dojeon-ni 564 ☎043 422 1887. Just the

treat for a Danyang morning – good coffee with a partial river view. Figure on W3000–5000 per cup; there are teas available too. Daily 7am–6pm.
Ssogari 쏘가리 Byeolgong-ni 564 ☎043 421 8826. River-facing restaurant that's the place to come for olgaengi haejanguk (see box, p.280); a bowl of the good stuff will set you back W8000. Daily 8am–7pm.

6

DANYANG TREATS

Danyang is famed for its **garlic**, which often fills the market in the town centre; there's even a festival related to the bulbs each July, which features a Miss Garlic contest. Don't miss the local dish, **maneul dolsotbap** (마늘 돌솥밥), in which four types of grain are served in a hot earthenware bowl speckled with chestnuts, dates, ginkgo nuts and a whole lot of garlic. Hunt around the market and you'll find a couple of places serving dumplings (*mandu*; 만두) with garlic mixed into the meat or veg filling. Another town speciality is **olgaengi haejangguk** (올갱이 해장국), a warming vegetable soup filled with tiny **river snails** from the lake outside. Finally, there are a few good **makgeolli** brands to hunt down in the town's shops and restaurants, including Sobaeksan Geomungong (소백산 검은공), a greyish, gloopy number made with black bean – probably the best such variety in the country.

★**Taeneung** 태능 Byeolgong-ni 603 ☎ 043 422 7088. In terms of presentation and taste, this restaurant has the best *maneul dolsotbap* (see box above) in town – and, commendably, it's the only one prepared to serve single diners. These gut-busting meals will set you back W15,000 a head, and they're worth every won. Daily 11am–9.30pm.

Guinsa

구인사 • Daily 24hr • Free • Buses from Danyang (40min), Seoul (hourly; 3hr) and a few others from elsewhere in Korea; note that most services dry up by 6pm

Shoehorned into a tranquil valley northeast of Danyang is **GUINSA**, one of Korea's more remarkable **temple** complexes. A great divider among Koreans, it's viewed by many as the most un-Korean temple, which is emphatically true – the colours and building styles are hard to find anywhere else in the country, and the usual elegant restraint of the traditional layouts has been replaced by a desire to show off. On the other hand, numbers alone bear witness to its importance – well over one thousand monks may reside here at any one time, and the kitchens can dish up food for twice that number on any given day.

Guinsa is the headquarters of the Buddhist **Cheontae sect**, once the most powerful in the country, and resuscitated in the 1940s (see box opposite). Here, the usual black slate of Korean temple roofing has occasionally been eschewed for a glazed orange finish reminiscent of that in Beijing's Forbidden City, and some buildings show hints of Lhasa's Potala Palace, with their use of height and vertical lines. Buildings swarm up the valley and connect in unlikely ways, with alleys and bridges crisscrossing like the dragons depicted around the complex; you'll often wander up a path, and on looking back discover three or four routes that could have brought you to the same place. Despite being infested with an almost plague-like number of dragonflies in late summer, it's one of the most scenic temples in all Korea.

The temple

Entry to the main body of the complex is through the **Gate of Four Heavenly Kings**, from where you'll head up to the five-storey **law hall**; this is one of the largest such facilities in Korea, and like many other buildings on the complex is elaborate both in terms of painting and structural design. Inside you'll find a golden Shakyamuni Buddha and two attendants – tempting as it may be, you are not allowed to take photos in this building. Further along the maze of paths is a courtyard, sometimes barely visible under the masses of *kimchi* pots used for making dinner, which is cooked up in colossal kitchens and served in the huge **canteen**. Close by are several buildings which serve as **living quarters**; the one with the sheer vertical face is the newest and largest structure in the still-growing complex. Head up alongside this on a wonderful pine-covered path and you come to the **Great Teacher Hall**, the achingly gorgeous golden crown of the complex, and a gleaming shrine to its creator, whose statue stands proud at the centre of the hall. Continuing on the uphill path will bring you to his well-tended gravesite, while further on are the western slopes of **Sobaeksan National Park** (see opposite).

THE CHEONTAE SECT

Cheontae (천태) is a Buddhist sect whose Korean followers number almost two million, making it one of the biggest in the country. As with other Korean sects, the school descended from China, where it was created in the sixth century and known as Tiantai (天台). On crossing the West Sea the sect's beliefs were polished into a local form deemed more logical, consistent and holistic than its Chinese predecessor; after wrestling with competitors during Unified Silla rule, the school became fully established in the eleventh century. Cheontae declined to near-extinction by the 1940s, but was given a second lease of life in 1945 by **Songwol Wongak**, a monk who put his overseas studies to good use by creating an altogether different temple – the Guinsa that you see today.

6

ACCOMMODATION AND EATING   GUINSA

Guinsa is one of the most interesting places in Korea to embark on a **templestay** programme (W40,000). Failing that, there are **minbak** at the foot of the complex (figure on W25,000), as well as plenty of **restaurants**. It's most enjoyable, however, to take a simple rice-and-spice lunch in the huge temple **canteen** (daily 11.30am–1.30pm) for a voluntary donation.

Sobaeksan National Park

소백산 국립 공원 • Daily from 2hr before sunrise to 2hr after sunset • Free • @ english.knps.or.kr

Far quieter than most Korean parks on account of its location, **SOBAEKSAN NATIONAL PARK** is an unheralded delight. It is best visited at the end of spring (around May or June), when a carpet of royal **azalea blooms** paints much of the mountainside a riot of pink, but at any time of the year the views are impressive – the park is traversed by a relatively bare ridge heading in an admirably straight line from northeast to southwest, crossing numerous high peaks. A steep three-hour uphill path runs from the main entrance at Cheondong-ri to **Birobong**, the park's highest peak at 1440m. After reaching the ridge most head straight back down, but if you follow it along in either direction you will be rewarded with a succession of amazing views. Many opt to head northeast to Gungmangbong (1421m), an hour or so away, but only the hard core continue all the way to Hyeongjebong. Southwest of Birobong are three peaks, confusingly, all named Yeonhwabong; on the central crest, taking advantage of the park's clean air and lofty elevation, is Korea's main **astronomical observatory**, though unfortunately it is closed to visitors. From here it's possible to exit the park to the south through the Huibang park entrance, the two-hour walk mopping up small waterfalls and a secluded temple on the way.

ARRIVAL AND DEPARTURE   SOBAEKSAN NATIONAL PARK

To Cheondong The Cheondong entrance is close to Danyang – just beyond Cheondonggul cave – and is best reached by taxi (W6000), though there are local buses every hour or so from the town's bus terminal. The park's other entrances aren't easily accessible without your own transport.

To Huibang The Huibang entrance is a 2km walk from Huibangsa train station (희방사); those travelling by rail from Danyang should note that the track at one point dives into the mountain, and makes a 360-degree turn before coming out again much further up.

ACCOMMODATION

Most visitors to Sobaeksan stay in Danyang, though there's plenty of choice around the park entrance. **Minbak** rooms cluster by the Cheondong entrance; the price goes down and the quality up the further away you get from the entrance. Both park entrances have **camping** grounds (from W1600 per person).

Carpe Diem 카르페 디엠 Darianno 569 ☎ 043 421 2155. The best rooms in the area are in this chic pension about 1km down the road from the Cheondong park entrance. It boasts a café and art gallery, rooms filled with modern art, plastic fruit strewn liberally about the place, and an incongruous statue of Marilyn Monroe at the entrance. W80,000

Jeju Island

JUSANGJEOLLI

Jeju Island

The mass of islands draped along Korea's southern coast fades into the Pacific, before coming to an enigmatic conclusion in the crater-pocked Jeju Island, known locally as Jejudo (제주도). This tectonic pimple in the South Sea is the country's number one holiday destination, particularly for Korean honeymooners, and it's easy to see why – the volcanic crags, innumerable beaches and colourful rural life draw comparisons with Hawaii and Bali, a fact not lost on the local tourist authorities. This very hype puts many foreign travellers off, but while the five-star hotels and tour buses can detract from Jeju's natural appeal, the island makes for a superb visit if taken on its own terms; indeed those who travel into Jeju's more remote areas may come away with the impression that little has changed here for decades. In many ways it's as if regular Korea has been given a makeover – splashes of tropical green fringe fields topped off with palm trees and tangerine groves – and while Jeju's weather may be breezier and damper than the mainland, its winter is eaten into by lengthier springs and autumns, allowing oranges, pineapples and dragon fruit to grow.

Jeju City is the largest settlement, and whether you arrive by plane or ferry, this will be your entry point. You'll find the greatest choice of accommodation and restaurants here, and most visitors choose to hole up in the city for the duration of their stay, as the rest of the island is within day-trip territory. Although there are a few sights in the city itself, getting out of town is essential if you're to make the most of your trip.

The eastern half of Jeju is wonderfully unspoilt – think unhurried fishing villages, stone walls and lush green fields. On the east coast is **Seongsan**, a sumptuously rural hideaway crowned by **Ilchulbong**, a green caldera that translates as "Sunrise Peak"; ferries run from here to **Udo**, a tiny islet that somehow manages to be even more bucolic. Inland are the **Manjanggul lava tubes**, evidence of Jeju's turbulent creation and one of the longest such systems in the world, and **Sangumburi**, the largest and most accessible of Jeju's many craters.

All roads eventually lead to **Seogwipo** on the south coast; this relaxed, waterfall-flanked city is Jeju's second-largest settlement, and sits next to the five-star resort of **Jungmun**. Sights in Jeju's **west** are a little harder to access, but this makes a trip all the more worthwhile – the countryside you'll have to plough through is some of the best on the island, with the fields yellow with rapeseed in spring, and carpeted from summer to autumn with the pink-white-purple tricolour of cosmos flowers. Those with an interest in calligraphy may want to seek out the remote former home of Chusa, one of the country's most famed exponents of the art.

Highlights

❶ Walking the Jeju Olle Trail A delightful walking trail now circumnavigates more or less the entire island – if you've no time for the whole lot, at least try a section. **See box, p.288**

❷ Udo by bike There are few more enjoyable activities in all Korea than gunning around this tiny island's narrow lanes on a scooter. **See p.298**

❸ Route 97 A rural day-trip along this road can see you take in a volcanic crater, a folk village and a culture museum, before finishing at the beach. **See p.299**

❹ Seogwipo Flanked by waterfalls, Jeju's second-largest city is a relaxed base for tours of the sunny southern coast. **See p.300**

❺ Teddy Bear Museum The moon landings and the fall of the Berlin Wall are just some of the events to be given teddy treatment at this shrine to high kitsch. **See p.303**

❻ Yakcheonsa Turn up for the evening service at this remote temple for one of Jeju's most magical experiences. **See p.304**

❼ Hallasan Korea's highest point at 1950m, this mountain dominates the island and just begs to be climbed. **See p.310**

HIGHLIGHTS ARE MARKED ON THE MAP ON P.286

JEJU ISLAND

N

0 kilometres 5

HIGHLIGHTS

1 Walking the Jeju Olle Trail
2 Udo by bike
3 Route 97
4 Seogwipo
5 Teddy Bear Museum
6 Yakcheonsa
7 Hallasan

---- Jeju Olle trail

ACCOMMODATION
Island Guesthouse 2
Ocean House Jeju 3
Red Sky Pension 1
Zen Hideaway Jeju 4

● **RESTAURANT**
Tamna Sikdang 1

Mainland

Byangdo

Biyangdo

Udo 2

Seongsan
Ilchulbong

Sinyang Beach

MAESONG ROAD

SEOGSENG ROAD

Pyoseon Beach

Jeju Folk
Village

TILL ROAD

Gimnyeong Beach

Gimnyeong
Maze

Manjanggul

Bijarim Forest

MID-MOUNTAIN ROAD

Seong-eup Folk
Village

Sangumburi

NAMJORO

ROUTE 97 | EAST TOURIST HIGHWAY

5.16 ROAD

Jeju City

Jeju Love
Land

HALLASAN
NATIONAL PARK
7
Hallasan
(1950m)

Seogwipo

1100 ROAD

4

Yakcheonsa
6

Airport

Sinjeju

MYSTERIOUS ROAD

Jungmun
5
Jungmun
Beach

Jusangjeolli

WEST TOURIST HIGHWAY

O'Sulloc Tea
Plantation

Jeju Art Park

Sanbanggulsa
Yongmeori

Hamel's
Ship
Songaksan Peak

Hyeopjae &
Geumneung
Beaches

Biyangdo

Jeoji Art Village

Bunjae Artpia

Peace
Museum

Chusa Exile Site

Daejeong

Moseulpo

Gapado

Marado

JEJU'S UNIQUE CULTURE

Around the island, you'll see evidence of a rich local culture quite distinct from the mainland, most notably in the form of the **hareubang** – these cute, grandfatherly statues of volcanic rock were made for reasons as yet unexplained, and pop up all over the island (see box, p.291). Similarly ubiquitous are the **batdam**, walls of hand-stacked volcanic rock that separate the farmers' fields: like the drystone walls found across Britain, these were built without any bonding agents, the resulting gaps letting through the strong winds that often whip the island. Jeju's distinctive **thatch-roofed houses** are also abundant, and the island even has a breed of miniature horse; originally brought across during the Mongolian invasions, these are of particular interest to Koreans due to the near-total dearth of equine activity on the mainland, and their meat also turns up on some local menus. Also unique to Jeju are the *haenyeo*, **female divers** who plunge without breathing apparatus into often treacherous waters in search of shellfish and sea urchins (see box, p.298). Although once a hard-as-nails embodiment of the island's matriarchal culture, their dwindling numbers mean that this occupation is in danger of petering out.

7

In the centre of the island is **Hallasan**, an extinct volcano and the country's highest point at 1950m, visible from much of the island, though often obscured by Jeju's fickle weather.

Brief history

Jejudo burst into being around two million years ago in a series of volcanic eruptions, but prior to an annexation by the mainland Goryeo dynasty in 1105 its history is sketchy and unknown. While the mainland was being ruled by the famed Three Kingdoms of Silla, Baekje and Goguryeo, Jeju was governed by the mysterious **Tamna kingdom** (see box, p.288). The *Samguk Sagi* – Korea's main historical account of the Three Kingdoms period – states that Tamna in the fifth century became a tributary state to the Baekje kingdom on the mainland's southwest, then hurriedly switched allegiance before the rival Silla kingdom swallowed Baekje whole in 660. Silla itself was consumed in 918 by the Goryeo dynasty, which set about reining in the island province; Jeju gradually relinquished autonomy before a full takeover in 1105. The inevitable **Mongol** invasion came in the mid-thirteenth century, with the marauding Khaans controlling the island for almost a hundred years. The horses bred here to support Mongol attacks on Japan fostered a local tradition of horsemanship that continues to this day – Jeju is the only place in Korea with significant equine numbers – while the visitors also left an audible legacy in the Jejanese dialect.

Under the Joseon dynasty

In 1404, with Korea finally free of Mongol domination, Jeju was eventually brought under control by an embryonic **Joseon dynasty**. Its location made it the ideal place for Seoul to exile radicals. Two of the most famed of these were **King Gwanghaegun**, the victim of a coup in 1623, and **Chusa**, an esteemed calligrapher whose exile site can be found on the west of the island (see p.306). It was just after this time that the West got its first reports about Korea, from **Hendrick Hamel**, a crewman on a Dutch trading ship that crashed off the Jeju coast in 1653 (see box, p.307).

The Jeju Massacre

With Jeju continually held at arm's length by the central government, a long-standing feeling of resentment against the mainland was a major factor in the **Jeju Massacre** of 1948. The Japanese occupation having recently ended with Japan's surrender at the end of World War II, the Korean-American coalition sought now to tear out the country's Communist roots, which were strong on Jeju. Jejanese guerrilla forces, provoked by regular brutality, staged a simultaneous attack on the island's police

THE TAMNA CREATION MYTH

Jeju's aloofness is no modern creation, for even during Korea's Three Kingdoms period, it conspired to be ruled by a fourth – the **Tamna kingdom**. With no historical record of Tamna's founding, it is left to Jeju myth to fill in the gaps: according to legend, the three founders of the country – Go, Bu and Yang – rose from the ground at a spot now marked by **Samseonghyeol** shrine in Jeju City (see p.290). On a hunting trip shortly after this curious birth, they found three maidens who had washed up on a nearby shore armed with grain and a few animals. The three fellows married the girls, and using the material and livestock set up agricultural communities, each man kicking off his own clan. Descendants of these three families conduct twice-yearly (in spring and autumn) ceremonies to worship their ancestors.

stations. A retaliation was inevitable, and the rebels and government forces continued to trade blows years after the official end of the **Korean War** in 1953, by which time this largely ignored conflict had resulted in up to thirty thousand deaths, the vast majority on the rebel side.

Recent times

Things have since calmed down significantly. Jeju returned to its roots as a rural backwater with little bar fishing and farming to sustain its population, but its popularity with mainland **tourists** grew and grew after Korea's took off as an economic power, with the island becoming known for the *samda*, or three bounties: rock, wind and women. Recently domestic tourist numbers have decreased slightly, with richer and more cosmopolitan Koreans increasingly choosing to spend their holidays abroad. However, Jeju still remains the country's top holiday spot, as well as a magnet for tourists from other Asian countries – the number of Chinese visitors, in particular, has ballooned since visa restrictions to the island were lifted.

ARRIVAL AND DEPARTURE   JEJU ISLAND

Note that, whichever way you arrive from the mainland, Jeju's special **visa rules** (it's open to Chinese and several other Asian nations who'd otherwise need a Korean visa) mean that it's necessary to bring along your passport.

By plane There are flights to Jeju from most mainland airports (usually around W85,000), as well as a fair few cities across eastern Asia; this has long been the preferred form of arrival for locals, and the resultant closure of ferry routes means that planes are generally the way to go for foreign travellers too.

By ferry Schedules have long been in a state of flux, but at the time of writing there were daily ferries to Jeju City from Mokpo (3 daily; 3hr–4hr 30min; W30,000–43,000) and Wando (3 daily; 1hr 40min–5hr; W25,000–35,000), as well as an overnight ferry from Busan (1 daily Mon–Sat; 12hr; W43,000).

THE JEJU OLLE TRAIL

One of the most pleasing recent additions to the Jeju tourism scene is the **Jeju Olle** trail (𝕎 jejuolle.org), a walking route that circumnavigates the entire island – 425km in total, along 26 marked sections. These take three to seven hours each, and if attempting one you're advised to get an early start – Jeju often clouds over in the afternoon, when there's also more chance of rain. It's also possible to book a trail **guide** to accompany you and provide useful information about the island (see website for details).

Most of the trail is walking only, though some routes do venture onto roads for stretches. One of the nicest sections is **#1**, which takes in beaches, fields and a couple of extinct volcanoes near Seongsan (see p.296); it's actually better to walk this route in the opposite direction to that recommended by the authorities. Another good route is **#8**, which hits the stunning temple of Yakcheonsa (see p.304), the Jusangjeolli basalt columns (see p.303) and Jungmun beach (see p.303), and a couple more mini-volcanoes.

GETTING AROUND

By bus Most of the island is easily accessible by bus; all routes start in Jeju City (see box, p.292 for details), and most finish down south in Seogwipo.

By car or bike Jeju is one of the few places in Korea where renting a car or bicycle makes sense (see p.293). Outside Jeju City, roads are generally empty and the scenery is almost always stunning, particularly in the inland areas, where you'll find tiny communities, some of which will never have seen a foreigner. Bicycle trips around the perimeter of the island are becoming ever more popular, with riders usually taking four days to complete the circuit – Seongsan, Seogwipo and Daecheong make logical overnight stops.

On foot It's now possible to make a circuit of Jeju on the island's excellent "Olle" trails (see box opposite).

Jeju City

제주시

JEJU CITY (*jeju-shi*) is the provincial capital and home to more than half of the island's population. Markedly relaxed and low-rise for a Korean city, and loomed over by the extinct volcanic cone of Hallasan, it has a few sights of its own to explore, though palm trees, beaches, tectonic peaks and rocky crags are just a bus ride away, thus making it a convenient base for the vast majority of the island's visitors.

7

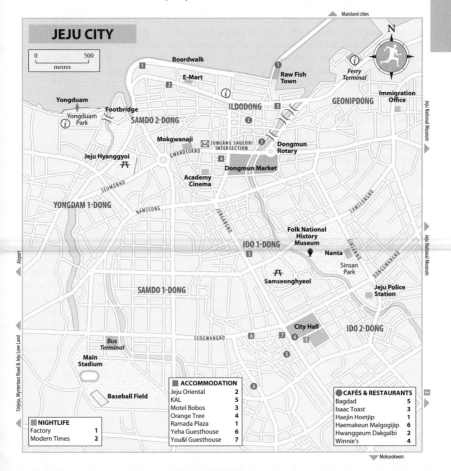

Jeju City was, according to local folklore, the place where the island's progenitors sprung out of the ground (see box, p.288); you can still see the holes at **Samseonghyeol**. While there are few concrete details of the city's history up until Joseon times, the traditional buildings of **Mokgwanaji**, a governmental office located near the present centre of the city, shows that it has long been a seat of regional power. Other interesting sights include **Jeju Hyanggyo**, a Confucian academy, and **Yongduam** ("Dragon Head Rock"), a basalt formation rising from the often fierce sea. Further east along the seafront, there's an appealing walk along the **promenade**; in bad weather the waves scud in to bash the rocks beneath the boardwalk, producing impressive jets of spray. There are also a couple of vaguely interesting **museums**, best reserved as a means of shelter on one of Jeju's many rainy days. Finally, south of the centre along the **Mysterious Road**, where objects appear to roll uphill, is the entertainingly racy **Love Land**.

Yongduam

용두암

Who'd have thought that basalt could be so romantic? The knobbly seaside formation of **Yongduam**, or "Dragon Head Rock", appears in the honeymoon albums of the many Korean couples who choose to celebrate their nuptials in Jeju, and is the defining symbol of the city. From the shore, and in a certain light, the crag does indeed resemble a dragon, though from the higher of two viewing platforms a similar formation to the right appears more deserving of the title. According to Jeju legend, these are the petrified remains of a regal servant who, after scouring Hallasan for magical mushrooms, was turned into a dragon by the offended mountain spirits. Strategically positioned lights illuminate the formation at night, and with fewer people around, this may be the best time to visit.

Jeju Hyanggyo

제주 향교 • Daily: March–Oct 8.30am–6pm; Nov–Feb 9am–5.30pm • Free

On the way back east from Yongduam towards the city centre, you may be tempted to take one of the gorgeous paths that crisscross into and over tiny, tree-filled Hancheon creek, eventually leading to **Jeju Hyanggyo**, a Confucian shrine and school built at the dawn of the Joseon dynasty in the late fourteenth century. Though not quite as attractive as other such facilities around the country, this academy is still active, and hosts age-old ancestral rite ceremonies in spring and autumn.

Mokgwanaji

목관아지 • Daily 8am–7pm • W1500

In the centre of the city are the elegant, traditional buildings of **Mokgwanaji**, a recently restored site that was Jeju's political and administrative centre during the Joseon dynasty; it's a relaxing place that makes for a satisfying meander. Honghwagak, to the back of the complex, was a military officials' office established in 1435 during the rule of King Sejong – the creator of *hangeul*, Korea's written text, and featured on the W10,000 note – and has since been rebuilt and repaired countless times. The place also provides evidence that vice and nit-picking are far from new to Korean politics – several buildings once housed **concubines**, entertainment girls and "female government slaves", while the pond-side banquet site near the site entrance was repossessed due to "noisy frogs".

Samseonghyeol

삼성혈 • Daily 8am–6pm • W2500

Jeju's spiritual home, **Samseonghyeol**, is a shrine that attracts a fair number of Korean tourists year-round. Local legend has it that the island was originally populated by Go,

GRANDFATHERS OF ROCK

What is it with Pacific islands and **statues**? The *moai* of Easter Island are the most famous, but similar relics have been found on Fiji, Tahiti, Hawaii and Okinawa, among other places. Jeju's own version is the *dolhareubang*, or "**stone grandfather**". Commonly abbreviated to **hareubang** (하르방), they can be found all over Korea – nowadays usually outside fish restaurants wishing to drum up custom. Bulgy-eyed and often cheery, they differ from their Polynesian counterparts by being quite expressive. Their hands rest on their tummies as if full of food; those with their left hands above their right are said to be military, as opposed to the more scholarly right-above-left brigade.

Like the *moai*, the origin and purpose of the statues remain shrouded in mystery, though it seems likely that they were placed at village entrances as a means of protection. Another theory, and one supported by their extremely **phallic appearance**, is that they served as sources of fertility – today, miniature versions are sold to women who are having trouble getting pregnant, as well as tourists wanting a souvenir of their trip to Jeju.

Today, only a few dozen **authentic** *hareubang* remain; the most accessible can be found in Jeju City, at the entrance to the Folklore and Natural History Museum, and outside Samseonghyeol.

Bu and Yang, three local demigods that rose from the ground here (see box, p.288). The glorified divots are visible in a small, grassy enclosure at the centre of the park, though it's hard to spend more than a few seconds looking at what are, in effect, little more than holes in the ground. The pleasant wooded walking trails that line the complex will occupy more of your time, and there are a few buildings to peek into as well as an authentic *hareubang* (grandfather statues; see box above) outside the entrance.

Folklore and Natural History Museum

민속 자연사 박물관 • Daily: March–Oct 8.30am–6.30pm; Nov–Feb 8.30am–5.30pm • W1100 • ⓦ museum.jeju.go.kr

Just east of Samseonghyeol, along Samseongno, you'll come to the **Folklore and Natural History Museum**. Local animals in stuffed and skeletal form populate the first rooms, before the diorama overload of the folklore exhibition, where the ceremonies, dwellings and practices of old-time Jeju are brought to plastic life. Unless you're planning to visit the two folk villages on Route 97 (see p.299 & p.300), there are few better ways to get a grip on the island's history.

Jeju National Museum

제주 국립 박물관 • Tues–Fri 9am–6pm, Sat & Sun 9am–7pm • Free • ⓦ jeju.museum.go.kr • A taxi will cost around W3000

As with all other "national" museums around the country, **Jeju National Museum**, 2km east of the centre, focuses almost exclusively on regional finds, but this particular institution – despite its size – has surprisingly little to see. Highlights include some early painted maps, a collection of celadon pottery dating from the twelfth century and a small but excellent display of calligraphy – be sure to take a look at the original **Sehando**, a letter-cum-painting created by Chusa, one of Korea's most revered calligraphers (see p.306). The upper floor is not open so you'll have to make do with staring up at the sprawling stained-glass ceiling from the lobby.

Mysterious Road

도깨비도로 • Best accessed by taxi (around W12,000 from Jeju City), or just off #740 bus route

A few kilometres southwest of Jeju City, a short section of Route 99 – christened the **Mysterious Road** – has achieved national fame. Though no scheduled buses run to this notorious stretch of tarmac, there's always plenty of traffic: cars and tour buses, or indeed pencils, cans of beer or anything else capable of rolling down a hill, are said to roll upwards here. Needless to say, it's a visual illusion created by the angles of the road and the lay of the land. Some people think it looks convincing, while others wonder why people are staring with such wonder at objects rolling down a slight incline, but it makes for a surreal pit stop.

Jeju Love Land

제주 러브 랜드 · Daily 9am–midnight · W9000 · ⓦ jejuloveland.com · Best accessed by taxi (around W12,000 from Jeju City), or just off #740 bus route

Right next door to the Mysterious Road, the tourists themselves constitute part of the attraction – **Jeju Love Land** is Korea's recent sexual revolution contextualized in a theme park. This odd collection of risqué sculpture, photography and art has been immensely popular with the Koreans, now free to have a good laugh at what, for so long, was high taboo. There are statues that you can be pictured kissing or otherwise engaging with, a gallery of sexual positions (in Korean text only, but the pictures need little explanation), several erotic water features, and what may be the most bizarre of Korea's many dioramas – a grunting plastic couple in a parked car. You may never be able to look at a *hareubang* in the same way, or see regal tombs as simple mounds of earth – maybe this park is the continuation of a long-running trend.

ARRIVAL AND DEPARTURE   JEJU CITY

By plane Domestic flights from several mainland destinations arrive every few minutes, landing at the island's airport a few kilometres west of the city centre – around W5000 by cab. In addition, six bus routes make the short run to Gujeju, the city centre, the most useful of which is #100 (W1200), which heads east every 15min or so to the bus terminal, then on to Dongmun Rotary in the city centre, or south to Sinjeju. Bus #600 runs at similar intervals to the top hotels in Jungmun and Seogwipo (both W5000), on the south of the island.

Destinations Busan (1–3 hourly; 55min); Cheongju (12 daily; 1hr); Daegu (13 daily; 50min); Gwangju (12 daily; 45min); Incheon (5 weekly; 1hr 5min); Jinju (2 weekly; 50min); Seoul Gimpo (every 5–15min; 1hr 5min); Ulsan (3 weekly; 1hr); Wonju (daily; 1hr 10min); Yeosu (2 weekly; 45min).

By ferry The terminal sits at the eastern edge of the city, and has connections from several mainland ports

---

JEJU BUS ROUTES

Public buses scoot across much of the island, with the bulk of routes running from Jeju City's bus terminal. The #780 route is the fastest means of travelling between Jeju City and the southern resorts of Jungmun and Seogwipo.

#701 – East Coast (every 15–25min)
Jeju City–Gimnyeong–Seongsan–Pyoseon–Seogwipo
#702 – West Coast (every 15–25min)
Jeju City–Hallim–Sanbangsan (not all buses)–Jungmun–Seogwipo
#710 – Seongsan (every 50–80min)
Jeju City–Sangumburi (not all buses)–Seongsan
#720 – Pyoseon (every 20–40min)
Jeju City–Sangumburi (not all buses)–Seong-eup Folk Village–Pyoseon (for Jeju Folk Village)
#730 – Seogwipo (every 20–40min)
Jeju City–Seogwipo
#740 – 1100 Highway (every 20–40min)
Jeju City–Yeongsil (Hallasan entrance)–Eorimok (Hallasan entrance)–Jungmun
#750 – Daejeong (every 20min)
Jeju City–Sanbangsan–Daejeong
#755 – Moseulpo (every 50–80min)
Jeju City–O'Sulloc Tea Museum–Moseulpo
#780 – Express Road (every 15–20min)
Jeju City–Seongpanak (Hallasan entrance)–Jungmun–Seogwipo

(see p.288 for an idea of prices). The Incheon service was discontinued following the tragic sinking of the *Sewol* in 2014 (see box, p.224), and is unlikely to return.

Destinations Busan (daily except Sun; 12hr); Incheon (daily except Sun; 14hr); Mokpo (2 daily; 3hr 10min–4hr 30min); Wando (3 daily; 1hr 40min–5hr).

By bus Jeju is not connected to the mainland by road (though there have been discussions about an undersea rail line), but a number of bus routes spread out across the island from Jeju City (see box opposite for details).

GETTING AROUND

By bus Jeju City is small and relaxed enough to allow for some walking, but you may occasionally need to hop on a city bus (W1200). The last services on all routes leave at 9pm or just after, and start again at around 6am.

By taxi Rides in the centre are unlikely to top W6000.

Bike rental Several outfits rent out bicycles in Jeju City, including Jeju Hiking (☎ 064 712 4400), within walking distance of the airport, and Yongduam Hiking (☎ 064 757 7777), in the town centre. You'll pay W8000–15,000 per day, depending upon the bike selected, and some places charge an extra W10,000 per day to keep your luggage. You may have to leave your passport behind as a security deposit.

Car rental Many companies jostle for business at the city airport. Rates start at around W35,000 per day.

Motorbike rental Mr. Lee's Bike Shop (☎ 064 758 5296, ⓦ jejubike.co.kr), near the bus station, has motorcycles and scooters to hire (W23,000–55,000 per day), and an English-speaking owner. Discounts are available for multi-day hires.

INFORMATION

Tourist information There are two information desks just metres apart from each other at the airport. At least one will be open from 8am to 10pm (☎ 064 742 8866), but both can supply you with English-language maps and pamphlets and help with anything from renting a car to booking a room. Another booth at the ferry terminal offers similar assistance (daily 10am–8pm; ☎ 064 758 7181). English-language help can also be accessed by phone on ☎ 064 1330.

Hiking equipment There are stores all over the city, especially in the shopping area around Jungang Sagori. Prices are higher than you might expect, but Treksta is a fairly safe choice.

Hospital The best place for foreigners is the Jeju University hospital (☎ 064 750 1234); call ☎ 119 in an emergency.

Post office Post offices across the island are open weekdays from 9am–5pm, with the central post office (☎ 064 758 8602), near Mokgwanaji, also open on Saturdays until 1pm.

ACCOMMODATION

Jeju's capital is firmly fixed on Korea's tourist itinerary; most visitors choose to base themselves here. However, many establishments were built when Korea's economy was going great guns in the 1980s, and are now beginning to show their age. All higher-end **hotels** slash their rates by up to fifty percent outside July and August, so be sure to ask about **discounts**. Often you'll be asked whether you'd like a "sea view" room facing north, or a "mountain view" facing Hallasan; the latter is usually a little cheaper. There are many cheap **motels** around the nightlife zone near City Hall, and in the rustic canalside area between Dongmun market and the ferry terminal.

Jeju Oriental 제주 오리엔탈 Tapdongno 47 ☎ 064 752 8222, ⓦ www.oriental.co.kr. Upper rooms have great sea views; few live up to the promise of the large reception area, but you'll be paying for the facilities anyway – a casino and four restaurants, internet in every room and courteous staff. Competition from the *Ramada* across the road means that discounts of fifty percent are not uncommon. **W240,000**

KAL KAL 호텔 Ido 1-dong 1691-9 ☎ 064 724 2001, ⓦ kalhotel.co.kr. An immaculate hotel and Jeju's tallest building, with 21 floors; friendly, white-suited staff buzz about the place, while the rooms are a bit small but pleasingly decorated. There's also a funky cocktail bar on the top floor. **W270,000**

Motel Bobos 모텔 보보스 Geonipdong 20 ☎ 064 727 7200. Don't be put off by the rather dingy reception area – the wood-floored rooms here are large and airy, and you'll get a free (instant) coffee in the morning. The motel is also within walking distance of the ferry terminal and seaside promenade, as well as some of the city sights. **W40,000**

Orange Tree 오렌지트리 Ildo 1-dong ☎ 064 755 8688. The motel-renovated-as-boutique-hotel craze is by no means confined to Seoul: the rooms at this one may be smallish, but they're attractive and certainly do the job, and a free breakfast is served too. A little beacon of serenity in an otherwise earthy part of town. **W88,000**

Ramada Plaza 라마다 프라자 Tapdongno 66 ☎ 064 729 8100, ⓦ ramadajeju.co.kr. A modern, cavernous hotel that's even bigger than it appears from outside. Vertigo-inducing interior views, plush interiors and some of Jeju's best food make it the hotel of choice for those who can afford it, though the atmosphere may be a little mall-like, especially when it hosts conventions. **W340,000**

7

Yeha Guesthouse 예하 게스트하우스 Seogwangno 278 ☎ 064 756 5506, ⓦ yehaguesthouse.com. The Yeha team have opened at a new location, very close to City Hall and Jeju's best bars. As with the original, it's a friendly and immaculately clean place, and within walking distance of the bus terminal. Dorms W19,000, doubles W50,000

You&I Guesthouse 예하유앤아이 게스트하우스 Yido 2-dong 1772-10 ☎ 064 753 5648, ⓦ uniguesthouse .com. A new hostel in the downtown area, boasting a gigantic kitchen area that's great for cooking. Staff are super-friendly, and local tangerines pop up in the free breakfasts. Dorms W19,000, doubles W60,000

EATING

Jeju prides itself on its **seafood**, and much of the city's seafront is taken up by fish restaurants. These congregate in groups, with two of the main clusters being the large, ferry-like complex at the eastern end of the seafront promenade, and another near Yongduam rock. There's plenty of non-fishy choice away from the water – the two best areas are the shopping district around Jungang Sagori, which contains some excellent chicken *galbi* restaurants, and the trendy **student** area west of City Hall.

★**Bagdad** 바그다드 Ido 2-dong 1188-16 ☎ 064 757 8182. Nobody's quite sure whether this attractive place is a café, a restaurant, or a bar – it seems happy to function as all three. The tasty curries, doled out by Nepali chefs, will set you back W10,000–15,000, and the laidback air is accentuated when the *shisha* pipes get fired up of an evening. Mon–Sat 11am–11pm.

Isaac Toast 이작 토스트 Ildo 1-dong 1477-5. In keeping with this cheapie chain's other branches across the country, *Isaac Toast* is a great little breakfast target for toast made the Korean way (that is mostly on a buttered-up hotplate). You'll rarely need to pay more than W3000, even with a small drink. Mon–Sat 9am–6pm.

Haejin Hoetjip 해진 횟집 Geonipdong 1319-31 ☎ 064 757 8889. Watch Jeju's air traffic glide over the sea at this fish restaurant, located on the lower deck of the ferry-like "Raw Fish Town" complex. A huge W100,000 mixed sashimi set meal could feed three quite easily – the sushi, sea squirts and sea snails come with a nice grilled fish, as well as a fish soup. Alternatively, try the delicious broiled sea bream with tofu for W10,000. Daily 10am–9pm.

★**Haemakeun Malgogijip** 해맑은 말고기집 Ido 2-dong 1378-36 ☎ 064 726 5073. Jeju is famed for its horses, and inevitably they also crop up on the menus of a few dedicated restaurants here. This place looks simple but the food is fantastic – try your horsemeat barbecued (말고기 구이), or raw and served with slices of Korean pear (말육회); these dishes will set you back W25,000 each. The place is a bit hard to find, but it's only 10min on foot from the bus terminal. Daily 11am–7pm.

Hwanggeum Dakgalbi 황금 닭갈비 Ildo 1-dong 1476-60 ☎ 064 758 9346. *Dak-galbi* is a chicken kebab cooked at your table in a hot metal tray (see box, p.142); here it costs around W9000 per portion, usually for a minimum of two people. When it's nearly finished, add some rice, noodles (or both) to the scraps for yet another meal. Daily 10am–9pm.

Winnie's 위니스 Ido 2-dong 1179-3 ☎ 064 8523 2930. This bright, sweet-looking brunch place is just what the city centre needed – and it's proven wildly popular with expats and locals alike. For tourists, it's simply a grand place for that all-important first meal of the day; try Vegemite toast (W6000), eggs Benedict (W10,000), ciabatta sandwiches (W9000) and more. They also sell beer. Daily except Wed 10.30am–midnight.

NIGHTLIFE AND ENTERTAINMENT

Most of the city's **drinking** takes place in the tightly crammed area west of City Hall. At the time of writing you could barely walk for five minutes without stumbling across a flavoured-beer and cheese-sticks bar – probably a passing fad, but perhaps worth giving a try.

BARS

★**Factory** 팩터리 Ido 2-dong 1180-1 ☎ 070 7575 1579, ⓦ facebook.com/jejufactory. One of the nightlife zone's quirkier bars, appropriately demarcated by a Warholes-que bendy banana. It hosts a whole bunch of events aimed at local expats, though live music is still the biggest draw – the host, Myeongae, is the island's go-to source of music information. Tues–Sun 7pm–3am.

Modern Times 모던 타임스 Yeondong 263-6 ☎ 064 748 4180. Good, locally brewed craft beer in a pleasant environment. As well as pints of the good stuff (around W7000), there's decent pub grub on offer. Daily 11am–1am.

CINEMA AND SHOWS

Academy Cinema In a large complex a short walk south of Mokgwanaji, this cinema is the best place to catch a film; tickets cost W7000.

Nanta 난타 Ido 2-dong 837-20 ☎ 064 723 8878. The Jeju outpost of Seoul's wacky kitchen-based musical (see p.111) has been going strong since opening up here. Tickets W50,000. Performances daily 5pm & 8pm.

The northeast coast

For one reason or another, most travellers making a circuit of Jeju do so in a clockwise direction. After escaping Jeju City's modest sprawl, rice paddies will suddenly be upon you, often bordered with the delightful stone walls for which the island is famed. **Gimnyeong** is the most pleasing of several **beaches** hereabouts, and makes a good place to stay the night; even if you don't, it's easy to mop up the area's other main sights – the lava tubes of **Manjanggul** and a neat little **maze** – on your way east to Seongsan.

Gimnyeong beach

김녕 해수역장 • On #701 bus route from Jeju City, Seongsan and Seogwipo

One of the island's most popular beaches on account of its exceptionally bright sand, **Gimnyeong beach** lies within easy swiping distance of Jeju City; it boasts the area's greatest concentration of restaurants and accommodation, and is accessible on the buses that run along the coastal road. There are three main swimming areas here, with the central one most conducive to swimming – best at low tide, since there are rocky outcrops at the top of the beach.

7

ACCOMMODATION   GIMNYEONG BEACH

★**Red Sky Pension** 레드 스카이 펜션 Dongbok-ni 671 ☎ 064 783 2887; map p.286. Modern, adventurously designed pension overlooking the ocean just west of Gimnyeong beach. The decor used in the rooms could be described as a little loud, with its floral wallpaper and zebra-print top sheets – all the more reason to open the windows of an evening, and gaze out towards a constellation of squid boats. W100,000

Manjanggul

만장굴 • Daily: April–Oct 9am–6pm; Nov–March 9am–5pm • W2000 • #700 bus from Jeju City or Seogwipo to Manjanggul stop, then 20min walk

Not too far in from the coast is **Manjanggul**, a long underground cave formed by pyroclastic flows – millions of years ago, underwater eruptions caused channels of surface lava to crust over or burrow into the soft ground, resulting in subterranean tunnels of flowing lava. Once the flow finally stopped, these so-called "**lava tubes**" remained. Stretching for at least 9km beneath the fields and forests south of the small port of Gimnyeong, Manjanggul is one of the longest such systems in the world, though only 1km or so is open to the public. This dingy and damp "tube" contains a number of hardened lava features, including balls, bridges and an 8m-high pillar at the end of the course – all in all, quite spectacular.

Gimnyeong Maze

김녕 미로 공원 • Daily 8.30am–8pm • W3300 • On #701 bus route from Jeju City, Seongsan and Seogwipo; 15min walk from Manjanggul stop (see above)

A neat little diversion from the beach or lava tubes is **Gimnyeong Maze**, created in the vague shape of Jeju Island by Frederic H. Dustin, a professor and long-term expat in these parts. There are four routes through the hedges, and it's actually pretty easy to get lost for a while – or it would be, were so many visitors not brazenly cheating with the aid of maps supplied at the entrance. While plotting your escape, be sure to take a closer look at some of the foliage, which has been brought to the site from all over East Asia.

Seongsan

성산

You're unlikely to be disappointed by **SEONGSAN**, an endearing rural town with one very apparent tourist draw looming over it: **Ilchulbong**, or "Sunrise Peak", so named as it's the first place on the island to be lit up by the orange fires of dawn. The town can easily be visited as a day-trip from Jeju City but many visitors choose to spend a night here, beating the sun out of bed to clamber up the graceful, green slope to the rim of Ilchulbong's crown-shaped caldera.

Besides the conquest of Ilchulbong, there's little to do in Seongsan bar strolling around the neighbouring fields and tucking into a fish supper, though the waters off the coast do offer some fantastic **diving** opportunities (see below). South of town is **Sinyang beach**, where the water depth and incessant wind make it a good place to windsurf; equipment is available to rent. Head the other way for the charming island of Udo (see opposite), which lies just offshore; this makes a better place to stay if you're not going to get up at dawn for the Ilchulbong sunrise.

Ilchulbong

일출봉 • Daily 1hr before sunrise to 8pm • W2000

From Seongsan town it's a twenty-minute or so walk to the summit of **Ilchulbong**, a delightfully verdant caldera. A steep set of steps leads up to a 182m-high **viewing platform** at the top, and although the island's fickle weather and morning mists usually conspire to block the actual emergence of the sun from the sea, it's a splendid spot nonetheless. Powerful bulbs from local squid boats dot the nearby waters; as the morning light takes over, the caldera below reveals itself as beautifully verdant, its far side plunging sheer into the sea – unfortunately, it's not possible to hike around the rim. If you turn to face west, Seongsan is visible below, and the topography of the surrounding area – hard to judge from ground level – reveals itself. Ilchulbong is an especially popular place for Koreans to ring in the New Year – a small **festival** celebrates the changing of the digits.

ARRIVAL AND DEPARTURE   SEONGSAN

By bus Seongsan lies on the #701 coastal bus route, which links Jeju City with Seogwipo (around 1hr 30min from either). From Jeju City, you'll save a little time by taking the #710 (1hr).

By ferry There are ferries to Udo (on the hour, 8am–4pm; 10min) from a small terminal a 15min walk from town – it's the terminus of the #710 bus route, but not on the #701.

ACTIVITIES

Diving Sungsan Scuba (☎064 782 6117), near *Haechon* restaurant, offers diving trips – these are at their most spectacular during May and June, when the summer rains are yet to hit and visibility is at its best. It'll set you back around W50,000 per small group for the boat out, and W40,000 for costume and equipment hire; they also run three-day PADI courses for W600,000.

ACCOMMODATION AND EATING

There's no higher-end accommodation in Seongsan, but **minbak** can be found in abundance – hang around for long enough and the *ajummas* will find you, and after a bit of haggling the price should drop to W20,000. For food, there are loads of **fish restaurants** around, and plenty of cafés and snack stands clustered around the Ilchulbong ticket booth; there are also some 24-hour convenience stores.

Dosirak Guesthouse 도시락 게스트하우스 Seongsan-ni 33-12 ☎010 5149 0400. Seongsan's hostel has okayish (if slightly noisy) dorms and a few private rooms. It's all cheerfully decorated, though as with hostels all over Korea, quite overpriced. Dorm beds W20,000,

private rooms W50,000

★**Haechon** 해촌 Seongsan-ni 399-10 ☎064 784 8001. This restaurant is simply fantastic. Not only does it have optimum views of Ilchulbong rising up above the waters (grab a seat as close to the windows as you can), but the seafood here is quite superb. They have the regular *hoe-deop bap* (sashimi on rice; W10,000) and grilled mackerel (W13,000), but think about trying the local speciality, cutlassfish, served on *bibimbap* – quite unusual, but very tasty (W11,000). Daily 8am–9pm.

Kondohyeon Minbak 콘도형 민박 Seongsan-ni

399-12 ☎064 784 8940. Sitting above a restaurant, this is the fanciest *minbak* in the area (not that this is saying much), and in fact is much closer to a pension in style. Rooms here are adequate, and some have internet access; try to nab one with a balcony facing Ilchulbong. **W60,000**

Udo

우도

Visible from Ilchulbong is **UDO**, a rural speck of land whose stacked-stone walls and rich grassy hills give it the air of a Scottish isle transported to warmer climes. Occasionally, the nomenclature of Korea's various peaks and stony bits reaches near-Dadaist extremes; "Cow Island" is one of the best examples, its contours apparently resembling the shape of resting cattle. This sparsely populated dollop of land is a wonderful place to hole up for a few days, and one of the best places to spot two of Jeju's big draws – the stone walls (밭담; *batdam*) that line the island's fields and narrow roads, and the **haenyeo**, female divers long famed for their endurance (see box, p.298). Bring enough money for your stay if possible – there's an ATM in the supermarket at the very centre of the island, but it's a bit of an uphill slog from the coast.

7

Sanho beach

산호 해수역장

Within walking distance of the main ferry terminal, westward-facing **Sanho beach** is the largest and most popular on the island, and boasts its greatest concentration of restaurants and accommodation (see p.298). Even if you're staying elsewhere on the island, be sure to come by for sunset if the weather's looking agreeable – these can be even more spectacular than the famed sunrises on Ilchulbong (a peak which is, in fact, the most conspicuous thing on the horizon).

Geommeolle beach

검멀레 해수역장

Geommeolle is a black-sand beach, located on the southeast coast of Udo. It's not exactly the best of places to work on your tan, but the rock formations backing it up are quite sumptuous. Rising up over the beach, **Lighthouse Hill** protrudes from the very far south of the island, and can make quite a spectacular sight when viewed from certain angles around the coast. Scampering up the hill will give you the best possible vantage point for viewing Udo, which looks thrillingly rural from up here.

Biyangdo

비양도

If Udo is an island-off-an-island, then minute **Biyangdo** is an island-off-an-island-off-an-island. Tethered to Udo by a bridge, there are often just two people resident here: the owners of *Deungmeoeul* guesthouse (see p.298). Biyangdo used to be one of the main jump-off points for Jeju's famed diving women (see box, p.298), though a few of its sparse collection of buildings have now fallen into disrepair.

ARRIVAL AND GETTING AROUND

UDO

By ferry Udo is reached on hourly ferries (8am–4pm; 10min; W4000, plus W1500 Udo entry fee) from Seongsan

port (see opposite). These dock at one of two terminals, so on arrival it may come in handy to note what time the ferries

JEJU'S DIVING GRANNIES

It may be hard to believe in a place that once was, and in many ways still is, the most Confucian country on earth, but for a time areas of Jeju had **matriarchal** social systems. This role reversal is said to have begun in the nineteenth century as a form of tax evasion, when male divers found a loophole in the law that exempted them from tax if their wives did the work. So were born the **haenyeo** (해녀), literally **"sea women"**; while their husbands cared for the kids and did the shopping, the females often became the breadwinners, diving without breathing apparatus for minutes at a time in search of shellfish and sea urchins. With women traditionally seen as inferior, this curious emancipation offended the country's leaders, who sent delegates from Seoul in an attempt to ban the practice. It didn't help matters that the *haenyeo* performed their duties clad only in loose white cotton, and it was made illegal for men to lay eyes on them as they worked.

Today, the *haenyeo* are one of Jeju's most famous sights. Folk songs have been written about them, their statues dot the shores, and one can buy postcards, mugs and plates decorated with dripping sea sirens rising from the sea. This romantic vision, however, is not entirely current; the old costumes have now given way to black wetsuits, and the *haenyeo* have grown older: even tougher than your average *ajumma*, many have continued to dive into their 70s. Modern life is depleting their numbers – there are easier ways to make money now, and few families are willing to encourage their daughters into what is still a dangerous profession. The figures peaked in the 1950s at around thirty thousand, but at the last count there were just a few hundred practising divers, the majority aged over 50. Before long, the tradition may well become one of Jeju's hard-to-believe myths.

return; if you're staying the night, your accommodation will advise on which terminal to head to for the return leg.

By bus Tour buses are the easiest way to get around the island; they meet the ferries, and cost W5000 for the trip around the island. They first stop at Geommeolle beach for half an hour or so, which allows just enough time to scamper up the lighthouse hill (see p.297), then at a small natural history museum (free with bus ticket, and not worth it otherwise); they then continue past Sanho beach (see p.297) before returning to the ferry terminal.

By rented vehicle Infinitely more enjoyable than the tour buses are the bicycles (W8000/2hr), scooters (W15,000/2hr) and buggies (W30,000/2hr) available for rent outside both ferry terminals. Udo is so small that it's hard to get lost for too long, and most people simply fire around the island's near-empty lanes until it's time to return their vehicle. Don't worry if you're a bit late – this is Udo, after all.

On foot Udo has its own segment of the Jeju Olle trail (route 1-1, if you must know). The 11.3km circuit takes 4–5hr to complete.

ACCOMMODATION AND EATING

Minbak are readily available on Udo, though the rural ambience comes at a slightly higher price than you'd pay in Seongsan; prices are around W30,000 per night, and few people speak English. Udo has become somewhat trendy of late – the cue for lots of samey **cafés** to open up and charge huge mark-ups. **Seafood** is king here, but those in the mood for something else will find a couple of other eating options dotting the coastal road; there's also a **supermarket** (daily 8am–10pm) in the very centre of the island. Udo has its own brand of **makgeolli**, made with the peanuts for which the island is famed. It costs a fair bit more than regular brands (W5000, even in shops), since Udo has no machinery enabling the oil to be removed from the nuts – they're exported to Chungcheong on the mainland, turned into *makgeolli*, then brought back here.

★**Deungmeoeul** 등머울Biyangdo ☎ 064 784 3878. The chance to sleep on tiny Biyangdo is something special – even if it's a full house here, the island's entire population for the night won't exceed a dozen, making for a truly end-of-the-world feel. Rooms are a little bare, but the floor-to-ceiling windows afford views of naught bar sky, sea and grass – except at night, when the horizon becomes a pearl-like chain of squid boats. The friendly couple who run the *minbak* speak a little English, and will collect you from the ferry terminal if you give them a call. W70,000
Green Jeju Pension 그린 제주 펜션 Udo-myeon

2471 ☎ 064 782 7588. The best value of the several places lining Sanho beach – rates will drop considerably on weekdays and during the off season. Rooms are all en-suite with lovely, warm showers, and there's cooking apparatus if you fancy making your own meals. W70,000
Haewa Dal Geurigo Seom 해와달 그리고 섬 Udo-myeon 78-5 ☎ 064 784 5740. Just off the Udo side of the bridge to Biyangdo is this simple seafood restaurant, which specializes in colossal, fist-sized sea snails called *sora* (소라; W20,000 per portion). Daily 10am–9pm.
★**Hoeyanggwa Guksugun** 회양과 국수군

Udo-myeon 2473 ☎ 064 782 0150. This place has been on TV a whole bunch of times, and certainly deserves the attention – not least because it stays open the latest of any place on the Sanho stretch. Their speciality is flatfish sashimi on spicy, cold noodles (화국수; W10,000 per person, minimum two people) – a surprisingly rare dish in Korea, and ever so refreshing in the summer. Daily 9am–9.30pm.

Route 97

With a volcanic crater to see and two folk villages to explore, rural **Route 97** – also known as the East Tourist Road – is a delightful way to cut through Jeju's interior. All three attractions covered below can be visited on a day-trip from Jeju City, or as part of a journey between the capital and Seogwipo on the south coast, though it pays to start reasonably early.

Sangumburi

산굼부리 • Daily 9am–7pm • W6000 • Bus #710 or #720 from Jeju City, though not all buses stop here – ask at the bus terminal

If you head south from Jeju City on Route 97 the first place worth a stop is **Sangumburi**, one of Jeju's many **volcanic craters** – possibly its most impressive, certainly its most accessible, though currently the only one you have to pay to visit. Hole lovers should note that this particular type is known as a Marr crater, as it was produced by an explosion in a generally flat area. One can only imagine how big an explosion it must have been: the crater, 2km in circumference and 132m deep, is larger than Hallasan's (see p.310). A short climb to the top affords sweeping views of some very unspoilt Jejanese terrain; peaks rise in all directions, with Hallasan 20km to the southwest, though not always visible. The two obvious temptations are to walk into or around the rim, but you must refrain from doing so in order to protect the crater's wildlife – deer and badgers are among the species that live in Sangumburi. Consequently there's not an awful lot to do here other than stroll and take pictures, though there's a small art gallery on site.

Seong-eup Folk Village

성읍 민속 마을 • Daily 24hr • Free • Bus #720 from Jeju City or Pyoseon

A twenty-minute bus ride south of Sangumburi lies dusty **Seong-eup Folk Village**, a functioning community living in traditional Jeju-style housing surrounded by an

---

JEJU TRADITIONS

Essentially a frozen piece of the past, Seong-eup Folk Village is a wonderful place to get a handle on Jeju's ancient **traditional practices**, but you'll see evidence of these age-old activities all over the island. Many locals still wear *galot* (갈옷), comfy Jejanese **costumes** of apricot-dyed cotton or hemp; these are available to buy in Seong-eup and Jeju Folk Village. Local homes are separated from each other with *batdam* (밭담), gorgeous **walls** of hand-stacked volcanic rock built with no adhesive whatsoever – ironically, this actually affords protection against Jeju's occasionally vicious winds, which whip straight through the gaps. The homes themselves are also traditional in nature, with **thatched roofs** and near-identical gates consisting of three wooden bars, poked through holes in two stone side columns. This is a quaint local **communication system** known as *jeongnang* (정낭), unique to Jeju and still used today – when all bars are up, the owner of the house is not home, one bar up means that they'll be back soon, and if all three are down, you're free to walk on in. Some houses still have a traditional open-air Jeju **toilet** in their yard; these were located above the pig enclosures so that the family hogs could transform human waste into their own, which could then be used as fertilizer. Needless to say, no locals now use these toilets – traditional, for sure, but some things are best left in the past.

7

immaculate town wall. Within its confines, you're free to wander at will among the thatch-roofed houses; the residents, given financial assistance by the government, are used to curious visitors nosing around their yards. Here you'll see life carrying on as if nothing had changed in decades – farmers going about their business and children playing while crops sway in the breeze. Most visitors spend a couple of pleasant hours here, and if you're lucky you'll run into one of the few English-speaking villagers, who act as guides.

Jeju Folk Village

제주 민속 마을 • Daily: April–Sept 8.30am–6pm; Oct–March 8.30am–5pm • W9000, audio guides W2000 • Folk performances daily 11.20am, 1.30pm & 3.30pm • Bus #720 from Jeju City, or #701 from Seogwipo

Route 97 terminates near the coast at the **Jeju Folk Village**. This coastal clutch of traditional Jeju buildings may be artificial, but provides an excellent complement to the Seong-eup village to its north. Information boards explain the layout and structures of the buildings, as well as telling you what the townsfolk used to get up to before selling tea and baggy orange pants to tourists. The differences between dwellings on different parts of the island are subtle but interesting – the island's southerners, for example, entwined ropes outside their door with red peppers if a boy had been born into their house. However, the buildings may all start to look a little samey without the help of an English-language **audio guide**, available from a hidden office behind the ticket booth. There are three daily **folk performances**, free with the price of your ticket.

EATING
ROUTE 97

Tamna Sikdang 탐라 식당 Seongeum-ni 1627 ☎ 064 787 0007; map p.286. Just outside the Seong-eup Folk Village perimeter walls, this restaurant is renowned for its black pork (yet another Jeju speciality food). Tasty set meals of black pork and side dishes (*heukdwaeji jeongsik*; 흑돼지 정식) go from W11,000 per head, while the restaurant also makes its own *makgeolli*. Daily 9am–7pm.

Seogwipo

서귀포

Sitting pretty on Jeju's fair southern coast, charming **SEOGWIPO** is Korea's sunny-side-up. Whereas days up north in Jeju City are curtailed when the sun drops beneath Hallasan's lofty horizon, there's no such impediment here; evidence of this extra light can be seen in a series of tangerine groves, famed across the land, which start just

ACCOMMODATION
Jeju Hiking Inn	6
KAL Hotel	5
Little France	2
Shinsegye	4
Slow Citi	1
Tae Gong Gak	3

RESTAURANTS & CAFÉS
Angeori Bakkeori	2
Geonchuk Café	1
Rose Marin	3
Saengsan Galbi	4

SEOGWIPO

outside the city. Seowipo is the most pleasant place to base oneself on the island, and while there's plenty to do – gorgeous waterfalls flank the city, and water-based activities range from diving to submarine tours – the real attraction here is the chance to kick back and unwind.

Lee Joong Seop Gallery

이중섭 미술관 • Tues–Sun: July–Sept 9am–8pm; Oct–June 9am–6pm • W1000

In the centre of the city is an interesting **gallery** devoted to the works of **Lee Joong-seop** (1916–56), who used to live in what are now the gallery's grounds. During the Korean War, he made a number of pictures on **silver paper** from cigarette boxes, which now take centre stage in a small but impressive collection of local modern art. Many of Lee's pieces echo the gradual breakdown of his private life, which culminated in his early demise. Just down the road from the gallery is *Geonchuk*, Seogwipo's most characterful café (see p.302).

7

Jeongbang waterfall

정방 폭포 • Daily 8am–7pm • W2000 • 10–15min walk from central Seogwipo

To the east of central Seogwipo is **Jeongbang**, a 23m-high cascade claimed to be the only one in Asia to fall directly into the ocean. Unique or not, once you've clambered down to ground level it's an impressive sight, especially when streams are swollen by the summer monsoon, at which time it's impossible to get close without being drenched by spray. Look for some Chinese characters on the right-hand side of the falls – their meaning is explained by an unintentionally comical English-language cartoon in an otherwise dull exhibition hall above the falls.

Cheonjiyeon waterfall

천지연 폭포 • Daily sunrise–10pm • W2000 • 10–15min walk from central Seogwipo

Seogwipo's western falls, **Cheonjiyeon**, are shorter but wider than Jeongbang, and sit at the end of a pleasant gorge that leads from the ticket office, a signposted downhill walk from the city centre. Many prefer to visit at night, when there are fewer visitors and the paths up to the gorge are bathed in dim light.

Saeseom Island

새 섬 • Daily sunrise–10pm • Free

The small islet of **Saeseom** sits across a bridge that you'll see poking up south of Seogiwo – certainly at night, when it becomes a light show of sorts. The uninhabited island itself has nothing more than a pleasant walking trail – a simple pleasure, maybe, but fully worth the walk here.

ARRIVAL AND GETTING AROUND   SEOGWIPO

By bus Numerous bus routes connect Seogwipo to Jeju City (see box, p.292). All stop in Seogwipo's large bus station, though this is inconveniently located several kilometres east of the city centre, near the World Cup Stadium. For central Seogwipo, you should get out at Jungmun Rotary stop, which is on all routes bar the #702.

Motorbike rental Several places rent motorbikes (from around W30,000 per day); your accommodation will have pamphlets directing you to the nearest.

INFORMATION, TOURS AND ACTIVITIES

Tourist information The main office (daily 9am–6pm; ☎ 064 732 1330) is at the entrance to the Cheonjiyeon falls (see above).

Tours Near Cheonjiyeon is the launch point for a submarine tour (every 45min; W50,000); the subs dive down to 35m, allowing glimpses of colourful coral and marine life, including octopus, clownfish and the less familiar "stripey footballer". Boat trips around the coast and offshore islets are also available; check with the tourist office for details.

Diving The islands just south of Seogwiop are popular with divers. Big Blue, a German-run operation (☎ 064 733 1733, ⓦ bigblue33.co.kr), offers a range of courses starting at W110,000 per person.

ACCOMMODATION

Seogwipo has a range of accommodation to suit all budgets, though things often get booked out on summer weekends – if you're stuck, you can try your luck in the motel area near the *Jeju Hiking Inn*. For a cheap and slightly bizarre place to stay, there's a **jjimjilbang** (W8000) in the World Cup Stadium to the west of the city.

Jeju Hiking Inn 등머울 Seogwidong 587-15 ☎ 064 763 2380. This quasi-hostel gets mixed reviews, but its rooms are comfy enough, with passable bathrooms, and you can rent bicycles for W10,000 per day; in addition, there are stunning views from the rooftop. **W30,000**

KAL Hotel KAL호텔 Chilsimni 242 ☎ 064 733 2001, ⓦ kalhotel.co.kr. This is a very businesslike tower that stands proudly over its surroundings. It's immaculate – a little too clinical for some – and the grounds are beautiful. There's also a tennis court, a jogging track and various on-site restaurants and cafés. Off-peak discounts can bring rooms down to under W90,000 – a bargain. **W170,000**

★**Little France** 리틀 프랑스 Seogwidong 486-1 ☎ 064 732 4552, ⓦ littlefrancehotel.co.kr. Vaguely European in feel, this chic hotel is a real find. Views aren't amazing but the rooms are bright and fresh, created with a warmth rarely evident in Korean accommodation. **W80,000**

Shinsegye 신세계Jeongbangdong ☎ 064 732 5800. Officially a hotel, but in reality a less-seedy-than-average motel, this is a great cheapie – this doesn't mean that you shouldn't try to haggle them down further. Some rooms have internet-ready computer terminals, and others boast pleasant ocean views. **W50,000**

Slow Citi 슬로 시티 Seogwidong 307-3 ☎ 064 732 1286. Attractive, modern hostel adept at making international guests feel welcome – queries about diving, sightseeing and the like are answered promptly, and they run great-value daily minibus tours of sights around the south coast (W15,000). Dorm beds **W18,000**, private rooms **W50,000**

★**Tae Gong Gak** 태공각 Seogwidong 823-1 ☎ 064 762 2623. Homely little place with simple private rooms and a kitchenette for making your own meals. The real bonus here is the super-friendly staff, who are full of handy advice; they'll also do your laundry for free, with any donations you make going to UNICEF. **W90,000**

EATING AND DRINKING

★**Angeori Bakkeori** 안거리밖거리 Seogwidong 584-3 ☎ 064 763 2552. This homely restaurant serves colossal set meals for W8000 – a small price to pay for a table near-covered with no fewer than fifteen delectable (and largely vegetarian) side dishes. Daily 10am–9pm.

★**Geonchuk Café** 건축 카페 Seogwidong 482 ☎ 064 762 2597. Opposite the Lee Joong Seop Gallery you may make out a small treehouse – this almost certainly constitutes Jeju's most distinctive coffee spot. This rambling café has an almost bewildering selection of indoor and outdoor tables, as well as exhibitions of modern art, in its various nooks and crannies; the coffee and teas are good, too (from W3000), and the curious layout may tempt you to return for a beer in the evening. Daily 10am–10pm.

★**Rose Marin** 로즈마린 Namseongjungno 13 ☎ 064 762 2808. Located down by the harbour near Cheonjiyeon waterfall, this is basically a shop with some cool seating areas attached to it – rather pleasingly, you pay shop prices (a bottle of *makgeolli*, beer or *soju* will set you back about W1500), then take your goodies outside to a seating area festooned with scuba gear, surfboards and goodness knows what. Give the pink-labelled *Jeju Makgeolli* a try – it's made with "friendly" bacteria, and is a cut above the island's other, oversweet brands. Daily noon–midnight.

Saengsan Galbi 생산 갈비 Seogwidong 650-2 ☎ 064 732 4001. Popular *galbi* joint overlooking the sea (though trees obscure the view from the tables). Their black-pig ribs (흑돼지 갈비) are very tasty (W15,000 per portion), and there are more meats available, though the whole thing is occasionally ruined by wretched service. Daily noon–10pm.

Jungmun

중문

Korea's most exclusive resort curls along a beautiful beach west of Seogwipo, a place where expense-account tourists come from the mainland and abroad to play a few rounds of golf, shop for designer bags or relax in five-star pools in between business conventions. However, to write off **JUNGMUN** on account of this would be a mistake – the surrounding area has the island's greatest and most varied concentration of sights, accessible on any budget, and can even credibly claim to possess the most distinctive temple, gallery and museum of Korea's inexhaustible collection – all this shoehorned amid beaches, gardens and waterfalls.

JUNGMUN

■ ACCOMMODATION	
Hyatt Regency	4
Lotte Hotel	2
The Shilla	3
The Suites	1

Jungmun Golf Club

Yeomiji Botanical Gardens

Teddy Bear Museum

Cheonjeyeon

Jungmun Beach

African Art Gallery

Jeju International Convention Centre

Jusangjeolli

● RESTAURANT	
Gecko's Island	1

Teddy Bear Museum

테디베어 박물관 • Daily 9am–8pm • W7000

Although it may sound like the epitome of Jeju tack, the **Teddy Bear Museum** impresses even its most sceptical visitors. The main building is filled with floors of bears, but the diorama room is the museum highlight, with furry depictions of historical events – one for every decade of the twentieth century. As the scenes move backwards in time, you'll encounter teddies bashing down the Berlin Wall and fighting in World War II. Then following on from the battle, what appears to be a roller-skating teddy Hitler races into view, though he's soon revealed to be a teddy Charlie Chaplin. Other delights include a teddy Elvis, a "Teddycotta" Army, and a vision of what teddies may be up to in the year 2050, as well as a shop (no prizes for guessing what's on sale here) and garden.

Cheonjeyeon

천제연 • Daily 8am–6.30pm • W2500

A short walk east of the Teddy Bear Museum you can stretch your legs on the paths around **Cheonjeyeon**, a string of three small **waterfalls** (not to be confused with the similar-sounding Cheonjiyeon falls in Seogwipo). Note the seven white nymphs painted onto the vermilion humpback bridge – these fairies were said to bathe in the falls in the moonlight; a performance in their honour is put on by the falls every May. The uppermost fall gushes into a pool of almost unnatural sapphire, from where paths head through subtropical flora.

Jungmun beach

중문 해수욕장

Summer crowds throng to **Jungmun beach**, which many deem the best in Korea – though be warned, the waves rolling in from the Pacific can often be fierce, and this short stretch of sand claims at least one victim a year. Every August the beach is the starting point for the **Ironman Korea Triathlon** when competitors thrash out a few kilometres in the ocean, followed by a 180km bike ride across the island, with a 42km marathon for dessert.

Jusangjeolli

주상절리 • Daily 8am–7pm • W2000 • A 2km walk from the resort, or a short taxi ride away (W4000 or so)

East of Jungmun beach, waves smash against the hexagonal basalt columns of

Jusangjeolli, which rise in angular beauty from the sea in formations similar to the Giant's Causeway in Ireland. These strange creations were created when lava from one of Jeju's many volcanic explosions came in contact with sea water, and they can be viewed from a loop platform that runs along the coast.

African Art Gallery

아프리카 미술 박물관 • Daily 9am–7pm • Musical performances Tues–Sun 11.30am, 2.30pm & 5.30pm • W8000 • A 2km walk from the resort, or a short taxi ride away (W4000 or so)

A stone's throw away from Jusangjeolli is the **African Art Gallery**, which was the brainchild of Mr Han, a traveller and interior designer who developed his collection into a museum. The collection was moved in 2004 from Seoul to a larger and more interesting building – a large faux-dirt structure peppered with logs on the outside, built to resemble the world's largest adobe building, the spectacular Grand Mosque in Djenné, Mali. Inside there's an interesting display of African photography on the ground floor, while the upper levels are mostly filled with sub-Saharan carved wood. Make sure your visit coincides with one of the entertaining **musical performances**; the groups are usually from the musical hotbeds of Ghana, Nigeria and Senegal.

Yakcheonsa temple

약천사 • Open 24hr • Free • Not on any bus routes; best accessed by rented scooter, or taxi from Jungman (up to W30,000 including waiting time)

A few kilometres east of Jungmun is the stunning temple of **Yakcheonsa**. Built in the 1990s, what it lacks in historical value it more than makes up for with its main building, a feast of intricate decoration despite its colossal size – the cavernous four-storey main hall is claimed to be the biggest in Asia, and is one of the most impressive in the country. The huge golden Buddha at the centre is best viewed from the encircling upper levels, which are themselves crowded with thousands of Buddhist figurines. Yet more (over five hundred, and all individually crafted) can be found in an exterior hall to the front of the complex; most are jovial (cheer up, no. 184) and many are individually interesting – take a look at no. 145's disturbing party trick, if you can find him. The best time to visit is 7pm on a summer evening, when worshipping locals **chant** under the interior glow with their backs to the sunset. Insect and bird calls add extra resonance to the bell rings that mark the beginning of the service, while squid boats out at sea shine like fallen stars on the horizon.

ARRIVAL AND DEPARTURE   JUNGMUN

By bus Limousine bus #600 (every 15min; 50min; W3900) runs directly from the airport to outside the top hotels listed below. There are also no fewer than four routes here from Jeju City's bus terminal (see box, p.292 for details).

ACCOMMODATION AND EATING

Standards are among the highest in the country at Jungmun. Accommodation caters almost exclusively to the well-heeled, especially in the resort area, where a slew of **hotels** have presidential suites with rack rates of W5,000,000. More affordable rooms are, of course, available, but travellers on low budgets are advised to stay in nearby Seogwipo. Given Jungmun's price levels, it's hardly surprising that most guests eat at their hotel, though there are a few **restaurants** at the top of the resort, near the Teddy Bear Museum.

Gecko's Island 게코즈 아일랜드 Iljuseoro 968-8 ☎ 064 739 0845, ⍟ geckosterrace.com. Related to a near-eponymous restaurant in Seoul (see p.108), this bar-like venue can make a nice change of pace if you've been in Jeju for a while – there's a range of Western comfort food, including burgers (W13,500), bangers and mash

(W17,000) or chicken with honey mustard and apricot (W13,000). Thanks to its distant location, however, it can feel awfully empty. Daily 10am–9pm.
Hyatt Regency 햐야트 리젠시 Jungmun Resort ☎ 064 733 1234, ⍟ hyattcheju.com. This is the most relaxed of the three major hotels, whose attention to detail

is much as you'd expect of this chain; a leaf-filled atrium leads to ample, muted-tone rooms, and the on-site bars and restaurants are top-notch. A health club, spa and nine-hole putting green can also be found on site, and there's a walking trail down to the beach. W320,000

Lotte 롯데 Jungmun Resort ☎064 731 1000, ⓦlottehotel.com. The *Lotte* prides itself on being the "finest resort hotel in the world", but can be a little overblown for some. Aimed squarely at designer-handbag-toting guests from Japan and Hong Kong, the busy interior resembles a shopping mall, with the outside a theme park where every evening is celebrated with a Vegas-style volcano show. Though the rooms are excellent, the outside bustle can often be hard to escape. W450,000

The Shilla 신라 Jungmun Resort ☎064 738 4466, ⓦshilla.net/jeju. Immaculately designed, the *Shilla* is the hotel of choice for Western tourists. Soft music tinkles through the lobby and plush corridors, and it's a big place – though it may look low-rise from the outside, there are seven large floors and 429 soothing rooms. W480,000

The Suites 더 수이츠 Jungmun Resort ☎064 738 3800, ⓦsuites.co.kr. This hotel is less busy and more minimalist in style than its nearby competitors, but the lack of clutter and less starchy attitude of the staff may come as something of a relief. Hefty discounts can usually be clawed from the rack rate. W300,000

Southwestern Jeju

7

Jeju's windswept **southwestern** corner boasts a collection of sights, three of them within walking distance of each other around the mountain of Sangbangsan: **Sangbanggulsa** is a temple hewn out of the peak itself, which looks down on **Yongmeori**, a jagged and highly photogenic coastline pounded mercilessly by waves; adjacent to this sits a replica of a Dutch vessel which came a cropper near these crags. In the distance lie the wind- and wave-punished islets of **Gapado** and **Marado**, the latter being Korea's southernmost point. Just north of Sangbangsan are a couple of arty attractions: fans for contemporary work may appreciate the large outdoor **sculpture park**, while traditionalists should head to the former exile site of **Chusa**, one of Korea's foremost calligraphers.

Sanbangsan

산방산 • Daily 8.30am–7pm • W1000, combined ticket with Yongmeori W2500 • Bus #750 from Jeju City, or #702 from Seogwipo

Jeju's far southwest is presided over by the mountain of **Sanbangsan**, which rises crown-like from the surrounding terrain. According to local folklore, this mountain once lay in what is now Hallasan's crater area, and was blasted to the edge of the island when the mountain erupted. Although the sharp cliffs that separate Sanbangsan's lower regions from its tree-flecked summit would make rock climbers go weak at the knees, the mountain has long been considered holy, and the highest you're allowed to go is the cave temple of **Sanbanggulsa** (산방굴사), about halfway up (there are, however, some challenging rock trails lower down). The holy grotto, created by a monk in Goryeo times, is bare but for a Buddha on its rear wall, while fresh, drinkable mountain water drips unceasingly from the ceiling near the entrance; slow as the flow is, try to catch the drops directly in one of the plastic cups provided, as the pool that they land in is hardly ever cleaned. After sweating up the hundreds of steps that lead here you'll have a superlative view of the ocean

---

THE HWASUN ISSUE

The community settled just east of Sanbangsan is **Hwasun** (화순), situated at what would be an idyllic place were it not for the ugly power station that was built by the shore to supply much of Jeju's energy. As if this blight were not enough, the depth of the bay (and its convenient location, as far as possible from Pyongyang) has now attracted the **South Korean navy**, which plans to move a number of destroyers into a purpose-built naval port by 2020. The residents' regular protests are doing little to block a deal apparently set in stone, which makes a mockery of Jeju's designation as the "Island of World Peace".

and the area's surrounding communities. This view is partially obscured by some ugly metal mesh at the top of the grotto opening, which provides important protection from falling rocks, a fact hammered home by several large indentations.

Yongmeori

용머리 • Daily 8.30am–7pm • W2000, combined ticket with Sanbangsan W2500 • Bus #750 from Jeju City, or #702 from Seogwipo

The dramatic, wind-swept cliffs of **Yongmeori** stretch into the sea beneath Sanbangsan. A fissure-filled walkway curls around the rocks, but be warned that it may be closed if the waves are coming in with a lot of force: the seas in this unsheltered corner of Jeju are notoriously unpredictable, so don't venture too near the edge. The rock formations are stunning, their beauty somehow heightened by the strong winds that usually race in from the South Sea, and once around the outermost tip the contrast between the golden horizontal strata of the cliffside and the vertical grey crags of Sanbangsan becomes apparent. Keep an eye out for naturally made water paths that surge through the rock, where small fish peek out and dash between the crevices. *Ajummas* sometimes set up stalls along here to sell freshly caught fish.

Hendrick Hamel Ship

하멜 상선 전시관 • Daily 8.30am–6pm • W1000 • Bus #750 from Jeju City, or #702 from Seogwipo

From Sanbangsan's slopes you should be able to make out what appears to be a marooned ship just inland from the coast. This, the **Hendrick Hamel Ship**, is a replica of a Dutch trading ship that crashed off Jeju's shores in 1653, with important consequences for Korea and its relationship with the West (see box opposite). An account of the ship and her crew's story is provided in an **exhibition** inside the vessel; some of this has, rather tenuously, been devoted to a more recent Dutch connection – South Korea's 2002 World Cup manager Guus Hiddink. In case you're wondering, the statue fighting the dinosaur outside the ship is also Guus, even if it does look more like Bill Clinton.

Jeju Sculpture Park

제주 조각 공원 • Daily 8am–7pm • W4500 • Bus #702 from Jeju City, Jungmun or Seogwipo

A few kilometres north of Sanbangsan – off Route 95 – is **Jeju Sculpture Park**, a large, open-air exhibition of contemporary sculpture from around the world. If you can imagine Copenhagen's Little Mermaid having a garden party with a bunch of oddly shaped friends, you're on the right track, but though metal sculptures are the predominant features around the park's grassy confines, there are several themed areas too, as well as a couple of indoor painting exhibitions.

Chusa's exile site

추사 적거리 • Daily 9am–6pm • W500 • Bus #702 from Jeju City, Jungmun or Seogwipo

The **exile site** of a calligrapher named **Chusa** sits a couple of kilometres west of Jeju Sculpture Park in the midst of some beautiful farmland. Kim Chun-hee, better known by his pen name, was exiled here in 1840 for his involvement in a political plot. Like a naughty boy sent to his room to consider his actions, he took to drawing on the walls, eventually honing his brushstrokes to such a degree that he is now revered as one of Korea's greatest artists and calligraphers. A letter-cum-painting named **Sehando** is his most famous piece, though the one on display is a replica, the original having been moved to Jeju National Museum (see p.291). The exhibition room is small with few actual articles, and there's no English-language information.

After you've seen the art you can wander around the nearby traditional buildings that Chusa once called home. While there's little here to detain any but ardent devotees of his work, the surrounding area – particularly that leading up to the distinctive mountain to the south – contains some achingly bucolic farming communities, a timeless land where elderly women sow grain, beasts plough the fields and mainland Korea feels a lifetime away.

Gapado and Marado

Several daily ferries from Moseulpo port, on the #755 bus route from Jeju City, and a 15min walk from the #702 buses linking Jeju City and Seogwipo • Bike rental W4000/hr

Off Jeju's southwestern shores lie the islets of **GAPADO** (가파도) and **MARADO** (마라도), home to tiny (and car-less) communities of just a few dozen people who somehow manage to eke out a living from land and sea. Low-lying **Gapado** was the unlikely conduit for the West's first contact with Korea, as it was where Hamel's ship ran aground (see box below); it's now apparently carbon-free, as part of a wider experiment intended to encompass the whole of Jeju by 2030. **Marado** is smaller, loftier and more popular than its twin, attracting fans of geographical extremities who come to stand at Korea's southernmost speck of land. The place achieved national fame in a popular TV commercial in which a parachutist floated onto the island asking who had ordered the *jjajang-myeon*, a black-bean noodle dish; now an essential part of any Korean tourist's visit, the dish is served in all of the island's few restaurants. From the ferry, you may notice caves in the cliffs – these were military storage cavities made by the Japanese during their occupation of Korea, in anticipation of American attacks on strategically important Jeju. Even today, getting to these islands can be tough – ferries are often cancelled due to inclement weather or sea conditions, so check with local tourist authorities to see whether they're running.

7

ACCOMMODATION   SOUTHWESTERN JEJU

Island Guesthouse 아일랜드 게스트하우스 Jungmun Resort ☏ 070 7096 3899, ⊛ islandguesthouse .kr; map p.286. It's possible to stay just a few hundred metres from Chusa's exile site at this surprisingly fresh hostel. It's almost literally in the middle of nowhere, which is what many Jeju travellers are looking for, but it'll be hard to find by yourself; staff will be willing to meet you at the nearest bus stop if you phone ahead. They'll also let you plonk a tent down. Dorm beds W20,000, double W70,000, tent pitch W10,000

Ocean House Jeju 오션 하우스 제주 Sagye-ri 123

☏ 064 794 4541, ⊛ hyattcheju.com; map p.286. Nestling between Sanbangsan and the sea, and therefore easy to find, this wood cabin sports cooking facilities in every room. W70,000

Zen Hideaway Jeju 젠하이더웨이 Sagyenamno 186-8 ☏ 064 794 0133, ⊛ zen2316.com; map p.286. One of the more distinctive places to stay on the southern coast, located near the seafront just southwest of Sanbangsan. The industrial-chic exterior carries through into the rooms, which are a bit overpriced – ask about discounts. There's a great café on site. W250,000

A PEEK INSIDE THE "HERMIT KINGDOM"

In 1653 a **Dutch trading ship** bound for Nagasaki in Japan encountered a fierce typhoon south of the Korean peninsula and ran aground on the tiny island of **Gapado**. Just half of its crew of 64 survived the shipwreck, but despite their obvious status as victims rather than aggressors, they had entered the "**Hermit Kingdom**" and found themselves treated with scant respect – Joseon-era Korea was a highly isolationist land, whose policy (one rarely triggered) was to bar any foreigners who washed ashore from returning to their homeland. Forced into servitude, the survivors made repeated attempts to escape, but it was not until 1666 that a group of eight managed to flee to Japan from Yeosu, a port city in what is now Jeonnam province. Unfortunately, the survivors found Japan little more welcoming, but one year later a second escape took them back to the Netherlands. The accounts of survivor **Hendrick Hamel** became a bestseller in his homeland, and gave the West its first real portrayal of the Korean peninsula; English-language copies of *Hamel's Journal: A Description of the Kingdom of Korea 1653–1666* have been published, but are hard to track down.

The western interior

Jeju's **western interior** is strikingly beautiful, and covered with the purples, pinks and whites of cosmos bloom from summer to autumn – Jeju at its rural best. Those who've been drawn to the island by promises of empty roads, bucolic villages and unspoilt terrain should look no further – to many, this is quintessential Jeju. Its remoteness is very much part of the appeal, but it also makes it harder to reach its sights, and if you have no **transport** you may have to resort to the occasional spot of hitchhiking. Those who make it this far can hunt down a **tea plantation**, a **bonsai park** and the underground tunnels and rusty munitions of a **peace museum**.

O'Sulloc Museum

오설록 차 재배단지 Daily: April–Sept 10am–6pm; Oct–March 10am–5pm • Free • On the #755 bus route between Jeju City and Moseulpo port

7

Tour buses descend en masse to the open plan **O'Sulloc tea plantation**, which is a pleasant pit stop for groups touring the west of the island. A café in the **visitor centre** serves a stash of green-tea-related goods: try *nok-cha* tiramisu, cookies, ice cream – or even have a cup of tea – before visiting the viewing deck on the top level. The big building on view is the factory itself, one of two that the company uses to make the nation's favourite tea (though to keep costs down, much of it is now grown in China). The real attraction here is the opportunity to walk through the **tea fields**. If you've been to Boseong in Jeolla (see p.228) you'll know what to expect, though the fields here are flatter, and despite the plantation's popularity with Korean tourists, a short walk will find you alone among the leaves.

Bunjae Artpia

분재 아트피아 • Daily 8.30am–6pm • W9000

Not so long ago the site on which the picturesque **Bunjae Artpia** bonsai garden now sits was wild, uncultivated land; nowadays, thanks primarily to the efforts of a lone botanist, this site claims to be the largest bonsai exhibition in the world. Though the English language uses the Japanese word, bonsai culture actually originated in China, where it was known as *penjing*, and hit Korea (known here as *bunjae*) before finally making it to Japan. There's lots of English information to read as you take a sweet-smelling walk around the gentle mounds of earth that make up the complex. A five-hundred-year-old juniper stands in tiny pride as the star of the show.

The Peace Museum

평화박물관 • Museum daily 8.30am–6pm • W3000 • Botanical garden daily 9am–5pm • W1000 • 10min walk from Cheongsu-ri bus stop on #900 route from Jeju City

Tucked away in countryside near the tea plantation is the **Peace Museum**, one of many such places in Korea. Like the others, it's entirely devoted to Japan's occupation of the Korean peninsula, and not so peaceful at all when groups of school kids are having nationalistic rhetoric barked at them through megaphones. If you're lucky enough to avoid these, you'll be rewarded with a modest but absorbing exhibition.

Deeming Jeju a strategically important hub between China, Korea and the Japanese mainland, Japanese forces established headquarters on the site of the museum during their occupation of Korea, and at one point planned to station up to seventy thousand soldiers on the island. Korean slaves were used to dig the 2km of **tunnels** that still snake underfoot, some of which are open to the public – cool, squat and dark, they're not for claustrophobes. There are relics from the occupation period on show in the main building

FROM TOP TEDDY BEAR MUSEUM (P.303); JUNGMUN BEACH (P.303) >

(guns, grenades and the like), where staff will be pleased to show you an English-language film. This contains interviews with survivors from the camp, and explains the site with a refreshing lack of vitriol, though as there are a few gory pictures, it's not really for kids.

Across the road is a **botanical garden**, which is a great place to reward yourself with a nice cup of herbal tea for getting this far.

Hallasan National Park

한라산 국립 공원

Arriving by ferry on a clear day, you can see the whole of Jeju tapering slowly to Mount Halla, known locally as **HALLASAN**, a dormant volcano at the centre of the island, and Korea's highest point at 1950m. Blanketed with pink azalea in the spring, and snow in the winter, the centre of the island has long been a **national park**, with four well-trodden hikes heading to Hallasan's crater, a grassy bowl pocked with grey volcanic rocks, and home to a couple of small lakes. As long as the weather cooperates, a climb up Hallasan is one of the main goals for adventurous visitors from the mainland. The **four main routes**, starting from the north and heading clockwise, are Gwaneumsa, Seongpanak, Yeongsil and Eorimok.

Gwaneumsa route

Entrance open daily: May–Aug 5–10am; Sept–April 6–10am • 8.3km; 4hr up • Around W30,000 by taxi from Jeju City

The **Gwaneumsa route**, heading to the peak from the north, is the best if you'd like to tackle the peak without the crowds. This path is more challenging and **less accessible** than others – there are no public buses here, and though it's only an 11km taxi ride from Jeju City, you may have to pay almost double for the trip, as the driver will have

HALLASAN NATIONAL PARK

HALLASAN HIKING PRACTICALITIES

Jeju's porous volcanic rock means that Hallasan's climbing trails provide more grip than your average Korean national park, even in wet weather. Though the climb is not a terribly difficult walk, hikers should take certain **precautions** if attempting to reach the summit. In order to stop lots of feet stomping indelible lines into the mountain, trail sections – or even whole routes – are regularly **closed off**; your first point of call should be one of Jeju's many tourist offices, or telephone the tourist information line (☎ 064 1330) for up-to-date information. To make sure that everyone gets down in time, routes may close earlier than expected, sometimes even at 9am. This also reduces the chance of getting wet, which becomes increasingly likely towards evening as the air cools – bear in mind, though, that even a sunny morning may degenerate rapidly into thick fog and zero visibility at higher elevations; **bad weather** is the number one cause of most failed attempts to the summit. Even if you avoid the rain, strong winds can bite – bring at least a few layers of decent clothing. Also remember to bring enough **water** – Halla's rock absorbs most of the rainwater, so there are very few springs on the trails. With the longer walks some energy-giving **snacks** are a must; cooking and camping are prohibited, though the usual snack shops can be found at the trailheads.

7

next to no chance of picking someone up for the return leg. The most important advice is to get to the entrance early. Initially, it's easy going, but things soon get steeper. There are a lot of steps on this route, so many hikers opt to use it for their **downhill** run. The park's only **campsite** is near the start of the trail – book from one of Jeju's tourist offices.

Seongpanak route

Entrance open daily: May–Aug 5–10am; Sept–April 6–10am • 9.6km; 4–5hr up • On #780 bus route between Jeju City and Seogwipo

The popular **Seongpanak route** heads to the summit from the east. It's longer than the Gwaneumsa trail, but the gradient is gentle and makes for a much **easier climb** – it's possible to complete it in a moderately sturdy pair of trainers, as long as the weather agrees. The route is especially popular in the spring, when the path is surrounded by pink azaleas and other flowers.

Yeongsil route

Entrance open daily: March, April, Sept & Oct 6am–2pm; May–Aug 5am–3pm; Nov–Feb 6am–1pm • 5.8km; 2hr 30min up • Near #740 bus route between Jeju City and Jungmun

The **Yeongsil route** is the easiest and **shortest** path up the mountain, although at the time of writing the final burst to the **summit** was closed – this will no doubt change at some point, so ask at a tourist office for advice. The picturesque course starts off higher up the mountain than other routes, heading past some impressive rock scenery on the way to the top. There's currently no **public transport** to the park entrance, which is at least an hour's walk uphill from the "Yeongsil" bus stop – get hold of an up-to-date schedule at a tourist office or the Jeju City bus terminal. Alternatively, you could try flagging down a car heading up from the main road.

Eorimok route

Entrance open daily: March, April, Sept & Oct 6am–2pm; May–Aug 5am–3pm; Nov–Feb 6am–1pm • 6.8km; 3hr up • #740 bus between Jeju City and Jungmun

At the time of writing, the **Eorimok route** also terminated before the summit, coming to an end at the same point as the **Yeongsil** route. It's a **moderately difficult** trail, approaching the park from the northwest, and passing through lush forest at the beginning before heading into bamboo. Many Koreans believe this to be the most beautiful of the park's paths.

North Korea

MANSUDAE GRAND MONUMENT

PYONGYANG SUBWAY

Basics

Getting there

First things first: yes, it is possible to enter North Korea (Democratic People's Republic of Korea, or DPRK), even for US citizens. However, you can't just pop in on a whim, and those permitted entry will only be able to visit government-approved sights, and even then only in the company of a local guide. The process is often lengthy and never cheap, but it can be surprisingly simple: a travel agency usually does all the hard work with visas, permits and suchlike. The price of your tour will include pretty much everything: transport (most commonly a flight from Beijing to Pyongyang and a flight or overnight train back out, as well as all internal travel), accommodation, meals and entry fees.

Note that you can actually enter the country **from South Korea**, if only for a minute or two: some of the DMZ tours from Seoul allow you to take a few highly guarded steps across the border in the Joint Security Area (see p.132). Though extremely enjoyable, this doesn't offer a true taste of the DPRK – for this, you'll just have to head to Pyongyang.

From China

While several routes into North Korea exist, almost all Western travellers start their journey in **Beijing**. From here you can either take a flight or an overnight train; which one you use will depend on your tour operator, and the cost will be factored into your tour price. Most tour groups fly into Pyongyang and take the train out, the latter leg giving a warts-and-all view of the North Korean countryside. Don't be too trigger-happy on the camera, however: some tourists have got into trouble after being reported as spies by local farmers (see p.319 for more on photography restrictions).

Flights into Pyongyang have improved dramatically since Air Koryo – the DPRK's flag-carrier – replaced their 1970s Soviet relics with a newer fleet of Russian Tupolevs (and Ukrainian Antonovs) in 2011. The EU lifted its travel ban for the most modern Koryo planes in 2010, though flights to Europe have yet to resume; at the time of writing, there were scheduled international flights from Pyongyang to Beijing (2hr; route also flown by Air China) and Shenyang (1hr 20min) in China, and to the Russian city of Vladivostok (2hr).

Train journeys take around 24 hours from Beijing, though with the permission of your tour company

you'll also be able to get on in Dandong, a Chinese city near the North Korean border; from here it's only a seven-hour trip to Pyongyang. Carriages are split into four-bed berths, with foreigners usually grouped together in the same carriage. There's also a restaurant car. Note that if you're crossing the border by train, you'll find that the **toilets** are often locked for hours: go before you reach Dandong on the way to North Korea, and before arriving at Sinuiju, a city just a few kilometres from the Chinese border, on the way out. At Sinuiju station, those able to escape the guards' attention may be able to take a quick look out over the town square.

Customs inspections are usually thorough, so expect to be questioned (see box, p.316 for information on what not to bring); procedures are far faster at Pyongyang airport than at Sinuiju train station.

Tours and packages

A surprising number of travel operators offer **tours** into North Korea (see below for a few of the best), most lasting for four to seven days. All visit the same core of Pyongyang-based sights, though some of the more expensive head to locations around the country. Group tours are cheapest – the size of the party can be anything from four to forty – but some also offer **individual packages**. These may sound appealing, but ironically you get more freedom on group trips – it's simply a lot harder for the two guides to keep tabs on twenty people than one or two, so those on group tours get far more leeway when walking around – more picture-taking opportunities, the occasional chance to wander off by yourself for a few minutes, and less official spiel. Many is the tale of woe from an individual traveller who has been marched around the same sights as group tourists, had no foreign company to bounce ideas, questions or frustrations off, and paid three times the price for the privilege.

To travel with the following operators, try to apply at least four weeks in advance.

TOUR OPERATORS

Explore Nelson House, 55 Victoria Rd, Farnborough GU14 7PA, UK ☎ 0870 333 4001, ⊛ explore.co.uk. This UK-based operator offers annual twelve-day tours, which include four nights in Pyongyang, two at other DPRK destinations and a few in Beijing, from £2675 per person, not including flights.

★ **Koryo Tours** Near Yashow Market, Sanlitun, Beijing, China ☎ 010 6416 7544, ⊛ koryogroup.com. This company takes more than half of the DPRK's foreign tourists, and its success is fully deserved – their tours are the best informed and most enjoyable ones available. The group has also made valiant efforts to open up as much of the country as possible to tourism, and to foster all-important cultural exchange with this reclusive nation. All tours head off from Beijing, and range from two nights (€790) to three weeks (€4490); their budget "Kimchi" tours, started in 2014, are a steal at €950 for five nights. Individual tours are available, as are visits to cities and sights inaccessible to any other company.

Regent Holidays Froomsgate House, Rupert St, Bristol, UK ☎ 020 7666 1244, ⓦ regent-holidays.co.uk. This agency has more than two decades of experience of sending travellers to North Korea and other far-out destinations. A standard tour gives seven nights in the DPRK for £1500 or so, not including flights, while shorter five-day trips cost around £1150.

Young Pioneers ⓦ youngpioneertours.com. Operating from the Chinese city of Xi'an, this group offers the cheapest visits to the DPRK – their shortest, cheapest tours give three nights in North Korea for just €745. Their tours have, thankfully, become more professional in recent years.

Getting around

Once inside North Korea you'll have precious little say in your day-to-day travels – all transport requirements will be arranged before you set foot inside the country, with the cost factored in as part of the tour price, and you'll be obliged to stick to the schedule.

Most travel is done by **tour bus** if you're in a group, and by **car** on independent tours, both within Pyongyang and for most trips to nearby destinations. Contrary to popular belief, the countryside around the highways hasn't been overhauled to present a false face to foreign tourists, and you'll see a great deal of poverty. The roads themselves are getting busier and busier – Pyongyang now has a few traffic lights to augment the semaphoring traffic ladies (see box, p.334), and even plays host to occasional traffic jams – quite an amazing change, considering the fact that roads across the land were near-empty as recently as 2008. There's also a **subway system** in Pyongyang, which figures on most tour schedules (see p.331), though the city's trams and buses are off limits on all but the most expensive tours. **Internal flights** also exist, and those heading to Paekdusan or other more remote locations will find themselves taking one.

Accommodation, food and drink

As with transportation, all of your accommodation and dining requirements will be taken care of and paid for prior to your arrival. While the country has occasional – and often severe – problems sourcing food, and leans heavily on the outside world for aid, try not to feel too guilty about eating here: the money you're paying is more than enough to cover what you eat, and at least part of it will be used to help feed the locals.

Most travellers spend every night of their tour in **Pyongyang**, where there are a few decent hotels (see p.333), but some tours include a night or two outside the capital; the two most common provincial bases are **Kaesong**, near the DMZ (see p.336), and **Paekdusan**, a mountain straddling the Chinese border (see p.339).

The quality of your own **food** will vary according to financial, political and climatic conditions, but most visitors emerge well fed. If you have special dietary requirements you should make them clear to your tour company on application. Local **specialities** include *naengmyeon* (a buckwheat noodle dish similar to Japanese *soba*, but served in a spicy cold soup) and barbecued duck.

There's more choice with local **drink**, as it's one of the only things that you'll have to pay for once inside the country; many travellers buy a few bottles of grog to take home (perhaps more for the bragging rights than the taste). Local hooches include some curious mushroom, ginseng and berry concoctions, as well as one apparently made from seal penis. **Soju** is tastier than it is in the South (see p.41) and available in most hotel bars, while the same can be said of some of the **beers** – Taedonggang is the most popular, but try to hunt down Ryongsong, which has a distinctive hoppy taste.

PLAN AHEAD, AVOID TROUBLE

Be careful when **packing your bags** for North Korea – with your trip likely to cost a pretty penny, it would be a shame to have to end it at **customs control**. Beware of taking anything that's very obviously American or South Korean – while K-pop on your music player is unlikely to be picked up, any clothing emblazoned with the stars and stripes surely will. Literature deemed to be of a subversive nature (including this guidebook) will also be confiscated.

The good news is that many restrictions on electronic devices have been lifted of late – almost all cameras and video recorders are fine, and tourists are now allowed to bring (and keep hold of) their **mobile phones**. You can even buy local SIM cards – a fun souvenir.

The media

While locals subsist on the *Nodong Shinmun* ("Workers' Daily"), North Korea also produces a surprising amount of English-language printed material, and is more than happy to offload it on foreign visitors. Of course, reportage by international media is usually a wee bit more grounded in fact, and there are a couple of DPRK specialist websites to choose from (see below).

In addition to the **books** written by Kim Jong-il – he was said to have authored well over a thousand, and many have been translated into various languages for foreign consumption – there are a few interesting **newspapers** and periodicals, some of which may be dropped into your lap on the flight from Beijing (pop these into your bag before stewardesses come around to collect them prior to arrival).

Once you get to your hotel, you'll be able to tune into **KCTV**, the state television channel. For locals, this is off-air for much of the day, but foreign visitors get a full 24 hours of looped North Korean news and period drama. The latter is mainly made up of patriotic heroes refusing to capitulate to foreign forces, the themes a mix of Japanese occupation period, Korean War times, and not much else. In addition, there's ⓦkcna.co.jp, the official news **website** of the DPRK; the near-daily stories (some real, some not) of South Korean unrest against American military presence bring to mind the news reports about Eurasian and Eastasian activity in Orwell's *Nineteen Eighty-Four*.

Periodicals to look out for include *Korea Pictorial*, a colourful, glossy A3 monthly – with the word "Korea" on the front – that focuses more on photography than reportage, though some stories are rather absorbing. *Korea Today* is a smaller, far wordier version, with a songsheet reading of the "Song of General Kim Il-sung" on the inside cover. The articles are rather insipid, but for the odd laugh-out-loud gem (do the laughing when you're back out of the country). The weekly **newspaper**, the *Pyongyang Times*, is not always easy to find inside the country, though its stories are fascinating ("School performs well"; "Factory increases shoe production"), and inevitably Kims-obsessed.

INTERNATIONAL WEBSITES

★**NK News** ⓦnknews.org. One of the best, and most up-to-date, sources of news pertaining to North Korea; they also include snippets from the official KNCA agency.

Yonhap News ⓦenglish.yonhapnews.co.kr. A huge news agency in the South, Yonhap's website has a dedicated section for articles related to North Korea.

Festivals

There's but one truly notable event on the North Korean travel calendar, but what an event it is. The Mass Games (see box, p.335) must count as one of the world's great spectacles, but contrary to popular belief, this colourful feast of song and dance is not aimed at tourists – almost all of the spectators are North Korean, and almost all citizens aim to see it at least once in their life: a kind of Juche rite of passage (see box, p.331 for more on Juche).

The timing of the games has been erratic of late, but the authorities are trying to make it a yearly celebration in **July and August**. Festival season normally lasts three or four weeks, with, usually, a performance every evening, lasting around ninety minutes, with tickets costing €50–300 depending on your desired level of luxury.

In addition to the Mass Games, special events are held on important anniversaries – there's usually something going on to celebrate the birth of long-dead leader Kim Il-sung each April, which is also the month the **Pyongyang Marathon** – now open to foreign entrants – takes place.

Culture and etiquette

The first rule when travelling through North Korea is this: do not disrespect the Kims. Disobeying could lead to dramatic consequences, but the sheer madness of the place makes acquiescence a hard line to toe – it's difficult not to pass comment on something that's likely to run contrary to your own upbringing. While the propaganda stuffed down your throat may be hard to stomach, it's unwise to react to it – asking questions or making accusations is not going to change the way that anybody thinks, much less the running of the country, and can only lead to trouble.

You'd be foolish to travel to North Korea with the intention of creating a stink, even after your visit:

GIFT GIVING

It's a good idea to bring **gifts**, not just for your guides and driver but for the locals who you're likely to run into along the way. Make sure that they're appropriate – nothing overtly capitalist, American or South Korean in origin. Western cigarettes go down well with local men and postcards from home with everyone, while balloons and small toys are always popular with children; try to ask a parent's permission before handing anything over.

while a critical blog or travel article will not be of any danger to its author, the North Korean guides tarnished by association may get into a lot of trouble, and travel agencies have been known to lose their licences.

Good behaviour is required in private as well as public places – rumours abound of hotel rooms being **bugged**, and these cannot be wholly discounted. Even seemingly innocent activity is not above suspicion – there's one oft-quoted tale of a traveller who got into serious trouble after stubbing out his cigarette on a newspaper, inadvertently desecrating the holy face of Kim Jong-il.

However frightening all of this may seem, note that the vast majority of travellers encounter no problems whatsoever, and most have a fantastic time. Simply do as you're told, don't go running off, don't take pictures when you've been told not to, and keep any frustrations bottled up until you're back in Beijing. The local **guides** are usually amiable folk; getting into their good books at the beginning of the tour by behaving yourself and asking permission to take pictures is likely to result in your gaining greater leeway as you make your way around. Neither should you fear the local North Korean people, who end up being the highlight of many a journey. Repeated contact with Western tour groups has convinced many Pyongyangers that foreigners are not to be feared; acting in a courteous manner will continue the trend.

Shopping

While staunchly anti-capitalist North Korea isn't exactly renowned for its shopping possibilities, there are a number of interesting things to buy, most of which are impossible to get anywhere else, and make fantastic souvenirs.

The race to stock up on as much North Korean material as possible often starts on the plane – wet-wipe packets, tissues, cutlery sleeves and even sick bags can be sold for a quick buck on the internet, though most people choose to hang on to these little mementoes. You may also be handed propaganda-filled North Korean periodicals during your flight (see p.317). Once you're in North Korea, you'll find plenty to purchase in Pyongyang (see p.335).

Travel essentials

Communications

There are now more than 2 million **mobile phones** in the DPRK, all connected to the local Koryolink network. These cannot be used to make international calls, or to call any foreigner inside the DPRK. Foreign visitors can buy a local phone, or a local **SIM card** to put in their own; if you are willing to pay more you can even get a 3G SIM card, which gets you unrestricted Internet use. You won't be able to call any North Koreans, but can make and receive international calls; this is the best way to stay in touch with friends and family while on a trip, and the SIM cards themselves make good souvenirs.

Bear in mind that whatever you say or read is likely to be monitored. This also applies to **post**, which will be read and understood, whatever the language; anything that seems cryptic or anti-establishment will likely be thrown away.

Costs and money

All accommodation and transport will be included in your tour fee, as well as two or three meals per day, but for drinks, snacks and souvenirs you'll have to use hard currency, as there are no ATMs or banks accessible to foreigners. Most prices for tourist goods are quoted in **euros**, though American dollars and Chinese yuan are just as widely accepted. Those in North Korea for the Mass Games (see p.335) will have to pay €80 for a ticket, which is quite a bargain for such a stupendous event.

The official currency of the DPRK is the **North Korean won**, but you're unlikely to have much contact with it as foreigners aren't allowed to use local money. There was a time when the won was pegged at 2.16 to the dollar, a fiscally ridiculous nod to Kim Jong-il's birthday on February 16, but this policy was abandoned in 2001.

Note that it's illegal to export **North Korean currency** out of the country – if you do manage to get hold of some (see p.335 for advice), keep your cache of cash well hidden when leaving – dirty socks may come in useful.

Entry requirements

Everyone needs a **visa** to enter North Korea, and though the process of obtaining one is lengthy, as long as you've got money and make your plans a couple of months in advance you should find it pretty easy to get in. **Journalists** can find it hard, though it's not impossible – it's the travel agency's responsibility to vet applicants, so if you say that you're a circus performer and they believe you, you're in. Many try to avoid fraud by asking for signed confirmation from your employer.

Your visa is organized prior to arrival by the travel agency, and forms part of your tour price. Unless you make out your own visa application in a country that has diplomatic relations with the DPRK, it will come on a slip of paper (not as an insert in your passport) that you'll only possess for a short time on entry to North Korea. You won't receive a stamp, so your passport will show no evidence of your visit – a good thing, since it would cause problems getting into many countries. If you really want a stamp, try to pick up your visa at a DPRK embassy – ask your tour company for information on how best to do this.

Insurance

It's wise to have **travel insurance** wherever you go, and North Korea is no exception. Most travel policies cover North Korea, but do check by making a quick call to your company; if they won't cover you, find one that will.

Photography

In terms of pictures taken per traveller per minute, North Korea must be one of the most photographed nations on earth, a hugely ironic fact given that most of it is closed off, and even official sights are subject to **photographic restriction**. This is a nation where even the mundane is incredible, and even on the shortest trips some visitors end up with over a thousand images.

Some of the photographic **rules** are those that apply worldwide: don't take pictures of military installations or soldiers (unless you're in the DMZ, where it is almost expected), and ask permission if taking any photographs of people. Others are a little harder to guess, many of them surrounding **the Kims** – if you're taking a picture of a statue, mural or painting of the great men, try to get the whole body into your shot, as anything else may be viewed as disrespectful. (This can be quite a feat when snapping the huge bronze statues at Mansudae; see p.328). It's also risky to photograph anything that might be taken as a **criticism of the country**: a picture of a peasant sitting by the roadside could be construed as a deliberate attempt to smear North Korea's stellar international reputation. In practice, though, these rules are hard to police, and customs officials simply can't sift through each and every picture.

Tipping

Tipping is not a Korean custom, but will obviously be appreciated in a country as poor as this. A representative from most tour groups will usually pass the hat around on your final day, then split the pooled money between the various guides and drivers, who are not well paid despite their regular contact with foreigners – North Korean convention tends to reward work on the basis of danger, so guiding tourists is not high on the list. A tip of €10 per day for each guide and driver is about right; they're also happy to receive cigarettes and alcohol as gifts – even if they don't drink or smoke, these can be sold easily on the black market.

Travellers with disabilities

Travellers with **disabilities** can travel to North Korea, but there are next to no access facilities laid on for wheelchairs, and there are far easier countries to visit. It's interesting to note that disabled locals are highly revered in North Korea, a country where brave resistance is the theme of most songs, films and TV dramas; many women, indeed, consider it their duty to marry injured soldiers.

Travelling with children

It's quite possible to travel to North Korea with **children**, but there are two points to consider. First, the sight-packed days can be hard even on adults – you'll spend a lot of time in a tour bus or taxi, and yet more standing at sights while being bombarded with the greatness of the Kims. Second, there are precious few facilities for children, either in the hotels or around the country – bring everything that your child will need. That said, every housing block in Pyongyang has a small playground area; while tightly planned group tours are unlikely to squeeze this in, independent tours should be able to work a quick play into the schedule.

North Korea

A riddle, wrapped in a mystery, inside an enigma – a cliché it may be, but North Korea is far more deserving of Churchill's famous quip than Russia ever was. This is, quite simply, the world's least-understood nation, with reams of international reporters, scholars and diplomats devoting their whole careers towards making some kind of sense of the place. Espionage, famine and nuclear brinkmanship; perpetrator-in-chief of an international axis of evil; a rigidly controlled population under the shadowy rule of a president long deceased... you've heard it all before, but North Korea's dubious charms make it the Holy Grail for hard-bitten travellers. A trip to this tightly controlled Communist society is only possible as part of an expensive package, but a high proportion of those fortunate and intrepid enough to visit rank it as their most interesting travel experience.

North Korea is officially known as the **Democratic People's Republic of Korea**, or the DPRK for short. However, of the world's five remaining Communist countries, this remains the most committed to the system, and real democracy is thin on the ground. Comparisons with the police state in Orwell's *Nineteen Eighty-Four* are impossible to avoid: in addition to a regime that acts as a single source of information, residents of Pyongyang, and many other cities, do indeed wake up to government-sent messages and songs broadcast through speakers in their apartments, which can be turned down but never off – the fact that this is often the cue for callisthenic exercises further strengthens associations with the book. (Messages are also often relayed into many South Korean apartments, though these tend to be about garbage disposal and missing children, and the speakers can be turned off.) Other Big Brother similarities include verified claims that the country is crawling with informants, each seeking to further his or her own existence by denouncing friends, neighbours or even family for such crimes as letting their portrait of the Great Leader gather dust, singing unenthusiastically during a march, or simply being related to the wrong person. Also true is the rumour that locals have to wear a **pin-badge** portraying at least one of the deceased leaders – **Kim Il-sung**, the country's inaugurator and "Great Leader", and the "Dear Leader", his eldest son **Kim Jong-il**. Interestingly, Kim Il-sung remains the country's official president, despite having died in 1994. Both Kims, as well as present-day leader **Kim Jong-un**, are revered almost as gods, by a people with precious little choice in the matter.

For all this, North Korea exerts a **unique appeal** for those willing and able to visit. Whether you're looking out over Pyongyang's oddly barren cityscape or eating a bowl of rice in your hotel restaurant, the simple fact that you're in one of the world's most inaccessible countries will bring an epic feel to everything you do. It's also important to note the human aspect of the North Korean machine. Behind the Kims and their carefully managed stage curtain live real people leading real lives, under financial,

THE MASS GAMES

Highlights

❶ Kumsusan Memorial Palace of the Sun
Pay a visit to the two dead Kims, who lie in state
beyond a labyrinthine warren of corridors,
elevators and moving walkways. **See p.328**

❷ Ryugyong Hotel Rising 105 stories into the
Pyongyang sky, this half-finished mammoth is
off limits to tourists and impossible to miss; it
may eventually reopen as one of the world's
largest hotels. **See p.329**

❸ Pyongyang subway Six stations are now
accessible to foreigners on the capital's subway
network; you'll certainly get a kick out of the
depth and design of these palaces of the
proletariat. **See p.331**

❹ Pyongyang Water Park One of the capital's
newest "sights", and a unique opportunity to
mingle with North Koreans in your swimming
togs. **See p.333**

❺ The Mass Games Unquestionably one of the
most spectacular events you'll ever see – try to
time your visit to coincide with it at all
possible. **See p.335**

❻ The DMZ Get a slightly different take on the
Korean crisis during a visit to the northern side
of the world's most fortified frontier. **See p.337**

HIGHLIGHTS ARE MARKED ON THE MAPS ON P.322 & P.327

nutritional, political and personal restrictions unimaginable in the West. Thousands upon thousands have found conditions so bad that they've risked imprisonment or even death to escape North Korea's state-imposed straitjacket. All the more surprising, then, that it's often the locals who provide the highlight of a visit to the DPRK – many, especially in Pyongyang, are extremely happy to see foreign visitors, and you're likely to meet at least a couple of people on your way around, whether it's sharing an outdoor *galbi* meal with a local family, chatting with the staff at your hotel, or saluting back to a marching gaggle of schoolchildren. This fascinating society functions in front of an equally absorbing backdrop of brutalist architecture, bronze statues, red stars and colossal murals, a scene just as distinctive for its lack of advertising or Western influence.

A visit to North Korea will confirm some of the things you've heard about the country, while destroying other preconceptions. One guarantee is that you'll leave with more questions than answers.

NORTH KOREA

N

C H I N A

Tuman River

Paekdusan

HAMGYEONGBUK-DO

Rajin

Chongjin

Hyesan

RYANGGANG-DO

▲ Chilbosan

CHAGANG-DO

Kanggye

Kilju

Amnok River

HAMGYEONGNAM-DO

Tanchon

Dandong
(China)

Huichon

Sinuiju

PYEONGANBUK-DO

Hamhung

Pakchon

MYOHYANGSAN

PYONGANNAM-DO

Pyongyang Sunan
International Airport

EAST SEA
(SEA OF JAPAN)

PYONGYANG

Wonsan

Nampo

KANGWON-DO

Kosong

HWANG-
HAEBOK-DO

Sariwon

KUMGANGSAN

DMZ

HWANGHAENAM-DO

Sokcho

Haeju

Kaesong

⑥

Panmunjom

SOUTH
KOREA

WEST SEA
(YELLOW SEA)

SEOUL

0   50
kilometres

HIGHLIGHTS
⑥ The DMZ

BUSTING MYTHS

A lot has been said and written about the current situation in North Korea, much of it true. These crazy truths, however, make it awfully easy to paint **rumours**, assumptions and hearsay as cast-iron fact. Political falsehoods have been detailed by excellent authors such as Cumings, Winchester and Oberdorfer, who take both sides' views into account (see p.364 for some recommended reading), but a few of the more straightforward rumours can be easily debunked.

The first great untruth to put to bed is that North Koreans are somehow **evil**; whatever their leader's state of mind, remember that the large majority of the population have no choice whatsoever in the running of the country or even their own lives, much less than other populations that have found themselves under authoritarian rule. Another myth is that you'll be escorted around by a **gun-wielding soldier**; it's true that you'll have guides with you whenever you're outside the hotel, but they're generally very nice people and it's occasionally possible to slip away for a few minutes.

Sometimes even the myths are myths. The tale of Kim Jong-il hitting **eleven holes in one** on his first-ever round of golf is bandied about in the West as evidence of mindless indoctrination; the so-called rumour itself is actually unheard of in North Korea.

Brief history

The Democratic Republic of Korea was created in 1948 as a result of global shifts in power following the Japanese defeat in World War II and the **Korean War** that followed (see p.350). The Korean War, which ended in 1953, left much of the DPRK in tatters; led by **Kim Il-sung**, a young, ambitious resistance fighter from Japanese annexation days, the DPRK busied itself with efforts to haul its standard of life and productive capacity back to prewar levels. Kim himself purged his "democratic" party of any policies or people that he deemed a threat to his leadership, fostering a personality cult that lasts to this day. Before long, he was being referred to by his people as *Suryong*, meaning "Great Leader", and *Tongji*, a somewhat paradoxical term describing a higher class of comrade (in North Korea, some comrades are evidently more equal than others). He also did away with the elements of Marxist, Leninist or Maoist thought that did not appeal to him, preferring instead to follow "**Juche**", a Korean brand of Communism that focused on national self-sufficiency (see box, p.331). For a time, his policies were not without success – levels of education, healthcare, employment and production went up, and North Korea's development was second only to Japan's in East Asia. Its GDP-per-head rate actually remained above that of South Korea until the mid-1970s.

The **American threat** never went away, and North Koreans were constantly drilled to expect an attack at any time. The US Army had, in fact, reneged on a 1953 armistice agreement by reintroducing **nuclear weapons** into South Korea, and went against an international pact by threatening to use such arms against a country that did not possess any; North Korea duly got to work on a reactor of their own at Yongbyon.

There were regular skirmishes both around the **DMZ** and beyond, including an attack on the USS *Pueblo* in 1968 (see p.332), assassination attempts on Kim Il-sung and South Korean president Park Chung-hee around the same time, and the famed "Axe Murder Incident" that took place in the Joint Security Area in 1976 (see box, p.131). During the 1970s at least three tunnels were discovered heading under the DMZ (see p.133), which if they had been left undetected could have seen Korean People's Army (KPA) forces in Seoul within hours.

Decline to crisis

Then came the inevitable **decline** – Juche was simply not malleable enough as a concept to cope with external prodding or poor internal decision-making. Having developed into a pariah state without parallel, North Korea was forced to rely on the help of fellow Communist states the Soviet Union and China – the latter busy solving problems of its own under the leadership of Chairman Mao. The economy ground almost to a halt during the

1970s, while in the face of an American-South Korean threat that never diminished, military spending remained high. It was around this time that **Kim Jong-il** was being groomed as the next leader of the DPRK – the Communist world's first dynastic succession.

During the 1990s North Korea experienced alienation, famine, nuclear threats and the death of its beloved leader. The break-up of the **Soviet Union** in 1991 nullified North Korea's greatest source of funds, and a country officially extolling self-sufficiency increasingly found itself unable to feed its own people. Despite the **nuclear crisis** with the US (see box opposite) the DPRK was making a few tentative moves towards peace with the South; indeed, it was just after examining accommodation facilities prepared for the first-ever North-South presidential summit that Kim Il-sung suffered a heart attack and died. This day in July 1994 was followed by a long period of intense public mourning – hundreds of thousands attended his funeral in Pyongyang, and millions more paid their respects around the country – after which came a terrible **famine**, a period known as the "Arduous March". Despite being dead, Kim Il-sung was elected "Eternal President", though his son, Kim Jong-il, eventually assumed most of the duties that require the authorization of a living body, and was made Supreme Commander of the army.

The Sunshine Policy

The year 1998 brought great changes to North-South relations. **Kim Dae-jung** was elected president of South Korea, and immediately started his "**Sunshine Policy**" of reconciliation with the North, which aimed for integration without absorption (assimilation having been the main goal of both sides up until this point). With US president **Bill Clinton** echoing these desires in the White House, all three sides seemed to be pulling the same way for the first time since the Korean War. The two Kims held a historic Pyongyang summit in 2000, the same year in which Kim Dae-jung was awarded the Nobel Peace Prize. The southern premier revealed to the Western media that Kim Jong-il actually wanted the American army to remain in the South (to keep the peace on the peninsula, as well as for protection from powerful China and an ever more militarist Japan), as long as Washington accepted North Korea as a state and pursued reconciliation over confrontation. Clinton was in fact set for a summit of his own in Pyongyang, but the election of **George W. Bush** in 2000 put paid to that. Bush undid much of the progress that had been made, and antagonized the DPRK, famously labelling it part of an "Axis of Evil" in 2002.

The **second nuclear crisis**, in 2002 (see box opposite), brought about a surprise admission from the North: Japanese prime minister **Junichiro Koizumi** went across for a summit expecting to be forced into saying sorry for Japanese atrocities during occupation, but instead it was Kim Jong-il who did the apologizing, admitting to a long-suspected series of **kidnappings** on the Japanese coast in the late 1970s and early 1980s, ostensibly as a rather convoluted way of teaching his secret service personnel Japanese. Though the number of abductions was probably higher, Kim admitted to having taken thirteen people, of whom eight had died; one of the survivors had married **Charles Robert Jenkins**, an American defector from the post-Korean War period. The belief that more hostages were unaccounted for – and possibly still alive – made it impossible for Koizumi to continue his policy of engagement with the DPRK.

In 2002 **Roh Moo-hyun** was elected South Korean president, and adhered to the precepts of the Sunshine Policy. While the course under his tenure was far from smooth – the US and the DPRK continued to make things difficult for each other, South Korean youth turned massively **against reunification**, and Roh himself suffered impeachment for an unrelated issue – there was still some movement, notably the symbolic reopening of train lines across the DMZ in 2007.

Return to crisis

In 2008, a South Korean tourist was **killed** after entering a high-security area on a visit to the Geumgang mountains. Seoul suspended these cross-border trips, choking off a much-needed source of income for Pyongyang, which eventually confiscated all South

NUCLEAR BRINKMANSHIP

Say this about North Korea's leaders: they may be Stalinist fanatics, they may be terrorists, they may be building nuclear bombs, but they are not without subtlety. They have mastered the art of dangling Washington on a string.

David Sanger, *New York Times*, March 20, 1994

Since the opening of a reactor at **Yongbyon** in 1987, North Korea has kept the outside world guessing as to its **nuclear capabilities**, playing a continued game of bluff and brinkmanship to achieve its aims of self-preservation and eventual reunification with the South. The folding of the Soviet Union in 1991 choked off much of the DPRK's energy supply; with few resources of their own, increasing importance was placed on nuclear energy, but the refusal to allow international inspectors in strengthened rumours that they were also using the facilities to create weapons-grade plutonium. **Hans Blix** and his crew at the International Atomic Energy Agency (IAEA) were finally permitted entry in 1992, but were refused access to two suspected waste disposal sites, which would have provided strong evidence about whether processed plutonium was being created or not; Blix was, however, shown around a couple of huge underground facilities that no one on the outside even knew about. North Korea was unhappy with the sharing of information between American intelligence (the CIA) and the independent IAEA, but after threatening to withdraw from the **Nuclear Nonproliferation Treaty** (NPT) they agreed in 1994 to freeze their programme in exchange for fuel. This only happened after an election within the White House – Bill Clinton was more willing to compromise than his predecessor George Bush Senior. North Korea continued to do itself no favours, at one point launching a missile into the Sea of Japan in 1993: though this was actually a failed attempt at launching a satellite, it was seen by many as practice for a future attack.

The second part of the crisis erupted more suddenly. In 2002, after making veiled threats about a possible resumption of their nuclear programme, North Korea abruptly booted out IAEA inspectors. Coming at the start of the war in Afghanistan, the timing was risky to say the least, but Pyongyang skated even closer to the line by admitting not only to having **nuclear devices** (and claiming that it did not know how to dismantle them), but also to being willing to sell them on the world market. All of these were bargaining ploys aimed at getting George W. Bush's administration to follow the "Sunshine Policy" pursued by Clinton and Kim Dae-jung. Regular six-party talks between China, Russia, Japan, the US and the two Koreas achieved little, and in 2006 North Korea conducted its **first nuclear test**, and sent another missile into the Sea of Japan. North Korea had shown it had yet another card up its sleeve, and talks continued with greater candour. In July 2007 Pyongyang finally announced that it was shutting down its Yongbyon reactor in exchange for aid, though it was only two years before they were cranking up the "permanently disabled" machinery once more, in response to UN criticism of a failed missile launch. More tests followed in 2012, and the following year's rhetoric warned of nuclear attacks against the South, as well as Japan and the USA – brinkmanship once more, most likely, but with North Korea one can never be fully sure.

8

Korean-owned property in the area. Tension remained high until 2010, when two catastrophic incidents brought inter-Korean relations to a postwar low (see box, p.354). First came the **sinking of the Cheonan**, a South Korean naval vessel; this was followed later in the year by the shelling of the West Sea island of **Yeonpyeongdo**, and retaliatory attacks by the South. Though North Korea continues to deny involvement in the sinking of the *Cheonan*, the attack may well have had something to do with the country's change of leadership – Kim Jong-il had been unwell for some time, and knew that elements of his military would be against yet another dynastic transfer of power to his son and mooted successor, Kim Jong-un. Many analysts suggest that the younger Kim may have ordered the attack on the *Cheonan* as a way of proving to the military that, despite his youth, he possessed the necessary fortitude for leadership of the country.

The day duly arrived in December 2011, when Kim Jong-il passed away. According to the state media, the ice on Paekdusan's lake (see p.339) cracked so loudly that it "seemed to shake the heavens and the Earth", while the prevailing snowstorm paused in order to allow a glowing red sunset. Kim Jong-il was posthumously given the title of "**Generalissimo**" or "**Grand Marshal**", and you are likely to hear him referred to as such on your tours.

Kim the Third

The third of North Korea's Holy Trinity, **Kim Jong-un**, ascended to power in April 2012, after a suitable period of national mourning. Little was known about Lil' Kim, bar the fact that he had spent part of his youth in Switzerland; only one verified picture of him existed, and even the year of his birth was a mystery, though it now seems that he was aged 30 when he attained leadership of the country. His relative youth, combined with his international upbringing, prompted hopes abroad that North Korea would finally crawl out of its hidey-hole. These were dashed as early as December 2013, when Kim's uncle **Jang Sung-taek** was executed, after a very public dismissal from his post as a chief of the Workers' Party. To compound the shock abroad, Jang had been seen as one of the more reform-minded elements of the North Korean elite. His crimes were, ostensibly, "counter-revolutionary" acts including cavorting, corruption and attempting to overthrow the leadership. It remains possible that the execution was ordered by the military, not Kim Jong-un himself, but the country's international reputation took another huge blow.

For all this, much has changed under Kim's leadership – incremental **improvements**, largely ignored by global media. Restrictions on business have been relaxed, and restaurants, bars and shops are now quite visible in Pyongyang and other cities; there are many more cars on the road now (including local brand Pyonghwa, many of whose models are based on those of Fiat); and agricultural reform has allowed farmers to keep a share of their produce for themselves. There's simply more bustle about the country now, and though these things are hard to measure, people do seem happier than they did a decade ago. Indeed, Chinese residents of Pyongyang have been heard to compare the pace of change to that of Beijing in the 1990s – except "they're changing even faster than we

8

2014: A DPRK ODDITY

The year 2014 was a bit of an odd one, even by North Korean standards. NBA legend **Dennis Rodman** set things rolling with his visit in January; after making a couple of visits to North Korea the previous year, he'd headed to Pyongyang again to enact some "sports diplomacy" with a cohort of basketball stars. The trip quickly descended into farce: Rodman was visibly inebriated during a shouty interview with CNN on January 7, and also while leading a "Happy Birthday, Mister President" sing-song at a basketball match the following day – the North Korean crowd clapped along diligently, despite not being familiar with the tune, or the fact that it was Kim's birthday (until that point something approaching a state secret). The entourage struggled to keep Rodman under control during the trip, and he also went on to drop the ball by revealing to international media about Kim's marital status, and the fact that he had a baby girl. Following his return to the US, Rodman was investigated for violating state sanctions by donating luxury goods, including vodka (his own brand, as it turns out) and watches, to the Kims. The whole shebang was covered in an entertaining documentary: Dennis Rodman's *Big Bang in Pyongyang*.

Next, in April, came the curious story of **Matthew Miller**, which may also be turned into a movie in due course. The 25-year-old Californian entered the country on a group tour, but destroyed his visa at the airport shortly after arrival, and demanded asylum in the DPRK; he also claimed that he would be able to disseminate US state secrets to the North Korean authorities. The authorities initially ignored Miller's requests, and attempted to get him onto the next flight back to Beijing; when Miller refused to leave his hotel room, insisting on being able to meet local people, he was eventually sent down for six years' hard labour. After doing some farm work, and enduring periods of isolation, Miller was released – and sent back to the US – in November of the same year.

Lastly, December saw the release of "**The Interview**", a comedy in which Seth Rogen and James Franco play hapless journalists sent into North Korea with orders to assassinate Kim Jong-un. The North Korean government had, six months previously, threatened the US with "merciless retaliation" were they to permit the film's release. The computer systems at Sony Pictures were hacked, and sensitive company information leaked, by the "Guardians of Peace", a cyber-terrorist group suspected by the FBI of having strong ties to North Korea – whose government, of course, denied all involvement. Promises to attack the premiere, and any theatres showing the film, came to nought; all publicity being good publicity, *The Interview* raked in the cash, despite not actually being very good.

did". This may turn out to be a false dawn, but at least there are reasons to be optimistic about the future of this most reclusive of nations, and its long-suffering populace.

Pyongyang

평양

A strange concrete and marble experiment in socialist realism, the North Korean capital of **PYONGYANG** stands as a showcase of North Korean might, its grey high-rises and wide boulevards a faint echo of Le Corbusier's visions of utilitarian urban utopia – albeit one with Communist slogans screaming from the tallest buildings. Every street, rooftop, doorway and windowsill here has been designed in keeping with a single grand vision, meaning that this could, credibly, claim to be the most distinctive capital on earth – a maze of huge monuments and high-rises, studded with bronze statues and colourful murals in honour of its idolized leaders. On closer inspection, however, you'll notice that the buildings are dirty and crumbling, and the people under very apparent control.

Hard as it may be to believe, Pyongyang's near three million inhabitants live a relatively privileged existence. Life here is far better than in the countryside, though you'll still see signs of poverty: power cuts are commonplace, and each evening the city tumbles into a quiet darkness hard to fathom in a capital city.

Recent years have, however, seen some seismic shifts in the cityscape – and, perhaps, in the minds of its populace. Following Kim Jong-un's loosening of rules regarding private business, there is more and more visible commerce on the streets. **Restaurants** and **bars** have been present in number for decades, but now most of them actually have signboards to mark their presence, and indeed many have gone for flashy LED numbers – the lineaments of China's first baby steps towards capitalism are not hard to recognize.

8

You'll be taken by around a selection of officially sanctioned sights during your stay. These include **Kumsusan Memorial Palace of the Sun**, where the bodies of Kim and Kim lie in state, and **Mansudae**, site of their colossal statues; the distinctive granite **Juche Tower** overlooking the Taedong river; and the **Pyongyang metro**, one of the world's most intriguingly secretive subway systems. Pyongyang is also the venue for the amazing **Mass Games** (see box, p.335), which take place at the May Day Stadium. However, all sights aside, whether you're simply eating at a restaurant or relaxing in your hotel, Pyongyang is always fascinating.

Kumsusan Memorial Palace of the Sun
금수산 태양궁전

The huge **Kumsusan Memorial Palace of the Sun** is a North Korean cathedral, labyrinth, palace and Mecca all rolled into one, and the single most important place in the country. It's here that the bodies of **Kim Il-sung** and **Kim Jong-il** lie in state, though only invitees, such as tour groups, are allowed to see them – you'll witness a lot of high-ranking military proudly wearing their medals and stripes. The official residence of Kim Il-sung until his death in 1994, it was transformed into his final resting place under the orders of his son, heir and future partner in rigor mortis, Kim Jong-il. While perceived disrespect to the leaders isn't advisable anywhere in the country, it will not be tolerated here – be on your best behaviour, dress smartly and keep any conversation hushed.

The tour

The walk around the palace and past the Kims is a long, slow experience, one that usually takes well over an hour. **Security** is understandably tight – you'll be searched at the entrance and told to leave cameras, coats and bags at reception. Then starts the long haul through corridor after marble corridor, some of which are hundreds of metres long; thankfully, moving walkways are in place, but stand on them, rather than walk – locals view this as an experience to be savoured for as long as possible, and you're likely to see many in tears – even the butchest of soldiers.

After accessing an upper floor by elevator, your proximity to **Kim Il-sung's body** will be heralded by a piped rendition of the "Song of General Kim Il-sung", composed after his death. Absolute silence is expected as visitors pass into the main room, which is bathed in a dim red light. A queue circles around the illuminated body – follow the North Korean lead, and take a deep bow on each side. After paying your respects, you'll be ushered through more corridors. In one room are Kim Il-sung's many medals, prizes, doctorates and awards – note that a few of the universities on his dozens of diplomas have never existed – while in others there's a wall map of the world showing the countries that he visited, and the train carriage and car that he did some of his travelling in.

After this, you do the same again for objects pertaining to **Kim Jong-il** – and the fella himself. At the end of the tour, after collecting your things, you'll usually be allowed out onto the adjacent park for a much-needed stroll.

Mansudae Grand Monument
만수대

At **Mansudae**, west of the river, huge **bronze statues** of Kim Il-sung and Kim Jong-il stand in triumph, backed by a mural of Mount Paekdu – spiritual home of the Korean nation (see p.339). Unlike the mausoleum, this was not originally a memorial – Kim Il-sung's statue was cast when he was still alive, a sixtieth birthday present to himself, paid for by the people and monies donated by the Chinese government (Beijing was said to be unhappy with the unnecessary extravagance of the original gold coating, and it was soon removed). In 2012 the authorities added a statue of the recently deceased Kim Jong-il, and replaced Kim Il-sung's original stern-looking statue with a jollier one, so that the two chaps are both beaming with benevolent smiles.

So important are the statues that, despite their size (a full 20m) they're given a thorough scrub with disturbing regularity – not a single bird poo is ever seen on them and if you ask your guide the reason why, they'll likely tell you that the birds respect them just as much as the people do. Indeed, said respect is also expected of foreigners: each individual, or every second or third person if it's a large tour party, will have to **lay flowers** at the divine metal feet (these will be purchased on the walk towards the monument, and you may be asked to chip in). Each group must also line up and perform a simultaneous bow – stay down for at least a few seconds. Note that taking any pictures that might be deemed "offensive", which includes those cutting part of the statue off may result in your phone or camera being confiscated. Guides also usually ask people to smarten up a bit here, and be on their best behaviour – no chewing gum, smoking or larking about.

Sloping up from the monument is **Moran Hill**, a small park crisscrossed with pleasant paths, and used by city-dwellers as a place to kick back and relax. While there's nothing specific to see, those who visit on a busy day will get a chance to see North Korean life at first hand – this is one of the best places in the country to make a few temporary friends. A simple smile, wave or greeting (in Korean, preferably) has seen travellers invited to scoff *bulgogi* at a picnic or dance along to traditional tunes with a clutch of chuckling grannies.

The Arch of Triumph

개선문

The huge white granite **Arch of Triumph**, at the bottom of Moran Hill, is on almost every tourist itinerary; you may even be taken here before checking in to your hotel.

8

THE WORLD'S LARGEST SHELL

The Ministry of Truth – Minitrue, in Newspeak – was startlingly different from any other object in sight. It was an enormous pyramidal structure of glittering white concrete, soaring up, terrace after terrace, three hundred metres into the air... the Ministry of Truth contained, it was said, three thousand rooms above ground level, and corresponding ramifications below.

George Orwell, *Nineteen Eighty-Four*

It's somewhat ironic that North Korea's most distinctive building seems to have had its design lifted from the pages of *Nineteen Eighty-Four*, a book banned across the country. In a Pyongyang skyline dominated by rectangular apartment blocks, the **Ryugyong Hotel** (류-공-호텔) is the undisputed king of the hill – a bizarre triangular fusion of Dracula's castle and the Empire State Building. Despite the fact that it sticks out like a sore and rather weathered thumb, a whole generation of locals have viewed it as a taboo subject – this was something that couldn't be painted over with the regular whitewash of propaganda.

Construction of the pyramidal 105-floor structure started in 1987, a mammoth project intended to showcase North Korean might. The central peak was to be topped with several revolving restaurants, while the two lower cones may have held smaller versions of the same. For a time, rather amazingly, Pyongyang was one of only three cities in the world that could boast a hundred-storey-plus building, the others being New York and Chicago. Kim Il-sung had expected the *Ryugyong* to become one of the world's most admired hotels, its near-3000 rooms filled with awestruck tourists; however, no sooner had the concrete casing been completed than the funding fell through, and the project was put on indefinite hold. It was left empty, a mere skeleton devoid of electricity, carpeting and windows.

Work only recommenced in earnest in 2008. By 2010, the crane that had maintained a lonely, sixteen-year vigil atop the structure had disappeared, and most of the naked exterior had finally been covered with tinted windows. At the time of writing everything was back on hold again, and tourists are still not allowed to enter its immediate area (though those who have the Victorious Fatherland Liberation War Square on their schedules will get quite near). All being well, in years to come the world's largest shell will finally become one of its most distinctive places to stay.

Modelled on the Arc de Triomphe in Paris, but deliberately built a little higher than its French counterpart, it's the largest such structure in the world. The arch was completed in 1982 to commemorate Korea's resistance to Japan, whose occupation ended in 1945. Despite the fact that it was actually Soviet forces that liberated the city, the on-site guide will tell you that **Kim Il-sung** did all the hard work. Just a minute's walk away, and easily visible from the arch, is a tremendous **mural** of the Great Leader receiving the adulation of his public, while set further back is the 40,000-seater **Kim Il-sung Stadium**. This is the venue for the start and finish of the Pyongyang marathon (see p.333).

Kim Il-sung Square

김일성 광장

South of Mansudae is **Kim Il-sung Square**, a huge paved area where the sense of space is usually heightened by a near-total dearth of people. First-time visitors may also get a sense of déjà vu – the square features in all the stock North Korean footage of goose-stepping soldiers that is shown whenever the country is in the news (incidentally, this act is far from a daily event, and not even an annual one – it's only performed on important military anniversaries). State propaganda peers down into the square from all sides in the form of oversized pictures and slogans. The message on the party headquarters on the north side of the square reads "Long live the Democratic People's Republic of Choson!" Others say "With the Revolutionary Spirit of Paekdu Mountain!" and "Follow the Three Revolutionary Flags!" – the red flags in question read "history", "skill" and "culture", and the horse rearing away from them is Chollima, a winged horse of Korean legend. Visible to the east across the river is the soaring flame-like tip of the Juche Tower (see below).

Grand People's Study House

인민 대학 습당

At the west of the square is the **Grand People's Study House**, effectively an oversized library and one of the few buildings in the city to be built with anything approaching a traditional style – a little ironic, considering its status as a vault of rewritten history. This isn't on all tour itineraries, but anyone given the chance to enter will doubtless be impressed by the super-modern filing system.

Juche Tower

주체 사상탑

While the Mansudae Grand Monument was Kim Il-sung's sixtieth birthday gift to himself, the **Tower of the Juche Idea** – as it's officially referred to – is what he unwrapped when he turned 70 in 1982: a giant, 150m-high candle topped with a 20m red flame, rising up from its site on the banks of the Taedong river. Named after the North Korean take on Communist theory (see box opposite) it's the tallest granite tower in the world, and one of the few points of light in Pyongyang's dim night sky. A kind of socialist version of Cheomseongdae in South Korea (see p.181), but without the astrological capabilities, it is made out of 25,550 granite slabs – one for each day of Kim's 70 years.

It's possible to take a **lift** to the torch level for stupendous views over Pyongyang. Alternatively, you could choose to stay behind, citing a fear of heights, for a guide-free walk around the area: your minder will have to go up with the group, leaving you alone to wander the riverside park. Given the slug-like speed of the lift, you may be on your own for a pleasantly long time. Take a look across the river, and to the right you'll see a sector of Pyongyang that some are now referring to as "**Mini Dubai**" (around Sungni subway station) – a slew of high-rise buildings, and rather attractive ones at that, which may well be a sneak peek into the architectural future of this city.

THE JUCHE IDEA

A local take on Marxist-Leninist theory, **Juche** is the official state ideology of the DPRK, and a system that informs the decision-making of each and every one of its inhabitants. Though Kim Il-sung claims the credit for its invention, the basic precepts were formed by *yangban* scholars in the early twentieth century, created as a means of asserting Korean identity during the Japanese occupation. The basic principle is one of **self-reliance** – both nation and individual are intended to be responsible for their own destiny. Kim Il-sung introduced Juche as the official ideology in the early 1970s, and the doctrines were put to paper in 1982 by his son Kim Jong-il in a book entitled *On the Juche Idea*. Foreign-language editions are available at hotels in Pyongyang, though the core principle of the treatise is as follows:

...man is a social being with independence, creativity and consciousness, which are his social attributes formed and developed in the course of social life and through the historic process of development; these essential qualities enable man to take a position and play a role as master of the world.

As one local puts it, "Juche is more centred around human benefit than material gain relative to the theories of Marx or Lenin. There's no time for asking why we don't have something, or excusing yourself because of this absence... if the state doesn't provide something, make it yourself!" In spite of this apparent confidence, there are some pretty serious flaws and contradictions evident in the DPRK's pursuit of its own creed – the country preaches self-reliance but has long been heavily dependent on the international community for aid, and though Juche Man is said to be free to make his own decisions, **democracy** remains little more than a component part of the state's official title.

Mangyongdae Schoolchildren's Palace

만경대 학생 소년궁전

Behind their strained faces, you sense all the concentration that goes into playing the music, and especially into trying to keep up those Miss World smiles…It's all so cold and sad. I could cry.

Guy Delisle, Pyongyang

The **Children's Palace** showcases the impressive talents of some of the most gifted youths in the country – you'll be escorted from room to room, taking in displays of everything from volleyball and gymnastics to embroidery and song. For some visitors, this by-product of Kim Il-sung's contention that "children are the treasure of the nation" is a sweet and pleasant part of the tour, for others the atmosphere can be more than a little depressing – while there's no denying the abilities of the young performers, it's hard to ignore the level of intensity required in their training. At the end of the tour is an impressive but brutally regimental **performance** of song and dance in the large auditorium, showcasing North Korean expertise to foreign guests; many leave wondering what the country would be like if similar efforts were put into more practical educational pursuits.

Pyongyang subway

평양 지하철

Many visitors find it incredible that a country as poor as North Korea has something as decadent as a functioning **subway system** (ⓦ pyongyang-metro.com), one that even has two lines; in fact, there are likely to be several more for government-only use, though details are kept well under wraps. Six of the sixteen known stations are now open to foreign visitors (though Koryo Tours, p.315, has occasional access rights for most of the rest).

The first thing you'll notice is the length of the escalator; Pyongyang has some of the world's **deepest** subway platforms, said to be reinforced and deep enough to provide protection in the event of a military attack. Marble-floored, with sculpted columns and bathed in the dim glow of low-wattage chandelier lights, these platforms look surprisingly opulent, and are backed by large socialist realist mosaics. The trains themselves are a mix of Chinese rejects and relics of the Berlin U-Bahn, the latter evident in the occasional bit of ageing German graffiti (there's none at all in Korean); all feature the obligatory Kim pictures in each carriage.

The journey between stations doesn't last long, but will give you the chance to make a little contact with the locals. Photos of the subway or the boards that mark it from the outside – "*ji*" (지) in Korean text, short for *jihacheol* – go down particularly well with South Koreans, most of whom are totally unaware that such a facility exists in the North.

The Victorious Fatherland Liberation War Museum

조국 해방전 쟁승리 기념관 • No photography allowed inside

If you have any say in your schedule, make sure that it includes a visit to the **Victorious Fatherland Liberation War Museum**. Right from the huge, cheery mural at the entrance, you'll be subjected to the most fervent America-bashing that you're likely to hear in North Korea; the terms "aggressors", "imperialists" and "imperialist aggressors" are used avidly. You'll be escorted through rooms filled with photos and documents relating to atrocities said to have been inflicted on Korea by the Americans, many of which were apparently seized after the liberation of Seoul during the Korean War. The important bits on the documents are underlined, which helps to steer the eye away from some suspiciously shoddy English – however obvious the forgeries may be (and there are some), don't be tempted to point it out, and just treat it as part of the game.

Outside the museum you'll see pieces of war machinery – several bullet-ravaged planes, a torpedo ship and some captured guns and trucks. Of most interest is a **helicopter** shot down over North Korean territory; next to the vehicle's carcass is an extraordinary photograph of the pilot surrendering next to his dead buddy. A statue of Kim Il-sung (looking, notably, for all the world like Kim Jong-un) greets you in the foyer; from here, you'll be led around three floors of exhibits. Perhaps most interesting is the **panorama room**, where the depiction of a battle in the Daejeon area – rendered on an apparently seamless 15m x 132m length of canvas – slowly revolves around a central platform. This latest incarnation of the museum dates back to 2013, and, in a sign of changing times, there are some computer terminals on which visitors can look at photos of the war. There are also three small coffee bars at which you can rest up if the rhetoric gets to you.

USS Pueblo

푸에블로 호 납치 사건

A piece of history floating on the Potong river, the **USS Pueblo** would count as a Pyongyang must-see were it not for the fact that you'll probably have to see it anyway – it's actually part of the War Museum complex (see above). On January 23, 1968, this small American research ship was boarded and captured by KPA forces in the East Sea – whether it was in North Korean or international waters at the time depends on who you ask. The reasons for the attack, in which one crew member was killed, also vary from one side to the other – the North Koreans made accusations of espionage, the Americans contend that the Soviet Union wanted an on-board encryptor – as do accounts of what happened to the 83 captured crew during their enforced stay in the DPRK; the misty cloak of propaganda makes it hard to verify tales of torture, but they're equally difficult to reject. What's known for sure is that Pyongyang spent months waiting for an **apology** which the Americans deferred for months, and it was only on December 23 that the crew finally crossed to safety over Panmunjom's "Bridge of No Return" (see p.132).

Mangyongdae

만경대

A visit to **Mangyongdae** – the purported **birthplace** of Kim Il-sung on April 15, 1912 – is almost guaranteed to feature on your itinerary. Despite the lack of things to see, the park-like area is pretty in a dull sort of way, and kept as modest as possible, its wooden buildings surrounded by greenery and meandering paths providing a nod to Kim's peasant upbringing. You'll likely be offered spring water from the on-site well, which supposedly gets visitors "into the revolutionary spirit of things". The nearby funfair is marginally more interesting, and features a coconut shy where you can hurl projectiles at targets dressed up as American and Japanese soldiers.

ARRIVAL AND DEPARTURE   PYONGYANG

Most visitors to Pyongyang are here to start a guided excursion, so whether you arrive by **plane** or **train** – your only two options – a bus or private car will be waiting. Given the tightness of the average itinerary, you're likely to visit at least one sight on the way to your hotel.

By plane The semi-decrepit Sunan International Airport (순안국제공항) received a thorough overhaul in 2015, and is now relatively pleasant. Customs inspections aren't usually too thorough; if you're bringing this guidebook, stuff it deep into your bag, or it'll get confiscated. The 20min journey from the airport to central Pyongyang is a fascinating one for first-time visitors, displaying as it does an impoverishment that the authorities have made surprisingly little effort to conceal.

By train Pyongyang station (평양역) is far more central than the airport. Before you leave, check out the pleasing 1920s-vintage architecture of the station.

GETTING AROUND

Getting around the city is usually as simple as waking up in time to catch your **tour bus** (those left behind will be stuck in the hotel until their group returns), but there are a few other ways in which to get around town – usually for locals only, though included on some tours.

By subway The city's subway system counts as a sight in its own right (see p.331), and forms part of most tours. The price will be included, but locals pay five won per ride – that's just a few cents.

By bus and tram Pyongyang's crammed public buses and trams feature on some tours. The buses are pretty photogenic, many of them Hungarian relics from the 1950s. Look out for the stars on their sides – each one represents 50,000 accident-free kilometres.

By taxi Pyongyang received its first-ever fleet of marked taxis in 2013. Rather interestingly, they're adorned with the word "Taxi" in English as well as Korean – a rare sign of globalization in this Juche-oriented society. Ask your tour company if you'd like to take one, and also if you'd like one of the prepaid cards that some locals are using to pay for their trips (see box, p.335).

INFORMATION AND ACTIVITIES

Guides There's no such thing as a tourist information office in North Korea, but your guide will be on hand to answer any questions. Most topics are fine, but asking anything that could be construed as disparaging of the regime could land you or your host in hot water. The guides are usually amiable sorts, and many of them are heaps of fun – especially if you can tempt them into the hotel bar after the day's touring is over. However, at some sights you'll be in the hands of specialists employed to bark out nationalistic vitriol (which, you'll notice, increases in force and volume when either of the Kims are mentioned).

Pyongyang Marathon Starting and finishing at the Kim Il-sung Stadium, this event takes place every April, and the guys at Koryo Tours (see p.315) lay on special tours for those wishing to take part in it.

★**Water park** Pyongyang now has a cool new water park, and to the surprise of many visitors, it's the equal of many similar facilities in the West. However, the main draw here is the chance to mingle with "normal" North Koreans, without your guide in attendance – you'll basically be left to your own devices for an hour or more, and will likely be asked to feature in a fair few local selfies. The park doesn't yet feature on many tours, but ask your operator or guides in advance, and you may be allowed to swing by – entry is €10, and it's usually only open to foreigners on weekends and holidays.

ACCOMMODATION

There are fewer than a dozen hotels in Pyongyang designated for foreigners, and which one you end up at will be organized in advance by your tour operator. Most groups stay at Pyongyang's **top hotels**, the *Koryo* and *Yanggakdo*; there's little between them in terms of service and quality. Both provide a memorable experience and are tourist draws in their own right, which is a good thing, considering the amount of time you'll be spending there – in the evening, when your daily schedule is completed, there's not really anywhere else to go.

TRAFFIC LADIES

At many major intersections in Pyongyang, you'll spot women in uniform directing, or supervising, the traffic. Chosen for their beauty by the powers that be, and evidently well schooled, these **traffic ladies** sport distinctive blue (sometimes white) jackets, hats and skirts, as well as regulation white socks. The traffic ladies are rather popular with some visitors, and one or two tour groups have persuaded their guides to stop by for a brief photo-shoot.

Haebangsan 해방산 호텔 This is the cheapest hotel for foreigners, and a recent renovation has made it a perfectly acceptable place to stay – at least in warmer months, since 24-hour running water is not guaranteed. Another drawback is a near-total lack of atmosphere or on-site activities.

Koryo 고려 호텔 The salmon-pink twin towers of this forty-storey hotel sit on a main thoroughfare, making for a decent appreciation of local life. Rooms are well kept and the on-site restaurants passable, while the ground-floor mini-market is stocked with foreign drinks, biscuits and other comestibles.

Moranbong 모란봉 호텔 A boutique hotel in Pyongyang – whatever next? There are just twelve rooms here, and the fitness centre and pool exude an atmosphere rather contrary to the rest of the country. However, it's popular with diplomats, and as such a little hard to book.

Potonggang 포통강 호텔 Just west of central Pyongyang, in a dull part of town, this is the only hotel to feed a couple of American TV channels into the rooms. Despite the acceptable facilities, few Westerners end up staying here; if you do, you'll find it hard to miss the huge Kim mural in the lobby.

Pyongyang 평양 호텔 The first official hotel in the country, this has benefitted enormously from recent renovations. Unlike the island-based *Yanggakdo* or the lofty *Koryo*, it's a low-level affair set right in the middle of things. If you're in a streetside room (highly recommended, if you have any say), look out of the window in the morning and you'll see locals heading to work; you may also hear fragments of quiet conversation drifting in from outside when you're falling asleep.

Yanggakdo 양각도 호텔 This 47-storey hotel sits on an islet in the Taedong, and commands superb views of both the river and the city from its clean, spacious rooms. The isolated location means that you'll be able to wander around outside without provoking the ire of guides or guards, though to be honest there's precious little to do. The on-site restaurants are excellent, as are the bars (see opposite). Also on site are a bowling alley, a karaoke room and a tailor.

EATING

As with accommodation, all your dining requirements will be sorted out in advance. The best restaurants are closed to all but foreigners and the party elite, and you'll probably eat at a different one on each day of your stay. The North Korean authorities seem to think that foreigners will only enjoy their meal if they're rotating slowly – both the *Koryo* and *Yanggakdo* hotels have **revolving restaurants**. You usually have **breakfast** in your hotel, and on some days will also have lunch or dinner there. Both the volume and the quality of food will depend on the prevailing food situation at the time of your visit – experienced diplomats suggest that it seems to improve when big groups or important folk are in town.

Austrian Coffee Shop Located on Kim Il-sung Square (see p.330), this offers some of the best coffee in the city – and, by extension, the whole country.

Chongnyu A popular choice with tour operators, particularly in colder months, this long-established restaurant specializes in Korean hotpot. It's opposite the Romanian and Iranian embassies – the latter featuring Pyongyang's only mosque.

Pyolmori Those staying at the *Koryo* should ask to be taken to this nearby café-cum-bakery – in addition to tasty snacks, it serves good coffee.

Pyongyang Best Barbecued Duck 평양 제일 오리고기 A popular tour stop, and only open when booked by an agency, this place serves duck and little else – though, on occasion, it may well be another kind of meat.

DRINKING

Drinking can be one of Pyongyang's most unexpected delights – while you won't exactly be painting the town red, many travellers stagger to bed from the **hotel bar** every single night of their stay (and then have to get up at 7am to catch the tour bus). There are also a handful of real **local bars** – a couple of classier joints, and some proletarian places – now licenced to allow foreign visitors; ask the guides to take you to one, since the chance to mingle with the locals is truly memorable.

Koryo 고려 호텔 There's a decent ground-floor microbrewery at this hotel, though the beer isn't quite as tasty as that at the *Yanggakdo*. The revolving restaurant up on the top level has better views, and also sells local *soju*.

Pyongyang 평양 호텔 Hunt down the fourth-floor bar if you're staying here – it's usually the most fun option of the several dotted around the establishment. You may well end up drinking with a Scottish lawyer, who has been living at this hotel for years.

Taedonggang #3 Beer Bar 태동강 재삼 맥주점 About 100m east of the Juche Tower, this impressive-looking bar is popular with Pyongyang's emerging middle-class, and has up to seven beers on tap (all made by the eponymous brewery; avoid the number five), plus cocktails, snacks and full meals.

Yanggakdo 양각도 호텔 This landmark hotel boasts two of the most interesting bars in town. One revolves slowly at the top of the tower, and makes a great place for a nightcap with a view of Pyongyang's galaxy of faint lights. The ground-floor bar brews its own beer, which can be quite delicious after a hard day slogging around sights.

SHOPPING

While staunchly anti-capitalist North Korea isn't exactly renowned for its **shopping** possibilities, there are a number of interesting things to buy in Pyongyang, most of which are impossible to get anywhere else, and make fantastic souvenirs.

Food and drink Your hotel is likely to have a shop at which you can buy North Korean booze – beer and *soju* are common purchases, though the bold can try some of the harder spirits, made with all sorts, from mushroom to seal penis. A few tours feature the fantastic new Kwangbok supermarket, in which purchases can only be made in North Korean money (there's a market-rate exchange booth at the front); the local honey's a sweet treat, while South Korean friends will get a kick out of the *naengmyeon* noodles (spelled "*raengmyeon*" in the North, and therefore clearly definable as contraband).

Kim-lit Imagine if your local bookstore only sold works from writers with the same surname – that's what it's like in the DPRK. Shops in hotels and various other places around Pyongyang sell books from the pen of Kim, Kim and Kim, the leaders holding forth on all sorts of subjects from cinema to social policy.

Kim suits The *Yanggakdo* has a tailor on the third floor, and it's often possible to make a special visit even if you're not staying at this hotel – ideal fodder for Hallowe'en parties. A variety of jackets and trousers are available, though most popular are the buttoned-up-to-the-collar "Kim suits", as popularized by Kim Jong-il; it's also possible to nab a green, military-style jacket with gold buttons.

Local money It's technically illegal for foreigners to use (and therefore, by extension, export) North Korean money, though there are certainly ways in which to get your hands on some. Those visiting in warmer months may spot women selling ice cream from tiny booths, most often a tasty stick-bar called an *Eskimo* – if you pay slightly over the odds in foreign currency you'll get some local change. The same goes at the snack kiosks you'll see streetside all over the city; you may be able to sneak to one when visiting certain sights, though don't let your guide see. In all cases, hard Chinese currency certainly goes down well – a case of yuan-won win-win.

Pre-paid cards These have become rather popular of late in North Korea, and can be used for all sorts from paying at grocery stores to taking local taxis. You may not actually ever get to use one, but ask your guide at the beginning of your trip and they may be able to fetch you one by the end of it – you'll need to pay, of course, though around $20 will do. The cards make fantastic souvenirs, and attempting to pay for something with one south of the border will provoke a fair bit of head-scratching, then wide-eyed astonishment as

8

THE MASS GAMES

The spectacular **Mass Games** are among the world's must-see events. Also known as the "Arirang Games", they take place in Pyongyang's 150,000-seater **May Day Stadium**; though this is not always full to bursting, there are, unbelievably, always more performers than there are spectators. Wildly popular with foreign tourists, the show is actually created for local consumption – this is a propaganda exercise extraordinaire, one used by the West as evidence of a rigidly controlled population in thrall to the Kim dynasty.

Even the warm-up will fill you with awe. Your entry to the stadium is serenaded by upwards of twenty thousand schoolchildren; filling the opposite stand, they scream out in perfect unison while flashing up the names of their schools on large **coloured flipbooks**, effectively forming human pixels on a giant TV screen that remains an ever-changing backdrop throughout the show. The performers themselves come out in wave after wave, relaying stories about the hardships under Japanese occupation, the **creation of the DPRK**, and the bravery in the face of American aggression, as well as less bombastic parables about farming life or how to be safe at the seaside. Among the cast will be thousands-strong teams of *chosonbok*-wearing dancers, ball-hurling schoolkids and miniskirt-wearing female "soldiers" wielding rifles and swords, their every move choreographed to a colourful perfection. The form of the displays changes – military-style marches give way to performances of gymnastics or traditional dance, and the cast are at one point illuminated in brilliant blue, forming a rippling sea. Visitors are often left speechless – you'll just have to see for yourself (see p.317 for details).

the poor cashier finally realizes where the card comes from. **Socialist realist stamps and badges** A visit to the stamp shop comes as part of many tours, and their socialist realist designs are really quite striking – a good purchase, even if you're not a philatelist. Your hotel's shop is also likely to stock a series of similarly cool badges.

Other sights in the DPRK

Most of the country is closed off to foreign visitors, but even the shortest tour itinerary is likely to contain at least one sight outside Pyongyang. The most common trip is to **Panmunjom** in the DMZ, via **Kaesong**, the closest city to the border, but there are other popular excursions to **Paekdusan**, the mythical birthplace of the Korean nation and its highest peak, and the wonderful "Diamond Mountains" of **Kumgangsan** near the South Korean border.

Kaesong

개성

Other than Pyongyang, **KAESONG** is usually the only North Korean city that foreign travellers get to see. From the capital, it's an easy ninety-minute trip south along the traffic-free **Reunification Highway**; the road actually continues all the way to Seoul, just 80km away, though it's blocked by the DMZ a few kilometres south of Kaesong. Kaesong's proximity to the border means that the surrounding area is crawling with soldiers, and it's hardly surprising that Kaesong's long-suffering citizens often come across as a little edgy.

The palpable tension, Kaesong – romanized as "Gaeseong" in the South – is actually a place of considerable history: this was once the capital of the **Goryeo dynasty**, which ruled over the peninsula from 936 to 1392, though thanks to wholesale destruction in the Korean War, you'll see precious little evidence of this today. One exception is **Sonjuk Bridge**, which was built in the early thirteenth century; it was here that an eponymous Goryeo loyalist was assassinated as his dynasty fell.

Kim Il-sung statue

The one sight guaranteed to catch the eye in Kaesong is a huge **statue of Kim Il-sung**. One of the most prominent such statues in the country, and even visible from the Reunification Highway on the way to Panmunjom, it's illuminated at night come what

---

SPECIAL EXCURSIONS

This section details a few of the most common DPRK sights outside Pyongyang. All regularly feature on tour itineraries, but new areas are opened up from time to time – largely thanks to Koryo Tours (see p.315), who take a hugely proactive stance in these regards. Here are a few lesser-visited places to look out for when choosing a tour:

Haeju (해주) A great side trip for history buffs: the city is home to a huge pavilion erected in 1500, while the surrounding area is home to a Goryeo-dynasty mountain fortress and a Joseon-era Confucian academy. It's possible to stay the night here.

Hamhung (함흥) This major east-coast city only opened to tourism in 2010 – your presence will cause quite a stir. It's visually interesting, with lots of buildings designed by East German architects, while attractions include factory tours and trips to local farms.

Nampo (남포) A major city just 45 minutes west of Pyongyang by bus. Sights are low-key, but interesting in their own way – most visitors get shown around the 8km-long West Sea Barrage, the steelworks and a couple of factories. Ask for a trip to the hot-springs resort.

Wonsan (원산) A large port city – visitors usually get shown around the docks, though more interesting is the chance to swim in the sea at Songdowon beach, just down the coast. On the way to or from Pyongyang (a 4hr drive) you may be able to stop at the gorgeous Ulim waterfalls – ask permission for a dip, if it's warm.

may owing to its own generator, which enables it to surf the crest of any power shortages that afflict the rest of the city.

The tomb of Wang Kon
왕건왕릉

There are a few officially sanctioned sights in Kaesong's surrounding countryside. West of the city on the road to Pyongyang is the tomb of **Wang Kon**, the first leader of Goryeo and the man responsible for moving the dynasty's capital to Kaesong, his home town. In the South, he's more commonly known as King Taejo, and his decorated grass-mound tomb is similar to those that can be found in Seoul (see p.91).

The tomb of Wang Jon
왕전왕릉

West of Wang Kon is another tomb, this one belonging to **Wang Jon**. Also known as King Kongmin, he ruled (1351–74) during Mongol domination of the continent; in keeping with the traditions of the time, he married a Mongol princess and was buried alongside her – the tiger statues surrounding the tomb represent the Goryeo dynasty, while the sheep are a nod to the Mongol influence. North of Wang Kon's tomb is **Pakyon**, a forest waterfall whose surroundings include a fortress gate and a beautiful temple.

ACCOMMODATION AND EATING	**KAESONG**

Groups heading to or from Panmunjom often have a **lunch stop** in Kaesong, which was famed for its cuisine prior to the division of Korea – there are plenty of restaurants south of the border named after the city. It's also possible to **stay** in Kaesong, which is provided as an interesting add-on to many tours.

Kaesong Folk Hotel A parade of traditional rooms running off a courtyard, set in a complex dotted with swaying trees and bisected by a peaceful stream. Rooms are basic, and sometimes fall victim to power outages, but it's a unique experience with an entirely different vibe from the big hotels in Pyongyang.

★**Tongil** The option favoured by most tour leaders, the "Unification" restaurant lays on a superb spread, apportioned into little golden bowls – perhaps the best food you're likely to encounter in the whole country.

Panmunjom
판문점

The village of **PANMUNJOM** sits bang in the middle of the **Demilitarized Zone** that separates North and South Korea (see p.131 for more information on how it can be reached from the South, where it's referred to as Panmunjeom). You'll see much the same from the North, but with the propaganda reversed – all of a sudden it was the US Army that started the Korean War and Kim Il-sung who won it. Interestingly, many visitors note that the cant is just as strong on the American side (though usually more balanced).

Into the DMZ

The route to Panmunjom follows the Reunification Highway from Kaesong. Your first stop will be at the **KPA guardpost**, which sits just outside the northern barrier of the DMZ; the southern flank is just 4km away, though it feels much further. After being given a short presentation of the site by a local soldier, it's time for the ride into the DMZ itself – note the huge slabs of concrete at the sides of the road, ready to be dropped to block the way of any invading tanks (this same system is in place on the other side). A short way into the DMZ is the **Armistice Hall**, which was cobbled together at incredible speed by North Korean soldiers to provide a suitable venue for the signing of the Korean Armistice Agreement, a document which brought about a ceasefire to the Korean War on July 27, 1953. Tucked away in a corner is what is said to be the weapon from the famed "Axe Murder Incident", an incident for which North Korea claims little responsibility (see box, p.131).

The Joint Security Area

From the Armistice Hall you are taken to the **Joint Security Area** (see p.131), where Panmun Hall looks across the border at a South Korean building of similar size. From here, you're led into one of the three halls that straddle the official line of control, and are permitted to take a few heavily guarded steps into South Korean territory. The whole experience is bizarre, but fascinating, and it's an oddly tranquil place, despite its status as one of the world's most dangerous border points.

Kumgangsan

금강산

Before partition, the **KUMGANGSAN** mountain range – which sits just north of the DMZ on Korea's east coast – was widely considered to be the most beautiful on the peninsula. The DPRK's relative inaccessibility has ensured that this remains the case. Spectacular crags and spires of rock tower over a skirt of pine-clad foothills, its pristine lakes and waterfalls adding to a richly forested beauty rivalled only by Seoraksan just across the border (see p.149). There are said to be more than twelve thousand pinnacles, though the principal peak is Birobong, which rises to 1638m above sea level.

Kumgangsan can be visited as part of a North Korean tour, and was indeed once visitable on **a trip from South Korea** (where it's spelled "Geumgangsan", but pronounced the same), until a South Korean tourist was killed in 2008 and the tours were put on indefinite hold.

Myohyangsan

묘향산

Many North Korean tours include a visit to **MYOHYANGSAN**, a pristine area of hills, lakes and waterfalls around 150km north of Pyongyang. Though it's about as close as the DPRK comes to a mountain resort, the main reason to come here isn't to walk the delightful hiking trails, but to visit the **International Friendship Exhibition** – a colossal display showing the array of presents given to the Kims by overseas well-wishers. After the exhibition you're likely to be taken to see **Pohyonsa**, an eleventh-century temple just a short walk away, and **Ryongmun** or **Paengryong**, two stalactite-filled limestone caves which burrow for a number of kilometres under the surrounding mountains.

The International Friendship Exhibition

국제 친선 전람관

The halls of the **International Friendship Exhibition** burrow deep into a mountainside – insurance against any nuclear attacks that come the DPRK's way. Indeed, such is the emphasis on preservation that you'll be forced to don a pair of comically oversized slippers before you enter the halls. Inside the exhibition hall, gifts numbering 200,000 and rising have been arranged in order of country of origin, the evident intention being to convince visitors that the Kims command immense respect all over the world – of course, this is not the place to air any painful truths.

The first rooms you come to are those dedicated to **Kim Il-sung**. For a time, gifts were pouring in from all over the Communist world, including a limousine from Stalin and an armoured train carriage from Chairman Mao. There are also a number of medals, tea sets, pots, cutlery and military arms, as well as more incongruous offerings such as fishing rods and a refrigerator. The **Kim Jong-il** rooms are less stacked with goodies, and instead feature heavily corporate treats and electronic gadgets. Perhaps most interesting is the **basketball** donated by former American Secretary of State Madeleine Albright, signed by Michael Jordan, of whom Kim was apparently a big fan.

ACCOMMODATION	MYOHYANGSAN
Chongchon Basic three-storey place with a bar and regular power cuts – good enough for one night, however, and a tour including this instead of the *Hyangsan* will be far cheaper.	**Hyangsan** Pyramidal hotel that's currently the best in the land, with an on-site health complex and stupendous pool, as well as the obligatory top-floor revolving restaurant.

Paekdusan

백두산

The highest peak on the Korean peninsula at 2744m, the extinct volcano of **PAEKDUSAN** straddles the border between North Korea and China, and is the source of the Tuman and Amnok rivers (Tumen and Yalu in Mandarin) that separate the countries. Within its caldera is a vibrant blue **crater lake** surrounded by a ring of jagged peaks; it's a beguiling place steeped in myth and legend. This was said to be the landing point for **Dangun**, the divine creator of Korea, after his journey from heaven in 2333 BC (see box, p.343). More recently, it was also the apparent birthplace of **Kim Jong-il**, an event said to have been accompanied by flying white horses, rainbows and the emergence of a new star in the sky – records seem to suggest that he was in fact born in Soviet Siberia, but who needs history when the myth is so expressive?

The main attraction for foreign visitors, however, is simple – extreme natural beauty. Paekdusan's ring of mountains is cloaked with lush forest, which is home to bears, wolves, boar, deer and perhaps even a small population of **Siberian tigers**. As long as the weather holds – and at this height, it often doesn't – you may be able to climb to the top of the Korean peninsula by taking a hike to **Jong Il peak**. A cable car also whisks guests down to the lakeside, where you can have a splash in the inviting waters in warmer months.

With Paekdusan being a place of such importance, every person in the country is expected to make the pilgrimage at some point; the journey is usually paid for in full by the government. Foreign tourists wishing to visit must take a **chartered flight** from Pyongyang, and then a car the rest of the way, though due to weather conditions the journey is usually only possible during warmer months. It's also possible to visit from the Chinese side, as thousands of South Koreans do each year (see box below).

8

NORTH KOREA FROM THE OUTSIDE

If budgetary constraints or possession of the wrong kind of passport make a trip to North Korea impossible, there are a number of ways to peer into the country from outside.

FROM SOUTH KOREA

The two Koreas share a 250km-long border, and though the area around the Demilitarized Zone that separates them is largely off limits, there are a number of vantage points from which you can look across. **DMZ tours from Seoul** are highly popular (see p.132); itineraries vary, but can include views of the North from an observatory, a trip inside tunnels dug by North Koreans in preparation for an attack on Seoul, as well as the chance to step onto **DPRK territory** in the Joint Security Area. Note that there's another observatory just north of **Sokcho** on the east coast (see p.146).

FROM CHINA

The large city of **Dandong** is right on the North Korean border, with only the Yalu river ("Amnok" in Korean) separating it from Sinuiju on the other side. The two cities offer a rather incredible contrast, with the tall, neon-seared skyscrapers on the Chinese side overlooking poor, low-rise Sinuiju across the water. On Dandong's riverside promenade you'll be able to buy North Korean banknotes and pin-badges, or take a boat trip to within a single metre of the North Korean shore; you can get just as close from **Tiger Mountain**, 25km east of the city and the easternmost section of China's Great Wall.

With the mountain and its crater lake straddling the border, it's also possible to visit **Paekdusan** (see above) from the Chinese side, a trip highly popular with South Koreans. The best form of access is Chiangbaishan airport, served by flights from most of China's largest cities.

INDEPENDENCE HALL OF KOREA

Contexts

History

With its two-millennium-long chain of unbroken regal rule interspersed by regular conflict, the Korean peninsula offers plenty for history buffs to get their teeth into. The country's early beginnings are shrouded in mystery, though events have been well documented since before the birth of Christ, a period when Korea's famed Three Kingdoms were springing into existence. Replacing Gojoseon – the first known Korean kingdom – these were Silla, Goguryeo and Baekje, three states that jostled for peninsular power for centuries, seeing off other nascent fiefdoms while dealing with the Chinese and Japanese states of the time. Even today, tangible evidence of all three kingdoms can still be seen. It was Silla that eventually prevailed, emerging victorious from a series of battles to bring the peninsula under unified control. Infighting and poor governance led to its demise, the slack taken up by the Goryeo dynasty, which lasted for almost five hundred years before folding and being replaced by Joseon rule. This was to last even longer, but was snuffed out by the Japanese at a time of global turmoil, bringing to an end Korea's succession of well over one hundred kings. World War II ended Japanese annexation, after which Korea was split in two in the face of the looming Cold War. There then followed the brutal Korean War, and in 1953 the Communist north and the capitalist south went their separate ways, each writing their own historical versions of the time – and in the case of North Korea, skewing historical events even prior to partition. The war was never technically brought to an end, and its resolution – either peaceable, or by force – will add the next chapter to Korea's long history.

The beginnings

Remains of *Homo erectus* show that the Korean peninsula may have been home to hominids for more than half a million years. The first evidence of habitation can be found in several clusters of Neanderthal sites dating from the Middle Paleolithic period (roughly 100,000–40,000 BC). The assortment of hand axes, scrapers and other tools made of stone and bone hauled from the complexes suggest a **hunter-gatherer** existence. **Neolithic** sites (8000–3000 BC) are far more numerous than those from the Paleolithic era, and in these were found thousands of remnants from the peninsula's transition from the Stone to the Bronze Age. In addition to the use of metal tools, from

2333 BC	7th century BC	c.109 BC
Founding of Gojoseon, Korea's first known kingdom, by semi-mythical bear-child Dangun	First mentions of Gojoseon in Chinese records	Demise of Gojoseon at hands of Chinese Han dynasty

KOREA'S MAJOR HISTORICAL ERAS

Gojoseon	c.2333 BC to c.109 BC
Three Kingdoms	c.57 BC to 668 AD
Silla	c.57 BC to 668 AD
Goguryeo	c.37 BC to 668 AD
Baekje	c.18 BC to 660 AD
Unified Silla	668–935
Goryeo	918–1392
Joseon	1392–1910
Japanese colonial period	1910–45
Republic of Korea (South)	1945–present day
Democratic People's Republic of Korea (North)	1945–present day

7000 BC **pottery** was being produced with distinctive comb-toothed patterns (*jeulmun*) similar to those found in Mongolia and Manchuria. Fired earth also came to play a part in death rituals, a fact made evident by small, shell-like "jars" into which the broken bodies were placed together with personal belongings; these were then lowered into a pit and covered with earth. An even more distinctive style of burial was to develop, with some tombs covered with large stone slabs known as **dolmen** ("*goindol*" in Korean). Korea is home to over thirty thousand burial mounds. Three of the most important sites – Gochang and Hwasun in the Jeolla provinces, and Ganghwado, west of Incheon – are UNESCO World Heritage Sites.

Gojoseon

The peninsula's first kingdom was known as Joseon, though today it is usually referred to as **Gojoseon** (고조선; "Old Joseon") in an effort to distinguish it from the later Joseon period (1392–1910). Its origins are obscure to say the least; most experts agree that it got going in 2333 BC under the leadership of **Dangun**, who has since become the subject of one of Korea's most cherished myths (see box opposite). Joseon initially functioned as a loose federation of fiefdoms covering not only parts of the Korean peninsula, but large swathes of Manchuria too. By 500 BC it had become a single, highly organized dominion, even drawing praise from Confucius and other Chinese sages. Accounts of the fall of Joseon are also rather vague, but large parts of its Manchurian population were squeezed onto the Korean peninsula during the Chinese **Warring States Period** (470–221 BC), and it seems likely to have fallen victim to a nascent Han dynasty in 109 BC. Joseon's historical name lives on: North Korea continues to refer to its land as such (and South Korea as Namjoseon, or "South Joseon"), while many South Korean tourist brochures use "The Land of Morning Calm" – a literal translation of the term – as a national motto.

The Three Kingdoms period

By 109 BC, after the fall of Gojoseon, power on the peninsula was decentralized to half-a-dozen fiefdoms, the most powerful of which – **Silla**, **Goguryeo** and **Baekje** – went

57 BC	**c.37 BC**	**18 BC**
Founding of Silla dynasty, first of Korea's "Three Kingdoms", by King Hyeokgeose, who supposedly hatched from an egg laid by a horse	Founding of Goguryeo dynasty by Jumong, another king hatched from an egg	Founding of Baekje dynasty by King Onjo

THE LEGEND OF DANGUN

The Korean peninsula has played host to some of the world's longest-running monarchies, and such regal durability has made for comprehensive records. However, much of what's known about the years preceding the Three Kingdoms period remains obscure, and Korea has resorted to mythology to fill in the gaps of its creation – primarily the legend of **Dangun**.

The story begins with **Hwanin**, the "Lord of Heaven", whose son **Hwanung** desired to live as a mortal being on Earth. Hwanin set his son down on Mount Paekdu (located in present-day North Korea) together with an army of three thousand disciples. Hwanung and his tribe took charge of the locals, and fostered celestial ideals of law, art and social structure. Two of his pets – a bear and a tiger – prayed to Hwanung that they be made human, just as he had been; they were each given twenty cloves of garlic and a bundle of mugwort, and told to survive on nothing else for a hundred days, before being sent to a cave. The tiger failed the challenge, but the bear prevailed, and on being made human soon bore Hwanung's child, Dangun, who went on to found **Joseon** in 2333 BC.

In 1993 North Korean officials announced that they had found Dangun's tomb in a location close to Pyongyang; unfortunately, they've been unwilling to share this evidence with the rest of the world.

on to become known as the Three Kingdoms. Though exact details regarding their beginnings are just as sketchy as those surrounding Gojoseon – two of the inaugurators are said to have hatched from eggs – this period saw the first definitive drawing of borders in Korean history, although it must be noted that none of them became fully fledged kingdoms for a couple of centuries, each existing initially as a loose confederation of fiefdoms. Several of those jostling for power after Gojoseon's demise are not included under the Three Kingdoms banner; most notably, these include the states of **Gaya**, which was absorbed by Silla, and **Buyeo**, parts of which were incorporated by Goguryeo and Baekje. The kingdom of **Tamna**, isolated on Jeju Island, also came under Baekje control.

Territorial borders shifted continuously as all three kingdoms jostled for power, and a number of fortresses went up across the land, many of which can still be seen today. Outside forces were occasionally roped in to help; interestingly, Baekje was closely aligned with Japan for much of its time, while Silla sided with the Chinese Tang dynasty, despite their positions on the "wrong" sides of the peninsula. Because of these close ties with China and Japan, Korea acted as a conduit for a number of customs imported from the continent: Chinese characters came to be used with the Korean language and the import and gradual flourishing of **Buddhism** saw temples popping up all over the peninsula. However, it was **Confucianism**, another Chinese import, that provided the social building blocks, with a number of educational academies supplying the *yangban* scholars at the head of the aristocracy. Great advances were made in the arts, particularly with regard to jewellery and pottery; wonderful relics of the time have been discovered in their thousands from the grassy hill-tombs of dead kings and other formerly sacred sites. After **centuries of warring** that saw the kingdoms continually changing allegiance to each other and to Chinese and Japanese dynasties, matters finally came to a head in the mid-seventh century. In 660, supplemented by Tang forces from China, Silla **triumphed in battle** against Baekje, whose people leapt to their

372	660	668
Buddhism introduced to Korea; it slowly starts to replace shamanism	Silla defeats Baekje	Silla defeats Goguryeo, unifies rule on peninsula by 676

death from a cliff in the city of Buyeo. Muyeol died just a year later, but within a decade his son King Munmu defeated Goguryeo, setting the scene for a first-ever **unified rule** on the peninsula.

Goguryeo

The kingdom of **Goguryeo** (고구려) covered the whole of present-day North Korea, a large chunk of Chinese Manchuria and much of what is now Gangwon-do in the South, making it by far the largest of the Three Kingdoms by territory. Because of its location, the majority of Goguryeo's relics are a little harder to come by today than those from the Baekje or Silla kingdoms, and the history even more vague; most guesses place the inauguration of the first Goguryeo king, Dongmyeong, at 37 BC. At this point Goguryeo was still paying tax and tribute to China, but when the **Han dynasty** started to weaken in the third century, Goguryeo advanced and occupied swathes of territory; they eventually came to rule over an area (much of which is now in the Chinese region of Dongbei) almost three times the size of the present-day Korean peninsula. Baekje and Silla forces mounted sporadic attacks from the south, and the Chinese Tang invaded from the north, squeezing Goguryeo towards the Tuman and Anmok rivers that mark North Korea's present boundary. The Tang also provided pressure from the south by allying with the Silla dynasty, and when this **Tang-Silla coalition** defeated Baekje in 660, the fall of Goguryeo was inevitable; it was finally snuffed out in 668.

Baekje

The **Baekje** (백제) dynasty, which controlled the southwest, was created as the result of great movements of people on the western side of the Korean peninsula. **Buyeo**, a smaller state not considered one of the Three Kingdoms, was pushed southward by the nascent kingdom of Goguryeo, and some elements decided to coalesce around a new leader – **Onjo**, the son of Dongmyeong, the first king of Goguryeo. Jealous of his brother's inheritance of that kingdom, Onjo proclaimed his own dynasty in 18 BC. Baekje is notable for its production of fine jewellery, which exhibited more restraint than that found in the other kingdoms, a fact often attributed to the dynasty's relatively early adoption of Buddhism as a state religion. Evidence of Baekje's close relationship with the **Japanese kingdom of Wa** can still be seen today – the lacquered boxes, folding screens, immaculate earthenware and intricate jewellery of Japan are said to derive from the influence of Baekje artisans. Unfortunately for Baekje, the Wa did not provide such protection as the Chinese Tang dynasty gave Silla, and much of its later history was spent conceding territory to Goguryeo. The capital shifted south from a location near present-day Seoul to Ungjin (now known as Gongju), then south again to Sabi (now Buyeo); after one final battle, fought in 660 against a Tang-Silla coalition, Baekje's small remaining population chose death over dishonour, and committed suicide from Sabi's riverside fortress.

Silla

Although it held the smallest territory of the Three Kingdoms, in the southeast, and was for centuries the most peaceable, it was the **Silla** (신라) dynasty that defeated Baekje and Goguryeo to rule over the whole peninsula. Unlike its competitors, it only

774	918	935
Completion of Bulguksa, still one of Korea's most revered temples	Inauguration of Goryeo dynasty by Wang Geon, later known as King Taejo	Official transfer of power from Silla to Goryeo

had one dynastic capital – Gyeongju – and many of the riches accumulated in almost a millennium of power (including over two hundred years as the capital of the whole peninsula) can still be seen today.

Silla's first king – Hyeokgeose – was crowned in 57 BC, but it was not until the sixth century AD that things got interesting. At this time, Silla accepted Buddhism as its state religion (the last of the Three Kingdoms to do so), and created a Confucian "bone rank" system in which people's lives were governed largely by heredity: Buddhism was used to sate spiritual needs, and Confucianism as a regulator of society. Following threats from the Japanese kingdom of Wa, they also began a rapid build-up of military strength; under the rule of King Jinheung (540–76) they absorbed the neighbouring **Gaya** confederacy, and started to nibble away at the other neighbouring kingdoms. Initially they sided with Baekje to attack Goguryeo, a dynasty already weakened by internal strife and pressure from the Chinese Tang to the north; a century later, Silla turned the tables on Baekje by allying with the **Tang**, then used the same alliance to finish off Goguryeo to the north and bring the Korean peninsula under unified rule.

Unified Silla

Following the quickfire defeats of its two competitor kingdoms in the 660s, the **Silla dynasty** gave rise to the Korean peninsula's first-ever unification, keeping Gyeongju as the seat of power. This was, however, no easy matter: small pockets of Baekje and Goguryeo resistance lingered on, and a new (perhaps necessarily) nationalistic fervour developed by the king meant that the Chinese Tang – allies previously so crucial to Silla – had to be driven out, an action that also sent a strong "stay away" message to would-be Japanese invaders. Silla also had to contend with **Balhae** to the north; this large but unwieldy successor state to Goguryeo claimed back much of that kingdom's former territory, and set about establishing favourable relationships with nearby groups to the north. Once the dust had settled, the Chinese officially accepted the dynasty in exchange for regular tributes paid to Tang emperors; King Seongdeok (ruled 702–37) did much of the work, convincing the Tang that his kingdom would be much more useful as an ally than as a rival.

Silla set about cultivating a peninsular **sense of identity**, and the pooling of ideas and talent saw the eighth century become a high-water mark of artistic development, particularly in metalwork and earthenware. This time also saw temple design reach elaborate heights, particularly at Bulguksa, built near Gyeongju in 751. Rulers stuck to a rigidly Confucian "bone rank" system, which placed strict limits on what an individual could achieve in life, based almost entirely on their genetic background. Though it largely succeeded in keeping the proletariat quiet, this highly centralized system was to lead to Silla's demise.

Decline and fall

The late eighth century and most of the ninth were characterized by **corruption and infighting** at the highest levels of Silla society. Kings' reigns tended to be brief and bloody – the years from 836 to 839 alone saw five kings on the throne, the result of power struggles, murder and enforced suicide. Tales of regal immorality trickled down to the peasant class, leading to a number of **rebellions**; these increased in size and

1145	1231	1248
Completion of the Samguk Sagi, a historical annal of the Three Kingdoms period	First of the inevitable Mongol invasions	Korea becomes a vassal state of Mongol Khaans

number as regal power over the countryside waned, eventually enveloping Silla in a state of perpetual civil war. With the Silla king reduced to little more than a figurehead, the former kingdoms of Baekje and Goguryeo were resurrected (now known as "**Hubaekje**" and "**Taebong**" respectively). Silla shrunk back beyond its Three Kingdoms-era borders, and after a power struggle Taebong took control of the peninsula. In 935 at Gyeongju's Anapji Pond, King Gyeongsun ceded control of his empire in a peaceful transfer of power to Taebong leader **Wang Geon**, who went on to become Taejo, the first king of the Goryeo dynasty.

The Goryeo dynasty

Having grown from a mini-kingdom known as Taebong, one of the many battling for power following the collapse of Silla control, it was the name of the **Goryeo** (고려) dynasty that eventually gave rise to the English term "Korea". It began life in 918 under the rule of **Taejo**, a powerful leader who needed less than two decades to bring the whole peninsula under his control. One of his daughters was to marry Gyeongsun, the last king of Silla, and Taejo himself wedded a Silla queen, two telling examples of the new king's desire to cultivate a sense of national unity; he was even known to give positions of authority to his enemies. Relations with China and Japan were good, and the kingdom became ever more prosperous.

Following the fall of Silla, Taejo moved the national capital to his home town, Kaesong, a city in present-day North Korea. He and successive leaders also changed some of the bureaucratic systems that had contributed to Silla's downfall: power was centralized in the king but devolved to the furthest reaches of his domain, and even those without aristocratic backgrounds could, in theory, reach lofty governmental positions via a system of state-run examinations. Despite the Confucian social system, **Buddhism** continued to function as the state religion: the *Tripitaka Koreana* – a set of more than eighty thousand wooden blocks carved with doctrine – was completed in 1251, and now resides in Haeinsa temple. This was not the only remarkable example of Goryeo ingenuity: 1377 saw the creation of *Jikji*, the world's first book printed with moveable metal type (now in Paris, and the subject of a tug-of-war with the French government), and repeated refinements in the pottery industry saw Korean produce attain a level of quality only bettered in China. In fact, despite great efforts, some **pottery techniques** perfected in Goryeo times remain a mystery today, perhaps never to be replicated.

The wars

Though the Goryeo borders as set out by King Taejo are almost identical to those that surround the Korean peninsula today, they were witness to numerous skirmishes and invasions. Notable among these were the **Khitan Wars** of the tenth and eleventh centuries, fought against proto-Mongol groups of the Chinese Liao dynasty. The Khitan had defeated Balhae just before the fall of Silla, and were attempting to gain control over the whole of China as well as the Korean peninsula, but three great invasions failed to take Goryeo territory, and a peace treaty was eventually signed. Two centuries later came the **Mongol hordes**; the Korean peninsula was part of the Eurasian landmass, and therefore a target for the great Khaans. Under the rule of Ögedei Khaan,

1251	**c.1350**	**1377**
Completion of *Tripitaka Koreana*, a carved set of Buddhist scripture	Mongols driven away from Korean peninsula as their Chinese Yuan dynasty crumbles	Creation of *Jikji*, world's first book made with moveable metal type

the first invasion came in 1231, but it was not until the sixth campaign – which ended in 1248 – that Goryeo finally became a vassal state, a series of forced marriages effectively making its leaders part of the Mongol royal family. This lasted almost a century, before **King Gongmin** took advantage of a weakening Chinese–Mongol Yuan dynasty (founded by Kublai Khaan) to regain independence.

The Mongol annexation came at a great human cost, one echoed in a gradual worsening of Goryeo's economy and social structure. Gongmin made an attempt at reform, purging the top ranks of those he felt to be pro-Mongol, but this instilled fear of yet more change into the *yangban* elite: in conjunction with a series of decidedly non-Confucian love triangles and affairs with young boys, this was to lead to his murder. His young and unprepared successor, King U, was pushed into battle with the Chinese Ming dynasty; Joseon's General **Yi Seong-gye** led the charge, but fearful of losing his soldiers he stopped at the border and returned to Seoul, forcing the abdication of the king, and putting U's young son Chang on the throne. The General decided that he was not yet happy with the arrangement, and had both U and Chang executed (the latter just 8 years old at the time); after one more failed attempt at putting the right puppet king on the throne, he decided to take the mantle himself, and in 1392 declared himself **King Taejo**, the first leader of the Joseon dynasty.

The Joseon dynasty

The **Joseon era** (조선시대) started off much the same as the Goryeo dynasty had almost five centuries beforehand, with a militaristic king named **Taejo** on the throne, a name that translates as "The Grand Ancestor". Joseon was to last even longer, with a full 27 kings ruling from 1392 until the Japanese annexation in 1910. Taejo moved the capital from Kaesong to **Seoul**, and immediately set about entrenching his power with a series of mammoth projects; the first few years of his reign saw the erection of the wonderful palace of Gyeongbokgung, the ancestral shrines of Jongmyo and a gate-studded city wall of which were. His vision was quite astonishing – the chosen capital and its palace and shrine remain to this day, together with sections of the wall. More grand palaces would go up in due course, of which another four were at some point home to the royal throne.

From the start of the dynasty, Buddhism declined in power, and **Confucianism** permeated society yet further in its stead. Joseon's social system became even more hierarchical in nature, with the king and other royalty at the top, and the hereditary **yangban** class of scholars and aristocrats just beneath, followed by various levels of employment, with the servants and slaves at the bottom of the pile. All of these social strata were governed by heredity, but the *yangban* became ever more powerful as the dynasty progressed, gradually starting to undermine the power of the king. They were viewed as a world apart by the commoners, placed great emphasis on study and the arts. Only the *yangban* had access to such education as could foster literacy in a country that wrote with Chinese characters. In the 1440s **King Sejong** (ruled 1418–50) devised **hangeul**, a new and simple local script that all classes could read and write; the *yangban* were not fond of this, and it was banned at the beginning of the sixteenth century, lying largely dormant until resurrected by waves of nationalist sentiment created by the end of Japanese annexation in 1945 (see box, p.8).

1392	1443	1592
General Yi Seong-gye executes last Goryeo kings and declares himself King Taejo of new Joseon dynasty	Creation of *hangeul*, Korea's official script, a project of King Sejong	Beginning of Japanese invasions of Korea

The Japanese invasions

In 1592, under the command of feared warlord **Hideyoshi**, Japan set out to conquer the Ming dynasty, with China a stepping stone towards possible domination of the whole Asian continent. The Korean peninsula had the misfortune to be both in the way and loyal to the Ming, and after King Seonjo refused to allow Japanese troops safe passage, Hideyoshi mustered all his military's power and unloaded the lot at Korea. After two relatively peaceable centuries, the Joseon dynasty was ill-prepared for such an assault, and within a month the Japanese had eaten up most of the peninsula; the advance was halted with forces from a Ming dynasty keen to defend its territory. By the time of the second main wave of attacks in 1597, Korean **Admiral Yi Sun-shin** had been able to better prepare Korea's southern coastline, now protected by a number of fortresses. The Japanese found themselves losing battle after battle, undone by Admiral Yi's "**turtle ships**", vessels proclaimed by Koreans as the world's first armoured warships.

The "Hermit Kingdom"

The Japanese attacks – together with the dynastic transfer from Ming to Qing in China in the 1640s, which led to Joseon becoming a vassal state forced to spend substantial sums paying tribute to the emperors in Beijing – prompted Korea to turn inwards; it became known as the "**Hermit Kingdom**", one of which outsiders knew little, and saw even less. When a Dutch ship crashed off Jeju Island in 1653 en route to Japan, the survivors were kept prisoner for thirteen years; when they finally managed to escape, the accounts of **Hendrick Hamel** provided the Western world with one of its first windows into isolationist Korea.

The Dutch prisoners had entered a land in which corruption and factionalism were rife, one that achieved little social or economic stability until the rule of **King Yeongjo** (1724–76), who authorized a purge of crooked officials. In 1767, inside the grounds of Changgyeonggung palace, he forced Sado – his son and the country's crown prince – into a rice basket, locked the flap and left him inside to starve rather than let the country fall into his hands. Sado's son **Jeongjo** came to the throne on Yeongjo's death in 1776; he went on to become one of the most revered of Korea's kings, instigating top-to-bottom reform to wrench power from the *yangban* elite, and allowing for the creation of a small middle class. The lot of the poor man gradually improved.

The end of isolation

Following Japan's **opening up** to foreign trade in the 1860s (the "Meiji Restoration"), Korea found itself under pressure to do likewise, not just from the Japanese but from the United States and the more powerful European countries – warships were sent from around the globe to ensure agreement. Much of the activity occurred on and around the island of Ganghwado, just west of Seoul: the French occupied the isle but failed with advances on the mainland in 1866, their battle fought partly as retaliation for the murder of several of their missionaries in Korea. Five years later, and in the same location, the Americans also attempted to prise the country open to trade; though they failed, the third bout of gunboat diplomacy – this time by the Japanese in 1876 – resulted in the **Treaty of Ganghwa**, which dragged Korea into the global marketplace on unfair terms. From this point to the present day, Korea would be a ship largely steered along by foreign powers.

1598	1653	1767
Invasions finally snuffed out, thanks in part to Admiral Yi Sun-shin's turtle ships	Dutch ship crashes off Jeju coast; Hendrick Hamel finally escapes to give West first account of "Hermit Kingdom"	Murder of Crown Prince Sado by his father, King Yeongjo

Through means both political and economic, the Japanese underwent a gradual strengthening of their position in Korea. Local resentment boiled over into occasional riots and protests, and peaked in 1895 after the Japanese-orchestrated **murder of Empress Myeongseong** – "Queen Min", to the Japanese – in Gyeongbokgung palace. After this event, **King Gojong** (ruled 1863–1910) fled to the Russian embassy for protection; in 1897, when things had quietened down sufficiently, he moved into the nearby palace of Deoksugung, there to set up the short-lived **Empire of Korea**, a toothless administration under almost full Japanese control.

In 1902 Japan forged an alliance with the British Empire, recognizing British interests in China in return for British acknowledgment of Japanese interests in Korea. Sensing shifts in power, Russia at this point began moving its rooks into Korea, though they ran into the Japanese on the way. To avoid confrontation, Japan suggested that the two countries carve Korea up along the **38th parallel**, a line roughly bisecting the peninsula. Russia refused to accept, the two fought the **Russo-Japanese War** in 1904–05, and after its surprise victory Japan was in a position to occupy the peninsula outright. They were given tacit permission to do so in 1905 by US Secretary of State and President-to-be William Taft, who agreed in a secret meeting to accept Japanese domination of Korea if Japan would accept the American occupation of the Philippines. Korea became a Japanese protectorate that year, and Japan gradually ratcheted up its power on the peninsula before a final **outright annexation** in 1910. Joseon's kings had next to no say in the running of the country during its last quarter-century under dynastic succession, and it was with a whimper that the book closed on Korea's near two thousand years of unbroken regal rule.

The Japanese occupation

After the signing of the Annexation Treaty in 1910, the Japanese wasted no time in putting themselves in all the top posts in politics, banking, law and industry with their own personnel; despite the fact that they never represented more than four percent of the peninsular population, they came to control almost every sphere of its workings. Korea was but part of the Empire of Japan's dream of **continental hegemony**, and being the nearest stepping stone to the motherland, it was also the most heavily trampled on. While the Japanese went on to occupy most of Southeast Asia and large swathes of China, only in Korea did they have the time and leverage necessary to attempt a total annihilation of **national identity**. Some of the most powerful insults to national pride were hammered home early. The royal palace of **Gyeongbokgung** had all the Confucian principles observed in its construction shattered by the placing of a modern Japanese structure in its first holy courtyard, while nearby **Changgyeonggung** suddenly found itself home to a decidedly unroyal theme park and zoo. Korean currency, clothing and even the language itself were placed under ever stricter control, and thousands of local women as "**comfort women**". were forced into sexual slavery. Korean productivity grew, but much of this was also for Japan's benefit – within ten years, more than half of the country's rice was being sent across the sea.

The local populace, unsurprisingly, objected to this enforced servitude. In 1919, the **March 1st Movement** saw millions of Koreans take to the streets in a series of non-violent nationwide protests. A declaration of independence was read out in Seoul's Tapgol Park, an act followed by processions through the streets and the singing of the Korean national anthem. The Japanese police attempted to suppress the revolt through

1895	1910	1919
Murder of Queen Min by Japanese	Japanese Empire annexes Korea	Mass protests against Japanese rule on March 1st

force; around seven thousand died in the months of resistance demonstrations that followed. The result, however, was a marked change of Japanese policy towards Korea, with Saito Makoto (the Admiral in charge of quelling the chaos) agreeing to lift the bans on Korean radio, printed matter and the creation of organizations, and promoting harmony rather than pushing the militarist line.

The pendulum swung back towards oppression on the approach to World War II. In the late 1930s, Japan began forcing Koreans to worship at Shinto shrines, speak in Japanese and even adopt a Japanese name (a practice known as *soshi-kaimei*), all helped by local **collaborators** (*chinilpa*). Thousands of these went across to Japan, but though many were there to do business and strengthen imperial ties, most were simply squeezed out of Korea by Japanese land confiscations.

The end of annexation

Throughout the remainder of the occupation period, the **Korean government-in-exile** had been forced ever further west from China's eastern seaboard, eventually landing near the Tibetan plateau in the Sichuanese city of Chongqing. Modern Korean museums and history books extol the achievements of what was, in reality, a largely toothless group. In doing this they gloss over the fundamental reason for Korea's independence: the **American A-bombs** that fell on Hiroshima and Nagasaki, thereby ending both World War II and the Empire of Japan itself. With Tokyo busy elsewhere, Seoul was little affected by the war: the main change in city life was the conscription of tens of thousands of Korean men, many of whom never returned. An even greater number of Koreans had moved to Japan prior to the war. Some, of course, were collaborators fearful of reprisals should they head home, but the majority were simply forced out of their impoverished homeland by the confiscation of their land. Many of these Korean families remain in Japan today, and are referred to there as "**Zainichi Koreans**".

The Korean War

Known to many as the "**Forgotten War**", sandwiched as it was between World War II and the war in Vietnam, the Korean conflict was one of the twentieth century's greatest tragedies. The impoverished peninsula had already been pushed to the back of the global mind during World War II; the land was under Japanese control, but the Allied forces had developed no plans for its future should the war be won. In fact, at the close of the war American Secretary of State Edward Stettinius had to be told in a meeting where Korea actually was. It was only when the **Soviet Union** sent troops into Korea in 1945 that consideration was given to the country's postwar life. During an emergency meeting on August 10, 1945, officials and high-rankers (including eventual Secretary of State Dean Rusk), with no in-depth knowledge of the peninsula, sat with a map and a pencil and scratched a line across the **38th parallel** – a simple solution, but one that was to have grave repercussions for Korea.

The build-up to war

With World War II rapidly developing into the **Cold War**, Soviet forces occupied the northern half of the peninsula, Americans the south. Both countries imposed their own social, political and economic norms on the Koreans under their control, thereby

1945	1948
American bombing of Hiroshima and Nagasaki effectively ends Japanese annexation	Two separate Korean republics declared, one either side of the 38th parallel: to the south the Republic of Korea; to the north the Democratic People's Republic of Korea

creating two de facto states that refused to recognize each other, the two diametrically opposed in ideology. The **Republic of Korea** (now more commonly referred to as "South Korea") declared independence on August 15, 1948, exactly three years after liberation from the Japanese, and the **Democratic People's Republic of Korea** (now better known as "North Korea") followed suit just over three weeks later. The US installed a South Korean leader favourable to them, selecting **Syngman Rhee** (ironically, born in what is now North Korea), who had degrees from American universities. Stalin chose the much younger **Kim Il-sung**, who like Rhee had been in exile for much of the Japanese occupation. The foreign forces withdrew, and the two Koreas were left to their own devices, each hellbent on unifying the peninsula by absorbing the opposing half; inevitably, locals were forced into a polarization of opinion, one that split friends and even families apart. Kim wanted to wade into war immediately, and Stalin turned down two requests for approval of such an action. The third time, for reasons that remain open to conjecture, he gave the nod.

War breaks out

Nobody knows for sure exactly how the Korean War started. Or, rather, everyone does: the other side attacked first. The South Korean line is that on June 25, 1950, troops from the northern **Korean People's Army** (KPA) burst across the 38th parallel, then little more than a roll of tape. The DPRK itself claims that it was the south that started the war. Indeed, both sides had started smaller conflicts along the line on several occasions, but declassified Soviet information shows that the main battle was kicked off by the North. With the southern forces substantially ill-equipped in comparison, Seoul fell just three days later, but they were soon aided by a sixteen-nation coalition fighting under the **United Nations** banner. The vast majority of troops were from the United States, but additional forces arrived from Britain, Canada, Australia, the Philippines, Turkey, the Netherlands, France, New Zealand, Thailand, Ethiopia, Greece, Colombia, Belgium, South Africa and Luxembourg; other countries provided non-combative support.

Within three months, the KPA had hemmed the United Nations Command (UNC) into the far southeast of the country, behind a short line of control that became known as the **Pusan Perimeter**, a boundary surrounding the (now re-romanized) city of Busan. Though the KPA held most of the peninsula, American general Douglas MacArthur identified a weak logistical spine and poor supply lines as their Achilles heel, and ordered amphibious landings behind enemy lines at **Incheon**, just west of Seoul, in an attempt to cut off Northern supplies. The ambitious plan worked to perfection, and UNC forces pushed north way beyond the 38th parallel, reaching sections of the Chinese border within six weeks.

At this stage, with the battle seemingly won, the **Chinese** entered the fight and ordered almost a million troops into North Korea; with their help, the KPA were able to push back past the 38th parallel. The UNC made one more thrust north in early 1951, and after six months the two sides ended up pretty much where they started. The lines of the conflict settled around the 38th parallel, near what was to become the **Demilitarized Zone**, but the fighting did not end for well over two years, until the signing of an armistice agreement on July 27, 1953. North Korea, China and the United Nations Command signed the document, but South Korea refused to do likewise, meaning that the war is still technically being fought today.

1950	1959	1962
Start of Korean War, in which over three million are killed	Founding of first national taekwondo body	General Park Chung-hee assumes power in coup and a course of rapid industrialization in South Korea

A land in ruins

In effect, both sides lost the Korean War, as neither had achieved the aims espoused at the outset. Seoul had fallen four times – twice to each side – and Korea's population was literally decimated, with over three million killed, wounded or missing over the course of the war; to this can be added around half a million UNC troops, and what may well be over a million Chinese. Had the war been "contained" and brought to an end when the line of control stabilized in early 1951, these figures would have been far lower. The war split thousands of families; in addition to the confusion created by a front line that yo-yoed up and down the land, people were forced to switch sides to avoid starvation or torture, or to stay in contact with family members. Though the course of the battle and its aftermath were fairly straightforward, propaganda clouded many of the more basic details, and the war was largely forgotten by the West. For all the coverage of Vietnam, few know that a far greater amount of **napalm** fell on North Korea, a much more "suitable" target for the material thanks to its greater number of large urban areas; also kept quiet is how close **nuclear weapons** were to being used in the conflict. After the war, General MacArthur was quoted as saying that he "would have dropped between thirty and fifty atomic bombs... strung across the neck of Manchuria". Since the end of the war there have been innumerable accounts of atrocities committed by both sides, many detailing beatings, torture and the unlawful murder of prisoners of war, others documenting the slaughter of entire villages. Korea lay in ruins, yet two countries were slowly able to emerge from the ashes.

To the present day

Considering its state after the war, South Korea's transformation is nothing short of astonishing. A rapid phase of industrialization, one often referred to as the "**Economic Miracle**" in the West, saw it become one of Asia's most ferocious financial tigers, and Seoul morph from battle-scarred wasteland into one of the world's largest and most dynamic cities. The country's GDP-per-head shot up from under US$100 in 1963 to almost US$30,000 in 2010. Thanks in large part to the bullishness of large conglomerates (known as *jaebeol*) such as Samsung, Hyundai and LG, it now sits proudly on the cusp of the world's ten most powerful economies. And, since flinging off its autocratic strait in the 1980s, it developed sufficiently to be selected to host some of the world's most high-profile events: the **Olympics** in 1988, the football **World Cup** in 2002 and the G20 Summit in 2010.

Problematic beginnings

The **postwar period** proved extremely difficult for South Korea: cities had been laid to waste and families torn apart, accusations and recriminations were rife, and everyone knew that hostilities with the North could resume at any moment. American-educated Syngman Rhee, who had been selected as president before the war, ruled in an

The following information refers to South Korean history after the Korean War. For details on North Korean events and information on North-South relations since the conflict, see pp.323–327.

1980	**1988**	**1994**
Massacre of student protestors in Gwangju; Seoul awarded Olympics the following year	Seoul hosts Olympic Games	North Korean leader Kim Il-sung dies; his son Kim Jong-il assumes leadership

increasingly autocratic manner, making constitutional amendments to stay in power and purging parliament of anyone opposed to his policies. In 1960 disgruntled students led the **April 19 Movement** against his rule, and after being toppled in a coup he was forced into exile, choosing Hawaii as his new home. One dictator was swiftly replaced with another: Yun Bo-seon came to office as a puppet of military general **Park Chung-hee**, who then swiftly engineered a coup and took the presidency himself in 1962. To an even greater degree than Rhee before him, Park's name became synonymous with corruption, dictatorship and the flouting of human rights – thousands were jailed merely for daring to criticize his rule. To his credit, Park introduced the economic reforms that allowed his country to push forward – until the mid-1970s, the South Korean economy actually lagged behind that of North Korea – and the country made great advances in automotive, electronic, heavy and chemical industries. This was, however, achieved at a cost, since Korean tradition largely went out of the window in favour of bare economic progress. These policies were a major factor behind the **loss of Korea's traditional buildings**: Seoul has almost none left.

Park's authoritarian rule continued to ruffle feathers around the country, and the danger from the North had far from subsided – Park was the subject, and Seoul the scene, of two failed **assassination** attempts by North Korean agents. It was, however, members of his own intelligence service who gunned him down in 1979, claiming that he was "an insurmountable obstacle to democratic reform". Those responsible were hanged the following year. Park's eventual successor, **Chun Doo-hwan**, was also from the southeast of the country, and the resultant Seoul-Gyeongsang tangent of power saw those parts of the country developing rapidly, while others languished far behind. The arrest of liberal southwestern politician Kim Dae-jung, as well as the botched trials following the assassination of Park Chung-hee, was a catalyst for mass uprisings across the land, though mainly concentrated in Jeju Island and the Jeolla provinces. These culminated in the **Gwangju Massacre** of May 1980, where over two hundred civilians died after their protest was crushed by the military.

The Olympic legacy

Incredibly, just one year after the massacre, Seoul was given the rights to host the **1988 Summer Olympics**: some estimates say the death count at Gwangju was similar to the Tiananmen Square massacre, but it's hard to imagine Beijing being granted a similar honour the year after those events. Although the Olympic plan had been Park Chung-hee's, Chun Doo-hwan followed it through in an apparent attempt to seek international recognition. Though he may have regarded the 1981 Olympic vote as a tacit global nod of acceptance, the strategy backfired when the country was thrust into the spotlight. Partly as a result of this increased attention, Korea's first free elections were held in 1987, with **Roh Tae-woo** taking the helm. During the same period Korean conglomerates, known as the *jaebeol*, were spreading their financial arms around the world. Korea's aggressive, debt-funded expansion only worsened the effect of the Asian Currency Crisis on the country in 1997.

In 1998, once-condemned liberal activist **Kim Dae-jung** completed a remarkable turnaround by being appointed president himself. The first South Korean leader to favour a peaceable reunification of the peninsula, he wasted no time in kicking off his **"Sunshine Policy"** of reconciliation with the North; some minor industrial

2002	2010	2011
Co-hosting of football's World Cup	North Korea sinks frigate from the South, and shells Yeonpyeongdo	North Korean leader Kim Jong-il dies; his son Kim Jong-un assumes leadership

projects were outsourced across the border, and new Seoul-funded factories were built around the city of Kaesong, just north of the DMZ. In 2000, after an historic Pyongyang summit with North Korean leader Kim Jong-il, he was awarded the **Nobel Peace Prize**.

Into the twenty-first century

South Korea's international reputation was further enhanced by the hugely successful co-hosting of the **2002 World Cup** with Japan. However, that same year a series of incidents gave rise to something of an anti-American (and, by extension, anti-Western) sentiment: most significant was the accidental killing of two local schoolgirls by an American armoured vehicle, which led to large protests against the US military presence. Late that year, **Roh Moo-hyun** was elected president on a slightly anti-American ticket; however, the fact that he sent Korean troops to Iraq so soon after taking office in early 2003 made him instantly unpopular, and he committed suicide in 2009, following a bribery scandal.

Roh's presidency coincided with **Lee Myung-bak**'s tenure as mayor of Seoul. In 2003, Lee announced plans to gentrify the **Cheonggyecheon** creek in the capital; the burden on local taxpayers made this a deeply unpopular project, though it has come to be loved by the public since. Lee was elected president in 2008, but as with Roh before him, there were almost immediate protests against his rule, this time thanks to a beef trade agreement made with the USA. Fears that mad cow disease would be imported to

---

THE SINKING OF THE CHEONAN, AND THE YEONPYEONGDO ATTACKS

On March 26, 2010, the **Cheonan**, a South Korean naval vessel, sank in the waters off Baengnyeongdo, killing 46 of its crew of just over one hundred, and claiming the life of one rescue worker. With the incident taking place in waters so close to the North Korean border, there was immediate worldwide suspicion that Pyongyang was behind the attack; Seoul refused to be drawn however, choosing instead to wait for the results of a full investigation. South Korean **conspiracy theorists** initially pointed fingers at an American submarine that had "gone missing", though such rumours were hurriedly put to bed when the sub resurfaced a few days later on the other side of the world. One rumour that refused to go away was that the attack may have been an internal show of force from **Kim Jong-un**, who was at the time being groomed for leadership in North Korea. It was suggested that Kim may have used the incident to prove himself to the country's military leadership, who were known to be unhappy with a dynastic transfer of power from his father, Kim Jong-il. Two months after the incident, an international team found that the *Cheonan* was sunk by a torpedo, most likely fired by a North Korean vessel.

Pyongyang continues to deny responsibility for the sinking of the *Cheonan*, but the attacks of November 23, 2010 were more directly attributable to North Korea. Almost two hundred shells and rockets were fired from North Korea's southern coast at the South Korean island of **Yeonpyeongdo**, in response to Seoul's refusal to halt a military training exercise in nearby waters. The Northern shelling appeared to be indiscriminate, killing two civilians and two soldiers from the South, which responded in kind with howitzers of its own. This was one of the most serious cross-border incidents since the Korean War, with many southerners formerly sympathetic to the North suddenly favouring a powerful military response to any future attacks.

2012	2014
Korea wins World Alphabet Olympics for the second time; declared eternal champion (see p.366)	Sinking of the *Sewol* ferry; hundreds of schoolchildren perish

this beef-loving land resulted in mass protests around the city, and **rioting** around the land; in Seoul, one man died after setting fire to himself in protest.

These political protests were small-fry compared to the **North Korean attacks** of 2010, in which a South Korean island was shelled, and a naval vessel sunk (see box opposite); cross-border relations have been frosty ever since. In 2014, South Korea's own internal politics were given a shake after the sinking of the *Sewol* (see box, p.235), a disturbingly tragic incident in which almost three hundred died – the vast majority of school age. The issue turned into a political hot potato, with opposition parties stoking widespread protests against president **Park Geun-hye**.

Religion

Korea has a long and fascinating religious history, one that has informed local life to the present day. Strewn with temples, the country is most closely identified with Buddhism, though Christianity actually has a greater number of followers. The rise of the latter is particularly interesting when laid over Korea's largely Confucian mindset, which is often diametrically opposed to Christian ideals and beliefs – priests and pastors preach equality at Sunday service but, outside church, relative age still governs many forms of social interaction, and women remain inferior to men.

Buddhism

Buddhism is a religion deriving from the teachings of the Buddha; also known as the Siddhartha Gautama or Sakyamuni, he lived in India sometime between the fourth and sixth centuries BC. Although there are two main schools of thought and several smaller ones, Buddhist philosophy revolves around the precept that karma, rebirth and suffering are intrinsic elements of existence, but that the cycle of birth and death can be escaped on what is known as the "Noble Eightfold Path" to nirvana.

An import from China (which had in turn imported it from the Indian subcontinent), Buddhism arrived in Korea at the beginning of the Three Kingdoms period. **Goguryeo** and **Baekje** adopted it at around the same time, in the last decades of the fourth century: Goguryeo king Sosurim accepted Buddhism almost as soon as the first Chinese monks touched down in 372, while Baekje king Chimnyu adopted it after taking the throne in 384. The **Silla** kings were less impressed by the creed, but a major change in regal thought occurred in 527 after an interesting episode involving an official who had decided to switch to Buddhism. He was to be beheaded for his beliefs, and with his final few gasps swore to the king that his blood would not be red, but a milky white; his promise was true, and the king soon chose Buddhism as his state religion.

Even in China, Buddhism was at this point in something of an embryonic phase, and Korean monks took the opportunity to develop the **Mahayana** style by ironing out what they saw to be inconsistencies in the doctrine. Disagreements followed, leading to the creation of several **sects**, of which the **Jogye** order is by far the largest, covering about ninety percent of Korea's Buddhists; other notable sects include **Seon**, largely known in the West as Zen, the Japanese translation, and **Cheontae**, which is better known under its Chinese name of Tiantai.

Ornate **temples** sprang up all over the peninsula during the **Unified Silla** period but, though Buddhism remained the state religion throughout the **Goryeo** era, the rise of Confucianism squeezed it during **Joseon** times. Monks were treated with scant respect and temples were largely removed from the main cities (thus there are relatively few in Seoul, the Joseon capital), but though the religion was repressed, it never came close to evaporating entirely. Further troubles were to come during the **Japanese occupation period**, during the latter years of which many Koreans were forced to worship at Shinto shrines. Mercifully, although many of the temples that weren't closed by the Japanese were burnt down in the Korean War that followed the Japanese occupation, reconstruction programmes have been so comprehensive that in most Korean cities, you will seldom be more than a walk away from an active temple.

Temples

Korea's many **temples** are some of the most visually appealing places in the country. Most run along a similar design scheme: on entry to the temple complex you'll pass through the *iljumun* (일주문), or "first gate", then the *cheonwangmun* (천왕문). The latter almost always contains **four large guardians**, two menacing figures towering on each side of the dividing walkway; these control the four heavens and provide guidance to those with a righteous heart.

The central building of a Korean temple is the **main hall**, or *daeungjeon* (대웅전). Initially, it was only Sakyamuni – the historical Buddha – who was enshrined here, but this was soon flanked on left and right by *bodhisattvas* (a term for those who have reached nirvana). Most of these halls have doors at the front, which are usually only for elder monks; novices, and visiting foreigners, use side entrances. Among the many other halls that you may find on the complex are the *daejeokgwangjeon* (대적광전), the hall of the Vairocana Buddha; *gwaneumjeon* (관음전), a hall for the Bodhisattva of Compassion; *geungnakjeon* (극락전), the Nirvana Hall and home to the celestial Amitabha Buddha; *mireukjeon* (미륵전), the hall of the future Maitreya Buddha; and *nahanjeon* (나한전), the hall of disciples. Some also feature the *palsangjeon* (팔상전), a hall featuring **eight paintings** detailing the life of the Sakyamuni Buddha, though these are more often found on the outside of another hall.

Somewhere in the complex you'll find the *beomjonggak* (범종각), a "**bell pavilion**" containing instruments to awaken the four sentient beings: a drum for land animals, a wooden fish for the water-borne, a bronze gong for creatures of the air, and a large bell for monks who have slept in. The bell itself can sometimes weigh upwards of twenty tonnes, and the best will have an information board telling you how far away they can be heard if you were to strike them lightly with your fist. Needless to say, you shouldn't test these contentions.

Confucianism

Like Buddhism, **Confucian thought** made its way across the sea from China. The exact date remains a mystery, but it seems that it first spread to Korea at the beginning of the Three Kingdoms era. Although Confucianism can't be classified as a religion – there's no central figure of worship, or concept of an afterlife – it is used as means of self-cultivation, and a guide to "proper" conduct, particularly the showing of respect for those higher up the social hierarchy. For centuries it co-existed with the state religion, informing not only political thought but also national ethics, and in many ways it still governs the Korean way of life today. Central to the concept are the **Five Moral Disciplines** of human-to-human conduct, namely ruler to subject, father to son, husband to wife, elder to younger and friend to friend.

During the Three Kingdoms period, the concepts of filial piety began to permeate Korean life, with adherence to the rules gradually taking the form of ceremonial rites. In the Silla kingdom there developed a "**bone rank**" system used to segregate social strata, one that was to increase in rigidity until the Joseon era. This was essentially a caste system, one that governed almost every sphere of local life – each "level" of society would have strict limits placed on what they could achieve, the size of their dwelling, who they could marry and even what colours they were allowed to wear.

At the dawn of the Joseon dynasty in 1392, King Taejo had the **Jongmyo shrines** built in central Seoul, and for centuries afterwards, ruling kings would venerate their ancestors here in regular ceremonies. At this time, Confucianism truly took hold, with numerous **academies** (*hyanggyo*) built around the country at which students from the elite *yangban* classes would wade through wave after wave of punishing examinations on their way to senior governmental posts. Buddhism had been on the decline for some time, with Confucian scholars arguing that making appeals to gods unseen had a detrimental effect on the national psyche, and that building ornate temples absorbed funds too readily. Some, in fact, began to clamour for the burning of those temples, as well as the murder of monks. As with other beliefs, some followers violated the core principles for their own ends and, despite the birth of great neo-Confucian philosophers such as **Yi-Yi** and **Toegye**, enforced slavery and servitude meant that the lot of those at the lower caste levels changed little over the centuries.

Confucianism today

It's often said that Korea remains the **most Confucian** of all the world's societies. In addition to several remaining academies and shrines – there's one of the latter at Inwangsan, just west of Gyeongbokgung – colourful ancestral ceremonies take place each year at Jongmyo in Seoul. The impact of Confucianism on everyday life is also clear: on getting to know a local, you'll generally be asked a series of questions both direct and indirect (particularly with regard to age, marriage, education and employment), the answers to which will be used to file you into conceptual pigeonholes. Though foreigners are treated somewhat differently, this world-view is the main reason why locals see nothing wrong in barging strangers out of the way on the

---

VILLAGE PRACTICES

Mountain rites By far the most common form of spirit worship in Korea, the *sansinje* remains a part of annual village festivals all across the country. The **Dano festival** (see box, p.153) in Gangneung – the biggest traditional event in the land – actually starts off with one of these in honour of General Kim Yu-sin, spearhead of the Silla campaigns that resulted in the unification of the country. Near Samcheok, just down the way, groups head to the hills for shamanistic *gut* ceremonies and animal exorcisms.

Rites to sea spirits Though these rites are held at points all along Korea's coastline, they are most numerous in Gangwon province on the east, particularly around the city of Gangneung. The spirit is often the ghost of a local female who perished tragically, often without having married (see "Phallicism" below); when finally placated by ceremonies and sacrifices, she becomes a patron of the village in question. One popular Gangwon tale regards a man who was prompted in a dream to rescue a travelling woman from a nearby islet; all he found on arrival was a basket containing the woman's portrait, and after carrying it home his village was blessed with a bumper crop. Villagers continue to pay respects to this day.

Rites to tree spirits Korea has many trees dating back five centuries or more, so it's understandable that many local Korean myths – including the Dangun legend, which details Korea's creation – include a sacred tree somewhere along the way. Trees of such repute are treated with enormous respect, as even to snap a twig is said to invoke a punishment of some kind from the spirit that lives within.

Rites to rock spirits As you make your way around Korea, you'll see English-language pamphlets pointing you towards rocks that are said to resemble turtles, tigers, sea dragons and the like. While some require an almost superhuman stretch of the imagination, many of these are still the subject of regular ceremonies for the spirits that are said to reside within the rock. You'll also see man-made stone mounds in and around certain temples, most notably wonderful **Tapsa** in Maisan Provincial Park (see p.250), which is surrounded by spires of rock that were all stacked by just one man.

Jangseung Having long served a range of purposes from protector to boundary marker, these carved wooden sticks may have jovial faces or snarling mouths full of blocky, painted teeth. You'll see the real things at the entrance to traditional villages – and replicas outside many traditional restaurants.

Phallicism Anyone who has seen the mysterious but rather phallic *hareubang* statues on beautiful Jeju Island will know that willy worship has long been popular in Korea. This usually takes the form of fertility rites, but the reasoning for some ceremonies is not so predictable: on a village south of Samcheok in Gangwon province once lived a young bride-to-be who was swept from the shore in a powerful storm. Her enraged spirit chased the fish from the seas until it was placated by a carved wooden penis; hundreds of the things now rise from the ground in the nearby **Penis Park** (see p.161).

street or showing no mercy on the road – no introduction has been made, and without knowledge of the "proper" behaviour in such a situation no moves are made towards showing respect.

Among those who do know each other, it's easy to find **Confucian traits**: women are still seen as inferior to men (their salary continues to lag far behind, and they're usually expected to quit their job on having a child, never to return to the workplace); the boss or highest earner will usually pay after a group meal; family values remain high; and paper qualifications from reputable universities carry more weight than actual intelligence. Also notable is **bungsu**, a concept that involves the moving of ancestral grave sites. Perhaps the most high-profile examples of corpse-shifting have been before general elections. After Kim Dae-jung lost the elections in 1987 and 1992, he decided to move the graves of his ancestors to more auspicious locations, and he duly won the next election in 1998. All that said, Confucian ideas are slowly being eroded as westernization continues to encroach, particularly as the number of Christians continues to grow.

Christianity

Practised by well over a quarter of the population, **Christianity** is now Korea's leading religion by number of worshippers, having surpassed Buddhism at the start of the twenty-first century. Surprisingly, the religion has been on the peninsula since the end of the eighteenth century, having been brought across the waters by missionaries from various European empires. At the time, the Confucian *yangban* in charge were fearful of change, hardly surprising considering how far apart the fundamental beliefs of the two creeds are. Christianity's refusal to perform ancestral rites eventually led to its repression, and hundreds of Christians were **martyred** in the 1870s and 1880s. A number of French missionaries were also murdered in this period, before Korea was forcefully opened up for trade. The numbers of Christians have been growing ever since, the majority now belonging to the Presbyterian, Catholic or Methodist churches.

Churches tend to be monstrous concrete edifices (many of them sporting rather frightening red neon crosses), and some are huge, with room for thousands of worshippers. In fact, Seoul's mini-island of Yeouido officially has the **largest church in the world**, with 170 pastors and over 100,000 registered deacons.

Film

For all of its efforts in finance, electronics and promoting its food and tradition, it's Korea's film industry that has had the most success in pushing the country as a global brand. While Korean horror flicks have developed an international cult following, and a number of esteemed directors have set international film festivals abuzz, special mention must also be made of the locally produced TV dramas that have caught on like wildfire across Asia. Like many of the movies, these are highly melodramatic offerings that don't seek to play on the heartstrings so much as power-chord the merry hell out of them. All of these form part of the Hallyeo movement, a "New Wave" of Korean production that has been in motion since cinematic restrictions were lifted in the 1980s. In the reviews that follow, films marked with a ★ are particularly recommended.

The beginnings

Film was first introduced to Korea at the very end of the **nineteenth century**; in 1899, just after making Korea's first-ever telephone call, King Gojong was shown a short documentary about the country put together by American traveller Burton Holmes, and Seoul's first cinema was opened shortly afterwards. Unfortunately, few examples from the prewar **silent era** have made it onto the international market; Korean produce was also scaled down, and at one point cut off entirely, during the Japanese occupation (1910–45). After **World War II**, and the end of annexation, there followed a short burst of films – many of which, understandably, had freedom as a central concept – but this was brought to an abrupt halt by the outbreak of the **Korean War** in 1950.

After the Korean War

Following the war, the film industries of the two Koreas developed separately; leaders on both sides saw movies as a hugely useful **propaganda tool**, and made immediate efforts to revive local cinema – see the box opposite for the continuation of the North Korean story. In the south, President Syngman Rhee conferred tax-exempt status on moviemakers, who got busy with works looking back at the misery of wartime and the occupation, and forward to a rosy future for non-Communist Korea. By the end of the 1950s, annual movie output had reached triple figures, the most popular being watched by millions, but the accession of **Park Chung-hee** to president in 1961 brought an end to what passed for cinematic freedom. In addition to the censorship and hard-fisted control over local produce, foreign films were vetted for approval and placed under a strict quota system, elements of which remained until 2006. As Park's rule grew ever more dictatorial, he inaugurated a short-lived era of "**governmental policy**" films; these were hugely unpopular, and cinema attendance dropped sharply. After Park's death, democratization and the gradual relaxation of restrictions gave rise to the Hallyeo movement.

The Hallyeo "New Wave"

Throughout the periods of governmental suppression, a clutch of talented directors were forced to keep their best ideas under wraps, or else be very clever about putting

CINEMA IN NORTH KOREA

Cinema is big business in **North Korea**: Kim Jong-il was pouring funds into the industry for decades before he became leader of the country, and in 1978 even went so far as to organize the kidnapping of **Shin Sang-ok** – a prominent South Korean director – in an effort to improve the quality of local produce. North Korea produces some of the world's most distinctive films; unfortunately, this niche in global cinema has remained almost entirely unexplored by the outside world. A few films have started to trickle onto the **international market**; to buy, go to ⓦ north-korea-books.com. The themes stick rigidly to brave North Korean resistance during the Korean War and the Japanese occupation, depicting Americans as unspeakably evil and South Koreans as their puppets.

them forward. With the loosening of the lid in the 1980s, the highest skilled came to the fore and finally gave Korea exposure in the West; foremost among these was **Im Kwon-taek**, a maverick who shrugged off his role as a creator of commercial quota-fillers to unleash striking new works on the world. The South Korean government continued to provide funding for films until the 1999 release of *Swiri*, the country's first fully independent film. Since then the industry has reached an ever-greater international audience, and a number of Korean directors such as **Kim Ki-duk** and **Park Chan-wook** are now globally acclaimed. The country's **dramas** have arguably been even more successful than its movies, though with an appeal largely limited to the Asian continent.

COMEDY

My Sassy Girl (2001) A mega-hit from Tokyo to Taipei, this tale doesn't add too much to the rom-com genre, but one scene was almost entirely responsible for a spate of high-school-themed club nights. It's worth watching, as is *My Tutor Friend*, a follow-up that hits most of the same buttons.

The President's Last Bang (2005) Korea has long been crying out for satire, particularly something to inject a little fun into its turgid political reportage, and this hits the nail squarely on the head (as demonstrated by the lawsuit that followed). It's based on a true story, namely the assassination of president Park Chung-hee in 1979; the portrayal of Park as something of a Japanese-sympathetic playboy certainly ruffled a few feathers.

DRAMA

3-Iron (2004) Korean movies about eccentric loners are ten a penny. In this Kim Ki-duk hit, the protagonist is a delivery boy who breaks into and then polishes up the houses that he knows to be empty. When he happens across one that's still home to a lonely girl, the couple begin a strange kind of silent relationship. Superbly acted, and an interesting take on the traditional love story.

The Crucible (2011) This is an account of physical sexual abuse in a school for the deaf, based on real-life occurrences which took place in Gwangju in the early 2000s – of six teachers found guilty, four were let off, and the other two were in jail for under a year. The public reaction which followed this story's journey to the big screen was to pave the way for a reform of the relevant legislation.

The Man From Nowhere (2010) A box-office hit in Korea, this tells the story of a recluse who has his only friend – a young neighbour – taken away from him as a result of gang warfare... cue lots of blood as the protagonist battles his way through said gangs.

Samaritan Girl (2004) Kim Ki-duk film with a storyline that's less explicit and far deeper than its premise may suggest. Two teenage girls looking to save up for a trip to Europe enter the murky world of prostitution, one sleeping with the clients, the other managing the affairs while keeping an eye out for the cops. Inevitably, things don't quite go according to plan.

★**Secret Sunshine** (2007) It's rare for government ministers to go into movie making, but so successful was Lee Chang-dong's effort that his film even won an award at Cannes. Focused on a woman entering middle age, it's a well-delivered interpretation of human suffering.

Spring, Summer, Fall, Winter... and Spring (2003) With just one set – a monastery in the middle of a remote lake – and a small cast, Kim Ki-duk somehow spins together a necessarily slow but undeniably beautiful allegory of human nature, one that relays the life of a boy nurtured to manhood by a reclusive monk.

HISTORY AND WAR

Chihwaseon (2002) Sometimes going under the title *Painted Fire*, this beautifully shot tale of Jang Seung-eop – a nineteenth-century Seoulite painter best known by his pen name Owon – won the Best Director award at Cannes for Im Kwon-taek, a maverick who had been around for decades but was previously ignored on the international stage.

Joint Security Area (2000) Any Korean film about the DMZ is worth a look, as is anything by acclaimed director Park Chan-wook. Here, two North Korean soldiers are killed in the DMZ; like *Memento* (which, incidentally, came out the following year), the story plays backwards, revealing the lead-up piece by piece.

Ode to my Father (2014) A look at Korea from the 1950s to the present day, through the eyes of an ordinary fella who gets caught up in the Korean and Vietnamese wars. The film was criticized by some for glorifying the country's dictatorial past; the fact that it was a huge hit demonstrates the local appetite for such selective nostalgia, and the politics that continue to divide South Korea.

Shiri (1999) Also known as *Swiri*, this was a landmark film in Korean cinema, marking the dawn of a Hollywood style long suppressed by the government. The mix of explosions and loud music is not of as much interest to foreigners as it is to Koreans, but the plot – South Korean cops hunt down a North Korean sniper girl – is interesting enough. The girl was played by Yunjin Kim, who later found fame on the American TV series *Lost*.

Silmido (2003) Loosely based on events in the 1960s, which saw South Korean operatives receive secret training on the island of Silmido to assassinate North Korean leader Kim Il-sung. The film broke Korean box office records, and provides a fascinating depiction of the tensions of the time.

★**The Admiral: Roaring Currents** (2014) The biggest selling film of all time in Korea, this big-budget blockbuster focuses on the attempts of Admiral Yi Sun-shin – one of the country's foremost national heroes (see box, p.224) – to rebuff a Japanese attack in the 1590s.

★**The King and the Clown** (2005) A period drama with homosexual undercurrents, this was an unexpected smash hit at the box office. Set during the reign of King Yeonsan – whose short rule began in 1494 – it tells of a pair of street entertainers who find themselves in Seoul's royal court. One of them fosters an ever-closer relationship with the king.

Welcome to Dongmakgol (2005) Too twee for some, but heart-warming to others and beautifully shot to boot, this tells of a motley assortment of American, South Korean and North Korean combatants from the Korean War who somehow end up in the same village, among people unaware not only of the conflict raging around them but of warfare in general.

THRILLERS AND HORROR

The Host (2006) The tranquil life of a riverside merchant is blown to smithereens when the formaldehyde disposed into the river by the American military creates a ferocious underwater creature. This comic thriller smashed box office records in Korea; the international reception was nowhere near as fervent, but it's worth a look nonetheless.

The Isle (2001) In the middle of a lake, a mute woman rents out small floating huts to men looking to escape city life for a while, sometimes selling herself to them, sometimes murdering them. This was the film that pushed Kim Ki-duk's unique style onto the world stage, a dark love story with a couple of nasty surprises.

Oldboy (2003) Part of Park Chan-wook's acclaimed "Vengeance Trilogy", this was the first Korean film to win big at Cannes, a dark and violent tale of a businessman mysteriously arrested after a night out, imprisoned for years then given three days to discover why he was put away and to hunt down those responsible.

★**A Tale of Two Sisters** (2003) This chiller seeks to petrify viewers not with lashings of ultra-violence but with that which cannot be seen. An adaptation of a Joseon-era folk story, it keeps its audience guessing, and some will find it Korea's best take on the horror genre.

Thirst (2009) Winner of the Jury Prize at Cannes, this was director Park Chan-wook's follow-up to his hugely successful Vengeance Trilogy. It's a romantic horror in which a priest, in love with his friend's wife, turns into a vampire – an odd concept that shouldn't work, but somehow Park pulls it off.

NORTH KOREA

A State of Mind (2004) On the surface, this is a documentary about two young girls training for the Arirang Mass Games in Pyongyang, but it amounts to a first-ever stab at a genuine portrayal of the average life of today's North Koreans. It was evidently a success: after the film was shown on DPRK state TV, locals complained that it was "dull", having merely filmed them going about their daily lives; little did they know how compelling this kind of realistic reportage is to the average foreign viewer.

★**Comrade Kim Goes Flying** (2012) Produced and directed by Nick Bonner of Koryo Tours fame (see p.315), this was the first foreign film to be made in North Korea, receiving the personal approval of noted cinephile Kim Jong-il. In the Korean language and with an all DPRK-cast, this light-hearted "commie rom-com" tells the story of an ambitious young trapeze artist.

Crossing the Line (2006) This fascinating documentary is the world's only peek inside the mind of "Comrade Joe" – James Joseph Dresnok – one of four American soldiers known to have defected to North Korea after the Korean War. With a candour that shows a genuine love of his new country, Dresnok tells of his journey from a troubled adolescence to old age in Pyongyang, including his crossing of the treacherous DMZ, a failed attempt at escape and his stint as a star on the North Korean silver screen.

The Interview (2014) This dumb comedy became a giant global news story even before its release. Its plot – two fools are sent to assassinate Kim Jong-un – angered the establishment in North Korea, and Sony Pictures had their systems hacked as an apparently direct result. The storyline of the film itself is less interesting, but it's still worth a watch.

Books

Despite Korea's long and interesting history, the East Asian sections in most bookshops largely focus on China and Japan. The majority of books that are devoted to Korea cover North Korea or the Korean War; far less biased than most newspaper or television reports, these are the best form of reportage about the creation and machinations of the world's most curious state. In the reviews that follow, books marked with a ★ are particularly recommended.

HISTORY AND SOCIETY

Michael Breen *The Koreans: Who They Are, What They Want, Where Their Future Lies.* Although the four main sections of this book – society, history, economy and politics – may seem dry, the accounts are relayed with warmth and a pleasing depth of knowledge.

Bruce Cumings *Korea's Place in the Sun: A Modern History.* The Korean peninsula went through myriad changes in the twentieth century, and this weighty tome analyses the effects of such disquiet on its population, showing that the South's seemingly smooth trajectory towards democracy and capitalism masked a great injury of the national psyche.

Euny Hong *The Birth of Korean Cool.* A good rundown of Korea's attempts to conquer Asia, and then the world at large, with its pop culture; as well as the more obvious effects on drama and music, it looks at how this impacted upon Korea's place at the global business table.

Keith Pratt *Everlasting Flower: A History of Korea.* This thoroughly readable book provides a chronicle of Korean goings-on from the very first kingdoms to the modern day, its text broken up with interesting illustrated features on the arts and customs prevalent at the time.

Daniel Tudor *Korea: The Impossible Country.* Written by Korea's former correspondent for the Economist, this book investigates how the country transformed from failed state to economic powerhouse in the space of a generation or two, and looks at what today's generation has in store.

★ **Simon Winchester** *Korea: A Walk Through the Land of Miracles.* This highly entertaining book details Winchester's walk from southern Jeju to the North Korean border. Written in the 1980s, it's now an extremely dated snapshot of Korean society, but this is actually a plus point: it is amazing to witness, even at second hand, how much has changed in such a short time.

NORTH KOREA AND THE KOREAN WAR

★ **Bruce Cumings** *North Korea: Another Country.* The US-North Korean dispute is far more complex than Western media would have you imagine, and this book provides a revealing – if slightly hard to digest – glance at the flipside. Cumings' meticulous research is without parallel, and the accounts of American atrocities and cover-ups both in the "Forgotten War" and during the nuclear crisis offer plenty of food for thought.

Guy Delisle *Pyongyang.* A comic strip describing his time as a cartoonist in Pyongyang, Delisle's well-observed and frequently hilarious book is a North Korean rarity – one that tells it like it is, and doesn't seek to make political or ideological statements. His illustrations are eerily accurate.

★ **Barbara Demick** *Nothing to Envy.* An admirably well-researched look at modern-day life in North Korea, based on the experiences of six residents of Chongjin, a major city in the northeast of the country. Gulags, the Kim cult, famine and poverty all get a mention, juxtaposed with the views of a seemingly unwavering believer in the regime.

Max Hastings *The Korean War.* A conflict is not quite a war until it has been given the treatment by acclaimed historian Max Hastings. With this book, he has provided more than his usual mix of fascinating, balanced and well-researched material; the account of the stand of the Gloucesters on the Imjin is particularly absorbing.

Kang Chol-Hwan *The Aquariums of Pyongyang.* Having fled his homeland after spending time in a North Korean gulag, Kang's harrowing accounts of squalor, starvation and brutality represent one of the only windows into the world's most fenced-off social systems. He's not a natural author, however, and the confused sermonizing at the end rather dilutes the book's appeal.

Bradley K. Martin *Under the Loving Care of the Fatherly Leader.* Almost 900 pages long – 200 of which are references – this isn't one to carry around in your backpack, but for an in-depth look at the Kims and the perpetration of their personality cult, it's hard to beat.

★ **Don Oberdorfer** *The Two Koreas: A Contemporary History.* Lengthy, but engaging and surprisingly easy to read, this book traces the various events in postwar Korea, as well as examining how they were affected by the actions and policies of China, Russia, Japan and the US. You'd be hard-pressed to find a book about North Korea more neutral in tone.

FICTION

Cho Se-hui *The Dwarf.* Even miracles have a downside: Seoul's economy underwent a truly remarkable transformation in the 1970s, but at what cost to its people and culture? This weighty, tersely delivered novel uncovers the spiritual decline of Seoul's nouveau riche, via twelve interconnected stories; *A Dwarf Launches a Little Bell* is particularly recommended, and has been reprinted hundreds of times in Korea.

★**Adam Johnson** *The Orphan Master's Son.* Winner of the 2013 Pulitzer Prize for fiction, this tells the story of an orphan who struggles through life in North Korea, and ends up employed as a kidnapper of Japanese citizens.

Park Wan-Suh *Who Ate Up All the Shinga?* A semi-autobiographical mother-daughter story from one of Korea's most highly acclaimed writers, set during the Korean War. Fans of Park should also check out *Sketch of the Fading Sun*, a collection of short stories.

★**Yi Munyeol** *Our Twisted Hero.* This tale of psychological warfare at a Korean elementary school has a deceptively twee plotline, managing to explore the use and misuse of power while providing metaphorical parallels to Korean politics of the 1970s.

Young Ha Kim *Your Republic is Calling You* and *I Have the Right to Destroy Myself.* Two books from a man whose international reputation is growing by the year, his popularity and his existentialist tendencies marking him out as a potential Korean Murakami. The first book revolves around a North Korean spy torn between his homeland and the South, while the second, set in Seoul, is the dark tale of a refined thinker with suicidal tendencies.

RECIPE BOOKS

Debra Samuels and **Taekyung Chung** *The Korean Table.* One hundred easy-to-follow recipes "from barbecue to *bibimbap*", accompanied by droolworthy photos, this will have you getting your kitchen stinky and covered with chilli paste in no time at all.

Marja Vongerichten and **Jean Georges Vongerichten** *The Kimchi Chronicles: Korean Cooking for an American Kitchen.* A very useful cookbook that takes account of the fact that its readers may not have access to a full Korean kitchen's-worth of utensils.

A–Z of contemporary Korea

A: Alphabet Olympics

Seoul hosted the Summer Games in 1988, and Pyeongchang is gearing up to host the Winter version in 2018. However, there's one festival at which Korea has been declared the eternal champion: the **Alphabet Olympics**. The first event was held in 2009, with Korea's *hangeul* beating off fifteen other national and international scripts. Lee Yang-ha, the (Korean) president of the World Alphabet Olympic Committee, explained with joy that while "the 26 letters of English can only express 300 or more sounds, the 24 Korean characters can theoretically express more than 11,000" – all rather odd, since the Korean script is very limited when transliterating words from other languages. The second event was held in 2012; with *hangeul* again the victor, the heads of the World Alphabet Academy (again all Korean, and with a manifesto to propagate *hangeul* and Christianity throughout the world) decided to make Korea the champion forever, because "scripts do not change as fast as language". Meanwhile, English teachers across Korea struggle to help students pronounce the letters Z or V, distinguish between L and R, or end syllables with most consonantal sounds.

B: Burberry man

What's generally known as a "flasher" in English is referred to as a **Burberry man** in Korea. These gents – dressed in a three-quarter-length jacket and little else – hang around universities in order to expose themselves to female students, most commonly when large crowds are gathered in the front enclosures. They're surprisingly common – most Korean girls will have seen at least one, and many schools see a Burberry man show up regularly. Korea's love of conformity means that even these sex pests have a uniform of sorts: while the Burberry label is not essential, most of their jackets are brown, and for some reason knee-length grey socks seem almost mandatory.

C: City branding

Cities and countries around the world have long attempted to rope in extra visitors with clever slogans, and in the early 2000s Korea took this idea and ran with it. Local consultants raked in the cash with a slew of **city branding**, which often verged on the comical. Some of the more "interesting" examples include "Aha! Suncheon", "Oh, Yeosu!", "Happy Citizen, Proud Jeongeup", "It's Daejeon", "Just Sangju", "Yes! Uiwang", "Hi-touch Gongju" and "Pyeongtaek Super". Then along came Psy, who did more for Korean branding with one silly dance than any city slogan ever achieved – the end of the gravy train for the aforementioned consultants.

D: Daeri-unjeon

In Korea, businessmen inevitably find themselves having to drink an awful lot as "social" job obligations, even if travelling with a car. To get round this situation Korea has **daeri-unjeon**, a network of drivers who drive both the customer and his car home, and who can be called from most bars; the telephone numbers usually end with 8282, digits whose pronunciation is almost identical to the Korean for "hurry, hurry!"

E: Eyelid surgery

In a country where appearance is not quite everything but pretty damn close, beauty is big business. The large and thriving plastic surgery industry sees women – and more than a few men – get all sorts from nose jobs to a nip and tuck, but the most popular alteration by far is **eyelid surgery**. This involves the creation of a crease in the upper eyelid, the results being apparently more beautiful to Koreans, but distinctly non-oriental.

F: "Fan death"

"**Fan death**" is a truly curious phenomenon – whereas around the world people fall asleep with a fan or the air conditioning left on, only in Korea does such folly regularly seem to result in fatalities. The reasons given include air currents starving the victim of air, reduced room temperatures inducing hypothermia, or even fan blades actually cutting the oxygen molecules in two. This is enough to convince most Koreans that the humble electric fan is an instrument to be feared – even broadsheet newspapers run fan-death stories, and the Korean government has issued warnings against using fans at night. Such beliefs are of much amusement to Korea's expat population (unless they find themselves sharing a room with a Korean in the summer).

G: Grandmother techno

While modern K-pop has swept across continental Asia, there's another strain of music that you're likely to come across on your way around Korea: "*bongjak*" songs – best described as a kind of **grandmother techno** – are fast-paced ballads, set to odd synthesized rhythms and crooned out in a semi-compulsory warble. Some of the best places to get a handle on *bongjak* are Korea's national parks: older locals are fond of drinking and listening to music both during and after their hikes, which makes it all the more likely that you'll get to see the accompanying dance (something like bouncing on a toilet seat while handling a steering wheel).

H: Homosexuality

Homosexuality has long been a bit of a taboo in Korea, but in line with the development of other countries, a couple of high-profile comings out have made such matters more acceptable to the wider populace. **Harisu** was born male, but flew in the face of a conservative society to become the country's first celebrity transsexual; she was also one of the first in the queue to change gender when it became legal to do so. Her big break was a cosmetics commercial, in which the camera focused on her Adam's apple. There was also the case of **Hong Seok-cheon**, an actor who lost pretty much all of his friends, family and money after coming out in 2000. After taking a risk by opening up a gay mingling spot in Itaewon, he now owns around a dozen bars and restaurants in the area, and appears on television pretty much every single day.

I: Internet deaths

Koreans are famed for their use of computers, most notably the amount of time they spend playing online games. In fact, there is a growing backlash among the non-Korean gaming community: such is the domination of the country's gamers that they are accused of taking over international gaming sites and tournaments. They even hit the international headlines with occasional **internet deaths**: stories of gamers making mammoth stints (one was measured at 92 hours) at PC bars have become less common since the government ordered tighter controls, but there's still the occasional death behind closed doors.

J: Jaebeol

Korean business is dominated by a troupe of gigantic business conglomerates known as **jaebeol**. A few of these organizations have achieved fame around the world, though most foreigners probably wouldn't know that the company is Korean even if the name is familiar to them. Some of the largest and most renowned *jaebeol* include Samsung, LG, Hyundai, SK, Lotte, Daewoo and Kumho Asiana. Most are still family-controlled, leading to enormous riches for the man at the helm; their power was a driving force behind Korea's "Economic Miracle". Times have changed; after the Asian Financial Crisis and the resultant reforms, many chose (or were forced) to break up into smaller units.

L: Louis Vuitton
Though the numbers are gradually starting to decline, patterned brown handbags from French designer **Louis Vuitton** have long been standard issue on female Korean arms. However, high prices – and increased expertise of counterfeiting in China – oblige many to invest in a fake bag instead. Watch what happens if it starts to rain.

M: Military service
South Korea still has compulsory **military service** for its young men. This was once 36 months, but is now around 24 months and likely to decrease further. Conscientious objectors will be jailed, but there are ways around the rule – many students manage to tie their service into university courses such as logistics and electronic engineering. Military service is also mandatory for men in North Korea, and women are actively encouraged to enrol as volunteers.

N: Nocheonnyeo
A **nocheonnyeo** is an "over-the-hill spinster", a woman who has gone past the perceived outer boundary of marriageable age; 30 has long been the feared number, though the Korean age-counting system (whereby children are born aged 1 and become 2 on the date of the next Lunar New Year) makes this 28 or 29 in international terms. While it remains much harder for a woman to marry after achieving *nocheonnyeo* status, societal shifts (notably an increase in divorce rates, and the slow decline of the resign-from-your-job-after-marriage path for females) mean that it's by no means impossible.

O: Oktapbang
Korea is the world's second most densely populated country of any substantial size, and as such there's understandable pressure for living space. From the 1980s on, many landlords increased the rents that they could accrue from low-rise buildings by making a tiny extra room on the roof; known as **oktapbang** ("home-top room"), these minuscule abodes are generally inhabited by students from the provinces.

P: Private tutoring
With Korea's mix of generous salaries and relatively oppr level of proficiency in foregn languages, there's a large and growing market for English teachers. Most of these go – at least initially – to teach children at after-school **private tutoring** institutes known as *hagwon*. These are not just for English lessons – the huge pressures inherent in Korea's educational system prompt an extremely high proportion of parents to push their kids into extra-curricular classes from ages as young as 5. In addition to language classes and "regular" school, the little mites may have violin lessons, computer training, art classes, dance groups and piano recitals crammed into their weekly schedule.

Q: Questionable English
Anyone spending time in Korea will see T-shirts splashed with **questionable English** all over the place – "Skinny Bitch" got to be popular with young girls, though "Hey Guy! Lay Me" was a mercifully short-lived fad. The mirth is not restricted to T-shirt slogans: Maeil Milk is available at every convenience store, there's an energy drink called Coolpis, a bakery chain called Gout, and children's clothing shops called Hunt Kids and Baby Hunt. There are also spelling mistakes galore: "crab" is spelt with a "p" on a surprising number of the country's menus, and a certain hamburger chain is often spelt "Bugger King" on English-language maps. Finally, don't be surprised to see rubbish bins in which to dispose of "pets"; this actually refers to certain plastic products.

R: Red Devils
Having casually pinched their nickname from England's Manchester United, the South Korean national football team is often referred to as the "**Red Devils**", as are their main

supporters' group. A noisy but friendly bunch, the latter were one of the highlights of the 2002 World Cup, an event half-hosted in Korea; most fans wore a T-shirt emblazoned with "Be The Reds!", perhaps the best-known example of "Konglish" (a hybrid of Korean and English which makes little sense in either language). The inventors of the logo initially neglected to copyright it, and it was eventually superseded by the official slogan of the supporters' club, the more grammatically correct "Reds Go Together".

S: Sogaeting
Many Korean couples meet through arranged blind dates, known as "**sogaeting**". Until recently, these were usually arranged by parents in anticipation of a happy marriage between friendly families, but in an increasingly liberal Korea *sogaeting* is now far more common as a way for boys and girls to find their own partners.

T: Table gifts
A first birthday party is a pretty special event wherever you are in the world, but Korea has added its own distinctive twist to proceedings – **table gifts**. At some point in the occasion, the baby will be seated on or dangled over a table laid out with money, rice, thread and a pencil, and pushed to make a selection that, it is said, will influence their future path. Money speaks for itself, but the selection of rice is said to lead to a comfortable life, thread to a long one, and a pencil to a scholarly career. Of course, this is not enough to satisfy many modern parents, who throw contemporary choices such as golf balls, footballs, DVDs or microphones onto the table too, often giving their young one precious little choice in the selection. Also interesting are the parties thrown to celebrate the hundredth day of a child's life – in times of high infant mortality, this was when the child was said to have "made it", and the special day continues to be celebrated with a feast of colourful rice cake.

U: Unconstitutional law
Koreans were, until recently, banned from marrying anyone of the same clan. This may have sounded like an extremely severe rule in a country with so few family names (around one-quarter of Koreans are named Kim, another fifteen percent Lee, and almost ten percent Park), but the ruling only in fact covered those who had both the same name and the same ancestral clan; some of these subdivisions, however, were over a million-strong in number. Same-clan marriages were termed incestuous, even if the pair were a dozen generations apart, but this law was found **unconstitutional** by the Korean court in 1997, and thousands have since taken advantage of this ruling.

V: VANK
The Voluntary Agency Network of Korea, also known as **VANK**, is an online club with over 120,000 members. Their remit is to promote Korea overseas, though the primary focus generally seems to be getting one over on arch-enemy Japan – any international organization that dares to use "Takeshima or Sea of Japan" on a map, rather than Dokdo or the East Sea, will likely be bombarded with emails by these cyber-nationalists.

W: Work meals
Work meals, known as *hoe-sik*, are the bane of many a Korean office worker's life. In the West, many employees would doubtless appreciate being treated to a big meal by their boss (not to mention the free booze); however, there's understandable resentment when it becomes a weekly occurrence that one can't back out of. It's common for bosses to announce the *hoe-sik* at the last minute, forcing the cancellation of any plans not involving the work team; in this determinedly Confucian society, it's also almost obligatory for the youngest female in the group to get drunk and be silly.

X: Xenophobia

Koreans tend to make foreigners feel very welcome, but this friendliness conceals a rampant **xenophobia**. Korea remains one of the most homogenous societies on Earth, and traces of the "Hermit Kingdom" remain, mainly thanks to history lessons that paint the motherland in virginal white while detailing every single injustice inflicted on her; most of the official ire is reserved for the Japanese, but anti-Americanism is also rife. It must be said that this very rarely results in anything approaching violence – Korea is simply seen as a world apart, and foreigners will always be viewed as such, even if they were born in Korea and speak the language fluently. This explains the surprise that many Koreans will show to Westerners able to use chopsticks – no matter how close you live to a Chinatown, it's simply not in your DNA.

Y: Yoo Jae-suk

It's quite possible that no person has ever clocked up more television hours than Korean chat show personality **Yoo Jae-suk**. Nicknamed "The Grasshopper" on account of his distinctive appearance, Yoo started life as one of Korea's many young, lower-level stand-up comedians, but soon made the transition from stage to small screen, and married a local beauty queen. His chat shows, often set in *jjimjilbang* (see p.35) and incorporating a distinct reality-TV element, are on television almost every single day of the year, and rope in washed-up A-listers like moths to a flame.

Z: Zodiac

Koreans are a superstitious bunch, and you'll see small tent-like fortune-telling booths in every city, most often attended by young couples looking for celestial approval of their relationship, or workers thinking about changing jobs. People's place in the **zodiac** may also be supplemented by palm-reading, teacup-gazing, craniology or Tarot cards.

Korean

The sole official tongue of both North and South Korea, the Korean language is used by almost eighty million people, making it one of the world's twenty most-spoken tongues. It's a highly tricky language to pick up – much to the chagrin of linguists, it remains stubbornly "unclassified" on the global language tree, its very origins something of a mystery. Some lump it in with the Altaic group (itself rather vague), which would put it on the same branch as Turkish and Mongolian, though many view it as a language isolate. Korean is therefore in the same boat as Japanese, its closest linguistic brother; both share a subject-object-verb syntax and similar grammar, though well over half of the Korean words themselves actually originate from China. Korea also used Chinese text for centuries, even after creating its own characters (known as *hangeul*; 한글) in the 1440s, but now almost exclusively uses the local system for everyday functions.

Native speakers of European languages will encounter some pretty significant **grammatical differences** when attempting to get a handle on the Korean tongue. Korean **nouns** remain unaffected whether they refer to singular or plural objects, very little use is made of **articles**, and **verbs** do not change case according to who or what they're referring to – *gayo* can mean "I go", "he/she/it goes" or "we/they go", the meaning made clear by the context. Verbs do, however, alter depending on which **level of politeness** the speaker desires to use, and the relationship between speaker and listener; the conversation will sound quite different depending on whether it's between a child and a mother, a boss and an employee, or even good friends of slightly different age. In general, it's pretty safe to stick to verbs with the polite **–yo** ending; the verb forms given here are in a formal style which should suffice for most travellers. Unfortunately, there are few good **books** from which to learn Korean; those from the *Teach Yourself* and *Colloquial* series fall short of the two companies' usually high standards, but are about as good as you'll find.

Korean characters

Though it consists of a highly distinctive scrawl of circles and Tetris shapes, many foreigners find Korean text surprisingly **easy to learn**. Koreans tend to assume that foreigners don't have the inclination or mental capability to decipher *hangeul*, so your efforts will not go unappreciated. Koreans are immensely proud of *hangeul*, which they see as the world's most logical written system (see box, p.372). While this is no great exaggeration, the efficiency also has a downside – user-friendly it may well be, but in reality *hangeul* is a very narrow system that cannot cope with sounds not found in the Korean language, a fact that partially explains the Korean people's occasionally curious pronunciation of foreign words.

Pronunciation

Pronouncing Korean words is a tough task – some sounds simply do not have English-language equivalents. You'll see from the *hangeul* box (p.372) that there's only one character for "l" and "r", with its actual sound some way in between the two

HANGEUL

Korean characters are grouped into **syllabic boxes** of more or less equal size, and generally arranged left to right – if you see a line of text made up of eighteen of these character-chunks, it will have eighteen syllables when spoken. The way in which the **characters** fall into the boxes is rather unique and takes a bit of figuring out – some have two characters in the top half and one at the bottom (the top two are read left to right, followed by the bottom one, so 한 makes *han*), while others have two or three characters arranged vertically (these are read downwards, so 국 makes *guk*). Thus put together, we have 한국 – *hanguk*, meaning "Korea". The basic building blocks are listed in the box below, though note that some of these symbols **change sounds** depending on whether they're at the beginning or end of a syllable or word (syllable-ending sounds are bracketed in the boxed text), and that "ng" is used as an initial null consonant for syllables that start with a vowel.

ㄱ	g (k)	ㅎ	h	ㅔ	e
ㄴ	n	ㅇ	ng	ㅐ	ae
ㄷ	d (t)	ㅏ	a	ㅖ	ye
ㄹ	r/l	ㅑ	ya	ㅒ	yae
ㅁ	m	ㅓ	eo	ㅟ	wi
ㅂ	b (p)	ㅕ	yeo	ㅞ	we
ㅅ	s (t)	ㅗ	o	ㅙ	wae
ㅈ	j (t)	ㅛ	yo	ㅘ	wa
ㅊ	ch (t)	ㅜ	u	ㅚ	oe
ㅋ	k	ㅠ	yu	ㅢ	ui
ㅌ	t	ㅡ	eu	ㅝ	wo
ㅍ	p	ㅣ	i		

– try saying both phonemes at the same time. The letters "k", "d", "b" and "j" are often written "k", "t", "p" and "ch", and are pronounced approximately halfway towards those Roman equivalents; unfortunately, the second set also have their place in the official system, and are usually referred to as **aspirated consonants**, accompanied as they are by a puff of air. Consonants are fairly easy to master – note that some are doubled up, and spoken more forcefully – but pronunciation guides to some of the tricky **vowels** and **dipthongs** are as follows (British English readings offer the closest equivalents):

a	as in "car"	**ye**	as in "yet"
ya	as in "yap"	**yae**	as in "yeah"
eo	as in "hot"	**wi**	as in "window"
yeo	as in "yob"	**we**	as in "wedding"
o	pronounced "ore"	**wae**	as the beginning of "where"
yo	pronounced as the British "your"	**wa**	as in "wag"
u	as in "Jew"	**oe**	as in the beginning of "way"
yu	pronounced "you"	**ui**	no English equivalent; add an "ee" sound to *eu* above
eu	no English equivalent; widen your mouth and try an "euggh" sound of disgust	**wo**	as in "wad"
i	as in "pea"		
e	as in "bed"		
ae	as in "air"		

TRANSLITERATION TROUBLES

Rendering the Korean language in Roman text is, simply, a battle that can never be won – a classic problem of square pegs and round holes. Numerous systems have been employed down the years, perhaps best exemplified in the Korean family name now usually romanized as "Lee": this has also been written as Rhee, Li, Ri, Lih, Rhi, Ree, Yi, Rii and more besides. Under the current system it would be "I", but the actual pronunciation is simply "ee" – it's amazing how much trouble a simple vowel can cause (especially when almost a fifth of the country has this name).

A Korean's age, schooling, family and even lifestyle influence the way that they'll romanize a given word, but official standards have long been in place. The **Yale** and **McCune–Reischauer** systems became widely accepted in the 1940s, and the latter is still much in evidence today; under its rules, aspirated consonants are marked with apostrophes, and certain vowels with breves. One problem – other than looking ugly – was that these punctuation markings are often neglected, even in language study books; though it remains the official system in North Korea, the South formulated its own system of **Revised Romanization** in the year 2000. While this is far from perfect, it's the official standard, and has been used throughout this book; exceptions include names of the many hotels, restaurants, universities and individuals who cling to the old ways. One other issue is the Korean syllable *shi*; this is now romanized as *si*, a rather ridiculous change since it takes Koreans years of language classes before they can pronounce the syllable without palatalizing it – "six" and "sister" will be pronounced "shix" and "shister". We've written it as *shi* in the language listings to help you achieve the correct pronunciation, but obeyed the official system in the rest of the book – Sinchon is pronounced "Shinchon", and so on.

Koreans themselves find it hard to render **foreign words** in *hangeul* as there are many sounds that don't fit into the system – the difficulties with "l" and "r" sharing the same character being an obvious example – but even when parallels exist they are sometimes distorted. The letter "a" is usually written as an "e" or "ae" in an unsuccessful effort to Americanize the pronunciation – "hat", for example, will be pronounced "het" by the majority of the population.

USEFUL WORDS AND PHRASES

BASICS

Yes	*ye/ne*	예/네
No	*aniyo*	아니요
Please (asking for something)	*…juseyo*	…주세요
Excuse me	*shillye hamnida*	실례합니다
I'm sorry	*mian hamnida*	미안합니다
Thank you	*gamsa hamnida*	감사합니다
You're welcome	*gwaenchan-ayo*	괜찮아요
What?	*muot?*	무엇?
When?	*eonje?*	언제?
Where?	*eodi?*	어디?
Who?	*nugu?*	누구?
How?	*eotteokke?*	어떻께?
How much?	*eolma-eyo?*	얼마에요?
How many?	*myeokke-eyo?*	몇 개에요?
I want…	*…hago-shipeoyo*	…하고 싶어요
Please help me	*dowa-juseyo*	도와주세요

COMMUNICATING

I can't speak Korean	*jeo-neun hangugeo-reul mot haeyo*	저는 한국어를 못 해요
I can't read Korean	*jeo-neun hangugeo-reul mok ilgeoyo*	저는 한국어를 못 읽어요
Do you speak English?	*yeongeo halsu-isseoyo?*	영어 할 수 있어요?
Is there someone who can speak English?	*yeongeo-reul haljul a-neun bun isseoyo?*	영어를 할줄 아는 분 있어요?
Can you please speak slowly?	*jom cheoncheonhi mal haejuseyo?*	좀 천천히 말 해주세요?

Please say that again	*dashi han-beon mal haejuseyo*	다시 한번말 해주세요
I understand/I see	*alasseoyo*	알았 어요
I (really) don't understand	*(jal) mollayo*	(잘) 몰라요
What does this mean?	*i-geot museun ddeushi-eyo?*	이것 무슨 뜻이에요?
How do you say (x) in Korean?	*(x) eul/reul hanguk-eoro eotteokke mal haeyo?*	(x) 을/를 한국어로 어떻게 말해요
Please write in English	*yeongeo-ro jegeo jushillaeyo*	영어로 적어 주실래요
Please wait (a moment)	*(jamggan) gidariseyo*	(잠깐) 기다리세요
Just a minute	*jamggan manyo*	잠깐 만요

MEETINGS AND GREETINGS

Hello; Good morning/ afternoon /evening	*annyeong haseyo*	안녕 하세요
Hello (polite)	*annyeong hashimnikka*	안녕 하십니까
How are you?	*jal jinaesseoyo?*	잘 지냈어요?
I'm fine	*jal jinaesseoyo/jo-ayo*	잘 지냈어요 / 좋아요
Nice to meet you	*bangapseumnida*	반갑습니다
Goodbye (when staying)	*annyeong-hi gaseyo*	안녕히 가세요
Goodbye (when leaving)	*annyeong-hi gyeseyo*	안녕히 계세요
What's your name?	*ireum-i eotteokke doeshimnikka?*	이름이 어떻게 되십니까?
My name is…	*ireum-i … imnida*	이름이... 입니다.
Where are you from?	*eodi-eso wasseoyo?*	어디에 왔어요?
I'm from…	*…eso wasseoyo*	에서 왔어요
Korea	*han-guk*	한국
Britain	*yeong-guk*	영국
Ireland	*aillaendeu*	아일랜드
America	*mi-guk*	미국
Australia	*oseuteureillia/hoju*	오스트레일리아 / 호주
Canada	*kae-nada*	캐나다
New Zealand	*nyu jillaendeu*	뉴질랜드
South Africa	*nam apeurika*	남 아프리카
How old are you?	*myeot-sal ieyo?*	몇 살이에요?
I am (age)	*(age)-sal ieyo*	(age)살이에요
Do you like…?	*…o-a haeyo?*	...좋아 해요?
I like…	*jo-a haeyo*	좋아 해요
I don't like…	*an jo-a haeyo*	안 좋아해요
Do you have (free) time?	*shigan-i isseoyo?*	시간이 있어요?

NUMBERS

Rather confusingly, the Korean language has two separate number systems operating in parallel – a **native Korean** system, and a **Sino–Korean** system of Chinese origin – and you'll have to learn according to the situation which one to use. To tell the time, you'll actually need both – amazingly, minutes and hours run on different systems. The native Korean system only goes up to 99, and has been placed on the right-hand side of the readings. Dates and months use the Sino–Korean system alone, with *il* (sun) used as a suffix for days, and *wol* (moon) for months: June 7 is simply *yuk-wol chil-il*.

Zero	*yeong/gong*	영/공
One	*il/hana*	일/하나
Two	*i (pronounced "ee")/dul*	이/둘
Three	*sam/set*	삼/셋
Four	*sa/net*	사/넷
Five	*o/daseot*	오/다섯
Six	*yuk/yeoseot*	육/여섯

Seven	*chil/ilgop*	칠/일곱
Eight	*pal/yeodeol*	팔/여덟
Nine	*gu/ahop*	구/아홉
Ten	*ship/yeol*	십/열
Eleven	*shib-il/ yeol-hana*	십일/열하나
Twelve	*shib-i/yeol-dul*	십이/열둘
Twenty	*i-shib/seumul*	이십/스물
Thirty	*sam-ship/ seoreun*	삼십/서른
One hundred	*baek*	백
Two hundred	*i-baek*	이백
Thousand	*cheon*	천
Ten thousand	*man*	만
One hundred thousand	*shim-man*	십만
One million	*baeng-man*	백만
One hundred million	*eok*	억

TIME AND DATES

Now	*jigeum*	지금
Today	*o-neul*	오늘
Morning	*achim*	아침
Afternoon	*ohu*	오후
Evening	*jeonyok*	저녁
Night	*bam*	밤
Tomorrow	*nae-il*	내일
Yesterday	*eoje*	어제
Week	*ju*	주
Month	*wol/dal*	월/달
Year	*nyeon*	년
Monday	*wolyo-il*	월요일
Tuesday	*hwayo-il*	화요일
Wednesday	*suyo-il*	수요일
Thursday	*mogyo-il*	목요일
Friday	*geumyo-il*	금요일
Saturday	*toyo-il*	토요일
Sunday	*ilyo-il*	일요일
What time is it?	*myo-shi-eyo?*	몇시에요?
It's 10 o'clock	*yeol-shi-eyo*	열시에요
10.20	*yeol-shi i-ship-bun*	열시 이십분
10.30	*yeol-shi sam-ship-bun*	열시 삼십분
10.50	*yeol-shi o-ship-bun*	열시 오십분

TRANSPORT AND TRAVEL

Aeroplane	*bihaenggi*	비행기
Airport	*gonghang*	공항
Bus	*beoseu*	버스
Express bus (terminal)	*gosok beoseu (teominal)*	익스프레스 (터미널)
Intercity bus (terminal)	*shi-oe beoseu (teominal)*	시외 버스(터미널)
City bus	*shinae beoseu*	시내 버스
Airport bus	*gonghang beoseu*	공항 버스
City bus stop	*jeong-nyu-jang*	정류장
Train	*gicha*	기차
Train station	*yeok*	역
Subway	*jihacheol*	지하철

Ferry	yeogaek-seon	여객선
Ferry terminal	yeogaek teominal	여객 터미널
Left-luggage office	jimbogwanso	짐보관
Ticket office	maepyoso	매표서
Ticket	pyo	표
Platform	seunggangjang	승강장
Bicycle	jajeon-geo	자전거
Taxi	taek-shi	택시

DIRECTIONS AND GENERAL PLACES

Where is (x)?	-i/ga eodi-eyo?	-이/가 어디에요?
Straight ahead	jikjin	직진
Left	oen-jjok (pronounced "wen-chok")	왼쪽
Right	oreun-jjok	오른쪽
Behind	dwi-e	뒤에
In front of	ap-e	앞에
North	buk	북
South	nam	남
East	dong	동
West	seo	서
Map	maep/jido	맵/지도
Entrance	ip-gu	입구
Exit	chul-gu	출구
Art gallery	misulgwan	미술관
Bank	eunhaeng	은행
Beach	haebyeon	해변
Department store	baekhwajeom	백화점
Embassy	daesagwan	대사관
Hot-spring spa	oncheon	온천
Museum	bangmulgwan	박물관
Park	gongwon	공원
Sea	haean/bada	해안/바다
Temple	Jeol/sachal	절/사찰
Toilet	hwajang-shil	화장실
Tourist office	gwan-gwang annaeso	관광 안내소

ACCOMMODATION

Hotel	hotel	호텔
Motel	motel	모텔
Guesthouse	yeogwan	여관
Budget guesthouse	yeoinsuk	여인숙
Rented room	minbak	민박
Youth hostel	yuseu hoseutel	유스 호스텔
Korean-style room	ondol-bang	온돌방
Western-style room	chimdae-bang	침대방
Single room	shinggeul chimdae	싱글 침대
Double room	deobeul chimdae	더블 침대
Twin room	chimdae dugae	침대 두개
En-suite room	yokshil-ddallin bang	욕실 딸린방
Shower	syaweo	샤워
Bath	yokjo	욕조
Key	ki	키
Passport	yeogwon	여권
Do you have any vacancies?	bang isseoyo?	방 있어요?

I have a reservation	yeyak haesseoyo	예약 했어요
I don't have a reservation	yeyak anhaesseoyo	예약 안했어요
How much is the room?	bang-i eolma-eyo?	방이 얼마에요?
Does that include breakfast?	achim-shiksa poham-dwae isseoyo?	아침식사 포함돼 있어요?
One/two/ three nights	haruppam/ i-bak/ sam-bak	하룻밤/이박/삼박
One week	il-ju-il	일주일
May I see the room?	bang jom bolsu- isseoyo?	방 좀 볼수 있어요?

SHOPPING, MONEY AND BANKS

Bank	eunhaeng	은행
Foreign exchange	woe-hwan	외환
Won	won	원
Pounds	pa-un-deu	파운드
Dollars	dalleo	달러
Cash	don	돈
Travellers' cheque	yeohaengja supyo	여행자 수표
How much is it?	eolma-eyo?	얼마에요?
It's too expensive	neomu bissayo	너무 비싸요
Please make it a little cheaper	jom kkakka-juseyo	좀 깎아주세요
Do you accept credit cards?	keurediteu kadeu gyesan dwaeyo?	크레디트 카드 계산 돼요?

POST AND TELEPHONES

Post office	uche-guk	우체국
Envelope	bongtu	봉투
Letter	pyeonji	편지
Postcard	yeopseo	엽서
Stamp	u-pyo	우표
Airmail	hanggong u-pyeon	항공 우편
Surface mail	seonbak u-pyeon	선박 우편
Telephone	jeon-hwa	전화
Fax	paekseu	팩스
Telephone	**card** jeonhwa kadeu	전화카드
Internet café	PC-bang	방
I would like to call...	...hante jeonhwa hago- shipeoyo	좀바꿔 주세요
May I speak to...	...jom baggwo juseyo	저는 아파요
Hello?	yeoboseyo?	여보세요?

HEALTH

Hospital	byeongwon	병원
Pharmacy	yak-guk	약국
Medicine	yak	약
Doctor	uisa	의사
Dentist	chigwa-uisa	치과의사
Diarrhoea	seolsa	설사
Nausea	meseukkeo-um	메스꺼움
Fever	yeol	열
Food poisoning	shikjungdok	식중독
Antibiotics	hangsaengje	항생제
Antiseptic	sodok-yak	독약
Condom	kondom	콘돔
Penicillin	penishillin	페니실린
Tampons	tampon	탐폰
I'm ill	jeo-neun apayo	저는 아파요
I have a cold	gamgi geoll-yeosseoyo	감기 걸렸어요

I'm allergic to...	...allereugi-ga isseoyo	...알레르기가 있어요
It hurts here	yeogi-ga apayo	여기가 아파요
Please call a doctor	uisa-reul bulleo juseyo	의사를 불러 주세요

FOOD AND DRINK

PLACES

Restaurant	sikdang	식당
Korean barbecue restaurant	galbi-jip	갈비집
Seafood restaurant	hoet-jip	횟집
Western-style restaurant	reseutorang	레스토랑
Italian restaurant	itallian reseutorang	이탈리안 레스토랑
Chinese restaurant	jungguk-jip	중국집
Japanese restaurant	ilshik-jip	일식집
Burger bar	paeseuteu-pudeu-jeom	패스트푸드점
Convenience store	pyeonui-jeom	편의점
Market	shijang	시장
Café	kape	카페
Bar	ba/suljip	바/술집
Club	naiteu-keulleob	나이트클럽
Expat bar	woeguk-in ba (pronounced "way-guk-in ba")	외국인 바
Makgeolli bar	makgeolli-jip	막걸리집
Soju tent	pojangmacha	포장마차
Where's (a) ... ?	...eodi isseoyo?	...어디 있어요?

ORDERING

Waiter/Waitress (lit. "Here!")	yeogiyo!	여기요!
How much is that?	eolma-eyo?	얼마에요?
I would like...	...hago shipeoyo	...하고 싶어요
May I have the bill?	gyesanseo juseyo?	계산해 주세요
I'm a vegetarian	jeo-neun chaeshikju uija-eyo	저는 채식주의자에요
Can I have this without meat?	gogi bbaego haejushilsu isseoyo?	고기 빼고 해주실수 있어요?
I can't eat spicy food	maeun-geot mot meogeoyo	매운 것 못 먹어요
Delicious!	mashisseoyo!	맛있어요!
Chopsticks	jeot-garak	젓가락
Fork	po-keu	포크
Knife	nai-peu/kal	나이프/칼
Spoon	sut-garak	숟가락
Menu	menyu	메뉴

STAPLE INGREDIENTS

Beef	so-gogi	쇠고기
Chicken	dak-gogi	닭고기
Duck meat	oti-gogi	오리고기
(Raw) fish	saengsun (hoe)/	생선(회)
Ham	haem	햄
Kimchi	kimchi	김치
Meat	gogi	고기
Noodles	myeon	면
Pork	dwaeji-gogi	돼지고기
Red-pepper paste	gochu-jang	고추장
Rice	bap	밥
Rice cake	ddeok	떡

Seaweed laver	*gim*	김
Shrimp	*sae-u*	새우
Squid	*ojing-eo*	오징어
Tuna	*chamchi*	참치
Vegetables	*yachae*	야채

RICE DISHES

Bibimbap	*bibimbap*	비빔밥
Fried rice (usually with egg and vegetables)	*bokkeumbap*	볶음밥
Marinaded beef on rice	*bulgogi (deop-bap)*	불고기 (덮밥)
Rice rolls	*gimbap*	김밥

MEAT DISHES

Barbecued ribs	*galbi*	갈비
Boiled beef rolls	*syabu-syabu*	샤부샤부
Dog-meat soup	*boshintang/yeongyangtang*	보신탕/영양탕
Marinaded beef	*bulgogi*	불고기
Pork belly slices	*samgyeopsal*	삼겹살
Spicy squid on rice	*ojingeo deop-bap*	오징어 덮밥
Steamed ribs	*galbi-jjim*	갈비찜

STEWS AND SOUPS

Beef and noodle soup	*seolleong-tang*	설렁탕
Beef rib soup	*galbi-tang*	갈비탕
Cold buckwheat noodle soup	*naengmyeon*	냉면
Dumpling soup	*mandu-guk*	만두국
Kimchi broth	*kimchi jjigae*	김치 찌개
Ginseng-stuffed chicken soup	*samgye-tang*	삼계탕
Noodles with vegetables and meat	*makguksu*	막국수
Soybean broth (miso)	*doenjang jjigae*	된장 찌개
Spicy fish soup	*maeun-tang*	매운탕
Spicy noodle soup	*ramyeon*	라면
Spicy tofu soup	*sundubu*	순두부
Tuna broth	*chamchi jjigae*	참치 찌개

SNACKS AND KOREAN FAST FOOD

Battered flash-fried snacks (tempura)	*twigim*	튀김
Breaded pork cutlet	*donkkaseu*	돈까스
Dumplings	*mandu*	만두
Fried dumplings	*gun-mandu*	군만두
Rice wrapped in omelette	*omeuraiseu*	오므라이스
Rice cake in red-pepper paste	*ddeokbokki*	떡볶이
Savoury pancake with vegetables	*pajeon*	파전
Steamed dumplings	*jjin-mandu*	찐만두
Stuffed sausage	*sundae*	순대

SEAFOOD

Broiled fish	*saengseon-gu-i*	생선구이
Fried baby octopus	*nakji bokkeum*	낙지 볶음
Raw fish platter	*modeum-hoe*	모듬회
Sliced raw fish	*saengseon-hoe*	생선회

WESTERN FOOD

Bread	*bbang*	빵
Cereal	*shiri-eol*	시리얼
Cheese	*chi-jeu*	치즈
Chocolate	*chokollit*	초콜릿
Eggs	*gyeran*	계란
Fruit	*gwa-il*	과일
Pizza	*pija*	피자
Spaghetti	*seupageti*	스파게티
Steak	*seuteikeu*	스테이크

TEA

Black tea (lit. "red tea")	*hong-cha*	홍차
Chrysanthemum tea	*gukhwa-cha*	국화차
Cinnamon tea	*gyepi-cha*	계피차
Citron tea		*yuja-cha* 유자차
"Five flavours" tea	*omija-cha*	오미자차
Ginger tea	*saenggang-cha*	생강차
Ginseng tea	*insam-cha*	인삼차
Green tea		*nok-cha* 녹차
Honey ginseng tea	*gyulsam-cha*	귤삼차
"Job's Tears" tea	*yulmu-cha*	율무차
Jujube tea	*daechu-cha*	대추차
Medicinal herb tea	*yak-cha*	약차
Plum tea	*maeshil-cha*	매실차
Wild herb tea	*ma-cha*	마차

ALCOHOLIC DRINKS

Baekseju	*baekseju*	백세주
Beer	*maekju*	맥주
Blackberry wine	*bokbunja*	복분자
Bottled beer	*byeong maekju*	병 맥주
Cocktail	*kakteil*	칵테일
Dongdongju	*dongdongju*	동동주
Draught beer	*saeng maekju*	생 맥주
Ginseng wine	*insamju*	인삼주
Makgeolli	*makgeolli*	막걸리
Plum brandy	*maeshilju*	매실주
Soju	*soju*	소주
Wine	*wain*	와인
Whisky	*wiseuki*	위스키

OTHER DRINKS

Coffee	*keopi*	커피
Orange juice	*orenji jyuseu*	오렌지 쥬스
Fruit juice	*gwa-il jyuseu*	과일 쥬스
Milk	*uyu*	우유
Mineral water	*saengsu*	생수
Water	*mul*	물

GLOSSARY

ajeossi an older or married man.

ajumma an older or married woman.

-am hermitage.

anju bar snacks.

-bang room.

-bawi boulder or large rock.

-bong mountain peak. The highest peak in a park is often referred to as *ilchulbong* ("Number One Peak").

buk- north.

buncheong a Korean style of pottery that became popular in Joseon times. The end product is often bluish-green in colour.

celadon a Korean style of pottery (also common in China and Japan), used since the Three Kingdoms period but largely overtaken by *buncheong* in Joseon times. The end product is often pale green in colour, with a cracked glaze.

cha tea.

-cheon stream or river of less than 100km in length.

Chuseok Korean Thanksgiving.

dae- big, large, great.

Dangun mythical founder of Korea.

DMZ the Demilitarized Zone that separates North and South Korea.

-do island.

-do province.

-dong city neighbourhood; part of a *–gu*.

dong- east.

dongdongju a milky rice wine much favoured by Korean students; very similar to *makgeolli*.

DPRK Democratic People's Republic of Korea.

-eup town.

-ga section of a major street.

-gang river of over 100km in length.

-gil street.

gisaeng Female entertainers popular in dynastic times.

-gu district of a city, subdivided into *–dong* neighbourhoods.

-gul cave.

-gun county.

-gung palace.

gwageo civil service examinations in the Joseon era.

Gyopo Koreans, or people of Korean descent, living overseas.

hae sea. Korea's East, West and South seas are referred to as *Donghae*, *Seohae* and *Namhae* respectively, though the international nomenclature of the first two (more readily referred to as the "Sea of Japan" and the "Yellow Sea" abroad) is a touchy subject with Koreans.

hagwon private academy for after-school study. Many expats in Korea are working at an English academy (*yeongeo hagwon*).

hallyu the "Korean New Wave" of pop culture, most specifically cinematic produce.

hanbok traditional Korean clothing.

-hang harbour.

hangeul the Korean alphabet.

hanja Chinese characters, which are still sometimes used in Korea.

hanji traditional handmade paper.

hanok a style of traditional, tile-roofed wooden housing.

-ho lake; also used for those artificially created after the construction of a dam.

hof a Korean-style bar.

insam ginseng.

jaebeol major Korean corporation.

-jeon temple hall.

jjimjilbang Korean spa-cum-sauna facilities, often used by families, youth groups and the occasional budget traveller (see p.35).

KNTO Korea National Tourism Organization.

KTX the fastest class of Korean train.

makgeolli a milky rice wine much favoured by Korean students; very similar to *dongdongju*.

minbak rented rooms in a private house or building, most commonly found near beaches and national park entrances.

mudang practitioner of shamanism; usually female.

mugunghwa Korea's third-highest level of train, one below a *saemaeul*. Named after Korea's national flower, a variety of hibiscus, also known as the "Rose of Sharon", which flowers punctually each July.

-mun city or fortress gate.

-myo Confucian shrine.

nam- south.

-ni village; sometimes pronounced – *ri*.

-no large street; sometimes pronounced – *ro*.

nocheonnyeo an "over-the-hill" female – Korean women have long been expected to marry by the age of thirty, though this is slowly changing.

noraebang a "singing room" often the venue of choice for the end of a night out.

oncheon hot-spring bath or spa.

ondol traditional underfloor system of heating, made by wood fires underneath traditional buildings, but replaced with gas-fired systems in Korean apartments and modern houses.

pansori Korean opera derived from shamanistic songs, sung by female vocalists to minimalist musical accompaniment.

-pokpo waterfalls.

pyeong Korean unit of measurement equivalent to approximately 3.3 square metres; still commonly used to measure the floors pace of housing or offices.

Red Devils a nickname for the South Korean national football team, or their noisy supporters.

-ri village; sometimes pronounced – *ni*.

-ro large street; sometimes pronounced – *no*.

ROK Republic of Korea.

-sa temple.

Saemaeul Korea's second-highest level of train, one faster than a *mugunghwa* but slower than a KTX. Also the name of the "New Community Movement" inaugurated by Korean president Park Chung-hee in the 1970s.

-san mountain; often used to describe an entire range.

sanseong mountain fortress.

seo- west.

Seon Korean Buddhist sect proximate to Zen in Japan.

seonsaengnim title for a teacher, which goes before the family name, or after the given name in the case of most expat teachers in Korea. Hence, a teacher named Martin will be referred to as "Martin *seonsaengnim*". It's also used as a version of "Mister".

seowon Confucian academy, most prevalent in Joseon times.

-si city, subdivided into *–gu* districts.

sijang market.

soju clear alcoholic drink (around 25 percent alcohol by volume) which is often compared to vodka, and usually cheaper than water at convenience stores up and down the land.

ssireum a Korean wrestling style inevitably compared to sumo, but far closer in form to Mongolian or Greco-Roman styles.

STO Seoul Tourism Organization.

taekwondo Korean martial art; now practised around the world.

tap pagoda.

tongil unification, a highly important concept on the divided Korean peninsula.

trot a very distinctive style of Korean music much favoured by older generations.

woeguk-in foreigner; pronounced "way-goog-in". *Woeguk-saram* is also used.

yangban the scholarly "upper class" in Joseon-era Korea.

yeogwan Korean form of accommodation, similar to a motel but privately run and almost always older.

yeoinsuk Korean form of accommodation, similar to a *yeogwan* but with communal toilets and showers.

Small print and index

A ROUGH GUIDE TO ROUGH GUIDES

Published in 1982, the first Rough Guide – to Greece – was a student scheme that became a publishing phenomenon. Mark Ellingham, a recent graduate in English from Bristol University, had been travelling in Greece the previous summer and couldn't find the right guidebook. With a small group of friends he wrote his own guide, combining a highly contemporary, journalistic style with a thoroughly practical approach to travellers' needs.

The immediate success of the book spawned a series that rapidly covered dozens of destinations. And, in addition to impecunious backpackers, Rough Guides soon acquired a much broader readership that relished the guides' wit and inquisitiveness as much as their enthusiastic, critical approach and value-for-money ethos.

These days, Rough Guides include recommendations from budget to luxury and cover more than 120 destinations around the globe, as well as producing an ever-growing range of ebooks.

Visit **roughguides.com** to find all our latest books, read articles, get inspired and share travel tips with the Rough Guides community.

Rough Guide credits

Editor: Claire Saunders
Layout: Ankur Guha
Cartography: James Macdonald and Swati Handoo
Picture editor: Aude Vauconsant
Proofreader: Susanne Hillen
Managing editor: Keith Drew
Assistant editor: Payal Sharotri
Production: Jimmy Lao

Cover design: Chloe Stickland, Ankur Guha
Editorial assistant: Freya Godfrey
Senior pre-press designer: Dan May
Programme manager: Gareth Lowe
Publisher: Keith Drew
Publishing director: Georgina Dee

Publishing information

This third edition published October 2015 by
Rough Guides Ltd,
80 Strand, London WC2R 0RL
11, Community Centre, Panchsheel Park,
New Delhi 110017, India
Distributed by Penguin Random House
Penguin Books Ltd,
80 Strand, London WC2R 0RL
Penguin Group (USA)
345 Hudson Street, NY 10014, USA
Penguin Group (Australia)
250 Camberwell Road, Camberwell,
Victoria 3124, Australia
Penguin Group (NZ)
67 Apollo Drive, Mairangi Bay, Auckland 1310,
New Zealand
Penguin Group (South Africa)
Block D, Rosebank Office Park, 181 Jan Smuts Avenue,
Parktown North, Gauteng, South Africa 2193
Rough Guides is represented in Canada by Tourmaline
Editions Inc. 662 King Street West, Suite 304, Toronto,
Ontario M5V 1M7
Printed in Singapore

© Rough Guides, 2015
Maps © Rough Guides
No part of this book may be reproduced in any form
without permission from the publisher except for the
quotation of brief passages in reviews.
392pp includes index
A catalogue record for this book is available from the
British Library
ISBN: 978-0-24120-132-9
The publishers and authors have done their best to
ensure the accuracy and currency of all the information
in **The Rough Guide to Korea**, however, they can accept
no responsibility for any loss, injury, or inconvenience
sustained by any traveller as a result of information or
advice contained in the guide.
1 3 5 7 9 8 6 4 2

MIX
Paper from
responsible sources
FSC
www.fsc.org   FSC™ C018179

Help us update

We've gone to a lot of effort to ensure that the third
edition of **The Rough Guide to Korea** is accurate and up-
to-date. However, things change – places get "discovered",
opening hours are notoriously fickle, restaurants and
rooms raise prices or lower standards. If you feel we've got
it wrong or left something out, we'd like to know, and if
you can remember the address, the price, the hours, the
phone number, so much the better.

Please send your comments with the subject line
"**Rough Guide Korea Update**" to ✉ mail@uk.roughguides
.com. We'll credit all contributions and send a copy of the
next edition (or any other Rough Guide if you prefer) for
the very best emails.

Find more travel information, connect with fellow
travellers and plan your trip on Ⓦ roughguides.com.

ABOUT THE AUTHOR

Norbert Paxton has been on the road almost non-stop since 2002 – the same year that he first pitched up in the Land of Morning Calm – and has now travelled to more than 100 countries. However, the Koreas remain hovering around the very top of his favourite-countries-on-earth list: he blames the eternal pleasures of *makgeolli*, *galbi* and *pajeon*; the otherworldly ridiculousness of North Korea; and, on both sides of the border, the wonderful Koreans themselves.

Acknowledgements

Norbert Paxton would like to thank all those who assisted him during his time in Korea, including Seoul chums Jason Strother and David Carruth for coming down to Jeju; Michael Spavor for his highly entertaining cameo appearance; sister Nicole for her own brief visit; Matt Crawford for letting me kip at his apartment for a couple of weeks; Mina Kim in Suwon; Eugene Hong for the feasts in Gwangju and Sokcho; Steven Borowiec for the chance meeting and copious bottles of mak in Danyang; Matt Baldwin for the night out in Daejeon; Yeongae Min and Woni for the fun drives out of town; the Seoul Tourism Organisation for their assistance in the capital; the Gangwon tourist authorities for their assistance in the north-east; and Nick, Simon and Eivind Thomassen for their assistance and company a bit further north again.

Readers' updates

Thanks to all the readers who have taken the time to write in with comments and suggestions (and apologies if we've inadvertently omitted or misspelt anyone's name):

David Brengelmann, Stephen P. Cahill, Daniel Crewe, Diane Cubey, Jill Fitzgerald, Glyn Garratt, Rolf Mattes, Prakash Menon, Brenda Patterson, Kara Richardson, Thorsten Schmidt, Flavia Woodwark.

Index

Maps are marked in grey

Map symbols

The symbols below are used on maps throughout the book

Point of interest	Lighthouse	Motorway	Beach
Information office	Gate	Main road	Park
Subway station	Memorial/statue	Minor road	National park
Subway line	Shrine	Tunnel	National park (marine)
Airport	Buddhist temple	Pedestrian road	Cemetery
Bus stop	Monument	Path	International boundary
Post office	Temple	Wall	Regional boundary
Hospital	Campsite	Ferry	Chapter boundary
Spring/spa	Palace	Railway	Demilitarized Zone
Observatory	Border checkpoint	High spreed railway	
Viewpoint	Beach	Cable car	
Museum	Mountain refuge/lodge	Building	
Mountain peak	Dam	Church (town maps)	
Mountain range	Cave	Stadium	
Waterfall	Picnic		
Crater	Observatory		
Gorge	Pagoda		

Listings key

- Accommodation
- Restaurant/café/tearoom
- Nightlife
- Shop